About the Authors

Mary F. Ray is a home economist and teacher. She earned a B.S. degree with a major in food and nutrition from Western Reserve University and an M.S. degree in home economics education from Florida State University. She taught at the high school and college levels and was Supervisor of Home Economics for the Broward County Schools, Fort Lauderdale, Florida. During this time, food service programs were initiated for the first time. Named as an outstanding home economist in *Who's Who Among American Women*, Mrs. Ray is a past president of the Florida Home Economist Association. She is coauthor of *Exploring Professional Cooking*.

Beda A. Dondi is a highly respected executive chef in Florida. Trained at the Cooks' Apprentice School in Montreux, Switzerland, he has worked in Canada and the United States as chef saucier, sous-chef, and executive chef. Most recently, he was food manager and executive chef for a large hotel complex in Fort Lauderdale, Florida. As a member of the Food Service Advisory Council, he has helped develop school programs.

Professional Cooking and Baking

Professional Cooking and Baking

MARY FREY RAY

BEDA A. DONDI

Bennett Publishing Company

Peoria, Illinois 61615

82 83 84 85   KP   5 4 3 2

ISBN 87002-328-4

Library of Congress Catalog Number 80-67648

Printed in the United States of America

TO THE STUDENT

You are beginning the study of food service, a study that can lead to a rewarding career. The pathway to success in food service is open to any ambitious young man or woman with the necessary skills. The course presented in PROFESSIONAL COOKING AND BAKING will help you develop those skills. You may find that you enjoy working with food. If this is so, and if you are willing to study and practice diligently the techniques of cooking, many interesting opportunities will become available to you.

However, no book can give you all the information you need for a career in food service. A book can never replace a good teacher. Your teacher will explain the concepts of food service. He or she will demonstrate techniques and supervise your skill development. Students learn more from a competent teacher than from any book, no matter how good it is.

Even so, when you graduate from this course, actual work experience is the only way to learn how to handle the stress of meeting meal deadlines. Only then may you discover if the vocation of food service is the career for you.

The purpose of this book is to help you understand the what, why, and how of professional cooking. Although some recipes are included in the book, it is not a cookbook. The recipes are intended to illustrate the principles of cookery. Your teacher will furnish you with most of the recipes you will use.

There are twenty-three chapters, grouped into six units. Each unit is based on specific concepts of food service. It emphasizes the development of skills and understandings you will need to find a job in food service. The charts, pictures, and recipes will help you better understand the concepts. At the end of each unit is a list of references. You may wish to learn more about the concepts and techniques.

These reference books and magazines may be checked for additional information.

Unit 1 is concerned with the professional cooks and where they work. Career opportunities are discussed. Stories of the lives of persons who earn their living in food service are included. This unit will also introduce you to the production kitchens and the equipment of food service.

Unit 2 takes you behind the kitchens to the areas where food is received and stored. You will learn the ways in which food is pre-prepared before being sent to the production kitchens.

Unit 3 starts you on the preparation of food for the customers. You will study the preparation of cold foods such as appetizers and salads.

Unit 4 is concerned with the preparation of hot foods such as meat, vegetables, sauces, and soups.

Unit 5 takes you to the bakery. Here, you will learn to prepare not only bread and rolls, but desserts also.

Unit 6 introduces you to the growing industry of fast foods.

To help your understanding of food service, each chapter begins with the objectives you should accomplish. This section is titled *What Will You Learn?* *Words to Remember* are included throughout the text to help you learn the vocabulary of food service. Terms that may be unfamiliar are set in *italics* and followed by a phonetic pronunciation.

The metric system of measurement is used along with the customary system throughout the book. The metric measurement is given first and the customary measurement follows in brackets, [ ]. This may seem confusing to you at first. However, the metric system is rapidly replacing the customary system. It is essential for you to become familiar with it.

Sanitation and safety are emphasized in sections marked *Caution.* Important information on cooking techniques is labeled as a *Cooking Tip.*

Preface

A section titled *How Much Have You Learned?* is at the end of each chapter. It contains questions to help you test yourself. How much did you learn by studying the chapter? Answering the questions may help you judge your understanding. But skill development can be tested only by *doing*. As you prepare the food under your teacher's direction, you will gradually develop the skills of cooking.

Becoming a chef, however, requires more than skill. It takes special talent and many years of experience. Becoming a chef demands a deep commitment to food preparation of the highest quality. Professional cooking is an art.

It is the sincere hope of the authors that this book will give you a sharp interest in food service. We hope you will go on to an enjoyable and lucrative career.

Acknowledgments

We wish to express our deep appreciation to the many persons, governmental agencies, and companies who assisted us in so many ways in the writing of *Professional Cooking and Baking*. We would especially like to thank the following:

- Evelyn Lewis, Supervisor of Vocational Home Economics, Broward County Schools, Fort Lauderdale, Florida. We turned to her for help with reference materials, curricular material, and consultant sources. She was always courteous and most helpful.
- Jeanne Brinkley, author, teacher, and friend, who gave us much advice, encouragement, and assistance.
- Tybe Kahn, food service teacher, who was especially helpful as a source of information for Chapter 11 ("Eggs and Cheese").
- Janet Raymond for the artwork that accompanies the text.
- Bill Snyder for many of the photographs.
- Kenneth Sullivan, owner/manager of Dan Dowd's Steak House, Fort Lauderdale, Florida, for checking the sections on meat and providing information on meat cuts.
- Ben Pollock, president of Angelo's Seafood Company, Deerfield Beach, Florida, and all of his employees for valuable assistance in writing Chapter 10 ("Finfish and Shellfish").
- The staff of Jacob's Bakery and Morrison's Cafeteria, Fort Lauderdale, Florida, who demonstrated techniques and answered countless questions.
- Our consultants, who introduce each unit. They spent many hours discussing food service with us and checking the accuracy of the information in this book.

We are especially indebted to the following persons and companies for their help in writing Chapter 22 ("Fast Foods"):

- The staff of Burger King University, Miami, Florida.
- Ottie Ladd, franchisee, Kentucky Fried Chicken, Tacoma, Washington.
- Robert Dennis, Yegen Foods (Arthur Treacher), Seattle, Washington.
- Robert Taft, Pizza Hut of Titusville, Fort Lauderdale, Florida.

The following companies and governmental agencies furnished needed information and illustrations. For their cooperation, the authors are most grateful.

Alto-Shaam, Inc.
American Egg Board
Blue Anchor, Inc.
Bunn-O-Matic Corporation
California Tree Fruit Agreement
Cecilware Corporation
Cleveland Range Company
Cory Food Services, Inc.
Crescent Metal Products, Inc.
EKCO
David W. Evans/Pacific, Inc.
Fitzgerald Advertising, Inc.
Florida Department of Natural Resources
Fresh Garlic Association
Frymaster Corporation
General Foods Corporation
Golden Dipt Company
Hamilton Beach, Division of Scovill
Hobart Corporation
Kentucky Fried Chicken
Land O'Lakes, Inc.
Thomas J. Lipton, Inc.
McDonald's
McGraw Edison Company
McIlhenny Company
Oscar Mayer and Company
Peter Mandabach Advertising
Merco Products, Inc.
Morrison, Inc.

Acknowledgments

Mr. Frosty Seafoods, Inc.
Frank C. Nahser, Inc.
National Live Stock and Meat Board
National Marine Fisheries Service
Newman, Saylor, and Gregory
Pizza Hut, Inc.
Polar Ware Company
Potato Board
Rubbermaid Commercial Products, Inc.
Russell Harrington Cutlery, Inc.
Caryl Saunders Associates
SCM Durkee Foods
J. R. Simplot Co.
Sparta Brush Company, Inc.
Taylor Freezer
Taylor Instrument Company
Thermo Pin Manufacturing Corporation

Thousand Springs Trout Farms, Inc.
Tupperware
Turkey Information Service
United States Department of Agriculture
Vollrath Company
Vulcan-Hart Corporation
Waring Products, Division of Dynamics
    Corporation of America
Wear-Ever Food Service Equipment
Wells Manufacturing Corporation
Western Iceberg Lettuce, Inc.

To all of the above and to any others we may have inadvertently omitted, we extend a sincere "thank you."

Mary F. Ray
Beda Dondi

Editor: Ed Zempel
Production Manager: Gordon Guderjan
Production Assistant: Carol Owen
Artist: Janet Raymond
Cover Design: William A. Seabright

Table of Contents

Table of Contents

The World of the Professional Cooks

Alex Martinez, Executive Chef, The Ogden Food Service Corporation, Houston, Texas.

MEET THE CONSULTANT

Alex Martinez, born in Houston, Texas, has a mixed heritage. One grandmother was a Cherokee Indian. The other grandmother was a Mexican. One grandfather was born in Spain. The other grandfather was born in Mexico.

Now in his forties, Alex says he has enjoyed his life as a chef. His only regret is that he left school after the sixth grade. School seemed to offer nothing to him. His lack of schooling made it harder to climb the ladder of success.

Even at that young age, he managed to pick up a few jobs peddling hot dogs at amusement parks. When he was sixteen, he became a dishwasher in a Mexican restaurant. Although a school dropout, he was interested in learning more about professional cooking. He learned the hard way—through experience. He watched and helped the cooks. He made many mistakes, but he was always willing to learn from his mistakes. When he was twenty-four, he began to cook.

When the Korean war began, he joined the Air Force. He was sent to the school for butchers where he learned to handle knives. Alex says that anyone who wants to succeed in food service must learn the importance of knives. He has a treasured set that go with him wherever he works. "Care of tools marks a real chef," says Alex.

After six years in the Air Force, three of them as mess sergeant, Alex returned to civilian life. With the Air Force experience behind him, Alex began a steady climb to the top of food service, working in many places.

"Food service is a good trade to learn," says Alex. "But you must be willing to start at the bottom. I began as a dishwasher, but I am still learning after twenty-five years in food service. Don't do anything halfway. Whatever you must do, do it all the way."

According to Alex, there are many cooks who can never become chefs because they are unwilling to accept responsibility for the cooking results in the station. The cooks are under the chef. The executive chef is responsible for the total production in the kitchen.

Alex Martinez accepts responsibility for the food service in the Albert Thomas Convention Center in Houston, Texas. He is responsible for breakfasts, lunches, and dinners. He oversees banquets served to thousands. He manages everything from simple beverage service to elaborate appetizers. For a dropout from school, he has accomplished a satisfactory career. He earns a good salary, but it hasn't been easy. He was saved, he says, by the Air Force.

Alex is sometimes afraid cooking is becoming a lost art. He says, "Convenience foods have caused a great change in food service. Sometimes it seems that everything is made up. All you have to do is heat and serve. But I think that young people should know foods. They should know what is in every dish they serve. Then they can improve it by adding their own touches."

The Professional Cooks

What Will You Learn?

When you finish studying this chapter, you should be able to do the following:

- Define the *Words to Remember*.
- Identify the individual ranks within the chain of command commonly accepted in food service.
- Explain the duties of each type of chef or cook and baker.
- List the qualities necessary to become a professional cook.
- Identify ways for career advancement.
- Pass the posttest.

CHAPTER

1

The purpose of this program is to introduce you to the methods of preparation used to prepare food for *food service*. Food service is the industry concerned with preparing food to be eaten. It is the third largest industry in the United States, feeding about 46,000,000 Americans over the age of seventeen. It is one of the few businesses where production and service are combined under the same roof.

FOOD SERVICE

Food service is divided into three sections. The part of the business concerned with the service of food is called the *front of the house*. The part of the business concerned with the production of the food is called the *back of the house*.

The third part, the *office*, is concerned with the management or administration of the whole enterprise.

In this book, you will study the activities of the back of the house—the receiving, storing, and cooking of food.

Words to Remember

WHO ARE THE PROFESSIONAL COOKS?

Food for food service is prepared by professional cooks. There are many cooks in this world. The *professional cooks* are those who have been trained for the job, receive money for it, and consider cooking for others as their vocation or career.

Professional bakers never call themselves cooks. They are proud to be known as *professional bakers* or pastry chefs. They are distinguished from the many who bake because they are professionals. Baking is their career or vocation.

The title "chef" (SHEF) has a proud meaning. A *chef* is a head cook, but the title has been earned by demonstrating superior techniques and artistry in cooking. There are many cooks but very few chefs.

Most cuisine in the Western World stems from that of Europe. *Cuisine* (kwee-ZEEN) comes from a French word for "kitchen" and means "the style of cooking." The most famous chefs have come from Europe, bringing the European cuisine with them. They were trained in the well-known *apprentice* schools of Switzerland, France, Italy, and Germany. An apprentice is a beginner studying a vocation under a master worker.

Words to Remember

THE BRIGADE

Just as the cuisine of most food service came from Europe, the names and ranks of the cooks or chefs also came from Europe. Large food service kitchens based on a European cuisine are something like an army. At the top is the executive chef (the general) and at the bottom are the cooks' helpers (the privates).

In this type of kitchen organization, the entire personnel is known as the *brigade*. The brigade includes the chefs, cooks, assistant cooks, cooks' helpers, and anyone else who works in the kitchens. They are a team. The chefs who actually do the cooking are sometimes called *working chefs*.

• *Executive chef.* The executive chef supervises all the food preparation and also works with the management. The duties of this top job include planning the menus, ordering the food, preparing the payroll, keeping the records, and planning special affairs. The executive chef also interviews prospective new cooks. The responsibility for the operation of the kitchens rests with the executive chef.

• *Sous-chef* (SOO-SHEF). The sous-chef is second in command. He or she assumes the responsibilities of the head chef when that chef is absent.

• *Chef saucier* (sos-cee-EH). Sometimes the head chef is also the chef saucier. This important chef prepares all of the sauces, and some of the fish dishes, sautées, stews, and hot appetizers.

• *Chef rotisseur* (roe-tee-SUR). The chef rotisseur is also known as the broiler chef. This chef presides over all meat and poultry preparation. The chef rotisseur is also usually responsible for fish preparation.

• *Chef entremetier* (on-tra-MEH-tee-ah). The chef entremetier is also known as the vegetable cook. This chef or cook prepares soups and eggs, as well as vegetables.

• *Chef garde-manger* (GUARD mon-ZHAY). The chef garde-manger prepares all cold foods such as appetizers, salads, cold sauces, garnishes, and cold buffet dishes. Sometimes this chef is called the pantry chef or salad cook.

• *Chef patissier* (pah-TEE-see-eh). The chef patissier is the pastry chef. All baked products and often all desserts are prepared by the pastry chef.

• *Chef tournant* (tur-NANT). The chef tournant is called the swing chef or swing cook. The chef tournant replaces other chefs as needed.

Other members of the brigade may or may not actually do any cooking. These are:

• *Boucher* (boo-CHEY). The boucher is the butcher.

• *Buffetier* (boo-FAH-tee-ah). The buffetier is the carver of meats and poultry for service.

A few very large French restaurants may have the following positions:

• *Potager* (poh-tah-ZHAY). The potager is the soup cook.

• *Poissonnier* (pwah-SOHN-ee-ah). The poissonnier is the fish cook.

• *Sugar chef.* The sugar chef is an artist who creates beautiful, edible art objects using sugar syrup.

Types of Food Service

The duties and responsibilities of the brigade vary with the size and complexity of the food service operation. Some restaurants are full-service. Full-service restaurants serve breakfast, lunch, and dinner. Such a restaurant would need two shifts of personnel. One would prepare breakfast and lunch. The other would begin work in the afternoon and prepare dinner.

Other operations may offer only limited service. They may serve lunch and dinner or dinner only. This type might have a full shift during the heavy service hours and a light shift to finish the evening.

The complexity of the menu also affects the type and number of workers. Some restaurants may serve *table d'hote* (TAHB-lah DOTE) featuring complete meals at a set price. Others may offer *á la carte* (AH LAH CART) service. Here, a wide variety of dishes are each priced separately. Most restaurants offer a combination of these two types of service. The wider the choice, the bigger the brigade.

Institutional food service such as is found in schools, hospitals, and nursing homes presents different problems. The brigade just described is seldom found in institutional service. Schools usually offer only lunch. The menu is simple. The workers are often part-time and drawn from homemakers. Supervision is under trained managers, rather than chefs.

Hospital kitchens are under the supervision of a *dietitian*. A *dietitian* is a professional person, highly trained in nutrition and in special diets needed by the ill. The workers in the kitchens are usually not professionally trained in cooking techniques.

Nursing homes usually offer set menus for breakfast, lunch, and dinner. A dietitian is often in charge of the food preparation.

Table 1-1 shows the brigade for a small food service operation. This particular one has a head cook and three assistant cooks. The head cook might also be the owner. The duties of each cook might be similar to those shown in Table 1-1.

A medium-sized restaurant might have a brigade similar to that shown in Table 1-2. The head cook in this restaurant might be a chef. A chef has much

Table 1-1. Duties of the Brigade in a Small Kitchen

Head Cook	First Cook	Second Cook	Third Cook
Plans menus Orders food May cook some foods Supervises cooks Pays bills Keeps records Trains new cooks	Short-order cooking	Meats Vegetables Soups Sauces	Salads Sandwiches Desserts

Table 1-2. Duties of the Brigade in a Medium-Sized Kitchen

Head Cook	Sous-Chef	First Cook	Short-Order Cook	Pastry Cook	Pantry Cook	Vegetable Cook
Plans menus. Orders food. Supervises cooks. Pays bills. Keeps records. Trains new cooks. Cooks when necessary.	Replaces head cook when necessary, but especially at night.	Soups. Sauces. Roasts.	Broils. Grills. Fries.	Rolls. Pastries. Cakes. Quick Breads. Desserts.	Appetizers. Salads. Hors d'oeuvres.	Pre-preparation and cooking of vegetables and fruits.

more training and experience in food service than a cook. A chef also commands a higher salary. Such a person is rightly proud of the title Chef.

The possible duties of each person in the medium-sized brigade are shown in Table 1-2.

The brigade for a large operation such as a hotel might include all of the jobs listed on pages 15–16. This type of food service might operate several different restaurants under one management. There may be a coffee shop offering quick breakfasts, lunches, and simple dinners. There may be a medium-priced restaurant open only for lunch and dinner. Some hotels might have a high-priced restaurant with a menu featuring expensive food. Banquet facilities might also be a part of the service.

Such an establishment would have a large brigade headed by an executive chef, always called by the title Chef.

Personal Qualifications

A professional worker in food service needs special physical, mental, and emotional qualities. Technical skill in food preparation is not enough. Equally important is the person's relationship to fellow-workers and the management. Many persons lose jobs because of their inability to get along with others.

PHYSICAL QUALITIES

A professional cook must have physical strength and endurance. He or she must also have the highest standards of personal cleanliness.

- *Physical strength.* Pots and pans used in food service are usually made of heavyweight stainless steel. A few may be made of aluminum. The pots are very large and heavy, especially when filled with food. A young person intending to make a vocation of food service must have the physical strength to handle such equipment.

- *Endurance.* A food service kitchen is no place for a person who tires easily. The hours are long, and the work is strenuous. The heat is often high, and the kitchens are seldom air-conditioned. During the service hours, the pace is fast and hectic. The cook must be able to perform under these conditions.

- *Personal cleanliness.* Cleanliness is a quality prized by everyone. All persons consider themselves clean, but the standards of cleanliness may vary. The standard of cleanliness for one job may not be high enough for food service.

Standards of cleanliness in many communities are set by the Board of Health. They are enforced by the management of the food service operation. A person who is not willing to abide by these standards should not attempt to become a professional cook.

High standards are enforced because you are cooking for others. The customers eat what you prepare. What you cook affects the health and well-being of the customers. You are working with food. Food can easily carry germs from the kitchen to the dining room. Your standards of personal hygiene must be exceptionally high. You should practice the following habits of cleanliness:

- *Clean body.* A daily bath or shower.
- *Clean hair.* Hair washed often and confined in a cap, if short, and a net, if long, during working hours.
- *Clean hands.* Nails trimmed short and kept clean. Wash hands before beginning work. Always wash hands after combing the hair, smoking, eating, or going to the toilet.
- *Clean clothes.* Change underwear daily after the bath or shower. Wear a clean uniform or apron daily. Most food service operations furnish clean uniforms.
- *Clean work habits.* No smoking in the kitchen. Never cough over food. Do not touch your nose, ears, or lips while preparing food. Do not work with food with an open cut on the hands or when wearing a bandage.

Cleanliness should be practiced until it becomes a habit, a way of life. When you automatically observe these rules, you will be on the way to becoming a professional cook.

In addition to physical strength and the highest standards of personal cleanliness, the professional cook must have a sense of orderliness. The French have a phrase for it—*mise en place* (MEES EN PLAS). It means "setup" or, in effect, "don't start cooking until you have assembled and pre-prepared all needed ingredients and equipment." It means complete organization for efficiency before you begin. It means cleaning up as you work so your work space is clear and clean. If you don't have this sense of orderliness, you can develop it through practice.

MENTAL SKILLS

A professional cook needs to read easily and be able to do simple arithmetic problems. Foreign phrases and words are used frequently in food service. The cook should be able to use these terms easily in conversation and writing.

- *Reading.* Recipes tell the cook the ingredients and equipment needed for each preparation. They tell how to combine the ingredients and prepare the food. The cook must be able to follow the recipes. Without reading ability, the cook is lost.

Professional cooks have a vocabulary of their own. The *Words to Remember* found in every chapter will help you understand and use the new words.

- *Foreign words and phrases.* Most European-trained chefs and cooks speak three or four languages fluently. They learned these in childhood. It is not necessary for you to speak another language, although it would be helpful. However, you must be familiar with certain words, terms, and phrases used constantly in food service. Most of them are French. You have already encountered some of them in this chapter.

- *Arithmetic.* It is essential to be able to measure ingredients in the correct amounts. Accurate measurement and weighing is a skill involving arithmetic. It is all-important in cooking. The results of the recipe will depend upon the cook's skill in measuring.

Many times, recipes must be increased or decreased. This involves skills in adding, subtracting, multiplying, and dividing.

EMOTIONS AND SOCIAL SKILLS

During the heavy service hours, cooks work under great stress. It is easy during those times to snap at fellow workers. All workers in any business need to keep tempers under control. It is especially important in food service, where close cooperation with fellow workers is essential.

Be pleasant and friendly, but businesslike, with

The Peoria Journal Star
1-1. This apprentice cuts steaks under the direction of a professional chef. The apprentice is sponsored by an association of professional chefs.

your companions during working hours. Fun is for after work hours.

Like a captain on a ship, when a chef gives an order, it is to be instantly obeyed. There is no time for a cook's helper to question the order.

Chefs, especially European chefs, are known to be difficult and temperamental. However, the chef must run a "tight" kitchen if the food is to be well prepared and properly served.

FURTHER EDUCATION

If you discover while studying this course that you really enjoy food work, you should consider more education. Every state in the United States has junior or community colleges in the larger towns or cities. Many of them offer courses in food service or culinary arts. *Culinary* means "relating to cookery or the kitchen." Many of the state universities offer a four-year program leading to a degree in hotel or restaurant management.

There are also many private cooking or culinary schools. Many of them are sponsored by well-known professional organizations. Fig. 1-1.

Opportunities for advancement are always there for the young man or woman who is truly interested. All you have to do is look for them.

PATHWAYS TO PROFESSIONAL COOKING

Many cooks and bakers were introduced to food service in the armed services. They continued the vocation when they returned to private life. Others were trained in the many fine vocational schools and colleges developed in the United States and Canada. A few learned through on-the-job training.

Some professional cooks have already led interesting and varied lives in food service. Others are young and just embarking on careers in food service. On the next few pages you will read some of the interesting ways a few professional cooks and bakers learned their trade.

For instance, *Charles Wagner* is now a teaching

Charles Wagner, sugar chef.

Joliet Herald News

chef at the Joliet Junior College in Illinois. How did he attain this job?

Charles Wagner is popularly known by his students as Chef Charlie. Charlie is a good example of a chef trained in the European tradition. He was born in the German-speaking part of Switzerland. Charlie didn't really want to become a chef. He preferred to work in an automobile factory. However, his father insisted that he become an apprentice in a pastry shop. Obediently, he entered one of the very fine trade schools in Switzerland. He worked in the pastry shop during the day and went to school at night.

"It wasn't easy," says Charlie, his German accent still very strong. "I was expected to work long hours, like ten to twelve hours every day. When holidays came, there was no holiday for me—only longer hours because I didn't go to school. Sometimes I worked twenty hours a day."

Even when he graduated from the school, Charlie wasn't sure he wanted to be a pastry chef. His first job was at St. Moritz, a famous Swiss ski resort. There he got what he describes as "the kick in the pants." He found out he could make really beautiful ice carvings and create lovely things from sugar syrup. He enjoyed this so much that he decided to become the best sugar chef in the whole world.

A sugar chef works with hot sugar syrup. When sugar is boiled with an acid, it becomes thick. As the syrup cools, it can be worked into different shapes. The shapes harden when cold. A sugar chef must have hands that do not sweat while working with the hot syrup. The chef also must develop thick skin on the hands so the hot syrup will not burn. His hands did not sweat, and he was able to develop the thick skin. Not everyone can be a sugar chef, but Charlie could.

Charlie won many prizes for his sugar artistry. The head chef on a large ship, the *Ile de France*, was impressed with his work. Although he was only twenty, Charlie was hired as sugar chef on the luxurious liner. He made thirty-six crossings on the Atlantic Ocean while he delighted the passengers with his creations.

On the last crossing, Charlie's patron, the head chef, died. The captain of the ship had never liked a

Swiss working on a French liner. He preferred an all-French crew. He told Charlie that when the ship returned to France, he would have to get another job.

Charlie had met an American on that last crossing. He did not want to go back to France and look for another job. And so he made a dive off the deck of the ship into the dark waters of New York harbor. His new friend was waiting for him on the shore. He helped Charlie get a job at a New York hotel. He worked in many different hotels, but he was an illegal alien in the United States.

Later, he met an American girl whom he wished to marry. The Swiss consul advised Charlie to go to Canada and reenter this country legally. He did this and was able to marry his American sweetheart. In 1940, he became an American citizen. He was thirty-one years old.

As happened to many young men in those days, World War II interrupted his life. He went first to the Great Lakes Naval Training School and then to the Cooks and Bakers School in New Orleans. He graduated with highest honors and remained there as an instructor.

After the war, he returned to the work he loved best—that of sugar chef. He has made his beautiful sugar creations for many famous people. For example, he made a globe out of spun sugar for Mayor Daly of Chicago.

He baked a huge cake for the astronauts and frosted it with blue icing. With white frosting, he added white waves to the blue sea. From sugar, he fashioned seagulls and mermaids. To top the cake, he made a replica of the Gemini capsule landing in the ocean.

When the King of Norway visited the hotel where Charlie was working, he duplicated the king's sailing yacht in sugar.

Such is the genius of Charlie Wagner. One president of the United States autographed Charlie's chef's hat because he was so delighted with his artistry. Because of his genius, he was sent to the International Culinary Olympics in Germany. He entered the same competition again a few years later. He proudly displays gold and silver medals he won for his creations in the competitions.

Several years ago, Charlie decided it was time to leave the profession of sugar chef. But being an active man, he could not let go completely. He began to teach the art of sugar creation and cake frosting at the Pontiac Correctional Institution in Illinois. One of his students won a prize for the beautiful, but edible, painting he created out of sugar and chocolate.

Now he is teaching the craft of baking pastry as well as the art of sugar cookery at the Joliet Junior College. He is a wonderful example to all the students, not only for his artistic ability, but also because of his hard work. Charlie is willing to come early and work late to accomplish his creations. The students constantly wander in and out to watch him at work in his kitchen. His genial smile, sparkling blue eyes, and friendly manner make him a favorite with all.

Charlie never fails to tell visitors of his love for America. He says, "Nowhere else in the world could a poor immigrant boy such as I was accomplish so much. The opportunities in this country are unlimited. I am proud to be an American."

Kathy Nagel wants to be a pastry cook. To accomplish her desire, she has taken a different route than Charlie.

She graduated from a high school in Aurora, Illinois, and entered college. She entered the home economics program because she liked to cook and bake. Then, after two years, she left college because she felt the program was not giving her what she wanted.

Although she worked for three years as a clerk, she never forgot her ambition to be a pastry chef.

One day, a friend told her about the culinary arts program at the Joliet Junior College and the great sugar chef who taught there. Kathy investigated other programs in food service. But she entered the one for pastry chef because of Charlie Wagner.

Now Kathy has graduated. She has enjoyed her courses and feels she has found her life's work. But she has many difficulties to overcome before she can call herself a pastry cook. She felt she needed work experience while studying at college, but she was unable to find work in baking. Baking has always been a man's field, and many bakers are reluctant to

Kathy Nagel, aspiring pastry cook.

to improve." With an attitude like that, Kathy is bound to succeed.

Scott Spieler is a bright young man in his middle twenties. Although he has worked at Dan Dowd's Steak House for only six months, he already is head broiler cook. Dan Dowd's is well-known for broiled meats, and Scott is responsible for all dinners on the menu. Broiling is his specialty, and all steaks and chops are broiled by him personally. In addition, he supervises the fry cook and the feeder cook. The feeder cook is the assistant to Scott and the fry cook. The feeder cook takes the meat out of the refrigerator and replenishes the supplies as needed. The busy cooks cannot take time to run to the refrigerator.

As Scott tells it, "One steak is easy. Anyone can broil one steak at a time. But when you have five, six, or more steaks broiling, you have to remember which one is rare, which one is medium rare, and which one is well done. You can't mix them up or you'll have dissatisfied customers. Then you have to remember that a steak continues to cook after it is

hire a woman baker. Kathy was determined. She found a job in a well-known hotel-motel chain which operates many resorts. She now works in the pastry department in one of the resorts. It is a large resort, with three restaurants. Although the pay is low, raises are frequent. The opportunities for advancement seem bright. Kathy is sure she will succeed.

She says the most important thing she learned in culinary arts is to take pride in everything she does. "Never settle for second best," she says. "Always try

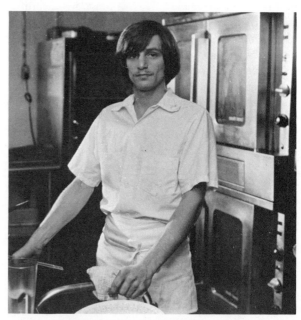

Scott Spieler, head broiler cook.

removed from the broiler. When I'm broiling, I don't talk. I don't do anything except pay attention to my broiling. Just last Saturday night, I broiled over 900 steaks. Only one was returned because it was too well done. I'm pretty proud of that record."

When Scott was fourteen, he looked around for an after-school job. Scott's father was a metal-worker, but Scott wanted to do something different. He had taken a home economics course and found that cooking was fun. He worked for a fast-food chicken chain and enjoyed it. He also noticed that there were plenty of cooking jobs, especially in South Florida. This was because of the tourist trade.

He took a job dishwashing in a restaurant. "I knew I wanted to be a cook, but I had to start at the bottom," he said. Although he was only fourteen, he was smart and mapped out a plan for himself to learn to cook. He noticed that the chefs were always willing to talk when they had a break. So Scott watched the chef and talked to him about cooking whenever possible. Soon the chef was taking an interest in him and teaching him the tricks of the trade. Gradually, he was permitted to make easy dishes for short order, such as soups, chili, and hamburgers.

He found employment in another restaurant as a short-order cook. There was a broiler in the station, so he began to broil.

On a trip north, he took a job as fry cook for seafood. He learned to work under stress. "When the going gets tough, when the waiters and waitresses are snapping orders at you, you have to keep your head," says Scott. A chef told him that a competent chef always had his own set of knives, so Scott bought the finest he could afford. "My knives are used only for meats," says Scott. "I have to watch them all the time or somebody will use them for slicing bread or something else."

When he returned to South Florida, he took a job at Dan Dowd's. He likes it because of the family atmosphere. He really enjoys cooking and never finds it monotonous.

"If you want a job at a particular restaurant," says Scott, "just walk in and take any job offered to you. Never mind if it seems lowly and unimportant. You are on hand, you have your feet in the kitchen.

Pete Ibias, head cook.

When an opening comes, you'll be Johnny-on-the-spot. Watch the chefs. Learn to cook under supervision. Before you know it, some cook will quit, and the job will be yours. Remember, people still eat three times a day. A good cook always can find a job."

Scott prefers to work the three to midnight shift. As head cook, he is the last one to leave the kitchens. Everything must be cleaned up, but he no longer has to do the cleaning himself. For a young man, Scott seems well started on a career in food service.

Pete Ibias is another example of a person who was helped on his way to a good profession by service in the armed forces. He was born and educated in the Phillipine Islands.

He joined the Coast Guard and was sent to the commissary school in San Diego. There he was trained to become a cook. However, after being discharged from the Coast Guard, he tried many different jobs. He was unmarried and free to move around. He thought he had plenty of time to decide what to do with his life.

But then something happened to him to make him think a little more seriously. He fell in love and

23

married. 'You know," he said, "when you become short of money and have the responsibility of a wife and children, you begin to look at life in a different way. I decided I needed a profession. Since I had had some training as a cook, I decided to make food service my career."

First, he worked as a dishwasher in an Oriental restaurant in Seattle. He was always looking for opportunities for advancement. He asked the chef to let him become an assistant to different cooks. By doing this, he could learn the trade. His brief training in the Coast Guard helped him learn the techniques faster.

He worked in several restaurants in Seattle and then moved to Juneau, Alaska. He thought he knew everything about food service, so he and his wife bought a restaurant. At last, they were in business for themselves—and very happy.

At first everything seemed to be going well. After a year, however, he discovered that being a cook in a restaurant and being the owner-manager were two different things. He and his wife were working long hours, but they never seemed to have any money for themselves. In fact, the two of them together had less money than Pete had made working for someone else.

Pete says, "No one ever told me that I should assign a salary to my wife and myself for our work. That should be part of the cost of running a restaurant. We just took home whatever was left at the end of a week, but there was never enough left for us to live on. I owed a lot of money, and I never had time for my children or for fun."

He sold the restaurant, paid what he owed, and looked around for a job. A friend suggested that he apply to the Alaskan ferry service. He applied for work on Friday and went to work on Monday as second cook.

Now, four years later, he is head cook with a second cook, salad cook, and baker working under him. The pay is very good, with many fringe benefits, such as good vacation time. The run from Juneau to Seattle and return takes seven days. Pete works seven days and is off seven days. Having seven days off gives him time to spend with his large family and to fish in the teeming Alaskan waters.

Pete had to join the union to work on the Alaskan ferries. He says that the seniority rules give him security and guarantee steady work.

The menus served on the ferries are planned in a central office in Juneau. All the ferries use the same menus, which must be approved by the union. Buying is also done through the central office. The supplies are put on the ships in Seattle and in Juneau.

The storeroom is in the hold of the ship, with a storekeeper in charge. Pete requisitions the supplies he needs to prepare the menu. The menus are repeated every two weeks, since there is a different set of passengers.

Pete does not seem to mind not planning the menus or supervising the buying. He says he did enough of that when he tried to operate his own restaurant. He is content to let the central office take that responsibility. He likes his job just the way it is. He plans to continue until he is old enough to retire.

Reginald Harris is a young man who proudly says he is self-motivated. He is one who does not need to be prodded into seeking opportunities.

When Reggie entered Batavia High School, he was like most high school students. He wanted a good job after he graduated, but he wasn't sure just what. In the last half of his junior year, he decided to take a course in food service at the vocational school—just for fun. Mid-Valley Vocational School was connected to his own high school. He continued his regular subjects at Batavia and studied the vocational subjects connected with food service at Mid-Valley. He discovered that he liked cooking and continued to take it through his senior year. He sought the help of the guidance counselor at Mid-Valley because he had decided he wanted to make food service his career. The guidance counselor suggested that he investigate the food service program at the junior college.

Reggie went to the junior college to look over the facilities and the two-year program. He liked what he saw. The instructors were excellent. The facilities were more than adequate, and the program could open up a promising career for him. He enrolled there when he graduated from high school.

He found that the culinary arts program com-

Reginald Harris, chef's assistant.

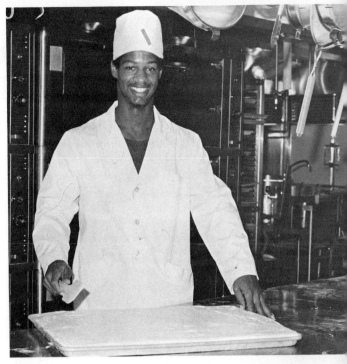

bined the practical and the theoretical sides of food service. He studied speech and other communication skills as well as business mathematics. He learned that getting along with others is essential to good management. He realized it is almost as important as knowing the necessary math. He watched professional demonstrations of many techniques that were as yet too difficult for him.

He learned about *mise en place,* the French phrase that soon becomes familiar to any student of food service. *Mise en place* is a watchword in the culinary arts program of Joliet Junior College. It has become a real slogan for Reggie.

In the school program, he developed skill in handling many different kinds of food preparations. He planned menus, operated the storeroom, and cut meat. He also garnished for beautiful service and assisted in preparing food for banquets and buffets.

To supplement his college training, Reggie decided he needed some work experience. Being self-motivated, he got a job first as assistant to the chef at a country club. Later, he worked in the restaurant of a large motel. He prepared all the food for quick service. Reggie found that these two jobs gave him the variety of experiences he needed. The pay helped with his college experiences.

Now ready for graduation, Reggie feels he is ready for a good position as assistant to a working chef. He is satisfied with the program he has followed. He is sure he will always be able to make a good living.

How Much Have You Learned?

Review this chapter. Answer the following questions to prepare yourself for the posttest. Check your answers with your teacher.

1. Define each of the *Words to Remember.*
2. From what part of the world did most American food come? Give examples how this has affected American food service.
3. What qualifications does a professional worker in food service need to succeed.
4. What is a brigade in food service? What types of food service have a brigade?
5. Who is in charge of the kitchens in a brigade? What are the duties? If that person is absent during the daytime, who takes over those duties?
6. Who is in charge of the kitchens at night?
7. By what title is the bake chef known in a brigade?
8. What is the garde-manger?
9. What are the duties of the swing chef or swing cook?
10. Name three ways a student of food service can get further education in culinary arts.

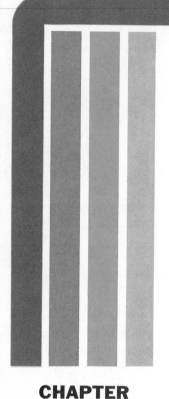

Basic Professional Cooking Equipment

What Will You Learn?

When you finish studying this chapter, you should be able to do the following:
- Define and use the *Words to Remember*.
- Identify the work areas in the kitchen, and name the chef responsible for each area.
- Identify the equipment commonly found in the food service kitchen.
- Pass the posttest.

The professional cooks work in a world of stainless steel and tile. Fig. 2-1. Both are used because they are durable and easy to keep clean. Although functional facilities may have their own beauty, food service kitchens are not designed to be beautiful. Color plays no part in their design. However, they are functional and efficient for the job for which they were designed. This job is to put out well-prepared food, attractively served, in the quantities needed, and ready to serve at the right time.

THE FOOD SERVICE KITCHEN

A well-designed food service kitchen should provide the following:
- An area for receiving and checking food and supplies.
- An area for sorting food according to type.
- Efficient flow of food from receiving to service.
- Centers of work for each type of food preparation.
- Needed equipment, conveniently placed.

Vulcan-Hart

2-1. Food service kitchens are designed for efficiency and ease of cleaning. This kitchen effectively employs stainless steel and tile in its design.

Words to Remember

controller	satellite kitchen
entrée	station

- Easy pickup and service of prepared food.
- Equipment for quick and thorough cleaning and sanitizing.
- Facilities for employees.

- Office for management.

The first two requirements will be discussed in detail in Chapter 3.

Food Flow Pattern

The food flow patterns for different types of food service are shown in Figs. 2-2 to 2-6. These are not actual floor plans. They are schematic drawings that show the different needs of various types of food service.

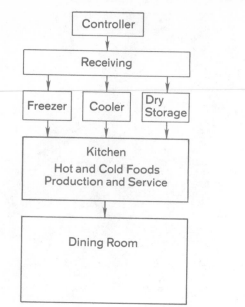

2-2. The possible food flow line for a small restaurant.

Figure 2-2 shows the possible food flow line for a small restaurant. The food is received, checked, and stored by the *controller,* also known as the storekeeper. From the controller, the food goes as needed to the kitchen for preparation. In a small restaurant, the prepared food is usually picked up directly from the cooks by the servers who take it to the customers.

Figure 2-3 shows the food flow for a large restaurant. Here, the food is sent to a pre-preparation area before being sent to the production kitchen. After the food is prepared, it goes to a separate service area, where it is made ready for service. It is then delivered for service as needed.

Figure 2-4 shows the food flow for a kitchen that services several dining areas. This type of food flow pattern might be found in a large hotel. After the food is prepared, it is sent to the *satellite kitchens.* A

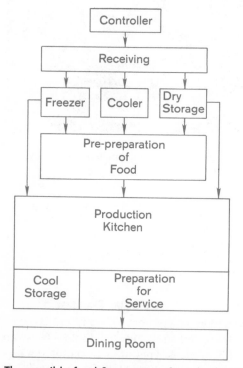

2-3. The possible food flow pattern for a large restaurant.

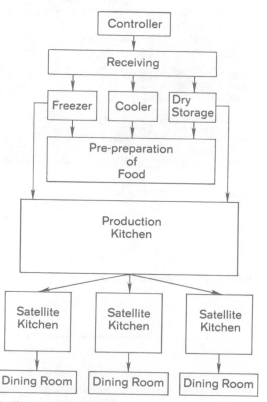

2-4. The possible food flow pattern for a kitchen that services several dining areas.

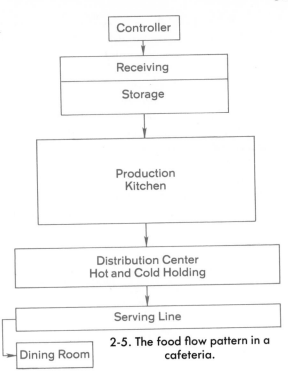

2-5. The food flow pattern in a cafeteria.

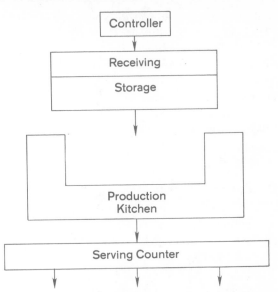

2-6. The food flow pattern for a fast-food restaurant.

satellite kitchen is a small kitchen designed to hold food for service to one of several dining rooms. It contains holding equipment for both hot and cold foods. Usually, no actual food preparation is done here. However, each kitchen may have equipment for fast foods. In the satellite kitchen, the food is made ready for service to the customers.

Figure 2-5 shows the food flow pattern in a cafeteria. The food flows from the production kitchen to a distribution center with hot and cold holding equipment. From here, the food on the serving line is replaced as needed.

Figure 2-6 shows the food flow pattern for a fast-food restaurant. Food service that features fast foods usually has the production kitchen open to the customer's view. The prepared food is passed to the service counter and then to the customer.

In food service, some facilities not directly connected with food preparation are also needed. There should be washrooms with hot and cold water for washing hands. Besides toilets, washrooms should be equipped with hot showers and a place for changing clothes. These facilities are more than just a convenience for the employees. They are necessary for sanitation and good grooming.

Employees also need a place for eating. The good health of the employees is protected by the provision of nutritious food. Employee morale is improved by an attractive place in which to eat.

Stations in the Kitchens

Each food service kitchen is divided into work centers, frequently called *stations*. Each station takes its name from the food prepared there or the cooking method used there. Thus, there are sauce, roast, broiler, and fish stations—plus others.

In kitchens based on the European cuisine, the stations may be the responsibility of the chef de partie. The chef de partie is responsible to the executive chef. There may be several assistant cooks and cooks' helpers under this chef. In Chapter 1, you studied the brigades found in kitchens serving different sizes and kinds of restaurants. The number of stations in any kitchen depends upon the following factors:

● *The menu.* A restaurant specializing in French cuisine would need many stations. In such a restau-

Unit 1: The World of the Professional Cooks

rant, the menu would feature a wide variety of food demanding much preparation.

- *The type of service.* A coffee shop featuring quick service would not need the work centers required for leisurely dining. The demands of the customers would be different.
- *The size of the kitchen.* The size of the kitchen limits the number of work centers. Since the number of work centers is limited, the menu might also be limited.

PLACEMENT OF THE STATIONS

The placement of the different stations in the production kitchen is determined by the food flow pattern. Look again at Figs. 2-2 to 2-6. The arrows show the general food flow from controller to stor-

age to pre-preparation area to kitchen to service. The work centers, or stations, are arranged along this line so that the cooks may work on the food. Usually, receiving stations and storage stations are at the beginning of the line. They are followed by meat and vegetable preparation stations. Cooking, holding, and service stations then follow in order.

Certain work centers are not part of the food flow pattern. Nevertheless, they are very necessary for food production.

- The *chef's office* is located where the food production can be easily supervised.
- The *potwashing area* is close to the equipment storage area.
- The *dishwashing area* is near the dining room and the storage areas for clean dishes and tableware.

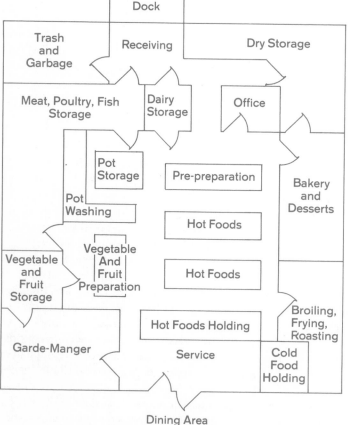

2-7. Possible work station locations in the production kitchen. Notice that the storage areas are close to the work stations.

• The *bakery* is frequently not part of the food flow line. Here, the work is usually completed before the peak hours of service. Baked goods and desserts may be served from the pantry.

Study Fig. 2-7. It shows the possible locations of work stations in the food production kitchen. This is only one plan of many possible ones. Notice that each food storage area is located close to the station using it most. For instance, the baking station has easy access to dry storage, where flour, sugar, and other dry ingredients needed in baking are stored.

The hot stations are close to the storage areas for meat, chickens, and fish. The hot stations use these products in food preparation.

The vegetable preparation station is in front of the entrance to the vegetable storage. The garde-manger is also close to this storage area. The chef garde-manger will need lettuce, celery, and the many other vegetables and fruits used in the preparation of salads. The station for the garde-manger is also close to the dining area, since the appetizers are served before the hot foods. Salads, also, are frequently served before the *entrée* (ahn-TRAY). The entrée is the main course on the menu.

FLOW OF WORK WITHIN THE STATIONS

Within the stations, the flow of work generally moves from the left to the right. For instance, the food will enter the station at the left. The finished food will be removed at the right.

The placement of equipment is all important in easing the flow of food. Arranging the equipment so that the work flows efficiently from production to service takes much study. As much as possible, small equipment used constantly should be within arm's reach of the worker. The larger pieces should be within a few steps.

Each station should be equipped with the equipment needed for the tasks. In addition, studies have shown that time and energy are saved if each station has its own water supply.

Many stations would benefit by such small appliances as can openers, scales, and small mixers. Even a station for cold food production needs a small cooking surface for food preparation.

The need for tables in the station is often overlooked. They should be close to the equipment so the worker will have a table closeby on which to set food. For instance, tables are needed next to such pieces of equipment as grinders, slicers, cooking tops, fryers, mixers, and scales.

In deciding the placement of each piece of equipment, the kitchen planner needs to know the following:

• How often each piece of equipment is used.
• The sequence in which pieces of equipment are used.
• The frequency of movement between pieces of equipment.
• How frequently the equipment will need to be moved.

Words to Remember

bain-marie	sauté pan
brasier	serrated
French (chef's) knife	skillet
China cap	stockpot
cleaver	tang
colander	whip
double boiler	

EQUIPMENT

Equipment needed for food production in the food service kitchen is generally divided into five groups.

• *Hand tools* are small items used in the hand, such as knives, mixing spoons, and forks.
• *Utensils* are containers for mixing, draining, cooking, or storage, such as bowls, saucepans, stockpots, and canisters.
• *Measuring tools* are tools and utensils needed for accurate measurement of ingredients, such as measuring spoons, cups, and scales.
• *Appliances* are easily portable and usually powered by electricity. Blenders, toasters, and small mixers are commonly used appliances.
• *Heavy-duty equipment* is equipment that is generally too heavy to be moved easily, such as ranges, refrigerators, ovens, and large mixers.

Tools

Tools are used for many kitchen jobs, especially for chopping, slicing, paring, sectioning, lifting, and turning. Some tools are designed for such jobs as sifting, rolling, scraping, and peeling.

BASIC TOOLS

Professional chefs have their own tools. They take great pride in them. If they leave one job for another, the tools go with them. They do not like anyone else to use them.

A young cook who aspires to become a chef requires a minimum of four basic knives. These are the:

- French knife.
- Paring knife.
- Slicer.
- Boner.

Others may be added from time to time as experience shows the need.

KNIVES

Of all the tools, professional cooks take the most pride in their knives. They are the most important tools in the kitchen. Some knives are made of high-carbon steel. This type of steel is very hard and durable. It may be sharpened to a fine edge. However, it stains easily and becomes unsightly if it is not scoured after use. For this reason, modern knives are usually made of stainless steel. Stainless steel does not discolor or rust, the blade stays sharp, and the knife lasts a long time.

If you look at the sharp edge of the blade on a fine knife through a microscope, you will see that it resembles a saw. For this reason, knives are used with a sawing motion. In some knives, the sawlike edge can be easily seen. These knives are said to be *serrated*.

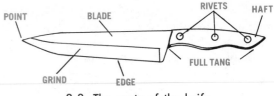

2-8. The parts of the knife.

The parts of the knife are the blade, including the tang, and the haft. Fig. 2-8. The *tang* is the metal extension of the blade that fits into the haft. *Haft* is another word for handle. The tang of the knife should run the entire length of the knife. It should be firmly riveted to the haft. The hafts of the finest knives used to be made from rosewood. Recently, boards of health in various communities have disapproved of wooden hafts. Wood may harbor bacteria. Plastic handles are preferred.

All knives may be classified into four groups.

- *French, or chef's, knives* are frequently used pieces of equipment. They are used constantly for slicing, chopping, mincing, and dicing. They are also used for splitting and boning poultry, lobsters, and fish. Fig. 2-9.

- *Butcher and boning knives* are used for cutting and boning meat. Butcher knives are usually slightly curved. Fig. 2-10. They are used for sectioning meats or cutting steaks. Sometimes a special steak knife is used for this job. Boning knives are used to remove meat from the bone. Fig. 2-11.

- *Slicers,* also called *utility knives,* usually have a distinct serrated or fluted edge. They are used for carving meat, slicing bread, among other jobs. They may have a pointed or rounded blade. Fig. 2-12.

- *Knives with flexible blades* do not have a sharp blade, and the tip is rounded. The blade is very flexible. Fig. 2-13. Spatulas are included in this cate-

Russell Harrington Cutlery, Inc.
2-9. The French, or chef's, knife.

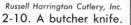

Russell Harrington Cutlery, Inc.
2-10. A butcher knife.

Russell Harrington Cutlery, Inc.
2-11. A boning knife.

Russell Harrington Cutlery, Inc.
2-12. A slicer.

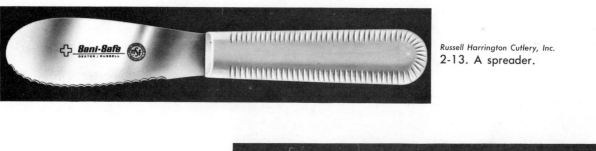

Russell Harrington Cutlery, Inc.
2-13. A spreader.

Russell Harrington Cutlery, Inc.
2-14. A paring knife.

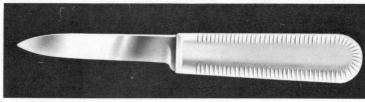

gory. Spatulas are used to remove food from flat pans. They are also used for spreading soft foods such as butter, salad dressings, and frostings.

• *Paring knives* have small blades, 6.5–9 cm [2½–3½ in] in length. The tip may be pointed or curved. Some may have a clip or spear point. Paring knives are used to prepare fruits and vegetables. Fig. 2-14.

• *Cleavers* have a very heavy, thick blade. They are useful for opening lobsters, splitting heavy

33

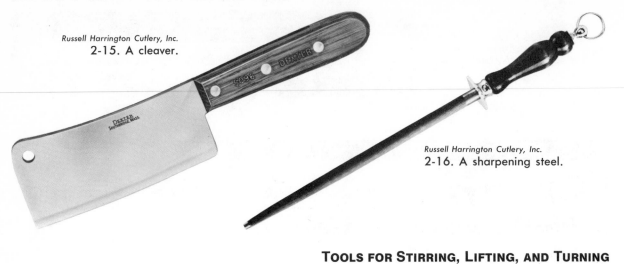

Russell Harrington Cutlery, Inc.
2-15. A cleaver.

Russell Harrington Cutlery, Inc.
2-16. A sharpening steel.

bones and joints, and cutting chickens into serving portions. Fig. 2-15.

- *Sharpening steels* may be flat, cylindrical, or oval. The most useful have a steel shaft. They are used to sharpen knives. Fig. 2-16.

Care of Knives

Store knives in slotted wood or rubber racks. The racks should be mounted on the wall in some easily accessible place. Never store knives in drawers. The blades will rub against each other and become dull.

CAUTION

Remember these safety tips:
- *Use the correct knife for the job.*
- *If you drop a knife, let it fall.*
- *Never put a knife where it cannot be seen. A knife in the dishwater or hidden under a pile of chopped vegetables can cause serious cuts.*
- *Always cut away from the body.*
- *Never cut vegetables in the palm of the hand.*
- *A dull knife causes accidents by slipping. Always keep knives sharp.*
- *Use knives only as intended, not to pry or open cans.*

TOOLS FOR STIRRING, LIFTING, AND TURNING

- *Turners* have a flexible blade. The blades may be slotted. Turners are sometimes called *offset spatulas*. They are used to slip under foods such as potatoes, pancakes and hamburgers and flip them over. Fig. 2-17.
- *Spoons* are used for mixing, stirring, and serving. They may be solid, slotted, or pierced. Fig. 2-18.
- *Wooden spatulas* are made of beech, cherry, or maple. Many chefs prefer a wooden spatula to a spoon for stirring, mixing, creaming, tossing, and folding. Fig. 2-19.
- *Ladles* come in assorted sizes holding from 58 g [2 oz] to 227 g [8 oz]. They are used to control portions when serving soups, sauces, dressings, or other liquids. Fig. 2-20.
- *Skimmers* are used to skim soups and remove unwanted pieces of food from liquids. They are always slotted to permit the liquid to flow back into the pan. Fig. 2-21.

Russell Harrington Cutlery, Inc.
2-17. A turner.

A

B

EKCO

2-18. Spoons. (A) A solid spoon. (B) A slotted spoon.

2-19. A wooden spatula.

EKCO
2-20. A ladle.

2-21. A skimmer.

Russell Harrington Cutlery, Inc.
2-22. A cook's fork.

Sparta Brush Company
2-23. A nylon paddle scraper.

EKCO
2-24. Tongs.

Sparta Brush Company
2-25. A short-handled spatula scraper.

• *Cook's forks* are two-tined forks, with the tines widely spaced. They are used to turn heavy pieces of meat. Fig. 2-22.

• *Paddles* are made of wood or metal with a very long handle. These long paddles are used frequently to stir food in deep pots and steam kettles. Fig. 2-23.

• *Tongs* are made of flexible, stainless steel with a sawtooth grip on the ends. They are used for re-moving hot foods such as corn-on-the-cob from the steamer or boiling water. They are also used to pick up and serve food without touching it with the hands. Fig. 2-24.

SCRAPERS

• *Plastic scrapers* are made of flexible, clear plastic. They are used to scrape down the bowl so all the ingredients are well mixed. They are also used to scrape the last bit of batter from the bowl. Fig. 2-25.

• *Scrapers,* or *dough cutters,* are made with a wide metal blade fastened in a wooden handle.

Unit 1: The World of the Professional Cooks

They are used for cutting dough into segments and for scraping worktables and meat blocks. Fig. 2-26.

WHIPS

• *French whips* are made of heavy piano wire firmly wound and fastened into a metal handle. They are used for heavy whipping jobs such as sauces and gravies. Fig. 2-27.

• *Wire whips* are made of lightweight piano wire fastened into a metal handle. They are used for light whipping jobs such as egg whites and cream. Fig. 2-28.

BRUSHES

Many kinds of brushes are used in food service.

• *Pot brushes* have metal bristles for cleaning food from pots and pans. Fig. 2-29.

• *Vegetable brushes* have stiff bristles for cleaning vegetables. Fig. 2-30.

• *Pastry brushes* have soft bristles for spreading thin mixtures such as melted butter or egg mixed with water. Fig. 2-31.

• *Bench brushes* have long soft bristles for brushing excess flour from the bench. Fig. 2-32.

• *Oven brushes* have soft bristles set in a very long handle for removing crumbs from oven floor. A scraper may be attached on the opposite side of the brush. Fig. 2-33.

Sparta Brush Company
2-27. A French whip.

EKCO
2-28. A wire whip.

Sparta Brush Company
2-29. A pot brush.

EKCO
2-30. A vegetable brush.

Sparta #751

Sparta Brush Company
2-31. A pastry brush.

2-26. A scraper, or dough cutter.

Sparta Brush Company
2-32. A bench brush.

Sparta Brush Company
2-33. Oven brush and scraper.

- *Kettle brushes* have stiff bristles in a very long handle for cleaning deep kettles. Fig. 2-34.
- *Grease brushes* have special bristles that attract grease. They are used for removing grease from soups, stocks, and sauces. Fig. 2-35.

TOOLS FOR OTHER PURPOSES

- *Tenderizers* are wooden or aluminum mallets with a toothed surface. They are used to break down and tenderize the tough fibers of meat. Fig. 2-36.
- *Melon ball cutters* (also called *Parisienne cutters*) are small metal scoops at each end of a plastic or wood handle. They are used for cutting small balls of soft fruits. They are also used to cut rounds of potatoes, cheese, butter, hard sauce, and vegetables. Fig. 2-37.
- *Peelers* have a double blade on a swivel attached to a metal handle. They are used to peel fruits and vegetables and to scrape carrots. Fig. 2-38.

2-36. An aluminum meat tenderizer.

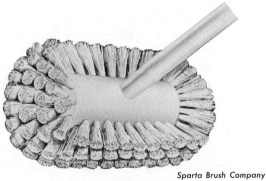

Sparta Brush Company
2-34. A kettle brush.

2-37. A melon ball cutter.

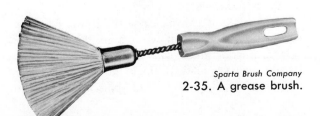

Sparta Brush Company
2-35. A grease brush.

2-38. A swivel peeler.

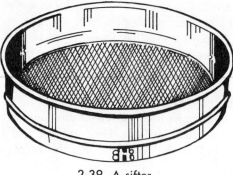

2-39. A sifter.

EKCO
2-40. A box-shaped grater.

EKCO
2-41. An egg slicer.

• *Sifters* are used to remove lumps, mix in air, and spread evenly such powdery ingredients as flour and powdered sugar. Fig. 2-39.

• *Graters* may be box-shaped or flat. The box grater has different shapes and sizes of slots or grids on each side. It is used for grating fruits, vegetables, and other ingredients. Fig. 2-40.

• *Egg slicers* are made of metal wires set in a frame. They are used for slicing hard-cooked eggs into round, even slices for garnishes. Fig. 2-41.

• *Skewers* are metal pins of different lengths. They are used to hold foods such as meats together while slicing. They are also used to conduct heat quickly into the inside of foods such as potatoes. Fig. 2-42.

• *Pastry bags* may be made of nylon, canvas, or plastic. Fig. 2-43. A wide variety of tubes are used to make shaped pastries, and decorations such as stars, rosettes, and ribbons. Fig. 2-44.

Utensils

MIXING UTENSILS

Utensils found in a food service kitchen are generally made of stainless steel or heavy plastic. Stainless steel is used in food preparation because it is durable, holds heat well, and is easy to clean. Bowls may be assorted sizes and shapes in stainless steel. Fig. 2-45.

DRAINING AND STRAINING UTENSILS

• *Colanders* are perforated, stainless-steel bowls. They are on a base to hold them level. They have handles on the sides for lifting. They are used for rinsing fruits and vegetables and for draining pastas such as spaghetti. Fig. 2-46.

• *China caps* are so called because they resemble the caps worn at one time by Chinese cooks. The cone-shaped bowl is made of heavy-duty, stainless-steel mesh. Fig. 2-47. It has a long handle and a hook so it can hang on the side of a pot. It also has a wooden mallet shaped to fit the bowl. Fig. 2-48. This mallet is used for forcing food through the mesh.

• *Strainers* come in assorted sizes and shapes. Meshes may be fine or coarse. Fig. 2-49.

COOKING UTENSILS

Most cooking utensils are called pots or pans. Pans are small and shallow. Pots are big and deep.

• *Frying, or sauté, pans* are also called *skillets*. Usually they are made of thick, heavy iron because iron heats evenly with no hot spots and holds the

EKCO

2-42. Skewers.

Wear-Ever

2-46. A colander.

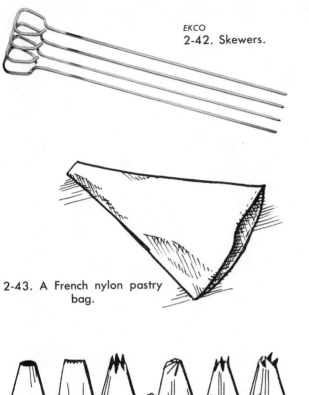

2-43. A French nylon pastry bag.

Wear-Ever

2-47. A china cap.

2-44. Tubes for pastry bags.

Wear-Ever

2-48. A wooden mallet for a china cap.

Polar Wear Company

2-45. A mixing bowl.

EKCO

2-49. A strainer.

Wear-Ever

2-50. Utensils commonly used in food service. Left to right on wall: frying pans and a large colander. Left to right, last row: heavy-duty brasier, stockpot, double boiler, stockpot, and colander. First row: Sauté pan, china cap, scoops, sauté pans, and saucepans.

heat for a long time. Frying, or sauté, pans come in assorted sizes, but they are always round. Most sauté pans have straight sides. Fig. 2-50.

- *Saucepans* vary widely in size. They are made of stainless steel with straight sides and riveted, long handles. Fig. 2-50.

- *Stockpots* have deep, straight sides and are made of heavy-gauge stainless steel. Handles are provided on both sides of the pot for lifting with both hands. Like saucepans, stockpots come in many sizes. Fig. 2-50.

- *Bain-maries* (BANE-MARIES) are deep pots for holding hot water into which other pots holding food may be placed. Often a sink is filled with boiling water. Pots filled with food are placed in the sink to keep the food hot without further cooking.

Bain-maries are also used for storage because they have close-fitting lids. Fig. 2-51.

- *Double boilers* are sometimes used instead of the bain-marie. A double boiler consists of two saucepans that fit together. One may be inserted into the other. The bottom pan holds the boiling water. The top one holds the food. Fig. 2-52.

- *Brasiers* are heavy pots with loop handles and close-fitting covers. Brasiers are used for cooking certain types of meats. Fig. 2-50.

- *Bake pans* are rectangular pans with straight sides and loop handles. They are used for many foods such as macaroni and cheese, baked apples, and meat loaf. They may be made of aluminum or stainless steel. They are similar in appearance to roasting pans.

- *Roasting pans* are rectangular pans with high sides. They are made of heavy-gauge stainless steel or aluminum. They are used for roasting meats. Usually, trivets or roasting racks are placed on the bottom to hold the meat out of the juices. Most roasters have covers. Fig. 2-53.

STORAGE UTENSILS

Heavy plastic is used more and more for storage utensils. Plastic covers snap on tightly, protecting the food from drying out. They also protect the food from infestation by ants, bugs, and vermin. The utensils may be deep or shallow, round, square, or oblong. They vary in size, holding from 1.9 L [2 qt] to 75.7 L [20 gal]. Fig. 2-54.

Measuring Tools

Measuring tools are used to measure ingredient amounts accurately. Successful food preparation depends in great part on having the correct amount of each ingredient in the recipe. Ingredient amounts

Polar Wear Company

2-52. A double-boiler.

Polar Wear Company

2-53. A roasting pan.

Polar Wear Company

2-51. A bain-marie.

Rubbermaid

2-54. Heavy plastic storage containers.

are measured by weight or by volume. Usually, solid ingredients are weighed, except for small amounts. Liquids may be weighed or measured by volume.

Temperature, also, must be carefully measured. Temperature may be increased, as in cooking, or reduced, as in refrigeration. Even if the correct amounts of food are carefully mixed, the final product can be ruined by the wrong application of heat. For example, a beef stew made with burned meat is no good, even if the ingredients have been carefully measured.

Words to Remember

agitators	paddles
baker's scale	portion scale
hooks	thermostat
metric system	volume

SYSTEMS OF MEASUREMENT

Until recently, all measurements in the United States were given in the *English*, or *customary*, sys-

tem. In this system, volume is measured by the cup (C), pint (pt), quart (qt), or gallon (gal). Temperature is measured by degrees on the Fahrenheit scale. Water freezes at 32° F. and boils at 212° F.

The English, or customary, system has been difficult to use because it is hard to remember. For instance, it is hard to remember that eight ounces equal one cup. Table 2-1 lists some of the equivalents in the customary system.

Another measuring system, the *metric* system, has been in use for nearly two hundred years. Because it is consistent and easy to remember, it has been adopted by scientists and manufacturers worldwide. The United States is now changing from the customary to the metric system. In this book, wherever measurements are given, the metric is given first, followed by the customary system in brackets, [ ].

Metric is easy to use because metric quantities are measured in multiples of 10, 100, and 1 000. (In the metric system, commas are not used in figures of four digits or more. A space is left instead.) In measuring mass (weight), the unit of measurement is the *gram* (g). A *kilogram* (kg) is 1 000 grams. In measuring volume, the unit of measurement is the *litre* (L).

Table 2-1. Table of Equivalents (Standard American Measures)

3 teaspoons	=	1 tablespoon	=	$\frac{1}{2}$ fluid ounce
2 tablespoons	=	1 jigger (small)	=	1 fluid ounce
1 jigger (large)	=	3 tablespoons	=	$1\frac{1}{2}$ fluid ounces
4 tablespoons	=	$\frac{1}{4}$ cup	=	2 fluid ounces
$5\frac{1}{3}$ tablespoons	=	$\frac{1}{3}$ cup	=	2.8 fluid ounces
8 tablespoons	=	$\frac{1}{2}$ cup	=	4 fluid ounces
11 tablespoons	=	$\frac{2}{3}$ cup	=	5.4 fluid ounces
16 tablespoons	=	1 cup	=	8 fluid ounces
24 tablespoons	=	$1\frac{1}{2}$ cups	=	12 fluid ounces
8 ounces (dry)	=	$\frac{1}{2}$ pound		
16 ounces (dry)	=	1 pound		
2 cups	=	1 pint	=	16 fluid ounces
2 pints (4 cups)	=	1 quart	=	32 fluid ounces
1 fifth	=	$\frac{1}{5}$ gallon	=	25 fluid ounces
8 cups	=	$\frac{1}{2}$ gallon	=	64 fluid ounces
4 quarts (16 cups)	=	1 gallon	=	128 fluid ounces
8 quarts (dry)	=	1 peck	=	32 cups
4 pecks (dry)	=	1 bushel		

	When you know:	You can find:	If you multiply by:
Length	inches	millimetres	25
	feet	centimeters	30
	yards	metres	0.9
	millimetres	inches	0.04
	centimetres	inches	0.4
	metres	yards	1.1
Mass	ounces	grams	28
	pounds	kilograms	0.45
	grams	ounces	0.035
	kilograms	pounds	2.2
Liquid Volume	ounces	millilitres	30
	pints	litres	0.47
	quarts	litres	0.95
	gallons	litres	3.8
	millilitres	ounces	0.034
	litres	pints	2.1
	litres	quarts	1.06
	litres	gallons	0.26
Temperature	degrees Fahrenheit	degrees Celsius	$\frac{5}{9}$ (after subtracting 32)
	degrees Celsius	degrees Fahrenheit	$\frac{9}{5}$ (then add 32)

Table 2-2. Comparing the Most Common Measuring Units (Approximate Conversions from Customary to Metric and Vice Versa)

One litre equals 1 000 *millilitres* (mL). Temperature is measured by degrees on the *Celsius* scale. Water freezes at 0°C and boils at 100°C. Table 2-2 lists some of the metric units used in food service, along with their customary equivalents.

MEASURING WEIGHT

An ingredient quantity is more accurately measured by weight than by volume. Thus, weight is most frequently used as a measurement in food service. Weight may be given in the metric system or the customary one—that is, in grams and kilograms, or ounces and pounds.

Several different types of scales are used in food service.

• A *heavy-duty scale* is used to check the weight of foods as they are received by the food service place. Examples of the types of food that would be weighed are sacks of potatoes, crates of fruits and vegetables, and cuts of meat.

• The *baker's scale* is described in detail on page 319. Although it is known as the "baker's scale," it is used in many other work stations.

• The *portion scale* is used to weigh servings accurately in grams or ounces. It is used especially in hospitals and other institutions where the servings to individuals must be carefully controlled. In a portion scale, the desired weight for the serving is set on the beam. The indicator shows whether the portion is over or under the desired weight. Fig. 2-55.

MEASURING VOLUME

Volume means the amount of space taken by a quantity of material. Volume is measured by litres in the metric system and by cups, pints, quarts, and

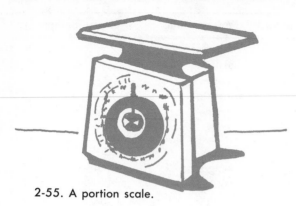

2-55. A portion scale.

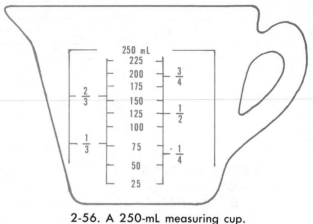

2-56. A 250-mL measuring cup.

gallons in the customary system. In the home, ingredients are usually measured by volume. In food service, volume measurement is used for measuring liquids. Volume measurement is sometimes used in measuring dry ingredients when absolute accuracy is not important.

• *Measuring spoons* are used to measure amounts of such dry ingredients as salt, spices, and baking powder. Metric measuring spoons are gradu-

ated in sizes of 1 mL, 2 mL, 5 mL, 15 mL, and 25 mL. Customary measuring spoon sizes are one-fourth teaspoon, one-half teaspoon, one teaspoon, and one tablespoon.

• *Measuring cups* are made of aluminum, stainless steel, heavy plastic, or glass. They are used especially for measuring liquids. Figure 2-56 shows the divisions on the 250 mL metric measuring cup. The customary measuring containers are usually gradu-

2-57. An assortment of scoops.
Hamilton Beach

Scoop Number	Weight		Measure	
	Metric	Customary	Metric	Customary
8	142 g	5 oz	125 mL	$\frac{1}{2}$ c
10	113 g	4 oz	100 mL	$\frac{2}{5}$ c
12	85 g	3 oz	83 mL	$\frac{1}{3}$ c
16	57 g	2 oz	62 mL	$\frac{1}{4}$ c
20	47 g	$1\frac{2}{3}$ oz	48 mL	$3\frac{1}{5}$ T
24	43 g	$1\frac{1}{2}$ oz	40 mL	$2\frac{2}{3}$ T
30	35 g	$1\frac{1}{4}$ oz	33 mL	$2\frac{1}{5}$ T

Table 2-3. Scoop Sizes, Weights, and Measures

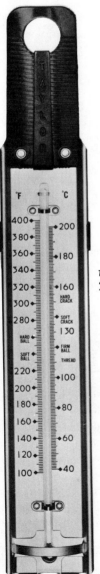

Taylor Instrument

2-58. A confectionary thermometer.

ated for one-fourth, one-third, one-half, two-thirds, three-fourths, and whole measurements.

● *Scoops* are metal half-ball cups with a movable strip on the inside of the cup. This strip scrapes out the food. It is operated by a clip on the side of the handle. Fig. 2-57. Scoops are used to fill muffin cups or drop cookie dough on baking sheets. They also measure serving portions. Scoops are numbered to indicate size. The larger the number, the smaller the amount. Table 2-3 gives scoop sizes.

MEASURING TEMPERATURE

Thermometers measure temperature. This is a very important function. For instance, the amount of heat in the oven governs the baking of bread or the roasting of meat.

In deep fat frying, different temperatures are used for different foods. If the fat is too hot, the food will brown before it is cooked through. If it is too cool, the food will become soggy with fat before it browns.

In making frostings and candy, the correct temperature is critical. Too high a temperature will cause the sugar syrup to harden before the frosting or candy can be made. If the temperature is not high enough, the frosting or candy will not harden at all. Fig. 2-58.

Refrigerators must be kept within a certain temperature range for proper storage of food. If the refrigerator is too warm, bacteria and molds will grow and the food may spoil. If it is too cold, the food may dry out and become icy.

45

Unit 1: The World of the Professional Cooks

As you study the different kinds of food preparation, you will use temperature control constantly.

Ovens, refrigerators, freezers, and fryers are equipped with *thermostats*. A thermostat is a device for regulating the temperature. Thermostats automatically measure temperature and maintain it at a certain level.

Thermometers are of two types. The *dial* type is used for recording the temperature of air. Fig. 2-59. The *probe* type is used to measure the internal temperature of an ingredient. Fig. 2-60. Some ovens have built-in probes for use in roasting meats.

Appliances

A few small appliances are frequently used in the food service kitchens. Some of these are listed below.

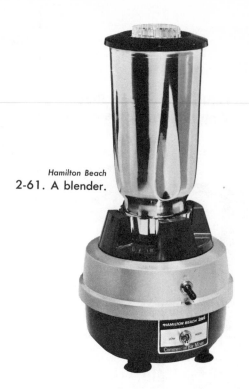

Hamilton Beach
2-61. A blender.

Taylor Instrument
2-59. An oven thermometer.

Taylor Instrument
2-60. A probe-type meat thermometer.

• *Blenders* are used to blend, mix, chop, grate, stir, crumb, shred, liquefy, and puree. Commercial blenders are made of stainless steel and have a 3.8 L [1 gal] capacity. Fig. 2-61.

• *Toasters* are used to toast bread. The toasters used in food service may toast from two to sixteen slices of bread at one time. Fig. 2-62.

• *Waffle irons* are made for one purpose—to cook waffles. The waffle is pressed and cooked between the top and bottom plates. The design in the plates is pressed into the surface of the waffle. Waffle irons may have single or double grids.

• *Coffee makers* are used to make fresh coffee and keep it hot. Although large coffee urns are still used, most food service places are now making coffee more often in smaller amounts. The most popular of these coffee makers filters the hot water through the coffee directly into the glass serving containers. Fig. 2-63.

• *Juice servers* continuously mix juice in a glass or plastic dispenser. Juice servers make an attractive

Wells Manufacturing

2-62. A toaster.

• *Food preparation equipment* such as mixers, cutters, choppers, and slicers.

• *Food cooking equipment* such as ranges, grills, broilers, steamers, fryers, and ovens.

• *Food warmers* for holding food in preparation for serving.

• *Refrigerators* and *freezers*.

FOOD PREPARATION EQUIPMENT

Three types of mixers are used in food service: the vertical, or upright mixer, the horizontal mixer, and the vertical cutter-mixer.

• *Vertical, or upright, mixers* come in different sizes to match the particular job. Size is determined by the capacity of the bowl. The smallest vertical mixer is 4.7 L [5 qt] and fits on the counter. The

Bunn-O-Matic

2-63. An automatic coffee brewer.

display on the counter and promote the sale of juices.

• *Small mixers* are used to mix small amounts of food. Some work stations may use a hand mixer. Others may need a small, stationary mixer.

• *Hot plates* are sometimes needed in a work station that is not equipped with a range.

Heavy-Duty Equipment

To any newcomer in food service, the huge, stainless-steel equipment is the most impressive sight. Heavy-duty equipment is considered stationary. Many pieces, however, have wheels to make them movable. This makes cleaning easier.

Heavy-duty equipment may be divided into categories according to the following uses:

Hobart

2-64. A vertical mixer.

Hobart

2-65. A horizontal mixer.

largest one is 37.8 L [40 qt] and stands on the floor. The large, stationary mixer has adapter rings so bowls of different sizes can be used with the same mixer. Fig. 2-64.

On small vertical mixers, the bowl is lifted by a crank to fit under the beater. On large, stationary models, this lifting is done by an electric motor.

Vertical mixers have many different types of beaters, or *agitators*. *Whips* are used for whipping cream, eggs, and other similar preparations. Flat beaters, or *paddles*, are used for most mixing jobs, such as mixing dough and mashing potatoes. *Hooks* are used for kneading dough.

Vertical mixers also have attachments that fasten on the front and are motor-driven. These attachments are used for grinding, chopping, slicing, shredding, and dicing.

- *Horizontal mixers* are used in commercial bakeries. Bakers in food service kitchens usually use a vertical mixer. A horizontal mixer is shaped like a

cylinder with a sliding door on the side. It makes it easy to add ingredients during the mixing. It is safer for the worker. Fig. 2-65.

- *Vertical cutter-mixers* are designed to cut and mix at the same time at a very high speed. The agitators are sharp blades that move very fast. This mixer is used to chop vegetables such as lettuce and cabbage. It is used to cut meat into small pieces. It is used to make pie dough and cake batter.

- *Food choppers* are used to chop or grind such products as meat, nuts, vegetables, bread crumbs, and similar foods. The particle size of the food can be varied by using plates with holes of different sizes. The food is pushed through the hopper against the blades, and through the holes using a wooden mallet. Food choppers are operated by hand or by electricity. Fig. 2-66.

- *Slicers* are used to slice meat, cheese, and vegetables. A slicer has a very sharp, rotating blade. The thickness of the slice can be adjusted as desired.

A slicer should have a guard to protect the hands of the user. It has a holder to press the food against the rapidly rotating blade. It has a receiving tray to hold the slices. Fig. 2-67.

> **CAUTION**
>
> *Mixers, choppers, and slicers can be very dangerous. Never scrape down the mixer bowl while the mixer is operating. Never use the slicer without the guard in place.*

Words to Remember

broiler	pass-through
convection oven	pumice brick
griddle	range
grill	stack oven
hearth oven	steamer
infrared lamp	steam table
magnetron	tilt-brasier
microwave oven	trunnion

COOKING EQUIPMENT

Food is cooked because cooking changes the taste, color, and texture of food. Cooking makes food taste better, easier to chew, and more attractive to serve. Cooking softens vegetables and fruits, but makes meat more firm.

In food service, gas, electricity, and occasionally charcoal are the usual sources of heat. Heat enters the food through the following mediums:

- Metal, such as pans.
- Moisture, such as water or steam.
- Hot fat.
- Heated air.
- Microwaves.

Each method of cooking requires its own equipment.

- *Ranges* usually are made of stainless steel with an oven under the top. A range may have four, six, or more burners on top. Some ranges have a solid plate on the top, instead of open burners. Fig. 2-68.

Ranges are usually equipped with thermostats. These thermostats control the temperature not only of the oven but also of the top burners.

The range was formerly the most frequently used piece of equipment in food service. Now steamers, fryers, brasiers, and convection ovens have largely taken over many of the jobs. The top of the range is used mostly for browning meats, cooking food in a

Hobart

2-66. A food chopper.

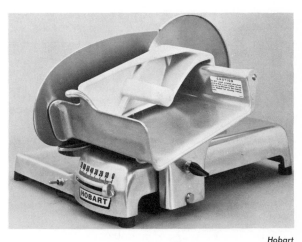

Hobart

2-67. A food slicer.

49

Vulcan-Hart
2-68. A grill, deep-fat fryer, and range.

small amount of fat, boiling, or cooking in a double boiler.

● *Grills,* or *griddles,* are words used interchangeably for the same piece of equipment. The equipment is usually called a grill if it is used for meat and a griddle if it is used for pancakes. A griddle, or grill, is a flat piece of stainless steel with burners under it to create even heat. The heat may be controlled by a thermostat. Fast foods such as hamburgers, pancakes, and French toast, are cooked on the griddle, or grill. Fig. 2-68.

Griddles are not washed, since this would destroy the finish and cause foods to stick. Instead, griddles are wiped clean with a grease mop and finished with a soft cloth. If some food has stuck, it is cleaned off with a *pumice brick* (also called a *pumice stone*). Pumice is a soft, volcanic rock. Since it cleans without scratching, it is frequently used for cleaning grills.

Griddles, or grills, should have a raised back, called splash backs, to keep the grease from spatter-

Vulcan-Hart
2-69. An open broiler.

50

ing on the wall. They should also have grease troughs and rounded corners for easy cleaning.

• *Broilers* apply heat directly to the food from underneath, from the top, or from both sides at the same time. Fig. 2-69. The source of heat may be electricity, gas, charcoal, or heated volcanic rock. In broiling, provision must be made for the juices and fat to drain away as the meat cooks.

Charcoal has long been considered the best source of heat for broiling. It gives the typical charcoal flavor. Some specialty houses still use charcoal, but it is expensive and smoky. The use of lighter fluid to set fire to the charcoal often gives an undesirable smell.

Heated volcanic rock is frequently used now instead of charcoal. Cleaner, cheaper, and safer than charcoal, it still gives the charcoal flavor. The rocks are heated by gas or electricity until they are white hot. The gas or electricity is then turned low. As the fat drips from the meat and hits the hot rocks, it flames. This produces the charcoal flavor.

Meat is also broiled in the broiler oven, using a broiler pan. This pan has grids in it to hold the meat out of the drippings. Fig. 2-70.

┌─── CAUTION ───────────────┐
│   │
│   *The drippings may catch fire. Have a con-* │
│   *tainer of salt or soda on hand. Sprinkle either* │
│   *of them on an open fire to extinguish it.* │
│   │
└────────────────────────────┘

• *Infrared lamps* are also used to broil meat. The meat passes through a battery of these lamps. The lamps broil the meat on both sides at the same time. This type of broiler is extremely fast and efficient. However, it does not give the charcoal flavor.

• *Steamers* use steam to cook food. Steam is used in food service because it cooks food quickly and economically. It also preserves the natural flavor and color. Cooking with steam preserves nutrients such as vitamins and minerals. Steam has other advantages, too. It cannot boil over like water. The food cannot stick or burn. Steam is used primarily for cooking vegetables. Fig. 2-71.

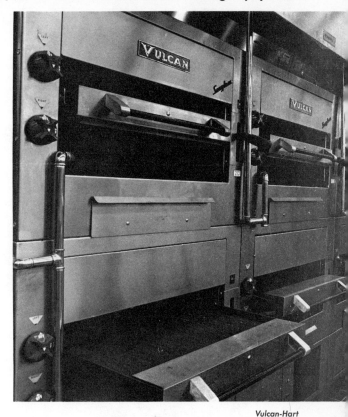

Vulcan-Hart

2-70. A closed broiler.

Steamers have perforated pans or baskets made of stainless steel mesh. This type of pan allows the steam to circulate freely around the food.

Steam may be free or under pressure. Free steam has about the same temperature as boiling water—100°C [212° F.]. Free steam is used occasionally for cooking vegetables, but the newest concept is for cooking meats. A perforated pan fits into another piece of equipment, called a *brazier* (or *brasier*). The steam circulates around the meat, slowly cooking it. Meat cooked in this way is juicy and tender.

Steam under pressure can develop much higher temperatures than boiling water. When steam is generated in a closed container, it builds up pressure. The pressure is measured in force per unit. In the metric system, it is measured in kilopascals

2-71. A pressure steamer.

Hobart

cycles. For instance, they can be set to defrost the food and then cook it for the correct length of time automatically.

The convection steamer is rather new, also. *Convection* means that the steam is driven by a fan. Thus, it circulates much faster than in other types of steamers. Because of the rapid circulation, the food cooks faster.

• *Steam-jacketed kettles* are used for cooking soups, stews, stocks, and other foods formerly cooked on top of the range. The steam enters the jacket surrounding the kettle. It circulates at 34–55 kPa [5–8 psi]. Fig. 2-72.

Some kettles are very large, holding as much as 568 L [150 gal]. Others are as small as 49.2 L [13 gal]. They usually have a gear-driven mechanism for tilting the kettle and pouring the food. Large kettles are used only where very large amounts of food are prepared. Because of their size and depth, they are cumbersome to use.

Smaller kettles may be mounted on a counter. These smaller kettles are sometimes called *trunnions* because they are mounted between two pivots

[kPa]. In the customary system, it is measured in pounds per square inch [psi]. As the pressure increases, the temperature also increases. See Table 2-4. Naturally, foods cook much faster at the higher temperatures.

Low-pressure steam, 34–69 kPa [5–10 psi] is used for cooking meats because meats tend to fall apart at higher temperatures.

High-pressure steam, 69–103 kPa [10–15 psi] is used especially for vegetables. Short cooking at high temperatures produces naturally colorful vegetables.

Pressure steamers, low or high, are stacked compartments, each compartment being about 203 mm [8 in] high. The doors are equipped with special gaskets and seals to keep the steam inside. The doors are tightly closed by clamps or wheels.

The newest pressure steamers are completely automated. They have preset timers with foolproof

Table 2-4. Steam Pressures and Temperatures

Pressure		Temperature	
kPa	psi	°C	°F.
0	0	100	212
13	2	103	218
27	4	106	224
41	6	110	230
55	8	113	235
68	10	115	240
103	15	121	250
137	20	126	259
172	25	130	267
206	30	134	274
275	40	142	287
344	50	148	298

Vulcan-Hart

2-72. Large steam-jacketed kettles.

(trunnions). These allow the kettle to be tilted for emptying. The smaller kettles are commonly used in food service because they are easy to handle.

Steam-jacketed kettles may have a draw-off valve on the lower front side for removing the liquid.

● *Fryers* are used for frying in deep fat. Fryers may be floor mounted or portable. Portable fryers are usually placed on a counter. Both types have wire baskets that can be lowered into the hot fat or oil. When the food is done, the basket is lifted out and rested on the lip of the fryer for a few seconds. This allows the fat to drain out. In very large fryers, the lowering and lifting may be done mechanically. Fig. 2-73.

Fryers are heated either with gas or electricity. The heat is controlled by a thermostat. Most fryers have automatic timers, also. A valve at the bottom of the fryer permits fat to be drained so the fryer can be cleaned.

Vulcan-Hart

2-73. Deep-fat fryers.

Vulcan-Hart
2-74. Convection ovens.

> ## CAUTION
>
> *Everyone knows that a range top or the inside of an oven is hot. However, everyone does not realize that steam is really super-hot water. Very serious burns result from contact with steam. Intelligence and extreme care are needed to operate steam equipment. Read and follow the manufacturer's directions exactly.*

• *Ovens* usually cook food by the circulation of heated air, a process called *baking* or *roasting*. By any name, the process is really the same. Therefore, the terms are interchangeable. For example, ham cooked in the oven is called baked ham, but oven-cooked beef is called roast beef. Chicken is sometimes called baked and sometimes roasted. Fish is always baked.

Heat is usually provided by electricity or gas. Infrared rays and microwaves are also used.

There are several different kinds of ovens: regular, stack, revolving or carousel, convection, hearth, and microwave.

Regular ovens located under the range top may be sufficient for a small restaurant. Fig. 2-67. Usually these ovens have two shelves, each holding a baking pan 46 × 65 cm [18 × 26 in]. For roasting a turkey or a tall beef roast, only one shelf is used.

Stack ovens are a series of baking shelves, one on top of the other, each with its own door. The temperature of each shelf is controlled by its own ther-

mostat. In a bakery, the shelves are about 22 cm [8 in] high. In the hot stations, the shelves are 30 cm [12 in] high to hold large pieces of meat.

Revolving, or *carousel, ovens* are described in Chapter 16 ("Ingredients and Equipment in the Bakery"), since they are used mostly in bakeries.

Convection ovens are used constantly in food service. They are fast, efficient, and do not dry out the food. Fig. 2-74.

The heat, provided by gas or electricity, is driven by a fan. The forced air speeds the cooking of all foods. Convection ovens also preheat faster. For instance, a regular oven takes about twenty minutes to preheat to a set temperature. A convection oven will preheat in five minutes.

Convection ovens come in many different sizes. The shelves may be placed close together because the forced circulation of air provides an even heat.

Because the shelves are close together, many more baking pans may be held in the same size area than in a regular oven. For instance, the regular oven holds two baking pans. The same size convection oven can hold approximately ten baking pans.

The fast circulation of heat also makes convection ovens useful for defrosting and heating frozen foods, especially ready-to-eat meals. Frozen prepared meals can be defrosted and uniformly heated to 260°C [500° F.] in twenty to thirty minutes.

Large convection ovens have big double doors for easy loading. They have windows and interior lights to allow full view of every shelf during operation.

Hearth ovens, or *brick-lined ovens,* are used in bakeries. They are described in Chapter 16.

Microwave ovens are in general use in most food service operations. Fig. 2-75. They are used mostly for defrosting and cooking frozen foods, or warming precooked foods for service. For instance, beef may be roasted to the very rare stage in a regular oven. As beef is ordered by the customer, it is sliced and heated in the microwave oven. Used correctly, microwave ovens maintain freshly prepared flavor and appearance.

Microwave ovens have an electron tube called a *magnetron.* The tube converts electrical energy to microwave energy.

In ordinary cooking, the heat is transferred to the food by the air or a heated pan. But microwaves are attracted to the fat, sugar, and moisture molecules of the food. They travel directly to the food without heating the air. The cooking dish heats only as the food inside it becomes hot.

When the microwaves encounter the molecules of food, they cause them to vibrate at a very high speed. The friction of the vibrating molecules generates heat. This heat, by chain reaction, moves from the outside edges to the center of the food. Even when the food is removed from the oven, the vibration continues for several minutes. This standing time must be considered when estimating the total cooking time.

Microwaves bounce off metal. The interior of the oven is made of metal so that the waves will bounce off and enter the food in the most efficient manner.

Hobart
2-75. A microwave oven.

Since microwaves always travel in a straight line, it is not possible to fill the oven area completely with microwaves. The food is cooked most efficiently in the center of the oven. It is cooked least efficiently in the corners. Consequently, recipe instructions tell you to rearrange the food about halfway through the cooking cycle so that it will cook evenly.

Because the waves bounce off metal, metal pans cannot be used in the microwave. Even casserole dishes cannot have metal trim or decoration. Fig. 2-76.

Microwaves, however, pass through glass, ceramic, china, paper, and plastic into the food. For instance, bacon can be cooked between two layers of paper towels. Food can be heated and served on the same dish.

Microwaves cook small amounts of food most efficiently. As the amount increases, the cooking time increases rapidly. Eventually, the cooking time might be more than if the same amount were cooked by conventional methods. This is one of the reasons microwave cooking is not used more in food service.

Microwave ovens for food service are very similar to those used in the home. Food service micro-

waves usually deliver 2000 watts and have a usable space 61 cm [24 in] wide by 61 cm [24 in] deep by 25 cm [10 in] high. They are constructed of stainless steel, with a large viewing window and interior light.

CAUTION

Microwave ovens are constructed so they cannot be operated unless the door is closed tightly. This protects you from exposure to microwave energy. Do not tamper with the safety interlocks. Do not place any object between the oven front face and the door. Do not allow soil to gather on the sealing surfaces. Do not operate the oven if the door does not close properly.

• The *tilt-brasier pan* can be used as a griddle, frying pan, kettle, steamer, and oven. Its special feature is a pouring lip and an upswinging cover. When the cover is swung up, the whole pan can be tilted by turning a wheel to the right of the pan. In

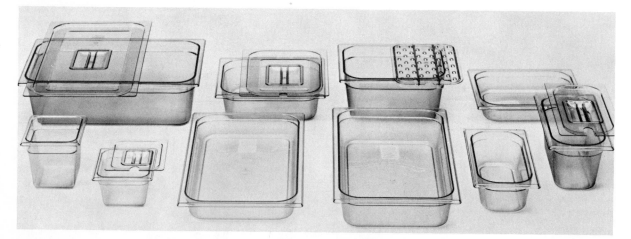

Rubbermaid

2-76. Microwave oven cookware.

Crown-X

2-77. A bank of four tilt brasiers.

this way, the cooking medium, such as water or cooking oil, can be poured off. Fig. 2-77.

The tilt-brasier is used in large production kitchens. It does the work of many small saucepans. If stew meat has just been sautéed in the tilt brasier, the vegetables, liquid, and seasoning can be added to it. The cooking is finished in the tilt-brasier, eliminating the use of other smaller pans. Tilt-brasiers are also used for other dishes, such as Swiss steak, pot roasts, and chicken in wine sauce.

Brasiers may be heated by gas, electricity, or steam.

• *Urns* are used for making coffee. Urns may vary in capacity from 9.5 L [2½ gal] to over 378.5 L [100 gal] to fit the size of the operation. Several

small urns are more useful than one large urn because the coffee will be freshly made. Coffee urns are discussed in detail in Chapter 23 ("Beverages").

The best urns are made of stainless steel. Urns have one container for hot water and two containers for coffee. The coffee is placed in a paper or cloth container. The hot water automatically filters through the coffee into the containers.

WARMERS

Keeping food warm without loss of quality is a difficult problem in food service. Some food warming equipment, such as the bain-marie, was discussed on page 40.

• *Steam tables* are used in cafeterias and buffets.

The table has compartments to hold 30.5- × 50.8-cm [12- × 20-in] pans. The pans have high domed covers to keep in the heat until service.

- *Pass-throughs* may be equipped with warming devices to hold hot food until service. Usually, infrared lamps are used. They diffuse a steady dry heat. Infrared lamps are especially good because they can be adjusted to keep food warm without cooking it further.

- *Heated carts* are used for transporting heated foods to the place of service. Commissaries use heated carts constantly. For instance, hot food is transported to airplanes in heated carts. On the plane, these carts are again plugged in to keep the food at serving temperatures.

- *Heated pellets* are placed under the tray to keep the food warm. They are used extensively in hospital service.

REFRIGERATORS AND FREEZERS

Refrigeration is most important in food service. Without proper refrigeration, food service as known today could not exist.

Refrigeration and freezing are based on *heat transfer*. In heat transfer, heat is removed from the food and conveyed by air currents to the evaporator. The evaporator is a series of tubes built into the walls. These tubes contain a colorless gas called Freon.® Freon® is the refrigerant. As the Freon® absorbs the heat, it expands and moves to the condenser. The condenser compresses the gas back to its original volume, forcing it to give up its heat. The heat is dispersed into the outside air by a fan. The cold gas then goes through the evaporator tubes, and the cycle begins again. The circulation of the gas is controlled by a thermostat, which keeps the refrigerator at an even temperature. The size of the operation and the type of menu determine the amount of refrigeration space that is needed.

There are four types of refrigerators and freezers generally used in food service—walk-in, reach-in, roll-in, and pass-through.

- *Walk-in refrigerators* and freezers are small rooms lined with slatted shelves.

- *Reach-in refrigerators* and freezers are usually placed at each station. The refrigerators are made of stainless steel, with pull-out shelves and double doors.

- *Roll-in refrigerators* and freezers are small refrigerated rooms into which prepared food on trays can be rolled. For instance, gelatin desserts may be prepared and garnished in the serving dishes. They are then placed on trays on carts. The roll-in refrigerator will store them at the proper temperature until serving time.

- *Pass-through refrigerators* have doors in the front and back. As the food is prepared, it is placed in the refrigerator. As needed for service, it is removed from the opposite door.

How Much Have You Learned?

Review this chapter. Answer the following questions to prepare yourself for the post-test. Check your answers with your teacher.

1. Define the *Words to Remember*.

2. Check the food service kitchen in which you are working. Does it meet the standards outlined in this chapter?

3. How many stations are there in the kitchen in which you are working? Identify each by name.

4. Give the name of the chef who would be in charge of each of the stations in the kitchen in which you are now working.

5. Check the storage areas for convenience and efficiency for work.

6. Practice naming each of the tools in the kitchen until you can say them easily.

7. Practice naming the utensils until you can name them easily.

8. Identify each piece of measuring equipment in the kitchen.

9. Identify the pieces of heavy equipment by name.

References

Folsom, Leroi, ed. *The Professional Chef.* Boston: CBI, 1974.

Haines, Robert G. *Food Preparation for Hotels, Restaurants, and Cafeterias.* Chicago: American Technical Society, 1973.

Kotschevar, Lendal H. *Standards, Principles, and Techniques in Quantity Food Production.* Boston: CBI, 1974.

Kowtaluk, Helen. *Discovering Food.* Peoria, Ill.: Chas. A. Bennett Co., Inc., 1978.

Kowtaluk, Helen, and Kopan, Alice. *Food For Today.* Peoria, Ill.: Chas. A. Bennett Co., Inc., 1977.

Morr, Mary L., and Irmeter, Theodore F. *Introductory Foods.* New York: Macmillan, 1974.

Ray, Mary Frey, and Lewis, Evelyn Jones. *Exploring Professional Cooking.* Peoria, Ill.: Chas. A. Bennett Co., Inc., 1980.

Sonnenschmidt, Fredric H., and Nicolas, Jean F. *Professional Chef's Art of Garde-Manger.* Boston: CBI, 1976.

Wolfe, Kenneth C. *Cooking For The Professional Chef.* Albany, N.Y.: Delmar Publishers, 1976.

Storage and Pre-preparation

Larry Sexton, Meat Cutter, Dan Dowd's Steak House, Plantation, Florida.

UNIT

2

MEET THE CONSULTANTS

Larry Sexton is an example of a man who did not really choose his vocation. He just happened into it.

Larry is a personable, friendly young man who earns a comfortable salary cutting meat for a well-known steak house. Dan Dowd's Steak House is one of several restaurants by the same name in Long Island and South Florida. The one in Plantation also has a butcher shop adjoining the restaurant. Larry is the head meat cutter. He has three young men working under him, learning the trade.

Since they all work in temperatures barely above freezing, they dress warmly under their white coats. They even wear warm, knitted caps on their heads.

Every week the manager of the restaurant and butcher shop estimates the meat needs and orders through a purveyor. The meat is brought by truck from the western states and delivered on Wednesday to the restaurant. It is hung by sides on a movable rack in the refrigerated room. Then Larry and the rest of the meat cutters go to work, cutting the sides into quarters and then into the wholesale cuts. Each wholesale cut must be cut again into portions for the restaurant or into retail cuts for the butcher shop.

"One thing I know," says Larry, "is the value of a sharp knife. We sharpen all of our knives once a week on a sharpening machine. Between times, we sharpen them on this sharpening steel. See?" He sharpened the knife quickly and competently. "Without a sharp knife, you can't cut meat," said Larry.

Like many young men, Larry began his meat cutting career by accident. When his father died, his mother married again. Her new husband happened to be a butcher. As a young teenager in junior high school, Larry went to the butcher shop, helping as he could. At first, he just cleaned up.

When his stepfather opened his own shop, Larry was allowed to bone out the meat for hamburger and chopped meat. He gradually began to do more complicated cuts.

While in high school, Larry took a job in another butcher shop, learning the trade under the butcher-owner of the store.

Construction of new homes was booming in Florida, and Larry was attracted by the high pay. He left the meat cutting trade to become a carpenter. For several years, he earned very good money, and he married. But as the building boom faded, he found it harder to get work.

Remembering his work as a meat cutter, he applied for a job at Dan Dowd's. He was employed as a busboy and also did a little carpentering around the restaurant. When the opportunity came, he talked to the owner-manager about his experiences as a meat cutter. Soon Larry was back cutting meat again.

Larry soon developed into an expert meat cutter. The owner-manager respects Larry's knowledge and boasts about his expert cutting of meat.

Larry says he enjoys his work. He makes a good salary and likes the working conditions. It is a family operation with a friendly atmosphere. He says he feels like a competent person who is respected, not just a cog in a machine. Meat cutting gives steady employment because there is always a demand for meat in restaurants and homes.

His only regret is that he did not finish high school. He feels that the vocational training available in many communities is a real opportunity for young men and women.

U. S. Jenkins, Fish Cutter, Angelo's Seafood and Frozen Foods, Deerfield Beach, Florida.

U. S. Jenkins was born in Waynesboro, Georgia, and named for Ulysses S. Grant, the famous general and president. Everybody calls him Jenks so he just uses the initials of his name.

Jenks is in his sixties now. He has been a fish cutter most of his life. During the Depression, Jenks came to South Florida. He was a young man without a job.

Standing on the street corner one day, he was approached by a man who asked him if he knew anything about cutting fish. Jenks didn't, but he had cut hogs and chickens on the farm in Georgia. So he said, "What I don't know, I can learn."

Fortunately, another worker at the fish market was willing to show him. Within three days, Jenks was an expert fish cutter. He has been cutting fish ever since.

Jenks has only a ninth-grade education, but he has six men working for him. Over the years, he has learned to identify the many different kinds of fish. He knows just how to cut each one. His employer, Angelo's Seafood and Frozen Foods, is the purveyor of fish products to the food service operations in South Florida.

Many fine restaurants in this area depend upon Jenks' expert cutting of fish to satisfy the demand for fish dinners.

Jenks has come a long way from the unemployed young man on the street corner in Fort Lauderdale. During World War II, he served in the Army as a cook on a troop train. He was horrified at the way chickens were being cut up for use by the Army. When he showed the mess sergeant the correct way to cut up a chicken for cooking, the mess sergeant put him to work teaching others. But when the war was over he went back to cutting fish.

He enjoys his work. "Lots of people don't want to cut fish. But fish are cleaner to handle than animals. Fresh fish don't smell, and there's very little blood. I'm my own boss here. The people are nice to work for, and I am happy with my job.

Ordering, Receiving, and Storing Food

- When you finish studying this chapter, you should be able to do the following:
- Define the *Words to Remember*.
- Weigh, record, and store correctly the foods as they arrive in the receiving area.
- Pass the posttest.

CHAPTER

3

Away from the dining room and the production kitchen is an area seldom seen by the customers. Even the cooks seem to pass it by. This area is the receiving area. It is one of the most important areas in food service. The food processing chain begins here, where the orders are placed. Here, the food is received and stored until needed in the production kitchens.

FOOD SERVICE BEGINS WITH THE MENU

The *menu* is the list of foods to be offered to the customer. Sometimes it is called the *bill of fare*. It may be simple or elaborate, but it has several important purposes.

The menu sells the food to the customer. It should be clean and present the food items to the customer in an appealing fashion. The customer reads the menu and makes the selection. The menu determines what foods are to be ordered and how much will be needed.

Who Sets the Menu?

In institutions such as hospitals and convalescent homes, the menu may be written by a dietitian. A dietitian is specially trained to meet the nutritional needs of the patients. Often the patients may not have a choice in their selection of foods.

Words to Remember

controller   purchase order
invoice   retail
menu   staples
purveyor   vendor
produce   wholesale

In cafeterias or other self-service operations, the menu may be set by the management team of the food chain. It may vary little from day to day.

In restaurants and hotels, the menu may be written by the executive chef in cooperation with the management. Many of the items on the menu may appear day after day, year after year.

Some restaurants specialize in regional foods or food specialties in the area where the restaurant is located. For instance, a restaurant located near the ocean may feature seafoods. A restaurant in the southern United States may specialize in southern fried chicken.

Many restaurants change the entrées every day or offer a special for the day. As defined in Chapter 2, an entrée is a main dish offered on the menu, such as fried chicken, roast beef, or spaghetti.

Finally, it is the customers who write the menu by choosing or refusing the offered items. If an item is not ordered for several weeks, it may be removed from the menu. An item that proves popular may become a permanent part of the menu. In the United States, roast beef and fried chicken are the most popular entrées. Apple pie is the most-ordered dessert.

The manager of a food service operation watches closely the popularity of the items on a menu. After all, pleasing the customers is the business of all food service.

ORDERING

Who Places the Order?

After the menu has been written, the order for the food must be placed. In a small operation, the head chef or cook may plan the menu, prepare the order, and place it. In a large operation, there may be a purchasing agent, a steward, or an executive chef who writes and places the order. The following sequence shows the usual route of food from the time the menu is written until the food is served to the customer.

1. The menu is written.
2. The chef gives the food order to the purveyors and vendors.
3. The purveyors and vendors deliver foods to the controller.
4. The controller sends food to the pre-preparation kitchens, the pastry chef, and the butcher.
5. The pre-preparation kitchens, pastry chef, and butcher send food to the main kitchen.
6. The various work stations in the main kitchen prepare the food.
7. The prepared food is delivered from the main kitchen to the dining area.

Certain items such as sugar, salt, flour, and canned goods are always kept on hand and reordered as the supply is depleted. These items are called *staples.*

Fresh fruits and vegetables are called *produce.*

Where Does the Food Come From?

Food travels from the producers or farmers by many different routes before reaching the consumers. Food processors or distributors along the route prepare the food to be eaten or cooked. For instance, the millers grind the flour. The produce distributors wash, sort, and package the fruit and vegetables. The meat processors slaughter and skin the animals. They also halve or quarter the carcasses.

Food reaches the consumer through the wholesale or retail route. Fig. 3-1. *Wholesale* businesses sell large quantities of food to such operations as food stores, restaurants, schools, hospitals, and hotels. *Retail* businesses sell food directly to the consumer through a store. Food is cheaper when bought in quantities. Wholesale prices are lower than retail prices.

Food is ordered wholesale through a purveyor or a vendor. A *purveyor* is a specialist in the wholesale selling of groceries, meats, poultry, and fish to food service. A *vendor* is any person or company selling merchandise wholesale or retail.

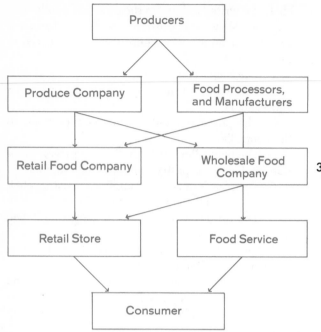

3-1. The way in which food reaches the consumer.

Orders are placed with several different purveyors and vendors. The person placing the orders quickly finds the reliable companies that will always deliver quality products. Wholesale companies usually specialize in one type of food. For instance, chickens may be ordered from one purveyor, fish from another, meat from a third, and fruits and vegetables from a fourth.

Just as among stores, prices will differ among purveyors and vendors. The person placing the order will shop among the purveyors and vendors for the best prices consistent with quality.

Purchase Order

Food is ordered through a *purchase order* with a reference number. Thus, there is a permanent record of the order. Fig. 3-2. Each purchase order should state the following:

- Date of order.
- Date of delivery.

- Description of each item.
- Quantity desired.
- Unit of purchase.

The date of order is the date the order was placed with the purveyor. The date of delivery is the date desired for delivery of the food to the food service operation.

Each item must be described in specific terms. The purveyor must be able to fill the order exactly from the description. For instance, it is not sufficient to order "flour." There are many different kinds of flour, such as white, whole wheat, or rye. Even white flour has many different qualities, depending upon the use. Is bread, pastry, or cake flour wanted? Is a specific brand desired? Should the flour be bleached or unbleached, enriched or unenriched?

As you study the foods used in food service, you will learn much about kinds and qualities. These standards will be discussed in detail in succeeding chapters.

The size of the food service operation and the storage facilities help decide the quantity to be ordered. The unit of purchase is the size package desired. For instance, the controller may want to order 22.7 kg [50 lb] of flour, but it is to be delivered in

PIER 66 COMPANY
HOTEL AND MARINA COMPLEX
(WHOLLY OWNED SUBSIDIARY OF PHILLIPS PETROLEUM CO.)
(A/C 305) 524-0566
DRAWER 9177, FORT LAUDERDALE, FLA. 33310

PURCHASE ORDER 00601

DATE *Jan. 15, 1981*

TO: *Alpine Gourmet Foods*
517 S.W. 12th St.
Fort Lauderdale, FL 33315

Please deliver to us, in good condition, the following named goods, together with invoice.

SHOW OUR ORDER NUMBER ON FACE OF INVOICE, MARK ALL PACKAGES WITH OUR ORDER NUMBER.

Item	QUANTITY	DESCRIPTION	AMOUNT	UNIT
1	1 Cs	Cream of Mushroom Soup Mix	72.00	$3 – lb
2	1 Cs	French Onion Soup Mix	72.00	$3 – lb
3	1 Cs	Cream of Leek Soup Mix	72.00	$3 – lb
4	1 Cs	Scotch Broth Soup Mix	72.00	$3 – lb
5	2 Cs	Culinate Vegetable Seasoning	168.00	$3.50 – lb
6	2 Cs	Lucul Chicken Bouillon	192.00	$4 – lb
7	1 Cs	Lucul Beef Bouillon	96.00	$4 – lb
8	1 Cs	Demiglace Mix (Brown Gravy Maker)	78.00	$3.25 lb
9	1 Cs	Clear Aspic Gelatin	102.00	$4.25 lb
10				
11				
12				

DELIVER TO: 2301 S.E. 17th STREET CAUSEWAY
FT. LAUDERDALE, FL 33316

Mailing Address: DRAWER 9177
FT. LAUDERDALE, FL 33310

__ HOTEL __ RESTAURANT X OTHER _____

☐ CHARGE FLORIDA SALES TAX AS REQUIRED BY LAW ☒ SALES TAX EXEMPT FOR RESALE CERT. #16-03-86887-08

F.O.B. _____

Terms: *30 Days*

By: *J. Jones.*

3-2. A purchase order, correctly filled out.

five 4.5-kg [10-lb] packages. The 4.5-kg [10-lb] package is the unit of purchase.

Wholesale food is cheaper in large amounts. Per kilogram or pound, one 22.7-kg [50-lb] sack of flour is cheaper than five 4.5-kg [10-lb] sacks of flour. However, some operations buy bread, rolls, cakes, and pies instead of baking them on the premises. Such operations may not be able to use up the larger sack of flour within a reasonable time. There may not be enough storage space, either.

Usually, the chef or controller places orders by telephone, giving the purchase order number.

RECEIVING

The receiving area is located close to the service entrance for trucks delivering supplies. Fig. 3-3. It is under the supervision of the *controller*. The controller is sometimes known as the receiver, storekeeper, or steward. By any title, this person is responsible for the food from the moment it arrives at the entrance until it is delivered to the production kitchens.

The purveyor or vendor delivers the raw food or merchandise to the controller. An *invoice* accompanies the order. An invoice is an itemized list of the goods shipped to the buyer. Fig. 3-4.

Words to Remember

freezer burn	lug
humidity	roll-in storage
inventory	walk-in storage

CHECKING THE INVOICE

When the merchandise arrives, the controller checks what is listed on the invoice against what has been received. The controller checks the quantity, weight, description, and quality. Fig. 3-5.

• *Quantity.* This check is a matter of count. How many cases of green beans? How many sacks of sugar? How many *lugs* of fresh peaches? A lug is a flat carton used to pack fruit that bruises easily.

• *Weight.* Close to the entry door and the desk of the controller stands a large platform scale. Some foods, such as meat, are purchased by weight. Meat is very expensive. An efficient controller checks to make sure that the weight on the invoice is the same as the weight received.

• *Description.* Occasionally mistakes are made, and the wrong merchandise is delivered. The controller checks the label against the invoice to catch any errors. For instance, if canned whole tomatoes are delivered instead of tomato puree, the cooks may be without a needed ingredient.

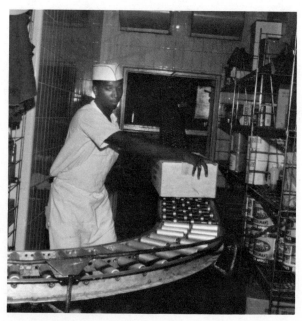

Morrison, Inc.

3-3. The receiving area of a large cafeteria.

SWISS ALPINE GOURMET FOODS

A 00751

SPECIALIZING IN...

SAUCES & SOUPS • WILD MUSHROOMS • TRUFFLES • BOUILLONS

LUCUL PRODUCTS   TEL. 305/524-4716

TO Pier 66 Hotel (Deliver to Restaurant Bldg.)

17 Street Causeway

Fort Lauderdale, FL 33310

ORDER NO. PO. 00601

DEPT. NO.

SHIP VIA Comp. Truck

ORDER NO.	DEPT.	VIA	TERMS Net 30 Days		ORD. COMPL.	BAL. TO FOLLOW	SALESMAN Peters	DATE 1/17/81

NUMBER	QTY.	DESCRIPTION	PRICE		EXTENSION		AMOUNT	
1 Cs 002	24 1b	Cream of Mushroom Soup Mix	3	00	72	00	72	00
1 Cs 023	24 1b	French Onion Soup Mix	3	00	72	00	72	00
1 Cs 003	24 1b	Cream of Leek Soup Mix	3	00	72	00	72	00
1 Cs 030	24 1b	Scotch Broth Soup Mix	3	00	72	00	72	00
*1 Cs 045	24 1b	Culinate Vegetable Seasoning Powder	3	50	84	00	84	00
2 Cs 040	48 1b	Lucul Chicken Bouillon	4	00	96	00	192	00
1 Cs 039	24 1b	Lucul Beef Bouillon	4	00	96	00	96	00
1 Cs 048	24 1b	Demiglace (Gravy Maker)	3	25	78	00	78	00
1 Cs 044	24 1b	Clear Aspic Gelatin	4	25	102	00	102	00
		Total———————					840	00
	(* Backorder 1	Cs Culinate Vegetable Seasoning)						

Thank You!

706

3-4. An invoice, correctly filled out.

INVOICE

• *Quality.* Standards of quality for some foods have been set by the United States Department of Agriculture (USDA). The best quality, of course, costs more than the lesser. The controller checks the quality of the delivered food against the quality charged for on the invoice. You will learn more about quality standards as you study the succeeding chapters.

After the invoice has been checked, it is filed for future reference. When the bill from the purveyor comes in, it is checked against the invoices for accuracy.

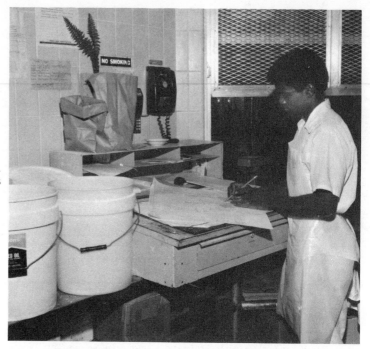

Morrison, Inc.
3-5. The controller must keep careful records of goods received.

Of course, the controller immediately notifies the purveyor of any mistakes found on the invoice. Checking makes sure that any mistakes have been corrected in the billing.

STORAGE

Once the food has been accepted by the controller, it is immediately stored until needed. Storage is also under the supervision of the controller.

Rules of Storage

An efficient controller will follow these rules for storage:

• *First in, first out.* Old merchandise should not have birthdays while new merchandise is used. The merchandise should be rotated by placing the new merchandise behind the old. The controller should make periodic checks on the length of time merchandise has been on the shelves.

• *Orderly storage.* Like is grouped with like. For example, canned peaches are stored together, not mixed with other canned fruits. The controller must know where everything is.

• *Exact count.* The controller must know what quantities are on hand. Most controllers keep a running, or perpetual, *inventory.* This inventory is a list of everything that is stored in each area. As new items arrive, they are added to the inventory. As items are removed to be sent to the kitchens, they are subtracted from the inventory. Each month, an actual count is taken to check against the running inventory.

Kinds of Storage

All foods are stored in either dry or refrigerated areas. Cases of canned food, large sacks of flour and sugar, and large amounts of fresh produce and meats must be stored. *Walk-in storage* or *roll-in storage* is generally used. Walk-in storage is a small room with shelves. Roll-in storage has no shelves. The foods are placed on rolling shelves and then rolled into the room.

In small operations, all food may be stored under refrigeration because the turnover is so rapid. Food is purchased in smaller amounts and bought more often. In a large operation, enough storage space is provided to store foods under the best conditions.

To maintain the highest quality, a wide range of temperature control is needed. Control of humidity is equally important. *Humidity* is the moisture content of the air. Table 3-1 shows the ideal temperatures and humidity for storing a variety of foods. Temperature control is important. Most storage areas have a thermometer on the outside, close to the door. Thus, the controller can easily check the temperature of the interior.

DRY STORAGE

If possible, dry storage should be provided for such items as canned goods, flour, sugar, salt, cereals, and crackers. In large operations, even the dry storage is kept slightly refrigerated at 18°C [65° F.].

Table 3-1. Optimum Temperature and Humidity for Storing Foods

Product	Temperature		Humidity Percentage
	°C	°F.	
Eggs and dairy products	3	38	75–85
Fresh produce	10	50	85–95
Frozen foods	−23	−10	75–85
Meats, poultry, fish	2	35	75–85

Humidity control is especially important because humidity causes cans to rust. It causes crackers and cereals to become soggy. High humidity and warmth cause mold and mildew to develop.

Slatted, instead of solid, shelves are best to provide a free flow of air around the stored items. Cases of canned foods might be stored on the floor. Sacks of flour, sugar, and salt, and boxes of crackers and cereals should be on the shelves to keep them dry.

REFRIGERATED STORAGE

To retain freshness, meat, poultry, fish, and produce must be kept under carefully controlled conditions of temperature and humidity. Temperatures for frozen food storage must also be exact to keep the food in the best condition.

Regulations in most communities require separate storage for produce, meat, poultry, fish, and dairy products. There is good reason for this. Each of these items needs different temperatures and humidity. Also, fresh produce may contain bacteria, molds, and yeasts that may contaminate other foods.

Dairy products readily absorb odors and tastes. For instance, if they were stored with fish or onions, they would quickly absorb the off-odor and taste. This would make them unusable.

As in dry storage, the shelves should be slatted to allow full air circulation. Large cuts of meat should be hung.

Refrigerated air is drying. Unless the item is to be used within a few hours, it should be securely wrapped in moisture-proof wrapping to prevent drying out.

Frozen items must be kept solidly frozen until ready for use. The controller must be aware of the usual shelf life for frozen foods. See Table 3-2. If the product is not securely wrapped, the shelf life will be much less than shown in the table. The lower the temperature, the more drying the air. Insecurely wrapped meat, poultry, and fish exposed to freezing temperatures for a period of time will develop *freezer burn.* Freezer burn gives the meat the appearance of being cooked in spots. The meat is also dried out. All frozen products must be securely wrapped in freezer paper or plastic film to avoid great loss of quality.

Product	Time
Baked Goods	
Bread and rolls	2–4 months
Cakes	2–4 months
Pies	2–4 months
Dairy Products and Eggs	
Butter	8–10 months
Whole eggs (out of shell)	8–10 months
Egg yolks	8–10 months
Egg Whites	10–12 months
Meat and Fish Products	
Beef, veal, and lamb (most cuts)	6–8 months
Hamburger and stew meat	4–6 months
Chicken and turkey	8–10 months
Ducks and geese	4–6 months
Pork (most cuts)	6–8 months
Sausage and bacon	3–4 months
Fish (fat)	1–3 months
Fish (lean)	4–6 months
Shellfish	4–6 months
Vegetables and Fruits	
Most vegetables (beans, peas, etc.)	10–12 months
Cauliflower	8–10 months
Mushrooms, cucumbers, green pepper	6–8 months
Most fruit	10–12 months

Table 3-2. Maximum Length of Time for Storing Frozen Products

How Much Have You Learned?

Review this chapter. Answer the following questions to prepare yourself for the post-test. Check your answers with your teacher.

1. Define the *Words to Remember.*
2. What is the purpose of the menu?
3. Who writes the menu in a hospital? A small restaurant? A large hotel?
4. Name two influences on the menu.
5. Trace the route of food from the time the menu is written until it reaches the customer.
6. Why are orders usually placed with several different purveyors?
7. What is a purchase order? What should appear on it?
8. What is an invoice? How does the controller use it?
9. Explain the two rules of storage.
10. Explain the importance of temperature and humidity in storage of foods.

Pre-preparation of Meat, Poultry, and Fish

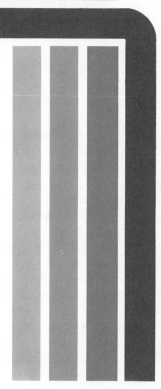

CHAPTER

4

What Will You Learn?

When you finish studying this chapter, you should be able to do the following:
- Define the *Words to Remember*.
- Describe the quality standards of meat, poultry, and seafood.
- Identify the wholesale cuts of meat and the retail cuts that come from them.
- Demonstrate the ability to portion meat, poultry, and fish.
- Store a variety of meats, poultry, and fish correctly.
- Pass the posttest.

Some foods may need pre-preparation before being stored or made into dishes to be served to customers. The pre-preparation of meats, poultry, fish, shellfish, fruits, and vegetables saves cooks much time. In a small operation, the pre-preparation is done by the cook or the cook's helper. Cook's helpers wash and trim the vegetables and fruits. They chop the onions and assist in cutting the meat.

In some restaurants, there may be very little pre-preparation because most foods are purchased ready to be cooked. The pre-preparation is already done when the foods are delivered by the purveyor.

In a large operation, a special area may be set aside for this purpose. The pre-preparation area may be located close to the receiving and storage areas. Sometimes it is in the production kitchen at the beginning of the food flow line.

Words to Remember

cells	kosher
collagen	marbling
conformation	muscle
connective tissues	mutton
cutability	yield
elastin	yield grades
finish	veal

MEAT

Strictly speaking, meat is the flesh of any animal used as food by human beings. However, to most people, meat is the flesh of mammals—steers, pigs, calves, and young sheep. Poultry is also considered to be meat.

- *Beef* comes from fully grown steers specially bred and fattened for meat.
- *Veal* comes from baby calves, still milk fed.
- *Pork* is the fresh or cured flesh of pigs or hogs.
- *Lamb* is the flesh of young sheep. *Mutton* is the flesh of fully grown sheep. Because of its strong flavor and odor, mutton is rarely used in food service in the United States.

Composition of Meat

All meat is made of muscle, connective tissues, and bone.

- *Muscle* is composed of very fine fibers. Perhaps you have noticed the fibers when you have eaten meat that is "stringy." The fibers are made of *cells*. These cells contain the proteins, fat, minerals, vitamins, and flavorings that make meat so nutritious and delicious to eat.
- *Connective tissues* bind the fibers together in bundles. Heavier connective tissues bind the bundles into a muscle. This light connective tissue is white and is called *collagen*. It becomes soft and dissolves in liquid during long cooking. The muscle is bound to the bone by even heavier connective tissue. This connective tissue is yellow and is called *elastin*. It cannot be softened by cooking.
- *Bone* forms the skeleton of the animal. The amount of bone varies with the cut. The color of the bone is a good indication of the age of the animal.

The bones will be tinged with red if the animal is young. Older animals have hard, white bones.

Quality Standards of Meat

- Quality beef is bright red, with firm, fine-grained flesh. The flecks of fat throughout the muscle are known as *marbling*. In quality beef, the flesh is well marbled.
- Quality veal is creamy pink with very little fat. The texture should be firm.
- Quality pork is light, grayish pink with large quantities of soft, white fat.
- Quality lamb is pinkish red with hard, white fat. Meat of a deep red color with hard, brittle fat shows an old sheep.

INSPECTION AND GRADING OF MEAT

The United States Department of Agriculture (USDA) has inspected and graded meat for many years. Grading began in 1916, when some standards were set for beef. Gradually, the grades have been developed and refined. Now, grading is exact and dependable. All meat shipped between the states must bear the round seal of wholesomeness. Fig. 4-1. This seal is rolled on the carcass by the USDA meat inspectors. It shows that the animal was healthy when slaughtered and was packed under sanitary conditions. When the meat left the packing house, it was fit for human consumption—it was *wholesome*.

The USDA also grades meat for quality. The quality stamp is shaped like a shield. It bears the words *Prime, Choice, Good, Standard, Commercial, Utility,* and *Cutter*. See Fig. 4-2.

Law does not require packers to have their meat graded. Nevertheless, many packers are glad to

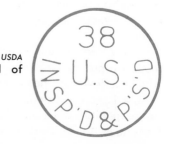

4-1. The USDA *USDA* seal of wholesomeness.

USDA

4-2. USDA quality grades.

have this service. Food buyers depend upon the USDA grading for buying quality meats.

Grade is the first consideration in the price of meat. It is expensive to feed an animal so it will qualify for the higher grades. Prime, the first grade, brings the highest price. The past few years, prime animals have become very rare because of the high cost of feed. Less than five percent of the total beef production is prime beef.

The second grade, Choice, is most often used in food service. The best restaurants, featuring fine steaks and roasts, will serve "high" or "top" Choice. It is a quality grade of the suppliers and packing houses. A person throughly trained in meat selection can go through rows of beef carcasses marked Choice and choose the "top" Choice from all.

The lower grades are also used in food service. Some of the steak houses featuring inexpensive steaks use Commercial or Utility grades.

Quality grades are based on these features:

• *Conformation*—the proportion of meat to bone and other less desirable or inedible parts.

• *Quality*—the expected "good eating" from the cuts. Marbling is the most important point in determining how flavorful the meat will be.

• *Finish*—the distribution of fat on the outside and throughout the meat.

In 1965, *yield grades* were adopted in addition to quality grades. Yield grades are concerned with the *cutability,* or *yield,* in boneless, closely trimmed cuts. Some top-grade restaurants, especially the chain operations, buy wholesale cuts and portion them for their own use. Cutability, or yield, grades are important to them. Yield grades are shown by the numbers 1, 2, 3, 4, and 5. Fig. 4-3. Grade 1 is the best. Food service operations that buy meat already portioned by the purveyor are interested only in the quality grade.

USDA

4-3. A USDA yield grade stamp.

Veal, pork, and lamb have similar quality and yield grades. Table 4-1.

Kosher beef, veal, and lamb is meat that has been slaughtered and processed according to the strict laws of the Jewish people.

Words to Remember

aging	wholesale cut
enzymes	primal cut
cryovac	dressed weight
tenderizing	side

Aging

Aging simply means hanging the meat under controlled conditions for a period of time. The time must be longer than it takes to transport the meat from the packinghouse to the customer. Pork and veal are not improved by aging. Beef and lamb are better when aged.

Meat from freshly slaughtered animals is called "green" meat. This is meat that hasn't had a chance to ripen. Ripening occurs during the aging process. Ripening occurs in many foods such as fruit, vegetables, flour, and meat. It occurs because foods con-

Kind	Grades
Beef 　Quality grades 　Yield grades	Prime, Choice, Good, Standard, 　Commercial, Utility, Cutter, Canner. Prime (1), Choice (2), Good (3), 　Standard (4), Utility (5).
Veal 　Quality grades 　Yield grades	Prime, Choice, Good, Standard, 　Utility. 1, 2, 3, 4, 5.
Lamb 　Quality grades 　Yield grades	Prime, Choice, Good, Utility, Cull. 1, 2, 3, 4, 5.
Pork 　Quality grades 　Yield grades	U.S. #1, 2, 3, 4; and Utility. 1, 2, 3, 4, 5.

Table 4-1. USDA Grades for Meat

tain *enzymes* (EN-zimes). An enzyme is an organic substance that gradually works changes in food. Enzymes soften food, tenderize it, and change the flavor. You have probably noticed the difference in the softness, flavor, and color of ripe and unripe fruit. The action of the enzymes makes the difference.

When an animal is slaughtered, the muscles stiffen, a process known as rigor mortis. As the carcass hangs under refrigeration, the muscles gradually relax. It takes about three to four days. Then the aging process can begin. Only the better grades of beef and lamb can be aged. They have the heavy layer of fat that is needed to protect the muscle against spoiling.

During aging, the enzymes soften the connective tissue. This makes the meat more tender. Some moisture also evaporates, causing a loss in weight. Aged beef costs more because of the time spent in aging and the loss of weight.

The rate of aging depends upon the temperature. The process takes ten to fourteen days at temperatures between 1°C [34° F.] and 4°C [40° F.]. At

these temperatures, meat may be held up to six weeks with further development of flavor.

Meat is sometimes aged at a higher temperature to cut down on the needed time. However, higher temperatures encourage bacterial growth. Some bacterial growth is good because it develops a desirable flavor—the "aged" flavor. Prime cuts of beef are often aged at the higher temperature to increase their market value.

As mentioned in Chapter 3, refrigerated air is drying. To prevent meat from drying and excess shrinkage during the aging process, the humidity is increased. A relative humidity of 70 percent to 95 percent is suitable. The higher the humidity, the less the shrinkage. However, bacterial growth is more rapid at the higher humidity.

Cryovac aging of meat is becoming more common. The meat is placed in a heavy plastic bag. The air is exhausted from the bag. Then the bag is tightly sealed and kept under refrigeration. During aging, the fluid drawn from the meat accumulates in the bag. These juices help keep the meat moist, but the loss of juices also causes some loss of weight. The meat is held in the cryovac bag until ready to be portioned.

Tenderizing

Some meat is *tenderized* by the injection of an enzyme. Just before slaughtering, the tenderizing enzyme is injected into the animal. The heart pumps it into all the muscles. After slaughtering, as the meat hangs, the enzymes break down the connective tissue, softening and tenderizing. Some persons object to this tenderizing process because it is cruelty to animals. They also say it ruins the texture of the meat. Others enjoy the increased "chewability" of the tenderized meat.

Slaughtering

The great majority of meat comes from animals especially raised for meat production. For instance, when the steers are fully grown, they are sent to feed lots to be grain fed. Grass-fed beef is stringy and tough. For about ninety days, the beef cattle are fed a carefully balanced feed. Exercise is restricted. The grain in the feedlots puts a layer of fat on the

outside of the muscles. It also develops fat throughout the muscle to make the meat well marbled.

When the steer has reached the weight of about 454 kg [1000 lb], it is slaughtered. A steer this size will yield about 218 kg [480 lb] of *wholesale cuts* of beef. Wholesale cuts of meat are large cuts sold to meat markets, restaurants, and institutions. Wholesale cuts are also called *primal cuts*. In beef, this is about 48 percent of *dressed weight*. Dressed weight is the weight of the animal after it has been bled, cleaned, and skinned.

Veal is slaughtered when about three months old and ready for regular feed. Veal gives a low percentage of meat. Only about 40 percent of dressed weight is usable for wholesale cuts.

Young pigs, however, have a very high proportion of usable meat. There is an old saying that everything can be used except the squeal. Pigs are slaughtered when they weigh about 100 kg [220 lb]. A pig this size will yield about 57 kg [125 lb] of wholesale cuts, or about 60 percent of dressed weight.

Young lambs are best when about six months old, weighing about 45 kg [100 lb]. A lamb this size yields about 16 kg [35 lb] of wholesale cuts. This is a very low yield—about 35 percent of dressed weight.

The yield in wholesale cuts is important in understanding the cost of meat. It explains in part the wide difference in the price of meat "on the hoof" and the price when delivered to the food service operation.

After slaughtering, the animals are skinned and the internal organs are removed or the animal is dressed. The carcasses are cut in half. Each half is called a *side*. The sides are hung under refrigeration. Fig. 4-4. For delivery to the food service operation, the sides of beef are usually quartered. Sides of veal, pork, and lamb are usually delivered whole.

Dan Dowd's Steak House
4-4. Beef sides are stored under refrigeration.

RETAIL CUTS OF BEEF

WHERE THEY COME FROM AND HOW TO COOK THEM

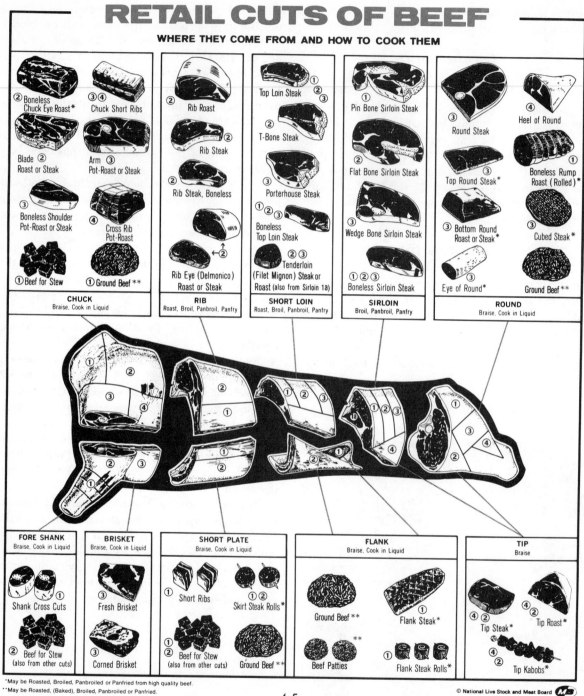

② Boneless Chuck Eye Roast*
③④ Chuck Short Ribs
② Blade Roast or Steak
③ Arm Pot-Roast or Steak
③ Boneless Shoulder Pot-Roast or Steak
④ Cross Rib Pot-Roast
① Beef for Stew
① Ground Beef**

CHUCK
Braise, Cook in Liquid

② Rib Roast
② Rib Steak
③ Rib Steak, Boneless
② Rib Eye (Delmonico) Roast or Steak

RIB
Roast, Broil, Panbroil, Panfry

Top Loin Steak ②③
T-Bone Steak ②
Porterhouse Steak ③
①②③ Boneless Top Loin Steak
②③ Tenderloin (Filet Mignon) Steak or Roast (also from Sirloin 1a)

SHORT LOIN
Roast, Broil, Panbroil, Panfry

① Pin Bone Sirloin Steak ②③
② Flat Bone Sirloin Steak
③ Wedge Bone Sirloin Steak
①②③ Boneless Sirloin Steak

SIRLOIN
Broil, Panbroil, Panfry

③ Round Steak
④ Heel of Round
③ Top Round Steak*
① Boneless Rump Roast (Rolled)*
③ Bottom Round Roast or Steak*
③ Cubed Steak*
③ Eye of Round*
③ Ground Beef**

ROUND
Braise, Cook in Liquid

FORE SHANK
Braise, Cook in Liquid

① Shank Cross Cuts
② Beef for Stew (also from other cuts)

BRISKET
Braise, Cook in Liquid

③ Fresh Brisket
③ Corned Brisket

SHORT PLATE
Braise, Cook in Liquid

① Short Ribs
①② Skirt Steak Rolls*
①② Beef for Stew (also from other cuts)
①② Ground Beef**

FLANK
Braise, Cook in Liquid

Ground Beef**
① Flank Steak*
Beef Patties**
① Flank Steak Rolls*

TIP
Braise

④② Tip Steak*
④② Tip Roast*
④② Tip Kabobs*

*May be Roasted, Broiled, Panbroiled or Panfried from high quality beef.
**May be Roasted, (Baked), Broiled, Panbroiled or Panfried.

4-5.

© National Live Stock and Meat Board

Words to Remember

brisket
Chateaubriand
chuck
filet mignon
forequarter
hindquarter
loin
plate
porterhouse
retail cut
rib

round
shank
short loin
sirloin
strip
T-bone
tenderloin
tip
tournedo
wholesale cut

BEEF CUTS

Figure 4-5 shows the *wholesale cuts* of beef from a side. The *chuck, shank, brisket, rib,* and *plate* are part of the *forequarter.* The *short loin, sirloin, flank, round,* and *tip* are part of the *hindquarter.*

The wholesale, or primal, cuts are divided into the *retail cuts.* The retail cuts are the familiar portions sold in the meat markets. The primal cuts are the most important cuts because you will encounter them in the production kitchens. Such understanding is a giant step toward knowing how to cook meat and why it is cooked that way.

Figure 4-5 is a drawing of a side of beef. It shows the primal cuts and the retail cuts. There is a big price difference from one cut to another. Generally, the most tender cuts are more expensive than the less tender cuts. The least tender cuts are also the cheapest.

There is also a difference in flavor. The less tender cuts have more flavor than the very tender cuts.

It is important for you to study this chart carefully. You will need to know what to order for a certain dish you are preparing.

For instance, you are to prepare braised brisket of beef. This is in the forequarter of beef. You can locate it on the chart. You would order by name. You would not order strip sirloin instead.

Another example is Yankee pot roast. If this is on the menu, you would order bottom round, which is a cut from the hindquarter. It will make a flavorful pot roast. You would not order top round. Top round is more expensive and not as flavorful.

However, if you are to prepare filet mignon, you would order tenderloin. You would not order a chuck eye roast.

Now that you know the importance of this information, read the following. Refer to Fig. 4-5 as you read.

Loin

Look at Fig. 4-6. Do you see where the *loin* is? It is in the hindquarter. It lies along the backbone in the midsection. It runs from the rib section almost to the tail.

The top section of the loin is called the *strip.* In the retail cuts, the strip is called the boneless top loin. Underneath the strip is the *tenderloin.* These cuts are the highest-priced items on the menu. On the menu, the strip is called the New York strip steak. The tenderloin is called *filet mignon* (fill-AY mean-YON). Twin, thick, round slices of tenderloin are called *tournedos* (TOOR-nuh-DOZE). A piece of tenderloin big enough to serve two persons is called *Chateaubriand* (Sha-TOE-bree-AHN).

The loin is divided vertically into two sections called the *short loin* and the *sirloin.* The short loin is in the middle of the back protected by the backbone. It gets very little exercise and is very tender. It has the most tenderloin.

If the strip is not separated from the tenderloin, the short loin is cut into steaks. They are called *T-*

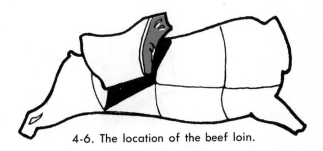

4-6. The location of the beef loin.

bone and *porterhouse*. These steaks are sold mostly in steak houses. They are seldom seen in luxury restaurants.

The sirloin runs from the short loin to the round. The top sirloin butt is closest to the short loin. On the chart, this is the boneless sirloin steak. All parts of the sirloin and top sirloin butt are excellent steaks and roasts. They are very expensive.

Words to Remember

bottom round	round
kabob	top round
knuckle	

Round

Just below the sirloin is the *round*. Fig. 4-7. It consists mainly of the *top round*, the *bottom round*, and the *knuckle*.

The top round is the section closest to the sirloin. It may be cut into roasts or steaks. The steaks need

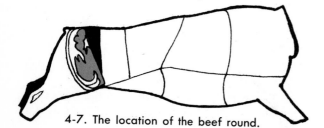

4-7. The location of the beef round.

to be tenderized in cooking. Top round may also be used for expensive stew meat. Tenderized chunks of top round may be used to make *kabobs*. A kabob is meat strung on a skewer and broiled.

The bottom round is less tender than the top round. It may be used for pot roast, steaks which will be tenderized, or stews.

The knuckle is the rounded muscle linking the hip to the leg bone. On the chart, it is called heel of round.

Words to Remember

chuck roll	hamburger
clod	muscle boning
club steak	prime rib
corned beef	shank
ground beef	trichinosis
ham	

Rib

In the forequarter, next to the short loin, is the rib section. Fig. 4-8. It may be divided into steaks and roasts. The rib eye and club steaks are taken from this cut.

The rib section is also the source of the famous *prime rib*. This is a time-honored name. Strictly speaking, the word "prime" should designate only meat of prime grade. However, if restaurants had to follow this meaning, a popular item, prime ribs, would disappear from the menu. The rib section is a very tender, expensive cut of beef.

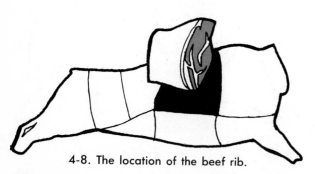

4-8. The location of the beef rib.

4-9. The location of the beef chuck.

Chuck

Next to the rib section in the forequarter is the *chuck*. Fig. 4-9. The chuck is a less tender, less expensive cut of beef.

The *clod* is chuck that has been muscle boned. In *muscle boning,* the shoulder and arm muscles are cut away from the beef in one solid piece. The clod is used for a less tender roast.

A *chuck roll* is a rolled, boneless cut from the chuck. The chuck roll may be roasted or used for stewing.

The best ground beef also comes from the chuck.

Brisket

Just below the chuck toward the foreleg lies the brisket. Although an excellent piece of beef, it is not as tender as the clod. The brisket is frequently cured to make the popular *corned beef.*

Other Cuts

The other cuts in the forequarter are the foreshank, short plate, and neck portions. These are among the least tender cuts. Most chefs use the foreshank for soup stock because it is very lean and flavorful. The plate, neck, and other secondary portions are used for soups, stews, and ground beef.

GROUND BEEF AND HAMBURGER

Ground beef must be 100 percent pure ground beef. It cannot contain any seasonings. Fat content is limited by law to 30 percent. Ground beef may be purchased in three categories. The category is determined by the amount of fat.

• Ground beef that is 70 to 75 percent lean is used for hamburgers, chili, and spaghetti sauce.

• Ground beef that is 75 to 80 percent lean was formerly called "ground chuck." It is used for meat loaf, meat balls, Salisbury steak, tamale pie, and casseroles.

• Ground beef that is 80 to 85 percent lean was formerly called "ground round." It is used for low-calorie patties and casseroles.

Hamburger is usually, but not always, ground beef. Unless it is labeled "pure ground beef" it may contain some pork.

USDA standards specify that hamburger may have seasoning and fat added. However, no extenders such as cereals or water may be added.

Most purchasers specify the amount of fat desired in the hamburger. About 25 percent seems to make a flavorable, moist hamburger, but not a greasy one.

Meat trimmings and unsaleable cuts of beef are used to make hamburger and ground beef. Bull meat, which is tough but flavorful, is often used.

Words to Remember ———————

cutlet   hindsaddle
foresaddle

VEAL CUTS

Figure 4-10 shows the cuts from veal. Note that veal, being a smaller animal, has fewer cuts. The forequarter is called the *foresaddle.* The hind quarter is called the *hindsaddle.* There are a few other differences in names of cuts.

Beef	Veal
chuck	shoulder
rib	hotel rack
plate and brisket	breast
round	leg

All veal is considered tender because of the youth of the animal. Some of the primal cuts, especially the breast, tend to be stringy.

Veal is a very much misused and abused term for a very special and versatile meat. It is the most delicately flavored of all meats. It combines well with sauces and other foods.

Veal has long been popular in Europe. Therefore, European-trained chefs know how to prepare veal in many different ways. It is most often found on the menu of luxury restaurants. Such restaurants usually feature the European cuisine.

Veal is graded as Prime, Choice, and Good. Like beef, the Choice grade may be subdivided into Top Choice. For food service either Prime or Top Choice is best.

In the United States, three types of veal may be purchased. These are bob veal, grain-fed veal, and

RETAIL CUTS OF VEAL
WHERE THEY COME FROM AND HOW TO COOK THEM

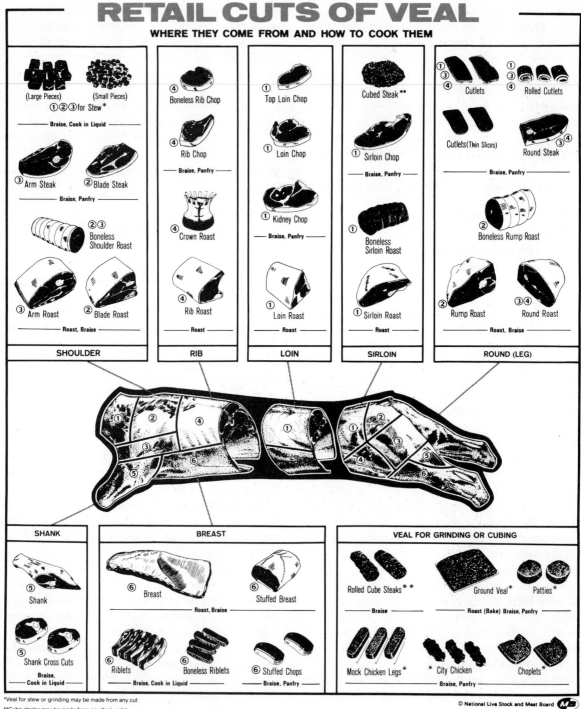

(Large Pieces)   (Small Pieces)
①②③for Stew*

— Braise, Cook in Liquid —

③ Arm Steak   ② Blade Steak

— Braise, Panfry —

②③ Boneless Shoulder Roast

③ Arm Roast   ② Blade Roast

— Roast, Braise —

SHOULDER

④ Boneless Rib Chop

④ Rib Chop

— Braise, Panfry —

④ Crown Roast

④ Rib Roast

— Roast —

RIB

① Top Loin Chop

① Loin Chop

① Kidney Chop

— Braise, Panfry —

① Loin Roast

— Roast —

LOIN

Cubed Steak**

① Sirloin Chop

— Braise, Panfry —

① Boneless Sirloin Roast

① Sirloin Roast

— Roast —

SIRLOIN

①③④ Cutlets   ①③④ Rolled Cutlets

Cutlets(Thin Slices)   ③④ Round Steak

— Braise, Panfry —

② Boneless Rump Roast

② Rump Roast   ③④ Round Roast

— Roast, Braise —

ROUND (LEG)

SHANK

⑤ Shank

⑤ Shank Cross Cuts

— Braise, Cook in Liquid —

BREAST

⑥ Breast

⑥ Stuffed Breast

— Roast, Braise —

⑥ Riblets   ⑥ Boneless Riblets   ⑥ Stuffed Chops

— Braise, Cook in Liquid —   — Braise, Panfry —

VEAL FOR GRINDING OR CUBING

Rolled Cube Steaks**   Ground Veal*   Patties*

— Braise —   — Roast (Bake) Braise, Panfry —

Mock Chicken Legs*   * City Chicken   Choplets*

— Braise, Panfry —

*Veal for stew or grinding may be made from any cut.

**Cube steaks may be made from any thick solid piece of boneless veal.

© National Live Stock and Meat Board

4-10.

specially-fed veal. Bob veal is from calves less than a week old. Since the animal is immature, the meat is pale and tasteless. It is plentiful.

Grain-fed veal is really baby beef. It does not have the creamy pink color.

Specially-fed veal has been fed a specially formulated milk diet. This produces the creamy pink color, slight marbling, and delicious flavor of quality veal.

A veal *cutlet* is a very thin slice of veal from the leg. It is usually pounded to make it even thinner. It is used to make many unusual and delightful dishes.

PORK CUTS

Figure 4-11 shows the pork cuts. You will notice that pork cuts also have some different names than beef cuts. Pork is usually sold as a side, instead of quartered. Below, the names for pork cuts are compared with those for beef cuts.

Beef	Pork
chuck	picnic ham
	Boston butt
	shoulder butt
	jowl butt
	hocks
head	head
plate	belly (bacon)
rib	spare ribs
round	ham

Pork is also very tender meat. In the United States, the quality of pork is high, although no grading has been set by the government. Pork that is shipped between states is always inspected carefully. This is because of the danger of *trichinosis* (TRICK-uh-NO-sus). Trichinosis comes from a microscopic worm that is found sometimes in the muscles of pork. It can be transmitted to man if undercooked pork is eaten.

Most pork comes from very young animals. Therefore, it is very tender.

Pork may be purchased fresh, cured, and smoked and salted. The cured pork is called *ham*. Today, hams are mild in flavor and not as salty as they were a few years ago. Sometimes they are partially or completely cooked. Both fresh and cured pork must be kept under refrigeration.

LAMB CUTS

Figure 4-12 shows lamb cuts. Lamb, being a very young animal, yields small primal cuts that are all tender. Like veal, it is divided into the *foresaddle* and *hindsaddle*. The cuts are similar to those of veal.

Lamb is graded Prime, Choice, Good, and Commercial. Choice lamb is usually used in food service. Most lamb is six weeks to ten months old. Such lambs are usually billed on the menu as "Spring Lamb."

Since lamb is a very young animal, it is also very tender. Lamb has a distinctive flavor and aroma. The flavor of the fat is often disliked. Thus, the fat should be trimmed as much as possible. Like veal, lamb is more popular in luxury restaurants featuring the European cuisine.

Meat Cut Identification

To aid the wholesale meat buyer, the USDA, in cooperation with the National Association of Meat Producers, has developed a coding system to identify each cut. This service is called the Institutional Meat Purchase Specifications (IMPS/NAMP). It is in use throughout the United States.

All beef cuts are numbered in the 100s. For instance, 100 is the whole carcass. The side is numbered 101, and the forequarter is numbered 102. Each cut in the forequarter is numbered consecutively to 154. The hindquarter is 155, and cuts from that quarter are numbered up to 200.

Veal cuts are numbered in the 300s.

Pork cuts are numbered in the 400s.

Lamb cuts are numbered in the 200s.

A manual is provided to meat purchasers. The manual lists and pictures each cut with its ordering number. This service helps the purchaser receive the exact cut of meat desired.

In addition, the following numbers are used:
- Cured, dried, and smoked beef products—600s.
- Edible by-products—700s.
- Sausage products—800s.
- Portion-cut meat products—1000s.

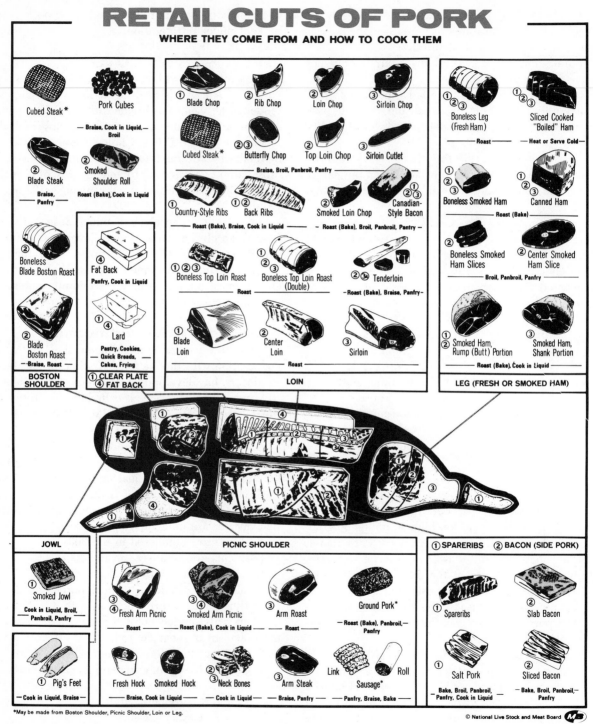

RETAIL CUTS OF PORK
WHERE THEY COME FROM AND HOW TO COOK THEM

*May be made from Boston Shoulder, Picnic Shoulder, Loin or Leg.

© National Live Stock and Meat Board

4-11.

RETAIL CUTS OF LAMB

WHERE THEY COME FROM AND HOW TO COOK THEM

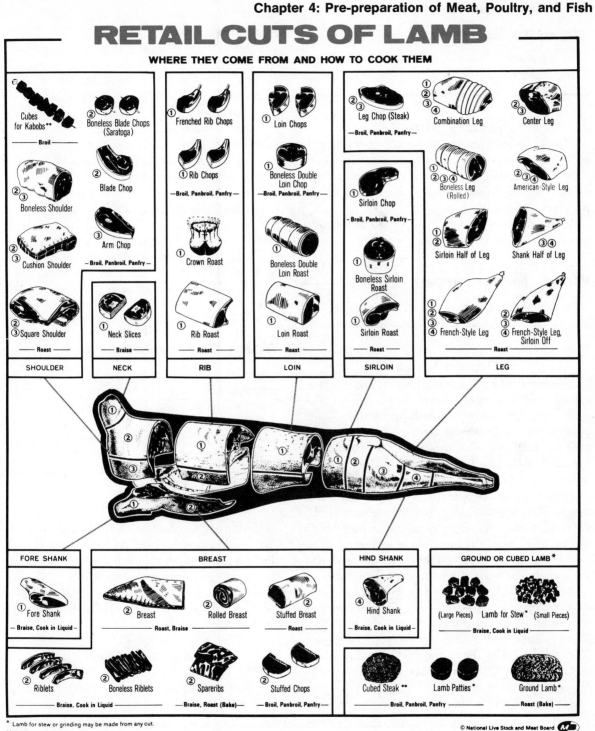

SHOULDER

Cubes for Kabobs**
— Broil —

② Boneless Blade Chops (Saratoga)

② Blade Chop

③ Arm Chop
— Broil, Panbroil, Panfry —

②③ Boneless Shoulder

②③ Cushion Shoulder

②③ Square Shoulder
— Roast —

NECK

① Neck Slices
— Braise —

RIB

① Frenched Rib Chops

① Rib Chops
— Broil, Panbroil, Panfry —

① Crown Roast

① Rib Roast
— Roast —

LOIN

① Loin Chops

① Boneless Double Loin Chop
— Broil, Panbroil, Panfry —

① Boneless Double Loin Roast

① Loin Roast
— Roast —

SIRLOIN

②③ Leg Chop (Steak)
— Broil, Panbroil, Panfry —

① Sirloin Chop
— Broil, Panbroil, Panfry —

① Boneless Sirloin Roast

① Sirloin Roast
— Roast —

LEG

②③④ Combination Leg

②③ Center Leg

②③④ Boneless Leg (Rolled)

②③④ American-Style Leg

①② Sirloin Half of Leg

③④ Shank Half of Leg

①②③④ French-Style Leg

①②③④ French-Style Leg, Sirloin Off
— Roast —

FORE SHANK

① Fore Shank
— Braise, Cook in Liquid —

BREAST

② Breast

Rolled Breast

Stuffed Breast
— Roast, Braise —   — Roast —

② Riblets

② Boneless Riblets
— Braise, Cook in Liquid —

② Spareribs

② Stuffed Chops
— Braise, Roast (Bake) —   — Broil, Panbroil, Panfry —

HIND SHANK

④ Hind Shank
— Braise, Cook in Liquid —

GROUND OR CUBED LAMB*

(Large Pieces) Lamb for Stew* (Small Pieces)
— Braise, Cook in Liquid —

Cubed Steak **
— Broil, Panbroil, Panfry —

Lamb Patties *

Ground Lamb*
— Roast (Bake) —

* Lamb for stew or grinding may be made from any cut.

**Kabobs or cube steaks may be made from any thick solid piece of boneless Lamb.

© National Live Stock and Meat Board

4-12.

Words to Remember

sweetbreads	variety meats
tripe	

Variety Meats

Variety meats include the organs of beef, veal, pork, lamb, and poultry. The organs are liver, heart, brains, kidney, tongue, tripe, and sweetbreads. *Tripe* is the stomach. *Sweetbreads* are the thymus or the pancreas of the calf.

Variety meats also include such parts as the tails, knuckles, feet, and jowls.

Words to Remember

portioned cuts	preportioned meat

Boxed Meat

In many food service operations, no pre-preparation of meats is actually done in the place itself. The meat is bought ready-prepared, preportioned, and packed in a box. *Preportioned* means that the meat is well-trimmed and cut into serving-size portions as specified by the purchaser. Nothing further need be done, except to cook it.

More food service operators are now using boxed meats. They are expensive, but they eliminate the need for a butcher. There is no waste with boxed meats. They also eliminate some customer complaints. Each customer who orders a club steak will get exactly the same size as any other customer.

For example, the buyer of Best Restaurant orders twenty-five 283-g [10-oz] steaks. They arrive in a box, each steak weighing almost exactly 283 g [10 oz]. Each one is the thickness ordered—say 38 mm [1½ in] thick. Each one has the same amount of fat covering. The specifications make sure the buyer gets what is wanted.

All kinds and cuts of meat including ground and chopped meat may be ordered boxed, preportioned, and ready to cook.

PORTIONED CUTS

Some restaurants prefer to order wholesale cuts and cut them into *portioned cuts*. Wholesale cuts are less expensive, but the management must figure in the labor of the meat cutter. The waste cut from the meat must also be costed.

Large restaurant chains often have their own meat cutters located in a central place. The restaurants in the chain order their meats only from the chain's central commissary.

Proper cutting of meat is very important to the restaurant trade. Since meat is usually the most expensive item on the menu, correct portioning can make or break the operation. Meat cutting must be exact. The expertise needed to be a meat cutter can be developed only through long experience. If you are interested in learning more about meat cutting, consult the references listed at the end of the unit.

Words to Remember

broiler	fleshing
capon	fryer
conformation	poultry
drawn	roaster
dressed	stewing hen
ducklings	tom turkey

POULTRY

Poultry are large domestic birds raised to supply food for human beings. The common poultry are chickens, turkeys, ducks, and geese. Chickens, turkeys, and ducks are often found on food service menus in the United States. Geese are seldom offered on the menu, except occasionally around the holidays.

Grades of Poultry

Like beef, pork, veal, and lamb, all poultry shipped between the states must be inspected and approved. The mark of approval may be a metal disk clipped to a wing, a paper tag stuck on the bird, or a printed emblem on the wrapping.

Table 4-2. Kinds of Poultry

Kind	Age	Weight		Characteristics
		Metric	**Customary**	
Chickens				
Broiler	8–10 weeks	0.45–1.2 kg	1–2½ lb	Small, no fat, little meat in proportion to bone.
Fryer	14–20 weeks	1.2–1.6 kg	2½–3½ lb	Meaty, thin layer of fat under skin. Fair portion of meat to bone.
Roaster	5–9 months	1.6–2.3 kg	3½–5 lb	Very meaty, excellent layer of fat. Chunks of fat inside body cavity. Good proportion of meat to bone.
Capon (castrated male)	7–10 months	1.8–3.2 kg	4–7 lb	Very meaty, excellent layer of fat. High proportion of white meat.
Stewing hen	Over a year	1.8–2.7 kg	4–6 lb	Heavy, meaty, fat. Large proportion of flavorful, but not so tender, meat.
Turkeys				
Broiler	8–12 weeks	1.4–3 kg	3–7 lb	Little fat. Little meat in proportion to bone.
Roaster				
Hen	3–9 months	3.8–7 kg	8–15 lb	Good layer of fat under skin and well distributed through meat. Smooth skin, flexible breast bone, few pin feathers.
Tom	3–9 months	3.8–11 kg	8–35 lb	Good layer of fat. Rough skin with pin feathers. Good proportion of white meat. Meat may be dry.

Poultry is graded by the USDA on a voluntary basis. Instead of descriptive words, the letters A, B, and C are used to denote quality. The highest quality is designated by the letter A. Federal grading involves the following five factors:

- *Conformation.* Conformation relates to the general form, shape, and body contour.

- *Fleshing.* The poultry should have plump, firm-looking flesh.

- *Fat.* There should be a thin layer of fat beneath the skin.

- *Cleanliness.* The skin should be free from pin feathers and down.

- *Condition.* The poultry should be free from

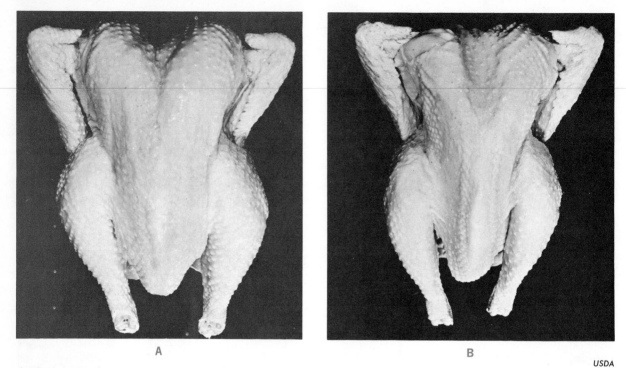

A   B

USDA

4-13. Stewing hens: A quality and B quality. Notice the heaviness of the flesh of the A-quality hen. Also, the B-quality hen has a slit in the skin.

4-14. The tangy taste of apple butter and mustard combine to add delicious flavor to broiled chicken.

National Broiler Council

tears, cuts, bruises, blemishes, or defects such as disjointed or broken bones.

Chickens

Chickens are classified according to the method used to cook them. There are *broilers, fryers, roasters, capons,* and *stewing hens.* Table 4-2 (Page 87) lists the characteristics of each type. Of these, the most important in food service are the fryers.

Figure 4-13 shows differences in A and B quality stewing hens.

PRE-PREPARATION OF CHICKENS

• *Broilers.* Broilers are halved, each half being a portion. They may also be quartered. Fig. 4-14.

• *Fryers.* Fryers are usually quartered, although in a family-service restaurant each chicken may be disjointed into ten to twelve pieces. Fig. 4-15.

• *Roasters.* Roasters are cooked whole.

- *Capons.* Capons are cooked whole. A *capon* is a male chicken that has been desexed. It has been especially bred and fattened for roasting.
- *Stewing hens.* Stewing hens are usually disjointed into ten to twelve pieces. The meat is removed after cooking and cut into chunks or diced.

Boxed Chickens

Many food service operations do not buy whole chickens and portion them. They order boxes of chickens already preportioned into servings. The buyer can order as many halves or quarters as needed. Whole pieces of white meat are frequently ordered for chicken salad or creamed chicken.

Many food service places receive the chicken portions breaded and ready to be fried. This is especially true of those featuring fried chicken.

Turkeys

Turkeys are either broilers or roasters. Table 4-2 lists the characteristics of each type. In food service, roasters are more frequently used. Figure 4-16

4-15. Most people prefer fried chicken to chicken prepared any other way.

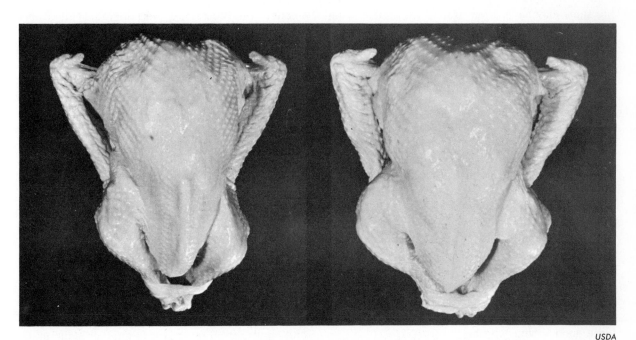

4-16. Roasting turkeys—B quality (left) and A quality (right).

shows the difference between A and B quality roasting turkeys.

The *tom turkey* (the male) is much larger than the hen. The tom is often used in food service because it is cheaper per kilogram. It also has more meat in proportion to bone. The larger the bird, the greater the net yield of meat. This is because the body cavity of a 9.1-kg [20-lb] bird is about the same as that of a 13.6-kg [30-lb] bird. The difference in weight is in the meat and the bone. In birds weighing over 8.2 kg [18 lb], only about 9 percent of the weight is bone. In frying chickens weighing about 1.4 kg [3 lb], almost 33 percent of the total weight is bone. A 13.6-kg [30-lb] turkey will serve about thirty persons.

PRE-PREPARATION OF TURKEYS

Turkey broilers are bigger than chickens. Thus, they are usually quartered, instead of halved.

The pre-preparation of roasting turkeys used to take a great deal of time because of the pinfeathers. These are small feathers that have not fully emerged from the skin. Today, methods of removing pinfeathers have been improved. Hens will have none, but toms may have a few around the legs or wing tips. Pull them out, using a sharp knife. Insert the blade under the feather. Place the thumb on top of the feather and pull.

Ducks

Ducklings, or young ducks eight to twelve weeks old, are best for roasting. Older ducks have stringy, strongly flavored meat. Ducks have only dark meat. Although there is little meat in proportion to bone, roast duckling is a popular item on the menu. Fig. 4-17.

Long Island and western ducklings are served in food service. In spite of the name, Long Island ducklings are raised all over the United States. They have very fine, moist tender meat because they are force-fed grain. Western ducklings are allowed to feed naturally. They are not quite so choice as Long Island ducklings.

Ducklings are usually quartered, a quarter making a good serving portion.

Geese

Young geese, the only kind used in food service, are less than six months old. They weigh from 3.6 kg [8 lb] to 4.5 kg [10 lb]. Geese have only dark meat. They have much fat. They are roasted whole or poached in water.

FROZEN MEAT AND POULTRY

Deep-frozen meat and poultry are plentiful on the market. Any cut of meat or any kind of poultry may be purchased frozen. Deep-frozen boxed meat, preportioned and ready for use, is served in many food service operations.

Chefs disagree on the relative merits of frozen raw meats and poultry versus fresh meats and poultry. Many believe that freezing ruins the quality by breaking down the fiber, causing loss of juices, and softening the texture. Others believe that any loss of quality is small and worth the convenience of having the food always on hand.

If thawing is needed, frozen meat and poultry should be removed from the freezer and placed in the refrigerator. The thawing time depends upon the weight of the piece of meat or poultry. Allow about 3 hours 20 minutes per kilogram [1½ hours per pound].

Poultry is usually cooked after thawing. Frozen meat roasts and steaks should be sent directly from the freezer to the chef for cooking. Frozen meat loses a great deal of juice in thawing and becomes dry during cooking.

CARE AND STORAGE OF MEAT AND POULTRY

There are three cardinal rules for the care and storage of fresh meat, meat products, and poultry.
1. Keep them clean.
2. Keep them cold.
3. Keep them moving.

Cleanliness

When meat and poultry are delivered from a reputable purveyor to the controller, they are as clean as possible. However, in the transfer of meat and poultry from one place to another, contamination is always possible. A reputable purveyor will prevent contamination by storing the meat and poultry in a clean, refrigerated place and transporting it in clean, refrigerated trucks.

Unfrozen quarters of meat are best left unwrapped. The heavy coating of fat protects them from drying. Cuts of meat should be lightly wrapped.

Since poultry does not have a heavy layer of fat, poultry should be *lightly* wrapped. The wrapping should not be tight enough to prevent circulation of air.

Once the meat and poultry have been delivered to the controller, they should be inspected. If boxed, the boxes should be unbroken. If wrapped, the wrapping should not be damaged.

To prevent contamination, the storage areas must be clean, sanitized, odor-free, well-ventilated, and free from litter. Meat, meat products, and poultry should be stored together and apart from any other type of food.

Refrigeration

Meat and poultry, being organic like all foods, contain bacteria. Meat and poultry at room temperature are perfect foods for bacteria. Only refrigeration will keep meat and poultry in top condition. Check again Table 3-1 for the best temperatures and times for holding meat and poultry. The temperature should never run over 4°C [40° F.].

Stock Rotation

This is the same rule discussed before—"first in, first out." Packages should be dated, and the older ones moved to the front. No product should be forgotten in the back of the refrigerator.

USDA
4-17. Ducks that carry the USDA Grade A mark are fully fleshed with a good layer of fat.

Words to Remember

butterfly	mollusk
crustacean	prawn
deveining	roe
fillet	scallop
finfish	shuck

FISH AND SHELLFISH

Seafood is a general term covering all edible fish and shellfish that come from water. Seafood may come from either salt or fresh water. It is classified as finfish or shellfish.

Finfish have fins and a bony structure as part of the backbone.

Shellfish have a hard outer shell covering a soft body with no spinal column. Some shellfish such as lobsters and crabs breathe through gills and have hard outer shells and jointed bodies. Such shellfish are called crustaceans (crus-TAY-shuns). Others, called *mollusks*, have hinged shells and undivided bodies.

Table 4-3 lists the names of finfish and shellfish often offered on the food service menu.

Many restaurants featuring seafoods depend upon local supplies. For instance, salmon is featured in Alaska and the Pacific Northwest, abalone in California, and shrimp and crayfish in Louisiana. In Florida, red snapper and spiny lobster are featured. In New England, Maine lobsters, cod, and halibut are expected. Clams and oysters are found along the Atlantic seacoast.

The Great Lakes are famous for lake trout, whitefish, and perch. Recently the coho salmon has become plentiful there. The rivers produce catfish,

Table 4-3. Finfish, Shellfish, and Mollusks

Finfish		Shellfish	Mollusks
Freshwater fish		Crab	Abalone
Catfish		Lobster	Clams
Frog Legs		Maine lobster	Conchs
Salmon		Slipper lobster	Mussels
Coho salmon		Spiny lobster	Oysters
Silver salmon		Shrimp	Scallops
Sockeye salmon		Brown shrimp	
Trout		Pink shrimp	
Brook trout		Rock shrimp	
Lake trout		White shrimp	
Whitefish			
Whiting			
Saltwater fish			
Bluefish	Pollock		
Cobia	Pompano		
Cod	Red snapper		
Dolphin	Sea bass		
Flounder	Sea trout		
Grouper	Sole		
Haddock	Tilefish		
Halibut	Turbot		
Kingfish	Yellowtail		
Mackerel			

mountain trout, brook trout, smelts, and many other fish. Each region is justly proud of its fish and seafood.

Quality Standards

The USDA inspects some fresh fish and grades according to standards that have been developed. As for meat and poultry, grading is a voluntary service. The quality standards for judging are:

- *Color.*
- *Elasticity of the flesh.*
- *Smell.*
- *Floatability.* Fish that are not fresh float; fresh fish sink.

The restaurants featuring local seafoods not under USDA jurisdiction depend upon the readily recognizable signs of freshness. Fresh finfish has the following qualities:

- *A fresh, mild odor.* A decided fish smell is a sign of a fish that is not fresh.
- *Appearance.* A fresh finfish has firm flesh, springy to the touch. The gills are red and free from slime. The eyes are bright, full, and clear, never sunken.

Some shellfish is purchased either live or already cooked. If purchased alive, they must be kept alive, usually in a tank, until ready to be cooked. Some seafood restaurants have a tank in the window with live lobsters in it as an inducement to the customers. Crab and spiney lobsters are cooked within a few hours of capture. They cannot live long outside the sea.

If purchased already cooked, lobsters and crabs should be a bright pink. The tail of the lobster should be curled and should spring back when straightened. This is a sure sign the lobster was alive when cooked.

Shrimp are sold either in the shell or without it. Shelled shrimp are more expensive. Raw shrimp may be white, pink, or brown, but all shrimp turn a beautiful pink when cooked. Shrimp vary greatly in size and are priced according to the number per kilogram or pound. The large ones, of course, are much more expensive. Large shrimp are sometimes called *prawns.*

Oysters and clams are also purchased live in the shell. The shell should be firmly closed. If the shell is slightly opened and does not close when touched, the mollusk is dead and not fit to eat. Oysters and clams are sold by the bushel, bag, or barrel.

Oysters and clams may be purchased *shucked*— that is, out of the shell. Fresh, shucked oysters and clams will look plump, shiny, and have a fresh odor. They are packed in their own thick, viscous juice. They are sold by the litre, quart, half gallon, and gallon.

A *scallop* is the muscle that opens and closes a certain type of shell. Scallops are always removed from the shell for the market. They should be almost white in color with a fresh smell. They are sold by weight or by the litre or quart.

Fish patties are usually made of cod. The chunks of cod are pressed into blocks and frozen. The block is cut into squares. Each square is breaded, ready for frying. Small pieces of cod are finely minced and pressed into fish sticks. These are also breaded, ready for frying.

Canned fish is also much used in food service. Tuna and salmon make excellent salads and sandwiches. Sardines are used as appetizers or in sandwiches. Herring may be pickled and mixed with sour cream for an appetizer. Fish *roe,* or fish eggs—especially the roe of the sturgeon—are used to make caviar, one of the most expensive appetizers. Caviar may be salmon roe—pink or black.

Pre-preparation of Finfish

Fish may be purchased in many different forms.

- *Whole.* As it came from the water. Fig. 4-18.

Florida Department of Natural Resources

4-18. Whole fish are marketed just as they come from the water. Before cooking, they must be scaled and eviscerated. Usually, head, tail, and fins are removed.

4-19. Drawn fish are marketed with only the entrails removed. They need to be scaled. Head, tail, and fins are removed before cooking.

4-20. Dressed fish are marketed with the scales and digestive tract removed. The head, tail, and fins are cut off.

4-21. A fish cut into steaks.

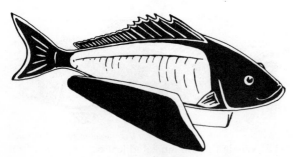

4-22. Fillets are cut from the sides of the fish.

- *Drawn.* Cleaned and scaled. Fig. 4-19.
- *Dressed.* Cleaned, scaled, with head, tail, and fins removed. Cleaning removes the organs and intestines. Fig. 4-20.
- *Steaks.* Large fish may be sliced crosswise into steaks. Each steak is a portion. Fig. 4-21.
- *Fillets.* Smaller fish may be cut lengthwise on each side of the backbone, giving two long fillets. These may be divided into portions, skinless and boneless if desired. Fig. 4-22.
- *Butterfly.* Very small fish, when filleted, have a piece of skin left on to hold the fish together in the shape of a butterfly. Fig. 4-23.
- *Sticks.* Large fish may be cut into uniform, stick-shaped pieces. The sticks may be breaded, ready for frying.
- *Chunks.* Large fish may be cut into chunks. Often the meat around the head and tail that cannot be cut into steaks makes up the chunk meat.

In some restaurants, fish and shellfish are completely prepared on the premises. In other food service operations, the fish may be purchased ready to cook.

Pre-preparation of Shellfish

To cook a live lobster, plunge it headfirst into a kettle of boiling water. Bring to a simmer and cook

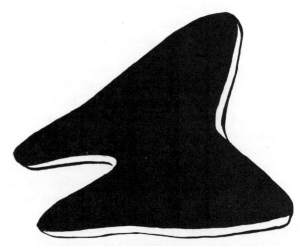

4-23. Butterfly fillets are boneless sides of small fish held together by belly skin.

for twenty minutes. Drain and chill unless it is to be further prepared immediately.

The meat is removed from a cooked crab.

Shrimp are usually deveined before cooking. In *deveining,* the sand vein is removed. The sand vein is a black strip just under the skin along the back of the shrimp. The shell must be removed first. It is very thin and peels off easily. With a sharp knife remove the sand vein and wash out any remaining material.

To cook shrimp, add about 115 g [4 oz] of salt to each 3.8 L [1 gal] of water. Bring the water to 88°C [190° F.]. Add shrimp and bring the water to the boiling point. Do not boil. Let the shrimp cool off in the water.

To prepare clams, soak first in salty water to cover the clams. Soak them for fifteen to twenty minutes to make them spit out the sand. Rinse repeatedly until they are free of sand.

To prepare oysters and clams for the half shell, open the shell with a clam or oyster knife at the thinnest part. Do this by inserting the tip of the knife where the shell meets. Twist the knife, forcing the shell to open. Cut the muscle at the hinge of the shell. Cut the muscle holding the mollusk to the shell. Place on a bed of ice and refrigerate. Be careful not to let the mollusks soak in the ice water. They should rest on the ice, not in it.

Care and Storage

Frozen fish should be kept at −18°C [0° F.] until ready to be defrosted. Many fish can be prepared without defrosting. If thawing is needed, place in the refrigerator and use immediately after the thawing is completed. Never refreeze fish that has thawed.

Fresh fish are packed by matching fillets, meat side to meat side. Place the fillets on top of ice and refrigerate. Allow proper drainage so the fish does not rest in water. For top quality, fillets and steaks should be used the same day they are cut.

Do not store fresh fish with any other product. The fishy taste and odor are readily picked up by other foods. Also, fish will absorb the taste and odor of other foods.

Smoked fish should be kept refrigerated. Canned fish should be kept in cool, dry storage. Once the can has been opened, the contents should be placed in a covered container and refrigerated. Canned fish should be used the same day the can is opened.

How
Much
Have
You
Learned?

Review this chapter. Answer the following questions to prepare yourself for the post-test. Check your answers with your teacher.

1. Define the *Words to Remember.*

2. From what animals do beef, pork, veal, and lamb come? Describe the quality standards for each.

3. What are the two seals placed on meat by the USDA? What do they mean to the buyer of meat?

4. Why is aging important to beef? Name two methods of aging.

5. Name the primal cuts of beef. Name the retail cuts from the primal cuts.

6. What is the difference among a rib-eye, T-bone, porterhouse, sirloin, and round steak?

7. Compare boxed meats with cut meats. What are the advantages and disadvantages of each?

8. What is the difference between a frying chicken and a stewing hen? What is a capon?

Unit 2: Storage and Pre-preparation

9. Compare a tom turkey with a hen turkey. Why is the tom turkey more commonly used in food service?

10. Name the three cardinal rules for storing fresh meat, meat products, and poultry. Briefly explain each one.

11. Why should steaks be cooked while still frozen?

12. How can the freshness of finfish be judged?

13. How are finfish pre-prepared? Demonstrate the pre-preparation of either a finfish or shellfish.

14. Why should fish fillets be packed on cracked ice?

Regardless of the size of the operation, the receiving area must be organized and well managed. Food service begins here.

96A

Iceberg lettuce is the main ingredient in each of these salads. The addition of cheese, fresh fruits, hardboiled eggs, or herring lends color and variety.

96B

The attractive presentation of food is important. Cut as shown above, the watermelon will serve as a colorful container for the fresh fruit shown in the foreground.

96C

Meat--whether beef, pork, veal, or lamb--is cut into steaks, chops, and roasts, as well as being ground. Notice the marbling in the beef steaks and pork chops in the center.

96D

Filled with marinated sliced cucumbers, sliced black olives, and sliced cold meats, pita bread can be used to make a nutritious sandwich.

Morrison, Inc.

Proper pre-preparation of large cuts of meat, such as those shown in the background, depends on the skill of the meatcutter. He or she must know the correct use for the retail cuts that can be obtained from each piece of meat.

96F

The pork chop has been pan-fried, sealing in its natural juices. The meat in the sandwich is roast beef. The small white dish holds the juice obtained in roasting. Potatoes, french-fried or sautéed, are nourishing accompaniments for both of these dishes.

J. R. Simplot Co.

Blue Anchor, Inc.
One characteristic of quality apples is a firm unbruised skin. Like most fruits, apples can be prepared in many ways. However, some apples, such as the Rome Beauty, are better for cooking. Here, they have been used in an apple tart.

Land O'Lakes, Inc.
Various cut or unwrapped cheeses are displayed against several cheeses covered with protective wax. Blue cheese is shown at the top. Mozzarella, two types of Swiss, Muenster, and brick are shown in the middle. The cut wheels of cheese at the bottom are Cheddar. The semicircular cheese resting on the Cheddar is colby.

96G

Served with candied sweet potatoes or in a sandwich, turkey is delicious with crisp lettuce and fresh tomatoes.

96H

Pre-preparation of Vegetables, Fruits, and Dairy Products

What Will You Learn?

When you finish studying this chapter, you should be able to do the following:
- Define the *Words to Remember*.
- Pre-prepare a variety of fresh fruits and vegetables.
- Store eggs, milk, butter and cheese correctly.
- Identify the types of cheeses and how they are used in cooking.

CHAPTER 5

Fresh fruits and vegetables are often called fresh produce. They are sold by produce purveyors. Fresh produce is important to food service. Fruits are popular as a menu item because of their beauty and flavor. Fruits are also used in the preparation of other foods and for decoration.

Vegetables are even more important. Most meat, poultry, and fish dishes require some vegetables in preparation. Complete meals on the menu usually offer several vegetable dishes.

Freezing, freeze-drying, and improved transportation methods have made possible a wide variety of fruits and vegetables the year round. Food service operations are no longer dependent on a local supply.

Frozen vegetables requiring little or no preparation are now widely available. You might question why you should need to study fresh produce at all. However, as a professional cook you will need to understand the cooking process. Professional cooking is more than just following the directions on a package of frozen peas. Professional cooking involves understandings that come only from handling fresh produce.

Dairy products include milk and all products made from milk. Butter, cheese, and yogurt are made from milk. Puddings, sauces, and other dishes are often based on milk. Although eggs are not a dairy product, they usually are included in a discussion of products requiring refrigeration.

Words to Remember

bulb vegetable	lug
carton	pod vegetable
flat	root vegetable
flower vegetable	seed vegetable
fruit vegetable	stalk vegetable
leaf vegetable	

FRESH PRODUCE
Fresh Fruits

Common fresh fruits, their quality points for selection, and how they are packaged for shipping are listed in Table 5-1. Fresh fruits bruise very easily and require careful packaging. They are packed in a carton, lug, or flat.

• *Carton.* Fruit separated according to size is packed in a carton—a large, heavy cardboard box. Apples, for instance, vary greatly in size, from seventy-two per carton to ninety-six per carton. Hand eating apples such as the Delicious variety are carefully graded for size, wrapped in paper, and packed in a carton.

• *Lug.* Small easily bruised fruits such as apricots, peaches, plums, and cherries are packed in a shallow cardboard or wooden box called a lug. A lug holds 13.6 kg [30 lb], loosely packed. Fig. 5-1.

• *Flat.* Berries that can be crushed very easily, such as strawberries and raspberries, are packed in small baskets. Each basket holds about 454 g [1 lb]. The baskets are placed in a flat, which holds twelve baskets.

• *Other packing.* Some solid fruits such as oranges and grapefruit are packed in a crate. A crate is a large, oblong box separated into two sections. The count in the crate depends upon the size of the fruit.

Cooking apples such as the McIntosh may be packed in a sack.

QUALITY POINTS

The USDA does grade some fresh fruit by number. Number one designates the best quality. However, if left unrefrigerated, fruit, like all produce, will deteriorate quickly in quality. Thus, the grading is often no indication of quality at the moment of delivery.

Blue Anchor, Inc.
5-1. Fresh grapes packed in a lug.

Table 5-1. Fruits—Kinds, Quality Points, Packaging

Kinds	Quality Points	Packaging	
		Type	Count
Apples			
Delicious (red)	Smooth yellow, brilliant red, eating,	Carton	#72 large,
Delicious (yellow)	both varieties should be crisp, good		#96 small.
	flavored, and firm.		
Jonathan	Deep red, eating.	Sack	
McIntosh	Red streaked, cooking.		
Rome Beauty	Large, deep red, baking.		
Apricots	Plump, juicy, golden orange. Flesh yields to gentle pressure.	Lug	13.6 kg [30 lb], loose packed. Medium, and large.
Avocados	Fully ripe, yield to gentle pressure, flesh soft green, no discolored spots.	Flat	#12 large, #18 small.
Bananas	Firm, bright yellow with brown flecks. Avoid green tips or mushy fruits.	Carton	40 lb or 20 lb. By single "hand."
Blueberries	Dark blue color with silvery sheen. Avoid dried berries or mushy ones. Look for mold.	Flat	12 baskets to flat, about 454 g [1 lb] each.
Cherries			
Bing	Dark red. Plump, full fruit.	Lug	13.6 kg [30 lb], loose packed.
Sour	Bright red, fully ripe. Look for moldy fruit, stained container.	Lug	13.6 kg [30 lb], loose packed.
Cranberries	Bright red, firm, no shriveled berries. Look for mold spots.	Lug	13.6 kg [30 lb], loose packed.
Grapefruit	Firm, good shape, heavy for the size, indicating juiciness. Avoid soft spots especially at the stem end.	Carton Crate	#36 largest, #64 smallest.
Grapes			
Emperor	Plump fruit that cling to the stem.	Lug	13.6 kg [30 lb].
Muskat	Deep red.		
Thompson	Pale green seedless.		

Table 5-1. Fruits—Kinds, Quality Points, Packaging (Continued)

Kinds	Quality Points	Packaging	
		Type	**Count**
Lemons and Limes	Bright yellow for lemons. Deep green for limes. Smooth, glossy skin with no soft spots or mold.	Carton	Select medium.
Melons Canteloupe	Pebbled, yellowish skin. Strongly aromatic. Blossom end will yield slightly to pressure. Avoid soft spots and mold.	Crate	#36 smallest.
Honeydew	Pale green with white underside. Good aroma.		
Nectarines	Rich peach color, plump fruit with a slight softening along stem.	Lug	Sized $\frac{6}{8}$, $\frac{6}{7}$.
Oranges Juice	Yellow orange with thin, smooth skin.	Crate	Count 100, 150, 200, etc., to the crate.
Navel	Deep orange with pebbled skin. Easy to peel.		
Peaches Clingstone	Flesh sticks to stone. Must be fully ripe. Avoid mushy, bruised fruit.	Lug	Sized $\frac{6}{8}$, $\frac{6}{7}$.
Freestone	Stone pulls free from flesh. Deep pink-orange. Gives slightly under pressure.		
Pears Bartlett	Pale yellow, bulb shaped. Soft to pressure.	Lugs	Medium to large.
Bosc	Small, brownish yellow.		
Pineapples	Developing yellow color and fragrant odor. Fresh looking spikes. No soft or decayed spots.	Flat	Count 4, 5, or 6.
Plums	Deep purple, soft, plump. Avoid shriveled fruit.	Lug	13.6 kg [30 lb].
Raspberries	Deep red. Avoid soft, mushy, pale pink fruit.	Crate or Flat	12 baskets per flat, about 0.45 kg [1 lb] each.
Strawberries	Bright pink.		
Watermelon	Firm, juicy, bright pink flesh. Smooth, shiny skin with creamy underside.		

As you look at Table 5-1, notice the descriptive quality points. Fruits are judged by appearance first and flavor second. Because of the high amount of sugar in fruit, it molds easily. Since fruit softens as it ripens, ripe fruit bruises and decays easily.

When fruit is delivered, the controller should inspect it for bruises, soft spots, and signs of decay. Wrinkled skin or dry-looking berries are signs of fruit held too long in storage.

PRE-PREPARATION OF FRUIT

Fresh fruit to be served whole needs no preparation except washing just before service. Some fruit will be pared, peeled, sliced, or diced. Because many fruits darken quickly when cut, they are usually not pre-prepared but go immediately into storage.

STORAGE OF FRUIT

Fresh fruit is very aromatic. The delightful smell is one of the reasons for the popularity of fruit. However, fruit should never be stored close to food that absorbs odors. Store fruit with the fresh vegetables.

Fresh fruit continues to ripen while in storage. During ripening, some of the moisture is drawn out of the fruit into the air. Fruit kept too long in storage will develop a wrinkled skin. The refrigerator should have a relative humidity of 85 to 95 percent. The temperature should be between 2–7°C [36–45° F.].

Vegetables

The service of fresh vegetables in food service, except for those used in salads, is now becoming less common. When Clarence Birdseye developed the method of successfully quick-freezing vegetables, he revolutionized food service. He made possible the service of fresh-tasting vegetables without the time-consuming pre-preparation.

KINDS OF FRESH VEGETABLES

Fresh vegetables are often identified by the part of the plant from which they are taken. Table 5-2 lists many vegetables and their source.

• *Root vegetables* are usually starchy since they are the storehouse of energy to grow new plants. Potatoes, carrots, and turnips are examples of root vegetables.

• *Bulb vegetables* such as onions, garlic, and shallots are related to the lily family. Most of them have a strong flavor and odor. They are often considered as herbs. They are used to add flavor to many dishes.

• *Stalk vegetables* such as asparagus, rhubarb, and celery are popular. They must be young and succulent.

• *Leaf vegetables* such as spinach, lettuce, chard, and romaine are often used as the base for salads. They must be young. Old plants are tough.

• *Flower vegetables* are cauliflower, Brussels sprouts, and broccoli. They are picked before the full flowering.

• *Seed and pod vegetables* are peas, beans, and corn. Green peas and beans are picked before they are fully ripe. Corn also is more flavorful and tender if not fully ripe. Corn may be on the cob or stripped from the cob.

• *Fruit vegetables* are squash, tomatoes, and eggplant.

PACKAGING OF VEGETABLES

Like fruits, vegetables are packed in cartons, lugs, and flats. Solid vegetables like potatoes and onions are usually packed in sacks. Some vegetables used mainly for garnish, such as parsley and watercress, are packed in bunches. Twelve bunches make a bundle.

Vegetables such as tomatoes that are packed in a lug are numbered by size. For instance, a lug of tomatoes marked 5/5 will have five tomatoes each way, or twenty-five tomatoes in a layer. The number 6/7 would mean six tomatoes one way and seven tomatoes the other, or forty-two tomatoes per layer. Lugs are packed with two layers.

QUALITY POINTS FOR SELECTION

Notice the descriptive words for vegetables in Table 5-2. Appearance is important, especially for those vegetables to be used raw in a salad. But texture is equally important. High-quality, fresh vegetables are young, crisp, and freshly colored. As veg-

Table 5-2. Vegetables

Kind	Source	Quality Points	Packaging	
			Type	Count
Artichokes	Flower	Bright green. Tightly closed.	Carton	Count #18 to #36.
Asparagus	Stem	Bright green. Unshriveled stems, fresh tops.	Crate	13.6 kg [30 lb], medium, large, jumbo.
Beans, green	Pod	Fresh green. Snappy and crisp.	Carton	13.6 kg [30 lb], loose.
Brussels sprouts	Leaf	Light green. Tightly closed. No spots.	Carton	13.6 kg [30 lb], loose.
Broccoli	Stem and Flower	Deep green. Tightly closed. No yellow flowers.	Carton	450 g [1 lb], loose.
Cabbage				
Red	Leaf	Purplish red. Tightly closed.	Carton	Loose, 18.1 kg [40 lb].
White	Leaf	Light green. Tightly closed.	Carton or sack	18.1 kg [40 lb].
Carrots	Root	Bright orange. Firm.	Sack	11.3, 22.7, 45.4 kg [25, 50, 100 lb].
Cauliflower	Flower	Creamy white, no brown spots.	Crate	Count: 12, 16, 18, 24.
Celery	Stems	Pale green on outside, creamy inside. Crisp, no brown streaks, fresh tops.	Crate	24 bunches.
Chard	Leaf	Deep green, Crisp and fresh looking.	Carton	24 bunches—450 g [1 lb] each.
Chives	Stems	Deep green, white tips.	Bunch	12 bunches make 1 bundle.
Eggplants	Fruit	Deep purple, shiny, smooth skin. Avoid wrinkled skin.	Crate	13.6 kg [30 lb], loose.
Garlic	Bulbs	Full, plump, creamy center with no brown spots when cut.	Bag	2.3–4.5 kg [5–10 lb] per bag.
Leeks	Bulb	White, cylindrical bulb with deep green, fresh leaves.	Bunch	24 bunches in carton.
Lettuce				
Bibb	Leaf	Deep green, small heads. Crisp but fragile.	Carton	13.6 kg [30 lb], loose.
Boston	Leaf	Delicate green, loosely formed heads. Crisp but fragile.	Crate	24 heads to crate.
Endive, curly	Leaf	Light green, crisp, free of brown streaks.	Crate	24 heads to crate.

Table 5-2. Vegetables (Continued)

Kind	Source	Quality Points	Packaging	
			Type	Count
Lettuce (Cont.) Head	Leaf	Light green, crisp, heavy for size, solid center.	Crate	24 heads to crate.
Romaine	Leaf	Deep green, coarse leaf, crisp.	Crate	24 heads to crate.
Mint	Leaf and stem	Deep green, strong minty aroma.	Bunch	12 bunches are one bundle.
Mushrooms	Stem and top of fungus	Creamy white tops with light brown to pink gils. Avoid shriveled tops. Look for moldy spots.	Basket	1.2 kg [2½ lb] per basket, 12 baskets per carton.
Onions	Bulb	Firm, white inside. Avoid soft spots.	Sacks	22.7 kg [50 lb]. 45.4 kg [100 lb]. Medium, large, jumbo.
Parsley	Leaf	Deep green, crisp.	Bunch	12 bunches are one bundle.
Potatoes Idaho	Root	Oval shaped, free from bad spots or cuts.	Sack	45.4 kg [100 lb]. Graded 227 g [8 oz] to 284 g [10 oz].
Maine	Root	Rounded, free from bad spots or cuts.	Sack	45.4 kg [100 lb].
Radishes	Root	Bright red, crisp.	Bunch	12 bunches are one bundle.
Scallions	Bulb	Round, small bulb, fresh tops.	Bunch	12 bunches are 1 bundle.
Shallots	Bulb	Dried, small, round bulbs.	Bag	2.3 kg [5 lb]. 4.5 kg [10 lb].
Spinach	Leaf	Deep green, fresh, crisp.	Bunch	24 bunches are 1 carton.
Squash Summer	Fruit	Bright yellow, bulb shaped. Look for soft spots.	Carton	13.6 kg [30 lb] loose.
Zucchini	Fruit	Deep green.	Lug	13.6 kg [30 lb] loose.
Tomatoes	Fruit	Bright red, ripe. Look for soft spots and mold.	Lug	Largest, 20 to lug. Smallest, 48 to lug.

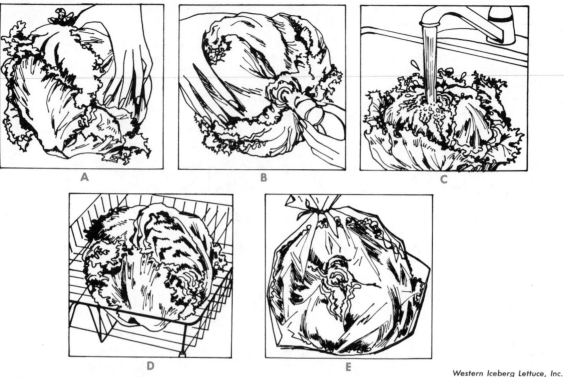

Western Iceberg Lettuce, Inc.

5-2. Washing lettuce. (A) Select heads that give slightly when gently squeezed. A firm—but not hard—head is a perfectly mature head. (B) Core lettuce by holding it core-end down. Whack it onto a countertop. Then lift or twist out the core with your fingers. You may cut out the core with a stainless steel knife. However, cut edges discolor sooner. (C) Rinse by holding head cored end up under running tap water. Allow the water to run all through the head. (D) Drain the rinsed head thoroughly with the cored end down in a rack or on a drainboard. (E) Store in refrigerator in a tightly closed plastic bag or a lettuce crisper.

etables ripen, they gradually lose flavor and become limp. The fresh color fades.

Like fruits, vegetables are graded by number, number one being the best grade. But such grading means nothing if the quality changes after grading. Only the best care can insure quality vegetables from the farmer to the consumer. Most buyers for food service rely on the integrity of the purveyor.

PRE-PREPARATION OF VEGETABLES

Fresh vegetables require more pre-preparation than fruits for several reasons. Vegetables grow close to the ground and are very likely to have dirt and grit clinging to them. Careful washing is needed. Vegetables such as carrots are often deliv-

Words to Remember

blanching	freeze-dried fruits and
canned foods	vegetables
chopping	French knife
dehydrated fruits and	mincing
vegetables	quick freezing

ered with unusable tops. Lettuce may have torn and brown outside leaves that must be discarded. Cleaning of bulky vegetables before refrigeration saves valuable storage space. Figure 5-2 shows the proper procedure for washing lettuce.

Some vegetables may require scraping, paring,

Table 5-3. Shaped Cuts of Vegetables

English Name	French Name	Operation
Dicing	Brunoise	Cutting into cubes.
	Mirepois	A mixture of chunks of vegetables.
Mincing		Chopping very fine.
Shredding	Julienne	Cutting into thin strips.
Slicing	Fermier	Slicing into square cuts.
	Paysanne	Slicing into triangular cuts.

chopping, or slicing if they are to be used the same day. Table 5-3 lists the operations used in their pre-preparation. The English name is given first, followed by the French. Since the French term is usually used by European-trained chefs, you should know both terms.

In some food service operations, the pre-preparation is done in a special area. In others, it is done in the work stations in the production kitchens.

Odds and ends of vegetables left over from the pre-preparation are put in the stockpot to add to the richness of the stock.

Table 5-4 (Page 106) lists the steps in the pre-preparation of a variety of vegetables. Vegetables are cut for many reasons. Some, such as potatoes to be fried, are cut in attractive shapes because they have more eye appeal after they are fried. Cutting also makes it easier to eat the vegetables. They are cut into bite-sized pieces, giving more eating pleasure. Chopping and mincing help release the flavor of vegetables. For instance, the flavors of onion and garlic mingle with and enhance the tomato flavor of spaghetti sauce.

USING THE FRENCH, OR CHEF'S, KNIFE

The method of sharpening a knife is shown in Fig. 5-3.

5-3. Steeling a knife. (A) Hold the sharpening steel in one hand and the knife in the other. (B) Beginning at the back of the blade, bring the knife blade across the steel, ending at the tip. The blade is always at a 45° angle to the sharpening steel. (C) Sharpen the other side in the same manner.

Table 5-4. Pre-Preparation of Vegetables

Vegetable	Pre-preparation
Root	
Beets	Leave on all of root and 2.5 cm [1 in] of stem on top. Wash off dirt.
Carrots	Cut off tops. Scrape. Shred, chop, or slice as needed.
Parsnip	Peel, trim, and rinse.
Potatoes	
Sweet	Wash thoroughly. Trim roots.
White	Scrub with water and a stiff brush before baking. For boiling, pare first. For deep-fat frying, pare and cut into desired shapes.
Rutabagas and Turnips	Pare. Trim ends and rinse.
Bulb	
Dry onions	Trim and peel outer skin with paring knife. Rinse. Cut in half from top to bottom. Chop, slice, or mince as needed.
Leeks and scallions	Cut off green tops about 2.5 cm [1 in] above white bulb. Cut off roots. Wash thoroughly.
Stem and Flower	
Asparagus	Cut off green stem above white part. Paring knife should easily cut through tender part. Strip off lower scales. Scrub thoroughly and peel. Slice.
Broccoli	Cut off tough ends of stalks. Strip away leaves. Split into serving pieces.
Cauliflower	Strip off leaves. Cut off tough ends. Break into flowerettes.
Celery	Trim off green tops and root end. Scrub each stalk with brush. Rinse well. Chop as desired.
Pods and Seeds	
Corn on the cob	Strip off husks and remove silk. Cut off immature tops and stems.
Green beans	Remove ends. Rinse and cut into 2.5 cm [1 in] sections. To French, cut beans lengthwise into two strips.
Peas	Shell. Rinse in colander.
Fruit	
Squash	
Acorn	Wash. Cut in half. Remove seeds and fiber.
Summer	Trim ends and wash. Slice into bite-sized pieces.
Tomatoes	Wash and remove stems. Cut or slice as needed.
Leaf	
Cabbage	Strip off wilted leaves. Quarter and core. Rinse. Cut into sections or shred as desired.
Brussels sprouts	Trim off yellowed leaves and bottom of stems. Soak in salted water for thirty minutes. Rinse and drain in colander.
Lettuce	Trim any brown outside leaves. For head lettuce, remove the core by rapping sharply on the side of the sink. Rinse leaves under running water. Drain in colander. For other lettuces, trim and rinse, following directions for spinach to remove grit.
Spinach	Remove any tough outer leaves, wilted leaves, and ends of stems. Place leaves in large pan filled with cold water. Lift leaves up and down several times. Lift leaves into colander. Pour out water and rinse grit from pan. Refill pan with fresh water. Replace spinach leaves in pan. Rinse leaves again. Continue to rinse and replace water until no grit is in bottom of pan. Drain leaves in colander.

As a beginning professional cook, one of the most important skills to learn is the proper way to slice, chop, dice, and mince all types of food. Fig. 5-4. For this important job, most chefs use the *French knife*, also called the chef's knife. The knife must be very sharp.

┌─ CAUTION ─────────────────────────┐
│ *Know where your hand and the knife are* │
│ *at all times. Take it easy. Work carefully.* │
│ *Speed will come with practice. It is more im-* │
│ *portant to do it right than to do it fast.* │
└────────────────────────────────────┘

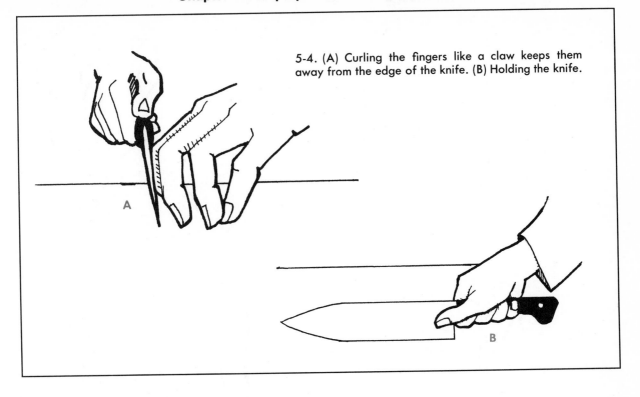

5-4. (A) Curling the fingers like a claw keeps them away from the edge of the knife. (B) Holding the knife.

As you read these steps, follow them in Fig. 5-4 and 5-5.

Chopping may be coarse, medium, or fine. Fine chopping is usually called mincing. Follow these steps to chop and mince an onion.

1. Peel the onion from the top to the root.

2. Cut a small slice on one side of the onion to make a flat side. Place the onion flat side down on the cutting board.

3. If you are right-handed, pick up the knife with the right hand. Hold the onion firmly to the board with the left hand. Curl the fingers like a claw, grasping the onion. This will hold the onion firmly and keep the fingers away from the edge of the knife. Fig. 5-5(A).

4. Make the first vertical cuts perpendicular to the cutting board. The cut pieces should be thin—about 2 mm [$\frac{1}{16}$ in] wide. Leave the root end of the onion uncut. Fig. 5-5(B).

5. Cut across the onion in two horizontal cuts. Fig. 5-5(C).

6. Make the second vertical cuts perpendicular to the first cuts. Fig. 5-5(D). Stop short of the root. The onion will now fall apart.

7. Mince finer if desired. Fig. 5-6.

Once you have mastered the techniques of chopping and mincing onions, the other cutting techniques will come easily. Figure 5-7 shows the techniques for chopping celery. Figure 5-8 shows the technique for slicing tomatoes. Potatoes are sliced as shown in Fig. 5-9.

STORAGE OF VEGETABLES

Fresh vegetables are usually purchased daily because the flavor, appearance, and texture can be easily damaged in storage. The shorter the time from picking to cooking or service, the better the quality. Vegetable storage should always be short-term.

Onions, squash, and sweet potatoes can be stored for a short time at room temperatures. Potatoes need a dark, well-aired room with temperatures

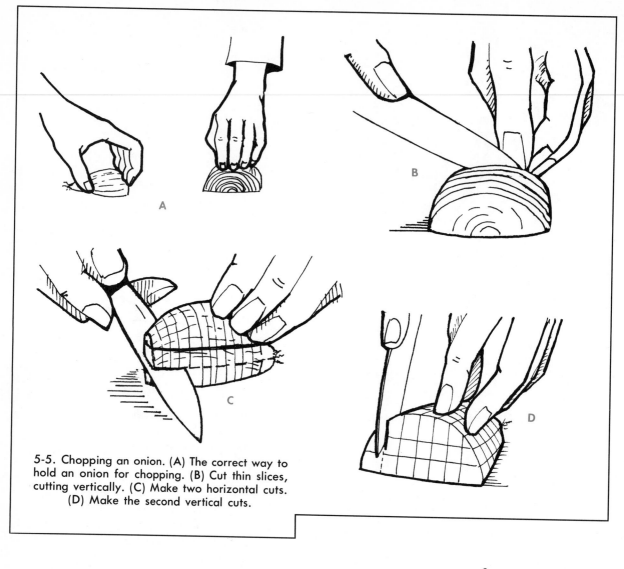

5-5. Chopping an onion. (A) The correct way to hold an onion for chopping. (B) Cut thin slices, cutting vertically. (C) Make two horizontal cuts. (D) Make the second vertical cuts.

between 13–16°C [55–60° F.]. All other vegetables require a high humidity and cold temperatures. The refrigerator should be kept between 2–7°C [36–45° F.] with a relative humidity of 85 to 95 percent.

FROZEN FRUITS AND VEGETABLES

Just about every fruit and vegetable now comes frozen. They may be cut, sliced, diced, or left

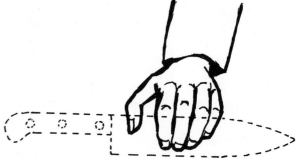

5-6. The position of the left hand when mincing.

A

C

5-7. Chopping celery. (A) Straighten the celery against the side of the French knife. (B) Form a claw with the left hand. This holds the celery firmly, but keeps the fingers away from the cutting edge of the knife. Chop the celery. (C) Study the position of the left hand.

B

5-8. Hold the stem end of the tomato with the left hand. Slice the tomato diagonally.

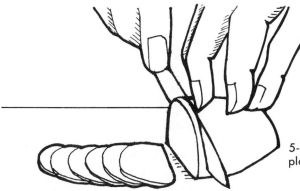

5-9. Peel the potato. Cut it in half lengthwise and place it flat side down on the cutting board. Slice the potato evenly.

whole. They may be combined with many sauces. Frozen foods are extremely popular in food service. They are as close to the natural state as possible, without all the time-consuming labor involved in preparing fresh fruits and vegetables.

The fruits are chosen from young, fully ripe fruits and berries. Rushed from the producer to the quick-freezing plant, they are at the peak of flavor and color. In the newest processing, portable freezers follow the workers. The fruits and vegetables are frozen as soon as they are picked, cleaned, and packed.

Fruits may be frozen with or without sweetening. Sugar adds to the flavor and helps the fruit keep its shape when it is thawed.

Vegetables are picked when young and slightly underripe—close to perfection. Quick-frozen immediately, they keep their bright colors and natural flavors. Vegetables are blanched before freezing. In *blanching*, live steam is applied to seal the outside of the vegetable and shorten the cooking time.

Frozen fruits and vegetables usually do not carry a quality grade because only Grade-A quality fruits and vegetables are frozen. There may be some quality differences among the brands.

Frozen vegetables and fruits must be kept deeply frozen until ready for use. They keep best at a temperature of −18°C [0° F.].

For food service, frozen fruits and vegetables are packaged in 1.1-kg [2½-lb] or 2.3-kg [5-lb] cartons. The cartons are sealed to prevent freezer burn and dehydration.

DRIED AND FREEZE-DRIED VEGETABLES AND FRUITS

Pod vegetables such as peas and beans are often dried. All varieties of dried beans may be purchased—kidney, navy, pinto, soy, or limas. Lentils and peas such as black-eyed peas and split peas are also used, especially for soups.

Dried beans and peas are graded U. S. #1, #2, and #3. The best-quality beans and peas are free of broken vegetables and foreign objects such as twigs, pebbles, and dirt.

Many fruits are also dried. Grapes are dried to make raisins. Plums are dried to make prunes.

Peaches, apricots, and apples are also dried. Dried fruits are graded the same as vegetables.

Dried (dehydrated) fruits and vegetables are soaked before cooking to restore the moisture lost through drying.

Dehydrated, low-moisture, and freeze-dried fruits and vegetables are used more and more in food service. When prepared correctly, they are almost as fresh-looking as frozen foods. Some herbs and vegetables such as garlic, parsley, onions, green peppers, and mushrooms are used in the dried state to add flavor and seasoning. To add even more flavor, onions and mushrooms are sometimes sautéed in butter before freeze-drying.

Dehydrated potatoes are used for making mashed potatoes and other potato dishes. Even the best food service operations use them. It is usually cheaper to use a dehydrated product than to prepare fresh produce, considering the labor cost involved.

Dried and freeze-dried fruits and vegetables should be stored in tightly sealed containers in a cool, dry place.

CANNED VEGETABLES AND FRUITS

The common sizes in canned foods are shown in Table 5-5. The No. 10 tin is most commonly used in food service.

Canned fruits and vegetables are used in food service because they are usually cheaper and easier to prepare than fresh or frozen products. Canned fruits and vegetables do not have the fresh color or flavor. The high heat necessary for sterilizing drains the color and flavor from many of them.

Signs of Spoilage

Although unusual, spoilage of canned foods does happen occasionally. Discard any cans showing the following signs:

- Bulging sides or top.
- Mushy contents.
- Gas bubbles coming through the liquid after the can has been opened.
- Spurting of liquid from the can during opening.
- Sour smell.

Table 5-5. Can Sizes

Name	Size Metric	Size Customary	Cups	Pack
Buffet	225 g	8 oz	1	Fruits, vegetables, sauces, and spaghetti.
Picnic	300–340 g	10½–12 oz	1¼	Soups, fruits, vegetables, fish and meat products.
Vacuum	340 g	12 oz	1½	Corn.
#300	400–450 g	14–16 oz	1¾–2	Baked beans, meat products, cranberry sauce, and blueberries.
#303	450–480 g	16–17 oz	2	Fruits, vegetables, meat, and soups.
#2	600 g	20 oz	2½	Juices, soups, pineapple, and apple slices.
#2½	765–850 g	27 oz–29 oz	3½	Fruits, tomatoes, tomato sauce, pumpkin, sauerkraut, and greens.
	1.3 kg	46 oz	5¾	Juices, whole chicken, pork and beans, and soups for food service.
#10	2.9–3.3 kg	6½–7¼ lb	13–14½	Fruits, vegetables, and entrées.

Grades of Canned Fruits and Vegetables

• *U. S. Grade A Fancy.* Excellent quality. Best color and flavor. Pieces of fruit or vegetables are perfect and uniformly sized.

• *U. S. Grade B Choice* (sometimes called Extra Standard). Good flavor and color. Pieces of fruits and vegetables may have some imperfections. Size of pieces may vary.

• *U. S. Grade C Standard.* Poor color and flavor. Pieces are imperfect and vary in size.

Canned foods, although sterile, need a cool, dry storage. Changes in color, texture, and taste occur at room temperatures or above. The best storage temperatures are between 7–15°C [45–60° F.]

Words to Remember

air cell	egg yolk
candling	emulsifier
chalaza	fresh eggs
clarifier	frozen liquid eggs
dried eggs	infertile eggs
egg white	permeable

EGGS, MILK, AND MILK PRODUCTS
Eggs

Eggs commonly used as food are the product of chickens bred and fed to be good layers of eggs. Most of the eggs sold in the stores or used in food service are *infertile*. Infertile eggs cannot develop into chickens.

Eggs may have white or brown shells, but the color of the shells is unimportant. It has nothing to do with the flavor of the eggs or the color of the yolks.

Eggs are extremely important in food service. Cooked in many ways for meals, they are also used in every work station in the production kitchen. They are important in almost every product made in the bakery. Eggs also are used in the following ways:

• *Garnish.* Hard-cooked eggs decorate salads, appetizers, sandwiches, casseroles, and other dishes.

• *Thickener.* Eggs thicken soufflés and other dishes such as sauces and puddings.

• *Binder.* Eggs hold food such as meat loaf together.

111

• *Coating.* Eggs coat food to be fried so the crumbs stick to the food.

• *Emulsifier.* An emulsifier holds fine droplets in suspension in a liquid. For example, eggs keep the oil in mayonnaise from separating.

• *Clarifier.* Eggs remove the cloudiness from clear soups.

GRADING OF EGGS

Eggs are graded in two ways—for size and quality. The size of eggs is based on the minimum weight per dozen. Table 5-6. Larger eggs command a premium price.

The quality of eggs is determined by a process called *candling.* To understand this process, you need to know something about the structure of an egg. Figure 5-10 is a drawing of an egg. The outer shell is *permeable,* that is, air and fluids can gradually pass through it.

Notice the *air cell* at the top of the egg. When the egg is newly laid, there is no air cell. Gradually, as the egg cools, some of the moisture evaporates through the shell. This forms the air cell. The older the egg, the larger the air cell. The *yolk* is well centered in a freshly laid egg. It is held firmly in place by the *chalaza*—twisted, cordlike strands of heavy egg white. The yolk is well developed with a round shape. The *white* in a fresh egg is very thick. It thins out as the egg ages.

In candling, the eggs are passed in rows over a light beam. The light shines through the thin shell as the egg is rotated. The candler can judge the fresh-

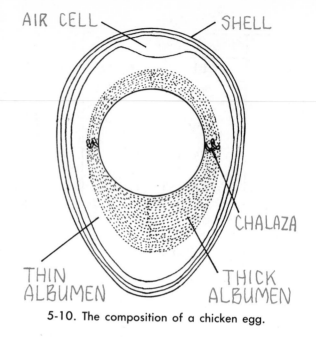

5-10. The composition of a chicken egg.

ness of the egg by the size of the air cell, the centering and shape of the yolk, and the thickness of the white. Blood spots can also be detected. Defective eggs are removed.

The candler grades the eggs by letter:

• *Grade AA.* Thick white, small air cell.

• *Grade A.* Not quite so thick white, larger air cell.

• *Grade B.* Thin white, flattened yolk, large air cell.

The best restaurants will serve only Grade AA eggs for cooking alone. Bakeries may use Grade A or Grade B.

The top and side views of Grade AA, Grade A, and Grade B eggs are shown in Figs. 5-11, 5-12, and 5-13.

PACKAGING OF EGGS

Before packaging, eggs are washed to meet the U. S. standard that eggs must be clean. The washing removes the natural protective coating on the eggshell. Remember, the shell of the egg has pores. It is permeable. To replace this protective natural coating, the eggs are sprayed with a fine mist of oil. The

Table 5-6. Egg Sizes and Weights

	Weight per Dozen	
Size	Metric	Customary
Jumbo	850 g	30 oz
Extra large	840 g	27 oz
Large	745 g	24 oz
Medium	650 g	21 oz
Small	560 g	18 oz
Peewee	470 g	15 oz

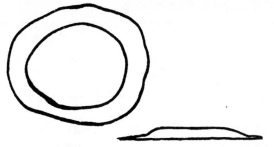

American Egg Board

5-11. Grade AA egg. The area covered is small. The yolk is firm and upstanding. The thick white is large in amount. It stands high and firmly around the yolk. There is only a small amount of thin white.

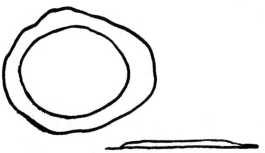

American Egg Board

5-12. Grade A egg. A moderate area is covered. The yolk is round and upstanding. There is a large amount of thick white. It stands fairly well around the yolk. There is a small amount of thin white.

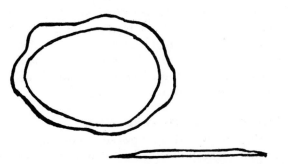

American Egg Board

5-13. Grade B egg, top view and side view. The area covered is wide. The yolk is somewhat flattened. The thick white is medium in amount and flattened. There is a medium amount of thin white.

coating reseals the pores and prevents loss of moisture through the shell.

Fresh, whole eggs are usually bought by the dozen. A box of eggs contains fifteen dozen eggs in six layers of thirty eggs each. The boxes are labeled for grade and size and carry the USDA emblem. Fig. 5-14.

Eggs may also be purchased as fresh liquid eggs, frozen liquid eggs, or dried eggs. These forms are described in detail in Chapter 16.

STORAGE OF EGGS

The treatment of egg shells described above has lengthened the storage life of eggs. Eggs will keep their fresh qualities for weeks at temperatures of 7–13°C [45–55° F.]. Eggs held at room temperature can lose more quality in one day than they will lose in one week under refrigeration. The eggs should be stored in the box in which they were delivered.

Words to Remember

butterfat	margarine
canned milk	pasteurization
cream	salted butter
dried milk	unsalted butter
homogenized milk	

USDA

5-14. An official grade mark for use on cartons or cases of eggs packed under continuous supervision.

Table 5-7. Milk and Cream—Butterfat Content, Packaging, and Use

Name	Butterfat Percentage	Container Size		Use
		Metric	Customary	
Cream				
Coffee	18	1 L	1 pt, 1 qt, 1 gal	Coffee, sauces, cream soups.
Half-and-half	12	1 L	1 pt, 1 qt, 1 gal	Sauces, cream soups, chowder, oyster stew.
Sour	18	0.50 L, 1 L	½ pt, 1 pt, 1 qt, 1 gal	Topping for vegetables, salads, salad dressings, special sauces.
Whipping	36	0.50 L, 1 L	½ pt, 1 pt, 1 qt	Topping for desserts, fruit salads, hot chocolate.
Milk				
Low-fat	2	0.25 L, 0.50 L, 1 L	½ pt, 1 pt, 1 qt, 1 gal	Beverage.
Whole	3.2–4	0.25 L, 0.50 L, 1 L	½ pt, 1 pt, 1 qt, 1 gal	Sauces, puddings, custards, soups, baking.

Milk and Cream

In the United States, "milk" means cows' milk. Other milks such as sheeps' or goats' are used for making cheeses and occasionally for drinking in special diets. Cows' milk, however, is the main product of the dairy industry.

Milk is important in food service because it is used for making many dishes such as sauces, puddings, and casseroles. It is also popular as a beverage by itself or in combination with ice cream or flavors such as chocolate.

Milk has been called the "most perfect food" because it contains so many nutrients in the right proportion for human beings. It is also a source of easy contamination because the "perfect" food for human beings is also the perfect culture for bacterial growth.

PASTEURIZATION AND HOMOGENIZATION OF MILK

Because milk is in general use throughout the United States, its wholesomeness is strictly controlled by the federal, state, and local governments. Pasteurization (PASS-chur-uh-ZA-shun) of milk is required almost everywhere. The word *pasteurization* came from the noted French scientist, Louis Pasteur, who developed the process to make milk safe.

Fresh milk is heated under controlled conditions to 74°C [165° F.], killing all harmful bacteria. It is cooled rapidly and packaged to protect the flavor.

Most milk is also *homogenized*. The milk is forced through a very fine mesh, breaking up the fat globules called *butterfat*. In unhomogenized milk, the cream rises to the top as the milk stands. In homogenized milk, the butterfat remains spread throughout the milk so no cream line develops.

BUTTERFAT CONTENT OF MILK

Milk is graded and priced according to the amount of butterfat in it. Ordinary milk has between 3.2 percent and 4 percent butterfat. Recently, low-fat milk has become very popular because it has fewer calories.

Cream is milk with a higher proportion of butterfat. Table 5-7 shows the butterfat content of milk and creams, their uses, and packaging.

CANNED MILK, DRIED MILK, AND MILK SUBSTITUTES

Canned milk and *dried milk* are used often in food service. They are cheaper and save refrigerated storage space. These types of milk are discussed in Chapter 16.

Coffee cream substitutes have been developed in recent years. These are used in food service. Some are made of nondairy substances such as soybean oil derivatives. Others are a blend of dried dairy products. They are usually packaged in small cups to be served with coffee.

Butter

Butter is the fat of cow's milk that separates from the cream while it is being churned. Butter may be salted or unsalted.

Unsalted butter is also called sweet butter. It is made from sweet cream. It is not graded because only sweet cream is used.

Salted butter may be made from either sweet or sour cream. Salt is added to lengthen the shelf life and to add flavor. Salted butter is graded by letter just like eggs.

- *U. S. Grade AA* is the best quality. It is made from sweet cream and lightly salted. It has a delicate, sweet flavor.
- *U. S. Grade A* is made from cream that has been soured. It is brought back to sweetness by the addition of a chemical neutralizer. It is a little saltier than Grade AA.
- *U. S. Grade B* is made from cream that has soured naturally. The cream has deteriorated in flavor and requires more neutralizer to sweeten. It is heavily salted.

Yellow coloring is often added to butter if needed.

Butter is important in food service, especially in places featuring European cuisine. To most European-trained chefs, nothing can take the place of fine butter.

Margarine

Although not strictly a milk product, margarine is considered a butter substitute. It is made from different oils—mainly vegetable in origin. Margarine is churned with pasteurized skim milk to give it a "butter" taste. The consistency is similar to that of butter. Margarine is colored to look like butter. Margarine has improved greatly the last few years and has won wide acceptance in the United States. The best margarine has a fresh, buttery flavor. No quality grades have been established for margarine.

PACKAGING

Butter and margarine are packed in 454-g [1-lb] bricks divided into quarters or 22.7-kg [50-lb] blocks. The latter is used especially for cooking.

Words to Remember

cold pack cheese	process cheese
curds	rennet
natural cheese	sharpness
pasteurized process cheese food	whey

Cheeses

Cheeses are made from fermented milk solids. Although some cheeses are made from the milk of sheep and goats, cow's milk is used for most cheeses. There are hundreds of kinds of cheeses, but all of them begin with milk and a starter.

The starter is a mixture of sterilized milk and *rennet* (REN-ut). Rennet is an enzyme taken from the fourth stomach of a suckling lamb or calf. It coagulates milk and causes it to separate into *curds*. Curds are the milk solids. The starter may also contain certain bacteria and/or molds. Each bacteria or mold produces a special flavor in the cheese.

After the milk has coagulated, it is cut with a special wire cutter. This causes the curds to separate from the liquid, or *whey*. The whey is drained off, and the curds are cut again. Salt is added for flavor and to help the whey to drain. The curds are then pressed into a metal or wooden frame that drains the last of the whey. The cheese must now ripen under carefully controlled conditions of temperature and humidity. It must ripen for a certain length of time. As the cheese ripens, it develops flavor, or *sharpness*. Sharp cheese is aged cheese with a well-developed flavor.

All these factors affect the flavor, consistency, and quality of cheese. In addition, the butterfat content is very important. All natural cheeses must have at least 36 percent butterfat to be called cheese. The butterfat content of some cheeses may run as high as 80 percent. This is close to the butterfat content of butter.

Kinds of Cheeses

Cheeses may be classified as *natural cheeses, process cheeses,* and *pasteurized process cheese food.*

• *Natural cheeses* are made from milk combined with a starter. Natural cheeses may be divided into three types—*hard, semihard,* and *soft*. Cheeses are classified according to these types in Table 5-8. Of the hard cheeses, Parmesan is the hardest. It may be grated and used in cooking. Parmesan cheese is the cheese sprinkled on spaghetti. Cheddar is softer and may be sliced. Cheddar cheeses are used for sauces, sandwiches, or sliced for serving. Fig. 5-15.

The semihard cheeses of the Fontina type may be sliced for serving. The blue-type cheese has blue veins formed by mold developed in the ripening process. This mold gives the cheese a sharp, distinctive taste. Blue cheeses are often crumbled in salads or mixed with salad dressings.

California Tree Fruit Agreement

5-15. Cheese is often served with fresh fruit for dessert.

The soft cheeses of the Brie type have a crust on the outside and a very creamy, sharp-tasting inside. They are served with crackers as an appetizer or as dessert. Cream-type cheeses such as cottage cheese have a fresh cream flavor. They are used in salads, as a spread, a dip, or in cooking.

• *Process cheeses* are made from a combination of cheeses that have been ground together and well-mixed. They often have seasonings or smoke flavor added. Process cheese that is the consistency of natural cheese is packed in large loaves or small packages. Some process cheese, called *cold pack*, is spreadable. It is sometimes spread on crackers as an appetizer.

• *Pasteurized process cheese food.* This product is not actually a cheese because it has about 10 percent butterfat, instead of the required 36 percent. Natural cheese is mixed with nonfat dry milk solids

Table 5-8. Natural Cheeses

Hard	Blue Mold	Semihard	Semisoft	Soft
Gorgonzola	Blue, American	American	Bel Paese	Brie
Parmesan	Blue, Danish	Cheddar	Brick	Camembert
Romano	Roquefort, French	Cheshire	Mozzarella	Cottage
		Edam	Muenster	Cream
		Emmenthaler	Provolone	Liederkranz
		Gruyère		Ricotta
				Stilton

and water. It makes a mild, soft, easily melted "cheese." It comes in bricks, rolls, slices, or links. This cheese may also be mixed with more moisture and flavorings to make an easily spreadable mix. This type is packed in jars. It usually has a sharp flavor because sharp, aged cheese is used as the base.

STORAGE OF MILK AND MILK PRODUCTS

Milk and most milk products are extremely perishable, requiring refrigeration for storage. The best temperatures are 3–7°C [38–44° F.]. Following are some additional rules for storage:

- Milk and milk products absorb odors and taste very easily. Store tightly covered or wrapped in plastic.
- Natural cheese molds very easily. Use it within a week of delivery.
- Cheese dries out very quickly. Always wrap it securely in plastic. Natural cheese also "oils off" at room temperatures. As cheese warms, some of the butterfat melts. This gives the cheese a greasy look. The dried cheese cracks and loses flavor. It can be used only for cooking.

How Much Have You Learned?

Review this chapter. Answer the following questions to prepare yourself for the post-test. Check your answers with your teacher.

1. Define the *Words to Remember*.
2. How should fresh fruits and vegetables be stored?
3. Explain how you pre-prepare lettuce.
4. Demonstrate how to chop onions.
5. How are eggs used in cooking?
6. How are eggs graded? What does each grade mean? How should eggs be stored?
7. How is butter graded? What does each grade mean? How should butter be stored?
8. What is the difference between natural cheese, process cheese, and process cheese food?

References

Folsom, Leroi. *The Professional Chef*. Boston: Cahners, 1974.

Haines, Robert G. *Food Preparation for Hotels, Restaurants, and Cafeterias*. Chicago: American Technical Society, 1973.

Kotschevar, Lendal H. *Quantity Food Production*. Boston: Cahners, 1966.

National Association of Meat Purveyors. *Meat Buyer's Guide*. Chicago: National Association of Meat Purveyors, 1966.

National Live Stock and Meat Board. *Meat in the Food Service Industry*. Chicago: National Live Stock and Meat Board in cooperation with the National Association of Meat Purveyors, 1975.

Pepin, Jacques. *La Technique*. New York: Quadrangle/New York Times Book Co., 1976.

Ray, Mary Frey, and Lewis, Evelyn Jones. *Exploring Professional Cooking*. Peoria, Ill.: Chas. A. Bennett Co., Inc., 1980.

Villella, Joseph A. *The Hospitality Industry, The World of Food Service*. New York: McGraw-Hill, 1975.

Wolfe, Kenneth C. *Cooking for the Professional Chef*. Albany: Delmar, 1976.

The Garde-Manger, or Pantry

Martha Gray Dubois, Salad Supervisor, Morrison's Cafeteria, Fort Lauderdale, Florida.

MEET THE CONSULTANT

Morrison's Cafeteria is noted for its good-looking salads. They are the first foods the customers see as they enter the serving line. Their beauty is the result of the expertise of Martha Dubois, salad supervisor.

Six years ago, Martha found herself in a difficult position. She was in the process of being divorced, had three children to support, and no training for a job. Martha had left school in the tenth grade. She married early and never expected to work outside the home. Her youngest child was four years old when Martha had to find a job.

Morrison's had a cafeteria close to Martha's home. Salad servers were needed to work the serving counter. Martha was hired part-time, although she had no experience.

While working the line, Martha became intrigued by salads. Born into a poor family in Virginia, she could not recall eating salads at home. To her they were something "classy," something the rich ate. She was interested in the great variety of ingredients used in salad making.

Sometimes the customers would ask her about the salads. What was in this one? What kind of dressing did that one have? Were salads fattening? In learning to answer the questions, she learned about making salads. She decided she would rather make salads than serve them.

After six weeks on the serving line, she was transferred to the kitchen. Two days after she started work in the pantry, the head salad maker cut the end of her finger while chopping lettuce. Martha had to take over.

She learned salad making the hard way. There was no one to teach her. She followed the recipes provided by Morrison's and began to add individual touches. From her experience on the salad line, she knew how salads were supposed to look. Studying the recipes and using her intelligence and sense of beauty, Martha quickly caught on. Now she has four persons working under her. The manager respects her skill as a salad maker and frequently consults her.

She has won the respect of the manager because she is always aware of the cost of food. With food costs going up all the time, the salad maker must always be looking for ways to cut costs. Less expensive food must sometimes be substituted for more costly items. For instance, in making a carrot-pineapple salad, more carrots and less pineapple cut the cost per serving. Expensive nuts are eliminated, or the amount of nuts is cut back.

Martha is also respected because she has learned to work against the clock. The serving line opens at 11:00 in the morning. Martha's salads are ready for service. She has discovered that mixing with the hand is quicker and more thorough than using a spoon. "Just be sure you scrub thoroughly—even above the elbow. Be sure to wear plastic gloves," cautions Martha. "Sanitation is very important in making salads."

Cafeterias serve many senior citizens because the food is good, clean, and inexpensive compared to table service restaurants. "Senior citizens are big salad and vegetable eaters," says Martha. "They like fresh fruit, also." Martha sometimes talks to them about their nutritional needs and encourages them to eat salads.

Martha enjoys her work. She takes great pride in the beautiful salads created at Morrison's. "It would have been easier if I had had some training," she says. "Every person should be trained for a job of some sort. Kids have lots of opportunities now that I didn't have."

Two of Martha's daughters also are salad makers. One works with Martha, and the other works at a neighboring cafeteria. They also enjoy the work. However, they are looking for ways to advance themselves.

Now that her children are older, Martha would like to go back to night school and complete her education. With her intelligence and drive, she will accomplish her aim.

The Seasonings

CHAPTER

6

What Will You Learn?

When you finish studying this chapter, you should be able to do the following:
- Define the *Words to Remember*.
- Identify the seasonings and the dishes in which each is commonly used.
- Pass the posttest.

Seasonings are ingredients that add flavor and zest to foods. They add interest and increase the variety of possible dishes. Seasonings are usually very potent. A little goes a long way, so they should be used lightly. Seasonings should *complement* food, not overpower it. To complement food means to complete its flavor.

Salt and pepper are the most used and best known seasonings. Herbs, spices, salts, extracts, and flavorings are very important in food service. As a professional cook, you need to know how to use them wisely and well.

HERBS
The Families of Herbs

An *herb* (URB) is any plant with a strong flavor and aroma that is used to season foods. Herbs have a stem that withers to the ground after the growing season. Herbs may live from year to year. However, they do not develop woody stems, as do some other plants.

It is difficult to describe the flavor of some herbs. Spend some time smelling and tasting small amounts of herbs. As you eat foods, try to identify the herbs used in their preparation. Then check your identification with the recipe. Only the recipe and experience can help you use herbs correctly in different preparations.

Herbs grow in families. You are familiar with the names of most of the families already. But the members used as herbs may be new to you.

121

Unit 3: The Garde-Manger, or Pantry

Words to Remember

anise	hot pepper
basil	leek
bay leaf	marjoram
caper	mustard
caraway	onion
celery leaves	oregano
celery root	parsley
celery seed	peppermint
chervil	rosemary
chives	saffron
cilantro	sage
comino	savory
coriander	scallion
cumin	sesame seed
dill	shallot
fennel leaves	spearmint
garlic	sweet pepper
herb	tarragon
horseradish	thyme

THE CARROT FAMILY

• *Anise* (ANN-us) is an herb with the taste of licorice. The seeds of the plant are used in baking cookies, cakes, or making pickles. The seeds may be used whole or crushed. Crushing the seeds lets out the full aroma and flavor.

• *Chervil* (SHUR-vil) has parsleylike leaves. Fresh or dried, they are used in sauces and salad dressings.

• *Coriander* (KOR-ee-AN-der) is used in gingerbread, pastries, curries, soups, and sauces. It is called *cilantro* (si-LAN-tro) in Spanish-speaking countries.

• *Cumin* (CUH-min) is called *comino* (CUH-me-no) in Spanish. Its seeds are used extensively in dishes from the Spanish cuisine.

• *Dill* is used in pickles, sour cream mixes, fish, and cabbage. Both the seeds and leaves are used. The dried leaves are called *dill weed*.

• *Fennel leaves* are used in fish dishes and with rice and potatoes.

THE LAUREL FAMILY

• *Bay leaves* are extremely pungent and flavorful. They are used in soups, sauces, stuffings, marinades, and in cooking meats and vegetables.

THE CELERY FAMILY

• *Celery leaves* are the fresh or dried leaves of the celery plant. They are used in soups, stews, and sauces.

• *Celery root* has a stronger flavor than the leaves. It is used in stocks and soups.

• *Celery seeds* have a powerful flavor. They are used in pickles and relishes.

THE ALLIUM FAMILY

The *allium* (AL-e-um) *family* includes the strong-tasting and smelling members of the lily family.

• *Chives* have the most delicate flavor of the allium family. The green, spearlike leaves are chopped or minced. They are then added to eggs, cheese, salads, and sauces.

• *Garlic* is the most powerful member of this family. It grows in small bulb clusters. The segments of each cluster are called *cloves*. The cloves are extremely pungent. Garlic is so strong that very little is needed. For instance, the salad bowl need only be rubbed with garlic for seasoning. Garlic is essential for many preparations from Italy, Greece, Spain, and the Near East.

• *Leeks* have a white bulb and a long green top. Only the bottom half is used. They are milder than onions. They are essential for the finest onion soup.

• *Onions* may be used to flavor almost any meat, poultry, or fish dishes. The different types of onions are described in Chapter 5. Yellow onions, having the strongest flavor, are used as an herb. Cooking onions first removes much of the strong flavor and smell. Thus, onions are usually sautéed before being added to a preparation.

• *Scallions* (SKAL-yons) are the small, green onions used in salads.

• *Shallots* (SHAL-lots) resemble garlic in appearance because the bulbs divide into clusters.

Unlike garlic, the flavor is very mild and sweet. Shallots are highly prized.

THE MINT FAMILY

The mint family includes other members besides the familiar spearmint grown in the garden.

- *Basil* (BAZ-il) is sometimes called the royal herb because it has been highly prized throughout the centuries. Basil is particularly good in tomato sauces, on fish, and in egg dishes.
- *Marjorams* (MAR-jor-ams) include sweet marjoram and oregano. They are very pungent herbs. Sweet marjoram is used in many meat, poultry, and vegetable dishes. *Oregano* (uh-REG-uh-no) is used in sausages, stews, and tomato dishes. It is essential in Italian, Greek, and Spanish dishes.
- *Rosemary* has a very pungent flavor. It is used in marinades, poultry, veal, and with peas and spinach. It is often used in pizza sauce.
- *Spearmint* and *peppermint* are the flavors most identified with the mint flavor. Mint has long been used to flavor candies, chewing gum, and jellies. Its pleasant flavor is much used in desserts. It is especially good when used with chocolate. Fresh mint leaves are used as a garnish for fruit cups, salads, and beverages.
- *Thyme* (TIME) is used in many meat dishes and in Creole cooking.

THE MUSTARD FAMILY

- *Horseradish* is a root. It is very hot when fresh, but gradually loses its flavor in storage. Ground horseradish is mixed with salad dressings, seafood cocktail sauces, and vinegar.
- *Mustard* may be hot or mild. The mustard seeds are used in pickles and to make prepared mustard.

THE PARSLEY FAMILY

- *Parsley* is used constantly in cooking and as a garnish. The flavor blends well with meat, poultry, and fish. Parsley adds flavor to soups, sauces, and vegetables. The roots, stems, and leaves may be used. The roots and stems have the stronger flavor.

Curly parsley is added in sprigs as a garnish. Minced, it is sprinkled on soups, potatoes, sauces, and other dishes. *Straight parsley*, or *Italian parsley*, has a much stronger flavor than curly parsley. It is used in soups, stocks, and sauces.

THE PEPPER FAMILY

- *Hot peppers* are long and slim with a pointed end. Their color may vary from deep green to yellow. The hotness varies greatly, also. Hot peppers are used especially in Mexican cooking and in curries.
- *Sweet peppers* are the deep green, bell-shaped peppers. The bell peppers gradually turn bright red as they mature, but they keep their sweet taste. Whole bell peppers may be stuffed with a meat and rice mixture. Minced or chopped sweet peppers are added to meat loaf, soups, sauces, and stews. They are often used raw in salads.

OTHER HERBS

- A *caper* (KAY-purr) is a flower bud from the Mediterranean area. Capers are pickled and used in sauces, salad dressings, and relishes. Their flavor adds piquancy to *tartar sauce*, a sauce often served with fish.
- *Caraway seeds* are often used in rye breads and cheeses. They also flavor stews, marinades, cabbage, and sauerkraut.
- *Saffron* comes from the stigma, or upper tip, of the crocus. Its delicate flavor and yellow color are highly prized, especially in Spain. Since saffron is very expensive, turmeric is often substituted.
- *Sage* is the best-known seasoning for poultry stuffing. It is also used for seasoning sausages.
- *Savory* has a slightly turpentine taste. It is relished as a flavoring for green beans, green bean salad, lentil soup, and deviled eggs.
- *Sesame seeds* give a nutty flavor to breads, cookies, rolls, and vegetables. Toasting brings out the nutlike flavor.
- *Tarragon* leaves are added to vinegar as a variation for salad dressings and sauces. It is used sparingly in egg dishes, sauces, and sweetbreads. As

mentioned in Chapter 9, a sweetbread is the thymus gland from a calf.

Words to Remember

allspice	mace
black pepper	nutmeg
cardamom	paprika
cayenne pepper	peppercorn
cinnamon	poppy seed
cassia	spice
clove	turmeric
ginger	white pepper

SPICES

Spices are taken from the seeds, stems, barks, fruits, roots, or leaves of plants and trees. Spices are generally grown in the tropics. They are very pungent, aromatic, and flavorful. Spices may be purchased whole or ground.

Spices are not the same as herbs, although both add authenticity to many foreign dishes. Spices are exotic. They come from such faraway places as India, Zanzibar, or Madagascar. Herbs are usually grown in more temperate climates. They are the comfortable country cousins growing in the backyard.

• *Allspice* is the ground berry of a West Indian tree. It blends the flavors of four other spices—cinnamon, cloves, nutmeg, and juniper. Its flavor gives the spice its name.

• *Cardamom* (CARD-uh-mum) is the dried fruit of a plant grown in India. It is used in baking. It is a delicious addition to coffee.

• *Cinnamon* is the bark of a tree that grows in the East Indies. It is used more than any other spice to flavor cookies, cakes, breads, sweet rolls, and pies. It is also used in some stews.

• *Cassia* (CASH-uh) is similar to cinnamon. The flavor and aroma are not as delicate. It is considered inferior to pure cinnamon. It is grown in most tropical countries.

• *Cloves* are the unopened buds of a tree that grows in Madagascar and Zanzibar. Cloves have a very strong flavor. Whole cloves are used to flavor and garnish baked hams. Ground cloves are used in cookies, cakes, and pies.

• *Ginger* is a sharp, peppery spice from the root of the ginger plant. Jamaica ginger is smooth and mild. Indian ginger is strong and hot. African ginger is bland. Ginger is used in curries and in cakes, cookies, and pies.

• *Nutmeg* and *mace* come from the same nutlike fruit of the nutmeg tree. This tree is grown in the East Indies. The inner kernel is the nutmeg. The outer shell is the mace. The inner kernel has the most flavor. Both are ground and used to flavor cakes, cookies, bread, sweet rolls, and pies. Freshly ground nutmeg is sprinkled on custards and eggnogs.

• *Paprika* (pap-REE-ka) is a ground, mild red pepper from Spain or Hungary. The bright red paprika from Spain is considered superior to the dark red paprika from Hungary. Paprika is used as a garnish. Sprinkled on stuffed eggs, casseroles, and salads, it adds a bright spot of color. It browns as it cooks. Therefore, it is often sprinkled on fish, chicken, or meats to aid in browning during frying or broiling.

• *Pepper* is a spice as well as an herb. The pepper that is a spice may be white, black, or red. These peppers come from the dried berries of pepper plants that grow widely in tropical countries.

White pepper is made from the fully ripe seed or berry. The outer shell is buffed away before the seed is ground. White pepper is used in sausages and canned meats. It is also used in white sauces where the specks of black pepper would be undesirable.

Black pepper is commonly used on the table. It is ground from the green, or underripe, whole, dried pepper berries. The berries are cured in the sun. This turns them black. They are called *peppercorns*. There is little difference in flavor between black and white pepper. However, freshly ground black pepper has more flavor than the purchased black pepper. Peppercorns are placed in a pepper mill to be ground as needed. Peppercorns may be crushed and added to soups, stews, and sauces. Crushing releases the flavor.

• *Cayenne* (ki-YEN) *pepper* is a very hot red

pepper ground from the dried fruit of the red pepper plant.

- *Poppy seeds* are the bluish black seeds from a poppy grown in Holland. They are used on top of rolls and bread. Ground, they are sometimes added to cakes.
- *Turmeric* comes from India. It is slightly hot and should be used with care. In small amounts, it may be substituted for saffron because the yellow color is similar. Turmeric gives the yellow color to curries.

Words to Remember

bouquet garni	fines herbes
curry powder	sachet bag
duxelles	spice bag

HERB AND SPICE MIXTURES

- A *bouquet garni* (bow-KAY GAR-nee) is a mixture of fresh herbs tied in a bundle for easy removal. Frequently, the cook will use a celery stalk to hold the herbs, tying them tightly in the stalk with a white string. Bouquets garnis vary widely, depending on the intended use. Two possible mixtures of ingredients are listed on page 127.
- *Chili powder* is a mixture of cumin (comino), ground hot peppers, oregano, and other spices.
- *Duxelles* (do-SELL) are a convenient way to add mushroom flavoring to sauces. The recipe is on page 128. Duxelles will keep for several weeks under refrigeration.
- *Curry powders* are a mixture of spices. They are associated with the cuisine of India. However, they vary widely with the regions of India. Curry powders may be fiery hot or they may be quite mild. Mild curry powders are a blend of ginger, coriander, cardamom, cayenne, and turmeric. Hot curry powders might contain all of these ingredients, plus ginger, peppercorns, ground dried hot peppers, and mustard seed.
- *Fines herbes* (feen-ZURB) is a mixture of parsley, thyme, oregano, rosemary, marjoram, and basil. It is purchased ready-mixed in a bottle or can. The

mixture may vary with the company producing it. Fines herbes is used to flavor egg and meat dishes.

- *Poultry seasoning* is a mixture of sage, thyme, marjoram, savory, pepper, onion powder, and salt.
- A *spice bag* is a name sometimes used for a mixture of spices and dried herbs sewn in bags. A spice bag is sometimes called a *sachet* (sa-SHAY) *bag*. Each bag may hold a different mixture to be used for different preparations. The bags prevent the contents from clouding the sauce or soup. The bag also makes it easy to remove the spices when cooking is done. A typical spice or sachet bag may contain parsley, thyme, marjoram, bay leaf, peppercorns, and whole cloves.

Words to Remember

beau monde	seasoned salt
dehydrator	smoked salt
iodized salt	table salt
kosher salt	
monosodium glutamate	

SALTS

Salt heightens the flavor of other foods. Even in candy and frostings, a pinch of salt brings out the flavor. Salt should be used sparingly. It can always be added by the customer at the table, if desired. European-trained chefs usually use less salt in preparation than do American-trained chefs.

- *Table salt* is a finely ground, free-flowing salt. It contains a *dehydrator*. A dehydrator is a mineral compound that removes moisture from surrounding materials.
- *Kosher salt* is a coarse, natural sea salt. It has a squarish grain. It is sprinkled on pretzels, rolls, and breads before baking.
- *Iodized salt* is seldom used in food service. It is a table salt containing minute amounts of iodine. The body requires iodine in the food or body to maintain normal body health. Iodized salt is used in regions where natural iodine is lacking in the water and soils.

• *Monosodium glutamate* (GLUE-tuh-MATE) is a chemical compound extracted from grains, beets, and soybeans. It has the power to intensify the flavor of food, although it has no flavor of its own. It is much used in Oriental cookery.

• *Seasoned salt* is a mixture of table salt, vegetable flavoring, spices, and monosodium glutamate. Examples are celery salt and garlic salt. *Beau monde* (bow-MAHND) is a seasoned salt containing a mixture of ground celery seed, ground dried onions, and salt. It is used on vegetables such as summer squash and zucchini.

• *Smoked salts* are flavored with hickory smoke or smoke from other scented woods. They give a barbecue flavor to meats.

Words to Remember

catsup	prepared mustard
chili sauce	seafood cocktail sauce
condiment	soy sauce
extract	steak sauce
prepared horseradish	Worcestershire sauce

EXTRACTS AND CONDIMENTS

An *extract* is the concentrated flavor and aroma of an ingredient. Some extracts are preserved in alcohol. The extracts most commonly used in food preparation are vanilla, almond, lemon, orange, and peppermint. These flavorings used to be extracted from natural sources. For example, vanilla extract was taken from the vanilla bean. However, chemists have duplicated many of the flavors. The imitations are cheaper, and they do not bake out. They do not lose their flavor during baking. Therefore, bakeries use the imitation flavorings most of the time.

A *condiment* (CON-duh-munt) is a seasoning or relish for food. You are familiar with many of these, such as mustard, catsup (also spelled ketchup and catchup), or steak sauce. They are offered to the customer at the table. They are also used in cooking.

• *Prepared mustard* is a condiment made from the mustard seeds described earlier in this chapter. It is called prepared mustard to distinguish it from mustard seed or mustard powder. Prepared mustards may be mild or hot. Hot mustards are made by mixing the ground seeds with water and vinegar. Mild mustards are also made from ground seeds, but the seeds have been treated with hot water before grinding. The water draws out the hot flavor from the seeds. They, also, are mixed with water and vinegar. Other spices may be added. The prepared mustards may be made smooth and thick by adding cornstarch.

• *Catsup* is a smooth mixture of tomato sauce, herbs, spices, and sugar.

• *Prepared horseradish* is ground horseradish mixed with vinegar, herbs, and spices. It may be thickened with starch to form a sauce. It comes in varying strengths.

• *Chili sauce* is a mixture of chopped tomatoes cooked with sugar, spices, and vinegar.

• *Steak sauce* is based on tomato sauce flavored with garlic, onions, raisins, herbs, spices, and sometimes orange peel.

• *Seafood cocktail sauce* is catsup or chili sauce spiced with horseradish, red peppers, onions, and herbs.

• *Worcestershire* (WOO-ster-shur) *sauce* is a famous sauce based on vinegar, with garlic, anchovies, spices, and other flavorings.

• *Soy sauce* is a mixture of wheat, soybeans, salt, and monosodium glutamate. It is used extensively in Oriental cooking.

PACKAGING OF HERBS, SPICES, EXTRACTS, AND CONDIMENTS

Spices and herbs should be purchased in small cans or bottles because they lose strength and aroma easily. They are expensive. A little goes a long way.

Extracts and flavorings are stored in dark bottles since they deteriorate in the light. Condiments are packaged in cans or bottles. If used extensively, the condiment is purchased in No. 10 cans.

CARE AND STORAGE

The controller, or storekeeper, should examine the spices and herbs when they are delivered. They should be judged by color, aroma, and freshness.

When rubbed between the fingers, herbs should have a fresh, pleasant smell. The aroma of spices should be apparent as soon as the package is opened.

Light and warmth cause herbs and spices to lose color, fragrance, and flavor. Keep tightly covered in a cool, dark room.

How Much Have You Learned?

Review this chapter. Answer the following questions to prepare yourself for the post-test. Check your answers with your teacher.

1. Define the *Words to Remember*.
2. Why are spices and herbs important in food service?
3. Name the families of herbs and at least one herb from each family.
4. Name at least six spices important in food preparation.
5. Describe a bouquet garni. Why is it important in food service?
6. Describe a sachet bag. How is it used in food service?
7. What are two kinds of prepared mustard?
8. Name three kinds of salt.
9. How does chili sauce differ from catsup?
10. How should spices be stored?

TWO BOUQUETS GARNIS

Yield: 1 bouquet garni per recipe

One		Two	
3 sprigs	Parsley	3 sprigs	Chervil
1	Bay leaf	3 sprigs	Parsley
2 sprigs	Fresh thyme	1	Bay leaf
1	Leek	2 sprigs	Fresh thyme
2	Cloves	1 stalk	Celery
1 stalk	Celery		

METHOD

1. **Place** herbs and spices in celery stalk.
2. **Bind** stalk tightly with white string.

DUXELLES

Equipment   **Yield:** 250 mL [1 c]
Cloth
Sauté pan
Wooden spoon
China cap
Jar with cover

Metric	Ingredients	Customary
250 g	Mushroom stems, chopped	½ lb
50 mL	Onions, chopped	¼ c
30 mL	Shallots, chopped	2 T
30 mL	Parsley, chopped	2 T
30 mL	Butter	2 T
45 mL	Olive oil	3 T
3 mL	Nutmeg, ground	½ t

METHOD

1. **Mix** mushrooms, onions, shallots, and parsley.
2. **Squeeze** mixture in cloth to take out as much moisture as possible.
3. **Melt** butter in sauté pan. Add olive oil.
4. **Stir in** mushroom mixture.
5. **Sauté** on high heat until golden brown.
6. **Stir in** nutmeg. Remove from heat.
7. **Force** mixture through china cap.
8. **Store** in covered jar in refrigerator. Mixture will keep for several weeks.
9. **To use, add** 30 mL [2 T] of duxelles to each 250 mL [1 c] of sauce.

Appetizers

What Will You Learn?

When you finish studying this chapter, you should be able to do the following:
- Define the *Words to Remember*.
- Demonstrate increasing proficiency in the use of the tools used in the garde-manger.
- Prepare a variety of appetizers that meet acceptable standards for flavor and eye-appeal.
- Prepare attractive garnishes and garnish a variety of appetizers.
- Pass the posttest.

EQUIPMENT AND TOOLS IN THE GARDE-MANGER

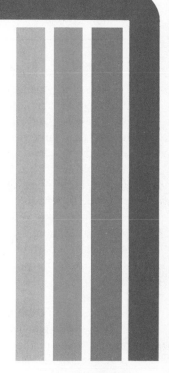

CHAPTER

7

The phrase *garde-manger* (GARD-mahn-JAY) is a French term. It originally meant a space for storage of food. Since cold storage was provided in this area, foods requiring refrigeration began to be prepared here. Now garde-manger means the station where all cold foods are prepared.

For instance, cold appetizers, fruit and fish cocktails, salads, and some sandwiches are under the supervision of the chef of the garde-manger. This station also prepares garnishes to decorate dishes for serving. If a cold *buffet* (buh-FAY) is to be prepared, the garde-manger station has the responsibility. A cold buffet is a form of service in which the guests serve themselves. Desserts prepared by the pastry chef are sometimes served from the garde-manger.

In many American restaurants, the garde-manger is known as the *pantry*. By any name, the work done there is the same. The garde-manger is the station where a worker can use imagination for new decorative ideas.

To function efficiently and artistically, the station of the garde-manger should meet certain requirements. These requirements will depend upon the amount of work to be done.

Words to Remember

appetizer	pantry
barquettes	pullouts
buffet	quiche
garde-manger	zesters
hors d'oeuvre	

Refrigeration

The garde-manger station cannot exist without sufficient refrigerators. In a small restaurant where only salads, sandwiches, and a few garnishes are prepared, a large reach-in refrigerator may be sufficient. However, if many appetizers and an elaborate cold buffet are to be prepared, walk-in, reach-in, roll-in, and pass-through refrigerators may all be needed. To refresh your memory, reread the section in Chapter 3 on refrigerated storage. Some garde-manger stations make good use of *pullouts*. Pullouts are portable, refrigerated drawers that can travel from the production station to the service area.

Cooking Facilities

The garde-manger produces only cold foods, although some of the ingredients may require cooking. Vegetables may need to be cooked and sauces made. Some garde-mangers may have a small cooking space. For others, food that needs cooking may be cooked in other stations. The garde-manger station will need the following equipment:

- *Ice maker,* or at least an *ice keeper.*
- *Blender.*
- *Bench mixer.*
- *Slicer.*
- *Buffalo chopper* for fine mincing and chopping. (It is called a buffalo chopper because it is shaped like the head of a buffalo.)
- *Worktables* with wooden or plastic tops.

Tools

Most of the knives described and pictured in Chapter 2 are needed in the garde-manger. Certain tools are needed for specialized jobs such as carving vegetables, fruits, and butter into fancy shapes. These tools are called *zesters.* Fig. 7-1. Figure 7-2 shows how one zester is used. Fancy cutters such as those used for cookies are necessary. Pastry bags with different tubes are also needed.

Perhaps the most important tools are your hands. The preparation of appetizers and salads requires much handwork. Fig. 7-3. Your hands will be in and out of water most of the time.

APPETIZERS

An *appetizer* is a small bit of food offered to tempt the appetite and prepare the diner for the heavier foods to follow. Appetizers should be:

- Attractive and tempting.
- Light.
- Very tasty, piquant, sharp, and savory.
- Glistening, with a fresh look.

There are hundreds of appetizers. They can be classified into the following five general groups:

- Hors d'oeuvres (hot or cold).
- Canapés (hot or cold).
- Relishes.
- Dips.
- Cocktails.

Salads and soups may also be appetizers. Salads are discussed in Chapter 8.

Cold Hors d'Oeuvres

Hors d'oeuvre (or-DURV) is another French expression. It means a bit of food served apart from

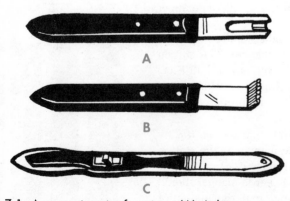

7-1. An assortment of zesters. (A) A lemon zester, (B) a citrus peeler, and (C) a citrus shell cutter.

7-2. Using a zester to cut thin slices of peel from an orange.

7-3. Scoring the peel on citrus fruit to make decorative slices. Start at the top and bring the scorer to the bottom.

the main course itself. (The plural is *hors d'oeuvres*— or-DURVS.) It is often finger food. Finger foods may be eaten using the fingers, instead of a fork or spoon. Some hors d'oeuvres may be served with very little or no preparation. Others require a great deal of work.

READY-MADE COLD HORS D'OEUVRES

Some examples of hors d'oeuvres purchased ready to serve are:

• *Cheese.* Small bits of sharp, piquant cheeses may be served on a toothpick. The smokey, flavorful cheese products described in Chapter 5 are often served this way. The soft Brie-type cheeses are placed in a dish with crackers and a small knife for spreading.

• *Fish.* Smoked salmon, oysters, or clams, pickled herring, and fish roe may be served with crackers.

• *Meat.* Smoked sausages, salami, ham, rare roast beef, and other meats may be sliced thin and arranged on a platter. Snack-sized bread or crackers may be served alongside.

PREPARED COLD HORS D'OEUVRES

Some examples of hors d'oeuvres requiring preparation are described here.

• *Eggs.* Deviled or stuffed eggs are attractive and very popular. Cook, cool, and peel the eggs. Halve them lengthwise. To hard-cook eggs, see Chapter 11. After cooking and cooling, remove the yolks and force through a sieve. Mix the yolks with mayonnaise and seasonings such as salt, Worcestershire sauce, hot pepper sauce, or mustard. Sometimes other ingredients such as tuna fish, chicken,

turkey, or cheese may be blended with the yolks and mayonnaise. The yolk paste should be smooth and soft. Fill a pastry tube. Fig. 7-4. Using a tip, fill the whites with the yolk mixture. Decorate with a slice of stuffed olive, chopped parsley, a black olive, a slice of radish, or another garnish. Fig. 7-5. Use your imagination.

• *Vegetables.* Any raw or cooked vegetable may be used. Raw vegetables should be very crisp. Celery may be stuffed with pimiento cheese, cream cheese blended with blue cheese, or Cheddar cheese mix. Cut the celery stalks into 5-cm [2-in] pieces. Using the pastry tube with a tip, fill the stalks. Cover tightly and refrigerate until firm. You may sprinkle with paprika before serving, if desired.

Another vegetable hors d'oeuvre might be artichoke hearts marinated in Italian dressing. Radishes can be carved to look like roses. Cherry tomatoes may be served whole. Quartered, they can be filled with a blend of cream cheese and blue cheese.

If cooked vegetables are used, they should still be slightly crisp. They may be served with a dip.

• *Fruit.* Any fruit sliced into small finger-food size may be used. Dried fruits such as apricots, prunes, or dates may be stuffed with cream cheese

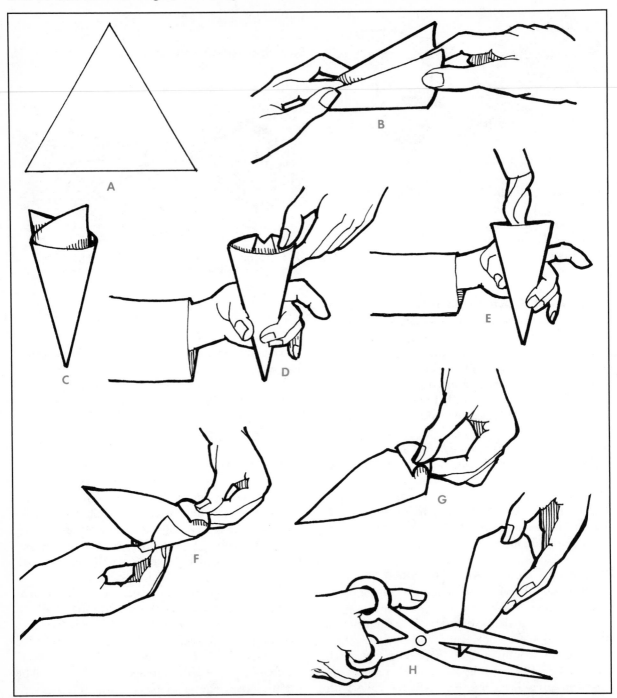

7-4. Making a pastry cone. (A) Cut a triangle with sides 25 cm [10 in] in length. (B) Roll the triangle into a cone. (C) Properly rolled, the cone should look like this. (D) Fold down the corners of the cone. (E) Fill the cone. (F) Flatten the top of the cone. Fold in each side to seal. (G) Fold the top again for a tight seal. (H) Clip off the point.

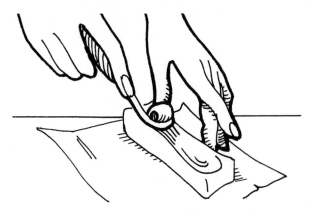

7-5. Making a butter curl for a garnish.

Sauces will come from the saucier station and vegetables from the entremetier station. Among some of the popular hot appetizers are the following:

- *Miniature pizzas.* Small bite-sized pizzas are made in the pastry station.
- *Angels on horseback.* Oysters are wrapped in bacon and broiled.
- *Meatballs.* Small bite-sized meatballs are browned in fat and simmered in a highly seasoned tomato sauce. They are served with toothpicks.
- *Pastries.* Small pastry boats, called *barquettes* (bar-KETS), may be filled with a tasty mixture of mayonnaise mixed with chicken or shrimp.
- *Quiches.* A quiche (KEESH) is a baked onion-cheese pie. It is served in small wedges.

and garnished with nuts. Fresh strawberries with fresh green hulls may be arranged around a bowl of powdered sugar.

- *Fish.* Arrange rolled anchovies, pearl onions, sliced cucumber, cherry tomatoes, or stuffed olives on a skewer. Marinate herring in sour cream. Serve with crackers on the side. Serve cold shrimp on a bowl of ice with spicy tomato sauce.
- *Meats.* Spread very thinly sliced ham with softened cream cheese. Sprinkle with chopped chives. Roll tightly. Chill and cut into 5-cm [2-in] lengths.

Dice ham, salami, smoked turkey, or other meats. Skewer by alternating cubes of meat with pearl onions and cubes of Cheddar cheese.

Slice salami thin and halve each circle. Spread with blue cheese mixed with cream cheese. Roll and fasten with a toothpick.

- *Cheese.* Grind Cheddar cheese in the food grinder. Form into small balls about the size of a walnut. Place clove in one end for a stem. Sprinkle with paprika to give a rosy blush.

Make a cheese ball of ground Cheddar cheese. Roll in chopped nuts. Serve with crackers and knife for spreading. (Cheese balls may be purchased ready-made.)

Hot Hors d'Oeuvres

Since the garde-manger prepares only cold food, the hot appetizers are prepared in other stations.

Words to Remember

aspic	punch
base	relish
canapé	rolled sandwich
dip	spread
garnish	tea sandwich
mousse	terrine
paté	truffles
pullman loaf	

CANAPÉS

Any garde-manger station will sooner or later have the task of preparing *canapés* (CAN-a-PAYS). A canapé is a small, eye-appealing, open-faced sandwich served as an appetizer before the main course. It may also be served at a tea or cocktail party. Canapés may be either hot or cold. They usually have three parts—the *base, spread,* and *garnish.* Sometimes there is a fourth part—the *aspic.*

BASE

Pullman loaves of bread are used for canapés. A pullman loaf is a long, square loaf of bread. The bread is sliced thinly lengthwise, and the crusts trimmed. The bread is usually toasted on one side before making into canapés. White bread is preferred, although whole wheat may also be used.

Occasionally, crackers, pastry, and wafers may be the base for canapés. However, since they quickly lose crispness, they are unsatisfactory.

SPREADS

Spreads are based on butter or margarine.

Spreads are often called "butters" because butter or margarine is the main ingredient. The butter may be mixed with mayonnaise, sharply flavored cheese, mustard, fish, or vegetables. Spreads should be soft enough to cover the bread easily. Their flavor should blend with the rest of the canapé.

The spread has the following purposes:
- It helps keep the base from becoming soggy.
- It helps prevent the bread from drying out.
- It adds flavor.
- It keeps the garnish from slipping.

The greatest help to the chef garde-manger is the butterbase spread. The recipe for this proven spread is found on page 141. Recipes for variations of the basic butter spread are found on page 141.

The recipe for another, more complicated, spread is found on page 141. This spread is called goose liver parfait. It is quite expensive to make. Canapés demand the choicest ingredients, and this recipe is a good example. Notice it contains a good liver mix. Either chicken or goose liver may be used. This mix comes in a can. It also contains whipping cream and truffles. *Truffles* are a very expensive

member of the mushroom family. They grow underground. They are greatly prized for their delicate flavor and aroma.

On page 142 is a recipe for chicken liver spread. This is a less expensive, but delicious, canapé spread.

A *paté* (pah-TAY) is a very fine paste of liver, meat, poultry, or fish enclosed in pastry and baked in the oven. Patés are served cold. They are used extensively on canapés in the best restaurants.

A *mousse* (MOOSE) is a mixture of meat or chicken paste, whipped cream, and gelatin. Because it is expensive, it is found only in luxurious restaurants.

A *terrine* (tuh-REEN) is similar to a paté. A finely ground meat mixture is placed in an earthenware mold and poached in the oven or bain marie. It, also, is served cold.

Herbs, such as finely minced garlic, or horseradish may be blended with butter as a base for sliced roast beef. Used alone, vegetable and cheese butters are delicious spreads.

If used for canapés, all these spreads should be applied to the lengthwise-sliced pullman loaf. Apply the spread to the untoasted side. Cover the slice evenly to the edges. After the slices have cooled, place in the refrigerator. When they are cold and the spread has hardened, they may be cut into any desired shape, as shown in Fig. 7-6.

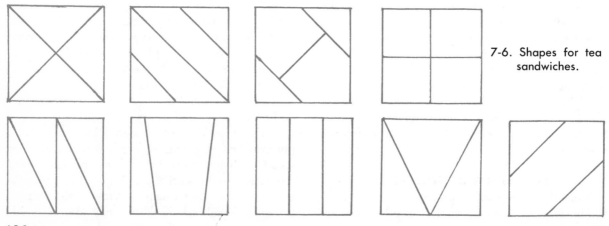

7-6. Shapes for tea sandwiches.

Durkee Foods

7-7. An attractive assortment of canapes.

GARNISH

The *garnish* is the decoration used to top the canapé to make it more attractive. The garnish must always be edible. Since canapés are open faced, the garnish is most important. It should add color, design, and flavor. The colors should never be unnatural or garish. Avoid such colors as purple, blue, or even bright green. Remember, the canapé must look appetizing. Fig. 7-7.

The garnish should also be compatible with the flavor of the butter. For instance, a strip of anchovy should garnish anchovy butter. Anchovies are small, very salty fish. Bits of fish and curls of meat may be used. Herbs such as parsley or mint and spices such as paprika and curry add color and flavor. Vegetables such as carrot curls, radishes, and green peppers can be used to add flavor and decoration to canapés. A garnish chopper is used to chop the garnishes. Fig. 7-8.

ASPIC

After the canapé is spread, cut into fancy shapes, and garnished, it is often covered with an *aspic* (AS-pic). Aspic is a jelly lightly flavored with bouillon or tomato. It contains gelatin to congeal the mixture. It is spread thinly on top of the canapé to hold the ingredients in place. It also helps keep the canapé from drying out. It forms a thin, glossy glaze when refrigerated.

KINDS OF CANAPÉS

• *Egg.* Cut slice of bread into triangles or other shapes as shown in Fig. 7-6. Butter with mustard butter. Place slice of hard-cooked egg on top and a

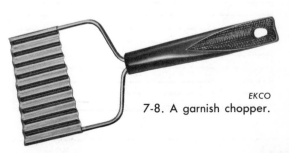

EKCO

7-8. A garnish chopper.

dab of mayonnaise on top of egg. Border sandwich with chopped eggs. Sprinkle chopped parsley in center.

- *Cheese.* Butter shapes of bread with unflavored butter. Mix cheese spread made of ground Cheddar cheese, Worcestershire sauce, grated onion, hot pepper sauce, vinegar, and mustard. Mix in softened cream cheese. Spread on bread. Decorate with half of a cherry tomato and parsley.

- *Fish.* Mix anchovy butter and spread on shapes of bread. Lay strip of anchovy lengthwise on butter. Decorate with pimiento.

- *Meat.* Mix garlic butter and spread on shapes of bread. Curl a very thin slice of rare roast beef around stuffed olive and place in center.

- *Poultry.* Spread shapes of bread with curry butter. Mix finely minced white meat of chicken with minced, crisp bacon and mayonnaise to moisten. Spread on bread. Decorate with cherry tomato and green pepper.

ROLLED SANDWICHES

For cocktail parties, teas, or receptions, *rolled sandwiches* are tasty, attractive, and popular. A rolled sandwich consists of a thin slice of bread spread with a tasty filling. It is rolled and sliced. Fig. 7-9. Long loaves of unsliced pullman bread are needed. Day-old bread is best, since it will not be so crumbly.

To make rolled sandwiches trim the crusts from the bread and slice lengthwise into fine slices. Roll each slice with a rolling pin to compress the bread. Spread each slice with a smooth filling such as is used for the spread on canapés. The filling should cover the slice. However, it should not be so thick that it oozes out when the sandwich is rolled. If desired, place three stuffed olives at the beginning

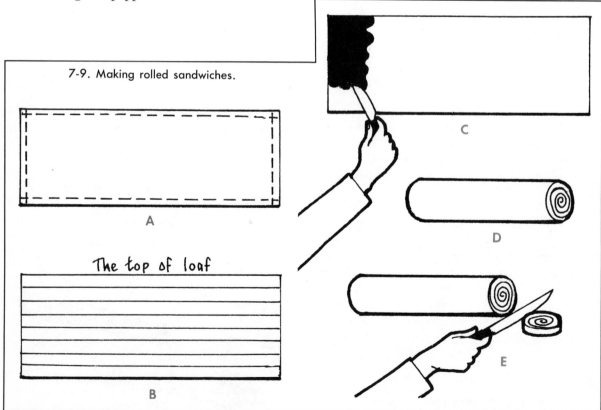

7-9. Making rolled sandwiches.

The top of loaf

of the roll to make an attractive center. Roll up firmly like a jelly roll. Wrap tightly in waxed paper and refrigerate. Slice into pinwheels just before serving.

A ribbon effect can be had by alternating slices of whole wheat and white bread. You will need a loaf each of white and whole-wheat bread. Trim the crusts and slice lengthwise into five slices. Make into two loaves by spreading the filling between alternate slices of whole-wheat and white bread. Divide each loaf into square chunks. Wrap and refrigerate. Slice thinly just before serving.

Tea Sandwiches

For teas and receptions, sweet sandwiches are often served. These sandwiches are known as *tea sandwiches*. Sweet breads such as date-nut, banana, or orange-nut may be spread with softened cream cheese. They may be decorated with a bit of marmalade or preserve. Sweet sandwiches may be closed or open faced.

Relishes

Relishes are crisp vegetables, pickles, or olives served at the table before the meal. In the finest restaurants, relishes are served on a bed of cracked ice in an attractive dish. Relishes must be ice cold.

Almost all crisp, raw vegetables make good relishes. The time-honored ones are celery hearts, green onions, and radishes. Less often used but just as good are sticks cut from carrots, zucchini, cucumber, broccoli, and other vegetables. Whole olives, either green or ripe, and both sweet and sour pickles add to the variety.

Some restaurants specialize in passing relish dishes containing sweet-sour relishes that require a fork for eating. Sauerkraut, sweet-sour corn kernels, miniature corn on the cob, pickled beets, and sweet-sour beans are among the popular relishes.

To prepare vegetables for relish service, first scrub the outside with a stiff brush. Be especially careful to scrub each stalk of celery. Dirt may stick to the ribs of the celery. Some raw vegetables will need further preparation as follows:

• Scrape carrots and cut into long strips about 5 cm [2 in] long.

• Use the stems of fresh broccoli, which are often discarded. Peel off the tough outer skin. Slice the inner, green section as you would carrots.

• Zucchini need not be peeled. Quarter and slice.

• Cucumber is prepared like zucchini. Sometimes it is sliced and placed in a sour cream dressing.

Vegetables should be placed in ice and refrigerated. The ice will keep them moist and crisp. Drain just before serving.

Dips

In recent years, *dips* have become increasingly popular. A dip is a tasty creamy mixture, thick enough to cling to vegetables, or crackers, when they are dipped into it. They are easy to prepare and economical to serve. Dips should always be very flavorful—piquant and savory.

Since guests serve themselves with the dip, the consistency is all important. If it is too thin, it will not cling to the cracker or vegetable. If too thick, the cracker or chip may break.

The cracker or chip should be chosen with care. Potato chips are often used with dips, but they must be sturdy enough not to break. Because of the popularity of dips, many snack foods have been developed besides potato chips. These snack foods are more sturdy than the usual potato chip.

Raw vegetables are also becoming popular with dips. A dip surrounded with colorful, crisp, bite-sized, fresh vegetables is always eye-appealing. Cauliflower, mushrooms, carrots, zucchini, broccoli, and cucumber are among the popular vegetables served with dips.

Sour cream, cream cheese, and mayonnaise are the usual bases for dips. The consistency seems about right. Many spices and herbs are used to add zest to the dips.

Following are a few primary ingredients used in dips:

• *Cheese.* Sharp Cheddar, Roquefort, or blue cheese is blended with sour cream, herbs, and spices.

• *Avocados.* Avocados are blended with cream cheese, onions, and a touch of garlic.

• *Fish.* Clams, anchovies, and shrimp are

137

blended with herbs, spices, and either sour cream or softened cream cheese.

Words to Remember

cocktail	grenadine
fruit cup	punch

Cocktails

Cocktails are another popular predinner food. Cocktails may be juices, fruit cups, or pieces of fish served in a stemmed glass. Offered before the meal, alcoholic beverages are also considered as cocktails. These drinks, however, are not the responsibility of the garde-manger.

All cocktails should be colorful, fresh-appearing, and ice-cold.

JUICES

Fruit and vegetable juices should be served in small, well-chilled glasses. The juice should be tangy, not too sweet, and brightly colored. Tomato juice is an example of a vegetable juice. Orange, pineapple, apricot, papaya, and cranberry are sources of fruit juices. A sprig of bright green mint adds a spot of color, making the juice more eye-appealing.

Juices may be combined for greater variety. Combinations of fruit juices are usually called *punch*. The addition of a carbonated beverage such as soda or ginger ale adds sparkle to the punch. Punch is frequently served at receptions from a large silver or glass bowl. Sometimes an ice ring with fruit and fresh mint leaves frozen in it is placed in the center of the punch bowl for added beauty.

Some mixtures for juices and punch are suggested here.

- *Tomato.* Add dash of Worcestershire or hot pepper sauce. Serve ice-cold. Tomato juice may be mixed with vegetable juices or clam juice for variety.
- *Cherry-apple.* Dissolve cherry gelatin in hot water. Mix with equal parts of apple juice and ginger ale. Serve ice-cold.

- *Tea and juice.* Mix strong tea with equal parts of orange juice, grape juice, pineapple juice, or ginger ale. Add lemon juice and sugar to taste. A few drops of red coloring add to the beauty of the punch.
- *Cranberry and ginger ale.* Mix in equal portions. Add lemon juice to taste.
- *Fruit punch.* Mix orange juice, pineapple juice, grapefruit juice, and ginger ale in equal portions. Add lime sherbet just before serving.

FRUIT CUPS

Fruit cups are cocktails made of pieces of fresh or canned fruit and served in stemmed glass bowls. The better restaurants serve fresh fruit. Although fresh fruit is delicious, canned fruit cocktails are the usual menu fare. They are less expensive, and easier to prepare and serve.

Canned fruit cocktail is served so often that the management seems to forget the appeal of fresh fruit. Consider these cocktail mixtures:

- Mix fresh cantaloupe balls with canned pineapple tidbits. Blend pineapple juice with mint flavoring and green coloring. Take care—a little flavoring and coloring goes a long way! Pour over fruit and chill. Garnish with a sprig of mint.
- Mix pitted Bing cherries, sliced bananas, and canned pineapple chunks. Pour a mixture of pineapple juice and orange juice over the fruit. Chill and serve.
- Mix canned pears, pineapple, and sliced bananas with lemon juice flavored with grenadine. Decorate with a red cherry. *Grenadine* is a syrup made with the juice of the pomegranate fruit and often used as flavoring with fruits and juices.

Fresh fruit is sure to please most customers. Wedges of cantaloupe, honeydew melon, or watermelon are attractive and eye-appealing. Bunches of seedless grapes are easy to serve and eat.

SEAFOOD COCKTAILS

Cocktails made of shrimp, crab meat, clams, oysters, or other seafoods are among the most popular items among the appetizers. They are usually served with lemon wedges or slices and a tomato sauce, spicy and piquant. Usually a few greens such as let-

Florida Department of Natural Resources
7-10. Oysters on the half shell.

tuce or watercress are placed in the cocktail glass as a base for the seafood.

• *Shrimp.* Shrimp may be large or small. Large shrimp, however, are very expensive. To make a larger cocktail shrimp may sometimes be combined with fruit or with other seafood, such as chunks of cooked halibut.

Some fine restaurants have special glass dishes for serving seafood. The glass is in two sections, the outer one for cracked ice, and the inner one for the food. The sauce is served alongside.

Sometimes the shrimp is hooked over the rim of the glass and the sauce served in a small bowl on the inside.

• *Crab meat.* Fresh or canned crab meat may be combined with avocado and vegetables such as celery. Carefully remove the fine, thin bones from the crab meat. Put aside a few large pieces for garnish. Mix the crab meat with mayonnaise and lemon juice. Place a slice of avocado and celery slices on a bed of lettuce. Top with crabmeat mixture. Garnish with a large piece of crabmeat and parsley.

• *Oysters and clams.* These popular mollusks may be served in a cocktail glass with tomato sauce or "on the half shell". Whole, large oysters, usually called bluepoints, are served on a half oyster shell. Six oysters usually make a serving. Fig. 7-10. The half shells are served on cracked ice with spicy tomato sauce alongside.

PRODUCTION OF APPETIZERS

Because the garde-manger is concerned with small units such as appetizers, much handwork must be done. The handwork requires skill and quickness on the part of the workers. Some appreciation for color and design is helpful. If the restaurant prepares food to order, some cocktails may be prepared ahead of time. Many must be made quickly on the spot as they are ordered. The worker must be able to work well under pressure.

Appetizers such as hors d'oeuvres and canapés are usually prepared for special occasions. The chef garde-manger knows how many to prepare. Rarely would they be prepared at the last minute.

Production Assembly of Appetizers

Workers in the garde-manger should know how to set up work centers to allow for fast, efficient work flow. Right-handed workers are most efficient when the work flows from left to right.

In making appetizers, follow these rules:

• Assemble everything completely before beginning to work (mise en place).

• Use both hands.

• Complete one operation before beginning another. For instance, fill all cups with fruit before pouring on the syrup or liqueur.

• Work quickly so food does not become warm.

• Keep a steady pace. Work for rhythm.

139

● Have someone on hand to resupply as needed.

● For two workers, work on opposite sides of the table, using the same supply dishes.

These rules apply whether you are making salads, forming rolls in the bakeshop, setting up desserts, or preparing any other food in quantity.

CARE AND STORAGE

Sanitation is very important in the garde-manger. Here, it is particularly important since you are working with small pieces of food, usually uncooked. Such foods are perfect for bacterial growth. The refrigerators in the kitchen must provide a constant temperature of 4°C [40° F.] or less. Do not allow food to stand out of the refrigerator any longer than necessary. Never allow it to stand out for more than four hours at room temperature. Cover when not in use.

--- CAUTION ---

Many operations insist on workers wearing plastic gloves when handling food by hand. Tongs, forks, spoons, and scoops should be used whenever possible. Remember, the human hand is always a possible source of contamination.

Cover appetizers such as cold hors d'ouevres and canapés with plastic film. Store in the refrigerator until serving.

How Much Have You Learned?

Review this chapter. Answer the following questions to prepare yourself for the post-test. Check your answers with your teacher.

1. Define the *Words to Remember.*

2. List equipment and tools most needed in the garde-manger.

3. What are the qualities of a good appetizer?

4. How does the amount of time needed for preparation affect the making of appetizers?

5. You have been told to prepare 250 crab meat cocktails containing avocado, crab meat, lettuce, and a lemon slice. Set up the production line.

6. Set up the production line for making rolled sandwiches.

7. What is the difference between a canapé and an hors d'oeuvre?

8. How do you store canapés and other appetizers?

9. Why does the garde-manger need so much refrigerator space?

10. Name three qualities a worker in the garde-manger should possess. Discuss each one briefly.

GOOSE-LIVER PARFAIT BUTTER

Equipment
Bench mixer
Paddle

Yield: 900 g [2 lb]

Metric	Ingredients	Customary
450 g	Butter, softened	1 lb
500 mL	Whipping cream	1 pt
900 g	Goose or chicken liver mix, canned	2 lb
50 mL	Cognac or brandy	$\frac{1}{4}$ c
30 g	Truffles	1 oz
Dash	Cayenne pepper	Dash

METHOD

1. **Cream** butter with mixer at medium speed until fluffy.
2. **Beat** in cream a little at a time.
3. **Add** other ingredients. Mix thoroughly.

BASIC BUTTER SPREAD

Equipment
Small mixer
Bowl

Yield: 450 g [1 lb]

Metric	Ingredients	Customary
450 g	Butter, softened	1 lb
30 g	Prepared mustard	1 oz
To taste	Vegetable seasonings	To taste

METHOD

1. **Place** butter in bowl of mixer. Cream on medium speed until light and fluffy.
2. **Add** mustard and seasonings. Mix thoroughly.

Variations for Basic Butter Spread

To basic butter spread recipe, add the following and blend in the blender:

- **Anchovy Butter:** 12 fillets of anchovies.
- **Crab Butter:** One 225-g [8-oz] can of crab meat and 225 g [8 oz] of Gruyère cheese.
- **Curry Butter:** 10 mL [2 t] of curry powder.
- **Garlic Butter:** 5 to 6 cloves of garlic pressed through a garlic press.
- **Mustard Butter:** 30 mL [2 T] of English mustard.
- **Paprika Butter:** 30 mL [2 T] of paprika.
- **Tuna Fish Butter:** One 225-g [8-oz] can of tuna fish and 225 g [8 oz] of Gruyère cheese.

CHICKEN LIVER SPREAD

Equipment
Sauté pan
Spoon
Blender

Yield: 25–50 canapés

Metric	Ingredients	Customary
225 g	Pork fat, chopped	8 oz
450 g	Chicken livers	1 lb
55 g	Onions, chopped	2 oz
120 g	Mushroom trimmings, chopped	4 oz
14 g	Salt	$\frac{1}{2}$ oz
To taste	Pepper	To taste
5 mL	Thyme	1 t
1	Bay leaf	1

METHOD

1. **Melt** pork fat in sauté pan.
2. **Sauté** chicken livers lightly. Remove while still rare.
3. **Sauté** onions and mushroom trimmings.
4. **Combine** all ingredients in blender. Blend until very smooth.
5. **Refrigerate** in covered dish.

Salads, Salad Dressings, and Sandwiches

What Will You Learn?

When you finish studying this chapter, you should be able to do the following:

- Define the *Words to Remember*.
- Compose a variety of salads that meet acceptable standards.
- Identify the best salad dressings for a variety of salads.
- Set up a production line for salads or sandwiches.
- Compose a variety of sandwiches that meet acceptable standards.
- Pass the posttest.

CHAPTER

8

SALADS

Salads vary in many ways. In food service, it is easiest to classify them according to the way they are used in the menu. Salads may be served as appetizers, side salads, entrées, or desserts. Fig. 8-1.

A *salad* is defined in the dictionary as a mixture of green herbs or vegetables served with a dressing. Sometimes it is a similar mixture made with meat, poultry, fish, or fruit. This is an accurate definition, but it cannot begin to describe the delicious mixtures called salads. Salads are especially popular in the United States. Nowhere else is such a delightful variety offered on the menu. Salads are distinctively American. They are, perhaps, the biggest contribution of the United States to the modern cuisine.

Some salads may be hot, but the great majority of them are served cold and crisp. A good cold salad should have the following qualities:

143

The California Iceberg Lettuce Commission
8-1. Many different ingredients can be used to vary the taste, texture, and color of salads.

Words to Remember

congeal	marinade
croutons	marinate
emulsifier	mayonnaise
emulsion	rancid
extender	salad
gelatin	vinaigrette

• *Balanced.* There should be a correct proportion of dressing to other ingredients. Each piece should be lightly coated with dressing, unless the dressing is served on the side.

• *Light.* Each piece should be distinct. The salad should not look overmixed and heavy.

• *Cold and crisp.* The salad should be refrigerated to preserve crispness.

• *Variety of texture.* Pieces should be bite-sized, some soft, some crisp.

• *Flavorful.*

• *Colorful.* The colors should be bright, clear, and fresh. The colors should go together.

Salads as Appetizers

An appetizer salad should be small with a sharp, appetite-provoking flavor. It should be colorful and light. Vegetables, meat, poultry, or fish to be used as an appetizer are frequently marinated. To *marinate* means to soak food in a *marinade* for several hours. A marinade is a mixture of liquids and seasoning. This soaking enables the food to absorb the flavor of the marinade.

The following are examples of salads used as appetizers:

• Small pieces of marinated herring mixed with sour cream. A few pieces are placed on lettuce and garnished with pimiento or chopped parsley.

• Thinly sliced smoked salmon, or lox, served on a piece of lettuce and garnished with parsley. Mustard sauce may be served alongside.

• Fresh fruit arranged on lettuce.

• Melon and avocado slices served on watercress. A thin, piquant dressing is served alongside.

• Raw mushrooms, green pepper, and small flowerets of cauliflower arranged on a bit of lettuce and served with curry mayonnaise.

Side Salads

Side salads are served with a meal. They are larger than an appetizer salad. They will contain more greens. Frequently, the side salad may be served first in the meal. Thus, it acts as both an appetizer and an accompaniment salad. Such salads should be light and refreshing. Side salads are made of vegetables or fruits. Meat, poultry, or fish make too heavy a salad. However, a small amount of cheese may be added for flavor. The following are examples of side salads:

• A variety of vegetables, including chopped lettuce, served in a bowl. This is known as a mixed vegetable, or garden, salad. Fig. 8-2.

• Mixed fruit arranged on a bed of lettuce or watercress.

• Head lettuce cut in a wedge and served on a plate with a choice of dressing.

Entrée Salads

Large, substantial salads may be served as the main course of a meal. These salads are known as entrée salads. They are especially popular as luncheon plates during the warm summer months. Such salads may be composed of greens, vegetables, and fruits. They may also contain more substantial foods such as meat, poultry, or fish. Following are some examples of hearty salads that might be served as an entrée:

• *Chef's salad.* Contains cheeses, meat, poultry, or fish cut in julienne strips. It is served on a bed of lettuce and vegetables. This popular salad is usually served in a large bowl with a choice of dressings.

• *Fruit plate.* Contains fresh and/or canned fruit. It is attractively arranged on a bed of greens on a large plate. Frequently, a scoop of cottage cheese is placed in the middle and the fruit arranged around it.

• *Tuna fish salad.* Tuna fish served with tomato slices, stuffed eggs, olives, and pickles.

• *Stuffed tomato.* Tomato stuffed with tuna fish, shrimp, chicken, or cottage cheese. The stuffed to-

8-2. Fresh and cooked vegetables are combined in an appealing salad.

Green Giant Company

8-3. A turkey salad with chili and tortillas.

mato is often served on a bed of greens and accompanied by olives, pickles, celery sticks, and sliced hard-boiled eggs.

Dessert Salads

Dessert salads are sweet, light, and fruit-filled. The fruits may be whole, sliced, diced, or set in gelatin. Whipped cream is frequently used as the dressing. The following are some examples of dessert salads:

- *Jellied fruit salad* containing any variety of fruit or a mixture of fruit. It may be molded with gelatin and served with whipped cream. Different flavors of gelatin may be used.
- *Wedges of cantaloupe* or other melons served on a plate.
- *Mixture of fresh fruit,* served in a bowl with cream.

Salad Bars

Recently, the salad bar has become increasingly popular. The customers enjoy it because they can concoct their own salads from a variety of ingredients. Food service operators find it profitable because it saves the labor cost of making the salads in the kitchen.

Salad bars may be simple or very elaborate. Some fine restaurants may include expensive items such as thinly sliced roast beef, fish, turkey, and a variety of cheeses. Other restaurants may offer only the bare necessities such as chopped greens, tomatoes, and canned vegetables, plus two or three dressings.

Whatever the offering, all ingredients should appear fresh and appealing. Wilted greens, soft celery, and dry-looking onions will quickly discourage the customer from visiting the restaurant again.

Parts of a Salad

The salad can be divided into four parts, each one requiring different ingredients. These parts are:

- The *base*, or underliner.
- The *body*, or main part.
- The *dressings*.
- The *garnish*.

THE BASE, OR UNDERLINER

The base of a salad is made from greens, mostly those from the lettuce family. Cup-shaped leaves may be used to nest the main part of the salad. A slice of lettuce may underline the body. Greens may also be chopped or shredded.

THE BODY, OR MAIN PART, OF THE SALAD

The body is the most important part of the salad. The main ingredient of the body often gives the salad its name, such as turkey, tuna fish, chicken, or egg salad. Fig. 8-3.

THE DRESSING

Most salads are served with a dressing that adds flavor and tartness. Because some persons may not wish a dressing, it is often served separately in a bowl. On a salad bar, several different kinds of dressing may be offered. Salad dressing may be poured or spooned. Fig. 8-4.

There are four types of dressings:

• *Oil and vinegar.* A thin, tart dressing used on greens, vegetables, and some fruit salads. *Vinaigrette* (VIN-uh-GRET) is the French word for this type of dressing.

• *Creamy.* A thick, creamy dressing made in many different flavors. It is very popular in the United States, but almost unknown in Europe. It is used on greens, vegetables, fruits, and other salads.

• *Mayonnaise.* A very thick, yellow, glossy dressing made with eggs, oil, vinegar, and seasonings. It is spooned on meat, fish, and poultry salads.

It is often mixed with chopped onion, eggs, cheese, and chopped pickle.

• *Cooked.* A very thick, yellow, tart dressing. It is used in potato salads, coleslaw, and many meat and fish salads.

GARNISH

A garnish adds beauty to the salad. The garnish should be edible, simple, and blend with the flavor and color of the salad. Garnishes are listed in Table 8-1.

Equipment

Equipment needs for the salad making area are simple. Most of them have already been described in Chapter 2.

• *Knives.* French knife, paring knife, and slicer. All must be very sharp.

• *Other tools.* Grater, zester, kitchen scissors, shredder, scoops, spatulas, rubber scrapers, mixing spoons, whips, forks, and possibly, fancy cutters.

Morrison, Inc.

8-4. Martha uses the pastry tube to put whipped cream dressing on a fruit salad.

Table 8-1. Garnishes for Salads

Sweet Salads	Tart or Piquant Salads
Red	**Red**
Whole cherries	Sliced or julienne beets
Whole, sliced strawberries	Red pepper slices or rings
Whole raspberries	Sliced or julienne pimiento
Pomegranate seeds	Stuffed olives
Red-colored coconut	Plain radishes
Sugared grapes	Whole cherry tomatoes
Currant jelly	Tomato slices or wedges
Sliced Delicious apple	Salmon roe
White	**White**
Grated coconut	Celery curls or sticks
Marshmallow	Cottage cheese
Other	Swiss cheese—sliced, shredded, grated, or julienne
Whole or chopped nuts	Crumbled blue or Roquefort cheese
Stuffed prunes or dates	Mushrooms
Sugared grapes	**Yellow-orange**
Yellow-orange	Sliced or chopped eggs
Stuffed apricots	Carrot curls or sticks
Sliced oranges	Cheddar cheese—sliced, shredded, grated, or julienne
Pineapple fans or fingers	Lemon slices
Melon balls	**Other**
Green	Ripe olives
Cherries	Caviar
Watercress	**Green**
Mint	Cucumber slices or curls
Sugared green grapes	Green pepper rings or strips
	Mint jelly
	Green olives
	Parsley
	Whole or sliced green onions
	Pickles

• *Utensils.* Large mixing bowls (dishpans are frequently used), pans (#200 size), storage containers, colanders, molds for gelatin salads, and possibly a wooden salad bowl with serving spoon and fork.

• *Small appliances.* Hand mixer, blender.

• *Large equipment.* Horizontal speed cutter, counter mixer with attachments for slicing and shredding, buffalo chopper for fine mincing and chopping. A buffalo chopper is often used in salad making. It stands on the workbench.

Ingredients

Table 8-2 lists the foods most commonly found in the body of the salad. You will note that almost any

Table 8-2. Body of Salads

Ingredient	Use
Cheeses	
Blue	Break into chunks and add to body of salad or blend with dressing.
Hard	Grate and add to body of salad or sprinkle over top for flavor.
Semisoft	Cut julienne and add to greens.
Fish	
Canned	Mixed with other ingredients as an entrée salad.
Fresh	Large pieces mixed with greens for an entrée salad.
Fruits, canned	Standard favorites for fruit plates.
Apricots	
Peaches	
Pears	
Pineapple	
Fruit, dried	Uncooked, dried fruit is often stuffed with cream cheese.
Fruit, fresh	
Apples	Peaches and pears, and bananas are peeled and sliced or served in
Bananas	halves. Apples, especially the Delicious variety, are often sliced un-
Peaches	peeled to add a bit of red color.
Pears	
Canteloupe	Slice in wedges or form into balls. Adds color, flavor, and freshness.
Citrus fruit	Orange, grapefruit, and tangerines must be peeled and sectioned. They are often purchased ready to serve to save time.
Honeydew	Adds a delicate, pale green to salads.
Pineapple	Sliced, cubed, served alone or in combination with other fruits. Sweet and flavorful.
Meats	Thinly sliced roast beef or ham. Meat may be cut julienne as an addition to greens.
Poultry	White meat of chicken or turkey, diced for chicken or turkey salad, sliced or cut julienne as an addition to greens.
Vegetables, canned	
Beans	Green beans, yellow beans, and kidney beans for the popular three-bean salad. Garbanzo beans are well liked at the salad bar.
Peas	Much used in meat, poultry, and fish salads as an extender.
Pickled Beets	Adds deep red color to salad plates.
Sauerkraut	The sour tang is liked by most people.
Vegetables, raw	
Avocado	The soft texture, yellow-green color, and nutty flavor add a ''touch of class'' to a salad.
Broccoli	Adds deep green color and texture to salad.
Cabbage	Shredded to make a slaw.
Carrots	Bright orange color and texture adds color, hardness, and flavor to salad. May be shredded or julienned.
Cauliflower	Crisp, white flowerets.

Table 8-2. Body of Salads (Continued)

Ingredient	Use
Vegetables, raw (Cont.)	
Celery	Add to most salads for crispness.
Cucumber	Sliced thin. Add refreshing coolness, as well as crispness and flavor.
Green pepper	For color, crispness, and flavor.
Mushrooms	Creamy white color, soft texture, and flavor.
Onion	Onions add crispness and interest in flavor. Bermudas—the sweet, purple onion. Spanish—the sweet, yellow onion. Green—the small bulbs on a green stem.
Radishes	Tangy, peppery flavor and bright red color add zest to a salad. May be cut into rosettes for interest.
Tomatoes	A very important vegetable. Add for color and softness. Large tomatoes may be sliced or quartered. Small cherry tomatoes may be halved or left whole.
Zucchini	Dark green skin and creamy inside add beauty and interest. Must be very young.

vegetable or fruit, canned, cooked, or raw, can be used to make the body of the salad. In addition most meat, poultry, and canned or fresh fish add to the variety. Frequently, small amounts of leftover food can be used in salads.

GREENS

The greens are the most important single ingredient in salads. Table 8-3 lists the greens commonly used in salad making. Also included is a description of their appearance, texture, and flavor, as well as the way each is used in a salad. Head lettuce is used the most, but the other greens are also important. You should be familiar with them.

VEGETABLES

The next most important ingredients are the vegetables. Fig. 8-5. Even fruit salads may contain some vegetables. Salads should be crisp and refreshing. Raw vegetables add these necessary qualities. Fig. 8-6. For instance, celery adds crunchiness and moisture to chicken salad.

8-5. A mixing bowl with stand.

Table 8-3. Salad Greens

Green	Description	Use
Endive		
Belgian	Straight tightly packed leaves. Pale green with creamy center. Bitter taste. Crisp texture.	Split in half for service.
Curly	Pale green outer leaves. Creamy centers. Wide-spreading head with curling edges. Slightly bitter taste. Crisp texture.	Blended with other greens.
Escarole	Broad, thick, deep green leaves. Elongated head. Bitter taste. Tough texture.	Blended with other greens.
Lettuce		
Bibb	Deep green leaves. Small loose heads. Slightly spicy flavor. Tender, fragile texture.	Because it is expensive, it is usually mixed with other greens.
Boston	Light green cups. Loose-cupped heads. Sweet, bland flavor. Tender, fragile texture.	Seldom used in food service because it is so fragile.
Garden, or leaf	Bright green with curly edges. Flat and long loose leaves. Sweet and tender.	A base for salads and sandwiches where a flat leaf is needed.
Head, or iceberg	Dark outer leaves. Bright to pale green inner leaves. Firm, tight, rounded heads. Sweet flavor. Tender and crisp, but sturdy. Does not wilt easily.	Torn to bite-sized pieces for salad body. Formed into cups for salad base.
Romaine, or cos	Dark green outer leaves. Creamy inner leaves. Long, loosely packed, elongated heads. Sweet nutty flavor. Not as crisp and tender as head lettuce. Does not wilt.	Used in the salad body more than any other lettuce.
Spinach	Dark green, small leaves. Spreading heads. Delicate flavor. Tough stems.	Mixed with other greens to add color and flavor.
Watercress	Dark green, rounded leaves. Comes in bunches. Peppery flavor. Tender.	Used especially with fruits and as a garnish.

GELATIN

The molded salad made with a gelatin base is popular. Either plain or flavored gelatin may be used. Gelatin salads are colorful and flavorful. They are very useful as a means to makeover odds and ends of food into appealing dishes. Fig. 8-7.

Gelatin is a by-product of the meat packing industry. Gelatin is extracted from the bones and connective tissue of animals. It is then dried. If you have made soup from meat or chicken bones, you might have noticed that the liquid *congeals* when refrigerated. To congeal means to solidify or thicken when cold. It is the gelatin found in bones that makes the liquid congeal. Gelatin may be purchased either in granular form or in sheets. When dissolved in water, it congeals as it cools in the refrigerator. It

151

Morrison, Inc.

8-6. Yvette feeds carrots into the grater attachment on the standing mixer.

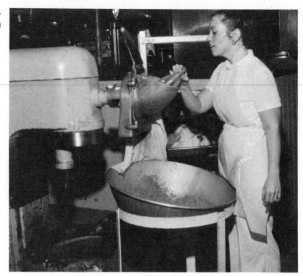

becomes liquid again when heated. Gelatin is sold by weight. It requires 0.45 kg [1 lb] of plain gelatin to set 26.5 L [7 gal] of liquid.

In Chapter 21, gelatin is discussed as it is used in desserts. The same principles apply for making molded salads. Refer to Chapter 21 for more information on gelatin.

EGGS

Eggs are often used in salad making. Only eggs of the highest quality will add the best flavor. Hard-cooked eggs are discussed in Chapter 11. Be sure and follow the directions exactly. This will ensure that the yolks will be bright yellow surrounded by a clear white.

Eggs are also used to make creamy dressings, mayonnaise, and cooked dressings. Perhaps you have noticed that when oil is mixed with a liquid, it separates and floats on top. That happens because oil is lighter than water. However, in creamy dressings and mayonnaise, even though oil is the main ingredient, the oil does not separate. Eggs make the difference. When beaten with oil, the eggs surround fine droplets of oil and hold them in suspension. This is called an *emulsion*. Used in this way, eggs are an *emulsifier*.

In a cooked dressing that contains no oil, eggs add color and flavor. They also help thicken the dressing.

OIL

In most salad dressings, oil is the most important ingredient. Oil adds gloss to the salad, improving the appearance. It also makes the ingredients slightly slippery so they are more palatable.

The oil must be of the best quality. It must be light, and fresh-tasting, since the flavor of the oil will spread through the entire salad. Oil that has deteriorated because of warmth and age is said to be

Morrison, Inc.

8-7. Gelatin salads are put into bowls that have already been garnished with lettuce leaves.

rancid. Vegetable oils from peanuts, cottonseeds, and corn are preferred. Their taste is sweet and bland, and they do not spoil easily. Olive oil is prized for its distinctive flavor. However, it is very expensive and easily becomes rancid.

OTHER INGREDIENTS

Vinegar is another important ingredient in salads. It adds tartness or acidity to a salad. It is essential in most salad dressings. Cider vinegar is a product of the fermentation of apple juice. It is brown and used more than any other type of vinegar. Wine vinegar is distilled from wine. White vinegar is fermented, distilled alcohol. It is less acid than cider vinegar. Vinegar may be seasoned with herbs such as tarragon. Lemon juice is sometimes substituted or used along with vinegar.

Many of the herbs and spices discussed in Chapter 6 add flavor and piquancy to salads. Paprika, dry mustard, pepper, garlic, onions, and oregano are just a few that lend variety.

Croutons (CROO-TAHNS) are cubes of bread, toasted and seasoned to make them crunchy and tasty.

Fresh bread cubes are sometimes added to expensive moist food such as crabmeat as an *extender.* Bread absorbs flavors easily, extending the apparent amount of crabmeat in the salad. Crabmeat is very expensive, but bread is cheap.

Crisp ham and bacon bits have long been used to add flavor and crunchiness to salads. Recently a substitute for these items has become available. Although the bits taste like ham or bacon, they are made from soybeans and other ingredients.

Words to Remember

hydrolize	smørrebrød
permanent emulsion	temporary emulsion
salmonella	weeping
sandwich	

Convenience Foods

Some food service operations prefer to order the salads ready to serve. This saves the cost of preparing the ingredients. A mixture of various greens packed in plastic bags may be purchased by the kilogram or pound. If desired, the cook may add personal touches such as croutons, fresh tomatoes, bacon bits, or anchovies. Ready-prepared fruits as well as molded salads are also available. The quality varies widely among the brands.

High-quality commercial salad dressings are used in almost all food operations. The chef may make a "house" dressing by adding such ingredients as minced chives, crumbled blue cheese, or chopped hard-cooked eggs.

Salad Production

The kind and size of the food service operation affects the salad production. A small restaurant such as a diner may offer two or three simple salads—a tossed salad, cole slaw, and perhaps a fruit or molded salad. The demand is fairly steady. The cook knows from experience the number of salads to prepare.

A larger, family-type restaurant may serve tossed salad with the dinner. If 300 people are expected for the dining hour, 300 salads will have to be prepared.

A cafeteria may take great pride in having a large selection of beautiful salads. The cook may prepare fewer salads of each kind, but there may be a wider variety. Fig. 8-8. For instance, one large

Morrison, Inc.

8-8. A tempting display of salads.

cafeteria offers nine different fruit and vegetable salads and eight gelatin salads, as well as several appetizers.

In a luxurious restaurant or a hotel dining room, many salads may be offered. Much pre-preparation may be done but the salad is assembled to order.

The floor plan of a salad station will depend upon the salad prepared there. Frequently, the station is divided into two sections. One section is for the preparation of individual salads and appetizers. The other is for dishing salads from a bowl or a pan.

The salad preparation may be for a luncheon or banquet where all guests are seated and served at the same time. Here, more room will be needed. As many as 1000 identical salads may have to be prepared ahead of time. Each situation demands a different floor plan and production schedule.

MISE EN PLACE

Perhaps you remember that mise en place means having everything prepared and ready for use before starting production. All needed equipment must be on hand. Ingredients should be pre-prepared and ready for assembly. The time element must be considered. For instance, if molded salads are on the menu, they should be prepared twenty-four hours ahead. This can be done in the late afternoon or evening, after the heavy work load is over. Such early preparation also allows plenty of time for a firm set of the gelatin salad.

Greens should be washed and prepared for serving during the early morning hours, before the busy mealtime starts. Other vegetables and fruits should be ready for the salads. Garnishes should be pre-prepared.

Each worker must know what goes into each type of salad and the amounts of each ingredient. The worker must know the measured amount for the body of the salad. He or she should know what the finished product should look like. A picture of each salad in front of the worker is helpful.

PREPARING THE GREENS

Table 8-4 lists the methods of cleaning the various greens. Study it carefully. Refer to it, as needed, when cleaning greens.

In a small restaurant, the breakfast cook may prepare the greens early in the morning. In a larger operation, the pantry cook will arrive several hours ahead of service to begin the preparation. Fig. 8-9.

Table 8-4. Preparation of Greens

Kind of Green	Preparation
Bibb lettuce Boston lettuce Curly endive Spinach Watercress	Fill sink with cold water. Break leaves off at the core. Trim stems as necessary. Rinse in cold water. Lift leaves into colander and drain water from sink. Refill and wash again in fresh water. Repeat until all dirt is removed. Drain in colander. Discard outer leaves of endive and stems of spinach and watercress. Bibb and Boston lettuce are very fragile. Handle gently.
Belgian endive	Trim end of core. Split in half and soak in cold water for thirty minutes.
Escarole Garden lettuce Romaine	Trim tough outer leaves. Wash repeatedly, removing all dirt and grit.
Head lettuce	Hold firmly and strike core against tabletop. Grasp core with fingertips and pull out. Soak lettuce in cold water for thirty minutes. If cups are desired, separate leaves into cups under running water.
Cabbage	Remove outer leaves. Quarter each head and cut out core. The core is slightly peppery and some cooks prefer to leave it in. Shred finely.

Morrison, Inc.

8-9. Martha trims spinach and places it in a pan of cold water.

After cleaning the greens, discard the outer leaves of escarole and endive. They are tough and bitter. In good condition, the outer leaves of Bibb, Boston, and head lettuce may be saved for the base of salads or appetizers. The outer leaves wilt fast and have a tough texture. They are not suitable for the body of the salad.

Bite-sized pieces may be needed for the body of the salad. If so, it is best to tear the inner, tender leaves into small pieces by hand. However, an expert may use a knife. Remember, the leaves bruise easily, causing the greens to wilt. Tear only enough greens for mealtime. If many tossed salads are to be made at one time, the greens may be shredded in a vertical cutter-mixer. However, the quality will not be the same. Figures 8-10 through 8-13 show the preparation of iceberg lettuce.

KEEPING THE GREENS CRISP

At the beginning of this chapter, you read that cold salads must be crisp and refreshing. The greens give this quality to salads. The following rules may help you keep the greens crisp.

- *Drain after washing.* Drops of moisture should still cling to the leaves. Some moisture must be present for crisping, but the greens should not stand in water.
- *Heap lightly* in clean, moistened cloth bags, baskets, or colanders. Bowls or plastic bags may also be used for short-time storage. Cover the greens with a clean, damp cloth.
- *Refrigerate* until service.

PREPARING THE BODY OF THE SALAD

In preparing the body of the salad, keep in mind its desired taste and appearance. Review Table 8-2, listing the ingredients that might be used for the body of the salad. In mixing these ingredients, remember the following principles of salad making.

- *All ingredients should be bite sized.* If not, the customer should be able to cut them easily. For instance, a wedge of head lettuce should be served on a plate with a fork so the customer can eat it easily.
- *Mix the textures.* There should be crisp, hard, and soft textures. A variety of textures makes a more interesting and more palatable salad. A salad that is palatable gives pleasure in eating. The word *palatable* refers not only to the taste but to the feel of the food in the mouth.
- *Work quickly.* If you work quickly, you will avoid wilting the ingredients. Also, do not over-mix the salad. This will bruise the greens.
- *Keep ingredients cold.* This is necessary for sanitation and to preserve crispness.
- *Add dressing as close to service time as possible.* Dressing causes loss of crispness.
- *Choose colors carefully for contrast.* Mix dark greens with light greens. Add a spot of bright color, such as a red tomato.
- *Garnish attractively.*
- *Arrange artistically.* Do not make the salad look contrived or worked on. A simple salad is better than an elaborate one.
- *Serve cold salads well-chilled.* Do not set out until just before service time.

Some salads require special handling. Fresh fruits add a "touch of class" to a salad. However, their use

The California Iceberg Lettuce Commission

8-10. Shredding iceberg lettuce. Cut head lengthwise into halves. Place cut side down on cutting board. Slice crosswise with a thin-bladed knife. You will get about four cups of shredded lettuce from one medium-sized head.

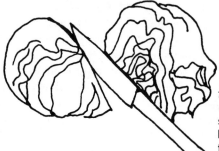

The California Iceberg Lettuce Commission

8-11. Cutting iceberg lettuce into wedges. Using a sharp, stainless knife, cut head lengthwise into halves. Place cut sides down. Cut each half-head into halves or thirds. For easier eating, cut wedges into halves crosswise.

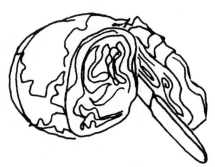

The California Iceberg Lettuce Commission

8-12. Cutting a raft from iceberg lettuce. Cut head crosswise into slices about 2.5 cm [1 in] thick. A medium-sized head will yield three or four rafts.

The California Iceberg Lettuce Commission

8-13. Cutting iceberg lettuce into chunks. Slice a medium-sized head crosswise into rafts about 2.5 cm [1 in] thick. Then cut the rafts length-wise and crosswise into chunks. This will give about four cups of bite-sized chunks.

may present some problems. For instance, bananas, apples, peaches, pears, and avocadoes begin to darken as soon as they are sliced.

Lemon juice contains ascorbic acid, or vitamin C. Ascorbic acid can help prevent the darkening, or oxidation, of fruit. When slicing apples, peaches, or pears, slice them into a pan of very cold water with salt and lemon juice. Marinate the fruit in the water until ready to assemble into the salads. See the recipe for Waldorf salad on page 166.

Avocadoes and bananas are too soft to marinate in water. Dip them in lemon juice or sprinkle the juice over the fruit.

PREPARING GELATIN SALADS

Molded salads are sometimes called congealed, or jellied, salads. Molded salads can be made from meat, poultry, fish, vegetables, fruits, or cheese. The aspic mentioned in Chapter 6 is made from gelatin.

Gelatin salads require special handling. Unflavored or plain gelatin usually should be hydrolyzed before it can be dissolved in liquid. To *hydrolyze* means to sprinkle the gelatin on cold liquid and let stand for about five minutes. The gelatin will absorb the liquid, swell, and become soft. It will then dissolve in boiling water, forming a clear liquid.

Flavored gelatin has been preconditioned. It dissolves easily in boiling water without being hydrolyzed first. It has been sweetened and flavored with fruit. The directions on the box may say to dissolve the flavored gelatin in hot water. However, most chefs agree it takes boiling liquid to dissolve it completely. Gelatin that is incompletely dissolved will be ropy or stringy when congealed.

Flavored gelatin often needs the addition of plain gelatin. This helps the salad hold up when it is molded in a large pan and cut into squares for serving. The more ingredients added, such as meat, vegetables, or fruit, the more plain gelatin must be used. Extra gelatin is also needed for salads molded with mayonnaise. This extra gelatin prevents *weeping*. Weeping is the seeping of liquid from a food as it stands.

Before adding any solid ingredients, chill dissolved gelatin in the refrigerator until it begins to thicken. Solid ingredients will either sink to the bottom or float on top if the gelatin is thin. If the gelatin has begun to thicken, the ingredients will remain suspended in the liquid.

The making of gelatin salads can be hastened by using ice water and crushed ice. Add half the water hot to dissolve the gelatin. Stir with a wire whip to dissolve thoroughly. Add half the remaining water in the form of ice water. Stir, using the hands. *Wash hands first.* Use plastic gloves. Using the fingers, feel for any undissolved gelatin. Rub it between the fingers. Add the vegetables or fruits according to the recipe. Measure the remaining liquid as crushed ice. Mix it in the gelatin, using the hands. Remove any large pieces of ice that do not melt. Stir, rubbing the mixture with the hands until all the ice is dissolved. Mold in a flat pan with 5-cm [2-in] sides, and refrigerate. The salad will congeal almost instantly, before the solids have a chance to sink to the bottom.

Let the gelatin set until very firm. If extra gelatin and the method outlined in the preceding paragraph are used, the salad will set in about three hours. If the usual recipe is followed, it will take twenty-four hours for a firm gel.

On pages 166 and 167 are two recipes for gelatin salads. One uses unflavored gelatin and the other flavored gelatin. Notice that the directions for making these salads follow the principles you have just read. Unmold gelatin just before serving. Just as gelatin becomes solid when it chills, it will become liquid again as it warms. Use this principle to unmold gelatin salads.

Fill the sink or a pan with hot water. It must be large enough to hold the mold. Place the serving plate for the salad close at hand.

Dip the bottom of the mold into hot water for about thirty seconds. Shake the mold slightly to see if the gelatin moves. This will indicate that it has loosened. Remove the mold from the water. Dry the outside, and place the serving plate on top of the mold. Flip over the mold and plate. Tap the mold lightly on top and remove. The gelatin should have slipped out quickly and cleanly. It may take a little practice to do it smoothly. Place the salad in the refrigerator until serving time.

Small molds made with extra gelatin slip out of the mold without using hot water. Run the index finger around the edge of the mold. The heat of your finger will loosen the edge of the mold slightly. Gently pry up the gelatin with your finger. Hold the mold in the left hand and pry with the right hand, if you are right-handed. The mold should free itself easily. It can then be placed on the serving dish.

Gelatin salads are often molded in a #200 size pan that holds 7.5 L [2 gal]. The gelatin is cut into twenty-eight servings. Slice in four sections lengthwise and seven sections horizontally. Each square can be removed cleanly by first dipping the spatula in hot water.

Preparing the Salad Dressing

Excellent commercial dressings are easily available and used freely in food service. You may seldom need to prepare a dressing. Nevertheless, as a professional cook, you need to know how to prepare all kinds of dressings. Many chefs garde-manger prefer to mix their own dressings, believing they will have a fresher taste.

Earlier you read that there are four types of dressings—oil and vinegar, creamy, mayonnaise, and cooked dressings. Table 8-5 lists variations of these types of dressings.

Preparation of oil and vinegar type dressing requires oil, vinegar, and seasonings. It is a thin dressing. On page 159 are recipes for many variations of this simple dressing.

Oil and vinegar dressing is a *temporary emulsion*. On standing, the oil separates from the liquid. It is simple to make. The ingredients are placed in a jar and shaken vigorously. To mix thoroughly, the dressing must be shaken again just before pouring onto the salad. See the recipe on page 168.

Both creamy and mayonnaise-type dressings are *permanent emulsions*. In a permanent emulsion, the oil will not separate from the liquid. As explained earlier, the addition of eggs makes the emulsion permanent.

On page 169 is a recipe for mayonnaise. Notice how the directions demonstrate the principles for making a permanent emulsion.

The egg yolks and whole eggs must be beaten until thick and lemon-colored. Only then should oil be added.

As the oil drops into the egg mixture, the beating disperses tiny droplets of oil, coating them with egg. This starts the emulsion. The oil must be added slowly until the emulsion is firmly set. Then the oil can be added faster.

The vinegar adds flavor and thins the emulsion. As the oil is added again, the emulsion thickens.

Mayonnaise should be very thick—not pourable. If the emulsion breaks it will become thin and the oil will separate. You will then have to start over, using more eggs and following the same procedure.

Creamy dressings are made with a mayonnaise base. Vinegar or lemon juice is usually added, as are seasonings. Sour cream is sometimes folded into creamy dressing for added richness. See page 168 for the recipe for creamy dressing.

Cooked dressing is thickened with flour or cornstarch as it cooks. No oil is used. Most cooks use the bain marie or double boiler for cooking this type of dressing. See the recipe on page 169 for this method.

Garnishing the Salad

See page 135 in Chapter 7 for information on garnishing appetizers. The garnishing of salads is very similar. It is best to garnish a salad using some of the ingredients found in the salad. For instance, a tossed salad can be garnished with a slice of tomato and thin strips of green pepper. The tomato and peppers in the garnish should not be the only ones in the salad.

Many salads are so pretty they require little or no garnishing. Others, such as potato salad, may be rather colorless. They are more appealing with a spot of color. As for canapés and appetizers, the garnish for salads must always be edible. Fig. 8-14.

Production Assembly of Salads

Salad production is no different than appetizer production. Refer to pages 139-140. The same production principles apply to salads.

SANDWICHES

The making of cold sandwiches is the responsibility of the garde-manger station. Sandwiches are especially popular for lunch. They are nutritious, fill-

Variation	Added Ingredients
Oil, Water, Vinegar Base	
French	Paprika, pepper, salt, dry mustard, sugar.
Italian	Oregano, minced garlic.
Blue or Roquefort	Crumbled cheese, salt, pepper.
Celery seed	Dry mustard, salt, celery seed.
Chiffonade	Chopped hard-cooked eggs, chili sauce, chopped sweet pickle, celery, parsley, pimiento, paprika.
Honey	Honey, sugar, paprika, dry mustard, celery seed, pepper, salt.
Vinaigrette	Parsley, onions, capers, chives, pimiento (for color), chopped hard-cooked eggs.
Mayonnaise Base (Creamy)	
Thousand Island	Chili sauce, chopped hard-cooked eggs, chopped sweet pickle, paprika.
Russian	Add caviar, omit pickle to Thousand Island dressing.
Louis	Horseradish, chopped dill pickle, chopped celery, pickled beet juice, lemon juice.
Green Goddess	Sour cream, tarragon vinegar, minced scallions and garlic, chopped anchovies, sugar, salt, pepper.
Tartar sauce	Chopped sweet pickles, capers, green pepper, parsley, celery, green onions.
Cooked Dressing Base	
Whipped cream	Marshmallows, eggs, pineapple juice, sugar, whipped cream.
Fruit	Orange, lemon, and pineapple juices, sugar, whipped cream.
Mustard	Evaporated milk, egg yolks, dry mustard, salt, pepper.

Table 8-5. Variations of Salad Dressings

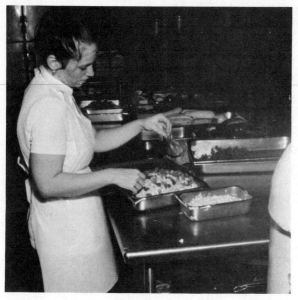

Morrison, Inc.

8-14. Yvette garnishes a cottage cheese salad with cherry tomatoes and parsley.

ing, and easy to eat. If made properly, they are delicious.

Standards for a Good Sandwich

A *sandwich* is a filling served on or between bread. A good sandwich should have the following qualities:

- *Fresh tasting.*
- *Easy to eat with the fingers or a fork.*
- *Firm in texture, but tender.* The bread should be firm enough to hold the filling, but never dry.
- *Moist filling with some crunchy ingredients.*
- *Flavorful.*
- *Neat looking, never messy.* Sandwiches should be cut cleanly in two, with no ragged edges. The filling should not hang over the edge of the bread.

Kinds of Sandwiches

Sandwiches may be hot or cold, but only cold sandwiches are made in the garde-manger. Hot sandwiches may be made in the meat and poultry station with the entrées or by the short-order cook.

There are four types of cold sandwiches:

- *Regular sandwich.* A filling between two slices of bread.
- *Open-faced sandwich.* A filling, attractively garnished, on one slice of bread. The Scandinavian people are famous for open-faced sandwiches called smørrebrød (SMAR-UH-brahd), or butter bread. Many Scandinavian restaurants offer a large variety of attractive open-faced sandwiches served as a buffet for lunch.
- *Decker sandwich.* Made with at least three slices of breads and two types of fillings. For instance, one layer may contain tomato and bacon. The other layer may be sliced turkey or chicken.
- *Specialty sandwich.* A filling placed in a sliced roll, usually a crusty roll. Often, a specialty sandwich is given an unusual name such as hoagie, submarine, poor boy, or Reuben. Fig. 8-15. Many specialty sandwiches reflect the tastes of other cultures. Fig. 8-16.

Equipment

Equipment needs for cold sandwich making are simple. Most sandwich makers prefer to work on a wood or plastic board. Such a board will not dull the knife and is easy to clean. Besides the board you will need:

- Spatulas.
- Spreaders.
- Slicing knives or a slicing machine.
- French knife for dicing.
- Container for trimmings (crusts, etc.).
- Bowls for ingredients.
- Trays or carts to hold sandwiches.

The Parts of a Sandwich

A sandwich consists of four parts: the *bread, spread, filling,* and *garnish.*

BREAD

All sandwiches are made with bread. White bread is the most common and popular. However, many persons prefer rye, pumpernickel, or whole wheat. Quick breads may be used, also, especially

Oscar Mayer & Co.

8-15. This submarine sandwich contains lettuce and slices of salami, bologna, tomato, and onion. It also contains slices of Swiss and Cheddar cheese.

Green Giant Company

8-16. Pocket bread, a delicacy from the Middle East, makes delicious sandwiches. These are filled with browned ground meat. The meat is first sautéed with beans, corn, peas, onions, and mushrooms.

for sweet sandwiches. White or rye rolls may be needed for specialty sandwiches.

As noted in the standards, bread for sandwiches should be firm, but tender. Some breads, especially white breads, are too soft and pasty for sandwiches. Bread fresh from the oven is always too soft. It is better to use day-old bread.

Bread that has been refrigerated is easier to spread because the cold firms the texture. Bread may also be frozen successfully to retard staling. Thaw it in the wrapper before using.

Crusts may be trimmed or untrimmed. Trimmed crusts make a daintier sandwich. However, the crusts are usually left on for luncheon sandwiches.

Customers are often given the choice between toasted or untoasted bread for sandwiches. Only sandwiches made to order can have toasted bread, since toast stales very quickly.

Bread easily absorbs odors and tastes. Remember how bread can be used to extend salad fillings because it absorbs odors and flavors? Keep bread well-wrapped and away from any foods with strong odors. Be particularly careful of any odors on your hands, such as cigarette or onion odors.

SPREADS

Spreads may be butter, margarine, or mayonnaise. Refer to page 134 for more information on spreads.

Spreads are often omitted in the making of sandwiches. They should not be. Spreads are important to prevent staling of the bread. They make a dry sandwich more palatable. They also seal the surface of the bread. Thus, the filling cannot soak in, making a soggy sandwich.

FILLINGS

The filling usually gives the sandwich its name, such as chicken, tuna fish, or cheese. It may be a *dry filling* such as sliced turkey, ham, or cheese. It may be a *moist filling* such as ham salad.

Meat or cheese for a dry filling should be sliced very thin. Several thin slices are better than a single thick slice. They make the sandwich tastier and easier to eat. It is also more economical. Many thin slices give the illusion of more meat or cheese in the

sandwich. Meat should be well-trimmed of fat and connective tissue. The dry filling should be portioned accurately, based on weight or a definite number of slices per sandwich.

Frequently, a thin slice of tomato or onion and a lettuce leaf are placed on top of the meat or cheese. These add moisture and crunchiness to the sandwich. Mustard, horseradish, ketchup, or mayonnaise may be served alongside.

Salad sandwiches may be made from fish, chicken, turkey, meat, or chopped cheese. The ingredients should be finely chopped, but not minced. Chopped celery, onion, and cucumber may be added for texture. Mayonnaise is usually needed to bind the ingredients together and to add flavor. Be careful to make the filling of the right consistency—moist, but not soggy. If lettuce is used with the salad sandwich, place the filling on the bottom slice of bread. Then add the lettuce and the top slice of bread.

Portion control is achieved by using a scoop (for example, #20) to measure the salad filling in each sandwich.

CAUTION

Moist fillings must be mixed under sanitary conditions and refrigerated until ready to use. Any mixture of a protein, such as meat, with mayonnaise can quickly become contaminated with salmonella. Salmonella (SAL-muh-NELL-uh) is a very toxic bacteria that can make human beings very sick.

Garnishes

Sandwiches made with two slices of bread are garnished very simply. Sliced pickles or olives held by toothpicks on top of the sandwich are often used. The garnish is frequently placed alongside. Such garnishes might be sliced tomatoes, a green pepper, egg slices, cucumber slices, radishes, or lettuce. Potato chips or shoestring potatoes also add interest.

Open-faced sandwiches require more elaborate garnishes. Stuffed olives may be sliced and spread on the filling. Chopped bacon or green pepper strips may be used. Radish roses, or a carrot curl also add to the beauty of the sandwich.

Methods of Production

A restaurant that offers sandwiches made to order must keep a supply of ingredients on hand under refrigeration. They must be wrapped in plastic sheets to prevent drying out.

The ingredients may be set out in utensils at the back of the cutting board. Mise en place must be observed. A cluttered work space will cause loss of time and a poor quality sandwich. Before the busy mealtime starts, all ingredients should be pre-prepared. The following should be done:

- Prepare and refrigerate salad fillings.
- Soften butter and prepare spreads.
- Slice meat and cheese.
- Wash, drain, and tear lettuce to correct size.
- Prepare garnish and accompaniments.

ONE SANDWICH WORKER

Figure 8-17 shows the normal work span for a person of average height. This work span is about 76 cm [30 in]. A person working in the center of a 1.8-m [6-ft] table would work most efficiently within that range. Anything over the comfortable range would make it necessary to reach.

Figure 8-18 shows how the ingredients should be efficiently arranged. The worker would have to reach to replenish the bread supply. He or she would also have to reach into the refrigerator for fresh ingredients.

Assuming the worker is right-handed, the flow of work would proceed from left to right. The worker would proceed as follows to make a salad sandwich. Notice that the worker uses both hands.

1. Place top slices of bread from bread stacks in front of the worker. Use the top slices first. Thus, the bread exposed to the air will be used first.

2. Place spread on both slices of bread, using the spatula.

3. Measure one scoop of salad filling in center of bread slice on right side. (Use right hand.)

4. Spread filling evenly with spatula to edges of bread. (Use left hand.)

5. Cover filling with lettuce leaf. (Use right hand.)

6. Cover with other slice of bread. (Use left hand.)

7. Cut diagonally. (Use right hand.)

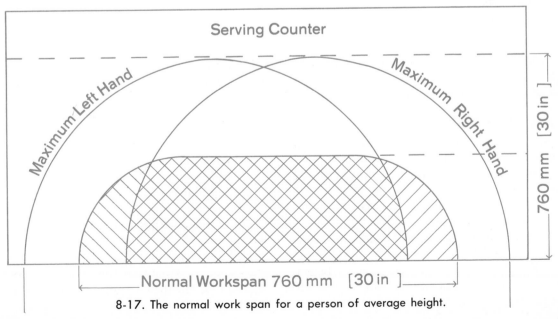

8-17. The normal work span for a person of average height.

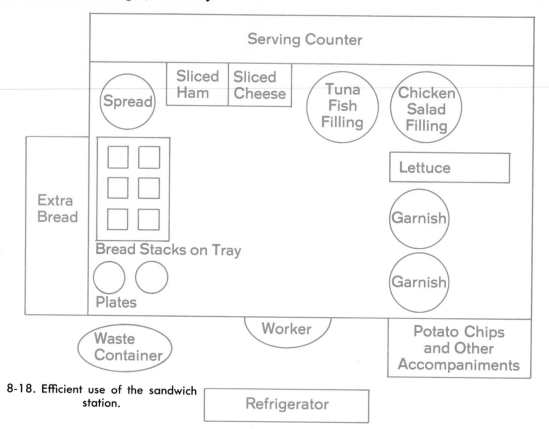

8-18. Efficient use of the sandwich station.

8. With left hand, move plate to center, place sandwich on it with right hand.

9. Garnish and add accompaniments with right hand.

10. Place on serving counter with left hand.

TWO OR MORE WORKERS

Two or more sandwich makers would need to cooperate to make sandwiches in quantity.

1. One worker would spread the bread and add filling.

2. The second worker would add lettuce, top the filling with the slice of bread, and add garnish.

3. A third worker, if needed, would wrap sandwiches.

The setup would be much the same. A bigger table would be needed to provide enough room for the workers.

If sandwiches are frequently made in quantity, the work area may move slowly on a motorized continuous belt past the workers. It would carry the sandwiches from one worker to the next.

Care and Storage

Observe the following rules:

• Keep work counter clean at all times.

• Prepare fillings for only one work period.

• Cover fillings before storing.

• Keep fillings refrigerated at no less than 7°C [45° F.].

• Wrap sandwiches to keep them from drying out.

• Store sandwiches at 7°C [45° F.].

• Sandwiches may be frozen, but the quality deteriorates. On thawing, the sandwich is apt to become soggy.

164

How Much Have You Learned?

Review this chapter. Answer the following questions to prepare yourself for the post-test. Check your answers with your teacher.

1. Define the *Words to Remember*.
2. List the qualities of a good cold salad.
3. Name four ways salads are used on the menu. Give one example of each.
4. List and describe the four parts of a salad.
5. Name and describe three greens used in salads. How do you clean greens for salads? Why is it best to tear greens instead of cutting them?
6. What is an emulsion? What part do eggs play in making an emulsion?
7. What happens to a green salad when the dressing is added an hour before serving time? Is it a good idea to set the salads on the table before the guests are seated at a large luncheon? Give the reasons for your answer.
8. Why is fruit sometimes marinated in a mixture of ice water, salt, and lemon juice?
9. What would happen if you mixed plain gelatin in boiling water? Why is flavored gelatin different?
10. Give at least five standards for a good sandwich and explain each one.
11. Since a sandwich should be fresh, why not use bread fresh from the oven to make it?
12. What is the difference between the two types of sandwich fillings?
13. Describe the setup of a sandwich-making counter for one person.

References

Beard, James, ed. *The Cook's Catalogue*. New York: Harper and Row, 1975.

Haines, Robert G. *Food Preparation for Hotels, Restaurants, and Cafeterias*. Chicago: American Technical Society, 1973.

Kotschevar, Lendel. *Standards, Principles, and Techniques in Quantity Food Production*. Boston: Cahners Books, 1973.

Kowtaluk, Helen. *Discovering Food*. Peoria, Ill.: Chas. A. Bennett Co., Inc., 1978.

Kowtaluk, Helen, and Kopan, Alice O. *Food for Today*. Peoria, Ill.: Chas. A. Bennett Co., Inc., 1977.

Medved, Eve. *The World of Food*. Lexington, Mass.: Ginn and Company, 1973.

Moor, Mary L., and Irmeter, Theodore F. *Introductory Foods*. 2nd ed. New York: Macmillan, 1974.

Ray, Mary Frey, and Lewis, Evelyn Jones. *Exploring Professional Cooking*. Peoria, Ill.: Chas. A. Bennett Co., Inc., 1980.

Sonnenschmidt, Frederick H., and Nicholas, Jean F. *The Professional Chef's Art of Garde Manger*. Boston: CBI, 1976.

Terrell, Margaret E. *Large Quantity Recipes*. Philadelphia: J. B. Lippincott, 1975.

Villella, Joseph A. *The Hospitality Industry—The World of Food Service*. New York: McGraw-Hill, Inc., 1975.

Wolfe, Kenneth. *Cooking for the Professional Chef*. Albany, N.Y.: Delmar Publishers, 1976.

WALDORF SALAD

Equipment   **Yield:** 25 servings
Large bowl
Fruit knife
Colander
French knife
Chopping board
Scale or measuring cups and spoons
No. 12 scoop

Metric	Ingredients	Customary
1.7 kg	Red apples	$3\frac{3}{4}$ lb
450 g	Raisins	1 lb
450 g	Celery	1 lb
57 g	Walnuts	2 oz
340 g	Cooked dressing	12 oz
60 mL	Lemon juice	4 T

METHOD

1. **Wash, core,** and **dice** apples. Do not peel.
2. **Marinate** in salted water.
3. **Chop** celery and walnuts.
4. **Drain** apples well in colander.
5. **Mix** apples, raisins, nuts, and celery in bowl.
6. **Thin** salad dressing with lemon juice.
7. **Fold** into salad.
8. **Scoop** on lettuce cup.

MOLDED PINEAPPLE AND CARROT SALAD

Equipment   **Yield:** 28 servings
Scale or measuring cups and spoons
Large stainless steel bowl
Mixer with shredder attachment
28 individual molds or #200 pan

Metric	Ingredients	Customary
280 g	Lemon-flavored gelatin	10 oz
1.25 L	Boiling water	5 c
340 g	Pineapple juice	12 oz
340 g	Shredded carrots	12 oz
680 g	Crushed pineapple, drained	$1\frac{1}{2}$ lb

METHOD

1. **Dissolve** gelatin in boiling water. Stir in pineapple juice.
2. **Cool,** and chill in refrigerator until mixture becomes thick.
3. **Add** shredded carrots and crushed pineapple.
4. **Mold** and chill for 24 hours until firm.

MOLDED PINEAPPLE AND CHEESE SALAD

Equipment
Saucepan
Bowl
Bench mixer with whip attachment
Baking pan, 30 × 46 × 5 cm
   [12 × 18 × 2 in]

Yield: 24 servings, 7.5 cm [3 in] square

Metric	Ingredients	Customary
625 mL	Crushed pineapple, drained	2½ c
57 g	Gelatin, unflavored	1½ oz
2.5 L	Pineapple juice	1 gal
125 mL	Green pepper, diced	1 c
250 mL	Celery, diced	1½ c
50 mL	Pimiento, diced	½ c
500 mL	Whipping cream	1 pt
680 g	Cottage cheese	1½ c
250 mL	Mayonnaise	1 c
250 mL	Lemon juice	1 c
150 mL	Sugar	⅔ c

METHOD

1. **Drain** crushed pineapple. Add juice to pineapple juice.
2. **Soak** gelatin in 500 mL [2 c] of juice.
3. **Bring** rest of juice to boil. Dissolve gelatin in it.
4. **Stir** until clear of gelatin granules.
5. **Cool** and refrigerate until it starts to thicken.
6. **Add** pepper, celery, and pimiento to gelatin.
7. **Whip** cream until thick, using bench mixer. Mix with cottage cheese and mayonnaise.
8. **Fold** whipped cream mixture into gelatin.
9. **Pour** into pan. Refrigerate overnight.

OIL AND VINEGAR DRESSING

Equipment
Bowl
Wire whip

Yield: 750 mL [1½ pt]

Metric	Ingredients	Customary
170 g	Onion, finely chopped	6 oz
170 g	Herbs, finely chopped (parsley, capers, and olives—pimiento, if desired)	6 oz
2	Eggs, hard-cooked, finely chopped	2
150 mL	Cider vinegar	⅔ c
500 mL	Salad oil	1 pt

METHOD

1. **Place** all ingredients in bowl.
2. **Whip** vigorously with wire whip.

3. **Mix** again before using.

CREAMY DRESSING (GREEN GODDESS)

Equipment
French knife and board
Blender
Bowl
Wire whip

Yield: 2 L [2 qt]

Metric	Ingredients	Customary
4 cloves	Garlic	4 cloves
250 mL	Chives	1 c
50 mL	Anchovies	¼ c
125 mL	Parsley	½ c
50 mL	Lemon juice	¼ c
50 mL	Tarragon vinegar	¼ c
10 mL	Salt	2 t
1 mL	Pepper	¼ t
1 L	Mayonnaise	1 qt
500 mL	Sour cream	1 pt

METHOD

1. **Mince** garlic, chives, and anchovies finely.
2. **Mince** parsley finely. Mix with lemon juice and vinegar.
3. **Place** parsley mixture in blender. Liquefy on high speed.
4. **Add** salt and pepper to mayonnaise.
5. **Blend** garlic, chives, anchovies, and parsley with mayonnaise.
6. **Fold** in sour cream. Refrigerate until used.

MAYONNAISE

Equipment
Bench mixer with whip attachment
Rubber scraper
4-L [1-gal] jar with lid

Yield: 3.8 L [1 gal]

Metric	Ingredients	Customary
4	Egg yolks	4
4	Whole eggs	4
10 mL	Dry mustard	2 t
3 mL	Paprika	$\frac{1}{2}$ t
30 mL	Sugar	2 T
10 mL	Salt	2 t
3.5 L	Salad oil	$3\frac{3}{4}$ qt
250 mL	Cider vinegar	1 c

METHOD

1. **Place** egg yolks and whole eggs in mixer bowl.
2. **Add** mustard, paprika, sugar, and salt.
3. **Beat** on second speed until thick.
4. **Add** one half the oil a little at a time beating on high speed. As the mixture thickens, the oil may be added in a thin stream.
5. **Add** the vinegar alternately with the rest of the oil beating all the time.
6. **Adjust** seasonings. Store covered in 4-L [1-gal] jar in refrigerator until needed.

COOKED SALAD DRESSING

Equipment
Double boiler
Wire whip

Yield: 1.9 L [2 qt]

Metric	Ingredients	Customary
10	Whole eggs	10
250 mL	Flour	1 c
125 mL	Sugar	$\frac{1}{2}$ c
5 mL	Salt	1 t
45 mL	Dry mustard	3 T
1.5 L	Milk	$1\frac{1}{2}$ qt
150 mL	Cider vinegar	$\frac{2}{3}$ c
125 g	Butter or margarine	$\frac{1}{4}$ lb

METHOD

1. **Break** eggs and place in top of double boiler.
2. **Blend** in flour, sugar, salt, and dry mustard with wire whip.
3. **Add** milk and blend.
4. **Place** top part of double boiler over hot water in bottom part. Cook, mixing constantly with wire whip until thick.
5. **Add** vinegar slowly.
6. **Remove** from heat. Beat in butter or margarine.
7. **Cool** and refrigerate.

169

The Hot Stations

Ernest Ishem, Sous-Chef, Tacoma Country Club, Tacoma, Washington.

MEET THE CONSULTANT

Ernest Ishem has become a professional cook "the hard way." With very little professional training, he is now sous-chef at a well-known country club in Tacoma, Washington. How he attained that position is an interesting story. It is a completely different route than that taken by Charlie Wagner or Kathy Nagel.

Ernie was born in poverty in a small town in Mississippi. School never interested him much, so he dropped out after the eighth grade. Since there wasn't much for a boy with little education to do, he "messed around" in Ernie's own words. The United States was in the midst of a depression. So, for a while Ernie was unemployed. Then he was offered the opportunity to go to Camp Shelby as part of the CCC (Civilian Conservation Corps). The CCC was a federal agency during the Depression. It was designed to train young persons for jobs. It was created to give them the opportunity to do constructive work. Ernie was placed in the cook's school of the CCC. He cooked for the people in the camp.

In 1941, he left the camp and returned to Mississippi. He still didn't have much interest in cooking, so he took a job helping to construct an air force base. Soon the United States was at war with Germany and Japan. Ernie was drafted into the Army. Because of his experiences with the CCC, he was placed in the cook's school and soon was shipped overseas. Ernie cooked all over Europe, but it was only basic cooking. There was no time for fancy frills in combat units.

At the end of the war, he returned home, still not interested in food service. He took a course in mechanics, tended bar, and finally returned to the Army as a cook.

He was assigned to Fort Lewis in Tacoma, Washington. For the first time he saw the Pacific Northwest. It left an impression—one he never forgot—of serenity and beauty. He thought it would be a good place to live.

Later, he served as mess sergeant in many parts of the United States and abroad. Since these units were no longer combat units, he could experiment with different kinds of cooking. Working in France and Germany, he had the chance to observe and taste different cuisines. He learned that cooking could be fun and challenging, too. He was convinced he could earn a good living as a cook when he retired from the Army.

He returned to Fort Lewis. Having served his country for twenty-five years, he decided to retire. He took a job as cook at a Tacoma restaurant. The restaurant catered to a discriminating clientele. For the first time, he learned the difference between cooking for the army and cooking to please paying customers. Each dish had to be carefully prepared and garnished to the customer's satisfaction. The restaurant was noted for its beautiful buffet service. Ernie quickly became an expert at preparing buffet foods that were a picture to the eye and a delight to the taste.

After a few years Ernie went to the Tacoma Country and Golf Club as sous-chef. When the head chef is not there, the sous-chef has the responsibility for food service. Ernie enjoys this job very much. He feels less pressure than in a public restaurant. He is encouraged to be creative in the preparation and garnishing of food. He especially enjoys setting up the Sunday evening buffet table. It is a beautiful picture, very pleasing to the club's members and guests.

Ernie says he wishes a vocational school had been available for him when he dropped out of school. He wasted so much time. He is grateful to the Army for his training as a cook. As he looks back on his life, he says, "Tell the young people not to be afraid to start at the bottom. Tell them to keep their eyes open for advantages such as extra schooling. Anybody can do what I have done. But if they're smart, they can do it a lot quicker."

Meats and Poultry

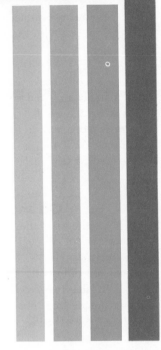

**What
Will
You
Learn?**

When you finish studying this chapter, you should be able to do the following:
- Define and use the *Words to Remember.*
- Identify the tender and less tender cuts of meat.
- Choose the best method to cook a wide variety of meats and poultry.
- Cook a wide variety of meats and poultry, meeting the standards of acceptable service.
- Pass the posttest.

The meat course is usually the center of the meal. The meat course includes either meat or poultry. When scanning the menu, the customer usually chooses the meat course first and then selects the other items to go with it. Because meat is so popular, the lessons on cooking meat are among the most important you will study.

The principles of cooking meat apply equally to the flesh of animals and birds. Therefore, meat and poultry are grouped together. The cooking of sea food is also governed by the same principles. However, fish and shellfish demand a separate chapter.

REVIEW OF MEATS AND POULTRY

You have already learned much about meats and poultry when you studied the pre-preparation of ingredients for cooking in Chapter 4. Reread parts of that chapter to refresh your memory about the following facts.
- The kinds of meats usually prepared for food service.
- The kinds of poultry usually prepared for food service.
- The grading of meat and poultry for quality.
- The primal cuts from each animal and the section of the animal each cut comes from.
- The retail cuts from each primal cut.
- The types of chickens featured on food service menus.

173

Words to Remember ———————

au jus	papain
caramelize	scoring
flavor enhancers	yield

If you are familiar with these facts, you are ready to proceed with the study of meats and poultry.

STANDARDS OF MEATS AND POULTRY

In cooking and serving meat and poultry, tenderness, juiciness, flavor, and appearance are the primary concerns. In food service, yield is also important. *Yield* means the number of servings to be expected from a certain amount of food.

Tenderness and Connective Tissue

In choosing the correct method for cooking a certain cut of meat or type of poultry, the natural tenderness is most important. Tender cuts are cooked differently than the less tender cuts.

In Chapter 4 you read that the structure of meat was made from fibers bound together with connective tissue. Heavier connective tissues bind the fiber bundles into muscles. Even heavier tissues fasten the muscles to the bone.

The amount and kind of connective tissue determine the natural tenderness of the piece of meat or poultry. Other factors that affect the tenderness are the location of the primal cut and the age and sex of the animal or bird.

As you read in Chapter 4, there are two kinds of connective tissue, white and yellow. The white is called collagen, and the yellow is called elastin.

Exercise develops the connective tissue. The legs have heavy muscles and much connective tissue because they are used the most. The back and ribs get very little exercise and so have little connective tissue. The breast of poultry also has little connective tissue.

Animals permitted to run the range will have more connective tissue than penned animals. Caged poultry will be more tender than birds that run the barnyard.

Because exercise develops connective tissue, the tender cuts come from the less exercised parts. The less tender cuts come from the heavily exercised muscles.

Older animals and birds have more connective tissue than younger ones. Lamb and pork always come from young animals. Thus, the flesh is tender.

Delft Blue Provimi

9-1. Veal and veal products. From left to right: shoulder slices, rib-eye slices, veal shank (from which Osso Buco is made), breaded veal steaks, ground veal steaks, and veal link sausages.

Veal is an exception. Fig. 9-1. It comes from a very young animal. Nonetheless, there is an abundance of fine connective tissue binding the fibers together. Beef, coming from older animals, has much connective tissue, especially elastin.

Male animals have heavier muscles and more connective tissue than females. Older males, the bulls, have so much elastin they are often called "baloney bulls." This is because their meat is ground up for baloney and wieners.

Males that have been castrated, or desexed, are called steers. Steers have finer, more tender meat than bulls.

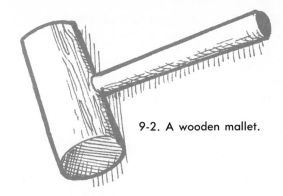

9-2. A wooden mallet.

Tenderizing of Meats and Poultry

Less tender cuts may be tenderized in many ways. All of the following tenderizing actions break down the connective tissues.

- *Chemical action* of acid or enzymes.
- *Cooking.*
- *Physical means.* A mallet with a sharp, uneven surface is used for pounding. Fig. 9-2. The sharp points on the surface break down the connective tissue during the pounding. Often, seasoned flour is pounded into the meat. Swiss steak is made from meat that has been pounded.

Cube steaks are an example of meat that has been tenderized through cutting. The meat is criss-crossed with shallow cuts called *scoring*. These cuts shorten the connective tissues and the length of the fibers. Flank steak is often cubed because the fibers are long and stringy. The name "cube steak" comes from the cube shape of the meat between the cuts.

Grinding and chopping also tenderize by breaking up the connective tissues. The yellow tissue, elastin, should never be ground up with the muscles. It cannot dissolve and will leave unchewable parts. You probably have had experience with hamburger containing unchewable bits.

- *Enzymes.* Papain may be used for softening and tenderizing meats. It is obtained from the papaya. People in Mexico, South America, and Central America have used papaya for many years for tenderizing. Now commercial products containing the enzyme are available and used in marinades.

The less tender cuts of beef may be tenderized through marinating. Lamb, veal, pork, and poultry may also be marinated for flavor. Tenderizing is not needed since these meats are naturally tender.

The meat is soaked or marinated in a solution containing the papain, spices, and herbs. The meat is first pierced thoroughly with a fork so the marinade can penetrate the meat.

- *Acids.* Tomato juice, lime juice, sour orange juice, or wine will also soften connective tissue. A marinade containing both papain and an acid will soften the tissues more quickly.
- *Cooking.* Collagen turns to gelatin during cooking. Thus, less tender cuts of meat are tenderized when cooked for a long time in liquid. If cooked too long, the meat or poultry will fall apart when served. This is because the connective tissue binding the fibers together has dissolved.

Flavor of Meats and Poultry

At one time it was thought most of the flavor of meat and poultry came from the lean parts. However, many other factors contribute to it, such as fat, bones, and the method of cooking.

- *Fat and flavor.* The fat of meat and poultry adds much flavor. Very lean cuts or meat from animals with very little fat will not be as flavorful. For the best flavor, the highest quality of meat must have 25 to 35 percent fat, mostly in marbling. Even hamburger needs fat. Government standards allow up to 30 percent.

• *Cooking and flavor.* The flavor of meat and poultry is developed by cooking. Browning enhances the flavor. It also enhances the aroma because the sugar and starch on the surface of the meat *caramelizes.* Browning sugar and starch is called caramelizing. During cooking, bone also adds flavor to the meat and to the gravy. Meat next to the bone is sweeter and more flavorful.

• *Exercise and flavor.* As an animal exercises, the blood flows into the muscle. This develops a better flavor in the meat. Less tender cuts are more flavorful than tender cuts. This is because they are cut from highly exercised muscles. It is common practice to restrict the movement of animals and poultry while they are being fattened for slaughter. Poultry, especially, are caged almost from birth. To many people, caging animals and birds is inhumane. It should also be noted that caged animals and birds are not as healthy as those allowed freedom of movement. The meat taken from such animals and birds may not be as good for human consumption. Several countries in Europe have outlawed such practices, but they serve the purpose of fast profit.

• *Feed and flavor.* Animals raised on corn have a mild flavor, but range-fed animals develop a stronger taste. Wild animals are gamy. Chickens fed a milk-mash diet will have a more delicate flavor.

• *Sex and flavor.* Females have a milder flavor than males. Steers are less flavorful than bulls, but the flavor of steers is better liked by most persons. Also, steers give a higher yield in servings per kilogram of meat.

• *Flavor enhancers.* Herbs, spices, salt, vegetables, and fruits are *flavor enhancers.* They are used to bring out the flavor of meat and poultry and to blend their own flavors with them. Refer to Chapter 6.

As you read in Chapter 6, monosodium glutamate, commonly known as MSG, is a protein salt. It has little flavor of its own. However, when added to meat or poultry, it strengthens the flavor. It is often used in Oriental cooking.

Appearance of Meat and Poultry

To most people, meat and poultry with a crisp, brown surface has more appeal than unbrowned

meat and poultry. Given a choice between fried or baked chicken and boiled chicken, most persons will choose the baked or fried chicken. Fig. 9-3.

Sauces also add appeal. Mint sauce may be served with lamb. Beef may be served *au jus* (O ZHUS) meaning "with natural juices." Such meats look more appetizing than meat served dry.

Garnishing also adds eye-appeal. A sprig of watercress with beef, applesauce or spiced apple with pork, cranberry with turkey add a bit of color and flavor.

Words to Remember

fork tender	skewer
medium	trichina
medium rare	trichinosis
medium well-done	very rare
rare	well done

COOKING MEAT AND POULTRY

Meat and poultry used to be cooked to preserve them. Cooking kills the bacteria naturally present. Before refrigeration was freely available, only cooking, salting, drying, and spices could preserve fresh meat and poultry.

Now, meat and poultry are cooked primarily to develop flavor, improve appearance, and tenderize. Table 9-1. Following are the effects of cooking on meat and poultry.

• During cooking, the fat melts, spreading throughout the meat or poultry. This adds flavor and juiciness.

• The heat coagulates the muscle fibers, making the texture more firm.

• The heat evaporates some of the moisture naturally present in the meat or poultry. This evaporation causes shrinkage during cooking. The heat and moisture soften the collagen, tenderizing the meat.

• Direct heat on the surface browns the meat or poultry. This improves the flavor and appearance.

Earlier you read that tenderness, juiciness, flavor, appearance, and yield are the primary concerns in

National Broiler Council

9-3. These boned chicken thighs have been stuffed with broccoli before being baked. Lightly browned, their color is complemented by the deep green of the vegetable.

Table 9-1. Methods of Cooking Meat

Dry Method	Fat Method	Moist Method
Broiling Grilling Oven frying (ovenizing) Roasting	Deep-fat frying Sautéing	Barbecuing Braising Fricasseeing Steaming Stewing

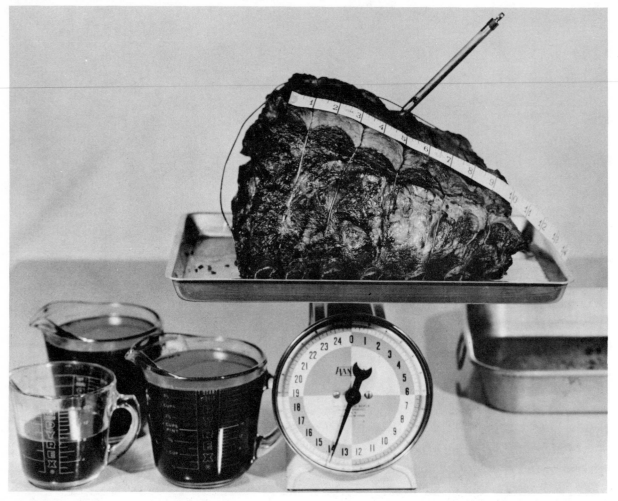

National Live Stock and Meat Board

9-4. A beef rib roast roasted at 232°C [450° F.] oven temperature to an internal temperature of 60°C [140° F.].

meat and poultry preparation. These four factors are influenced by the cooking time and temperature. Temperature and time are the two most important elements in meat and poultry cookery. One cannot be separated from the other.

Temperature

A high temperature over a long period of time will harden the meat fibers and the connective tissues. It will evaporate the natural moisture and burn the fat, causing great shrinkage. Study Figs. 9-4 and

9-5. The beef roast shown in Fig. 9-4 was cooked at a high temperature. The roast shown in Fig. 9-5 was cooked at a low temperature. The roasts were identical in shape and weight. They were cut from the same animal. However, the one cooked at a low temperature weighs 2.5 kg [5½ lb] more than the one cooked at a high temperature. Meat or poultry cooked at a low temperature gives a higher yield and has a better flavor. It is juicier and more tender than one cooked at a high temperature.

A low temperature also means cleaner ovens.

National Live Stock and Meat Board

9-5. A beef rib roast roasted at 121°C [250° F.] to an internal temperature of 60°C [140° F.].

The fat spatters less and does not smoke. This makes the oven easier to clean.

As the meat cooks, the temperature inside the cut gradually rises. The internal temperature of a cut of meat or poultry is measured by a meat thermometer. Fig. 9-6.

Time

The amount of time needed to cook meat depends upon the following factors:

- *The size, shape, and weight of the meat or*

Taylor Instrument

9-6. A pocket meat thermometer. The diameter of the dial is 2.4 cm [1 in]. The stem has a length of 12.7 cm [5 in]. This thermometer is calibrated in degrees Fahrenheit. However, thermometers calibrated in degrees Celsius are available.

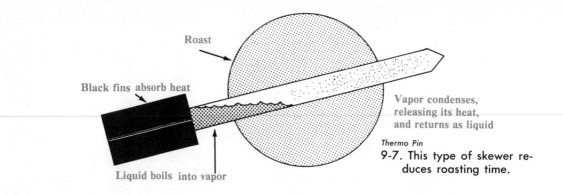

Roast

Black fins absorb heat

Liquid boils into vapor

Vapor condenses,
releasing its heat,
and returns as liquid

Thermo Pin
9-7. This type of skewer reduces roasting time.

poultry. The larger and heavier the cut or bird, the longer the needed time. However, a thick cut will take longer than a thin cut. This is true even if the weight is the same.

• *The amount of bone.* Bone conducts the heat to the center of the meat or poultry. A boneless rib roast will take longer to cook than a standing rib roast of equal weight.

• *The natural tenderness.* Long, slow cooking tenderizes meat and poultry. The less tender cuts require lower temperatures and longer cooking times. Also, meat that has been aged properly will cook faster than "green" meat.

• *The amount of fat cover.* A heavy layer of fat will act as an insulator, lengthening the cooking time. However, marbling will shorten the cooking time. The melting fat will carry the heat throughout the meat. A light covering of fat underneath the skin of poultry shortens the roasting time.

• *The temperature of the meat when cooking begins.* A cut at room temperature will cook more quickly than one right from the refrigerator. A frozen roast or poultry will take about three times as long to cook as one at room temperature. It will take about twice as long as one at refrigerator temperature.

• *The cooking temperature.* The oven temperature is controlled by the thermostat. A *thermostat* is a device that automatically raises and lowers the temperature as needed. Meat and poultry cooked at a high temperature will take less time.

• *The distance between the meat or poultry and the heat source.* This distance is particularly important in broiling.

• *Skewers.* Skewers are metal pins that reduce the roasting time. The metal conducts the heat to the center of the roast. A new type of skewer is more efficient in conducting heat. Fig. 9-7. It has a hollow, pencillike tube in the center filled with a special liquid. Black, aluminum fins at the end of the skewer absorb the oven heat. The heat causes the liquid to vaporize. The vapors rise within the pin and condense. This releases the oven heat inside the roast. The roast cooks from the inside out as well as from the outside in. Use of these skewers can cut the roasting time in half.

Doneness of Meat and Poultry

Overcooked meat becomes dry, stringy, and flavorless. It is less tender and nutritious than meat that has been properly cooked. Some people prefer a well-done steak. Nonetheless, a medium-rare steak is juicier, more flavorful, and also more tender. "Cook meat until it is just done" is a good principle to follow. However, what is doneness?

BEEF AND LAMB

Beef, and occasionally lamb, may be served rare, medium, and well-done. Study Tables 9-2 through 9-5 (pages 184–189). They show the times and temperature for broiling and roasting meat. Although three stages of doneness are shown in the charts, six stages are generally recognized.

• *Very rare.* The heat has barely penetrated to the center of the cut. The inside is still raw and cool. The juices are very red and bloody. The meat is soft and jellylike. Few persons relish very rare roast beef. However, there are some who want it burned on the outside and raw on the inside. Lamb is not served very rare, especially in the United States. The internal temperature of very rare beef is 49–52°C [120–125° F.].

• *Rare.* Rare means that the heat has penetrated to the center of the meat. The inside and the juices are red, but not bloody. The meat has begun to co-agulate and develop some resistance to finger pres-sure. Internal temperature for rare meat is 57°C [135° F.].

• *Medium rare.* The interior is bright pink, not red. The juices are also pink. The meat feels more firm to the touch. Medium rare is preferred by the majority of beef eaters. The internal temperature for medium rare is 57°C [135° F.].

• *Medium.* The interior is a light pink. The juices are slightly pink. The meat feels quite firm to the touch. Lamb rack or chops are often cooked to the medium stage. The internal temperature for medium is 60°C [140° F.].

• *Medium well-done.* The pink color has disap-peared. The juices are clear, not pink. The meat feels firm to the touch. The internal temperature for medium well-done is 65°C [150° F.].

• *Well-done.* The meat is gray-brown from the exterior to the center. The meat is hard and dry to the touch. The internal temperature for well-done meat is 71°C [160° F.].

PORK AND VEAL

Overcooking is very common with pork, which must be cooked beyond the well-done stage. Pork may harbor a parasite, a microscopic worm called *trichina* (trik-EYE-nuh). It causes a disease called *trichinosis* (TRIK-uh-NO-sis) in humans who eat in-fected pork. Improved care of hogs and pigs has made trichinosis rare. However, since the parasite is killed by heat, pork should always be cooked a little beyond the well-done stage. The temperature should be 74°C [165° F.]. The meat should be white, the juices clear, with no hint of pink around the bone. Be careful not to overcook. Otherwise, the meat will be tasteless, dry, and stringy. Pork is very fat. Thus cooking to the well-done stage makes it more digestible by melting much of the fat.

Because veal has so much connective tissue, it is also cooked to the well-done stage. The internal temperature should be 77°C [170° F.]. Long cook-ing softens the connective tissue, making the meat more palatable.

POULTRY

Like pork and veal, poultry is always served well done. There should be no hint of pinkness in the flesh or around the bones. The thigh joint where it joins the leg bone should move easily. The meat should be *fork-tender.* This means that a fork should pierce the meat easily to the bone at the thigh joint. The internal temperature should be 82°C [180° F.] at the thigh joint to the leg bone.

Words to Remember ──────

barding	prime ribs
basting	rack
deckel	roasting
frenched	sauté
larding	truss
mirepoix	

METHODS OF COOKING

Meat may be cooked with dry or moist heat. Dry heat is used for the tender cuts. Less tender cuts containing more collagen require moist heat to ten-derize the meat.

Meat may also be fried in deep fat or *sautéed* in a small amount of fat. *Sauté* (saw-TAY) is a French word meaning to cook in a small amount of fat. Only tender cuts may be cooked by these methods because the cooking is too fast to tenderize.

In the French brigade, cooking by the dry meth-ods is under the chef de rotisseur. In the American brigade, there may be a fry cook, broiler cook, roast cook, or even a short-order cook.

Roasting

Roasting means cooking in the oven by direct heat without added moisture. By common usage, ham is baked, but most other meats and poultry are roasted. The process is the same.

Unit 4: The Hot Stations

Roasted meats are preferred by customers over meats cooked with liquids. The fat and small amounts of carbohydrates in meat brown as the meat and poultry roasts. This develops the flavor and aroma preferred by most people.

CUTS OF MEAT FOR ROASTING

Roasting is a dry method of cooking. Thus, only tender cuts or tenderized cuts can be roasted. The cut must be thick enough to permit browning on the outside before the inside is overcooked. A thinner cut, such as a steak, cannot be roasted successfully.

In beef, the ribs, usually called the *prime ribs,* are the most popular. The filet, or beef tenderloin, is occasionally roasted. It is the exception to the principle of long, slow cooking because it is so small. It is roasted at a high temperature, 246°C [475° F.] for twenty-five to thirty minutes. It is the most expensive beef roast. The whole New York cut from the sirloin is also roasted at a slightly lower temperature, 204°C [400° F.].

From pork, the loin, fresh ham, and smoked ham are usually roasted. Leg of veal, loin of veal, and saddle of veal are also roasted. Leg of lamb is popular in the United States. *Rack of lamb* is more popular in restaurants featuring the French cuisine. The racks are the center cuts from the loin. They are often *frenched.* The meat from the ends of the ribs is completely removed so the bone is bare. At serving time, the bare bones are covered with a frill of crepe paper.

Turkey, chicken, duck, and goose may also be roasted. A roasting bird is a little older than a fryer. It has a heavier layer of fat between the skin and the meat.

PRE-PREPARATION OF MEAT AND POULTRY FOR ROASTING

Some roasts need little pre-preparation. If the meat has very little fat cover, fat must be added to prevent the meat from drying out. *Barding* is the laying of strips of fat on top of the meat. In *larding,* the strips of fat are pulled through the meat using a larding needle. Veal almost always has to be barded or larded since it contains very little natural fat.

Some chefs do not salt roasts before cooking. They believe that salt cannot penetrate more than 1.2 cm [½ in] and can make no difference in the fla-

National Turkey Federation

9-8. Roast turkey with cranberries.

vor. However, other chefs claim salting makes a big difference in the flavor. They rub the salt over all the meat parts, except the fat. They do this a short time before beginning to roast.

Boned roasts should be tied with string or enclosed in netting to keep the roast together. The string or netting is removed before serving.

Some chefs like to lay a *mirepoix* (meer-PWA) on the bottom of the roasting pan shortly before the end of the roasting period. A mirepoix is a mixture of coarsely chopped vegetables. The vegetables add flavor to the gravy.

Chickens and turkeys to be roasted are trussed first. To *truss* means to tie down the wings and the legs close to the body of the bird. This keeps them from drying out during cooking. Skewers or a trussing needle are used. Ducks and geese are not trussed because the legs are so short.

In food service, large tom turkeys, rather than hens, are usually chosen for roasting. Fig. 9-8. They are cheaper and have a greater yield. The drumsticks and thighs are often separated from the breast. They are roasted separately, since the bird will not be served whole. Legs and thighs take longer to cook than the breasts.

EQUIPMENT FOR ROASTING

Roasting meat and poultry requires very simple equipment. The roasting pan should be large enough to hold the meat. The roast should almost fill the pan. The sides should be high, to hold the juices. A rack to hold the roast above the drippings, and a meat thermometer are needed. The oven may be either the conventional, deck, convection, or halo type. (These ovens are described on pages 54–55.) A halo oven has heating elements in the sides as well as the top and bottom. Fig. 9-9. It is used for very long, slow roasting.

METHODS OF ROASTING

To roast beef, pork, veal, or lamb in a deck oven, follow these rules:

1. Preheat the oven to 135°C [275° F.].

2. Place the *deckel* on top of the roast. The deckel is the thick piece of fat trimmed off by the butcher.

Alto-Shaam, Inc.

9-9. A halo heat oven.

3. Rub salt and pepper on top and bottom of roast.

4. Place the roast fat side up, with the deckel in place, on the rack in the roasting pan.

5. Insert thermometer so the pointed end is in the center of the roast. Make sure it does not rest on a bone or a strip of fat. Bone and fat conduct heat quickly. A thermometer resting on bone or fat may not give an accurate reading. Experienced chefs do

183

not use a thermometer. They have learned exactly how long a roast of a certain size will take.

6. Set both top and bottom heat-intensity knobs on high at the indicated temperature. The top heat provides excellent browning.

7. Roast to desired doneness. For roasting in a conventional oven refer to Table 9-2. A 9–10.4-kg [20–23-lb] rib roast will reach a very rare internal temperature in about three and one-half hours. To prevent the roast from cooking in its own fat, pour off the accumulated fat after two hours.

To roast meat in a convection oven, follow the manufacturer's directions. The roasting temperature is the same, but the roasting time is shorter. Table 9-3.

On a halo oven, a large piece of beef is roasted at 82°C [180° F.] for eight hours to a very rare internal temperature. Some chefs do not approve of using a temperature this low. They believe it allows bacterial growth for several hours before the internal temperature is high enough to kill the bacteria. Table 9-4 lists the times and temperatures for roasting meat and poultry in the halo heat oven.

CARE AFTER ROASTING

Roasts will continue to cook for some time after removal from the oven. The length of time depends upon the size and weight of the roasts. The internal temperature will rise 3–6°C [5–10° F.]. Allowance must be made for this setting time before the roast is carved. Usually one-half hour setting time is allowed. As it sets, the roast will become more firm. This makes it easier to slice. Cover the roast with a sheet of aluminum foil or clean cloths to prevent rapid cooling.

In food service, roasts are usually cooked to the

Table 9-2. Time and Temperature for Roasting Meat and Poultry in a Conventional Oven

Meat and Cut	Weight		Roasting Temperature		Time (in hours)	Internal Temperature	
	kg	lb	°C	°F.		°C	°F.
Beef							
Rib roast, standing							
seven-rib	8.2	18	121	250			
Rare					$4\frac{1}{2}$–5	54	130
Medium					5–6	60	140
Well-done					6–$6\frac{1}{2}$	66	150
Top round	6.8	15	121	250			
Rare					5–6	54	130
Medium					6–$6\frac{1}{2}$	60	140
Well-done					7–8	66	150
Capon	2.3–2.8	5–6	121	250	3–4	82	180
Lamb leg	3.6	8	149	300	4	74	165
Pork ham							
Fresh	6.8	15	149	300	8	74	165
Smoked	6.4	14	149	300	3–$3\frac{1}{2}$	68	155
Turkey	8.2	18	121	250	8	82	180
Veal Rump	2.4	5	121	250	3–4	82	180

r Roasting Meat and Poultry in
n Oven

K...				Time	Internal Temperature		Load Control Setting
					°C	**°F.**	
Beef							
Rib							High
Ra...				? hrs	54	130	
Me...				hrs	60	140	
We...				hrs	66	150	
Top F...							High
Rar...				hrs	54	130	
Med...				hrs	60	140	
Well				hrs	66	150	
Lamb							
Leg				..hrs	74	165	High
Pork							
Ham, Fresh	7	15	164	325	3 hrs	77	170	High
Ham, smoked	8.2	18	164	325	2½ hrs	68	155	High
Turkey							
Whole	8.2	18	149	300	3 hrs	78	170	High
Veal							
Rump	2.4	5	149	300	2 hrs	77	170	High

Recommended temperatures, times, and load control settings are intended as a guide only. Adjustments must be made to compensate for variations in recipes, ingredients, and personal preference in product appearance.

Roasting of beef, lamb, poultry, and ham is most satisfactory at temperatures of 108–164°C [225–325° F.]. For fresh pork, the recommendation by the USDA and the American Meat Institute is 164–177°C [325–350° F.]. A pan of water approximately 30 × 50 × 2.5 cm [12 × 20 × 1 in] may be placed in the oven bottom. This water supplies humidity to reduce shrinkage. Water should be added to the pan during roasting, if necessary Closing the manual damper will help retain moisture in the oven.

Roasting pans should be no deeper than necessary to hold the drippings.

Cooking time and shrinkage vary with roasting temperature, cut, grade of meat, and degree of doneness. At a given temperature, smaller cuts generally show greater time savings than larger cuts.

very rare stage. They are then placed in a holding oven at a constant 60°C [140° F.] until ready to serve. The microwave oven is often used to cook the serving a little longer, if desired. For instance, a customer may want a well-done slice of beef. The microwave oven can quickly cook a rare slice of beef to the well-done stage. Fig. 9-10.

In most food service places, the slice of beef is slipped under the broiler for a few minutes. There, it is cooked to the desired degree of doneness.

Poultry is roasted like meat. However, it needs to be basted more often. *Basting* means occasionally to spoon the juices and fat over the bird or meat as it roasts. The breast has very little fat and tends to dry out as it roasts. Some chefs prefer to roast first with the breast side down. To brown the breast, the bird is turned breast side up about halfway through the roasting period. This eliminates some of the need for basting.

The thermometer should be placed deep into the joint connecting the thigh to the leg. This is the thickest part of the bird. It takes the longest to cook through.

In food service, turkeys are usually not stuffed

Table 9-4. Time and Temperature for Roasting Meat and Poultry in a Halo Heat Oven

Kind and Cut	Weight		Oven Temperature		Time	Holding Temperature		Internal Temperature	
	kg	lb	°C	°F.		°C	°F.	°C	°F.
Beef									
Rib Roast, standing	8.2	18	108	225		60	140*		
Rare					3½ hrs			54	130
Medium					4 hrs			60	140
Well-done					4½ hrs			66	150
Top Round	11.5	15	108	225		60	140*		
Rare					3½ hrs			54	130
Medium					4 hrs			60	140
Well-done					4½ hrs			66	150
Lamb									
Leg	4.2	8	149	300	1½ hrs	60	140**	74	165
Pork									
Ham, fresh	7	15	136	275	4 hrs	65	150**	74	165
Ham, smoked	6.4	14	136	275	3½ hrs	65	150	68	155
Turkey									
Whole	8.2	18	136	275	3½ hrs	65	150**	170	170
Veal									
Rump	2.4	5	149	300	3 hrs	65	150**	170	170

*Hold four hours before serving. Check internal temperature after one hour on hold.
**Hold one hour before serving.

before roasting. The stuffing is prepared separately. However, a turkey that is to be served family style is carved at the table. Then the bird would be stuffed before roasting.

The turkey may have been partially disjointed. Then, the breast and the rest of the carcass, except the legs and thighs, are placed in a roasting pan. Fig.

9-10. In food service kitchens, the microwave oven is often used to finish the cooking of certain foods.

National Turkey Federation
9-11. A roast turkey breast garnished with parsley and a lemon slice.

Oscar Mayer & Co.
9-12. The T-bone steak is a popular steak for broiling.

9-11. The tip of the breast is at the bottom of the pan to promote self-basting. It is roasted at 163°C [325° F.] for about two and one-half hours. The drumsticks and thighs are placed skin side up in another pan. They are roasted at a higher temperature, 177°C [350° F.], for the same length of time.

Words to Remember

blanche	noisette
brochette	satays
broiling	shashlik
grid marks	shish kabob

Broiling

Broiling is cooking meat directly by radiant heat. Warmed air cooks meat in roasting. In broiling, the meat is exposed directly to the heat source. This heat may be a gas flame, charcoal, or an electric burner. Broiling is under the direction of the short-order cook or the broiler cook.

Broiling is considered one of the finest ways to prepare meat, especially beef. Broiled steak is the most popular meat in the United States. The entire surface of the cut is browned, increasing the flavor and enhancing the appearance.

CUTS OF MEAT FOR BROILING

Broiling is used to prepare small, individual cuts such as steaks and chops. Fig. 9-12. Occasionally, a larger steak for two or four may be broiled. Only the most tender cuts of meat can be used because the cooking time is short and the temperature high. Study Fig. 4-5. Note the kinds of beef steaks. All of

187

these can be broiled. Chopped steaks made of ground round or sirloin can also be broiled. Sufficient tenderizing can make broiling possible for even less tender cuts, such as chuck or rump.

Cuts for broiling must be thick. A thin steak will dry out before the outside is brown. Steaks cut thicker than 5 cm [2 in] will brown on the ouside before the heat penetrates the interior.

The New York strip steak is a popular steak cut from the beef sirloin. It is a thick steak. Filet mignon is a thick steak cut from the tenderloin of beef. Chateaubriand is cut from the center of the beef tenderloin. It is big enough to serve two persons. It may be broiled and served as a steak or roasted.

Chops, either lamb or pork, may be broiled. Sometimes the eye of the meat (the round muscle) of the loin lamb chop is removed and broiled. It is called *lamb noisette* (nwa-ZET). A *noisette* is a small piece of lean meat. An *English lamb chop* is cut from the saddle and served with lamb kidney.

A mixed grill is any group of broiled meats. A popular mixture contains a lamb chop, a veal sausage, a slice of filet mignon, a slice of veal filet, a strip of bacon, and one-half a tomato.

Chicken may be broiled if very young. Broilers are usually cut in half, each half being a serving.

EQUIPMENT

Broilers are described in Chapter 2. They may be open, closed, or infrared.

An open broiler has the heating element below the meat. The heat may come from gas, gas-fired lava stone, or charcoal. The fat and juices drip into the fire as the meat broils.

A closed broiler is equipped with a broiler pan. A grid fits on the shallow broiler pan. This grid holds the meat above the drippings. The heating element is either electric or gas. It is above the meat.

Many of the newer restaurants broil by infrared heat. Both sides are broiled at once. It is clean, efficient, and quick.

Tongs or a turning fork are needed to turn meat and poultry. Most chefs prefer tongs. A fork would pierce the meat, causing some loss of juices.

PRE-PREPARATION OF MEAT FOR BROILING

Meat to be broiled usually has a heavy layer of fat on one edge. As the fat melts during cooking, the steak may curl up on the edges. To prevent this, cut slits through the fat to the muscle. Do not cut the meat or juices will be lost during cooking. Poultry for broiling is halved since the birds are small.

Excess fat should be trimmed. The best restaurants also trim the "tail." The tail is the long piece of less tender beef that is part of the end of the porterhouse and T-bone steak.

All meat and poultry should be lightly oiled before broiling. This prevents it from sticking to the grid. The oil also keeps it moist. The meat or poultry may be dipped in oil, or the oil may be brushed on. The oil should drain off before the food is placed on the grid.

Poultry is often dipped in an oil, vinegar, and seasoning mix. This mix is similar to a vinaigrette dressing.

Salt draws the juices from the meat if it is applied far ahead. This drys out the meat. For this reason, chefs differ on the salting of meats and poultry before broiling. Some do not salt until after broiling. Others believe all meats should be seasoned before broiling, but never more than fifteen seconds before placing the meat on the grid. These chefs believe the salt adds much flavor.

BROILING METHODS

As in all cooking of meats and poultry, temperature and time are the critical elements. A thermometer can be used for roasting, but this is impractical for broiling. Broiling temperatures are very high— 260°C [500° F.]. The high heat must be maintained. Temperature is controlled by the distance the meat is placed from the flame. The grids on most broilers are adjustable for the thickness of the meat.

COOKING TIP: *The thinner the piece of meat, the closer it should be placed to the heat. The thicker the piece of meat, the farther it should be placed from the heat.*

Table 9-5 is a timetable for broiling meat. Notice that it takes more than twice as long to broil a thick

Table 9-5. Timetable for Broiling Meats

Cut of Meat	Thickness of Cut		Total Cooking Time (in minutes)			Distance from Heat	
	cm	in	Rare	Medium	Well-done	cm	in
Beefsteak	2.5	1	10	15	20	5	2
	3.8	1½	18	20	30	7.6	3
	5	2	25	35	40–50	10.2	4
Lamb Chops	2.5	1		15	20	5	2
	3.8	1½		20	30–35	7.6	3
Ham Slice, Smoked	2.5	1			16–20	7.6	3
Pork Chops	2.5	1			25–30	7.6	3
Bacon					4–5	5	2
Half Chickens					40–50	10.2	4

steak as it does a thin one. A thick steak cannot be cooked to the well-done stage without drying the meat. A well-done steak cannot be juicy.

RULES FOR BROILING

1. Place grids at recommended distance from the heat.

2. Preheat broiler. *Grid marks* are a sign of quality in steaks and chops. Preheating the broiler brands the grid marks on the meat.

3. Place the meat on the broiler grids. Thick steaks should be about 13 cm [5 in] from the heat source. Thin steaks should be about 5 cm [2 in]. Judgment comes with experience.

4. Broil one side about half the estimated time or until well-browned. It is best to turn the meat just once. However, you may have to check the brown-

ing. If you do, remember the grid marks. The new grid marks made when you return the meat to the broiler should be at right angles to the old ones. Fig. 9-13. A steak with many crisscrossing grid marks of no particular pattern looks unprofessionally cooked.

5. Broil the second side to the desired doneness. (See Table 9-6 for testing doneness with the fingers.)

6. Many items may need to be broiled at once, as for a banquet. In this case, place the meat close to the flame and broil each side quickly. Chefs say they *blanche* the steak. To blanche means to cook the outside very quickly. The inside will be very rare and bloody. Some cooks use the microwave oven for

9-13. Grid marks should be at a 90° angle on steaks that are turned twice.

TURNED ONCE　　**TURNED TWICE**

Degree of Doneness	Meat
Very Rare	Meat feels very soft when pressure is applied.
Rare	Meat feels like the softness of your lips when pressure is applied.
Medium	Meat feels like the point of your nose when pressure is applied.
Well done	Meat feels like your chin when pressure is applied.

Table 9-6. Checking the Doneness of Broiled Meat—Using the Touch of a Finger

finishing the steaks just before serving. The more usual procedure is to place them on a sheet pan and slip under the broiler once more before serving.

Pork chops and chicken should be broiled at least 13 cm [5 in] from the flame to allow plenty of time for cooking.

CAUTION

The fat dripping from the meat into the broiler pan can catch fire. Remember, water spreads a grease fire. Baking soda, milk, or very damp rags will put out a grease fire. When broiling on an open broiler, a bottle filled with a mixture of water and baking soda may be used to douse the flames as needed. Flames char the meat and give it a sooty, burned look and flavor. Many nutritionists believe charred meat is unhealthy.

To clean the broiler grids, use a wire brush and wipe clean with paper towels.

The following are specialty broiled items:

Brochette (bro-SHET) is the French word for "skewer." The ends of tenderloin steak are strung on a skewer. The meat may be interspersed with vegetables. This dish is called Beef en Brochette.

Shish kabobs are tender chunks of lamb strung on a skewer with onions, cherry tomatoes, and mushrooms.

Satays are a dish from India made of curried meats broiled on a skewer.

Shashliks are the Russian version of brochettes.

Words to Remember

griddle	panfrying
grill	parboiling
grilling	variety meats
panbroiling	wok

Grilling or Panbroiling

Grilling and *panbroiling* are different names for the same process of cooking. Sometimes it is called *panfrying*. In this method, meat is placed in a hot pan or directly on the solid surface of the grill. Usually no additional fat is needed. Ground meat, hamburgers, sausages, minute steaks, veal steaks, ham, bacon, and thin chops are grilled. Fig. 9-14.

INGREDIENTS

Ground beef to be grilled is often extended with ground soybeans, cereal flours, and bread crumbs. These extenders may be purchased in dry or frozen form. They may be flavored or unflavored, colored or uncolored. Recently, they have become available for home as well as food service use. Perhaps you have noticed them on the supermarket shelves. The quality of the extenders is governed by regulations from the USDA. Because of the high price of meat, extenders are in general use.

Seasoning is mixed with ground meat along with the extender. Whole cuts of meat are usually seasoned after cooking or by the customer.

As you read in Chapter 4, the term *variety meats* refers to the edible parts of the animal, other than the regular primal and retail cuts. For instance, the heart, liver, kidneys, tongue, sweetbreads, tripe, and brains are known as variety meats. The term also refers to products made from the odds and ends of meat leftover from the primal cuts. Wieners are made in this way. Many of the variety meats are panbroiled or grilled because they are tender, having no connective tissue. They cook quickly.

Bacon comes from the cured and smoked belly of the hog. High-quality bacon should contain not more than 40 to 45 percent fat. It may be sliced thin or thick.

EQUIPMENT

The *grill*, or *griddle*, is pictured on page 50. Notice that it has a solid heating surface instead of grids. The amount of heat is controlled by a thermostat in the electric models or by lowering the flame in gas models. This type of grill or griddle is often found in places specializing in fast foods. Many chefs prefer to use a heavy frying pan made of cast aluminum or iron. In addition, a fork or turner is needed.

PRE-PREPARATION

Grilling is used extensively for breakfast items. To speed the cooking time, some pre-preparation is helpful.

Grill thick ham steaks ahead of time. Keep warm in steam table with a small amount of water.

Partially bake bacon on baking sheets in the oven. Pour off grease. Stack bacon in pan to be grilled as needed.

Parboil sausage. To parboil means to place food in cold water and bring the water to a boil. Drain and hold sausage for grilling as needed. Parboiling prevents sausage from splitting and overcooking. Overcooked sausage is hard and dry.

Veal liver, calve's liver, and lamb's liver may be sliced and grilled. Beef and pork liver should be parboiled before slicing and cooking. Parboiling is needed to remove the strong flavor.

RULES FOR GRILLING, OR PANBROILING

1. Preheat the pan or grill until a few drops of water sprinkled on the grill sizzle and evaporate. Brush with oil if cut is very lean.

2. Place meat in hot pan or on grill.

3. Turn item often for even cooking. Grilling is faster than broiling. However, the meat requires frequent turning. Do not pat or press meat with flat side of turner. It will cause loss of juice.

4. Use a moderate temperature to prevent smoking.

5. Scrape or pour off excess fat as it accumulates. Grills are equipped with grooves on the sides to drain grease into a grease cup. If a pan is being used, pour off the grease.

6. Cook to desired degree of doneness. Grilled meat will cook almost twice as fast as broiled meat.

7. After use, wipe grill with paper towels and clean any stuck spots with pumice stone (lava stone).

Oscar Mayer & Co.

9-14. Panbroiling is an excellent way of preparing ground meat patties.

Sautéing

Sautéing is often a preliminary step to another method of cooking. You will meet this word often as you study the other chapters.

Only small, thin, tender strips of meat or poultry can be sautéed. Sautéing is used for such delicious dishes as beef Stroganoff and cordon bleu. The recipe for cordon bleu is on page 201.

Figure 9-15 shows a sauté pan. Sauté pans are made of heavy-gauge aluminum or copper lined with stainless steel. It usually has sloping sides for easy turning of items being sautéed. The Oriental name for a sauté pan is *wok*.

To sauté, follow these directions:

1. Season meat with salt and pepper.
2. Preheat pan with a small amount of fat until it sizzles.
3. Add meat. Brown first on one side, and then on the other.
4. Use a moderate temperature.
5. Do not cover or meat will steam.
6. Do not overcook.

Words to Remember ————————

batter dipping   dough wrapping
breading   smoking point
croquette   tempura
deep-fat frying

Deep-Fat Frying

Deep-fat frying means cooking items in hot fat deep enough to float them. Sometimes, as in sautéing, it is a preliminary step to brown the meat before the final cooking by another method. Deep-fat frying is growing rapidly in popularity. Most people enjoy the flavor it gives to food. The fry cook is in charge of deep-fat frying. Deep-fat frying is also called French frying. The Oriental version is called *tempura*.

Ingredients

Since deep-fat frying is a dry method of cooking, only small, tender items may be fried. Fried chicken

is extremely popular, as is fried seafood. The frying of seafood will be discussed in the next chapter. Ground beef, pork, lamb, or poultry may be mixed with bread crumbs and cream sauce and fried in deep fat. This type of dish is called a *croquette* (crow-KET).

Of all the ingredients used in frying, the most important is the fat. Fat and oil are the same chemical compound. However, oil is liquid at room temperatures. Fat is a delicate product. It requires much care to keep it in prime condition. When melted, it does not boil away or evaporate as water does. Instead, it breaks down under use. At high temperatures, it gives a sharp, acrid odor. Then, it may give an undesirable flavor to food.

Fat suitable for deep-fat frying should have the following characteristics:

• *High smoking point.* Deep-fat frying must be done at high temperatures. Refer to Table 9-7. Notice that most foods are fried at 177°C [350° F.]. The fat must withstand these high temperatures without breaking down. Fats and oils from vegetables are used because they have high *smoking points*. The smoking point is the temperature at which fats disintegrate. The smoking point of vegetable-based fat and oil is over 204°C [400° F.]. Cottonseed, corn, peanut, soy, coconut, and palm oil are common vegetable oils.

• *Low moisture content* to insure that the compound is all fat and to reduce spattering.

• *Flavorless* and *odorless.*

• Contains an *antioxidant* to retard spoilage. Oil or fat becomes rancid when certain compounds unite with the oxygen in the air. Antioxidants prevent this union.

• Contains a *stabilizer* to reduce breaking down under high temperature.

Wear-Ever
9-15. A sauté pan.

Bread crumbs, flour, eggs, milk, and seasonings are other ingredients used in deep-fat frying. Breading and batter mixes are used constantly in food service. Many are of very high quality. They absorb less oil than ordinary crumbs and meals. They adhere better and resist burning. Due to the high cost of labor, ready-made coatings often are cheaper than those made on the premises.

EQUIPMENT

Figure 9-16 shows a deep-fat fryer. Notice the heavy construction to withstand the high temperatures of frying. Notice, too, that it has a basket for lowering the food into the hot fat and lifting it out to drain after frying. The fryer is equipped with a thermostat that controls the temperature of the fat. Its accuracy is all-important and should be checked

Table 9-7. Deep-Fat Frying Temperatures and Times

Food	Temperature		Time (in minutes)
	°C	°F.	
Chicken			
Precooked	177	350	3–4
Raw	163	325	12–15
Seafood			
Clams, breaded	177	350	1
Fish, sliced	177	350	6–8
Fish fillets, fresh	177	350	3
Fish fillets, frozen	177	350	4
Oysters, breaded	177	350	3–5
Scallops, breaded	177	350	4
Shrimp, breaded	177	350	3
Shrimp, frozen	177	350	4
Vegetables and Fruits			
Apple rings	149	300	3–5
Cauliflower, breaded	177	350	3
Corn on the cob	149	300	3
Eggplant, breaded	177	350	3
Onions	190	375	2–3
Potatoes, blanch	177	350	$2\frac{1}{2}$
Potatoes, brown	182	360	2
Tomatoes	182	360	2–4
Zucchini	182	360	3–5
Bakery Items			
Doughnuts, cake	177	350	1–3
Doughnuts, yeast-raised	177	350	1–3
Miscellaneous			
Croquettes	177	350	3–4
Fritters	177	350	3
Meat turnovers	177	350	5–7
Veal cutlets, breaded	177	350	3–4

Frymaster Corp.

9-16. A deep-fat fryer. This fryer has six frying baskets.

frequently by a hand thermometer. If a thermometer is not available, you can gauge temperature by the time it takes to fry a cube of bread golden brown. See Table 9-8.

Recently, a pressure deep-fat fryer has been offered on the market. The fat is heated under pressure, shortening the heating time and helping to reduce the deterioration of the fat. They are used in fast food operations featuring fried chicken. Pressure fryers are extremely dangerous and are seldom used in the usual restaurant.

PRE-PREPARATION FOR FRYING OF MEAT AND POULTRY

Meats and poultry require pre-preparation to shield them from the intense heat of the fat. This pre-preparation may be breading, batter dipping, or wrapping in dough.

Breading usually has three steps—flouring, moistening or washing, and crumbing. The first step uses flour. Dipping the item in flour absorbs the moisture and gives a good base. The second step is dipping in

a wash made of egg slightly diluted with water. Milk is sometimes used, but the final product will not be as crisp. The third step uses paprika with seasoned crumbs made from bread, crackers, cereals, or prepared mixes. The crumbs should be fine and even.

To bread, follow this procedure:

1. Using the left hand, pick up item and dip both sides in flour. Shake off excess.

2. Still using the left hand, immerse item in egg and water wash. Wet it thoroughly and let it drain.

3. With the left hand, dip item in crumbs, coating it well.

4. With the right hand, press crumbs evenly into item. The final product will be evenly coated with crumbs, covering the flour and wash completely.

5. Place on rack to dry for at least fifteen minutes before frying. In practice, breading is done

early in the morning. The items are refrigerated until needed.

Notice the use of the left hand until the last step. The left hand will become covered with flour and wash. The left hand does not touch the crumbs. Crumbs are pressed into the food with the right hand.

Breading is much preferred to *batter dipping,* although some preparations specify batter dipping. Batter is messy. It causes burning while frying because the batter drips into the fat. The frying basket cannot be used in batter frying because the batter sticks to the basket.

Use a batter made of flour, eggs, and water or milk. Prepared mixes are in general use. The batter must be thick enough to stick to the item and give a good coating. Allow the excess batter to drip off before placing item in the hot fat.

Food is sometimes wrapped with dough and then fried in deep fat. A dough richer in fat and eggs than biscuit dough but not as rich as pie crust dough is used. The dough should be carefully wrapped around the item and sealed by crimping with the fingers or a fork. *Dough wrapping* is used mostly for hors d'oeuvres and desserts.

METHODS OF DEEP-FAT FRYING

The primary purpose of deep-fat frying is to brown the item with the least fat absorption. Greasy food is unappetizing, unpalatable, and hard to digest.

The temperature of the fat controls the amount of fat absorption. A temperature that is too cool will allow the fat to penetrate the item before it is browned. Fat that is too hot will brown the item before it is cooked through. A temperature that is just right will instantly convert the coating into a crust. This will prevent the fat from entering. You can understand how important temperature control is.

To fry successfully, follow these procedures:

1. If oil is used, it may be poured directly into the fryer. The amount needed is specified in the instructions for use with each fryer. There is also a mark on the fryer to indicate the needed depth of oil. Never exceed this mark.

If fat is used, it is best to melt it on low heat before putting it in the fryer. However, many newer fryers have a setting for melting the fat before the heat is turned on high.

2. Set thermostat for proper temperature and turn on heat.

3. When proper temperature is reached, a light will come on. Shake off the excess breading and place items in the basket. Lower the basket into hot fat and fry until golden brown. Do not let the items become dark brown or they will be tasteless, dry, and tough. Sometimes, items will float to the top. These must be turned for even browning.

4. When items are golden brown on both sides, lift the basket. Hook it on the side so the food can drain.

COOKING TIP: *Do not overload the basket. Overloading causes the temperature of the fat to fall when the items enter the fat. Remember, a fat temperature that is too low causes fat absorption. Baskets should not be more than half full.*

Table 9-8. Temperature Test for Deep-Fat Frying (Time for Browning 2.5-cm [1-in] Cube of Bread)

Temperature of Fat		Time	Color
°C	°F.		
177–182	350–360	1 min 15 sec	Light brown
182–188	360–370	1 min	Light brown
190–196	375–385	40 sec	Light brown
196–204	385–400	20 sec	Light brown

CARE OF FRYING OIL AND FAT

The fry cook must be aware of the cost of fat and oil for frying. It is very expensive. Proper care will extend the life of the fat.

Fat has broken down and become unusable when it smokes and emits an unpleasant, acrid odor. Follow these rules and procedures to conserve fat and oil used in deep-fat frying.

1. Clean and scrub out fry kettles once a week.
2. Filter fats daily. Some fryers have automatic filters. Automatic filtering has proven to be very successful. If there is not an automatic filter, the fat should be filtered through a cheesecloth. This will remove any particles of food. These particles burn and cause disintegration of the fat or oil.
3. Add sufficient fresh fat to the kettles everyday. In the course of normal frying, foods will absorb some of the fat. The fat must be kept at the proper levels for correct frying. Do not add leftover suet or other fats. Only fresh fat or oil should be used. The fat or oil should be of the same type and quality as the original.
4. Skim off any loose particles of breading during the frying period. Loose particles cause smoking.
5. Hold temperatures at correct heat. With high recovery, fat will quickly regain loss of heat. High temperatures are the biggest cause of loss of quality in cooking fats and oils.
6. Turn down thermostat in off-peak periods.
7. Cover fat at night to protect from air and dirt.
8. Do not salt food over the fryer. Salt causes disintegration of the fat.

CAUTION

Make sure there is no drip from the exhaust hood into the fat. Keep hood clean. A dirty exhaust hood is the biggest cause of fires in food service.

CARE OF FRY KETTLES

Fry kettles should be cleaned once a week. Use the following procedure:

1. Drain fryer while still warm.

2. Rinse with hot water to remove all food particles.
3. Thoroughly flush kettle with hot water. Inspect for signs of overheating.
4. Use commercial cleaner, following manufacturer's instructions.
5. Remove any stuck deposits with stiff brush.
6. Rinse thoroughly with tap water. Rinse then with a solution of one part vinegar to twenty parts water. The vinegar will neutralize any cleaning compound that may remain.
7. Rinse again to remove vinegar.
8. Dry thoroughly. The kettle must be *absolutely dry* before being refilled with fat. Water will cause spattering and also break down the fat.

CAUTION

The thermostat consists of two wire probes. Be very careful not to harm these when cleaning the fry kettle.

Words to Remember

barbecuing	goulash
blanquette	oven frying
braising	ovenizing
dredging	ragout
fricassee	roulade

Barbecuing

Barbecuing is broiling meat or poultry over an open fire or in a specially constructed pit. The meat or poultry is basted with a tangy sauce while cooking and served with more sauce poured over it. Any meat or poultry may be barbecued. Pork spare ribs, beef short ribs, lamb riblets, and chicken are favorites. Barbecuing is a specialized art. It is found in restaurants emphasizing this type of meat preparation. Some restaurants are not equipped for barbecuing. They combine broiling and baking meat for an acceptable substitute. For instance, the recipe for barbecued spare ribs, found on page 201, demonstrates this method.

Oven Frying

Oven frying is also called ovenizing. It is a process of baking breaded meats or poultry in the oven. Fat is drizzled over the breaded items while baking. This causes them to look and taste very much like they were fried in deep fat. Oven frying is used when large quantities of food are to be prepared. (See the recipe on page 202 for oven-fried chicken.)

Braising

Braising is cooking meats in their own juices with perhaps a small amount of added moisture. *Fricasseeing* is another name for braising. It is applied especially to chicken and veal.

CUTS OF MEAT FOR BRAISING

Since braising is a moist method of cooking, it is suitable for the less-tender cuts of meat. The round and flank in the beef hindquarter are often braised. In the forequarter, the chuck, plate, brisket, and shank may be braised. Three types of meat may be cooked by this method.

1. Large cuts such as pot roasts.
2. Individual portions such as chops and Swiss steak.
3. Cubes, chunks, or ground meat.

Some veal cuts are braised to soften the stringy connective tissue. In pork, the picnic ham, Boston butt, jowl butt, and hocks may be braised. Lamb shanks, shoulder, and necks are cooked by this method. Older chickens, known as stewers, may be fricasseed.

OTHER INGREDIENTS

Meats to be braised are often dipped in flour, or *dredged*, before browning. Gravy is very important in braised meats. Thus, a mirepoix of vegetables is frequently cooked with the meats to add flavor. Many times, whole or cut-up vegetables such as carrots and onions may be cooked and served with the meat and gravy. Herbs such as garlic, bay leaves, basil, and thyme also add their flavors.

EQUIPMENT

Braising requires a heavy pan for long, slow cooking. The pan must have a tight-fitting cover to keep in the moisture. The tilt-brasier described on pages 56–57 is used in most quantity kitchens. Small kitchens may braise in a heavy-gauge, covered frying pan on top of the range. A covered brasier or roaster may be used in the oven.

PRE-PREPARATION OF MEATS AND POULTRY

Most meat and poultry are browned before braising. It improves the flavor and color of the meat and gravy by caramelizing the surface. Browning may be done on top of the range, in the oven, or in the tilt-brasier.

To brown on the top of the range, add fat to cover the bottom of the pan. Heat fat to sizzling and add the meat or poultry. Turn meat or poultry until richly browned.

To brown in the oven, heat oven to 204°C [400° F.]. Place meat or poultry in an oiled brasier or casserole. Brown in oven for fifteen to twenty minutes, turning as needed.

To brown in the tilt-brasier, add fat to kettle. Cover and turn steam on high. When fat is hot, uncover, and add meat or poultry. Brown, uncovered, turning frequently.

Marinating is used to tenderize and to add flavor to such dishes as sauerbraten. The meat is marinated for eight to seventy-two hours. The marinade is made from vegetables, spices, salt, and a mixture of half red wine and half vinegar.

METHOD OF BRAISING

Follow these rules for braising:

1. Brown seasoned meat or poultry in brasier in hot oil or fat. Do not use butter or margarine. They burn too easily. Make sure all sides are brown. Remove meat and set aside.
2. Add mirepoix (see page 183) to hot fat and brown.
3. Add tomato paste to vegetables to give a good flavor and color. Stir and brown.
4. Add chopped garlic, if desired.
5. Add small amount of water or broth. Cover tightly.
6. Reduce heat to 149°C [300° F.]. *Simmer* until tender. See Table 9-9. To simmer means to cook just below the boiling point.

Table 9-9. Timetable for Braising

Cut	Weight or Thickness		Time
	Metric	**Customary**	**Time**
Beef			
Flank steak	1.3 cm	$\frac{1}{2}$ in	45 min–1 hr
Pot roast	1.4–2.3 kg	3–5 lb	3–4 hrs
Pot roast	2.3–6.8 kg	5–15 lb	3–5 hrs
Short ribs	5 × 5 × 5 cm	2 × 2 × 2 in	$1\frac{1}{2}$–2 hrs
Stuffed steak	1.3–1.9 cm	$\frac{1}{2}$–$\frac{3}{4}$ in	$1\frac{1}{2}$ hrs
Swiss steak	2.5–5 cm	1–2 in	2–3 hrs
Lamb			
Lamb breast, rolled	0.7–0.9 kg	$1\frac{1}{2}$–2 lb	$1\frac{1}{2}$–2 hrs
Lamb breast, stuffed	0.9–1.4 kg	2–3 lb	$1\frac{1}{2}$–2 hrs
Lamb riblets	1.9 × 6.3 × 7.6 cm	$\frac{3}{4}$ × $2\frac{1}{2}$ × 3 in each	2–$2\frac{1}{2}$ hrs
Lamb shanks	0.2 kg each	$\frac{1}{2}$ lb each	1–$1\frac{1}{2}$ hrs
Pork			
Pork chops	1.9 × 2.5 cm thick	$\frac{3}{4}$–1 in thick	45 min–1 hr
Veal			
Veal birds	1.3 × 5 × 10 cm	$\frac{1}{2}$ × 2 × 4 in	45 min–1 hr
Veal breast, stuffed	1.4–1.8 kg	3–4 lb	$1\frac{1}{2}$–2 hrs
Veal cutlets	1.3 × 7.6 × 14 cm	$\frac{1}{2}$ × 3 × $5\frac{1}{2}$ in each	45 min–1 hr

7. Remove meat or poultry and make gravy. (See page 295.)

VARIATIONS OF BRAISED MEAT

There are hundreds of ways of preparing and serving braised meats. Only a few of them are listed and described below.

Beef pot pie. Braised beef chunks with vegetables served under a piecrust.

Swiss steak. Round steak pounded, browned, and braised in tomato sauce.

Pepper steaks. Thin slices of round steak browned and cooked in a sauce made of green peppers, onions, and celery, flavored with soy sauce.

Braised short ribs of beef. Short ribs cut from the end of the rib roast, browned, and braised with tomato paste added to liquid.

Beef roulade (ru-LAHD). Thin slices of round steak stuffed with ham, hamburger, onions, and bread crumbs. The steaks are rolled around the stuffing and fastened with toothpicks. They are cooked in a sauce of Burgundy wine and tomato paste.

Beef ragout (ra-GOO). Beef and vegetables in a wine sauce. *Ragout* is the French word for "stew."

Stewing Meat and Poultry

In this method, the meat or poultry is covered with water or some other liquid. The meat or poultry is simmered, or stewed. Meat or poultry is never boiled. The high temperatures make meat and poultry stringy and hard to cut.

The cuts of meat and poultry that are braised may be stewed, since both are moist methods of cooking. The very least tender cuts of meat and the older hens (stewers) may be successfully stewed. Variety meats such as beef heart, tongue, and tripe may also be cooked by this method.

Vegetables are almost always added to meat to be stewed. The gravy made by this method is very flavorful and nutritious. It is usually served with the meat.

EQUIPMENT

Stews may be cooked in the tilt-braisier, a stockpot, or in a heavy pot on top of the range. A tight-fitting cover is needed to keep in the moisture.

METHODS OF COOKING

There are two types of stews: brown and white. White stew is sometimes called blond. Chefs often have their own way of making a flavorful stew. In general, however, follow these rules in making a brown stew.

1. The meat should be cut in small, uniform chunks—about 5 × 2.5 cm [2 × 1 in]. Chicken is dismembered into joints.

2. Season and dredge well with flour. Some recipes omit this step. Flour adds to the flavor and helps thicken the stew.

3. Brown chunks of meat or poultry in a small amount of fat. Meat or poultry should be well-browned on all sides. Remove meat or poultry from fat.

4. Brown mirepoix in fat. You probably remember that a mirepoix is a mixture of cut vegetables.

5. Return meat or poultry to fat. Cover with liquid. Water, vegetable juices, stocks, and tomato paste are used.

6. Cover pot and simmer until meat or poultry is tender. The amount of time depends upon the type of poultry or the cut of meat and the size of the chunks. Generally, stew takes from two to four hours.

7. Vegetables to be served with the stew should be added toward the end of the stewing period. Do not overcook the vegetables. (See Table 12-3 for the cooking time of vegetables.) Vegetables for stews may be whole or cut attractively. They must be easy to eat. Small white onions may be left whole, but

carrots should be in bite-sized pieces. Some chefs prefer to cook the vegetables separately, adding them to the stew just before serving.

8. When vegetables and meat or poultry are tender, remove them to a pan. Use a perforated spoon so the gravy can run back into the pot. Keep hot while making the gravy. (See page 295.)

VARIATIONS OF STEWED MEAT

Ordinary stew does not have much appeal on the menu. It is usually sold under more appealing names.

Goulash. A famous Hungarian dish that may have a beef or veal base. The meat is not browned first. It contains paprika, garlic, onions, parsley, and caraway seed. Sour cream is added just before serving.

Blanquettes (blon-KETTS). A white fricassee, usually veal or lamb with white sauce.

Irish stew. Lamb, browned with bacon, flavored with garlic, and served with peas, small new potatoes, and carrots.

Chicken fricassee. Browned pieces of chicken stewed and served in a rich chicken gravy.

Brunswick stew. Chicken or turkey meat cut into chunks and stewed with tomatoes, corn, lima beans, spices, and seasoning.

Boiled Meats and Poultry

Poultry and many cuts of meat are "boiled" to prepare them to be served cold. Corned beef, ham, pastrami (beef cured like ham), chicken, and turkey may be covered with water. They are simmered with appropriate seasonings and spices until tender. Meat or poultry cooked in this manner is cooled in its own broth if to be served cold. The meat or poultry may be sliced for sandwiches and salads. It may be cubed for salads, ground for sandwich fillings, or cut into pieces for pot pies or creamed dishes.

Steamed Meats

Many chefs do not steam meats or poultry, especially with steam under pressure. They believe that steam overcooks meat and takes flavor from it. Under pressure, the outside of the meat and poultry is exposed to a temperature of 121°C [250° F.]. This shrinks meat and causes drying. Nevertheless, steaming under pressure is frequently used commercially because it saves time.

Free steam, or steam not under pressure, is used often in cooking meats. Free steam cooks meat slowly, leaving it juicy and tender. Meat should be steamed over a richly flavored broth to give it more flavor.

How Much Have You Learned?

Review this chapter. Answer the following questions to prepare yourself for the post-test. Check your answers with your teacher.

1. What makes some cuts of meat tender and others not so tender? How can meat be tenderized?

2. What effect does cooking have on meat? What does high temperature over a long period of time do to meat?

3. Describe the six stages of doneness for meat. Give the approximate internal temperatures for each stage.

4. Why is pork often overcooked? How can you be sure that pork is well done, but not overdone? Why is veal always cooked to the well-done stage?

5. What are the three general methods of cooking meat? How can you tell which way to cook a piece of meat?

6. Which cuts of beef may be roasted? Which cuts of veal, lamb, and pork may be roasted?

7. Why is a meat thermometer used in roasting? How is it placed in the roast?

8. Give the steps for roasting in a deck oven.

9. Give the steps for roasting a partially disjointed turkey.

10. What cuts of beef are suitable for broiling? What cuts of veal, lamb, and pork are suitable for broiling? What kinds of poultry may be broiled?

11. How do you pre-prepare steak and poultry for broiling?

12. How can you control the temperature and time in broiling?

13. Give the rules for broiling. Give the rules for pan-broiling or grilling.

14. What are the qualities needed in a fat suitable for deep-fat frying.

15. What is breading? Why is it needed in deep-fat frying? Give the rules for breading.

16. Give the rules for deep-fat frying. How do you care for fat after frying?

17. What cuts may be braised or stewed? Give the steps for braising. Give the steps for stewing.

18. What large cuts of meat may be boiled or simmered?

CORDON BLEU

Equipment
Cleaver   Sauté pan
Mallet   Turner

Yield: 6 servings

Metric	Ingredients	Customary
12 thin slices	Veal cutlets	12 thin slices
	Salt and pepper	
6 thin slices	Swiss cheese	6 thin slices
6 thin slices	Ham	6 thin slices
	Flour	
3	Eggs	3
175 mL	Bread crumbs	$\frac{3}{4}$ c
340 g	Butter	12 oz

METHOD

1. **Flatten** veal cutlets with cleaver.
2. **Sprinkle** with salt and pepper.
3. **Place** 1 slice ham and 1 slice cheese on each of 6 veal slices.
4. **Cover** with remaining veal slices.
5. **Pound** edges together with mallet.
6. **Dip** in flour and roll in bread crumbs.
7. **Melt** butter in sauté pan to sizzling.
8. **Fry** meat for 8 minutes on each side.

BARBECUED SPARERIBS

Equipment
Stockpot   Colander
Slicing knife   Baking pan

Yield: 50 servings
Temperature: 177°C [350° F.]
Time: 1 hr 45 min

Metric	Ingredients	Customary
17 kg	Pork spareribs	37–38 lb
As needed	Oil	As needed
As needed	Paprika	As needed
7.6 L	Barbecue sauce	2 gal

METHOD

1. **Divide** spareribs into 50 portions, each about 340 g [12 oz].
2. **Place** spareribs in stockpot, cover with water.
3. **Simmer** 30 minutes.
4. **Preheat** oven to 177°C [350° F.].
5. **Drain** spareribs in colander.
6. **Place** in baking pans.
7. **Brush** with oil.
8. **Sprinkle** with paprika.
9. **Place** under broiler and brown each side.
10. **Cover** each portion with barbecue sauce.
11. **Bake** for 1 hour until very tender.

OVEN-FRIED CHICKEN

Equipment
Stainless steel bowl
Breading pan
Baking pan

Yield: 50 servings
Temperature: 190°C [375° F.]
Time: 1 hour

Metric	Ingredients	Customary
340 g	Salad oil	12 oz
125 mL	Lemon juice	½ c
200 g	Fine bread crumbs	7 oz
15 mL	Poultry seasoning	1 T
5 mL	Pepper	1 t
5 mL	Salt	1 t
11.4 kg	Frying chickens, quartered	25 lb (50 quarters)

METHOD

1. **Preheat** oven to 190°C [375° F.].
2. **Mix** salad oil and lemon juice in bowl.
3. **Mix** bread crumbs, poultry seasoning, salt and pepper in breading pan.
4. **Dip** each piece of chicken in oil mixture. Drain.
5. **Roll** each piece of chicken in bread crumbs.
6. **Place** on baking pan, skin side up.
7. **Bake** 1 hour. Chicken should be very brown and tender.

Finfish and Shellfish

When you finish studying this chapter, you should be able to do the following:
- Define the *Words to Remember.*
- Prepare a variety of finfish, meeting the standards of acceptable service.
- Prepare a variety of shellfish, meeting the standards of acceptable service.
- Prepare a variety of dishes using processed fish, meeting the standards of acceptable service.
- Pass the posttest.

CHAPTER

10

In Chapter 4, seafood was defined as all edible fish and shellfish that come from water. Perhaps you remember there are two types of seafood—finfish and shellfish. Finfish have a bony structure and fins. Shellfish have a soft body with no spinal column.

Reread that section of Chapter 4 that relates to seafood. That information will prepare you for the information in this chapter. You should understand how to judge the quality of seafood. You must be able to pre-prepare seafood for the cook in the kitchen. Remember, too, that seafood is very perishable. It requires constant refrigeration.

Seafood has never been as popular as beef and other meats. Nonetheless, it has many advantages in food service. It is available throughout the United States because of modern refrigerating and freezing techniques. It is easy and quick to prepare. It is easily portioned for serving. Perhaps the most important advantage is the great variety. Few people realize how many different kinds of finfish and shellfish are available.

Fish is also gaining rapidly in popularity. As some customers become more calorie conscious, they consider the amount of fat in beef compared to fish. They are more apt to choose low-calorie, low-fat fish.

Words to Remember

amandine

butterflied

court bouillon

fillet

fish poacher

meunière

poaching

turbots

FINFISH

Finfish have been an important source of food for as long as history has been recorded. Fig. 10-1. Fish are referred to many times in the Bible. The remains of fish have been found in the ancient tombs of the pharaohs of Egypt.

Finfish are found in salt or fresh water. Some fish like salmon are migratory. They are born in fresh water but migrate when very young to the salt water. However, they return to the fresh water for spawning, or laying eggs. Saltwater fish are served much more frequently in food service than freshwater fish. They are cheaper and have fewer, but larger, bones.

Table 10-1 lists the finfish most often featured on the menu. Notice how many more of them are in the saltwater grouping than in the freshwater list.

Perhaps one of the reasons fish has never been as popular as beef is fear of bones. Small fishbones can make fish difficult, unpleasant, and even dangerous to eat. Modern methods of preparing saltwater fish have almost eliminated the possibility of bones.

Figure 10-2 shows the technique for boning cooked trout. The flesh of fish is almost free of connective tissue. Therefore, it is always tender and can be cooked by quick methods. The flesh of raw fish is very pale. Fish that are fat will have a slightly yellow tinge. However, salmon and trout, which are fat

McIlhenny Company

10-1. Delicious, freshly caught seafood.

Saltwater Fish	Migratory Fish	Freshwater Fish
Bluefish	Salmon, Atlantic	Catfish
Cobia	Salmon, silver	Northern pike or
Cod	Salmon, sockeye	pickerel
Dolphin	Rainbow trout	Salmon, coho
Flounder,		Smelts
northern		Trout, brook
Grouper		Trout, lake
Haddock		Yellow perch
Halibut		Walleyed pike
Kingfish		Whitefish
Mackerel,		
Spanish		
Plaice		
Pollock		
Pompano		
Red snapper,		
American		
Red snapper,		
Venezuelan		
Sea bass		
Sea trout		
Sole		
Whiting		
Yelloweye snapper		
Yellowtail snapper		

Table 10-1. Finfish Commonly Prepared in Food Service

fish, are a delicate pink. Fish with little fat will be blue-white.

The fat in fish varies from one to twenty percent. The fat is very soft and spread throughout the flesh with no marbling effect. Some fat fish are salmon, mackerel, shad, and trout. Some lean fish are flounder, halibut, and cod. In beef, the method of cooking is determined by the amount of connective tissue. However, there is no such thing as a less tender piece of fish. The method of cooking fish is influenced by the amount of fat.

Pre-preparation of Fish for Cooking

Fish almost always comes to the cook ready for cooking. As described in Chapter 4, the fish may be cut into steaks or fillets. A *fillet* (FIL-it) is a *boneless* piece of meat or fish. A fillet may be thick or thin. It may be the whole side of a small fish or a thick portion of a large fish.

Only large fish are suitable for steaks. As mentioned in Chapter 4, steaks are sliced crosswise. The backbone is often left in.

Only small, thin fish can be *butterflied*. When a small fish is filleted, a piece of skin holds the two sides together. This gives the fish the shape of a butterfly. The technique for butterflying trout is shown in Fig. 10-3.

Sticks, squares, rectangles, and fillet-shaped pieces of fish are made by cutting them from frozen blocks of fillets. These items are breaded and pre-portioned when purchased. They may be raw and

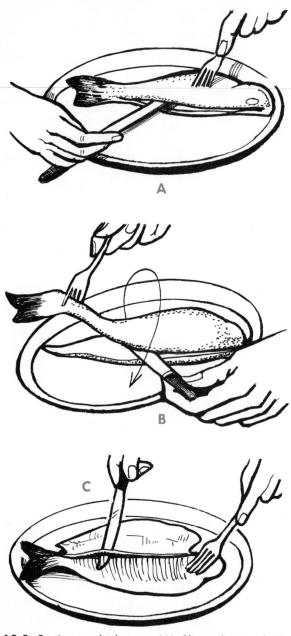

10-2. Boning cooked trout. (A) Slip a boning knife along the entire length of the backbone. Steady the fish with a fork. (B) Gently lift tail section and bones away from the bottom fillet. Using the knife, separate the head from the bottom fillet. Lay top fillet skin side down on plate. (C) Remove tail, bones, and head. Be careful to remove bone structure in one complete section.

ready to cook or precooked and ready to heat. Keep them frozen until ready to be prepared.

To thaw unbreaded fish, place frozen packages in the refrigerator. Allow twenty-four to thirty-six hours for defrosting a 454-g [1-lb] package. Allow forty-eight to seventy-two hours for a 2.3-kg [5-lb] package. If quicker thawing is needed, place package under cold running water. Allow one to two hours for the 454-g [1-lb] package. Allow two to three hours for the 2.3-kg [5-lb] package.

> **CAUTION**
>
> *Do not thaw at room temperatures or under warm water. Remember, warm fish spoils very quickly. Do not refreeze. Keep in a refrigerator in the original package and use within twenty-four hours.*

Fish to be fried in deep fat must first be breaded or batter dipped. Follow the directions on pages 194–195. Many food service places prefer to purchase prebreaded fish portions.

For buffet service, dressed fish may be cooked whole with the head and tail still on. Salmon is often cooked and served in this manner.

Equipment

The equipment used in meat cookery is also used for preparing fish. However, if a whole fish is to be poached, a narrow pan long enough to hold the whole fish is needed. It is called a *fish poacher* and is equipped with a trivet with handles. Fig. 10-4. The trivet keeps the fish out of the liquid. The handles make it easy to lift out the cooked fish.

Principles of Cooking

Seafood cooks more quickly than most other foods. All fish have delicate flesh and must be treated gently. *The most important rule is simple—don't overcook.* Overcooked fish is dry, tasteless, and tough. Cooking time varies with the thickness of the fish. Fillets about 2.4 cm [1 in] thick will take longer than very thin fillets.

Fish is done when the flesh becomes opaque and

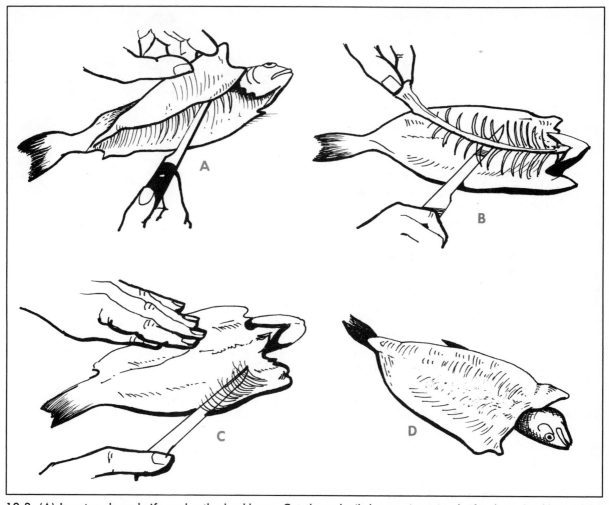

10-3. (A) Insert a sharp knife under the backbone. Cut through rib bones, inserting knife above backbone from head to tail. Repeat, inserting knife above backbone. (B) Work entire backbone free with tip of knife. Sever at head and tail with kitchen scissors. Pull out in one complete piece with fingers. (C) Remove the fine bones, scraping them away from the center of the fish. (D) The butterflied trout is now ready for cooking. It can be dipped in batter and cooked open. It can also be stuffed and roasted.

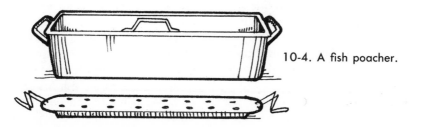

10-4. A fish poacher.

flakes easily. Raw fish is translucent, like frosted glass. As the fish cooks, the flesh becomes more dense, solid, and opaque.

Because of the delicate flavor of seafood, use a light hand in seasoning. The seasoning should help develop the flavor, not smother it.

Fish must be served immediately after cooking. It cannot be held, even at low temperatures, without serious loss of quality.

Methods of Cooking

Fish are cooked by baking, poaching, steaming, broiling, sautéing, and deep-fat frying. The method is influenced by the size and thickness of the piece and the amount of fat. Fig. 10-5.

Fish with a high percentage of fat are best cooked by broiling, barbecuing, and baking. Lean fish are better for steaming, sautéing, and deep-fat frying. Whole, large fish are suitable for stuffing and baking. As mentioned before, they may be steamed or poached whole and served cold for buffets. Small, whole fish are excellent for sautéing or panfrying. Steaks and fillets may be broiled, sautéed, and baked.

BAKING

Baking in the oven is especially good for thick fillets and whole, large fish. Fig. 10-6.

To bake fish fillets, follow these directions:

1. Oil baking pan and arrange fillets in it.

2. Preheat a conventional oven to 190°C [375° F.].

3. Brush fillets with butter, sprinkle with paprika.

4. Bake for twenty-five to thirty minutes. Flesh should flake easily when touched with a fork.

If using a convection oven, preheat oven to 163°C [325° F.]. Bake for fifteen to twenty minutes.

The following are variations of baked fillets.

• Dip portions in milk. Roll in fine bread crumbs. Brush with butter, and bake.

• Place portions in oiled baking pan. Spread each portion with cheese sauce. Sprinkle with crushed cornflakes, and bake.

• Dip each fillet in a mixture of lemon juice, salt, and pepper. Let stand one hour. Arrange in oiled

Thousand Springs Trout Farms, Inc.

10-5. Baked stuffed trout. The trout has been stuffed with sautéed mushrooms, chopped onions, and bread crumbs.

baking pan. Place a tablespoonful of sautéed onions on top of each fillet. Sprinkle with chopped parsley, and bake.

• Place a #20 scoop of crab meat stuffing (see page 221) on each fillet. Press stuffing to cover fillet completely. Brush with butter, and bake. Serve with Creole sauce.

• Sauté shallots in butter. Add white wine. Place fillets in baking dish. Arrange a slice of tomato, green pepper, and onion on top of each fish portion. Cover with sauce. Cover with greased brown paper, and bake.

Turbots (TUR-buts) are flat, thin fish that may be rolled and baked with stuffing. In Europe, turbot is a large, flatfish highly prized for its flavor. In the United States, halibut is usually used.

The thin slices of fish are dipped in a mixture of lemon juice and oil with salt, and pepper. Use about 30 mL [2 T] of lemon juice for each 250 mL [1 c] of oil. The fish slices are placed in an oiled baking pan, and a scoop of dressing (#20 scoop) is spread on top of each slice. The fish slice is rolled up, fastened with a skewer, and baked in the oven.

To bake a whole fish follow these directions:

1. Wash inside and out. Dry carefully. Salt inside.

208

2. Stuff, if desired. If fish is stuffed, close cavity with skewers. Preheat oven to 163°C [325° F.].

3. Place flat in oiled baking pan.

4. Spread lightly with bacon fat or margarine.

5. Bake for one hour for small fish, two hours for larger fish.

To prepare a whole baked fish for buffet, follow these directions. After baking, remove skin gently so fish does not break. Leave head and tail intact. Place fish on platter, and chill. Garnish with stuffed olives, parsley, and slices of lemon, hard-cooked egg, and cucumber.

POACHING

Poaching is cooking in a small amount of liquid below the boiling point. The temperature of the liquid should be about 93°C [200° F.]. The fish is placed in the fish poacher on the trivet. Poaching is usually done on top of the range. However, the oven may occasionally be used.

Fillets, steaks, or whole fish may be poached. The fish may be poached in the steamer basket instead of the fish poacher. A whole fish is usually wrapped in cheesecloth to hold it together. Sprinkle the inside of a whole fish with salt and pepper first.

The liquid for poaching fish may be milk, water, wine, fish stock, or court bouillon. *Court bouillon* (COURT BOO-yon) is a mixture of celery, onions, carrots, water, salt, pepper, spices, herbs, vinegar, or lemon juice. The sauce is cooked for thirty minutes, then strained.

To poach fish in a fish poacher, follow these directions:

1. Pour enough liquid to cover bottom of poacher to depth of 0.6 cm [$\frac{1}{4}$ in]. Oil trivet and place in pan.

2. Place fillets, steaks, or whole fish on trivet.

3. Sprinkle with salt and pepper.

4. Cover, place on range, and bring liquid to a simmer.

Florida Department of Natural Resources
10-6. Baked bluefish with apple and onion stuffing.

5. Cook slowly, allowing about twenty minutes per kilogram, or nine minutes per pound of fish.

6. Lift fish on trivet out of water. Slide off onto a platter. Use the liquid to make sauce by thickening with a roux (page 280).

7. A whole fish poached for buffet service should cool in its own stock. Follow directions for skinning and service on page 209.

STEAMING

Steaming under pressure is an excellent way to cook thick fillets in quantity.

To steam fillets, follow these directions:

1. Place fresh or thawed fillets in a single layer on a strainer in a standard third, half, or full-sized pan of a steamer.

Florida Department of Natural Resources

10-7. A broiled red snapper dinner.

2. Sprinkle fish with salt and paprika. Place pan in steam cooker.

3. Set timer for correct time. Allow one to four minutes in a steam cooker at 103 kPa [15 psi]. Follow the manufacturer's directions.

4. When timed cycle is complete, open door, and remove pan.

5. Brush fillets with butter. Place under the broiler for thirty seconds, or until lightly browned.

> **CAUTION**
>
> *Be sure pressure has been completely reduced before opening steamer. Be careful of escaping steam.*

BROILING

Broiling is a particularly good way to cook fat fish. Fig. 10-7. Fat fish will not dry as easily as lean fish. However, all fish, fat or lean, should be oiled before being broiled. More oil is required for lean fish. Oil is better than butter because it does not burn as easily.

Fish to be broiled are often placed in a hand rack or double broiler rack. The fish are placed on one rack. Another rack is placed on top. The fish can be turned without breaking apart.

To broil fish, follow these directions:

1. Grease broiler rack. Lay fish portions skin side down on rack. Fillets, steaks, or butterflied fish may be broiled.

2. Brush fish with oil and lemon juice. Season and sprinkle with paprika, if desired.

3. Place rack about 5 cm [2 in] from the source of heat for small, thin fish so they will not dry out. Small fish are not turned. Place thick fish closer to the heat and turn once.

4. Serve immediately.

COOKING TIP: *Cook only until the flesh can be flaked with a fork. Broiling must be done to order. Overbroiled fish is dry and tasteless.*

Because of the drying effect of broiling, some chefs like to dip the fish in oil. They then drain the fish and sprinkle soft bread crumbs on top. Broil until lightly browned. Finish in oven.

SAUTÉING

Small fillets and small whole fish such as brook trout are best for sautéing. Sole is a small, flat, thin fish highly prized for its delicious flavor. It is usually sautéed. Sole is very expensive. Thus, thin slices of halibut, plaice, or flounder can be substituted for sole in some recipes. Fish to be sautéed is usually dipped first in milk and then in seasoned flour.

To sauté fish, follow these directions:

1. Place fat in sauté pan and heat. Many chefs like to use a mixture of oil and butter. The melted fat should just cover the bottom of the pan.

2. Pass fish through milk and dip in flour. Shake off excess flour.

3. When fat is sizzling, immediately sauté fish. Never leave fish lying in flour before sautéing. The flour will absorb the milk. The fish will not brown.

4. Place fish skin side up. Sauté about three to four minutes until brown. Turn and sauté on other side for three to four minutes until golden brown.

5. Serve immediately with butter sauce or other sauce. (See pages 294–295.)

COOKING TIP: *The fat should be sizzling hot when fish is put in. This will keep fish from sticking. Reduce heat after putting in fish. Thus, fish will not become too brown before it is cooked through. Be careful of hot, spattering fat.*

The following are variations of sautéed fish:

• *Fish sautéed meunière* (mun-YAIR). Fish sautéed and served with a few drops of lemon juice in hot butter becomes fish sautéed meunière. In English, this would be called "miller's-wife style." (*Meunière* means "miller's wife.") To make it fish sautéed belle meunière, add a few sautéed mushrooms.

• *Sautéed fish with lemon butter.* Work 114 g [4 oz] butter until soft. Work in 25 mL [1½ T] lemon juice, 1 mL [¼ t] grated lemon rind, and 15 mL [1 T] chopped fresh parsley. Heat gently and pour over fish.

• *Sautéed fish with anchovy butter.* Work 30 mL

Morrison, Inc.

10-8. Golden brown fried fish from the deep-fat fryer.

[2 T] anchovy paste into 114 g [4 oz] soft butter. Mix in 5 mL [1 t] lemon juice. Heat gently and pour a small amount over each fish.

• *Fish amandine* (AH-mon-DEAN), or fish with almonds. Toast almonds in browned butter. Spoon over fish.

DEEP-FAT-FRIED FISH

Deep-fat frying has done more to popularize fish than any other method of cooking. Prebreading of fish portions and easy-to-use, dependable frying kettles have taken the guesswork out of deep-fat frying. The fry cook does not need to be an expert to turn out a quality product. Fish and chips, fish sandwiches, and fish platters—all are prepared through deep-fat frying techniques. Fig. 10-8.

Lean fish are best for deep-fat frying. Fig. 10-9. Cod, flounder, ocean perch, pollock, and whiting are the fish most often selected. Most prebreaded,

211

Florida Department of Natural Resources

10-9. Fried mullet. The garnish makes the fried fish more appealing.

flakes of breading left in the fat will give a fishy taste to other foods. Fat used for fish should not be used for any other foods.

MICROWAVE COOKING

Because fish cooks quickly, it is particularly adaptable to microwave cooking. Fish fillets are more successfully cooked than whole fish or steaks. Follow these rules:

1. Place fish on paper, glass, or china plate. Place thicker ends of fillets toward the outside of the dish.

2. Brush fillets generously with butter. Sprinkle with salt, pepper, and paprika.

3. Cover with waxed paper, tucking the paper under the dish.

4. Place in microwave and cook on high for six to seven minutes.

5. Let stand five minutes. Serve immediately.

ready-to-cook fish squares, oblongs, and sticks are made from these fish. The portion size may be specified from a small 57-g [2-oz] portion to a large 340-g [12-oz] serving.

To fry fish in deep fat, follow these directions:

1. Preheat frying fat to 177°C [350° F.].

2. If fish is not prebreaded, dip in milk and then in breading or batter. Do not thaw prebreaded portions.

3. Fill fry baskets to one-half their capacity. Do not overload.

4. Fry fish three to six minutes until golden brown.

5. Lift basket to drain. Serve immediately.

COOKING TIP: *Fish cooks very quickly. It can overcook very easily in deep-fat frying. Follow the timing suggested on the package.*

Care of the fat used for deep-fat frying of fish is especially important. Filter fat thoroughly. Any

Words to Remember

chicken lobsters	langustinos
coral	langustos
crawfish	prawns
crayfish	quarters
extruded shrimp	scampi
fan-tailed	selects
glacage	spiny lobsters
gourmet	tomalley
jumbos	

SHELLFISH

Shellfish are spineless animals with a shell that live in the water. As mentioned in Chapter 4, there are two types of shellfish—crustaceans and mollusks. Crustaceans breathe through gills and have hard outer shells and jointed bodies. Shrimp, crabs, lobsters, and crayfish are crustaceans. Mollusks are water animals with soft, unjointed bodies. Most of them are enclosed in a hard, hinged shell. Oysters, clams, mussels, and snails have hard shells. Squid and octopus do not, although they are considered a part of the mollusk family. Scallops are the muscle that opens and closes the shell of a certain mollusk.

Shellfish usually command high prices on the menu. Shellfish are considered a great delicacy, the finest of foods, fit for the tastes of a gourmet. A *gourmet* (gore-MAY) is a person who enjoys and appreciates the fine differences in the flavor and quality of food.

Shrimp

As you read in Chapter 4, shrimp are graded by size. The size of the shrimp determines the price and also the method of cooking. The largest shrimp, numbering 33 or less per kilogram [15 per pound], are called jumbo. They are usually fried or boiled. The next largest number 35 to 44 per kilogram [16 to 20 per pound], are usually boiled or steamed. They are then served whole and cold as shrimp cocktail or on a salad. Smaller shrimp are used in casseroles or salads.

Very small shrimp may number from 220 to 1320 per kilogram [100 to 600 per pound]. The very small, white shrimp are often called "popcorn" shrimp.

The directions for boiling, deveining, and peeling shrimp were given in Chapter 4. Besides being boiled, shrimp may be prepared for service by frying or sautéing.

DEEP-FAT FRYING OF SHRIMP

Fried jumbo shrimp are extremely popular and also very expensive. When the shrimp are peeled and deveined, the tail is often left on. The tail adds to the apparent size of the shrimp. It also makes it easier to eat the shrimp by hand. The shape is more interesting.

Shrimp are often butterflied, or *fan-tailed*. The peeled and deveined shrimp are split down the middle and pressed open. They are still held together by the back strip and tail. Butterflied, or fan-tailed, shrimp appear to be twice as large as regular shrimp.

Shrimp are always breaded before frying. The intense heat of the fat would toughen shrimp without the shield of the breading. Most food service places purchase prebreaded shrimp ready to cook. The percentage of breading can be specified, such as "under 30 percent breading." Some prebreaded shrimp are coated very heavily with breading mixture. This increases the apparent size of the shrimp but decreases the quality of the finished product. The taste of the heavy breading overwhelms the delicate flavor of the shrimp. If the breading exceeds government regulations (50 percent), the word *imitation* must be used.

Very large shrimp are sometimes called *prawns*. They may be stuffed with a mixture of bread and crab meat, breaded, and fried. A recipe for crab meat stuffing may be found on page 221.

Extruded shrimp are made from shrimp parts and coated with batter. To extrude means to shape by forcing through a hole. Extruded shrimp are much less expensive than whole shrimp.

To fry shrimp, follow these directions:

1. Preheat fat to 177°C [350° F.].

2. Place breaded shrimp in fry basket. Do not fill basket beyond one-half its capacity.

3. Lower basket into fat and fry shrimp for three minutes until golden brown. Butterflied shrimp will take four minutes. Stuffed shrimp will take about five minutes.

4. Lift basket and drain. Serve immediately.

COOKING TIP: *Do not overcook. Shrimp cooks very quickly. Overcooking will toughen them and make them tasteless and dry.*

SAUTÉING SHRIMP

Deveined and peeled shrimp, either raw or cooked, may be sautéed. Since shrimp cook so quickly, there is little advantage in using cooked shrimp. Raw ones add much flavor.

Sautéed shrimp are the basis of many delightful dishes such as shrimp meunière, shrimp Creole, and shrimp pizzaola.

To sauté shrimp, follow these directions:

1. Use butter or margarine. Although these fats burn easily, their flavor blends well with shrimp.

Shrimp cook quickly. With care, the butter will not burn.

2. Heat butter in sauté pan until sizzling.

3. Add shrimp. Reduce heat and cook, stirring gently until shrimp turn pink and opaque. Cook three to five minutes.

4. Serve with garlic butter or just with lemon and chopped parsley. To make garlic butter, mix 115 g [4 oz] of melted butter with one minced clove of garlic. Allow to stand thirty minutes. Strain before using.

Scampi (SCAM-pe), in the United States, are large greenish shrimp. The true scampi are members of the lobster family and come from the Mediterranean Sea. Scampi are served in a garlic butter sauce or in Creole sauce. Creole sauce, a spicy tomato sauce, comes from the Spanish-French cooking of Louisiana.

Lobster

The delicate flavor of lobster has made this crustacean one of the most desirable seafoods. The white meat is tinged with pink. The delicate, slightly sweet taste is highly prized by all gourmets of seafood.

The lobsters most often served in food service weigh about 454 g [1 lb] each. They are often called *chicken lobsters*. Large lobsters are called *quarters*. The largest lobsters are called *selects* and *jumbos*.

Lobsters with claws are taken from the icy waters of the North Atlantic. Each of them has a very large claw, called the fighting claw, and a smaller claw. In the United States, lobsters with claws are called Maine lobsters.

Spiny lobsters are much smaller. They are taken from the warm waters of the Atlantic Ocean around Florida. They are also found in the Caribbean Sea, the Pacific Ocean along Mexico and Southern California, and the Indian Ocean. Fig. 10-10.

Spiny lobsters are sometimes called *langustos*. Rock lobsters are smaller and are sometimes known as *langustinos*. They have no claws. The tails of these lobsters are large in proportion to the rest of the body. The tails contain all of the meat.

Crawfish, or *crayfish*, are the freshwater cousins of the spiny lobster. They are much smaller and

10-10. Spiny lobster thermidor.

abound in the bayous of Louisiana. They are famous in Creole cooking.

Lobsters may be boiled, broiled, stuffed and baked, sautéed, or fried in deep fat. The meat is used in many famous dishes.

BOILED LOBSTER

Maine lobster must be alive when plunged into the boiling water. Death is instantaneous. The shell turns a brilliant red almost as soon as the lobster hits the boiling water. If the boiling is a pre-preparation for further cooking, boil for only five to six minutes. If the lobster is to be served cold, as in a salad or appetizer, boil for twelve to fifteen minutes. A large lobster (select or jumbo) will take about twenty minutes. Chill the cooked lobster under cold, running water.

To remove the meat for further preparation, crack the shell of the claws with a cracker. Pull out the meat. Remove the flat, thin cartilage. Leave the claw meat in large sections. Crack the body by splitting the middle of the soft underbelly with a knife.

The stomach, or *lady,* lies just behind the head. The intestinal vein runs the length of the body. Both of these should be discarded. In female lobsters, there may be eggs, or *coral,* bright orange in color. They are considered a great delicacy. The dark green liver, or *tomalley,* should be removed, but saved. It is mixed with stuffing for lobsters. The tail meat should be removed and placed with the claw meat.

Spiny lobsters are purchased already cooked and cleaned. Since the tail contains all the meat, that portion is often purchased alone. The rest of the carcass is discarded.

Variations

Lobster meat may be mixed with rich sauces and baked in a casserole. At one time the empty lobster shells were refilled with the lobster meat and sauce. The red lobster shells made a spectacular showing. However, because of the danger of contamination, many health departments no longer permit this practice.

The two most famous lobster casserole dishes are lobster Newburg, and lobster thermidor. Many people prefer them to broiled lobster.

Lobster Newburg is made with a rich cream sauce flavored with lemon juice and sherry wine. The lobster is mixed with the sauce and placed in the casserole dish. It is topped with buttered crumbs and slipped under the broiler until hot and bubbling.

Lobster thermidor is made with rich cream sauce, white wine, diced mushrooms, and sautéed shallots. The lobster meat and sauce are placed in the casserole dish. They are then topped with a light cheese sauce, sometimes called a *glacage* (glah-SAHGE). The flavor of the cheese sauce should be delicate so the sweetness of the lobster is not overpowered. The casserole is slipped under the broiler to brown the cheese sauce.

Lobster cardinal is lobster thermidor with slices of truffles. Truffles are a rare, very expensive type of mushroom.

BROILED LOBSTER

Frozen, prestuffed, ready-to-broil lobster may be purchased. The quality varies widely with the purveyor. Many chefs prefer to prepare their own.

Lobster may be split and broiled without stuffing. However, the meat may become tough and flavorless because of the high heat. Lobster slightly cooked and stuffed before broiling is now commonly accepted. The meat remains tender, moist, and sweet because it does not have to be broiled so long.

To broil lobster, follow these directions:

1. Lobster to be broiled is first boiled for five minutes. After boiling, remove from water. Insert a sharp knife between the body and the tail. Split the lobster in two, but do not separate the sections. Remove claws and set aside. Remove the stomach, intestinal vein, and tomalley. Bend back the tail sharply until it snaps. This will prevent the tail from curling during broiling.

2. Prepare stuffing from buttered bread crumbs mixed with crab meat, shrimp, and seasoning.

3. Fill cavity with stuffing. Spread lobster meat with melted butter. Place on baking pan.

4. Broil until brown.

5. Finish by baking in the oven at 205°C [400° F.] for fifteen minutes.

6. While lobster is broiling, heat claws in the oven with a little water to keep them moist.

7. Serve immediately with the claws alongside. Lobsters are always broiled to order.

Words to Remember

bisque	quahog
chowder	scalloped
escalloped	timbale
escargot	

Crabs

Because the white meat of crab is sweet, tender, and juicy, it is almost as popular as lobster. It, too, can be used in many delightful menu items.

Four kinds of crab are available.

Blue crabs are found along the shores of the Atlantic Ocean. The blue crab is the most plentiful. About 75 percent of all crab meat sold commercially comes from blue crabs. They are small crabs, weighing about 140 g [5 oz]. In the spring of the year, blue crabs *molt* (shed their hard shells). If caught while growing the new shell, they are called soft-shell crabs. Some blue crabs are sold live. However, the meat is picked from most, then frozen or canned.

Stone crabs are a delicacy from the Gulf of Mexico. They have beautiful white shells with black and red markings. They are boiled and served in the cracked shell as an appetizer. They are also served as a main course.

Dungeness crabs are larger than blue crabs. They come from the Pacific Ocean from Mexico to Alaska. They weigh from 0.9–1.8 kg [2–4 lb]. When cooked, the shell of the Dungeness turns bright red. The meat is white tinged with pink. It is sweet, tender, and juicy. It is often cooked, frozen, and sold whole.

King crabs are caught in the icy waters around Alaska. They are truly the king of crabs, being the largest of all. One crab can weigh from 2.7–9.2 kg [6–20 lb]. The largest measure as much as 1.8 m [6 ft] from the tip of one leg to the tip of the opposite leg. The meat is similar to that of the Dungeness crab in taste and appearance. The crab legs are often disjointed, cooked, and frozen. They are usually sold in sections because the legs are so long.

CRAB MEAT

Crab meat contains flat, thin cartilage that is difficult to remove. The cartilage in the legs is easy to find. Here, the meat may be in chunks. The cartilage in the body is small, and the meat is usually stringy. Body meat without cartilage is called *picked crab meat.*

Variations

Picked crab meat may be mixed with sauces and served as crab thermidor or crab Newburg. Crab meat may also be served with a spicy Creole tomato sauce. There are several crab meat dishes that are justly famous.

• *Crab meat imperial* is crab meat in a thickened, rich cream sauce. Mushrooms and egg yolks are usually added to increase the richness. The mixture is placed in a casserole dish and topped with bread crumbs and toasted almond slivers. The casserole is placed under the broiler until brown and bubbly.

• *Deviled crab meat* is a popular menu addition. The crab meat is mixed with sautéed onions, green pepper, celery, and a seasoned cream sauce. Fig. 10-11. It is usually baked in a shell-shaped, individual casserole dish. Buttered bread crumbs are spread on top of the casserole. The casserole is then baked in the oven until browned.

DEEP-FRIED SOFT-SHELL CRABS

To dress soft-shell crabs for deep-fat frying, follow these directions:

1. Cut off the face of the crab just behind the eyes.

2. Remove the underside of the body, called the *apron.*

3. Remove the gills, stomach, intestine, and all spongy parts.

4. Rinse thoroughly in cold water and drain.

To fry in deep fat, follow these directions:

1. Dip crabs in egg-milk mixture (equal proportions) and then in flour. The soft shell is not removed. Toss flour over crabs and pat firmly in place. The meat is fragile, so be gentle but firm.

2. Place in basket and fry at 177°C [350° F.] until golden brown. Do not overcook.

3. Drain and serve immediately.

• *Crab cakes* are popular and inexpensive. Picked crab meat is mixed with sautéed mushrooms, onions, celery, and green pepper. Add seasoning, flour, and cream. Blend together and cook for fifteen minutes, stirring all the time.

The mixture is formed into cakes, using a #24 scoop for measure. The cakes are dredged in flour and fried in deep fat like the soft-shell crabs.

• *Crab fingers* are bits of crab compressed into fingers and fried in deep fat. Because crab meat is so expensive, it may be mixed with other fish, shaped, and breaded. It is sold as imitation crab sticks or fingers.

Scallops

As you read in Chapter 4, scallops are the muscle used to open and close the scallop shell. The scallop shell is very beautiful. Many food service places specializing in seafood serve the scallops in the shells or in porcelain replicas of the shells.

The meat of scallops is very white and solid. The flavor is sweet and delicate. There are two types of scallops.

Bay scallops come from shallow bay waters. They are sweeter and more tender than the larger scallops. Being small and tender, bay scallops are frequently sautéed.

Sea scallops are larger than bay scallops. They are taken from deep waters. Usually they are fried in deep fat.

Florida Department of Natural Resources
10-11. Deviled crab.

COQUILLES SAINT JACQUES

The most famous dish featuring scallops is *coquilles Saint Jacques* (coe-KEEL SAN ZHOCK). The scallops are served with a rich cream sauce in the scallop shell. To prepare *coquilles Saint Jacques,* follow these directions:

1. Cook scallops in white wine with shallots. When scallops become opaque, remove from liquid. Be careful not to overcook.

2. Reduce liquid by boiling down to one-third the volume.

3. Mix with a rich cream sauce and sautéed mushrooms.

4. Add poached scallops. Some chefs also add king crab meat.

5. Fill the scallop shells and top with cheese sauce or grated cheese. Slip under the broiler until brown and bubbling.

6. Duchesse potatoes may be served bordering the scallop shell. (See page 253.)

FRIED SCALLOPS

To fry scallops, follow these directions:

1. If scallops are not prebreaded, they must be coated with breading before frying.

2. Wash scallops and drain. Cut to a uniform size.

3. Pass through an egg wash and dip in seasoned breading. Press crumbs into scallops.

4. Fry in deep fat at 177°C [350° F.] for two to three minutes or until brown. Drain and serve.

Clams

Clams belong to the mollusk family. There are eight species used for food service.

• *Hard-shell clams* are often called *quahogs* (COE-hogs), the Indian name for clams. Quahogs are abundant along the Atlantic coast south of Cape Cod. The large quahogs are rather tough, so they are chopped and used for chowder. They may also be sliced thin, dipped in batter, and fried in deep fat.

• *Cherrystone, or littleneck, clams* are a small hard-shell clam. They are often served raw. (See page 139.)

• *Surf clams* are small with a hard shell and a

sweet flavor. They are very tender but difficult to clean because of the sand.

- *Long-neck clams* have a soft shell. They are used in the popular and famous New England clambakes.
- *Butter clams* are found along the Pacific coast. These are hard-shell clams prized for their delicious flavor.
- *Razor clams* are so named for the hard razor-sharp shell.
- *Pacific littleneck clams* are similar to cherrystone clams.
- *Pismo* are famous in the Pismo, California, area.

The pre-preparation and shucking of clams were discussed in Chapter 4. Clams are usually served in chowder or fried in deep fat.

CHOWDER

Clam chowder is a soup—the most famous and popular way to prepare clams. A *chowder* is a hearty soup thickened with potatoes. There are two varieties of clam chowder—New England and Manhattan. Both are prepared from chopped quahogs.

New England clam chowder is made from a milk-cream base with salt pork and onions for added flavor. It is thickened with potatoes. It is smooth, creamy, and lightly salted.

Manhattan clam chowder has a tomato base. It is flavored with salt pork, onions, celery, and spices. Like New England chowder, it is thickened with potatoes.

There are several kinds of fried clams. Like shrimp, all are breaded to shield them from the intense heat of the fat. When soft-shell clams are in season, they may be breaded, fried in deep fat, and served whole. Surf clams may be cut into strips, breaded, and fried. Diced quahogs may be shaped and breaded to resemble whole clams in appearance and taste. Follow the directions for frying shrimp in deep fat.

Oysters

Almost 90 percent of all oysters come from the eastern coast of the Atlantic Ocean and the Gulf of Mexico. They are raised, carefully tended, and kept free of contamination in large oyster beds. These beds are close to the shore. Small oysters, called Olympias, are taken from the Pacific Ocean. The very large Japanese oysters are now being cultivated and sold in the United States.

Raw oysters in the shell were discussed as an appetizer in Chapter 7. They are sold by the bushel basket. Shucked oysters, as you read in Chapter 4, are sold by the litre, quart, half-gallon, and gallon. Prebreaded oysters for deep fat frying are also available.

SCALLOPED OYSTERS

Smaller oysters may be *scalloped.* Sometimes, this term is written *escalloped.* Either way, it means to bake in a casserole with milk and broken crackers. Fig. 10-12. By whatever method they are cooked, only enough heat should be applied to heat

Florida Department of Natural Resources
10-12. Scalloped oysters.

the oyster through. They should still be plump and juicy. Thoroughly cooked oysters are also thoroughly tough.

Cracker crumbs, oysters, oyster liquid, cream, butter, and seasonings are layered in a casserole. The casserole is baked at 175°C [350° F.] only until thoroughly heated. The edges of the oysters should ruffle.

OYSTER STEW

Cook the oysters lightly in butter until the edges ruffle. Mix with a slightly thickened and seasoned cream sauce. Serve immediately, before the oysters toughen.

OYSTER BISQUE

A *bisque* (BISK) is a rich soup made with cream instead of milk. Any crustacean may be used in a bisque.

FRIED OYSTERS

Choose the largest oysters for frying. Follow these directions. If the oysters are prebreaded, omit the first two steps.

1. Wash oysters. Remove any bits of broken shell and dry thoroughly between paper towels.

2. Dip in egg wash and roll in lightly seasoned cracker crumbs. Press crumbs into oyster for a good coating.

3. Fry at 180°C [360° F.] until just browned. Serve immediately.

OYSTERS ROCKEFELLER

Oysters Rockefeller is a very famous gourmet dish served as an appetizer or an entrée. Follow these directions:

1. Poach large oysters in white wine with shallots until oysters curl or ruffle along the edge.

2. Place each oyster in half an oyster shell.

3. Reduce wine stock to about one half. Mix with oyster juice, chopped cooked spinach, and cream sauce.

4. Add a few drops of Pernod liqueur. Spoon the sauce over each oyster.

5. Broil until lightly browned.

Snails, Squid, and Octopuses

Snails, squid, and octopuses are popular in Europe and appreciated by gourmets in the United States. On the menu, snails are called *escargots* (es-car-GO). They are bought in cans with the shells in a separate package. They are baked in the shell with an herb butter, usually garlic. Squid and octopuses are extremely popular in Italy. The arms are sliced, breaded, and fried in deep fat.

CAUTION

Never forget that seafood, especially shellfish, spoils very quickly. Keep refrigerated until ready to be cooked. Shellfish combined with a sauce such as Newburg or thermidor is especially easy to contaminate and spoil. Take such preparations from the refrigerator directly to the oven. Then take them immediately to the table for service.

PROCESSED FINFISH AND SHELLFISH

Canned seafood is often used in food service. It is usually less expensive than fresh seafood. The use of processed seafood permits a wider choice on the menu. Tuna fish, salmon, crab meat, lobster, shrimp, and sardines are just a few of the seafoods available.

Many of the ways of cooking fresh seafood can be applied to processed seafood. Canned fish is especially good for fish cakes, patties, creamed dishes, casseroles, fish loaves, and croquettes. Canned tuna may be substituted for ground or chopped meat in many Americanized Chinese dishes such as chow mein and chop suey.

A *timbale* (TIM-bahl) is a custard-like, highly flavored dish of meat, poultry, or fish baked in small molds. Canned salmon is often used in timbales. Timbales may also contain vegetables.

Although fish is not inexpensive, it deserves a more prominent place on food service menus. It requires little labor in preparation and is easy to serve.

Unit 4: The Hot Stations

How
Much
Have
You
Learned?

Review this chapter. Answer the following questions to prepare yourself for the post-test. Check your answers with your teacher.

1. Define *seafood, finfish,* and *shellfish.* Name three finfish and three shellfish.
2. In what ways do a fish fillet, a fish steak, and a butterflied fish differ?
3. How should frozen fish be thawed? What precautions should be observed in thawing fish?
4. Name the primary principle to be observed in cooking seafood.
5. Demonstrate one method of baking fish.
6. Describe two variations of sautéed fish.
7. Describe how to cook fish in the microwave oven.
8. Why are shellfish always breaded for deep-fat frying? How do you care for fat used in deep-fat frying of fish?
9. What are prawns? What are scampi?
10. What is the difference between the Maine lobster and the spiny lobster?
11. Why are lobsters cooked live?
12. In what way does lobster Newburg differ from lobster thermidor?
13. Name four kinds of crabs. Demonstrate the preparation of one crab dish.
14. What are scallops? How are they cooked?
15. What is the main difference between New England clam chowder and Manhattan clam chowder?
16. What are escargots?
17. Describe one method of cooking oysters.
18. Name four kinds of clams.

CRAB MEAT STUFFING

Equipment
Sauté pan
Stirring spoon
Chopper
Small bowl
Large bowl

Yield: 5.4 kg [12 lb]

Metric	Ingredients	Customary
450 g	Onions, finely chopped	1 lb
450 g	Celery, finely chopped	1 lb
450 g	Butter or margarine	1 lb
2.3 kg	Bread, day-old, diced	5 lb
14 g	Salt	½ oz
10 mL	Pepper	2 t
2 L	Chicken broth	2 qt
225 g	Olives, stuffed, sliced	8 oz
30 mL	Lemon juice	2 T
15 mL	Worcestershire sauce	1 T
500 mL	Eggs, slightly beaten	2 c
1 000 mL	Crab meat or shrimp, minced	1 qt

METHOD

1. **Chop** onions and celery.
2. **Melt** butter or margarine in sauté pan. Sauté onions and celery until tender.
3. **Mix** bread crumbs with seasonings and sautéed vegetables.
4. **Mix** lemon juice and Worcestershire sauce with broth.
5. **Add** broth, tossing lightly until bread crumbs are moistened.
6. **Add** eggs and toss.
7. **Add** crab meat and olives. Mix thoroughly.

Eggs and Cheese

What Will You Learn?

When you finish studying this chapter, you should be able to do the following:

- Define and use the *Words to Remember*.
- Prepare eggs in a variety of ways for use as the entrée, meeting the standards for acceptable service.
- Identify the kinds of cheeses and the way they are used in cooking.
- Prepare cheese in a variety of ways for use as an entrée, meeting the standards for acceptable service.
- Pass the posttest.

CHAPTER

11

When you read Chapter 4, you studied much of the information you need to know about eggs and cheese. Chapter 14 will tell you about the kinds of eggs used in baking. In this chapter you will study how to use eggs and cheese in entrées.

EGGS

In 1965, a study was made to determine when eggs were eaten the most. Over half the eggs eaten that year were eaten for breakfast. For many persons, breakfast is not complete without an egg in some form. However, since 1965, egg consumption in the United States has fallen steadily. Were the same survey to be made today, it would probably show that Americans are eating fewer eggs for breakfast.

Eggs also appear on the brunch and luncheon menu. Sometimes they may be the main dish. Other times, they may be a part of it—such as deviled eggs on a salad plate.

Egg Quality

Table 11-1 gives the quality grades of eggs according to USDA standards. The quality of eggs is most important when they are served whole. Then, flavor and appearance are very noticeable. Eggs to be served whole for breakfast, brunch,

222

Table 11-1. Grades of Eggs

Grade	Description	Use
AA (fresh fancy)	Thick, high white, upstanding yolk	Poaching, frying, cooking in shell.
A	Slightly thinner white, yolk spreads slightly	Scrambled, omelet, soufflé.
B	Thin white, spreading yolk	Baked products.

Words to Remember

egg rings   poaching dish
Florentine   ramekin
mornay   shirred
omelet

or lunch should be Grade AA or A. Eggs to be mixed with other ingredients before cooking may be Grade A or B.

Egg sizes and weights are given in Table 5-6.

How To Recognize A Fresh Egg

As the cook responsible for cooking eggs, you should learn to judge the freshness of eggs. Break an egg into a saucer. Look for the following characteristics:

- *Entire egg* holds together with little spreading.
- *Yolk* is firm and upstanding.
- *White* stands high and firmly around the yolk. There may be a very small amount of white that spreads.

Remember, if the white spreads over a wide surface and the yolk is somewhat flattened, the egg is not as fresh as it should be for cooking whole. Use it for scrambled eggs or an omelet.

Egg standards are detailed in Chapter 4.

Egg Cookery

In food service, most eggs are prepared by the breakfast cook. There are hundreds of ways to prepare eggs. However, they can all be grouped under six general methods: frying, poaching boiling, bak-ing, scrambling, and omelet. Fig. 11-1 shows baked, poached, soft-boiled, scrambled, and fried eggs. Omelets are shown in Figs. 11-6 and 11-8.

American Egg Board

11-1. Various ways of cooking eggs. Clockwise from top: baked eggs, fried eggs, scrambled eggs, soft-boiled egg, and poached eggs.

Unit 4: The Hot Stations

A breakfast cook must know how to cook eggs in all these different ways quickly. Many persons are most particular about the way their eggs are cooked. For example, if a customer orders a three-minute egg, the egg should be cooked exactly three minutes. Otherwise it may be returned.

The basic prinicple of cooking eggs is simple: *Always cook eggs at low temperature until just done.* As in meat cookery, control of time and temperature is essential.

As eggs are heated, they gradually coagulate, or become firm. The longer they are cooked, the harder they become. Cooking eggs at high temperatures or cooking too long at any temperature causes the white to become rubbery. The yolk turns a greenish gray color. A greenish ring may be deposited around the yolk. When opened, the egg gives off an unpleasant sulfur smell.

FRIED EGGS

In food service, more eggs are fried than cooked by any other method. Definite terms are used to indicate the ways eggs are to be fried.

• *Sunny-side-up* or *"eyes open"* means the yolks are bright yellow and well-rounded. The yolk runs when broken. The white should be firm without brown edges.

• *Over-easy* means the white is firm. The yolk is soft and covered with a thin film of firm egg white.

• *Hard-fried* means the white and yolk are firm, but never rubbery.

• *Basted* means the white is firm and the yolk pink and soft. When eggs are cracked and cooked whole in a pan, the yolk is covered with a thin film of egg white. Basting makes the egg white translucent. The yolk of a fresh egg will turn a soft, salmon pink—not yellow.

Only grade AA eggs and butter should be used for fried eggs.

Eggs may be fried on the grill or in a frying pan. Most hotel breakfast cooks will use a frying pan. Places specializing in fast foods will use egg rings on the grill. *Egg rings* are metal rings placed on the grill to hold the egg whites in a round, compact shape.

To fry eggs on the grill, follow these rules:

American Egg Board

11-2. The yolks of these basted eggs are translucent, rather than yellow.

1. Brush grill with butter. Set temperature at 120°C [250° F.].
2. Place rings on grill.
3. Crack eggs and fill rings.
4. For sunny-side-up eggs, cook about two minutes. Test whites for firmness and serve. For over-easy eggs, slip rings off eggs. Turn eggs over, being careful not to break yolks. Fry a few seconds more and serve.

For hard-fried eggs, follow steps 1, 2, and 3 for over-easy. Continue as follows:

4. Fry about two minutes ten seconds to harden the yolk bottom.
5. Slip frying rings off eggs.
6. Flip egg over and fry about twenty to thirty seconds.
7. Test yolk to be sure it is solid. Serve immediately.

To baste eggs:

1. Follow directions for sunny-side-up eggs.

J. R. Simplot Co.

Not all sandwiches have a top covering. This open-faced roast beef sandwich served with its own gravy is only one example of the many ways in which sandwiches can be varied.

J. R. Simplot Co.

Lemon slices are a traditional garnish for broiled fish. The careful preparation and arrangement of such garnishes can lend much to the appearance of a dish.

224A

Although usually prepared in a skillet in the home, bacon is often partially baked in an oven in food service. It is then grilled as needed. This helps ensure uniform texture and appearance.

Oscar Mayer & Co.

The cooking method depends on the cut and grade of meat. Being naturally tender, this tenderloin steak taken from Prime beef has been broiled.

224C

Florida Department of Natural Resources

In the United States there are many regional specialties, such as corn bread, a traditional southern dish. Here it is shown topped with a shrimp Creole sauce.

224D

Arroz con pollo, or chicken with rice, is a tasty dish from the Hispanic culture. Containing chicken with tomato sauce, rice, peas, and mushrooms, such a one-dish meal is popular in food service.

General Foods

2. Spoon hot fat over egg until yolk turns pink. The following is another method of basting eggs:
1. Place butter in frying pan and heat to sizzling.
2. Break eggs into pan. Fry two minutes.
3. Add one teaspoon water and cover.
4. Steam a few seconds. When egg yolk becomes translucent, egg is done. Do not overcook. Fig. 11-2.

Variations

Serve fried eggs with pancakes.

Serve fried eggs with fresh fruit. Fig. 11-3.

Serve fried eggs with fried chicken livers and onions.

Make a round hole in a slice of bread. The hole should be the size of the egg yolk. Place bread and round on grill. Brown one side quickly. Break egg into hole and fry for two minutes. Place browned round of bread on top yolk and serve.

POACHED EGGS

To *poach* means to cook in a small amount of water below the boiling point. For poaching, Grade AA eggs are required. If lower grades are used, the white will spread too much. Vinegar in the water helps harden the whites before they spread in the

American Egg Board

11-3. Fried eggs served on toast with sliced oranges. Watercress has been added as a garnish.

11-4. An egg poaching dish.

water. Rinse off the vinegar in hot water before serving.

To poach in a skillet, follow these rules:
1. Fill pan two-thirds full of water. Add small amount of vinegar.
2. Bring to a simmer.
3. Crack egg in saucer and slip egg into the water.
4. Remove pan from heat, cover, and let stand five minutes. Test white for firmness. Rinse off vinegar, and serve immediately.

Although eggs can be poached in water alone, a poaching dish makes it easier. A *poaching dish* is a skillet fitted with an inset with small cups. Fig. 11-4. Each cup holds one egg. The cups control the shape of the eggs.

To poach in a poaching dish, follow these rules:
1. Fill skillet two-thirds full with water.
2. Put in cup inset and bring water to a simmer.
3. Place a small amount of butter in each cup.
4. Break egg into saucer and slip into cup when butter is melted.
5. Cover and steam for five minutes. Test white for firmness. Serve immediately.

Variations

Eggs Benedict are poached eggs served on a toasted English muffin with a slice of Canadian bacon. Hollandaise sauce is spooned over the top. (See page 294.) For an extra-special touch, top with a slice of truffle.

Western-style poached eggs are served with a spicy tomato sauce.

Eggs Florentine are poached eggs on a nest of cooked spinach, topped with cheese sauce. *Florentine* is a term used to describe any dish using spinach.

BOILED EGGS

Although boiling is the common term used for unshelled eggs cooked whole in water, eggs should never be boiled. Nevertheless, you will often see them boiled in food service. A better way is to cook them at temperatures below boiling. As you read earlier, high temperatures will turn the yolks greenish and make the whites rubbery.

Grade AA eggs are best for boiled eggs.

A saucepan deep enough to cover the eggs with water is often used. However, the automatic egg cooker is much more common. It automatically times the eggs. Most breakfast cooks are too busy to time eggs accurately.

To soft-cook or hard-cook eggs in a saucepan, follow these directions:

1. Fill pan with enough water to cover the eggs.
2. Gently place the eggs in the water.
3. Heat almost to boiling. Remove pan from heat and cover.
4. Let stand five to eight minutes, depending on customer's preference. For hard-cooked eggs, allow to stand for twenty minutes.
5. Cool slightly under running water before serving.

To soft-cook eggs in the automatic cooker, follow the instructions of the manufacturer.

COOKING TIP: *Many cooks forget about the necessary cooling period. Hard-cooked eggs will continue to cook and become rubbery unless cooled immediately.*

Hard-cooked eggs, already peeled, may be purchased. These are very popular in food service because it is difficult to peel hard-cooked eggs smoothly. Many are wasted because they do not look good enough to serve on a salad.

Hard-cooked eggs may be extruded into a long, sausagelike form for slicing. This form is also used in food service because it saves time.

Variations

Hard-cooked eggs may be served in endless variety. For instance:

Eggs a la goldenrod. Chop whites and add to cream sauce. Force yolks through sieve. Serve cream sauce over toast and sprinkle egg yolks on top. *Goldenrod* is a term used to describe any dish with chopped egg yolks sprinkled on top.

Deviled eggs. Peel eggs and slice in half. Remove yolks and mash through sieve. Mix with seasoning and mayonnaise. Stuff whites with egg yolks, using a pastry bag.

Eggs and peas. Chop eggs. Cook frozen peas and drain. Add peas and chopped eggs to cream sauce. Serve on toast.

Eggs and cheese on toast. Toast bread and butter it. Chop hot hard-cooked eggs and spread on toast. Top with slice of cheese. Slip under broiler for a few minutes until cheese melts.

BAKED EGGS

Baked eggs are called *shirred* eggs. Baking is a convenient way to cook many eggs at once. Baked eggs may be plain or fluffy. Fig. 11-5.

Since eggs are one of the most heat-sensitive foods, it is important to bake them at the exact temperature specified in the recipe. The temperature may be 163–195°C [325–375° F.]. However, the egg itself will not get any hotter than 60–65°C [140–149° F.] if cooked the correct length of time. The correct length of time depends upon the customer preference for hardness or softness of the egg. Experience will teach you how to test for doneness with the touch of the finger.

• *Ingredients.* Cooking fat may be butter, margarine, bacon fat, or cooking oil. Grade AA or Grade A eggs should be used. Allow two eggs per serving. Salt, pepper, bread crumbs, milk, cream, and other ingredients may be needed, depending on the recipe.

• *Equipment.* Eggs may be baked in a shallow ceramic baking dish with a handle called a *ramekin* (RAM-a-cun). For some variations, muffin cups, or a flat baking dish may be needed.

For plain baked eggs, follow these rules:

1. Preheat oven to 163°C [325° F.].
2. Butter ramekins or baking dishes.
3. Slip two eggs into each dish.
4. Season with salt and pepper.
5. Cover with buttered, seasoned crumbs if desired.

11-5. Baked, or shirred, eggs must be carefully cooked. These baked eggs are served with corn sticks and strawberries.

6. Bake fifteen to twenty minutes until white is firm. The time depends upon customer preference.

7. Serve in ramekin or baking dish.

For fluffy baked eggs, follow these directions:

1. Trim crusts and toast slices. Butter toast and place on flat baking pan. Allow one piece of toast for each customer.

2. Separate egg whites from egg yolks, placing whites in a bowl. Keep yolks in half shell, set upright.

3. Beat whites until stiff, but not dry.

4. Pile whites on toast. Make a depression in whites and slip yolk into depression.

5. Bake at 175°C [350° F.] about ten to twelve minutes. Whites should be lightly browned and yolk soft.

6. A slice of luncheon meat may be placed on toast before piling on the beaten egg white.

Variations

Line greased muffin tins with luncheon meat, ham, or cooked bacon. Break egg into each cup. Bake at 175°C [350° F.] until whites are firm. Serve on slice of toast.

Bake eggs in cheese sauce, sprinkling grated cheese on top of eggs before baking. This dish is called shirred eggs Mornay. *Mornay* is a term meaning "with cheese sauce."

Bake eggs on minced chicken with cream.

Peel tomatoes, cut off tops, and scoop out centers. Break eggs in each center. Cover each tomato with buttered crumbs. Bake at 175°C [350° F.] until egg is set.

SCRAMBLED EGGS

Scrambled eggs are second only to fried eggs in popularity for breakfast. They are quick and easy to prepare and can be varied in many delightful ways.

They are often served with fried ham, sausages, or crisp bacon.

- *Standards.* Just as people like different degrees of doneness in steaks, they also differ in just how scrambled eggs should be. Some like them soft and creamy. Others prefer them more solid and slightly browned. The cooking method determines the end result. Some standards for scrambled eggs do not change. They should be soft yellow, tender, and never watery. High heat and overcooking will cause scrambled eggs to "weep," or water.

- *Ingredients.* Grade A or even Grade B eggs may be used for scrambled eggs because the fresh appearance of the egg is not so important. Recipes for the four methods of preparing scrambled eggs are given on pages 237–239. Notice that the ingredients are almost the same.

Water added to eggs gives a tender product. Milk or cream adds more body and makes creamy, soft scrambled eggs. A cream sauce is used when the scrambled eggs are to be made in quantity to be held on the steam table for a length of time. (See page 300 for the recipe for making a cream sauce.) Salt and pepper are needed for seasoning.

Chopped ham, parsley, chives, mushrooms, and many other ingredients may be mixed with scrambled eggs. They lend a variety of flavor and texture.

A short-order cook will make the scrambled egg mixture ahead of time and hold it in a pitcher for use as needed. From experience, the cook knows just about how many orders for scrambled eggs will need to be filled in any morning.

• *Equipment.* Each method given in the recipes for scrambled eggs requires different equipment. A short-order cook, cooking scrambled eggs to order, will use a small sauté pan with sloping sides or cook directly on the grill. For quantity work, the cook will use a double boiler, or a bain-marie for Method 2, and a large sauté pan, or the brasier for Method 3. A few cooks may use Method 4. This requires a shallow baking pan.

For mixing, a fork is often used for individual portions since the eggs are only slightly beaten. For larger quantities a whip, eggbeater, or hand mixer may be used.

For stirring in the pan, a turner, spatula, or spoon is needed.

• *Methods of Cooking.* Compare the methods of mixing shown in the recipes on pages 237–239. Each method gives a different type of scrambled eggs. If the eggs are barely mixed with a fork, the product will have streaks of cooked white in the yellow of the yolk. If the eggs are beaten thoroughly, the product will be soft, creamy, and fluffy.

Method 1 produces layered, solid, but tender eggs.

Method 2 produces eggs with fine, soft particles, rather than large pieces. This is because they are stirred with a spoon.

Method 3 produces soft, large pieces of egg that stand up well on the steam table for a long time.

Method 4 produces soft, chunky eggs that must be served immediately. Cooks sometimes choose this method because the eggs do not have to be watched as closely.

Variations

Lightly sauté mushrooms. Add to egg mixture in the sauté pan.

Add chopped cheese when eggs begin to thicken.

Add a dash of curry powder to the egg mixture before cooking.

Shred dried beef. Sauté lightly in butter. Mix with scrambled eggs as they begin to thicken.

Mix scrambled eggs with a spicy tomato sauce as they thicken or pour the hot sauce over the eggs just before serving.

OMELETS (FRENCH SPELLING—OMELETTE)

An *omelet* is a mixture of eggs, salt, and pepper cooked in a sauté pan. Although it is often served for breakfast, it is popular as a luncheon dish, also. Omelets are made one at a time. Two eggs make a basic serving for one person. Ten eggs make the big-

Oscar Mayer & Co.

11-6. A folded omelet garnished with crumbled bacon.

11-7. These frying pans are made of heavy-gauge metal and have sloping sides. The smaller ones are used for omelets.

Wear-Ever

Oscar Mayer & Co.

11-8. This omelet has been filled with strawberry jam.

gest omelet that can be handled successfully. A two-egg omelet, takes only about two minutes to cook. Thus, it is better to make many small omelets than to attempt one large one.

• *Kinds of omelets.* An omelet may be plain or fluffy. The plain omelet is also called a classic, or French, omelet. It is the type most often served in food service. The French omelet is cooked on top of the range. The fluffy omelet is started on top of the range and finished in the oven.

• *Standards for omelets.* The French omelet should be firm but moist on the inside. It should be tender, with a delicate flavor. It should be lightly browned and rolled or folded. Fig. 11-6. The shape should be rounded and uniform.

A foamy omelet should be puffy with a good volume. It should have a delicate texture that is firm but never dry. It should be lightly browned and cooked through. There should be no runny egg mixture in the center. Puffy omelets are usually folded when served.

• *Equipment.* A good omelet pan for one serving should have a bottom diameter of 18–20 cm [7–8 in]. The interior should be very smooth with gently sloping sides that round into the bottom. Fig. 11-7. This design makes it easy to fold or roll the omelet. The ideal pan is made of heavy-gauge metal. Aluminum is preferred by Americans. French chefs prefer dark stainless steel with a well-seasoned interior. Omelet pans must be *seasoned*. In seasoning, the interior is coated with vegetable oil and the pan is gently heated until the oil smokes. The pan is rubbed with salt and allowed to cool.

Then the remaining oil and salt are wiped clean. After seasoning, the pan should never be washed with soap and water. These would remove the finish. A fork is needed for mixing and turning.

Omelets are important. They are considered the test of the expertise of a chef. It requires some practice to turn out a perfect omelet. To cook an omelet, follow the cooking methods compared in the recipes on page 236.

An omelet is cooked on high heat because it cooks so quickly. The pan should be hot enough to sizzle a drop of water before the butter goes in. Enough butter is needed to coat thoroughly the bottom and sides of the pan. When the eggs are poured in, they immediately begin to set around the sides of the skillet.

Variations

There are many ways to serve omelets. Omelets with ingredients folded inside are called *filled omelets*. All fillings should be prepared before the omelet is cooked. Almost any tasty food can be used to fill an omelet. Fig. 11-8.

229

Just before folding the omelet, sprinkle with jelly, chopped meat, poultry, seafood, vegetables, or chopped herbs. Creamed chicken, mushrooms, or crab meat may also be used as a filling.

Omelette savoyarde (salve-WAH-YARD) is a hearty omelet for luncheon. Potatoes, cheese, cubed ham, and leeks are cooked in water. They are then drained and spread on the omelet before folding. Corned beef hash may be used in the same way.

Care, Storage, and Service

Most egg dishes require immediate service. Thus, care and storage are not a problem. Hard-cooked,

unpeeled eggs may be kept for several weeks in the refrigerator and used as needed.

Words to Remember

au gratin	quiche
chafing dish	Reuben
cordon bleu	soufflé
fondue	Welsh Rarebit
process cheese	

CHEESE

As you have studied the preceding chapters, you may have noticed that cheeses are used in many different ways in food service. There are hundreds of varieties of cheeses. Each one is slightly different in texture and flavor from any other. The climate, water, temperature during ripening, the kind of milk used—all make each cheese unique.

Some cheeses are used mostly for appetizers, desserts, and salads. Such cheeses as Roquefort, blue, Brie, Camembert, Gorgonzola, Gouda, Edam, Liederkranz, Limburger, and Stilton are delicious cheeses. However, some of them have very strong flavors that make them unsuitable for cooking. Others do not melt and blend in cooking.

A good cheese for cooking should have these characteristics:

• *Meltable.* When heated, the cheese will melt into a soft mass. Fig. 11-9.

• *Blendable.* The cheese will blend with the other ingredients.

• *Definite cheese flavor.* The flavor should be definite, but not strong. It should not overpower the flavor of the other ingredients.

Because of these needed characteristics, process cheese was developed. It was first developed in Germany and Switzerland, and later in the United States. *Process cheese* is a blend of two or more varieties of cheese. An emulsifying agent is added to make the mass more plastic. Lactic acid, cream, salt, coloring, and seasoning are added for flavor. The best process cheeses have a definite cheese flavor. They melt easily without curdling.

Oscar Mayer & Co.

11-9. The omelet has been filled with Cheddar cheese. The pizza has been topped with mozzarella cheese. Both of these cheeses melt easily.

Table 11-2. Cheeses Used in Cooking

Kind	Color	Texture	Flavor	Uses
American. (Also known as Colby, Cheddar, daisy, longhorn.)	Pale to dark yellow.	Solid and semihard.	Mild to sharp.	Grilled cheese, garnishes, Welsh rarebit, cheese sauce, cheese platters.
Brick. (Strictly an American cheese.)	Creamy to pale yellow.	Firm, semisoft, small pinholes.	Mild and sweet.	Sandwiches and cheese platters.
Cheddar. (Most used cheese.)	Yellow.	Semihard, slices easily.	Mild to very sharp.	Welsh rarebit, fondue, soufflé, sandwiches, all cooking needs.
Cheshire. (Made only in England.)	Natural white to deep yellow.	Semihard, slices easily.	Slightly salty, sharp.	Welsh rarebit and fondue.
Gruyère. (Swiss origin.)	Pale yellow.	Semihard with small holes.	Mild, nutty.	Fondue, veal cordon bleu.
Mozzarella. (Italian origin.)	Creamy white.	Semisoft.	Mild.	Pizza, lasagna.
Parmesan. (Italian origin.)	Yellow.	Very hard and granular, grates well.	Sharp.	Onion soup, spaghetti, macaroni, lasagna.
Process.	Yellow.	Soft, melts easily.	Mild.	Cheese sauce, grilled cheese.
Provolone. (Italian origin.)	Light yellow.	Semisoft, can be cut without crumbling.	Mild to sharp, smokey.	Pizza and other Italian dishes.
Ricotta.	White.	Very smooth and creamy.	Bland, sweet like cream.	Lasagna, manicotti.
Romano. (Italian origin.)	Yellow with black rind.	Very hard and granular, grates well.	Sharp.	Topping for au gratin dishes, Italian dishes.
Swiss (Emmentaler). (Second most popular cheese.)	Pale yellow	Semihard, rubbery with large holes.	Mild, nutty.	Fondue, stuffings, grilled cheese.

Process cheese food contains some natural cheeses mixed with milk solids, water, and seasoning. It is very mild and easily melted. It never becomes stringy or curdled. Both processed cheese and cheese food are used extensively in food service because they are cheaper. They also keep well, even on the shelf before opening. They produce a smooth cheese dish with very little trouble.

Kinds of Cheeses

Table 11-2 lists the name, characteristics, and uses of the cheeses commonly used in cooking. *Cheddar* cheese was originally made in England. However, only American-made Cheddar cheese is used in the United States. It is the cheese most used in cooking. Cheddar is a deep yellow, almost an orange. Next in use is Swiss cheese, or *Emmentaler*. It has large holes caused by the gas during fermentation. Emmentaler is pale yellow. Study Table 11-3. Use as many of the cheeses as you can in cooking. Cheese is to milk as wine is to grape juice. A cook must become familiar with the use of both in cooking before being considered a chef.

Cheese Cookery

Like meat, milk, and eggs, cheese coagulates when heated. High heat and prolonged cooking turn it into a rubbery, stringy mass. Both temperature and time must be controlled. Remember these four rules of cheese cookery.

- Cook at low temperatures.
- Cook for a short time.
- When adding to other ingredients, cut cheese into small pieces. Then, it will melt quickly and blend into other foods.
- Use the correct cheese for the dish you are producing.

Cheese may be used in broiling, grilling, baking, or cooking on the top burners. By whatever method, the basic principles hold true. Cook at a low temperature for as short a time as possible.

GRILLING AND BROILING

Cheese sandwiches are often grilled or broiled. When two slices of bread are used in grilling, the cheese is protected from the high heat of the grill by the bread. A grilled cheese sandwich is usually creamy and tender.

A broiled, open-faced sandwich may become tough and rubbery because the cheese is exposed to the high heat of the broiler. Watch the time very carefully. A slice of tomato and strips of bacon broiled on top of the cheese help shield the cheese from the direct heat.

The short-order cook is usually in charge of making grilled and broiled cheese sandwiches.

- *Ingredients.* American, Cheddar, Swiss, or processed cheeses may be used. The bread type may be specified by the customer such as white, whole wheat, or rye. Usually such condiments as mustard are served alongside.
- *Equipment.* Needs are simple—a grill or broiler, and a turner. Some short-order cooks may use an electric grill that compresses the sandwich and cooks both sides at once.

- *Standards.* By whatever method the sandwich is cooked, the bread should be well-browned on the outside. The cheese should be completely melted, but never rubbery or stringy. There should be enough cheese in the sandwich to give it a distinctive, but mild cheese taste.

To grill a sandwich, lightly grease the grill with butter or margarine. Place the sandwich on it. As it cooks, press down the cheese to compress it, using the turner. When one side is brown, turn and brown the other side. Serve immediately.

To broil a sandwich, lightly butter bread on the outside of the sandwich. Make sandwich. Slip under broiler until bread is browned and cheese is melted. For an open-faced sandwich, toast the bread on one side and place filling on untoasted side. Toast until cheese is melted under the broiler. Serve at once.

Variations

Hero sandwich. In several places, slice a thick, hard roll almost to the bottom. Fill slices with luncheon meat and Swiss cheese. Slip under the broiler or bake in the oven at 220°C [425° F.] until the cheese is melted.

Cheeseburger. Place a slice of Cheddar or Swiss cheese on top of a hamburger on a bun. Slip under the broiler until cheese is melted.

Reuben. Spread rye bread with a tablespoonful of French dressing. Place corned beef, sauerkraut, and Swiss cheese on top. Slip under the broiler and broil until cheese is melted. Top with another slice of rye bread.

Bacon, tomato, and cheese. Toast one side of bread. Place cheese, tomato, and slices of bacon on untoasted side. Broil until cheese is melted and bacon is crisp.

BAKED CHEESE DISHES

Cheese soufflé (sue-FLAY) is the most famous baked cheese dish. It is a true delicacy, a gourmet's delight. A *soufflé* is a delicate, light, fluffy egg mixture baked in the oven. A cheese soufflé should be light in proportion to size. It should be golden yellow with a lightly browned crust. The crust should form a "hat." This means the soufflé should rise sharply above the dish with a distinct break similar to the oven spring of bread. The flavor should be very cheesy, but delicate.

- *Ingredients.* Cheddar cheese, thick white sauce, eggs, cream of tartar, and seasonings are all that are required.
- *Equipment.* A soufflé dish is a ceramic or porcelain dish with high, straight, fluted sides and a flat bottom. It is important to choose a dish of the correct size. The size is usually specified in the recipe.

French chefs insist on copper bowls for beating the egg whites. American chefs usually accept stainless steel.

Most chefs prefer a wire whip for beating and blending.

To make a cheese soufflé, follow the recipe on page 237.

COOKING TIP: *Cheese soufflés are so delicate they fall very easily. Do not open the oven door until you are sure the soufflé is almost done. Do not jar oven shelves. Do not overcook or the soufflé will be dry. Serve immediately.*

A *quiche* (KEESH) is a cheese pie flavored with onions, bacon, spinach, or other ingredients. It is a custard mixture baked in a piecrust. The classic is *quiche Lorraine.* It contains onions and cheese and bacon in an egg and cream custard mixture. Quiche is extremely popular as a luncheon dish. Cut in small pieces, it is popular as an appetizer.

Baked fondue is an American dish, similar to a soufflé. It is usually flavored with sautéed onions and peppers. Baked fondue is thickened with bread crumbs, as well as eggs. It is not as delicate as a true soufflé and will not fall as quickly.

Au gratin (O GRAH-tin) is a French term that describes casseroles topped with cheese or bread crumbs. Such a topping improves appearance and flavor. Bread crumbs are mixed with grated cheese such as Parmesan cheese. As the casserole bakes, the crumb topping browns. This adds to the eye-appeal of the dish and keeps the casserole moist.

Cordon bleu (CORE-DOON BLEW) is a famous veal dish made with Gruyère cheese and ham. See recipe on page 201.

TOP-BURNER COOKING WITH CHEESE

Welsh rarebit, or *Welsh rabbit,* is another famous cheese dish that is a gourmet's delight. Welsh rarebit is smooth, never stringy, with a sharp cheese flavor. Rarebit is always made to order in small amounts.

- *Ingredients.* A true Welsh rarebit consists of cheese melted in beer. Cheddar cheese is usually chosen because it is readily available. In Wales, the home of Welsh rarebit, Cheshire cheese is used as the base. Frequently, a process cheese is substituted for the real cheese. It melts easily and does not curdle or become stringy.

The cheese sauce is flavored with salt, pepper, Worcestershire sauce, dry mustard, and hot pepper.

- *Equipment.* The experienced chef can make Welsh rarebit in a heavy-gauge saucepan. For beginners, a double boiler is a better choice. It is easier to control the temperature. Use a wire whip for stirring.

On page 235 is a recipe for Welsh rarebit.

- *Variations.* Place a slice of tomato on toast. Cover with the rarebit. Garnish with two slices of crisp bacon.

Substitute tomato juice for beer to make tomato rarebit. When made hot with spices, this becomes *chili con queso* (CONE KAY-so).

Place a slice of ham and a spear of broccoli on the toast. Spoon rarebit over it.

Cheese fondue. A true fondue is made from one-half Emmentaler and one-half Gruyère cheese, melted in wine and flavored with kirsch (a liqueur made from black cherries). The fondue is seasoned with garlic, salt, and pepper. It is kept warm in a chafing dish or fondue pot. Cubes of hard crusted bread are served along with it for dipping. It may be an appetizer or a luncheon dish. A *chafing dish* is a pan with a heating element under it to keep the food warm. Often it is made like a double boiler. Thus, the water in the bottom pan is kept hot. See the recipe for Cheese Fondue on page 235.

COOKING TIP: *Fondue burns very easily. This will give it a scorched taste. Do not let the wine boil. Otherwise, the cheese will become rubbery and stringy.*

Care, Storage, and Service

Like egg dishes, cheese dishes cannot be stored and reheated successfully. Thus, storage is not a problem. All cheese dishes should be served immediately.

How Much Have You Learned?

Review this chapter. Answer the following questions to prepare yourself for the post-test. Check your answers with your teacher.

1. Define the *Words to Remember*.
2. What are the signs of a fresh egg?
3. What is the basic principle of egg cookery?
4. Describe the four basic variations of fried eggs. Demonstrate how you would cook each type.
5. Give the steps to be followed in hard cooking eggs.
6. Describe the steps for poaching an egg in a poaching dish.
7. What is a ramekin? When is it used in cooking eggs?
8. If eggs are to be cooked at below boiling temperature, why are eggs baked at 163°C [325° F.]?
9. Compare the four methods of scrambling eggs.
10. What are the standards for a French omelet?
11. Why is process cheese often used in cooking?
12. Name the four basic principles of cheese cookery.
13. What precautions should you observe in making a cheese soufflé?
14. What cheese is used to make a true fondue?
15. What precautions should be observed in making a cheese fondue?

WELSH RAREBIT

Equipment   **Yield:** 4 servings
Saucepan or double boiler
Wire whip
Measuring spoons and cups
Toaster

Metric	Ingredients	Customary
1 mL	Mustard (dry)	$\frac{1}{4}$ t
1 mL	Salt	$\frac{1}{4}$ t
1 mL	Worcestershire sauce	$\frac{1}{4}$ t
1 mL	Hot pepper sauce	$\frac{1}{4}$ t
Few grains	Cayenne pepper	Few grains
250 mL	Beer	1 c
225 g	Cheese, chopped	$\frac{1}{2}$ lb
4 slices	Toast	4 slices

METHOD

1. **Mix** seasonings in saucepan or top of double boiler.
2. **Stir** in beer.
3. **Place** on low heat if using saucepan. Place over hot water if using double boiler.
4. **Heat** to simmering.
5. **Add** cheese slowly, stirring all the time.
6. **Stir** until cheese is melted and blended with beer.
7. **Pour** over toast points and serve at once.

CHEESE FONDUE

Equipment   **Yield:** 4 servings
Fondue pot   Bowl
Grater   Wire whip

Metric	Ingredients	Customary
1 clove	Garlic, crushed	1 clove
500 mL	White wine	1 c
200 g	Emmentaler cheese	7 oz
400 g	Gruyère cheese	14 oz
30 mL	Cornstarch	2 T
75 mL	Kirsch	5 T
Dash	White pepper	Dash
Dash	Nutmeg	Dash

METHOD

1. **Rub** garlic on sides of fondue pot.
2. **Add** the wine and heat to bubbling.
3. **Grate** cheese. Stir into wine gradually until mixture starts to boil. Remove from heat.
4. **Mix** cornstarch with kirsch until smooth.
5. **Stir** cornstarch into wine-cheese mixture.
6. **Bring** to a boil and serve immediately.

FRENCH OMELET

Equipment

Bowl	Sauté pan
Wire whip	Fork

Yield: 1 serving

Metric	Ingredients	Customary
2	Eggs	2
5 mL	Butter	1 t
1 mL	Salt	$\frac{1}{4}$ t
Pinch	Pepper	Pinch

METHOD

1. **Beat** eggs with salt and pepper in bowl, using a wire whip.
2. **Place** butter in pan and melt over high heat until it is foamy. Do not brown.
3. **Pour** in the eggs as soon as the foam subsides but before the butter begins to brown.
4. **Tilt** the pan briskly to spread eggs around bottom of pan. Shake the pan vigorously with the left hand. Spread the eggs evenly with the fork in the right hand.
5. **Tilt** the pan sharply away from you as the eggs begin to thicken. Fold the omelet over on itself.
6. **Slip** the folded omelet onto a warm plate and serve immediately.

PUFFY OMELET

Equipment

Two bowls	Sauté pan
Eggbeater	Turner
Wire whip	

Yield: 1 serving
Temperature: 177°C [350° F.]
Time: 15 minutes

Metric	Ingredients	Customary
2	Eggs	2
5 mL	Butter	1 t
1 mL	Salt	$\frac{1}{4}$ t
Pinch	Pepper	Pinch

METHOD

1. **Preheat** oven to 177°C [350° F.]
2. **Separate** eggs and place in separate bowls.
3. **Beat** egg whites to a stiff foam.
4. **Beat** egg yolks with salt and pepper until thick and lemon-colored.
5. **Fold** whites into yolks. Mix thoroughly so there is no unmixed egg white.
6. **Melt** butter in sauté pan over high heat until it foams. Do not brown. When foam subsides, pour in eggs.
7. **Brown** bottom side quickly.
8. **Place** in oven and bake about 15 minutes until top is lightly browned. Mixture should feel dry and firm to the touch.
9. **Crease** the omelet and fold it over on itself away from you.
10. **Slip** folded omelet onto a warm plate and serve immediately.

CHEESE SOUFFLÉ

Equipment
Saucepan   Soufflé dish
2 Bowls   Baking pan
Wire whip

Yield: 10 servings
Temperature: 177°C [350° F.]
Time: Approximately 1 hour 15 minutes

Metric	Ingredients	Customary
115 g	Butter	4 oz
140 g	Flour	5 oz
500 mL	Milk	2 c
9	Egg yolks	9
140 g	Cheese, grated	5 oz
To taste	Salt and pepper	To taste
9	Egg whites	9

METHOD

1. **Preheat** oven. Grease and flour soufflé dish.
2. **Make** a roux with butter and flour. Cool.
3. **Heat** milk. Stir in roux. Stir with wire whip until thick and smooth.
4. **Beat** egg yolks until thick. Stir hot mixture into egg yolks. Return to saucepan.
5. **Stir** in cheese and seasoning. Cook on low heat until cheese is melted. Cool.
6. **Beat** egg whites until stiff just before baking.
7. **Fold** beaten egg whites into egg-cheese mixture.
8. **Half-fill** baking pan with hot water.
9. **Pour** egg-cheese mixture into soufflé dish. Smooth top. With spoon, make an indentation in soufflé about 2.5 cm [1 in] from sides of soufflé dish.
10. **Place** soufflé dish in water in baking pan.
11. **Bake** until light, puffy, and lightly browned.
12. **Serve** at once.

SCRAMBLED EGGS (METHOD NO. 1)

Equipment
Bowl   Sauté pan
Wire whip   Turner

Yield: 1 serving
Temperature: 120°C [250° F.] if using grill

Metric	Ingredients	Customary
2	Eggs	2
30 mL	Water or milk	2 T
1 mL	Salt	$\frac{1}{4}$ t
Pinch	Pepper	Pinch
5 mL	Butter	1 t

(Method found on following page)

SCRAMBLED EGGS (METHOD NO. 1)—Continued

METHOD

1. **Beat** eggs slightly with water or milk, salt, and pepper, using wire whip.
2. **Melt** butter to sizzling in sauté pan or on grill.
3. **Pour** eggs into pan or on grill.
4. **Lift** eggs as they thicken, using turner. Allow uncooked portion to flow under thickened portion.
5. **Remove** from pan or grill. Do not overcook.
6. **Serve** immediately.

SCRAMBLED EGGS (METHOD NO. 2)

Equipment
Bowl
Eggbeater
Double boiler
Wooden spoon

Yield: 1 serving

Metric	Ingredients	Customary
2	Eggs	2
30 mL	Milk or cream	2 T
1 mL	Salt	$\frac{1}{4}$ t
Pinch	Pepper	Pinch
5 mL	Butter	1 t

METHOD

1. **Beat** eggs with milk or cream, salt, and pepper in bowl, using eggbeater.
2. **Heat** water in bottom of double boiler to boiling. Reduce heat.
3. **Melt** butter in top of double boiler.
4. **Pour in** egg. Place over boiling water.
5. **Cook,** stirring occasionally, until thick and chunky.
6. **Serve** immediately.

Note: Eggs overcook very easily by this method, causing them to weep and curdle.

SCRAMBLED EGGS (METHOD NO. 3)

Equipment
Bowl
Eggbeater
Saucepan
Sauté pan
Turner

Yield: 1 serving

Metric	Ingredients	Customary
2	Eggs	2
5 mL	Butter	1 t
1 mL	Salt	$\frac{1}{4}$ t
Pinch	Pepper	Pinch
30 mL	Medium cream sauce	2 T

METHOD

1. **Beat** eggs with salt and pepper, using eggbeater.
2. **Make** medium cream sauce.
3. **Heat** butter in sauté pan to sizzling.
4. **Pour in** eggs. Cook, stirring vigorously until hardened. If making a large amount, cook one-third of the eggs at one time.
5. **Place** eggs in container from steam table. Stir in cream sauce. Place in steam table for serving.

SCRAMBLED EGGS (METHOD NO. 4)

Equipment
Bowl
Eggbeater
Baking pan
Turner

Yield: 1 serving
Temperature: 177°C [350° F.]

Metric	Ingredients	Customary
2	Eggs	2
30 mL	Milk or cream	2 T
1 mL	Salt	$\frac{1}{4}$ t
Pinch	Pepper	Pinch
5 mL	Butter	1 t

METHOD

1. **Preheat** oven.
2. **Beat** eggs with milk or cream, salt and pepper.
3. **Heat** butter to sizzling in bake pan.
4. **Pour in** eggs, place in oven. Cook, stirring occasionally, until thick and chunky.

Vegetables

What Will You Learn?

When you finish studying this chapter, you should be able to do the following:

- Define the *Words to Remember* and use them correctly.
- Classify vegetables according to their color family.
- Identify the best cooking method for each vegetable family.
- Prepare a wide variety of vegetables in different ways, meeting the standards for acceptable service.
- Pass the posttest.

In your classroom, you probably have some magazines published for food service. As you thumb through them, notice how little space is devoted to vegetable preparation compared with the space given to meat, poultry, and fish. Many menus merely mention a "vegetable of the day."

In many restaurants, vegetables are poorly cooked and served without imagination. Why should this be—especially with the present emphasis on natural food? Vegetables add nutrition and much enjoyment to the meal. If cooked correctly, they add flavor, excitement—and most of all—color. The varying textures and many kinds of vegetables make any meal more interesting.

Vegetables are not difficult to cook if you remember a few simple principles. As you study the preparation of vegetables, remember that the cost of meat is rising. Thus, more and more vegetables will be served. These lessons on vegetable cookery will be important to you and your future in food service.

KINDS OF VEGETABLES

Perhaps you remember reading in Chapter 5 that vegetables may be classified by the part of the plant from which they are taken. Roots, bulbs, stalks, leaves, flowers, fruit, pods, and seeds contribute to the great variety of vegetables. Other

Words to Remember

acid	chlorophyll
alkali	flavone
anthocyanin	pigment
carotene	

ways of classifying vegetables are important to the method of cooking. Vegetables are classified by color, flavor, and moisture content.

The Color Families of Vegetables

The beauty of vegetables comes from their brilliant coloring. The color comes from the *pigment*. Vegetables are white, yellow, red, or green—their color families. Fig. 12-1. One of the concerns in cooking vegetables is to preserve and enhance their coloring. The color family of the vegetable determines, in part, the cooking method. Study Table 12-1. It classifies vegetables according to color families.

ACIDS AND ALKALIS

The color of vegetables is affected by the water in which they are cooked. Everything in nature is either *acid, alkali* (AL-cuh-LIE), or *neutral*. Acids have a sour taste like lemons and vinegar. Alkalis, or bases, have a bitter taste like baking soda. The colors of some vegetables are greatly changed by the amount of acid or alkali in the cooking water. Tap water is normally slightly alkaline.

RED VEGETABLES

The red color in vegetables comes from the pigment *anthocyanin* (AN-thuh-SIGH-uh-nun).

Red cabbage is a good example of the way acids and alkalis affect the color of vegetables. As red cabbage cooks in water, the red color gradually turns a bluish purple. However, a little acid will turn the cabbage red again. This acid can come from lemon juice, vinegar, or a cut-up apple. Red cabbage is much more appealing than bluish-purple cabbage. Perhaps you have also noticed that the red color of beets is enhanced by vinegar.

WHITE VEGETABLES

Flavone (FLAY-VONE) is the white pigment in such vegetables as cauliflower and onions. During the cooking, flavone gradually turns yellow. The longer the vegetable is cooked, the deeper the yellow. Eventually, the vegetable will turn brown. Acids help preserve the white color. However, the sharp, acid taste they give is not always desirable. Cauliflower, for instance, is a beautiful white vegetable. Lemon juice or vinegar would ruin the natural flavor. To preserve the white color, cook cauliflower as quickly as possible, uncovered, in a small amount of water.

Green Giant Company

12-1. Tostados Olé, a hot Mexican sauté. The dish is topped with lettuce, green onions, tomatoes, olives, and sour cream. The vegetables add color and flavor.

Table 12-1. Cooking of Fresh Vegetables according to Color Family

White	Yellow	Red	Green
Asparagus, white	Carrots	Beets	Artichokes
Artichokes, Jerusalem	Corn	Cabbage, red	Asparagus, green
Beans, dried	Potatoes, sweet	Peppers, red	Beans, green
Cauliflower	Pumpkin	Pimiento	Beans, wax
Eggplant	Rutabagas	Radishes	Broccoli
Fennel	Squash, winter and	Tomatoes	Brussels sprouts
Kohlrabi	summer		Cabbage, green
Leeks	Yams		Celery
Mushrooms			Cucumber
Onions			Kale
Parsnips			Lima beans
Potatoes			Okra
Turnips, white			Peas
			Peppers, green
			Spinach
			Swiss chard
			Zucchini
Cooking Method	**Cooking Method**	**Cooking Method**	**Cooking Method**
• Uncovered. • Small amount of water unless strong flavored.	• Covered. • Water to cover.	• Covered. • Small amount of water with lemon juice or vinegar.	• Uncovered. • Small amount of water.

GREEN VEGETABLES

The green color in vegetables is caused by *chlorophyll* (CLOR-uh-FILL). Chlorophyll is easily destroyed by acids. Vinegar on spinach will turn the brilliant green a dull, unappetizing mustard green. Most vegetables contain some acid that will dissolve in the cooking water. The acids can be driven off in the steam if the vegetable is cooked uncovered. Thus, the green color is not affected. However, if the cover is kept on during cooking, the acids will increase in intensity. They will dull the green color. Cook green vegetables, uncovered, in a small amount of water.

YELLOW VEGETABLES

The pigment in most yellow vegetables is *caro-tene* (CAR-uh-TEEN). It is very stable. This means it is not affected by either acid or alkali. Perhaps you have noticed that carrots keep their bright orange color even after cooking. Yellow vegetables can be cooked covered.

Flavor and Moisture Content

Table 12-2 classifies vegetables according to flavor and moisture content. Flavor is closely related to smell. For instance, vegetables of the cabbage family have a strong smell when cooking. They have a strong taste, too.

HIGH-MOISTURE VEGETABLES

Vegetables such as spinach, summer squash, and beets have much natural water and a mild flavor.

Table 12-2. Flavor and Moisture Content of Vegetables

High Moisture		Low Moisture		Dry
Mild Flavor	**Strong Flavor**	**Mild Flavor**	**Strong Flavor**	
Asparagus	Broccoli	Beans, Lima	Parsnips	Beans, dried
Beans, green	Brussels sprouts	Okra		Peas, dried
Beets	Cabbage	Potatoes, sweet		Lentils
Carrots	Cauliflower	Potatoes, white		Vegetables, freeze-dried
Corn	Onions	Squash, acorn		
Eggplant	Rutabagas	Yams		
Kohlrabi	Turnips			
Lettuce				
Mushrooms				
Peas, green				
Peppers				
Pumpkin				
Radishes				
Spinach				
Squash, summer				
Swiss chard				
Tomatoes				
Zucchini				

They need little water for cooking. They may be cooked covered, except those with deep green coloring.

Vegetables such as broccoli and cabbage are strongly flavored, Fig. 12-2. Always cook strongly flavored vegetables with the cover off. This allows the strong smell to be driven off by the steam.

LOW-MOISTURE VEGETABLES

Low-moisture vegetables such as potatoes and winter squash require more water if they are to be boiled. However, this type of vegetable bakes well. Dried vegetables such as peas and beans must soak up additional water before they can be cooked.

Freeze-dried vegetables, rapidly becoming very popular, also must soak up moisture. When the water is absorbed they resemble the fresh product.

National Turkey Federation

12-2. Sauerkraut is a cabbage product, made from cabbage that has been pickled and shredded. Here, it is served with turkey franks.

Words to Remember ──────

cellulose	glace
en casserole	stir-frying
fat-soluble	vaporizing
fritter	water-soluble

MINERALS AND VITAMINS IN VEGETABLES

A professional cook should be interested in the nutritional content of the food. Vegetables are a major source of minerals and vitamins. The cook should be aware of the effect cooking can have on these valuable nutrients.

Most minerals and some vitamins are *water-soluble*. This means they will dissolve in water. If vegetables are soaked in water prior to cooking, many of the minerals and vitamins will be lost. The same is true if a large amount of water is used in cooking vegetables.

Some vitamins are *fat-soluble*. This is not usually a problem, since few vegetables are fried.

Some vitamins are destroyed by prolonged heat. Vitamin C is particularly easy to destroy. Green vegetables are a major source of this important vitamin.

PRINCIPLES OF VEGETABLE COOKERY

What you have just read should help you understand the reasons behind the following principles of vegetable cookery.

• Use as little water as possible, except for strongly flavored vegetables.

• Cover yellow and red vegetables. Do not cover white and green vegetables.

• Cook as quickly as possible. Keep vegetables just a little crunchy. *Cellulose* (CELL-yah-lows), a member of the carbohydrate family, forms the structure of vegetables. It is softened by cooking. Overcooking is the greatest enemy of vegetables. It drains color and flavor, causing soggy vegetables.

• If possible, cook in small amounts or to order. Holding vegetables causes overcooking.

• Drain and save cooking water. It contains minerals, vitamins, and flavor. It may be used in soups, sauces, and gravies.

• Season before serving.

MARKET FORMS OF VEGETABLES

In Chapter 5, you became acquainted with the forms in which vegetables are sold. You probably remember that they are sold frozen, dried, dehydrated, freeze-dried, and canned. Although canned vegetables are often used, frozen vegetables are the overwhelming choice for food service. To understand why, look at Table 12-3. It states the labor required to prepare fresh vegetables and frozen vegetables. It also gives the percentage of waste in each. Notice, too, the difference in cooking time. Frozen vegetables cook faster because they have already been blanched, or partially cooked. The cellulose has been softened by the freezing process. Also, frozen vegetables seldom cost more per serving than fresh vegetables. Frequently, they cost less. They are readily available, thanks to modern refrigerated transportation. The quality is universally high.

METHODS OF COOKING VEGETABLES

Before most fresh vegetables are cooked, they should be blanched, or slightly precooked. Green vegetables are blanched to enhance the green coloring. Strongly flavored vegetables are blanched to tone down the flavor. Blanching reduces the final cooking time of the vegetables. To blanch, follow these directions:

1. Bring to boil enough water to cover the vegetables.

2. Place vegetables in boiling water. Bring again to a boil, drain, and cool.

Vegetables are cooked to soften the cellulose, improve the appearance, and develop the flavor. They are also cooked to provide variety. They may be boiled, steamed, baked, sautéed, fried in deep fat, broiled, or served *en casserole*. Fig. 12-3. *En casserole* is a French term meaning that the food is served in the casserole in which it was baked. The method of cooking must be suitable for the vegetable to be

Table 12-3. Frozen Foods Portion and Cooking Comparison Chart

Product	Type	Unit of Purchase	Portions per Unit	Portion Served	Labor Required	Percentage of Waste	Approximate Cooking Time (in minutes)		
							Boil	Pressure Cooker	Free Steam
Asparagus									
Jumbo Spears	Frozen	1 133-g [40-oz] carton	17	3 stalks	30–35 min	54%	7–9	1½	12–15
	Fresh	13.6-kg [30-lb] crate	75	4 stalks			21	1–2	20–25
Cuts and tips	Frozen	1 133-g [40-oz] carton	16	71 g [2½ oz]	35–40 min	54%	7–9	1½	12–15
	Fresh	13.6-kg [30-lb] crate	88–90	71 g [2½ oz]			21	1–2	20–25
Broccoli									
Spears	Frozen	907-g [32-oz] carton	14	2 stalks			6–8	2	15–20
Cuts	Frozen	907-g [32-oz] carton	13	71 g [2½ oz]			5–7	1½–2	18–20
	Fresh	21.7-kg [48-lb] crate	165–170	71 g [2½ oz]	1½ hrs	45%	15–25	2–3	28
Brussels sprouts	Frozen	907-g [32-oz] carton	13	71 g [2½ oz]			8–12	2	17–20
	Fresh	11.3-kg [25-lb] drum	88–90	71 g [2½ oz]	1½ hrs	45%	10–15	3	25
Cauliflower clusters	Frozen	907-g [32-oz] carton	13	71 g [2½ oz]	30–40 min	65%	7–9	1	14–17
	Fresh	15.9-kg [35-lb] crate	78–80	71 g [2½ oz]			12–15	2	20–25
Corn									
Cut whole kernel	Frozen	1 133-g [40-oz] carton	20	57 g [2 oz]			3–6	1	9–11
	Fresh	22.6-kg [50-lb] crate	60	57 g [2 oz]	1 hour	85%	8–10	1–2	16–18
On the cob	Frozen	12 ears	12	1 ear			3–6	2–3	4
	Fresh	1 crate (60 ears)	57	1 ear	30 min	5%	10	3–5	15
Green beans									
Regular or French cut	Frozen	907-g [32-oz] carton	16	57 g [2 oz]			8–10	1–1½	20–25
	Fresh	12.7-kg [28-lb] bushel	165–170	57 g [2 oz]	1¼ hrs	25%	15–25	3–4	35
Lima beans									
Baby Green or Fordhook	Frozen	1 133-g [40-oz] carton	20	57 g [2 oz]			12–14	2	-25–30
	Fresh	12.7-kg [28-lb] bushel	82–85	57 g [2 oz]	2 hours	63%	20–30	2–3	40
Peas	Frozen	1 133-g [40-oz] carton	20	57 g [2 oz]			4–6	1	11–14
	Fresh	12.7-kg [28-lb] bushel	88–90	57 g [2 oz]	1¾ hrs	60%	10–15	1–2	25
Spinach	Frozen	1 360-g [48-oz] carton	19	71 g [2½ oz]			8–10	1	15–20
	Fresh	9-kg [20-lb] bushel	70–72	71 g [2½ oz]	30 min	45%	15	1–3	20–25

Winter Garden, Inc. 1977

NOTE: Loose frozen vegetables need not be defrosted before cooking. Block frozen vegetables and cob corn should be defrosted one hour at room temperature before being placed in a pressure cooker.

Green Giant Company

12-3. Brussels sprouts with cream sauce served *en casserole*.

cooked. For instance, leafy greens may be boiled, steamed, or baked en casserole. Solid vegetables such as eggplant and potatoes may be sautéed or fried in deep fat. Tomatoes may be broiled.

Look again at the principles of cooking vegetables and apply them to the specific method of cooking.

Boiling

More vegetables are boiled than are cooked by any other method. Boiling can be used for fresh, frozen, dried, or dehydrated vegetables.

To boil *fresh vegetables*, follow these directions:

1. Bring salted water to a boil in a saucepan. Leafy green vegetables require only the water that clings to the leaves. Other vegetables should be barely covered with the water.

2. Add vegetables.

3. Bring to a boil and cook just until tender. Consult Table 12-3.

To boil *frozen vegetables*, follow these directions:

1. Bring to a boil the amount of water suggested on the carton. Frozen vegetables have already been blanched. They require less water because they take less cooking time. Also, the ice crystals provide some of the water.

2. Add frozen vegetables. Vegetables should never be defrosted before cooking.

3. With a fork, break the vegetables from the ice pack as it melts.

4. Boil for the time specified on the package or follow the times in Table 12-3.

To boil *dehydrated* or *freeze-dried* vegetables, follow the directions on the package.

To boil *canned vegetables*, follow these directions:

1. Drain off juices in saucepan and reduce volume by one half. This concentrates the flavor and nutrients.

2. Add vegetables and seasoning.

3. Reheat to boiling and serve. Remember, canned vegetables have already been cooked. They only need reheating.

4. A little sugar added to vegetables enhances the flavor, especially if the vegetables are a little old.

To boil *dried vegetables* such as beans, peas, and lentils, follow these directions:

1. Cover vegetables with cold water. Allow about 7.6 litres per 454 g [2 gallons per pound] of dried vegetables.

2. Bring to a boil and add a *bouquet garni*. As you read in Chapter 6, bouquet garni is a mixture of spices and herbs in a bag.

3. Simmer until tender, usually for several hours. Add more water, if needed.

4. After boiling, vegetables may be drained and placed in a baking pan with a sauce and small pieces of meat. For instance, lima beans may be mixed with ham. Navy beans may be mixed with a rich brown sauce and salt pork. This last dish is known as Boston Baked Beans. Bake in the oven at 165°C [325° F.] for several hours until the beans are brown and mealy.

Steam-jacketed Cooking

For cooking vegetables in quantity, the steam-jacketed kettle may be used. Steam-jacketed cooking is faster than boiling. The steam does not touch the vegetables, since it circulates around the pot.

To cook in the steam-jacketed kettle, follow these directions:

1. Place water in kettle. Bring to a full boil.
2. Pour in vegetables. Bring to a boil.
3. Reduce heat. Cook until tender. Do not cover green or white vegetables.
4. Remove vegetables as soon as they are done.
5. Season and serve at once.

Cooking with Steam under Pressure

Steam under pressure is used for cooking most vegetables in food service. It is fast and uses very little water. It preserves the color, flavor, and nutrients. Fig. 12-4. It is usually not used for such delicate vegetables as spinach, kale, or Swiss chard. These vegetables cook very quickly.

North Pacific Canners and Packers

12-4. Cauliflower, broccoli, green beans, and asparagus can be steamed under pressure. Care must be taken that the proper cooking time is observed.

To cook vegetables under pressure, follow these directions:

1. Place vegetables in basket.
2. Add small amount of water if solid basket is used. No water is needed for perforated basket.
3. Place basket in steamer and lock tight.
4. Turn on steam.
5. Set pressure for 34–41 kPa [5–6 psi]. Set timer according to manufacturer's directions. Table 12-3 gives you the time needed for both fresh and frozen vegetables.

CAUTION

Timing must be exact. One minute of overcooking under pressure can drain the color from green vegetables. Do not attempt to open the door until pressure has been reduced to zero.

Free Steam

Vegetables may also be cooked in baskets by free steam. The free steamer is described on page 51. The timing for free steam is shown in Table 12-3. Green vegetables tend to lose color under free steam because of overcooking.

Microwave Cooking of Vegetables

Although not used extensively in food service, vegetables cook quickly and easily in the microwave oven. Only a few tablespoonsful of water are needed. Microwave cooking is quick. Thus, it preserves color, texture, and nutrients. Always cover the vegetables.

To cook vegetables in the microwave oven, follow these directions:

1. Place vegetables in ceramic casserole. Vegetables must be cut evenly into small pieces.
2. Add two tablespoons of water to fresh vegetables. Frozen vegetables require no water. The ice crystals will supply enough.
3. Cover the vegetables.
4. Cook on high for the suggested time. When

247

half the time has elapsed, stir vegetables to distribute the heat evenly.

5. Cook in small amounts.

The microwave can also be used for reheating vegetables without loss of color, flavor, or nutrients.

VARIATIONS OF BOILED OR STEAMED VEGETABLES

Seasoning is important. Table 12-4 suggests some seasonings that will add variety to the flavor.

- Serve with salt, pepper, and browned butter.
- Serve with cream sauces. The flavor of the sauce may be enhanced by Worcestershire sauce, dry mustard, or curry. Try adding sautéed onions and/or green peppers to the cream sauce. A bit of

MSG perks up the flavor. Melt a little cheese in the cream sauce. Use your imagination!

- Combine different vegetables such as whole kernel corn and small, whole carrots; peas and sautéed mushrooms; tomatoes, okra, and onions; summer squash and tiny white onions.
- Cook carrots, turnips, or pearl onions in a heavy saucepan with butter, sugar, water, and seasoning. To cook vegetables in this way is to *glace* (glah-SAY) them. Simmer, covered, until the sauce is cooked down and the vegetables are done.

Baking

Whole, solid, low-moisture vegetables such as potatoes and yams may be baked whole. Acorn

Table 12-4. Seasoning for Vegetables

Green Vegetables	Red Vegetables	White Vegetables	Yellow Vegetables
Asparagus	Beets	Cauliflower	Carrots
Chili powder	Cinnamon	Beau monde	Black pepper
Curry	Ginger	Parsley flakes	Onion flakes
White Pepper	Onion flakes	Sweet basil	Thyme leaves
Corn	Savory	White pepper	Summer squash
Nutmug	Red Cabbage	Onions	Beau monde
Onion flakes	Black pepper	Curry	Cilantro
White pepper	Caraway seeds	Parsley flakes	Parsley flakes
Green beans	Tomatos	Sweet basil	
Mace	Black pepper	White pepper	
Onion flakes	Cumin		
White pepper	Garlic powder		
Green peas	Oregano		
Celery salt	Sweet basil		
Garlic powder			
Onion flakes			
Lima beans			
Allspice			
Black pepper			
Dry mustard			
Spinach			
Black Pepper			
Nutmeg			
Onion powder			
Zucchini			
Beau monde			
Onion flakes			

squash and winter squash are usually cut into serving-size pieces. Other types of vegetables may be baked en casserole or au gratin in many delightful ways. Potatoes will be discussed later in this chapter.

To bake squash, follow these directions:

1. For acorn squash, allow one-half squash per person. Cut winter squash into serving-size pieces.

2. Preheat oven to 190°C [375° F.].

3. Cut squash and remove seeds.

4. Place, cut side down, on baking sheet.

5. Bake forty minutes or until squash is very soft.

6. Turn cut side up. Brush cavity with melted butter. Sprinkle with salt, pepper, and brown sugar.

7. Bake in oven until sugar is melted and browned.

To braise vegetables, follow these directions:

1. Sauté chopped vegetables (a mirepoix) with chopped bacon for five minutes.

2. Layer blanched vegetables in baking dish with bacon-vegetable mixture.

3. Cover with hot bouillon.

4. Place heavy paper over baking pan. Hold down the paper with some heavy object such as a cover or an ovenproof plate.

5. Bake in oven at 190°C [375° F.] until tender.

To vary scalloped or au gratin vegetables, try these suggestions:

• Bake eggplant in Italian tomato sauce topped with bread crumbs and Parmesan cheese.

• Place cooked asparagus in baking dish. Pour curried cream sauce over it. Top with bread crumbs. Brown under broiler.

• Pour Creole sauce over zucchini. Top with bread crumbs and brown under broiler.

• Mix a variety of vegetables with cream sauce in baking dish. Top with buttered bread crumbs and brown under broiler.

• Mix spinach with cream sauce. Top with sliced hard-cooked eggs, buttered bread crumbs, and grated cheddar cheese. Brown under broiler.

• Pour Mornay sauce over cauliflower. Top with buttered bread crumbs and brown under broiler.

• Place boiled asparagus, celery roots, or Swiss chard in baking dish. Mix well with Mornay sauce,

hollandaise sauce, or brown sauce. Bake in oven until hot and bubbling.

Sautéed Vegetables

Some vegetables are delicious sautéed in a small amount of butter, margarine, or oil. In Chinese cooking, most vegetables are *stir-fried*—in other words, sautéed. Stir-frying is quick, and gives vegetables a different flavor. Flavor the stir-fried vegetables with soy sauce.

Sautéing is often a preliminary step in the preparation of other dishes. You will probably notice that the directions in many recipes begin with the words "Sauté the onions until lightly browned." Mushrooms are sautéed before being used as a topping for vegetables.

Cooked vegetables such as green beans may be lightly sautéed in butter to add flavor before being served.

Vaporizing (French: *Étuver* —AY-too-vay)

This method is especially suitable for mushrooms and other white vegetables. Follow these directions:

1. Chop shallots or onions and slice mushrooms.

2. Place shallots, butter, and a little wine with lemon juice in sauté pan. Reduce in volume by one half.

3. Add mushrooms, cover, and let cook in own juices over low heat until tender.

4. Do not use this method for green vegetables. The acid of the wine and lemon juice will blanch the color.

Deep-Fat Frying of Vegetables

A few vegetables may be fried in deep fat. Potatoes are among the most popular. They will be discussed later in this chapter. Other vegetables such as onions, eggplant, cauliflower, and broccoli are sometimes dipped in batter and fried in deep fat.

A *fritter* is a small amount of batter mixed with vegetables or fruits and fried in deep fat. In the United States, corn fritters are a well-known southern dish. They are served with syrup, crisp bacon, sausages, or fried ham. They may be offered for breakfast or as an accompaniment for luncheon. The recipe for corn fritters is on pages 256–257.

Broiling Vegetables

Very few vegetables are broiled. Thick slices of large tomatoes may be topped with buttered crumbs and slipped under the broiler until browned. Some scalloped vegetables may also be broiled briefly, just to brown the top.

Vegetables as an Entrée

A vegetable plate or platter is one of the more spectacular ways to show off the beautiful colors of vegetables. It is seldom offered on the food service menu because of the belief that it might not prove popular.

However, a low-calorie luncheon is often offered. It usually consists of a ground beef patty and a cottage cheese and half-peach salad. Many customers might welcome a vegetable platter if it were well-cooked and carefully arranged with an eye for beauty. Try some of these.

• Deep green broccoli, snowy white cauliflower, pale green sautéed celery, orange rounds of carrots with a light glaze, green lima beans. Serve with hollandaise sauce on the side. (See page 294).

• Bright yellow corn on the cob, buttered Brussels sprouts, broiled slice of red tomato with buttered bread crumbs, marinated slices of raw mushrooms.

• Uncut bright green beans, fried eggplant, buttered yellow summer squash, Harvard beets in sweet-sour sauce.

Soufflés and Timbales

In Chapter 11 you read about soufflés. Perhaps you have even tried your hand at making one. Pureed vegetables make delicious soufflés. Spinach soufflé is perhaps the most well known. When carefully made with fresh or frozen spinach, it is a fresh green color. Light and fluffy, it can be delightfully seasoned with a bit of nutmeg. Even persons who do not like spinach accept spinach soufflé. It is a popular dish.

Other soufflés may be made using rutabagas, carrots, and sweet potatoes. The method of mixing and baking described in Chapter 11 is used. (See page 237.)

Timbales were described in Chapter 10. Vegetables may be baked in a custardlike mixture with cheese. Garnished with a slice of tomato, a serving of timbale is very attractive.

Casseroles

Vegetables may be combined with meat to make an entrée. For instance, eggplant combined with a tomato sauce, oregano, and ground lamb is used in the Greek dish *moussaka*.

Broccoli may be combined with sliced turkey and cheese sauce for a casserole known as turkey divan.

Words to Remember

duchesse	rissolé
Franconia	tuber
ricing	

POTATOES

Potatoes, as well as bread, are often called "the staff of life." For many people, a dinner is not complete without potatoes. If potatoes are slipping at all in popularity, it is because of the mistaken idea that potatoes have many calories. A medium potato contains no more calories than a cup of orange juice or a large apple.

The Spanish brought potatoes to Europe from Peru in the sixteenth century. Their cultivation and use were particularly promoted in Italy. In France, it was prepared in so many exotic ways that it became a gourmet food.

The potato early became the staple food of Ireland. Many people call white potatoes "Irish potatoes." So important was the potato that the failure of the potato crop in Ireland in 1845–46 caused widespread famine. Many of the Irish emigrated to the United States during the famine.

By 1719, the potato had come back to the New World. Increasingly popular, it deserves an important place in the study of food service.

Table 12-5. Kinds and Uses of Potatoes

Kind	Appearance	Cooked Texture	Use
Red, round	Red, thin skin. Small, round shape.	Slightly firm.	Whole with meat, riced.
Russett	Red, thin skin. Large oval shape.	Slightly firm.	Boiling, hashed brown.
White, long California Idaho	Brown, textured, thick skin. Long and oval.	Firm, mealy. Breaks up easily.	Best for baking, deep-fat frying, mashing.
White, round	Brown, smooth, thin skin.	Firm.	Boiling, mashing, frying.

Kinds of Potatoes

Table 12-5 shows the four recognized types of white, or "Irish," potatoes. Each potato type cooks to a different texture. Each has its own specialized use in cooking.

Sweet potatoes are more like a squash in consistency and flavor, although they are *tubers*. Tubers are vegetables that grow in the ground. They are an enlargement of the root.

Sweet potatoes and yams are similar. Both are especially popular in the southern United States.

Market Forms of Potatoes

Table 12-6 shows the market forms for potatoes. The versatile potato comes in many processed, convenient forms—canned, dehydrated, frozen, and chips. Potatoes are also available in potato combinations, casseroles, soups, and other dishes. All of

Dehydrated	Canned	Frozen	Chips
Diced	Small whole	French fries	Barbecue
Flakes		Crinkle cut	Onion
Granules		Ranch or country fries	Regular
Slices		Regular or straight cut	Ridged
		Shoestring	Ruffled
		Hashed brown	Shoestrings
		Shredded	Snacks manufactured
		Southern ranch-style	from dehydrated
		Potato rounds	potatoes
			Sour cream

Table 12-6. Market Forms of Processed Potatoes

The Potato Board

these are convenient to store. They are quickly prepared. These advantages have made processed potatoes most useful in food service. Dehydrated potatoes, particularly, are used in food service. Mashed potatoes are often made from this form. The use of dehydrated potatoes saves labor and time.

Frozen potatoes are especially used for deep-fat frying. They are purchased ready-cut and ready to fry. Canned potatoes are not used to any great extent in food service. The canning process changes the color and the flavor.

Methods of Cooking

All potatoes are grown in the ground. Therefore, they must be thoroughly scrubbed with a brush or cellulose sponge to remove the dirt.

Potatoes are often peeled before cooking. The eyes and any discolored spots must be removed. Sometimes the potatoes may look green on one end. This indicates they were not quite ripe. The green part should be removed.

Peeled potatoes will turn dark if not cooked right away. To protect their whiteness, toss them with an ascorbic acid mixture or a little lemon juice. Do not allow them to soak in water. This will cause some loss of nutrients.

Potatoes are cooked by boiling, steaming, baking, or frying. There are many variations of each method.

BOILING

Boiling is a very common method of cooking potatoes. It is a preliminary step to many other preparations.

1. Place potatoes in a heavy pot with a close-fitting lid. The steam-jacketed kettle is often used for cooking in quantity.

2. Add salted water to a depth of about 2.5 cm [1 in] for the steam-jacketed kettle. For boiling in a pot, add enough water to cover.

3. Boil until tender according to the following schedule:

- Whole—about thirty to forty minutes, depending upon size.
- Cut-up—about twenty to twenty-five minutes.

STEAMING

Steaming under pressure is a common practice in food service. It is quick, easy, and gives the same results as boiling.

To steam potatoes, follow these directions:

1. Place potatoes in wire basket.
2. Place basket in steamer and lock tight.
3. Turn on steam.
4. Set regulator for 34–41 kPa [5–6 psi]. Set time for twelve minutes. Check timetable for the steamer you are using. Potatoes will cook more evenly if they are cut to equal size.
5. Reduce pressure and remove at once.

Thermo Pin
12-5. The use of liquid-filled skewers cuts in half the baking time of potatoes.

Variations

Boiled or steamed potatoes may be used in potato salad. They may also be creamed or prepared in any of the following ways.

Mashed, or whipped. The recipe for making mashed potatoes the conventional way is on page 257. The recipe for making mashed potatoes using dehydrated flakes is on page 258. You will quickly see why dehydrated flakes are preferred in so many food service places.

Duchesse (dew-SHEZ). Mashed or whipped potatoes are blended with egg yolks and a small amount of nutmeg. The potatoes are placed in a pastry bag with a star tube. They may be pressed out around a meat, poultry, or fish dish to give it an extra "touch of class." The potatoes are spread with an egg wash and slipped in the oven along with the meat to brown lightly before serving.

Oven-roasted. Small, uniformly shaped and sized potatoes are rubbed with oil and seasoned. They are baked on a baking sheet in the oven until browned and tender. Oven-roasted potatoes are usually made from uncooked potatoes. They may also be placed around the roast for browning.

Franconia (franq-CONE-e-ah). These potatoes are made just like oven-roasted potatoes. However, the potatoes are boiled until almost tender before being put in the oven.

Potatoes rissole (ree-SAH-lay). Potatoes are cut in an oval shape and boiled. After draining, they are browned in butter and sprinkled with chopped parsley.

Riced. Potatoes are pressed through a coarse sieve called a *ricer*. This is often done as a preliminary step to mashing. Ricing eliminates any lumps.

BAKING

It is a toss-up whether baked or french-fried potatoes are the most popular in the United States. With the present emphasis on low-calorie, low-fat foods, baked potatoes seem to be the favorite. The Idaho is the super baking potato. Its development has had much to do with the gaining popularity of the baked potato.

Baked potatoes may be purchased already baked and stuffed. To be served, they require only reheating. The quality may not be as high as freshly baked potatoes.

To bake potatoes, follow these directions:
1. Wash and scrub potatoes well.
2. Pierce end with fork to prevent bursting. Most food service places insert a stainless steel skewer in the potato. This speeds the baking time. A constant supply of freshly baked potatoes is needed when the specialty is steaks or roast prime ribs.
3. Grease or oil potatoes lightly.
4. Place on baking sheet.
5. Bake at 204°C [400° F.] for one hour. If a skewer is used, reduce baking time to about thirty minutes. Fig. 12-5. Potatoes are done when they yield to finger pressure.

Recently, it has become the fashion to wrap potatoes in foil before baking. This practice steams the potatoes, instead of baking them. The skin will be soft, instead of crisp.

To bake stuffed potatoes, follow these directions:
1. Choose large Idaho baking potatoes. Bake in the oven, following the directions for baking potatoes.
2. When potatoes are tender, remove from the oven and slice in half.
3. Scoop out the soft insides into a bowl.
4. Mash, following directions for mashed potatoes.
5. Refill potato shells. Sprinkle with paprika and Parmesan cheese if desired. Spread lightly with butter.
6. Reheat by placing in hot oven for about ten to fifteen minutes until browned and hot.

As an alternate method, put potato pulp through ricer. Mix with butter, salt, pepper, egg yolks, and hot milk. Fill potato shells, using pastry bag with star tip.

To scallop potatoes, follow these directions:
1. Scalloped potatoes are baked in buttered baking pans 30 × 51 × 5 cm [12 × 20 × 2 in].
2. Preheat oven to 175°C [350° F.].
3. Peel potatoes and slice very thin. Use the attachment on the mixer for slicing. Do not let potatoes stand, as they will turn brown very quickly. Have all ingredients ready so you can proceed immediately with the rest of the preparation.

The Potato Board

12-6. Sautéed potatoes topped with fresh onion rings.

pared. The possible discoloration of the potatoes is eliminated. Follow the directions given on the package.

For potatoes au gratin, follow these directions:

1. Butter baking pans.

2. Peel and boil small red potatoes. Refrigerate overnight.

3. Chop potatoes coarsely.

4. Preheat oven to 175°C [350° F.].

5. Make cheese sauce.

6. Mix cheese sauce and potatoes thoroughly. Place in baking pans.

7. Top with buttered crumbs. Sprinkle with paprika.

8. Bake in oven for thirty minutes until lightly browned. If necessary, slip baking dish under broiler to complete browning.

Potatoes au gratin may also be purchased in the dehydrated form.

Variations

• For *scalloped potatoes,* add sliced onions in layers with the potatoes. Sprinkle grated Parmesan cheese on each layer with the salt and pepper.

• For *baked stuffed potatoes,* mix Parmesan cheese with the potato pulp when mashing it. Add a touch of nutmeg and chopped chives to the potato pulp with the milk, salt, and pepper.

FRYING POTATOES

Fried potatoes may be prepared in a small amount of fat or in deep fat. Deep-fat fried potatoes are universally known as french fries. They are commonly offered with steaks and prime ribs by even the best restaurants. In the fast food chains, they are always on the menu with fried chicken, fish, or hamburgers.

Potatoes fried in a small amount of fat are usually precooked. Russet or small red potatoes are a good choice for sautéed potatoes. Frozen potato slices or

4. Put a layer of potatoes on bottom of a greased baking pan. Season with salt and pepper. Dot with butter. Add another layer of potatoes and season and butter as before. Continue until all potatoes are used.

5. Pour on hot milk, even with top layer of potatoes. About 2.4 L [2½ qt] of milk will be needed for each baking pan of potatoes.

6. Cover with greased paper to prevent browning. Bake potatoes for thirty minutes.

7. Remove paper. Continue baking for thirty minutes or until potatoes are tender and top is lightly browned.

An excellent product can be made using dehydrated potatoes. The product is more quickly pre-

hash browns may be purchased for use in sautéing. Potato slices may be plain or with a corrugated surface. Hash browns may be diced or shredded.

Sautéed potatoes are usually called American-fried, cottage, or home-fried potatoes. There are many variations. Fig. 12-6.

To sauté potatoes, follow these directions:

1. Slice pared potatoes to medium thickness.

2. Heat fat in skillet to sizzling. Use oil, margarine, or bacon fat.

3. Add potatoes and fry to golden brown, turning as needed. Be careful not to break up the potatoes.

Variations

Hashed brown potatoes are made from chopped cooked potatoes. The potatoes are browned well on the bottom. They are then turned so the entire mass browns on the other side.

Potatoes O'Brien are hashed brown potatoes with diced onions, green peppers, and pimientos.

POTATOES FRIED IN DEEP FAT

Choose Idaho baking potatoes for deep-fat frying. They keep their shape and do not become mushy during frying. Most food service places use ready-to-fry potatoes because of the great saving in time and labor. The quality is very high.

Perhaps you remember reading in Chapter 8 that steaks sometimes are blanched, or precooked before being broiled. Potatoes for deep-fat frying are often blanched, too. It prevents the darkening of potatoes and cuts the frying time. It also prevents overcooking and drying out. In food service, frozen, blanched potatoes are commonly used, especially when the volume served is high.

Frozen potatoes may be purchased cut for regular french fries, thin or "shoestring" size, straight cut or crinkle cut. They may also be ordered "thick steak" size in straight-cut, crinkle-cut, or wedge-cut styles. Potato rounds are shredded potatoes formed into bite-sized log shapes.

If preparing your own potatoes, cut them into ice water to keep them crisp and white. However, do not let them soak. Soaking allows the potato to absorb water. This prolongs the cooking time. The potatoes will be oily and soggy. Dry potatoes before frying.

Frozen potatoes should be kept in the freezer until ready for use.

To fry potatoes in deep fat, follow these rules:

1. Blanch first if desired. To blanch, heat the fat to 190°C [375° F.]. Cook potatoes until tender, but not browned. Drain and put aside. Blanched potatoes may be held in the refrigerator up to two days. Bring to room temperature before proceeding to the next step.

2. For blanched potatoes, preheat fat to 193°C [380° F.]. For unblanched potatoes, heat fat to 190°C [375° F.].

3. Fill basket no more than half full. Don't overload.

4. For blanched potatoes, lower into fat and fry for one and one-half to two and one-half minutes until golden brown. Unblanched potatoes will take about seven minutes.

5. Shake basket lightly to drain.

6. Salt just before serving. Do not salt over the fryer. Salt will break down the fat and also make the potatoes less crisp.

7. If necessary, hold for two minutes under the infrared holding lamp. Do not hold longer than that. Crispness is fleeting.

COOKING TIP: *Do not forget to filter shortening and clean equipment daily. Check accuracy of the thermostat regularly.*

Variations of Deep-Fat-Fried Potatoes

Lightly salt potatoes with herbs and spices such as curry, barbecue salt, chili powder, oregano, thyme, garlic, or onion salt.

Sprinkle hot fried potatoes lightly with grated Parmesan cheese.

Prepare duchesse potatoes. (See page 253.) While mixing, add cornstarch to thicken. Form into rounds, using a scoop. Fry in deep fat until golden brown. Potatoes fixed this way are called *croquettes*.

Oven Finishing

Frozen french-fried potatoes may be finished in the oven if desired. See Table 12-7.

Table 12-7. Oven Finishing of Deep-fat-fried Potatoes

Product Type	Approximate Heating Time (in minutes)	
	Range Oven or Deck Oven at 232°C [450° F.]	Convection Oven 204–218°C [400–425° F.]
Regular french fries		
Oven-style (crinkle cut)	15–20	12–18
Straight and crinkle cut	20–30	15–25
Thin and shoestring		
Oven-style (crinkle cut)	20	8–9
Straight and crinkle cut	16–22	14–20

How Much Have You Learned?

Review this chapter. Answer the following questions to prepare yourself for the post-test. Check your answers with your teacher.

1. Why is it important to learn to cook vegetables properly? Give at least three reasons.

2. Name the color families of vegetables. How should you boil the vegetables in each family?

3. Name three strongly flavored vegetables. How should you cook these vegetables?

4. Name and describe the market forms of vegetables.

5. Name four reasons for cooking vegetables.

6. Suggest four ways to vary boiled or steamed vegetables.

7. Name four vegetables that may be baked. Describe the baking of one vegetable.

8. Name the four types of potatoes. How is each one used in cooking?

9. In what forms can frozen potatoes be purchased for food service?

10. How can you keep potatoes from turning dark during their preparation for cooking?

11. Describe three variations for baked potatoes.

12. How are potatoes blanched? Why are they blanched?

13. Describe the process of frying potatoes in deep fat.

CORN FRITTERS

Equipment
Deep-fat fryer
Sifter
Bowls for mixing
Eggbeater or wire whip
Saucepan for melting fat
Spoon for mixing

Yield: 50 servings
Temperature: 182°C [360° F.]
Time: 10 minutes

CORN FRITTERS (Continued)

Metric	Ingredients	Customary
1.9 kg	Yellow corn, drained	4 lb 2 oz
2.3 kg	Flour, pastry	5 lb
67 mL	Salt	4½ T
120 mL	Baking powder	8 T
60 mL	Sugar	4 T
67 mL	Nutmeg	4½ T
800 g	Eggs	1¾ lb
2½ L	Milk	2½ qt
200 g	Margarine	7 oz

METHOD

1. **Heat** fat to 182°C [360° F.]. Observe the fat level mark on fryer.
2. **Drain** corn. Set aside.
3. **Sift** flour with dry ingredients into mixing bowl.
4. **Beat** eggs slightly. Mix with milk.
5. **Combine** egg-milk mixture with dry ingredients.
6. **Add** melted fat and corn.
7. **Drop** the batter into the hot fat using a #20 scoop.
8. **Fry** about 10 minutes until golden brown.

MASHED POTATOES (CONVENTIONAL METHOD)

Equipment
Stockpot
Colander
Vertical mixer
Paddle and whip attachments

Yield: 50 servings
Time: About 50 minutes

Metric	Ingredients	Customary
7.7 kg	Potatoes, peeled	17 lb
225 g	Butter or margarine	8 oz
To taste	Salt	To taste
To taste	Pepper	To taste
470 mL	Light cream (optional)	1 pt
As needed	Hot milk	As needed

METHOD

1. **Boil** potatoes in salted water until tender.
2. **Drain** well.
3. **Place** in mixer. Break up with paddle.
4. **Replace** paddle with whip.
5. **Whip** on low speed until free of lumps.
6. **Add** butter, salt and pepper. Whip to thoroughly mix.
7. **Add** cream if desired. Whip.
8. **Add** enough boiling milk to give desired consistency.
9. **Adjust** salt and pepper to taste.
10. **Whip** on high speed until light and fluffy.

MASHED POTATOES (DEHYDRATED FLAKES METHOD)

Equipment
2 large saucepans
Whip

Yield: 50 servings
Time: About 5 minutes

Metric	Ingredients	Customary
3.8 L	Water	1 gal
45 mL	Salt	3 T
115 g	Butter or margarine	4 oz
1.25 L	Milk	$1\frac{1}{3}$ qt
910 g	Flakes	2 lb

METHOD

1. **Bring** water, salt, and butter to a boil.
2. **Stir** in flakes gently.
3. **Bring** milk to a boil.
4. **Add** to flakes.
5. **Whip** for 1 minute.
6. **Let stand** for 5 minutes. Serve.

Cereals and Pastas

What Will You Learn?

When you finish studying this chapter, you should be able to do the following:
- Define the *Words to Remember*.
- Identify the major cereals of the world.
- List and explain the principles of cooking cereals.
- Cook a variety of dishes based on cereals and pastas that meet acceptable standards.
- Pass the posttest.

Cereals and cereal products such as pasta and bread are the sustaining, or staple, foods of the world. They are the cheapest form of body energy, store easily, and keep well. Throughout the world, people depend upon cereals to keep them alive. When the cereal crop fails, famine may result.

CEREALS

Cereal is the common name for all grains grown for humans to eat. In Roman mythology, the goddess Ceres ruled over the growth and harvesting of grains. The word *cereal* comes from her name.

People generally like best the cereals that grow best in the climate in which they live. For instance, the climate of Europe is suited to growing wheat. Therefore, Europeans are accustomed to wheat and wheat products. Wherever Europeans settled throughout the world, they carried the preference for wheat with them.

The three most important cereals are wheat, corn, and rice. Most of the peoples of the world depend upon these three cereals for their food.

Wheat is the major crop in Europe, Canada, the United States, Argentina, Chili, Australia, and the Soviet Union.

Corn is the major crop in Mexico, Central America, the northern part of South America, and parts of Africa.

259

Words to Remember

barley	oats
brown rice	pilaf
cereal	pilau
coated rice	polished rice
converted rice	precooked rice
farina	wild rice
millet	

Rice is the major crop in India, China, Japan, and Malaysia.

Oats, barley, and millet are less important cereals. Nevertheless, they are used in many places where wheat is considered the primary grain. *Oats* are especially liked in Scotland because they grow well in a damp, cold climate. *Barley* is popular in the Near East. *Millet* is a small grain used for food in parts of Europe, Asia, Africa, and South America.

Use of Cereals

Cereals are used in four ways:
1. As breakfast food, either cooked or uncooked.
2. Ground into flour or meal.
3. As a thickener.
4. As a filler or extender for entrées.

Principles of Cooking Cereals

Since cereals are starchy foods, the general principles of starch cooking apply to their cooking. Read Chapters 15 and 21 for a discussion of the principles of starch cookery in using starch as a thickener.

The purpose of cooking cereals is to cause the cereal grains to absorb water and swell without making sticky lumps. To do this follow these principles.

1. Separate fine cereal grains with cold water before cooking.

2. Add the separated cereal grains slowly into the hot liquid.

3. Cook until the cereal grains absorb the water and become soft.

Farina (fa-REE-nah) is a fine-grained wheat cereal. If you were to dump farina directly into boiling water, the cereal grains would swell immediately and become very lumpy. Inside the lumps would be uncooked farina. To prevent this, farina is mixed with a little cold water. This separates the starch particles before they are stirred into the boiling water.

Less fine grains or whole grains such as rice may be stirred slowly into boiling water without mixing first with cold water.

As the cereal grains cook, they gradually swell and absorb water. They become soft and form a gel. If cooked too long, cereal grains will become mushy.

BREAKFAST CEREALS

The ready-to-eat cereals for breakfast are very popular. They are quickly and easily prepared. Many adults were raised on the well-known prepared cereals. In the past few years, presweetened cereals have been introduced. Recently, 55 percent of those polled in the United States chose ready-to-eat cereals over cooked cereals. Of this percentage, 31 percent preferred the unsweetened type. The presweetened variety was preferred by 24 percent. In the same survey, 33 percent chose cooked cereal. Cooked cereals were most popular in the South and the West.

There are two types of cooked cereals. There are fine-grained cereals such as farina and cornmeal. There are coarse-grained cereals such as oatmeal. Some cereals have been pretreated to cook faster with less water. Both types may be boiled or steamed.

Table 13-1 shows the proportion of water to cereal and the methods of cooking. Notice that the fine-grained cereals take almost three times as much water for the same amount of cereal. Notice, too, that the directions say to mix the fine-grained cereals with a little cold water first. Pretreated cereals may take different proportions. Check the manufacturer's directions for proportions and cooking time.

CEREAL AS FLOUR AND THICKENER

Cereals ground into flour or meals are discussed in detail in Chapter 16. Cereals as thickeners are discussed in Chapter 21 as they are used in pud-

Table 13-1. Cooking of Breakfast Cereals

Kind	Cereal		Water		Salt	
	Metric	Customary	Metric	Customary	Metric	Customary
Farina	454 g	1 lb	6.6 L	$1\frac{3}{4}$ gal	14 g	$\frac{1}{2}$ oz
Grits	454 g	1 lb	2.4 L	$2\frac{1}{2}$ qt	14 g	$\frac{1}{2}$ oz
Oatmeal (quick)	454 g	1 lb	2.8 L	3 qt	14 g	$\frac{1}{2}$ oz
Rice	454 g	1 lb	1.2 L	$1\frac{1}{4}$ qt	14 g	$\frac{1}{2}$ oz

Method of Cooking

Farina: Mix cereal with 0.5 L [2 c] of the cold water. Bring the rest of the water to a boil with the salt. Stir farina into boiling water. Cook 15 minutes, stirring frequently to prevent lumping. **Yield:** 20 servings.

Oatmeal: Bring water to boil with the salt. Slowly stir in the oatmeal. Reduce heat. Simmer for 5 minutes. Remove from heat, cover, and let stand 5 minutes. **Yield:** 20 servings.

Grits: Bring water to boil with the salt. Slowly stir in grits. Reduce heat. Simmer for 5 minutes. Remove from heat, cover, and let stand for 20 minutes until water has been absorbed. **Yield:** 20 servings.

dings. They are discussed in Chapter 15 as they are used to thicken sauces.

Rice

Of the cereals, rice is used the most in entrées. Rice is the staple food of the Orient. Thus, more people are dependent upon rice than upon any other cereal. Meat and poultry are expensive, and fish is not cheap. Rice adds nutrients and extends the flavor of these foods. This makes a less expensive, but enjoyable, flavorful dish.

KINDS OF RICE

Before processing, a grain of rice is similar to wheat. It has an outside hull and a brown skin covering the starchy interior.

• *Brown rice* has the outside hull removed, but the brown skin has not been polished off. It is more nutritious and has more flavor than polished rice. However, it is not as popular.

• *Polished rice,* or *white rice,* has been buffed to remove the brown skin. Many of the nutrients, especially the vitamins and minerals, are lost in polishing. Polished rice comes in many varieties. Long-

grained, or head, rice is considered the choicest. Its long, slender grains cook well and do not become sticky. Medium-grain is used occasionally but the cooked rice is apt to be sticky. Short-grain is less expensive, but becomes sticky when cooked. It seldom is used in food service.

• *Converted rice* has been processed before polishing. The nutrients are driven into the kernel of the rice. They are not lost through polishing. Converted rice is better nutritionally. It also retains its shape and texture during cooking.

• *Coated rice* has been treated with glucose and talc to heighten the polish and keeping qualities. The glucose and talc are washed off before cooking.

• *Precooked rice* has been partially dry cooked. Thus, it cooks quickly—in just a few minutes. It is often used in home cooking but not in food service. It loses quality if kept warm for long periods.

• *Wild rice* is not really a rice, although it resembles it somewhat. It is a grayish brown, long, pointed seed of a grass. This grass is not extensively cultivated. Wild rice is very difficult to harvest. This accounts, perhaps, for its very high price. When served, it usually is blended with long-grain rice.

This gives the dish an unusual, nutlike flavor and a different appearance.

USES OF RICE

Like other cereals, rice is occasionally served hot as a breakfast cereal. It is also frequently added to soups. However, it is most often served as an accompaniment to meat, poultry, or fish. It may be one of the main ingredients in baked dishes. Rice may also be used in desserts. (See Chapter 21.)

METHODS OF COOKING

Like other cereals, rice may be boiled or steamed. Recipes for the three traditional methods for cooking rice are on pages 269–270. Rice may be used in a *pilaf* (pe-LAHF) or *pilau* (pe-LOW). These are different words for the same dish. For pilaf, the rice is first sautéed with chopped onions in butter, margarine, or some other fat until the rice is well coated. The preliminary sautéing prevents the rice from sticking together in lumps. It also adds a nutlike flavor. It is generally best for dishes to be used as an entrée. Fig. 13-1. Boiling or steaming is

acceptable for preparing rice for desserts or breakfast cereal. Rice should never be stirred during steaming or boiling. Stirring breaks the grains and makes mushy, sticky rice.

VARIATIONS OF RICE AS AN ENTRÉE

• *Tomato and rice pilaf* is made from sautéed rice cooked in chicken stock. After cooking and draining, it is stuffed into hollowed-out tomato shells. The top is sprinkled with grated cheese. The pilaf is baked in a hot oven until the tomatoes are hot and the cheese browned. Be careful not to overbake. The tomatoes will collapse if cooked until soft.

• *Rice and cheese amandine* is a casserole of rice mixed with sautéed onions and mushrooms. It is baked in chicken stock and topped with grated cheese, sliced stuffed olives, and chopped parsley. A sprinkling of slivered almonds gives the dish its name—amandine.

• *Rice Valencienne* is a casserole of rice baked in the style of Eastern Spain. The sautéed rice is mixed with sautéed onions, garlic, green peas, mushrooms, and bits of ham. The mixture is covered with chicken stock and baked in the oven until the rice is tender.

• *Spanish rice* is a casserole of sautéed rice, onions, garlic and browned ground beef. The mixture

Green Giant Company

13-1. Broccoli Chicken Divan, a combination of rice pilaf, chicken breasts, cooked broccoli, and cheese sauce.

Table 13-2 Pastas

Kind	Name	Description	Use
Flat	Mafalda	Flat, thin.	Salad, with sauce.
	Riccia	Flat, wide, curly edges.	
Macaroni	Elbow	Curved, hollow tube.	Salads, casseroles.
	Manicotti	Large hollow tube.	Stuffed.
	No. 9	Cut or uncut.	With sauce or in casseroles.
	Ringli	Slices of straight macaroni.	Soups, salads.
	Straight	Straight, hollow tube.	Salads, casseroles.
Noodles (egg)	Broad	Variable width and length.	Casseroles.
	Fettucine	Wide, short.	Baked dishes.
	Fine	Sliced very fine.	Soups.
Spaghetti	Fuselli	Curly.	Thick cream sauces.
	Linguini	Medium fine.	
	Rotini	Spirals.	
	Vermicelli	Very fine.	Soups and casseroles.
Others	Alphabet	Large and small.	Salads, casseroles, soups.
	Bows	Small.	Salads, casseroles.
	Seashells	Large.	Stuffing.

is baked in a Spanish tomato sauce (see page 298) until the rice is soft.

• *Chicken and rice* is based on sautéed rice with onions, green pepper, and mushrooms. The rice mixture is layered with sliced chicken in a casserole dish and covered with hot chicken stock. It is baked until the rice is soft.

• *Curried shrimp* is made the same way as chicken and rice. Shrimp is substituted for the chicken slices. Curry powder gives it an exotic flavor.

Words to Remember

al dente	pasta
durum wheat	Riccia
fettucine	ricotta cheese
lasagna	spaetzle
macaroni	spaghetti
Mafalda	spaghettini
manicotti	vermicelli
mostacciola	

PASTAS

Starchy foods made from a dough of flour and water are called *pasta*. *Pasta* is an Italian word meaning "dough."

Pastas include spaghetti, macaroni, lasagna, ravioli, large pastas to be stuffed, and noodles. There are many varieties of each type. Table 13-2 shows only a few of hundreds.

The best pastas are made from *durum wheat*. This is a wheat containing a very high proportion of gluten. (See Chapter 16.) When durum wheat is mixed with water, the gluten becomes very elastic. The dough can be stretched and cut into many interesting shapes.

Pasta dishes are the "inflation fighters" for food service. They are high profit entrées. They are extremely popular, easily made, and quickly served.

Spaghetti

Spaghetti is the long, round, solid pasta identified by most Americans with Italian cooking. If it is long and thin, it is called *spaghettini* (spah-geh-TEE-

Pizza Hut, Inc.

13-2. A platter of spaghetti (left) and a platter of cavatini.

knee). Very thin, twisted, short spaghetti is called *vermicelli* (VUR-muh-CHEL-e).

The thickness of spaghetti is shown by numbers, number one being the thinnest. Number nine is the average thickness. It is the size usually cooked for spaghetti dinners. Fig. 13-2.

METHODS OF COOKING

All pastas are cooked by the same method. Notice how these principles are followed in the recipe on page 270.

1. The water must be boiling. Salt is needed for flavor. Most chefs like to add a little oil to keep the pasta from sticking together as it cooks.

2. For long pasta such as spaghetti, be careful not to break the strands as you put them in the water. The strands will bend in the boiling water. Push them down slowly so they will not break.

3. Do not overcook spaghetti. It should be cooked *al dente* meaning "to the teeth." In other words, pasta should have a firm, chewy texture.

4. Drain pasta well and shake off any remaining moisture. Moisture left on the pasta will dilute the sauce and make it watery.

5. Most chefs add butter chips or olive oil to pasta after draining to prevent it sticking together. Other chefs mix it with a little sauce.

Houses that specialize in spaghetti modify the procedure to insure fresh, hot spaghetti as needed. Figure 13-3(A–H) shows the steps for operating one type of automatic spaghetti cooker. After the spaghetti has been cooked *al dente,* follow these directions. Refer to Fig. 13-3(A–H) as you read the directions.

1. Rinse immediately with cold water until thoroughly cooled.

2. Mix with a small amount of oil—just enough to coat the spaghetti.

3. Store in the refrigerator in plastic tubs. Use within forty-eight hours. If held longer, spaghetti will turn sour.

4. To heat, portion spaghetti in 285-g [10-oz] portions in plastic baskets with covers.

5. As needed, lower portions into an automatic timer basket lift or bain-marie. The automatic basket will reheat the spaghetti portion in about thirty seconds. The bain-marie will take longer.

6. Place hot spaghetti on serving dish, pour on sauce, and garnish. The recipe for one spaghetti sauce is on page 271.

VARIATIONS

- *Spaghetti with clam sauce* may be made in two ways. Chopped clams may be added to a cream sauce, or chopped clams may be added to a spicy tomato sauce. Either sauce may be served on hot spaghetti.

- *Ham and spaghetti* is made from hot spaghetti, sautéed ham pieces, and bacon strips mixed with egg. Grated Parmesan cheese is sprinkled over the top.

- *Deep-dish spaghetti* is a casserole of cooked spaghetti and tomato sauce, topped with Parmesan cheese and slices of sausage.

Lasagna

Lasagna (la-SAHN-ya) is a flat ribbon noodle of pasta dough. The thin type is called *mafalda* (ma-FAL-da). The wide strip with curly edges is called *riccia* (REE-CEE-a). Riccia is the most common type of lasagna. Lasagna also gives its name to a casserole dish.

Lasagna is rapidly becoming very popular, in

third place after pizza and spaghetti. The typical lasagna is made with *ricotta* (rye-COT-uh) *cheese*. This is a smooth, sweet, unfermented cheese made from whole milk. It is rather expensive, so cottage cheese is often substituted for it.

Lasagna is layered with the cheese and Italian tomato sauce. Browned, ground beef or sausage may also be added. It is usually topped with slices of mozzarella cheese and then baked. A recipe for lasagna is given on page 271.

Methods of Cooking

Lasagna is cooked like spaghetti. It takes a little longer, but be careful not to overcook. Stir occasionally during the cooking, so it will not stick together.

In places serving much lasagna, individual serving-size casseroles may be used. They are filled with lasagna mixture and refrigerated the day before serving. If it is to be reheated in the microwave oven, be sure to put sauce in the casserole dish first. Then layer the lasagna with cheese, meat, and more sauce. Do not compress the layers. Be sure to surround the lasagna with sauce. Microwave ovens require liquid for even heating without drying.

To reheat in the microwave oven, place refrigerated lasagna in the oven and heat for five minutes. Just before serving, heat again for three minutes. Invert lasagna on heated serving dish. It will retain its molded shape.

Variation

Lasagna with spinach is an interesting variation. Ricotta cheese, blended with cooked, chopped spinach becomes a soft green. It is layered with the lasagna, tomato sauce, and cheese to make a casserole. After sprinkling with grated cheese, the casserole is baked in the oven for an hour.

Noodles

Noodles are different from other pastas because they contain eggs. In the United States, by federal standards, noodles must contain not less than 5.3 percent eggs by weight. The egg softens the gluten. This makes the noodles more tender, and also adds flavor. Noodles are served in most countries. In the United States, they are particularly identified with German and Pennsylvania Dutch cooking.

Kinds of Noodles

Noodle dough is rolled flat, cut into long strips, and then dried. The strips may be very fine, very thick, or any width in between. Fine noodles are suitable for soups. Wide noodles are usually used in baked dishes.

Very fine noodles are called *fettucine* (FET-uh-CHEE-knee). Sometimes they are fortified with spinach which turns them green.

Spaetzle (SHPET-sluh) is a small dumpling made with milk and a very high proportion of egg to flour. Commercial spaetzle are hard and look something like irregular noodles. Spaetzle may be made by mixing a stiff batter and dripping it immediately into boiling water to cook for a few minutes.

Methods of Cooking Noodles

Noodles are usually boiled before being used in other dishes. Following the principles of cooking starchy ingredients, stir the noodles slowly into boiling water. Stir occasionally to prevent the noodles from sticking together. Because noodles contain eggs, they cook very quickly—in about four to five minutes.

COOKING TIP: *Do not overcook. Noodles should be slightly firm—not mushy.*

Variations

• *Chicken and noodles* is a mixture of chopped chicken, cream sauce, chicken gravy, and cooked noodles. It may also contain sautéed green peppers and mushrooms. The mixture is placed in a casserole dish and topped with buttered bread crumbs and grated cheese. It is baked in the oven until brown.

• *Italian noodles* is another casserole dish made from cooked noodles. The noodles are combined with browned, tender beef chunks, sautéed onions, green peppers, and parsley. An Italian tomato sauce with canned, whole kernel corn is added. The mixture is placed in a casserole dish and topped with buttered crumbs and grated cheese. It is baked in the oven for an hour.

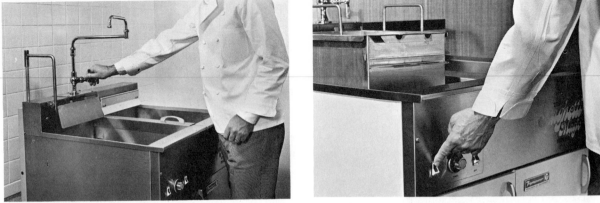

A

B

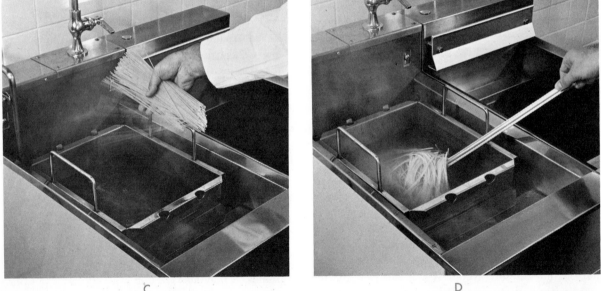

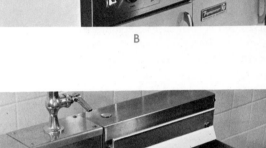

C

D

Frymaster Corp.

13-3. An automatic spaghetti cooker. (A) Fill the cooking side with water. (B) Turn on cooker and press two-position button to boil mode. When water begins to boil, you are ready to cook. Set timer. (Time will depend on type of pasta.) Lower bulk spaghetti basket into boiling water. (C) Load 2.7 kg [6 lb] of dry spaghetti as shown. (D) Stir gently as needed to keep strands separated. When cooking time is completed, the product should be *al dente*. The basket will raise automatically. (E) Hang the spaghetti basket over the storage side. Wash spaghetti thoroughly with cold water to remove starch. This rinsing will also stop the cooking. (F) Portion cooked spaghetti into servings, using plastic cups. Store spaghetti in clean cold water in storage tank until ready to reconstitute. Spaghetti may also be held in bulk in clean cold water or refrigerated. The storage method will depend on the holding time required. (G) To reconstitute, push two-position button to simmer mode. Place plastic cups with pre-portioned servings into holding rack. Set timer for thirty seconds. Spaghetti will lower with the touch of the timer button. It will reheat and then raise automatically. (H) Shake spaghetti onto serving plate. Add sauce. Garnish, and serve.

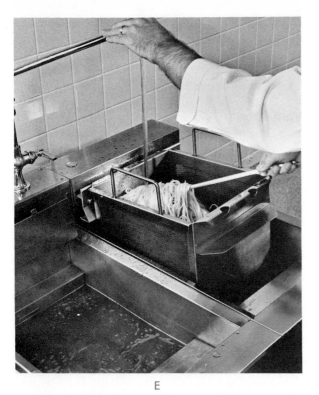

E

F

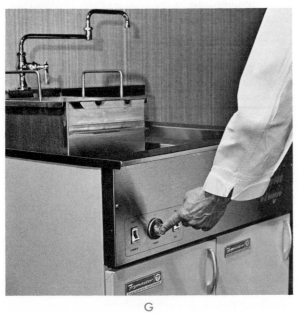

G

H

• *Spaetzle and frankfurters* is a German casserole. Sautéed onions are layered with the cooked spaetzle, sauerkraut, and sliced frankfurters. The casserole is baked about one hour.

• *Fettucine and mushrooms* is served like spaghetti. The sauce is made from sautéed fresh mushrooms added to a marinara sauce. (See page 298.) The dish is topped with grated Parmesan cheese.

Macaroni

Macaroni is a hollow tube. It may be long, bent (called elbow), cut into short pieces, or sliced into rings. When cut diagonally, it is called *mostaccioli* (MAHS-tah-CHO-lee). When large enough to be stuffed, it is called *manicotti* (man-uh-COT-ee).

Although macaroni came from Italy with other pastas, the many dishes made from it have been Americanized. Like other pastas, it is boiled first and then used in many delightful dishes. It may be chilled and made into a salad. It may be cooked in soup to add substance. However, it is most often used as the base for entrées in many baked dishes.

Macaroni should be cooked five to seven minutes. Some chefs like to add a few tablespoons of oil to the boiling water. The oil coats the macaroni and keeps it separated. Drain in a colander and rinse in warm water before mixing with sauce.

VARIATIONS

• *Macaroni and cheese* is the most famous macaroni dish.

• *Macaroni and vegetables* combines cooked macaroni with cream sauce, cooked cauliflower and broccoli. The macaroni is mixed with the cream sauce and poured over the vegetables in a casserole dish. The casserole is topped with buttered crumbs and grated cheese. It is baked in the oven for about thirty minutes until browned.

• *Macaroni and meat* is a combination of cooked macaroni, browned ground meat, sautéed onions, green pepper, and mushrooms. It is covered with tomato sauce and topped with buttered crumbs and grated cheese. It is baked about one hour.

How Much Have You Learned?

Review this chapter. Answer the following questions to prepare yourself for the post-test. Check your answers with your teacher.

1. Why are cereals and pastas important foods?

2. Name three of the most important cereals. In what parts of the world is each important?

3. Name four ways cereals are used in cooking.

4. Name and explain the three principles of cereal cooking. Do these principles apply to cooking pastas?

5. Give two ways of separating the cereal grains before cooking. Why is this important?

6. What happens to starch as it cooks?

7. What is converted rice?

8. Would you cook wild rice as a breakfast cereal? Explain your answer.

9. Describe the cooking of rice for pilaf.

10. From which kind of wheat are pastas made? What is the difference between this kind of wheat and other kinds?

11. What is the difference between noodles and other pastas? How does this affect the cooking of noodles?

12. How is the thickness of spaghetti shown?

13. How do you keep pastas from sticking together after cooking?

RICE RISOTTO, OR ITALIAN STYLE

Equipment
Sauté pan
Saucepan
Long fork

Yield: 10 servings

Metric	Ingredients	Customary
55 g	Oil	2 oz
170 g	Chopped onions	6 oz
450 g	Rice	1 lb
2 L	Broth	2 qt
140 g	Butter	5 oz
280 g	Parmesan cheese	10 oz

METHOD

1. **Sauté** onions in oil until transparent.
2. **Add** rice and coat well with oil.
3. **Bring** broth to boil. Stir in rice. Reduce heat.
4. **Cover** and simmer for 16 minutes or until rice is tender. Do not stir.
5. **Add** butter and cheese. Stir with fork.

RICE PILAF STYLE

Equipment
Sauté pan
Baking pan
Long fork
Saucepan

Yield: 10 servings
Temperature: 200°C [400° F.]
Time: 30 minutes

Metric	Ingredients	Customary
55 g	Oil	2 oz
170 g	Chopped onions	6 oz
450 g	Rice	1 lb
1.5 L	Broth	1½ qt
140 g	Butter	5 oz

METHOD

1. **Preheat** oven.
2. **Sauté** onions in oil until transparent.
3. **Add** rice and coat well with oil.
4. **Bring** broth to boil. Stir into rice using fork.
5. **Pour** into baking pan. Bake until rice is tender.
6. **Place** butter in chips on top of rice. Stir with fork.

RICE CREOLE STYLE

Equipment
Saucepan
Baking pan
Colander
Long fork

Yield: 10 servings
Temperature: 177°C [350° F.]

Metric	Ingredients	Customary
8 L	Water	2 gal
30 mL	Salt	2 T
450 g	Rice	1 lb

METHOD

1. **Bring** water and salt to a boil.
2. **Stir** in rice, using fork.
3. **Boil** 12 to 16 minutes without stirring. Rice should be almost tender.
4. **Drain** in colander. Rinse well with cool water.
5. **Drain** thoroughly. Place in flat baking pan with cover.
6. **Heat** in oven until hot and tender.

SPAGHETTI

Equipment
Stockpot
Cook's fork
Colander

Yield: 50 servings

Metric	Ingredients	Customary
21.5 L	Water	6 gal
90 mL	Salt	6 T
90 mL	Oil	6 T
2.8 kg	Spaghetti	6 lb
90 mL	Butter chips	6 T

METHOD

1. **Bring** water to boil with salt and oil in large stockpot.
2. **Push in** spaghetti and bend them slowly as they soften.
3. **Stir** with cook's fork to keep them moving until water again comes to full boil.
4. **Reduce** heat to prevent boiling over.
5. **Boil** 5 to 7 minutes until just tender. Do not overcook.
6. **Drain** and rinse lightly with warm water. Do not let spaghetti get cold.
7. **Shake** off excess moisture. Return to pan.
8. **Mix** with butter chips to prevent the spaghetti from sticking together.

SPAGHETTI SAUCE

Equipment
Stockpot   Stirring spoon
French knife

Yield: 50 servings

Metric	Ingredients	Customary
1.8 kg	Ground beef	4 lb
450 g	Onions, chopped	1 lb
4 cloves	Garlic, minced	4 cloves
225 g	Green pepper, chopped	8 oz
5.4 kg	Tomatoes, canned	12 lb
450 g	Tomato paste	1 lb
60 g	Sugar	2 oz
115 g	Salt	4 oz
60 g	Oregano	2 oz
6	Bay leaves	6
10 mL	Pepper	2 t

METHOD

1. **Brown** meat. Add onions, garlic, and green pepper. Drain off grease.
2. **Place** tomatoes and tomato paste in stockpot.
3. **Add** meat mixture and rest of ingredients.
4. **Simmer** 3 hours.

LASAGNA

Equipment
Sauté pan   Colander
Stockpot   Cook's fork
2 baking pans

Yield: 48 servings (24 servings each pan)
Temperature: 177°C [350° F.]
Time: 1 hour

Preparing the Pasta

Metric	Ingredients	Customary
8.5 L	Water	$2\frac{1}{4}$ gal
55 g	Salt	2 oz
55 g	Oil	2 oz
680 g	Lasagna	$1\frac{1}{2}$ lb

METHOD

1. **Add** salt and oil to water and bring to a boil.
2. **Add** lasagna slowly, stirring with cook's fork to prevent sticking together. Water must not stop boiling.
3. **Boil** uncovered for 12 minutes.
4. **Drain** in colander and rinse with warm water.
5. **Return** to pot and stir in enough oil to coat lasagna.

(Continued on next page)

LASAGNA (Continued)

Preparing the Sauce

Metric	Ingredients	Customary
55 g	Oil	2 oz
680 g	Onions, chopped	1½ lb
4 cloves	Garlic, minced	4 cloves
450 g	Mushrooms, sliced	1 lb
1.8 kg	Ground beef or sliced Italian sausage	4 lb
680 g	Tomato paste	1½ lb
900 g	Tomato sauce	2 lb
55 g	Oregano	2 oz
10 mL	Basil	2 t
21 g	Salt	¾ oz
1.8 kg	Ricotta cheese	4 lb
225 g	Parmesan cheese, grated	8 oz
1.1 kg	Mozzarella cheese, thinly sliced	2½ lb

METHOD

1. **Sauté** onions, garlic, and mushrooms in oil for 5 minutes. Drain and set aside.
2. **Brown** meat. Mix in sautéed vegetables.
3. **Place** tomato paste, tomato sauce, seasonings, and salt in stockpot. Add sautéed mixture with meat. Bring to a boil. Reduce heat.
4. **Simmer,** stirring occasionally, for 30 minutes.
5. **Grease** baking pans.
6. **Layer** the bottom of the baking pans with strips of lasagna. Spread ricotta cheese on strips. Cover with sauce. Place slices of mozzarella cheese on top. Continue layering lasagna, ricotta cheese, sauce, and mozzarella cheese until there are four layers of lasagna.
7. **Sprinkle** with Parmesan cheese.
8. **Bake** for 1 hour.

Stocks and Soups

What Will You Learn?

When you finish studying this chapter, you should be able to do the following:
- Define the *Words to Remember*.
- Identify the basic kinds of stocks and be able to prepare each one.
- Identify the basic types of soups.
- Make a variety of soups that meet the standards for acceptable service.
- Pass the posttest.

Chapters 14 and 15 are concerned with stocks, soups, and sauces. Stock is the basis for soups and sauces. You cannot produce a fine soup or sauce without good stock.

STOCK

Stock is also called *fond,* the French word for stock. Stock is a thin liquid made by extracting the flavor and many of the nutrients from the bones and meat scraps of animals.

In the old days, the stockpot simmered on the back burner all the time. All the meat scraps, bones, trimmings, bits of vegetables, and leftovers went into the stockpot. Sometimes it was a good stock. Many times, it was not. The results were unpredictable.

Today, most restaurants save few bones and scraps of meats and vegetables. The use of convenience foods and preportioned meat cuts has done away with the always simmering stockpot.

Because the preparing of the stock takes much time and labor, most restaurants no longer make it. Fine stock base is available for use in a convenient form. Nevertheless, you, as a student, need to understand the proper procedure for making fine stock. It is fundamental to professional cooking.

CHAPTER

14

273

Words to Remember

bouillon
clarification
clarify
consommé
consommé double
decant
deglaze

fond
fumet
game
raft
stock
venison

Kinds of Stocks

Four stocks are the basis for most soups, sauces, and gravies. They are *white stock, brown stock, chicken stock,* and *fish stock.* Each is made from different ingredients and by different methods of cooking. Each is used to make different kinds of soups, sauces, and gravies.

Principles of Stock Cookery

The basic principles of stock cookery are the same for all types. They are:

• Cook the stock slowly—simmer, *never* boil. Boiling makes a cloudy stock.

• Never cover stock while it is cooking. You need to evaporate some of the stock to concentrate the flavor.

• Carefully skim and defat the stock.

• Cool the stock quickly.

• Refrigerate promptly.

Equipment for Making Stock

The preparation of all stocks requires the same equipment.

• *Stockpot* or *steam-jacketed kettle.* Select the right size for the amount of stock you are making. The stockpot should be one-half to three-quarters full. It is not efficient to make a small amount of stock in a large pot.

• *Cleaver* or *meat saw* for cutting the bones. This will be needed unless the bones have been cut by the purveyor.

• *Long-handled spoon* for stirring.

• *Skimmer* for removing the scum.

• *China cap with cheesecloth* for straining the stock.

• *French knife* and *chopping board* for preparing the vegetables.

White Stock

White stock is very pale in color. It is also lightly flavored. A recipe for white stock is given on page 287.

INGREDIENTS

The finest white stocks are made from the bones of veal. However, pork and chicken bones may also be used. White stock from chicken is particularly important because it is used as a base in so many dishes.

Besides the bones, white stock requires bouquet garni, mirepoix, and salt. Chefs like to wrap the ingredients for the bouquet garni in the green leaves of leeks. The package is tied with a string. The mirepoix consists of chunks of lightly colored vegetables such as celery, onions, mushroom trimmings, and perhaps a few carrots.

Water dissolves the nutrients and dilutes the flavor of the bones and vegetables. The strength of the stock depends upon the proportion of water to the ingredients.

METHOD OF COOKING

The method of cooking is clearly outlined in the recipe. The recipe follows the principles of cooking for stocks. Notice that stocks, except for fish stocks, take four to six hours of simmering. This is needed to bring out the full flavor of the ingredients.

During the cooking process, a scum forms on the top of the stock. Use the skimmer to remove this. Discard the scum.

Beef Stock

Many soups are made from beef stock. For beef stock, use beef bones, rather than veal bones. For 11.4 L [3 gal] of stock, use 5.4 kg [12 lb] of beef bones. Use 900 g [2 lb] of mirepoix. These measurements are approximate. In making stocks, accurate measurement is not so important. The bouquet garni and salt add flavor to stocks.

Chicken Stock

Chicken stock should be pale yellow with the sheen of chicken fat. It should have a rich chicken flavor.

INGREDIENTS

For chicken stock, use chicken bones, gizzards, necks, and wing tips. A bouquet garni, mirepoix, spice bag, salt, and water are the other ingredients. The proportion of bones and mirepoix to water is the same as for beef stock.

METHOD OF COOKING

Both beef and chicken stock are made by the same method as white stock made with veal.

Brown Stock

A fine, brown stock will have a deep, reddish brown color with a hearty flavor. On page 285 is a recipe for brown stock. Brown stock is the basis for brown sauces.

INGREDIENTS

Like white stock, the finest brown stocks are made from veal bones. Pork, chicken, and lamb may also be used. As for white stock, a bouquet garni and mirepoix are needed. Tomato paste helps give the necessary deep, rich color.

A *spice bag*, also called a *sachet bag*, is needed to flavor brown stock. The spices are placed in a cheesecloth bag, making a little packet. They are easily discarded when the cooking is completed.

METHOD OF COOKING

To give the rich, brown color and flavor, the bones and meat scraps are deeply browned in the oven. Place the bones and meat in a baking pan with a little fat. Notice that a hot oven is needed. The usual temperature for browning is 220°C [425° F.]. Stir the bones frequently during the browning. This will ensure even browning. Brown, but do not burn.

After the bones and meat are removed from the baking pan, the vegetables are put in for browning. These add to the flavor and color.

To *deglaze* the roasting pan, add hot water after removing the ingredients to the stockpot. Scrape the bits of browned material from the bottom of the pan and add to the stockpot. Deglazing adds to the stock all the flavor and color of the meat juices. It also makes it easier to wash the pan.

For cooking, follow the same directions as for white stock.

Fish Stock

Fish stock is very pale, with a rich fish flavor. It is more highly seasoned than white, brown, or chicken stock. The recipe for fish stock is on page 286.

INGREDIENTS

• *Fish.* Only the freshest fish should be used for fish stock. Remember, fish that is really fresh has no odor.

The heads, tails, backbones, and skin from lean saltwater fish make the finest fish stock. Cod, halibut, haddock, grouper, whiting, pollock, and flounder are preferred. Stocks made from fat fish such as salmon, mackerel, and kingfish will have a heavier flavor and darker color.

A bouquet garni and mirepoix are used for flavor. Do not use any carrots in the mirepoix.

The finest chefs use white wine in fish stock.

METHOD OF COOKING

Simmer fish stock for only thirty minutes, since fish cooks very quickly.

Fish Fumet

A fish *fumet* (foo-MAY) is a double-strength fish stock. Use twice as much fish bones, and mirepoix as for a fish stock. The recipe for fish fumet is on page 286.

Stock for Game

Game is any wild animal or bird used as a food. The stock for game is a special stock made from *venison*. Venison is the culinary term for deer.

Care and Storage of Stocks

> **CAUTION**
>
> *Since the protein nutrients of the meat are dissolved in the water, stock is a good culture for the growth of bacteria. Bacteria will cause the stock to spoil, turning it sour. The growth of bacteria is retarded or held back at temperatures around 4°C [40° F.]. Stock should be refrigerated as soon as possible.*

Follow these directions for storing stock:

1. Drain stock through a china cap covered with cheesecloth into a clean pot.

2. Cool immediately by setting pot on a trivet in a cold running water bath. The stock will cool faster if the water can flow under the pot, as well as around the sides.

3. Stir occasionally. Cover between stirrings.

4. Place covered pot in walk-in refrigerator as soon as cool.

5. As stock cools, the fat will rise to the top. It will harden in the refrigerator. Remove fat when the stock is to be used.

6. Maximum storage time for stock should be 7 to 10 days at 4°C [40° F.].

Gelling of Stock

Long periods of cooking dissolve into the liquid much gelatin from the bones and meat. The gelatin will set as the stock cools, making a gel. (See page 151.) The gelling of stock is considered a mark of quality. It shows there was a high proportion of bone and meat to water.

Instant Soup Base

Instant soup beef base contains salt, vegetable protein, sugar, oil, caramel color, and monosodium glutamate (MSG). It also contains natural and artificial flavorings, beef extract, spices, and several chemical additives.

Instant soup chicken base contains the same ingredients, plus chicken fat and dehydrated chicken meat.

To make 11.4 L [3 gal] of soup stock you will need 190 g [6 oz] of soup base. Since the soup base contains salt, use less salt in the recipe.

Manufactured bases are time and labor savers. Now that you have read how long it takes to make stock, you can understand why prepared stocks are used in most food service operations.

SOUPS

Soup is a popular item on the menu. Many restaurants are offering a soup bar as well as a salad bar. In some restaurants, lunch customers make their own sandwiches and salads. They also help themselves to a cup of soup. Student centers on college campuses also are selling more soup. The students appreciate heavy chowders and hearty meal-in-a-bowl soups. Smart merchandising pays off because soups are a high-profit item. They can spread a little meat, vegetables, and cereals a long way. Fig. 14-1.

National Turkey, Federation

14-1. This nourishing turkey soup contains celery, carrots, and beans—as well as chunks of turkey.

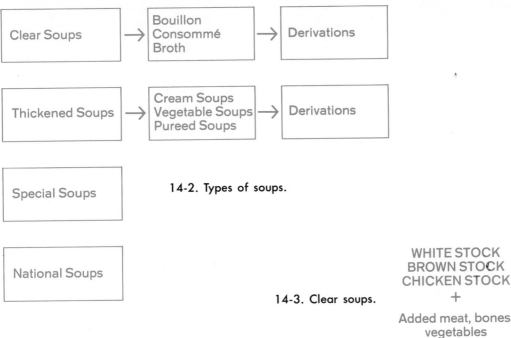

14-2. Types of soups.

14-3. Clear soups.

Soups can be divided into two general types—clear and thickened. Most soups are derived from them. Fig. 14-2. However, there are also special soups and regional soups. Many regions and countries have developed soups that are identified with them.

• *Clear soups* are thin and flavorful, but without substance. They are often served as a first course to a luncheon or dinner because they perk up the appetite. Fig. 14-3.

• *Thickened soups* have substance because they are thickened with flour, cereals, potatoes, or other vegetables. A small cup may be served as a first course. A large bowl with rolls, a sandwich, or a salad may make a complete meal. Fig. 14-4.

Clear Soups

BOUILLON

Bouillon (boo-YON) is the base from which all other clear soups are made. Bouillon is the French word for broth. There are different kinds of bouillon—beef, chicken, and lamb. Each type of bouillon is used for many different types of soups. Court bouillon is used only in the preparation of fish dishes. A recipe for bouillon is given on page 284. Follow it as you read the following explanation.

The same equipment is used for all types of bouillon. You will need a *stockpot with a faucet*, a *long spoon* for stirring, a *skimmer*, a *French knife*, a *chopping block*, a *sauté pan*, a *fork*, and a *china cap* with *cheesecloth*.

The recipe calls for lean beef and bones. The knowing chef chooses the lower grades of beef. Not only is the meat less expensive, but it has more flavor. Only lean meats such as the shank should be

277

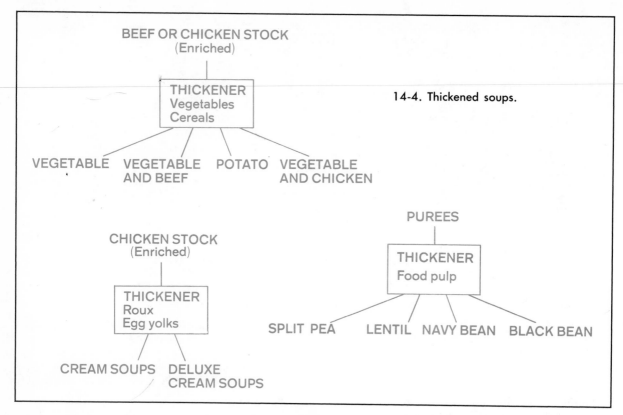

14-4. Thickened soups.

used for bouillon. The fat has to be skimmed from the top.

For chicken bouillon, use chicken stock and additional meat and bones from stewing chickens. The older chickens are fatter, but they have more flavor.

For lamb bouillon, the shank, neck, or less desirable cuts may be added to white stock.

All bouillons need a bouquet garni and onions for flavor.

As you read the method of cooking, notice that the directions say to brown the onions. Browning develops the flavor and adds color to the bouillon. About four hours of simmering are needed to bring out the full flavor.

CONSOMMÉ

Consommé (con-so-MAY) is a clear, sparkling broth made from bouillon. It is the most important clear soup because it is served constantly in fine restaurants. The recipe for consommé is on page 287.

The equipment for making consommé is as follows. *Stockpot with faucet, grinder,* and *china cap* with *cheesecloth.*

For the ingredients, you will need ground lean beef, ground vegetables (use the tops from celery and leeks), egg whites, ice water, and beef or chicken broth.

Clarifying

The making of consommé involves a very important technique called clarifying. To *clarify* means to remove all sediment so the soup is clear and sparkling. As you read the explanations, follow the recipe on page 287.

Perhaps you remember that protein coagulates when heated. This important principle of cooking is used in making many dishes. It is also used to clarify bouillon in making consommé. The proteins used in clarifying are the egg whites and ground meat. They are mixed with ground vegetables and ice water. This mixture is called the *clarification*. It is best to make it the day before using.

Before proceeding with the clarifying, the bouillon is *decanted*. To decant means to pour off the liquid gently without stirring up the sediment.

The clarification is mixed with the cold, decanted bouillon liquid and placed in the stockpot. It is important to bring the whole mixture to a boil slowly and then reduce the heat. As the mixture simmers, the proteins gradually coagulate. They gather all the sediment and ground vegetables into a mass. This mass is sometimes called a *raft* because it floats in the bouillon. It takes about two hours to clarify consommé.

When the bouillon is strained through a china cap lined with cheesecloth, it will be clear and sparkling. It will be consommé. Excess fat will rise to the top as the consommé cools. It should be removed.

Variations of Consommé

Consommé double (DUBE-lah) is extra rich. It is made with double the amount of ground meat for clarifying.

Consommés are served natural or with many kinds of garnishes. The consommé takes its name from the garnish.

Note: Vegetables or a cereal such as rice or noodles may be added to a consommé. Cook vegetables and cereals separately before mixing with the consommé. Otherwise, the starch from them will cloud the consommé.

Here are a few of the many consommés with garnish.

• *Consommé julienne.* Consommé with vegetables cut in long thin strips.

• *Consommé royale.* Consommé with unsweetened, baked custard cut into attractive shapes.

• *Consommé Madrilene.* Consommé with diced tomatoes, Madeira wine, brandy, and cayenne pepper.

• *Consommé aux vermicelli.* Consommé with fine noodles.

Words to Remember

beurre manie	puree
broth	roux
brunoise	slurry
liaison	velouté
potage	whitewash

BROTH

Broth is the English name for bouillon. It is a thin soup that can be served with many different garnishes.

Some broths are described here.

• *Chicken broth brunoise.* Chicken stock with diced vegetables. *Brunoise* (brune-WAZ) means "with vegetables."

• *English beef broth.* Brown beef broth with beef chunks, vegetables, barley, and tomatoes.

• *Lamb broth.* Lamb broth with barley, vegetables, and tomato puree.

Thickened Soups

Thickened soups include vegetable soups, creamed soups, and purees. Thickened soups are called *potage* (po-TAHZH) in French.

VEGETABLE SOUPS

Vegetable soups contain a liberal amount of diced or cubed vegetables. They may contain cereals and, perhaps, meat. They are considered a hearty, or filling, soup. The soup may be thickened with flour or potatoes. Potatoes are starchy and make a good thickener. The recipe for vegetable soup is on page 288.

Ingredients

The following ingredients are used in vegetable soups:

• *Stock.* Vegetable soups may be made without any meat flavor. Most professional cooks, however, believe a beef stock improves the flavor of vegetables. The strength of the stock may be doubled by adding additional meat and bones. This is sometimes done for the best soups. After the stock has been strained, cubes of beef may be added, if desired.

- *Bacon fat* is sometimes used to replace oil or fat for sautéing. It adds flavor.
- *Vegetables.* All kinds of vegetables may be used, such as potatoes, carrots, celery, and onions. However, strongly flavored vegetables should not dominate 'the flavor, unless the soup is named for that vegetable (for instance: cabbage soup or onion soup). The vegetables must be carefully washed to remove any dirt or sand. The proportion of vegetables to stock should be about 28–40 L [7–10 gal] of vegetables to 11.4 L [3 gal] of stock.
- *Thickeners.* Potatoes will help thicken the soup because they are starchy.
- *Garnish.* Sprinkle chopped parsley, chives, or chervil on top of the soup before serving.

If pieces of beef or chicken are to be added to the soup, simmer them with the vegetables.

Notice that the vegetables are sautéed in the bacon fat or oil before the stock is added. This practice increases the flavor.

CREAM SOUPS

Cream soups are among the most popular soups. They should be the consistency of thick cream, smooth and velvety—never curdled. The cream soups are usually named for the flavoring ingredient. Thus, we have cream of asparagus, cream of mushroom, and cream of chicken. A recipe for cream of vegetable soup is on page 288. Cream soups are made from a chicken or beef stock base. They may be thickened by a *roux* (ROO).

A roux is a mixture of *equal* parts of flour and fat. It is a basic preparation in food service. You will need to learn to make it properly. You will be using it often.

Making a Roux

- *Equipment.* Heavy sauté pan, wooden spatula, or whip.
- *Ingredients.* Fat and flour. Any good fat may be used. Chicken fat is preferred for soups or sauces with chicken flavor. Bacon fat is good for some other preparations. Any neutral fat such as margarine or butter is acceptable. Either rice flour or all-purpose flour may be used. Rice flour is particularly good for cream soups. It makes a smooth soup that does not curdle easily.
- *Method of Cooking.* To make a roux follow these directions:

1. Melt fat in heavy sauté pan.
2. Stir in flour. Stir well so there are no lumps.
3. Cook over low heat for ten minutes until mixture is frothy and leaves the bottom of the pan. If the roux is not cooked long enough, the final product will be grainy and taste of raw starch.

Some recipes will direct you to brown the flour before mixing it with the melted fat. The browning may be very slight, medium brown, or well-browned. Browning gives a toasted flavor to the roux. Browned flour loses some of its thickening power. Thus, more flour will be needed to thicken the same amount of liquid.

Roux may be used hot or cold, but remember this rule: *Never mix hot roux with a hot liquid.* You may mix cold roux with hot liquid. You may mix hot roux with cold liquid, or cold roux with cold liquid. However, hot roux with hot liquid will make lumps.

Roux may be kept a long time under refrigeration. Professional cooks keep roux always on hand for instant use.

Whitewash

A *whitewash* is a thin paste of flour and water. It is often called a *slurry*. The water separates the starch particles. The slurry must be absolutely smooth. Any lumps in the slurry will be lumps of uncooked starch in the sauce.

When using a slurry, mix some of the hot liquid with it to warm it. Then, pour it slowly into the hot liquid, stirring vigorously. Whitewash thickening adds no flavor. The texture may be slightly grainy.

Beurre manie

A *beurre manie* (BURR man-YEE) is made of equal parts of cold butter and flour kneaded together. Bits of this may be broken off for thickening sauces that are not quite thick enough.

Equipment for Cream Soups

Cream soups are made in a saucepan. They are kept warm in the bain-marie or a double boiler. A wire whip is used for stirring to make the soup smooth. A food mill and china cap remove any lumps that might form.

Ingredients

The recipe for cream of vegetable soup is on page 288. Chicken or beef stock is preferred for the base. However, a fine white stock may be used.

Cream soups are thickened by flour or a roux. If the recipe calls for fresh potatoes, less starch (flour) will be needed for thickening.

A *liaison* (LEE-uh-zahn) makes the soup flavorful and rich. A liaison is a mixture of cream and egg yolks. It is added to the hot soup just before serving. Cream soups made with a liaison are called *deluxe cream soups*. A deluxe cream soup made from shellfish such as oysters, shrimp, crab, or lobsters is called a *bisque*.

The vegetable pulp used to make the cream soup gives the soup its name.

Method of Cooking.

Look at the recipe for cream of vegetable soup on page 288. There are two methods for cooking cream soups. The first is preferred.

The methods differ in the way they are thickened. In the first, the vegetables are sautéed in fat or oil. Then the flour is mixed with them and cooked for ten minutes. The cold stock is added, and the stock thickens as it cooks. In the second method, a roux is made to thicken the stock. Then the sautéed vegetables are added. This doubles the fat content of the soup and increases the chance of curdling.

After the thickened stock is seasoned with vegetables, it is placed in a double boiler or bain-marie to be kept warm. The liaison is added just before serving.

Curdling

Curdling is a frequent problem with cream soups. For a smooth, uncurdled soup, follow these suggestions.

- Curdling may be caused by not cooking the roux long enough. The flour separates from the fat, causing a curdled look.
- High acid content will cause curdling. For example, if making cream of tomato soup, cook the tomato separately before adding it to the stock. Cooking it will reduce the acidity.
- Use all-purpose flour or rice flour. Cake or pastry flour will cause curdling.
- Do not cook the soup after the liaison has been added.

Once you have learned to make a basic cream soup, you can easily make many different varieties such as cream of mushroom, cream of celery, cream of asparagus, cream of tomato, and cream of chicken.

Purees

Puree (pure-AY) is the French word for mashed. Any ingredient forced through a food mill or china cap is pureed. When you made the vegetable pulp for cream soup, you made a puree. A recipe for green pea soup is on page 289.

EQUIPMENT FOR MAKING A PUREE

The equipment for making a puree includes the following:
- *Heavy stockpot.*
- *Long-handled spoon.*
- *Skimmer.*
- *Wire whip.*
- *Food mill, blender, or china cap.*

INGREDIENTS

The following ingredients are used in vegetable purees:
- *Stock.* The stock will depend upon the type of soup. Beef or chicken is the usual choice. Ham hock is sometimes added to the stock for the ham flavor.
- *Vegetables.* The vegetable puree gives the soup its name. The vegetables are usually dried, such as beans, peas, or lentils. About 900 g [2 lb] of dried vegetables are needed for each 4 L [1 gal] of soup. Always add fresh potatoes to a puree of dried vegetables. It makes a much smoother soup.
- *Liaison.* Cream may be added just before serving.

- *Spice bag.*
- *Bouquet garni,* if needed.
- *Seasoning.*

METHODS OF COOKING

Some chefs prefer to soak the dried vegetables overnight. If dried vegetables are to be used, place them in the stockpot with the stock, vegetable mirepoix, bouquet garni, and spice bag. Bring to a boil, reduce heat, and simmer for two to four hours or until vegetables are tender. Remove bouquet garni with skimmer, and force ingredients through food mill or china cap. A blender may be used to puree, if desired. Season to taste. Thicken with a roux, if needed. Reheat and serve.

> **COOKING TIP:** *The thickened mixture scorches very easily. Use a low heat, and stir frequently.*

For puree of fresh vegetable soup, sauté vegetables with onions in fat. The fat from salt pork adds flavor. Cook the vegetables with potatoes in stock until tender. Proceed as for other purees.

Words to Remember

borscht	mulligatawny
boula boula	olla podrida
bouillabaise	petite marmite
gazpacho	vichyssoise
gumbo	wonton

Special Soups

Mulligatawny (MUL-eh-guh-TAW-knee). Mulligatawny is a cream of chicken soup flavored with curry powder and diced apples. Some chefs also add diced green pepper and eggplant.

Petite marmite (puh-TEET mar-MEET). *Petite marmite* is a combination of beef and chicken stock with a variety of vegetables cut into *batonettes* (BA-tone-ETTS). A batonette is an oblong about 2.5 cm long by 0.7 cm wide [$2 \times \frac{1}{4}$ in]. It is served with croutons, Parmesan cheese, and slices of mar-

row. It is sprinkled with finely chopped parsley and chervil.

Boula boula (BOO-la BOO-la). *Boula boula* is a combination of beef stock and turtle soup thickened with a puree of fresh, cooked green peas. Sherry wine and brandy are added for flavor. A spoonful of whipped cream garnishes the top. The soup is glazed briefly under the broiler before serving.

Note: Green turtles are used for turtle soup. These large sea turtles are considered an endangered species. Only those raised specifically for food are used in most civilized countries.

- *Chicken gumbo creole.* A chicken soup with tomatoes, okra, green pepper, and rice. A *gumbo* is a soup thickened with okra pods.

National Soups

- *French onion soup.* This onion soup is the most popular and the simplest to prepare of all the French soups. It consists of diced or sliced onions sautéed and cooked in beef and chicken stock. Place the soup in an individual earthenware soup casserole. On top of the soup, place slices of crusty French bread. Sprinkle with Parmesan cheese or Swiss cheese. Place under the broiler for a few minutes to gratinee it. Presto! You have the best-selling soup in the United States.

Bouillabaisse (boo-yah-BAZ). *Bouillabaisse* is a soup famous in Marseilles, France, and in New Orleans. It is a solid meal in itself because it contains chunks of saltwater fish, lobsters, oysters, and possibly shrimp. It also contains leeks (a white onionlike vegetable), onions, spices, and herbs. After sautéing the vegetables, the fish and shellfish are added and simmered gently in white wine and fish stock. It is served on crusty, French bread with a sprinkle of parsley.

Olla podrida (O-ya po-DREE-dah). *Olla podrida* is a well-known soup of Spain. It is a puree of black beans with hot sausages, chicken, and ham.

Sopa de albondigas (SOAP-ah day al-bon-DEE-gahs). *Sopa de albondigas* is a popular, inexpensive Mexican soup. Fig. 14-5. *Albondigas* means "meatball." Hamburger is seasoned with salt, pepper, and minced garlic. The hamburger is fashioned into round meatballs and browned in hot fat. The

14-5. Sopa de albondigas served with garlic-cheese butter. The butter can be spread on crusty bread. It can also be used to season the soup.

browned meatballs are dropped into hot, rich brown stock with chunks of carrots and celery, and garbanzo beans. *Garbanzo beans* are round beans with a nutlike flavor. They may be either canned or dried. The soup is flavored with fresh garlic and sliced onions. Crusty bread with garlic-cheese butter is served on the side. For the authentic Mexican touch, place a small bowl of hot chili on the table.

Wonton (WAHN-TAHN). *Wonton* is a chicken, shrimp, and spinach soup from China. Each cup of rich chicken soup contains scallions, minced pork, a sliced strip of omelet, a pastry called wonton, one shrimp, and a leaf of spinach.

Cold Soups

For most people, soup must be hot or it is not soup. However, chilled soups are becoming more popular, especially in the summertime.

Jellied consommé. As you have read, a rich stock will gel when refrigerated because of the gelatin extracted from the meat and bones. Jellied consommé is often served in the summertime as a first course for dinner. To make sure the gel stays firm, unflavored gelatin is dissolved in the stock while hot. Usually, a slice of lemon is served as a garnish for the consommé. The stock may be mixed with tomato juice and gelatin for jellied tomato

283

bouillon. When served, the consommé is cut loosely to add sparkle. Always serve in chilled cups, surrounded by chipped ice.

Gazpacho (gaz-PACH-o). *Gazpacho* is a cold soup from the Spanish culture. It is a mixture of beef stock and tomato juice, simmered with onions, celery, green peppers, and garlic. It is highly seasoned with cumin (cominos), hot red pepper sauce, Worcestershire sauce, and tarragon vinegar. The stock is sieved with the vegetables and mixed with chopped cucumbers and fresh tomatoes. It is served ice-cold with a slice of cucumber as a garnish.

Vichyssoise (VISH-e-SWAHZ). *Vichyssoise* is a smooth, velvety soup made with a cream base. Potatoes, onions, leeks, bay leaf, and peppercorns are simmered in a chicken stock until tender. The bay leaf is removed. After being put through a food mill,

the puree is chilled and then mixed with chilled cream. It is served in a very cold cup with a sprinkle of finely chopped chives as a garnish.

Borscht. The beautiful color of borscht comes from the beets used in its preparation. Canned beets are drained. The juice is simmered with diced onions, vinegar, sugar, and water. The beets are run through a grinder and then mixed with the beet juice. The mixture is refrigerated until very cold. It is served with a spoonful of sour cream as a garnish.

Fruit soup. A cold soup from Norway, fruit soup is a mixture of lemons, oranges, and chopped dried fruits. The fruit is cooked in pineapple juice or apple juice and thickened with a slurry. It is sweetened to taste with sugar. Butter is added to give a sheen and flavor. It is served ice-cold in chilled cups surrounded by cracked ice.

How Much Have You Learned?

Review this chapter. Answer the following questions to prepare yourself for the post-test. Check your answers with your teacher.

1. What is a stock? Why are stocks important in food preparation?
2. What are the two basic kinds of stocks? Name the ingredients in each. Name three other kinds of stock.
3. How should stock be stored after cooking?
4. Describe the process of clarification.
5. Name and describe three types of clear soups.
6. Name and describe three thick soups that are not thickened with flour.
7. Name three regional or national soups.
8. Name and describe three cold soups.
9. Describe how to make a cream soup.
10. What is a roux? How is it made? If flour is to be browned before making it into a roux, will you need the same amount, a lesser amount, or more flour for the same measure of liquid? Why?

BEEF BOUILLON

Equipment
Stockpot
Sauté pan
China cap and cheesecloth

Yield: 20 L [5 gal]

BEEF BOUILLON (Continued)

Metric	Ingredients	Customary
4.5–6.4 kg	Beef bones, cut-up	10–14 lb
0.9–1.4 kg	Lean beef, cut-up	2–3 lb
17 L	Brown stock	4½ gal
3	Onions	3
450–900 g	Bouquet garni	1–2 lb
To taste	Seasoning	To taste

METHOD

1. **Cut** and wash bones and meat.
2. **Place** bones and meat in pot. Cover with cold water. Bring to a boil and skim.
3. **Cut onions** in half and brown in a little fat. Add to beef mixture.

4. **Add** bouquet garni or mirepoix.
5. **Simmer** for four hours. Strain through china cap lined with cheesecloth and refrigerate.

BROWN STOCK (BROWN FOND)

Equipment
Baking pan
Tongs
China cap with cheesecloth

Yield: 11.4 L [3 gal]
Temperature: 218°C [425° F.]

Metric	Ingredients	Customary
14 kg	Veal, pork, or chicken bones	15 lb
450 g	Mirepoix	1 lb
110 g	Fat or oil	4 oz
85 g	Tomato paste	3 oz
13 L	Water	14 qt
1	Spice bag	1
55 g	Salt	2 oz

METHOD

1. **Preheat** oven to 218°C [425° F.].
2. **Place** bones with oil in baking pan. Brown in oven until very dark brown. Turn frequently, using tongs.
3. **Remove** bones and place in stockpot.
4. **Add** mirepoix to baking pan. Brown in oven, but do not burn. Add to stockpot.

5. **Deglaze** baking pan by adding tomato paste. Stir and scrape. Add liquid to stockpot. Add water, spice bag, and salt.
6. **Bring** to a boil slowly. Reduce heat and simmer 5 to 6 hours.
7. **Strain** through china cap, cool, and refrigerate.

FISH STOCK

Equipment   **Yield:** 11.4 L [3 gal]
Stockpot
Skimmer
China cap with cheesecloth

Metric	Ingredients	Customary
7 kg	Fish	15 lb
11.4 L	Water	3 gal
225 g	White mirepoix	8 oz
500 mL	White wine	1 pt
1	Spice bag	1

METHOD

1. **Cut** fish into small pieces. Place in stockpot. Cover with water. Bring to a boil and skim, using skimmer.
2. **Add** mirepoix, wine, and spice bag.
3. **Reduce** heat and simmer for 30 minutes.
4. **Strain** through china cap lined with cheesecloth. Cool and refrigerate.

FISH FUMET

Equipment   **Yield:** 11.4 L [3 gal]
Stockpot
Sauté pan
China cap and cheesecloth

Metric	Ingredients	Customary
225 g	White mirepoix	8 oz
7 kg	Fish	15 lb
170 g	Butter or oil	6 oz
480 mL	White wine	1 pt
11.4 L	Fish stock	3 gal

METHOD

1. **Sauté** mirepoix lightly in butter or oil.
2. **Place** in stockpot. Add fish, wine, and stock.
3. **Simmer** for 30 minutes.
4. **Strain** through china cap with cheesecloth.

CLASSIC WHITE STOCK (WHITE FOND)

Equipment
Stockpot
Colander
Skimmer
China cap with cheesecloth

Yield: 11.4 L [3 gal]

Metric	Ingredients	Customary
4.5–6.8 kg	Veal bones	10–15 lb
1 bundle	Bouquet garni	1 bundle
900 g	Mirepoix—mostly onion, celery, carrots	2 lb
55 g	Salt	2 oz
13 L	Water	3½ gal

METHOD

1. **Crack** or chop bones if necessary. Wash in cold water.
2. **Put** bones in pot. Cover with cold water. Blanche, drain in colander, and rinse.
3. **Place** bones in pot, and add rest of ingredients. Cover with cold water.
4. **Simmer** for four hours. Skim as necessary, using skimmer.
5. **Strain** through china cap lined with cheesecloth.

CONSOMMÉ

Equipment
Stockpot
China cap with cheesecloth

Yield: 11.4 L [3 gal]

Metric	Ingredients	Customary
1.8–2.3 kg	Ground, lean beef	4–5 lb
6–8	Egg whites	6–8
1.9 L	Ice water	2 qt
450–900 g	Ground vegetables	1–2 lb
15 L	Meat bouillon	4 gal

METHOD

1. **Mix** ground beef, egg whites, water, and vegetables together thoroughly. Place in refrigerator overnight.
2. **Add** cold bouillon and vegetable-beef mixture to large pot and mix.
3. **Bring** to a boil. Reduce heat to simmer.
4. **Simmer** for two hours.
5. **Strain** through china cap lined with cheesecloth.
6. **Remove** excess fat.

VEGETABLE SOUP

Equipment   **Yield:** 11.4 L [3 gal]
Stockpot
Long-handled spoon

Metric	Ingredients	Customary
3.2–4.5 kg	Vegetables, including potatoes and onions	7–10 lb
285 g	Bacon slices, diced	10 oz
11.4 L	Beef stock	3 gal
To taste	Salt	To taste

METHOD

1. **Clean** and chop all vegetables.
2. **Sauté** diced bacon in stockpot. Add onions, vegetables, and potatoes. Sauté about 20 minutes. Do not brown.

3. **Add** stock. Simmer until vegetables are tender.

CREAM OF VEGETABLE SOUP

Equipment   **Yield:** 5 L [5 qt]
Stockpot   Food mill
Sauté pan   China cap

Metric	Ingredients	Customary
900 g	Vegetables	2 lb
140 g	Fat or oil	5 oz
170 g	Flour, rice or all-purpose	6 oz
4 L	Chicken or beef stock	4 qt
680 g	Potatoes, peeled and chopped	1½ lb
1	Bouquet garni	1
45 g	Garnish, according to flavor of soup	1 lb
500 mL	Cream	2 c
4	Egg yolks	4

METHOD 1

1. **Sauté** vegetables lightly in fat.
2. **Add** flour. Cook for 10 minutes, stirring all the time.
3. **Stir** in hot stock. Add potatoes and bouquet garni. Simmer until vegetables are tender.
4. **Put** through food mill. Strain through china cap.
5. **Cook** vegetables for garnish.
6. **Add** to soup.
7. **Blend** egg yolks with cream.
8. **Bring** cream to boil. Add to soup just before serving.

CREAM OF VEGETABLE SOUP (Continued)

METHOD 2

1. **Make** roux with butter and flour.
2. **Cook** vegetables.
3. **Add** stock to roux. Cook until thick.

4. **Add** vegetables, potatoes and bouquet garni. Proceed as for Method 1.

GREEN PEA SOUP

Equipment
Stockpot
Long-handled spoon
Sauté pan
Food mill
China cap

Yield: 11.4 L [3 gal]

Metric	Ingredients	Customary
900 g	Mirepoix	2 lb
140 g	Fat or oil	5 oz
11.4 L	Beef stock	3 gal
225 g	Ham hocks	8 oz
1.4 kg	Split peas	3 lb
1.4 kg	Potatoes, peeled and chopped	3 lb
1	Spice bag	1

METHOD

1. **Sauté** mirepoix in sauté pan until lightly browned.
2. **Place** stock and all ingredients in stockpot.
3. **Bring** to a boil. Reduce heat and simmer for about 2 hours. Stir frequently so it does not stick and burn.

4. **Force** through food mill. Strain through china cap.

Note: Add 1 L [1 qt] cream if desired just before serving.

Sauces

What Will You Learn?

- Define the *Words to Remember.*
- Identify the basic sauces and the small sauces made from each.
- Prepare a variety of sauces that meet the standards of acceptable service.
- Pass the posttest.

Sauces add to the flavor of the food. They improve its appearance and make it more interesting. Fig. 15-1. The art of cooking, like everything else, has not stood still during the past few decades. Sauces used to be very heavy and rich. The emphasis today is on lighter sauces—less cream, less butter, fewer calories.

CHAPTER

15

WARM SAUCES

A *sauce* is a richly flavored liquid used to complement another food. Sauces can be very confusing because there are so many of them. In the French cuisine, the *saucier* (saw-see-EH), or *sauce chef,* is very important. Because most sauces came from France, you will become acquainted with many French terms. For Americans, the French names add to the confusion. You will learn to make five basic warm sauces while studying this chapter. They are brown sauce, tomato sauce, white sauce, cream sauce, and butter sauce.

- *Brown sauce.* Made from brown stock.
- *Tomato sauce.* May be made from brown, white, or chicken stock. Sometimes, it has no meat stock.
- *White sauce.* Made from chicken stock or milk base.
- *Cream sauce.* Made from a rich chicken stock and milk or cream.
- *Butter sauce.* Made from egg yolks and butter.

These basic sauces are also called *foundation sauces,* or *mother sauces.* From these basic sauces, many *secondary sauces* are derived. From the secondary sauces, hundreds of *related sauces* are made. So, if you learn to make the basic

Fresh Garlic Association

15-1. The mushrooms, garlic, and herbs added to this sautéed chicken have combined with the natural juices of the chicken to form a tasty sauce.

Words to Remember

brown sauce	mother sauce
cream sauce	sauce
egg sauce	secondary sauce
foundation sauce	tomato sauce
marinara sauce	white sauce

sauces, you can easily make the secondary sauces and derivatives, or related sauces. All you need to do is change a few ingredients.

Equipment for Warm Sauces

For almost all cooked sauces, you will need the following equipment:

• A *heavy-gauge sauce pot* or *pan*, the right size for the amount of sauce you are making. Most sauces are made in small amounts. Fig. 15-2.

• A *sauté pan.*

• A *French knife and chopping board.*
• A *spatula, stirring spoon, and wire whip.*

Words to Remember

béarnaise	glace
béchamel	glaze
demiglace	hollandaise
espagnole	velouté
gastric	

Brown Sauce

The recipe for brown sauce is on page 299. Brown sauce is also called *espagnole* (es-spahn-YOL), meaning "Spanish."

Ingredients

The basis for brown sauce is brown stock. As you look at the recipe, you can see that the stock is strengthened with added bones, mirepoix, and spices. Tomato paste deepens the color and adds flavor. White wine gives the final touch. It is always used by the best cooks.

Method of Cooking

Brown sauce is made by the same method as that used for brown stock. After the bones and mirepoix have been browned, the tomato paste is used to deglaze the pan. All ingredients are simmered until the volume has been reduced to about 11.4 L [3 gal]. After straining through the china cap, the sauce may be thickened with a little cornstarch, if necessary. Mix the cornstarch with a little water before adding to the hot stock.

Brown sauce reduced to one-half the volume is

Wear-Ever

15-2. A heavy-gauge saucepan.

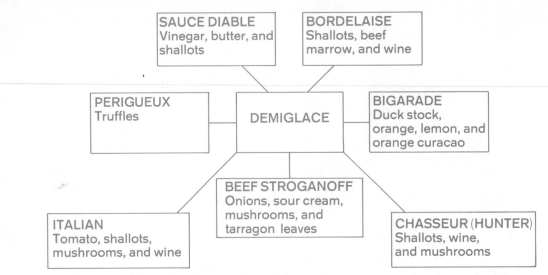

15-3. Some of the related sauces derived from a brown sauce reduced to a demiglace.

called a *demiglace*. Brown stock reduced to a paste is called *glace de viande* (gla-SAY duh VEE-ahn). The glace is spooned into small glass jars with lids. It is used to reinforce the flavor of gravies and sauces. It may be kept under refrigeration for several weeks.

RELATED SAUCES OR DERIVATIVES

Some of the related sauces derived from a demiglace are shown in Fig. 15-3. There are others, but these are the most important.

Tomato Sauce

Although the French cuisine makes tomato sauce from a stock base, the American taste prefers a more natural tomato sauce. It is better known as *marinara sauce*. It originated in Italy. The recipe for marinara sauce is on page 298.

INGREDIENTS

The ingredients are simple. They are canned, whole tomatoes, chopped shallots or onions, chopped garlic, white wine, and herbs and spices. Oregano is a must for marinara sauce.

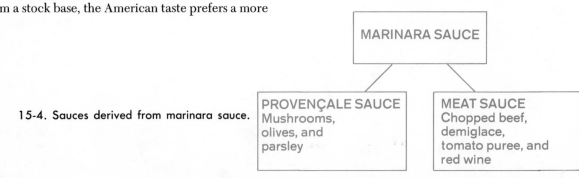

15-4. Sauces derived from marinara sauce.

METHOD OF COOKING

Notice in the recipe, that the liquid is drained from the tomatoes. It is then reduced to one-third its volume. This keeps the sauce from being soupy.

The method of sautéing also lends flavor and thick consistency to the sauce. The chopped shallots or onions and the garlic are sautéed lightly, but not browned. Then the white wine is added. The mixture is reduced to a thick syrup.

The tomatoes are lightly chopped and added to the tomato liquid. Spices and some glace de viande complete the sauce. Very little cooking is needed since most of the liquid has already been evaporated. It may be necessary to thicken it slightly with a little cornstarch mixed with water.

Two sauces are derived from marinara sauce, as shown in Fig. 15-4.

White Sauces

There are three basic white sauces, each is called a *velouté* (veh-LOU-tay). *Velouté* is the French word for "velvety". These sauces are velouté of veal, velouté of chicken, and velouté of fish. Veloutés

are really nothing but stock thickened with a roux. On page 300 is a recipe for a basic velouté.

You will notice that each of the basic veloutés has a secondary sauce. Fig. 15-5. The secondary sauces are made by the addition of a liaison of heavy cream and egg yolks. With the liaison, velouté of veal becomes sauce Allemande. Velouté of chicken becomes sauce supreme. Velouté of fish becomes sauce vin blanc (white wine sauce).

Each secondary sauce makes many related sauces with the addition of a few ingredients. Some of the related sauces are also shown in Fig. 15-5.

Béchamel

Béchamel (BAY-sha-MEL) is a cream sauce made from milk thickened with a roux. It is probably the most widely used sauce in the kitchen.

INGREDIENTS

Béchamel sauce may be thin, medium or thick. The use of the sauce determines its thickness. For example, the medium sauce would be needed for creaming vegetables, chicken, and other foods.

VELOUTÉ OF VEAL + LIAISON ↓ SAUCE ALLEMANDE	VELOUTÉ OF CHICKEN + LIAISON ↓ SAUCE SUPREME	VELOUTÉ OF FISH + LIAISON ↓ SAUCE VIN BLANC
RELATED SAUCES Caper Chaud-froid Curry Mushroom Poulette Tarragon	RELATED SAUCES A la King Albufera Mushroom Toulouse	RELATED SAUCES Anchovy Bercy Caper Cardinal Chaud-froid Crevettes Fine Herbes Lobster Rich Victoria

15-5. The three basic veloutés, or white sauces, and their secondary and related sauces.

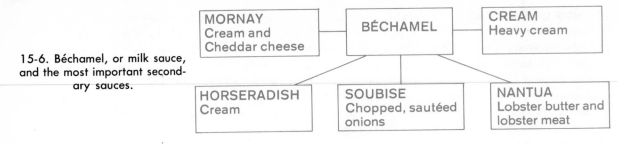

15-6. Béchamel, or milk sauce, and the most important secondary sauces.

In addition to the roux and hot milk, some cooks like to add an onion spiked with whole cloves. The sauce is seasoned with salt, pepper, and a dash of nutmeg.

METHOD OF COOKING

Remember the precautions when using roux? Cook the roux ten minutes to ensure that the flour is thoroughly cooked. Cool the roux before adding the hot milk. Cook the sauce for thirty minutes. Strain the sauce through a china cap to remove any lumps.

Béchamel has many secondary sauces of great importance in the kitchen. The most important are shown in Fig. 15-6.

Butter Sauces

The butter sauces are hollandaise (hol-an-DAYZ) and béarnaise (bar-NAYZ). The recipe for hollandaise Sauce is on page 301. They are the most difficult sauces to make—a true test of the expertise of the sauce chef.

HOLLANDAISE

Hollandaise sauce is an emulsion. It consists of butter, egg yolks, and lemon juice. Be careful to follow the directions exactly. Use a stainless steel double boiler. Be careful not to let the water in the bottom of the double boiler touch the upper pan. This will overcook the eggs. You will have scrambled eggs, instead of a sauce. Stir lightly but thoroughly while cooking. Stir down from the sides and up from the bottom so the sauce will cook evenly. When the eggs are like heavy cream, remove from

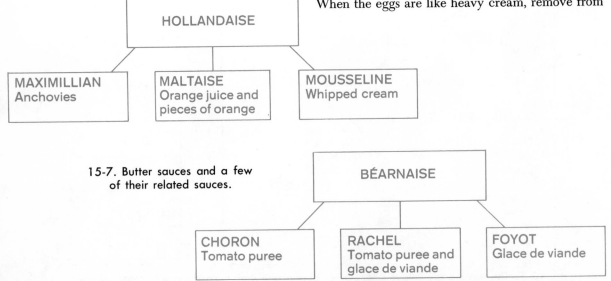

15-7. Butter sauces and a few of their related sauces.

the heat and take the upper pan off the bottom pan. Cool by stirring frequently.

Pour in the butter very slowly. Whip after each addition. Adding too much butter at one time will curdle the sauce. Season with lemon juice and cayenne pepper.

There are related sauces derived from the basic hollandaise sauce. Some are shown in Fig. 15-7.

BÉARNAISE

Béarnaise sauce is made with minced shallots, crushed peppercorns, and tarragon vinegar. The juice from this mixture is held in an emulsion with butter by the eggs. The juice is called a *gastric* (gahs-STREEK) by French chefs. It is prepared by cooking the mixture until almost all of the liquid is evaporated. The gastric is squeezed through a piece of fine cheesecloth. The gastric is added to the egg-oil emulsion in place of the lemon juice. In fine restaurants, béarnaise sauce is sprinkled with finely chopped tarragon leaves or parsley before serving.

CAUTION

Hollandaise and béarnaise sauce cannot be refrigerated because the butter will harden. Because the eggs will curdle, they cannot be cooked at a temperature high enough to kill bacteria. Thus, these sauces are a perfect culture for growing bacteria. To protect the customers, follow these precautions:

- *Never put hollandaise or béarnaise sauce on the buffet line where customers can help themselves. By helping themselves, they can also contaminate the sauce.*
- *Never add a new batch of sauce to one that is leftover.*
- *Do not hold sauces longer than one and one-half hours.*

BUTTERS

Butters give a sheen to vegetables, making them look fresh and moist.

Browning the butter greatly enhances the flavor.

Words to Remember

beurre noir	maitre d'hotel
black butter	meunière
chaud-froid	noisette
gravy	

Brown slowly over very low heat. Never permit butter to smoke. After browning, skim off the butter to be used as the sauce. Leave the particles in the bottom of the pan. Discard them.

The following are examples of the different types of butters:

- Cold butter with chopped chives, parsley, or shallots is called *maitre d'hotel* (MET-ruh do-TEL).
- Lightly browned, melted butter is called *noisette* (nwa-SET) because of its nutlike flavor.
- Darkly browned, melted butter is called *beurre noir* (BUR-NWAR), or *black butter*.
- *Meunière* (me-ne-AIR) is a lightly browned butter sauce with lemon juice and chopped parsley.

GRAVIES

Gravies are meat-flavored sauces to accompany the meat when served. They are made from brown sauce matching the flavor of the meat. As meat roasts, the fat melts and drips with some of the juices to the bottom of the roasting pan. Less experienced cooks may use the fat and the drippings to make the gravy. This is acceptable, but not approved by the best chefs. It is better to remove the fat from the drippings. What is left is added to the sauce or gravy to accompany the meat.

Au jus is defined in Chapter 12. It simply means "with the meat juices." The clear unthickened liquid that comes from the meat while it is roasting is served with the meat. It usually accompanies prime rib. Because there is seldom enough natural juice, reduced beef stock is actually what is served.

COLD SAUCES

Cold sauces are usually prepared from a tomato base or a mayonnaise base. Fig. 15-8. They are served with appetizers, hors d'oeuvres, dips, and sal-

Fresh Garlic Association

15-8. Three cold sauces, each having garlic as an ingredient. In the foreground is pasta with pesto, a cold sauce made of olive oil, fresh basil, pine nuts, and garlic. In the middle is aioli, a mayonnaise-based sauce. Bagna couda, meaning "cold bath" is in the back.

ads. There is very little difference between cold dressings and cold sauces. Sauces are associated with meats, poultry, fish, and vegetables. Dressings are served on salads.

Tomato-based Sauces

Seafood cocktail sauce may be purchased ready-prepared or commercially made catsup and chili sauce may be mixed with tomato puree for the base.

Many other ingredients may be added for variety, such as:

- Minced green pepper.
- Prepared horseradish.
- Minced onions.
- Minced olives.
- Capers.
- Spicy, hot additions such as hot red pepper sauce and Worcestershire sauce.

Mayonnaise-based Sauces

- *Tartar sauce.* Mayonnaise mixed with chopped parsley, dill pickles, onions, capers.
- *Dill sauce.* Mayonnaise mixed with sour cream, dry mustard, minced onion, dill seed, chopped cucumbers, and thinned with white vinegar.
- *Remoulade sauce.* Mayonnaise mixed with capers, sour gherkins, anchovies, shallots, English mustard.
- *Chantilly sauce.* Mayonnaise mixed with whipped cream.
- *Piccadilly sauce.* Mayonnaise mixed with Worcestershire sauce, lemon juice, and chopped fennel.
- *Indian sauce.* Mayonnaise mixed with curry, chopped chives, and a bit of prepared horseradish.
- *Mustard sauce.* Mayonnaise mixed with prepared mustard.
- *Oriental sauce.* Mayonnaise mixed with soy sauce, tomato paste, and chopped green peppers.

Chaud-Froid

Chaud-froid (sho-FRWAH) is a French word meaning "hot-cold." Chaud-froid sauce is prepared hot, but used cold. The sauce is used to coat meat products, especially poultry, for display on the buffet table. The sauce also enhances flavor.

Chaud-froid is made from a velouté of veal containing dissolved gelatin and cream.

Because chaud-froid is difficult and time-consuming to make, a substitute is often used. This substitute is made of heavy cream thickened with a roux with gelatin dissolved in it. Wine is sometimes added for flavor.

Mayonnaise chaud-froid is often used to coat fish. Hot gelatin is dissolved in mayonnaise and chilled.

Chaud-froid is ladled over a cold food such as a whole ham, turkey, capon, or fish. The food to be coated must be very cold. The chaud-froid must be at the point of congealing. Usually two or three coatings are needed to make a smooth surface. Refrigerate between each coating. Foods covered with chaud-froid are decorated elaborately. Because of the time and labor involved, the art of chaud-froid is almost a thing of the past.

CARE AND STORAGE OF SAUCES

It is best to use sauces immediately. However, the mother sauces, except hollandaise, are usually made in advance. They are chilled under running water and refrigerated until needed. Remember that sauces are very perishable. They can easily become contaminated with bacteria if not handled carefully.

How Much Have You Learned?

Review this chapter. Answer the following questions to prepare yourself for the post-test. Check your answers with your teacher.

1. Name the five mother sauces. Describe the stock used, and the ingredients of each one.
2. What precautions are necessary to make a successful hollandaise sauce?
3. How do you brown butter for a butter sauce?
4. Describe the method for making gravy from beef drippings.
5. Name two bases used most for cold sauces. Describe one sauce made from each base.
6. What is a chaud-froid? When is it used?
7. Describe the care and storage of sauces.

References

Culinary Institute of America. *The Professional Chef*. Boston: Cahners Books International, 1976.

Haines, Robert G. *Food Preparation for Hotels, Restaurants, and Cafeterias*. Chicago: American Technical Society, 1973.

Kotschevar, Lendel. *Standards, Principles, and Techniques in Quantity Food Production*. Boston: Cahners Books International, 1973.

Kowtaluk, Helen. *Discovering Food*. Peoria, Ill.: Chas. A. Bennett Co., Inc., 1978.

Kowtaluk, Helen, and Kopan, Alice Orphanos. *Food for Today*. Peoria, Ill.: Chas. A. Bennett Co., Inc., 1977.

Medved, Eve. *The World of Food*. Lexington, Mass.: Ginn and Company, 1973.

Morr, Mary L., and Irmiter, Theodore F. *Introductory Foods*. New York: Macmillan Co., 1974.

Ray, Mary Frey, and Lewis, Evelyn Jones. *Exploring Professional Cooking*. Peoria, Ill.: Chas. A. Bennett Co., Inc., 1980.

Ser-Vo-Tel Institute. *Grill Cooking and Fry Cooking*. Boston: Cahners Books International, 1974.

Terrell, Margaret. *Large Quantity Recipes*. Philadelphia: J. B. Lippincott Co., 1975.

Villella, Joseph A. *The Hospitality Industry—The World of Food Service*. New York: McGraw-Hill, Inc., 1975.

Wilkinson, Jule. *Selected Recipes for IVY Award Winners*. Boston: Cahners Books International, 1976.

Wolfe, Kenneth. *Cooking for the Professional Chef*. Albany: Delmar Publishers, 1976.

MARINARA SAUCE

Equipment
Strainer or colander
2 large saucepans
Stirring spoon

Yield: 4.8 L [5 qt]

Metric	Ingredients	Customary
4 No. 10 cans	Whole tomatoes	4 No. 10 cans
85 g	Shallots or onions, chopped	3 oz
140 g	Bacon fat	5 oz
750 mL	White wine	3 c
55 g	Garlic, chopped	2 oz
15 mL	Oregano	1 T
To taste	Salt	To taste
55 g	Meat glaze	2 oz
As needed	Cornstarch	As needed

MARINARA SAUCE (Continued)

METHOD

1. **Drain** canned tomatoes in colander. Reserve drained liquid.
2. **Pour** liquid from drained tomatoes into saucepan. Reduce by boiling to about one-third its volume.
3. **Sauté** shallots or onions in bacon fat. Do not brown.
4. **Add** wine. Reduce by simmering to a thick syrup.
5. **Chop** tomatoes lightly and add to shallots or onions.
6. **Simmer** for about 20 minutes.
7. **Add** tomato liquid. Season with garlic, oregano, and salt.
8. **Bring** to a boil and add meat glaze. If necessary, thicken with a little cornstarch.

BROWN SAUCE (ESPAGNOLE)

Yield: 4.8 L [5 qt]

Metric	Ingredients	Customary
450 g	Onions	1 lb
225 g	Celery	8 oz
225 g	Carrots	8 oz
285 g	Fat	10 oz
285 g	Flour	10 oz
4.8 L	Brown stock	5 qt
225 g	Tomato paste	8 oz
1	Bay leaf	1
To taste	Salt and pepper	To taste

METHOD

1. **Medium-dice** onions, celery, and carrots.
2. **Sauté** in fat until onions are soft.
3. **Add** flour and cook, stirring all the time, for 10 minutes.
4. **Stir** in stock and tomato paste.
5. **Bring** to a boil in stockpot. Stir until thickened and smooth.
6. **Add** bay leaf, salt, and pepper. Stir until vegetables are soft.
7. **Force** through a food mill or puree in blender.
8. **Strain** through china cap.

VELOUTÉ SAUCE

Yield: 3.8 L [1 gal]

Metric	Ingredients	Customary
285 g	Butter or margarine	10 oz
285 g	Flour	10 oz
3.8 L	Stock (chicken or fish)	1 gal
To taste	Seasoning	To taste

METHOD

1. **Heat** butter or margarine in heavy saucepan.
2. **Stir** in flour. Cook, stirring all the time for 10 minutes.
3. **Heat** stock to boiling.
4. **Slowly stir** stock into roux, stirring constantly. Cook until thick and smooth.
5. **Season,** reduce heat and cook for 30 minutes, stirring occasionally.
6. **Strain.**

BÉCHAMEL SAUCE (CREAM OR WHITE)

Yield: 3.8 L [1 gal]

	Thin			Medium			Thick	
Metric	Ingredients	Customary	Metric	Ingredients	Customary	Metric	Ingredients	Customary
170 g	Butter	6 oz	225 g	Butter	8 oz	340 g	Butter	12 oz
170 g	Flour	6 oz	225 g	Flour	8 oz	340 g	Flour	12 oz
3.8 L	Milk or cream	1 gal	3.8 L	Milk or cream	1 gal	3.8 L	Milk or cream	1 gal
15 mL	Salt	1 T	15 mL	Salt	1 T	15 mL	Salt	1 T

METHOD

1. **Melt** butter in heavy saucepan.
2. **Stir** in flour. Cook, stirring all the time for 10 minutes.
3. **Heat** milk almost to boiling in double boiler. Stir gradually into the roux. Stir briskly with wire whip until sauce is thick and smooth.
4. **Season** with salt. Simmer for 30 minutes, stirring occasionally. Strain.
5. **Thin** with rich chicken stock if desired.

Note: Cream may be substituted for part of the milk.

HOLLANDAISE SAUCE

Equipment
Double boiler
Sauté pan
Wire whip

Yield: 2.4 L [10 c]

Metric	Ingredients	Customary
900 g	Clarified butter	2 lb
10	Egg yolks	10
85 g	Water	3 oz
To taste	Salt	To taste
60 mL	Lemon juice	4 T
Dash	Cayenne	Dash

METHOD

1. **Fill** bottom pan of double boiler with water. The water level must be below the bottom of the upper pan. Heat to steaming.
2. **Clarify** butter by heating in sauté pan until liquid and solids sink to the bottom and oil rises to the top. Do not brown. Pour off butter, discard residue.
3. **Place** egg yolks and water in upper part of the double boiler. Mix well.
4. **Place** upper part on bottom part of double boiler.
5. **Stir** eggs vigorously until eggs are very thick. Remove from double boiler.
6. **Cool** slightly. Slowly, drop by drop, work the butter into the eggs, beating with the wire whip.
7. **Whip in** salt, lemon juice, and cayenne.

The Bakery

Jacob Tiefenbach, Master
Baker, Miami, Florida.

MEET THE CONSULTANT

"How did I get to be a baker?" asked Jake, his blue eyes sparkling. "Well, Missy, I'll tell you. My father died when I was very young, but he gave me one piece of advice I never forgot. He said, 'Be sure you learn how to do something and do it well. Choose something that people will always want.' I looked around and decided people would always want to eat bread, so I became a baker."

Now in his fifties, Jake has never regretted his decision. "When you bake, you create something," he says. You look at all the long line of perfect loaves of bread, and you sniff that delicious smell. You've made something you can be proud of."

Jacob Tiefenbach was born in a small town, Baka Palanka, on the Danube River in Yugoslavia. Heeding his father's advice, he apprenticed himself to a baker when he was fourteen years old. As an apprentice, he agreed to work for the baker for three years. He put in long hours, seven days a week, with time out only to go to school three times a week. In return, the baker gave him room and board. The baker also taught him the necessary skills to be a baker.

When his apprenticeship was over, he worked as a baker for three more years before he was drafted into the Yugoslavian army. During World War II, Germany occupied Yugoslavia, and Jake was captured. He escaped by convincing his captors that he was really German. Jake spoke fluent German.

Jobs were hard to find in Yugoslavia, but Jake heard that bakers were needed in Germany. He fled to Germany and worked in a pastry shop.

Jake always wanted to improve himself and his chances to get ahead. He had learned much about baking while in the army and while working in the pastry shop. Now he wanted a shop of his own. A course in bakery management was being offered at a nearby college. He completed courses in bookkeeping and other skills needed to manage a bakery. When he completed the program in 1945, he was awarded a certificate. Now he had the right to call himself a Master Baker.

Soon the war was over. An American he had met agreed to sponsor Jake as an immigrant to the United States. He worked in a bakery in Iowa for a while and then went to New York City where he opened his own shop.

After several years, he sold that bakery and moved to Hollywood, Florida. There, he worked as a pastry chef with a well-known hotel chain. As pastry chef, he saw the need for a bakery specializing in the hotel and restaurant trade. The Fort Lauderdale-Hollywood area was growing fast. Tourists were pouring in, and people were eating out more and more. Many places were finding it difficult to serve high-quality baked goods. Jake saw the opportunity and acted on it. He opened his own shop.

Now he employs thirty-two bakers and serves many of the fine hotels and restaurants in the area. He also does a brisk retail business.

Jake trains new employees himself. They begin by working with yeast dough. Jake says, "The only way to understand yeast is to work with it by hand. Using a mixer won't tell you. You have to feel the yeast come alive and the strength of the flour develop as you knead. Only then will you understand that yeast is a living thing and must be treated gently."

Eventually, he lets them weigh the ingredients and bake the products. "You never know everything there is to know about baking," says Jake. "Some of these young people—they work for me for a month, and they think they know baking. I have been baking for over forty years, and I am still learning. That's what makes it so interesting."

Is baking still a good business to join? "Yes!" says Jake emphatically. "People must eat, and bread is still the staff of life. Even when times are tough, people seem to eat more bread. Young women and men who want to become bakers must be willing to work hard at odd hours because much of the baking is done at night to provide fresh bread in the morning. Baking is satisfying work. If I could do it all over again, I would still want to be a baker."

Ingredients and Equipment in the Bakery

What Will You Learn?

When you finish studying this chapter, you should be able to do the following:

- Define the *Words to Remember*.
- Identify the ingredients used in baking, giving the purpose of each.
- Identify on sight the equipment found in bakeries and describe the use of each.
- List the sanitary procedures in bakeries and explain the reasons for each procedure.
- Pass the posttest.

How many bakeries are there in your town? A check of the Yellow Pages of the telephone directory might surprise you. If you live in a large city, you probably have hundreds of bakeries of different sizes. Some may be very large bakeries supplying bread and rolls to supermarkets. Smaller bakeries may supply baked products only to local neighborhoods. Some (like that of Jake Tiefenbach) may specialize in baking for hotels, restaurants, and institutions. Others may be located inside the kitchens of food service places. The products they bake are served only in that place. In this book, the equipment, ingredients, and techniques of baking for food service will be studied.

Words to Remember

bran	gluten
break	green flour
bromated flour	middlings
cake flour	milling
clears	patent flour
cracked wheat flour	soft flour
endosperm	whole wheat flour
germ	

INGREDIENTS IN BAKING

Baking requires few ingredients, but each has a specific use. Although the same ingredients are used in the home, those for food service baking must meet different specifications. A professional baker needs to be familiar with the special qualities of the ingredients needed for commercial baking.

Table 16-1 shows the ingredients for four products commonly made in the bakery—bread, cake, biscuits, and piecrust. What are the ingredients found in all of them? It is easy to see that flour, salt, and shortening are common to all.

Flour

Flour is a powdery substance produced by finely grinding grain through a process called *milling*. Although many grains may be ground, flour usually means the finely ground meal of wheat. Flour is used in every baked product. For this reason, it is important to understand the composition of flour and why it behaves the way it does.

THE WHEAT KERNEL

The wheat kernel is composed of three parts: the *bran*, the *endosperm*, and the *germ*. Fig. 16-1.

The *bran* is the rough, outer portion of the wheat kernel. It contains much of the minerals and the vitamins. Minerals and vitamins are nutrients essential for good health.

The *endosperm* is the starchy, inner portion of the wheat kernel from which the white flour is milled.

The *germ* is located at the bottom of the kernel. It is the part from which the new plant grows. It contains oil, minerals, and vitamins.

In milling white flour, all of the germ and most of the bran is removed. The germ is removed because the oil it contains causes the flour to spoil easily. The bran is removed because flour milled with bran would be brown and coarse.

Flour milled from the entire wheat kernel, including bran and germ, is called *whole wheat flour*. It is high in vitamins and minerals, but spoils easily. *Cracked wheat flour* is white flour mixed with the whole wheat kernel chopped into coarse particles, rather than ground.

MILLING OF WHEAT

Study Fig. 16-2. It shows how flour is milled. The first grinding, or *break*, in milling opens the wheat

Table 16-1. Ingredients Used in Baking

Bread	Cake	Biscuits	Piecrust
High-gluten flour	Cake flour	All-purpose flour	Low-gluten flour
Sugar	Sugar	Sugar	Salt
Yeast (dried)	Baking powder	Baking powder	Shortening
Salt	Salt	Salt	Ice water
Shortening	High-ratio shortening	Shortening	
Nonfat dried milk	Milk	Milk	
Water	Eggs		
	Vanilla		

kernel and exposes the endosperm. It reduces some of it to smaller particles. The particles are sifted, separating the coarse from the fine. The coarsest material contains most of the bran. The following grinding and sifting removes most of the bran from the endosperm, leaving particles called *middlings*. Subsequent grindings and siftings reduce the middlings to flour. Because of oil in the germ, the large particles containing germ will stick together. These are removed.

White flour always contains a little bran. *Patent flour* is the whitest flour with the least amount of bran. The next whitest flour is called first *clears*. Second clears and third clears have more bran than first clears. Second clears and third clears are used in commercial baking for hard rolls, crusty breads, and rye breads.

AGING

After grinding, flour needs to be aged. During aging, enzymes naturally present in the flour cause it to whiten gradually. They also change the flour so it is easier to mix. Unripened flour is called *green flour*. Green flour is yellowed, difficult to work, and makes a tough product.

Natural aging requires about six weeks. However, the mills speed up the process by adding chemicals. These chemicals do not affect the taste or nutritional qualities of the flour. However, they do improve the baking qualities. The mills also bleach some of the flour. Very white flour is preferred by most persons.

GLUTEN

Flour is composed of starch, protein, and small amounts of fat, sugar, and minerals. The protein in flour is called *gluten* (GLUE-ten). It forms the framework of the baked products.

The gluten in flour makes the dough sticky. As the mixing of the dough proceeds, the gluten in the flour becomes elastic and pliable. The more the dough is mixed, the more elastic the gluten becomes. When the dough is baked, the gluten coagulates, or becomes firm. It forms, along with the starch, the structure of the product.

All flours do not have the same amount of gluten.

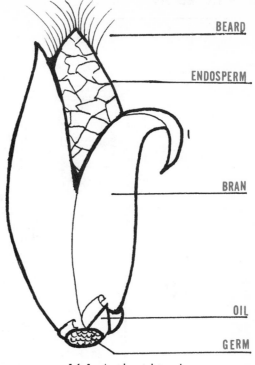

16-1. A wheat kernel.

Flour with very little gluten is desirable for products with a soft, tender structure, such as cake. High-gluten flour is best for bread and rolls because a firm texture is needed. For example, cake made from high-gluten flour would be tough. Bread made from low-gluten flour would be flat and dense.

Look again at Table 16-1 showing the ingredients commonly used in baked products. Notice that a different flour is used for each product. High-gluten flour is used for bread. Low-gluten flour is used for pastry. Cake flour is used for cakes, and all-purpose flour for biscuits. The amount of gluten in the flour determines its use. The amount of gluten depends upon the kind of wheat from which the flour was milled. Flour with a low gluten content is called soft. Flour with a high gluten content is called hard.

BROMATED FLOUR

One of the chemicals sometimes added to flour is potassium bromate. Flour containing this chemical

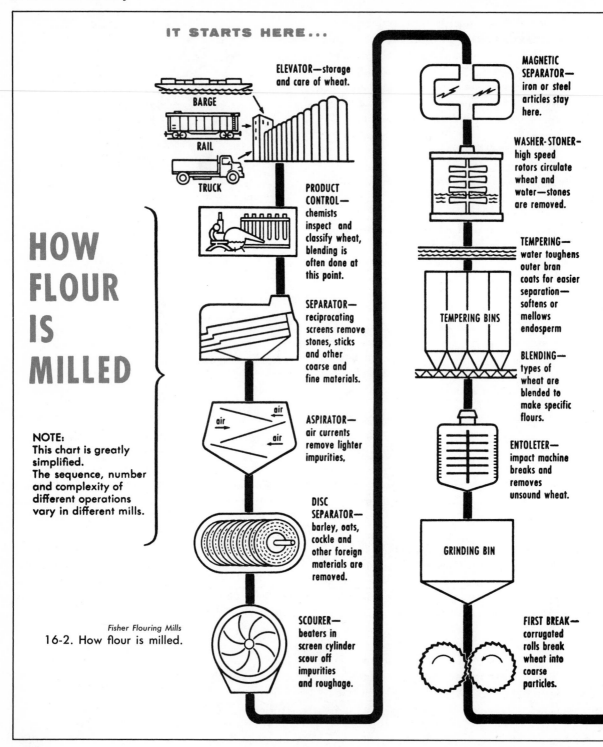

IT STARTS HERE...

ELEVATOR—storage and care of wheat.

BARGE

RAIL

TRUCK

MAGNETIC SEPARATOR—iron or steel articles stay here.

WASHER-STONER—high speed rotors circulate wheat and water—stones are removed.

HOW FLOUR IS MILLED

PRODUCT CONTROL—chemists inspect and classify wheat, blending is often done at this point.

TEMPERING—water toughens outer bran coats for easier separation—softens or mellows endosperm

TEMPERING BINS

SEPARATOR—reciprocating screens remove stones, sticks and other coarse and fine materials.

BLENDING—types of wheat are blended to make specific flours.

NOTE:
This chart is greatly simplified.
The sequence, number and complexity of different operations vary in different mills.

air

air

air

ASPIRATOR—air currents remove lighter impurities,

ENTOLETER—impact machine breaks and removes unsound wheat.

DISC SEPARATOR—barley, oats, cockle and other foreign materials are removed.

GRINDING BIN

Fisher Flouring Mills
16-2. How flour is milled.

SCOURER—beaters in screen cylinder scour off impurities and roughage.

FIRST BREAK—corrugated rolls break wheat into coarse particles.

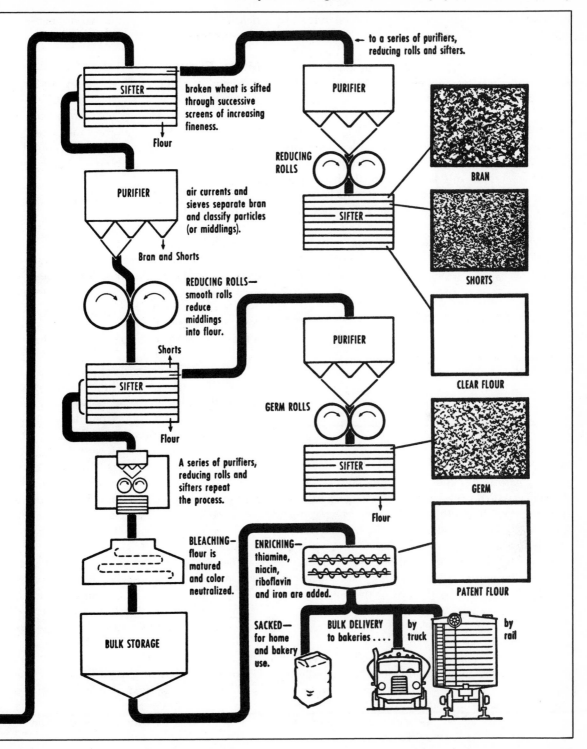

is known as *bromated flour*. When this chemical is added, the flour becomes elastic, stretchy, and easy to work during mixing. These are needed qualities for a good bread flour. Bromated flour may be marketed directly after milling. This eliminates the costly aging process.

SOFT FLOUR

In the United States, *soft flour* is milled from soft white wheat grown in the Midwest and parts of the South. Sometimes this flour is described as weak because the products made from it will be more tender with a delicate texture. Since it is used for cakes, it is also known as *cake flour.*

Soft flour is clear white in color and velvety to the touch. It sticks together when squeezed in the hand.

Words to Remember

bread flour	rice flour
enriched flour	rye flour
hard flour	self-rising flour
meal	strong flour
mixed flours	

HARD FLOUR

Hard flour is also known as *strong flour* or *bread flour.* It is milled from hard red winter or hard red spring wheats. In North America, it is grown in the northern plains. Hard flour has a high gluten content and so is used for breads.

Hard flours are creamy in color. They feel rather rough and granular between the fingers. An experienced baker can tell by the feel of the flour if it is suitable for breadmaking.

ENRICHMENT

When flour is milled, removing the bran and the germ, most of the minerals and vitamins are lost. To replace the lost nutrients, the vitamins thiamin, niacin, and riboflavin are added after milling. The mineral iron is also added. As nearly as possible, *en-riched flour* is equal to whole wheat flour in vitamins and minerals.

MIXED FLOURS

Flours can be built to specifications for the baking job to be done. They can be built by mixing soft and hard flours in different proportions. For instance, an all-purpose flour is a mixture of hard and soft flours. They are mixed in such proportions that all-purpose flour is suitable for almost any baking purpose.

OTHER FLOURS

Rice flour contains no gluten and is seldom used in baking.

Rye flour has a distinctive flavor many people like. It contains no gluten, so it must be mixed with hard flour to make bread. Second or third clears are usually blended with rye flour, making a rye-blend flour. Coarse rye flour that is unbolted (not finely sifted) is used to make pumpernickel bread.

Self-rising flour has baking powder and salt added to it. Its use eliminates one step in mixing and assures thorough mixing of the dry ingredients. It is frequently cheaper to use self-rising flour than to buy flour, salt, and baking powder.

Some flours are really not flours at all. Grated potatoes, ground soybeans, and finely grated nuts are frequently called flours. However, they do not have a grain base. Potato and soybean flours are used in making specialty breads. Nut flour adds flavor to cookies, pies, and cakes.

MEALS

Meal is coarsely ground cereal. It has limited uses in the bakery. So-called health breads include meals to add chewiness. Cornmeal is spread on the baking pans for hard breads to prevent sticking. Oatmeal adds variety to the flavor and texture of breads.

CARE AND STORAGE OF FLOUR

To maintain the good baking qualities of flour, follow these storage rules:

• Store flour in a room separate from the work

area. The room should be clean, dry, well lighted, and well ventilated.

• Keep flour at least 20 cm [8 in] off the floor to help maintain good air circulation.

• Temperature should be maintained as close to 18°C [65° F.] as possible.

• Flour absorbs odors. Keep it well away from products with strong aromas such as spices, onions, and apples.

• Use the oldest flour first. Remember the old saying, "First in, first out." Whole wheat flour and rye flour have a shorter storage life than white flour.

• Control of insects and vermin is essential. Absolute cleanliness and an adequate pest-control program must be practiced.

Words to Remember

creamability	plasticity
high-ratio shortening	shortening
hydrogenization	waxiness

Shortening

Shortening is another word for the fat used in baking. Perhaps you noticed that all the products listed in Table 16-1 contain shortening. Shortening is important because it affects the finished product in so many ways. For instance:

• During mixing, it surrounds the gluten in the dough. It shortens the strands and makes a more tender product.

• Shortening coats the gluten strands so they slip, rather than stick. This slippage helps the dough rise evenly, with a smoother shape.

• When creamed or beaten, shortening traps air in the dough. During baking, the air expands. This makes a lighter product with greater volume. This is particularly important in cake baking.

• Layered between moistened flour, shortening leaves the baked dough in soft, tender flakes. Many pastries are made in this way.

• Shortening oils the structure of the product so it is easier to chew and swallow.

• The amount of shortening can determine the kind of baked product. For instance, Danish pastry is made from a sweet yeast dough used for many other rolls. However, Danish pastry has much extra shortening rolled into it.

DESIRABLE QUALITIES FOR SHORTENING

To give best results, shortening for baking must have the following characteristics:

• *Plasticity*—readily mixed, worked, or spread.

• *Waxiness*—soft, smooth, and lustrous.

• *Creamability*—traps air when beaten, a quality related to plasticity.

• *Pleasant odor*—or no odor at all.

• *Pleasant flavor*—or no flavor at all.

BUILT SHORTENINGS

In 1900, butter, lard, chicken or goose fat, and some oils were the shortenings generally used in baking. Then in 1911, an important discovery was made. Vegetable oils would solidify into fats when the element hydrogen was passed through them. This is the process of *hydrogenation* (hi-dra-juh-NAY-shun). This process allows shortenings to be built to meet the exacting specifications for professional baking.

For instance, the amount of hydrogenation controls the plasticity and waxiness of the shortening. Bakers can order the type of shortening needed for the specific job. A piecrust requires a waxy, plastic, but firm fat. However, a cake requires a very different kind—a soft, creamable fat. *High-ratio shortenings* were developed especially for cakes. They are named high-ratio because they can be creamed to a high volume. They absorb much more sugar than regular shortenings. They make a sweeter, more tender, and more finely grained cake with a higher volume. Their use has simplified mixed methods and reduced the mixing time. At the same time they give a better product with longer shelf life.

Of course, butter is still used in baking because nothing can replace its flavor. Its use adds quality to baked products. Although it is expensive, quality bakeries use butter in small amounts for the flavor it adds.

Lard is still used by those bakers who believe nothing makes a better piecrust than lard.

Cooking oils are used in certain cakes and for deep frying doughnuts.

Margarine is used frequently for sweet yeast rolls, frostings, and desserts. It is close to butter in flavor and consistency and keeps well when refrigerated.

Words to Remember

confectioners' sugar	sugar
molasses	sugaring
refining	syrup

Sugar

Most baked products contain sugar. As shown in Table 16-1, only pie dough has no sugar.

Sugar is the sweet substance from the juice of the sugar cane or sugar beet. The process of purifying the juice and turning it into crystals is called *refining*. To many people, sugar means the sweet, white crystals found on the table or used in cooking. However, to the professional baker, there are many different sugars. Each has a specific use.

KINDS OF SUGAR

Dry sugars are purchased according to the fineness of the crystals.

- *Ultrafine*—for cakes and cookies. Sometimes this sugar is called "baker's special."
- *Very fine*—for puddings, gelatins, and fruits. Frequently, it is called "fruit sugar."
- *Fine*—the sugar commonly found on the table and in the home.
- *Medium coarse*—for making syrups and candies.
- *Coarse*—for sprinkling on cookies, doughnuts, and other baked products.

Sugar crystals may be pulverized, or ground to a powder. The fineness of the sugar determines its use. Fineness is shown by the letter *X*. The more Xs, the finer the sugar. Powdered sugar is frequently called

confectioners' sugar because it is used so much in making frostings and candies.

Following are the grades of powdered sugar:

- *Ultrafine (10X)*—used for uncooked frostings and icings.
- *Very fine (6X)*—used for the final coating on sweet rolls, some cakes, and other baked goods. This is the powdered sugar commonly found in the home.
- *Medium coarse (4X)*—used on doughnuts, cookies, crullers, and other similar products.

Brown sugar is often called "soft sugar" because it is very moist compared to the granulated kind. Its color may vary from light brown to dark brown. The dark brown has a very strong molasses flavor. Brown sugar is used in cakes, cookies, candies, and icings where a caramel or molasses flavor is desirable.

SYRUPS

Syrups are sweet liquids. They are frequently used in bakeshops.

Molasses is a by-product in the sugar refining process. When most of the sugar has been crystallized, the remaining juice is molasses. Like brown sugar, it varies from light brown to dark brown. The strength of the flavor increases as the color deepens. It is used in cakes, cookies, candies, and frostings for its distinctive flavor.

Malt syrup is made from barley grain. It is used especially in yeast breads and rolls because it starts the yeast growing quickly.

Honey is made by bees from the nectar of flowers. The kind of flower determines the color and flavor of the honey. For instance, clover honey is light and delicate in flavor. Buckwheat honey is very dark and strong in flavor. Honey is used in cakes, cookies, sweet rolls, frostings, and candies.

Corn syrup is extracted from the juice pressed from corn. It may be almost colorless or a light brown. Corn syrup is used extensively in candies, frostings, and icings because it gives a smooth texture.

Maple syrup comes from the sap of the sugar maple tree. It is highly prized for its delicious flavor.

However, it is rarely used in bakeries because of its high cost.

PURPOSES OF SUGAR IN BAKING

Sugar is used in baking because of its sweet taste. However, it also has the following effects on the quality of baked goods:

- It tenderizes the gluten.
- It makes a browner, crisper crust.
- It aids in the creaming process by increasing the plasticity of the shortening.
- It helps baked products stay fresh longer because it retains moisture.
- It forms a ready food for yeast.
- It adds greatly to the caloric value.

STORAGE OF SUGAR AND SYRUP

Sugar should be stored in tight containers in a dry place. This is particularly true of brown sugar. It tends to become lumpy and hard if allowed to dry out. Since sugar attracts ants, any spills should be wiped up immediately.

Syrups may be stored in glass bottles on a shelf in a cool room. Do not refrigerate, as this may cause the formation of sugar crystals. This process is called *sugaring*.

Words to Remember ─────────

baking ammonia	dry yeast
baking powder	fresh yeast
baking soda	leavener
cake yeast	single-action baking
compressed yeast	powder
double-action baking	yeast
powder	

Leaveners

A *leavener* is a substance used in baking to make a product rise so it is light in proportion to its size. Although only a small amount of leavener is used, it must be measured very accurately. It has a powerful effect on the finished product. Too much leavener will give a coarse product that will dry out easily. Too little leavener produces a fine grain with small volume and rough crust.

Leaveners work by producing a gas that expands when heated, causing the structure to rise. There are four kinds of leaveners—air, steam, chemical, and yeast. Some react slowly, rising over a period of several hours, others react so quickly that speed is essential in mixing and baking.

Yeast and baking powder are the leaveners in three of the products listed in Table 16-1. In pie-crust, the leavener is air.

AIR

Air works as a leavener because it expands when heated. It can be incorporated into the product in the following ways:

- Beating air into the mixture by hand or with a mixer.
- Folding in beaten egg whites. The air will expand when heated. Angel food cake is leavened by air from beaten egg whites.
- Mixing in whole beaten eggs increases the lightness of such products as shortened cakes.
- Sifting flour makes a lighter product because of the addition of air.
- Creaming shortening with sugar traps air in the mixture, making a lighter product.

STEAM

Steam is a powerful leavener. Water changes to steam when heated, causing the mixture to rise. All mixtures contain some water, which will turn to steam during baking. Some mixtures, such as popovers, contain a great deal of water. They are leavened by steam alone.

CHEMICAL LEAVENERS

Certain chemicals react with moisture and heat to form carbon dioxide, a gas. Carbon dioxide, like air, expands on heating. Such compounds, suitable for use in foods, are called chemical leaveners. They are baking soda, baking powder, and baking ammonia.

Baking soda is a compound that reacts with acid

to produce carbon dioxide. The acid may be sour milk, buttermilk, vinegar, molasses, brown sugar, or honey. Baking soda reacts very fast with the acid. To help delay the reaction, the baking soda is mixed first with the flour and salt before adding the acid. When the product is baked, the heat of the oven causes the gas to expand and the product rises. Soda is often used to leaven products that contain chocolate because it gives a deep red-brown color. Special care must be taken in measuring baking soda. Too much baking soda will cause the product to sink in the middle. It also may leave an undesirable aftertaste.

Baking powder is the most widely used leavener because of its convenience and sure results. It is a mixture of soda, an acid salt, and a dryer such as starch. The dryer prevents caking.

Baking powder may be single-action or double-action. In *single-action baking powder,* the acid salt reacts with the soda when the moisture is added. The reaction increases rapidly when heat is applied. Because of the speed of the reaction, single-action baking powder is seldom used in commercial baking.

Double-action baking powder acts much more slowly. It contains two acid salts. One salt reacts with the soda at room temperature. The other salt requires heat. About one-third of the carbon dioxide is formed during mixing. The rest is released during baking. Thus the name double-action. Most bakeries use this type of baking powder because it is more reliable.

All baking powders gradually lose strength with age because they absorb moisture in storage. Thus, baking powder should be bought in small amounts and used promptly.

Baking ammonia is the common name for ammonium bicarbonate. It decomposes rapidly when heated. Thus, it is used for cookies and puffs where rapid expansion is desired. It releases carbon dioxide and ammonia gas when heated. It disappears completely on baking, leaving no aftertaste or discoloration.

YEAST

Yeast is a single-celled plant that feeds on starch and sugar. It is completely different from the other leaveners because it is alive. It grows best at temperatures between 25–29°C [78–85° F.]. It dies at temperatures over 60°C [140° F.].

Yeast grows by the process of budding. One cell grows out of the previous one, forming branches. When moistened and given adequate food and correct temperatures, the yeast grows. It produces carbon dioxide. As it grows, the gluten stretches, causing the dough to rise. The growth is slow and steady, taking several hours.

Two types of yeast are commonly used in baking—*compressed yeast* and *dry yeast.*

Compressed yeast is also called *fresh yeast* or *cake yeast.* It is purchased in 0.46–2.3 kg [1–5 lb] blocks. Good compressed yeast should have these characteristics:
- Firm, crumbly, springy consistency.
- Uniform, creamy gray color with no discolored or moldy spots.
- Fresh, pleasant, yeasty odor.

Before using, crumble compressed yeast into a small amount of lukewarm water 25–29°C [78–85° F.]. Let stand for a few minutes before mixing. The yeast will disperse evenly and mix better with the other liquid.

Compressed yeast will keep four to five weeks under refrigeration. However, it spoils rapidly at temperatures above 15°C [60° F.].

Dry yeast is granular and darker in color than compressed yeast. It is purchased in sealed envelopes, dated to insure freshness.

Usually, dry yeast is sifted with the dry ingredients and then mixed with other ingredients. Sometimes, it is sprinkled in lukewarm water with a little sugar. It is allowed to stand for a few minutes. It is then added to the rest of the liquid. This method speeds the growth of the yeast.

Dry yeast does not require refrigeration. It may be stored on the shelf in a cool, dry room.

Liquids

All the baked products listed in Table 16-1 contain a liquid. Milk or water are the usual liquids used in baking. Other liquids such as potato water or fruit juices may be used occasionally.

Words to Remember

buttermilk
cocoa butter
dried eggs
dry milk
evaporated milk

fortified eggs
frozen eggs
scalding
sour milk

WATER

Water gives a different texture to baked items, especially bread and rolls. When water is used instead of milk, the texture will be coarse and chewy. The crust will be crisp. Thus, water is used for such items as French and Italian bread and hard rolls.

Water may be hard or soft, depending upon the amount of minerals it contains. Very soft water weakens the gluten strands, causing them to collapse before the dough has risen to its full height. Professional bakers add some minerals to the water if the bakery is in an area with very soft water.

MILK

Milk has a definite function in baking, besides adding nutritional value.

• It helps the product stay fresh longer.
• It assists gluten formation.
• It gives a finer, more velvety grain.
• It adds flavor.
• To many people, the use of milk indicates a quality product.

Many different kinds of milk may be used in baking. Each one gives equally good results.

Fresh, pasteurized milk is used for such products as custards and cream fillings. If fresh milk is used for products made with yeast, the milk must be scalded. In *scalding*, milk is heated just under the boiling point. This kills any bacteria or wild yeasts that may be present. These very small organisms could interfere with the action of the yeast and produce a flat product or one with an off-flavor. The milk is cooled to lukewarm before the yeast is added. Remember, hot milk will kill the yeast.

Evaporated milk has half the water volume of fresh milk. An equal amount of boiled water is added to bring the volume up to that of fresh milk.

Cans of evaporated milk may be kept on the shelf in a cool room. However, once a can has been opened, it requires refrigeration just like fresh milk.

Buttermilk and *sour milk* give a special flavor and texture to many products. They are used in combination with soda as a leavener.

Originally, buttermilk was the liquid left after churning butter. Sour milk was milk that had turned sour. Today, both are made by adding a certain bacteria. Buttermilk is made from skim milk. Sour milk is made from whole milk. Sometimes, vinegar is added to fresh milk to turn it sour.

Dry milk is used in bakeries more than any other form of milk because it is cheaper and easier to handle. The dry milk is measured and sifted with the other dry ingredients. Water is used as the liquid.

Dry milk requires no refrigeration. It may be kept on the shelf in a cool dry room.

OTHER LIQUIDS

Fruit juices may be used in cakes to give a special flavor. Since fruit juices are acid, the leavener would be baking soda.

Fruit juices are frequently used in pie fillings, cake frostings, and desserts. Lemon, orange, strawberry, and other juices add a variety of flavors.

Eggs

Of the products listed in Table 16-1, only cakes always contain eggs.

Eggs are used in yeast products mainly for flavor and color appeal. However, in cakes and similar products, they are considered the most important ingredient. In cakes, the cost of the eggs may be almost one-half the total cost of all the other ingredients.

PURPOSE OF EGGS

Eggs perform several important functions in cakes that other ingredients cannot do. Eggs are essential because:

• *They maintain structure.* Cakes use very little flour in proportion to the liquid. Thus, eggs are essential to help maintain the tender structure of the cake. They hold together the other ingredients during mixing and baking.

• *They aid in leavening.* When they are beaten, eggs take in air to make a lighter, more desirable product. They also add moisture to form steam, adding to the leavening action. A coarse cake would result if only chemical leaveners were used.

• *They help to shorten the product.* The yolks contain almost one-third fat, adding to the shortening already present.

• *They add color.* Their golden color is associated with richness and quality.

• *They add food value.* They increase the nutritional quality of baked products.

FORMS OF EGGS

Eggs may be purchased fresh in the shell, fresh in liquid form, frozen, or dried.

• *Fresh eggs in the shell* are seldom used in bakeries because of the time involved in cracking them. There is also the danger that some pieces of shell may end up in the finished product. See Chapter 5 for quality grades of fresh eggs.

• *Fresh eggs in liquid form* may be purchased in cans. They may be purchased as liquid whole eggs or yolks and whites alone. A 14-kg [30-lb] can will hold about 300 whole eggs, 670 egg yolks, or 540 egg whites. Liquid eggs may also be bought in different proportions of yolks to whites. For instance, a mixture of two-thirds egg yolks to one-third egg

whites is used for sponge cakes. *Fortified eggs* are a mixture containing more egg yolks than egg whites.

Since liquid eggs are fresh eggs, they must always be kept under refrigeration and used promptly.

• *Frozen eggs* are often an economical way to insure quality eggs the year around because the eggs may be purchased and frozen when the price is low. Hence, frozen eggs are often cheaper than liquid whole eggs.

Like liquid eggs, frozen eggs may be purchased whole, yolks alone, or whites alone. They may also be purchased in combinations of yolks and whites in different proportions. See Table 16-2.

Frozen eggs must be kept frozen until ready to be thawed and used. Thaw by placing the can in a tank of cool, running water for five or six hours. Stir before using.

CAUTION

Government standards have not been set for frozen eggs. The baker must be particularly careful to buy only from a reputable dealer.

• *Dried eggs* are available whole, yolks only, or whites only. Dried whole eggs and yolks are usually

Table 16-2. Processed Eggs—Weight and Equivalent in Fresh Eggs

Type of Egg	Weight		Water Needed to Reconstitute		Fresh Eggs Needed
	Metric	Customary	Metric	Customary	
Liquid or frozen	13.6 kg	30 lb	0	0	300
Liquid whole eggs	450 g	1 lb	0	0	9–11
Liquid or frozen egg yolks	450 g	1 lb	0	0	22–24
Liquid or frozen egg whites	450 g	1 lb	0	0	15–17
Dried whole eggs	450 g	1 lb	625 mL	5 c	36
Dried yolks	450 g	1 lb	425 mL	$1\frac{3}{4}$ c	47
Dried whites	450 g	1 lb	2.5 L	10 c	100

sifted with the dry ingredients. Extra water is added to the liquid in the recipe. Egg whites are mixed with a specified amount of water and allowed to stand for a few minutes. When whipped, they increase in volume and become fluffy, like fresh eggs.

Dried eggs are *vacuum-packed*—that is, packed in a can without air. After opening the can, keep the eggs under refrigeration in a tightly covered container. Although popular at one time, dried eggs have been largely replaced by frozen or liquid eggs. These give a better flavor and higher leavening action.

Salt

Salt is needed in baked products and desserts to improve the flavor. To most people, food without salt is flat and uninteresting.

Salt is essential in producing a satisfactory yeast product. It regulates the activity of the yeast and strengthens the gluten structure. It gives a finer texture to bread and helps the crust develop a deeper color. Be sure to measure salt accurately. It has an important effect on the taste and structure of the product.

Flavorings and Spices

Many different ingredients are used to add flavor, aroma, and color to baked products. Spices and extracts were discussed in Chapter 6. Chocolate and cocoa are important because chocolate flavor is the most popular flavor for many baked products. Chocolate cake is the most popular of all cakes.

CHOCOLATE AND COCOA

Chocolate comes from the cacao bean, which is grown in Central and South America. Chocolate is about 58 percent fat. The fat is called *cocoa butter.* Cocoa is made from ground chocolate with at least half the fat removed. Both cocoa and chocolate are highly prized for their flavor, aroma, and deep brown color.

The chocolate color of cake may vary from light brown to a deep reddish brown, depending upon the leavener and liquid. Since chocolate is slightly acid, it will react with baking soda to help leaven the cake. Chocolate cakes made with baking soda

will have a deep red color because soda is alkaline. Baking powder is neutral—neither acid nor alkaline. Cakes leavened with it will be light brown.

Cocoa and chocolate should be stored in a cool, dry place.

Words to Remember

baker's scale	fermentation room
bench	proofer
bench knife	rounder
bread strap	sheeter
dough trough	staphylococcus

Tools and Equipment

TOOLS

• *Bench knife,* or *dough scraper.* Used to scrape dough from the table or to cut dough. Fig. 16-3.

• *Bun dividers.* Nickel-plated steel cutters mounted on a roller with a handle. Used for dividing dough into equal portions. Fig. 16-4.

• *Cutters.* Individual cutters used to shape biscuits, cookies, and doughnuts. More common in bakeries is a roller type with shapes mounted on it. The roller is passed over the rolled dough, cutting

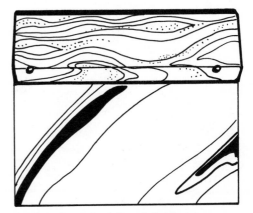

16-3. A bench knife.

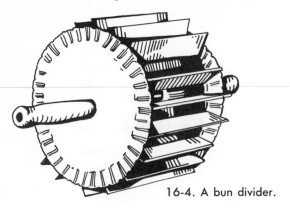

16-4. A bun divider.

the shapes. It is operated either singly or by two persons. Fig. 16-5.

• *Flour brush.* A soft brush for brushing loose flour from the table or rolled dough. Fig. 16-6.

• *Flour sifter.* Usually made of tin or aluminum. May have a side crank for agitating the flour. Most bakers use a flat pan with a sieve bottom that is agitated by hand. Used for sifting and mixing dry ingredients. Fig. 16-7.

• *Pastry brush.* A small brush with soft bristles used for spreading shortening or liquids on baked products. Fig. 16-8.

• *Rolling pin.* A hardwood roller with ball bearings for easier rolling. Used to flatten dough for rolls, biscuits, cookies, or pastry. Fig. 16-9.

• *Scraper.* Made of either plastic or rubber and used for scraping the last bit of dough or batter from the bowl. Fig. 16-10.

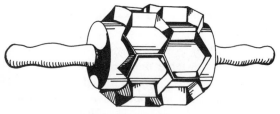

16-5. A biscuit cutter.

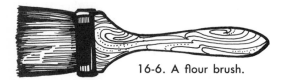

16-6. A flour brush.

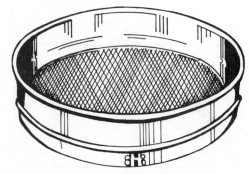

16-7. A flour sifter.

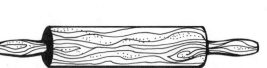

Sparta Brush Co.
16-8. A pastry brush.

16-9. A rolling pin.

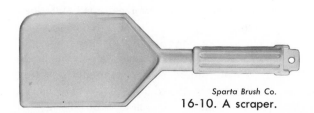

Sparta Brush Co.
16-10. A scraper.

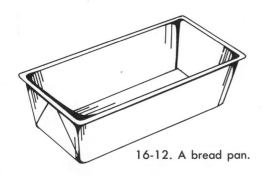

16-11. A baker's scale.

SMALL EQUIPMENT

• *Baker's scale.* A beam scale with twin platforms for weighing ingredients before mixing. Also used for weighing dough before shaping it for the pans. Fig. 16-11.

• *Bread pans.* Usually made of tin. Small bakeries use individual pans. Fig. 16-12. Larger bakeries use *bread straps.* Fig. 16-13. Bread straps are four or six pans strapped together for quantity baking.

• *Bun pan liners.* Silicone-treated paper cut to fit the pan. Eliminates greasing, sticking, scorching, and much pan washing.

• *Bun pans.* Made of aluminum or tin for baking rolls, biscuits, cookies, and other similar products. Fig. 16-14.

• *Cake pans.* Usually made of aluminum in different sizes and depths according to use. Fig. 16-15.

• *Muffin frames.* Made of tin or aluminum with twelve or twenty-four cups to the frame. Used for muffins and cupcakes. Fig. 16-16.

• *Pie pans.* Made of tin, aluminum, or heavy aluminum foil. May be purchased in different sizes or depths according to use. Fig. 16-15.

LARGE EQUIPMENT

• *Bench.* The baker's word for worktable. Used for kneading, rolling, cutting, and other similar processes.

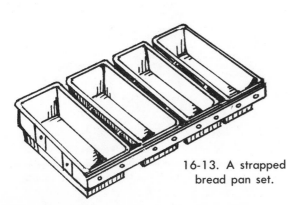

16-12. A bread pan.

16-13. A strapped bread pan set.

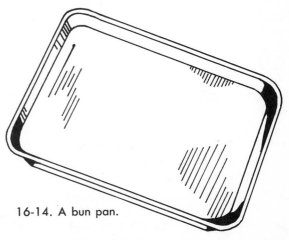

16-14. A bun pan.

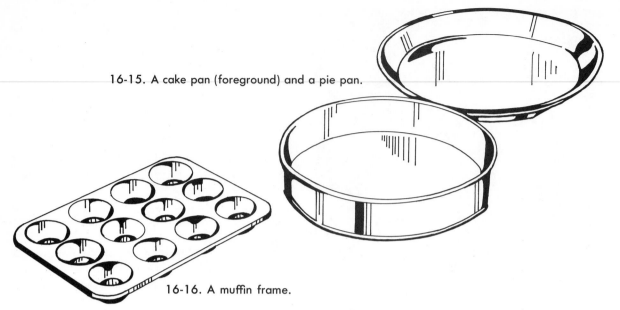

16-15. A cake pan (foreground) and a pie pan.

16-16. A muffin frame.

nates the need for rolling. It mechanically trims the dough and crimps the edges.

• *Proofer*. A cabinet with controlled warmth and high humidity for the final proofing of the dough. Fig. 16-18.

• *Cutter*. Cuts biscuits, rolls, cookies, or other similar products into desired shapes. Fig. 16-17.

• *Divider*. Mechanically cuts dough to desired sizes. Fig. 16-17.

• *Dough trough*. A large, deep, oblong stainless steel pan for the first rising of the dough. **Note:** The word *trough* is often pronounced *trow* by professional bakers.

• *Mixers*. Mixers may be the bench, floor, or horizontal types. These have been described in Chapter 2.

• *Ovens*. Although some bakeries use a conventional oven, the revolving tray, or carousel, oven is very popular. The trays revolve inside the oven like seats on a Ferris wheel. As each tray comes to the long, narrow oven door, the pans are placed on it. It then moves up and the next tray is filled. The trays revolve while the products are baked, thus assuring a constant, even temperature.

• *Pie presser*. A press with a low-temperature heater in the presser and a disk platform to hold the pie pan. The heated presser softens the dough and presses it into the shape of the pie pan. This elimi-

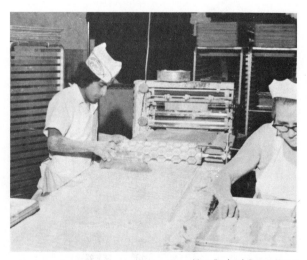

New England Oyster House

16-17. An automatic roller, cutter, and divider for rolls.

Cres-Cor

16-18. A movable proofing cabinet.

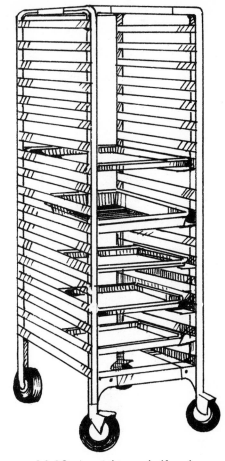

16-19. An eighteen-shelf rack.

• *Racks.* Hold pans of dough or finished products. Fig. 16-19.

• *Rounder, or molder.* Mechanically smooths and rounds divided pieces of dough.

• *Sheeter, or roller.* Rolls dough mechanically into sheets of desired thickness.

SANITATION IN BAKING

Products in a bakery are baked at a high heat, killing all very small organisms. Sanitation is, nevertheless, of great importance. Bakers have a constant fight against weevils, roaches, ants, mice, and rats. These pests relish the ingredients bakers use, especially the flour. In most cities, ordinances require bakeries to maintain a constant extermination program to keep such pests under control.

As discussed in Chapter 3, flour and sugar should be stored on shelves above the floor level for free circulation of air. Once these sacks have been opened, the ingredients should be stored in tightly covered containers. Any spilled sugar, flour, or other ingredients should be cleaned up immediately.

Spices attract small insects called weevils. Buy spices in small quantities so they are used up quickly. Keep tightly covered in a cool, dark place.

Since the bench is in constant use, it is scrubbed twice a week. Saturday afternoon or Sunday morning is usually cleanup time, since the baking is finished. Between cleanups, the bench is scraped with the dough scraper. Excess flour and dough particles are brushed off.

The dough troughs, mixer bowls, beaters, and other equipment are washed with a hot detergent solution. They are rinsed thoroughly. Invert on a rack to dry.

Danger lurks in the cream fillings used in pies, cream puffs, and eclairs. The *staphylococcus* bacteria, commonly called *staph* grow very fast in products made with eggs, milk, and sugar. As they grow, they develop a poisonous toxin that will make people very sick. All baked products containing cream fillings must be refrigerated until serving time.

How Much Have You Learned?

Review this chapter. Answer the following questions to prepare yourself for the post-test. Check your answers with the teacher.

1. What is gluten? Why is it important in baking?

2. Name the purposes of shortening in baking. Does shortening help or hinder gluten formation?

3. What makes yeast completely different from other kinds of leaveners? How does this affect the way yeast is handled?

4. Can a satisfactory cake be made without eggs? Why?

5. Is sweetness the only reason for adding sugar to baked products? Explain your answer.

6. What effect does salt have on bread?

7. Does the use of milk or water as the liquid affect the results in baking? Explain your answer, giving examples.

Baking with Yeast

What Will You Learn?

When you finish studying this chapter, you should be able to do the following:
- Define and use the *Words to Remember*.
- Prepare and bake a variety of yeast breads and rolls that meet acceptable standards of excellence.
- Prepare and bake a variety of sweet rolls and Danish pastries that meet acceptable standards of excellence.
- Achieve a passing grade on the posttest.

Many persons regard fresh, hot breads and rolls as a mark of quality in restaurants and other food service places. The aroma of freshly baked goods tempts the diner's appetite. Customer satisfaction builds repeat business for a restaurant that promotes freshly baked products.

High labor costs and lack of skilled workers have forced many places to use the services of outside bakeries. If the products are high quality and served hot and fresh, the effect will be the same as though they were baked on the premises.

Some food operations may purchase bread, but use a quality mix to prepare rolls. In many cases, rolls made from mixes are equal in quality to freshly made rolls. However, rolls made from mixes cost less to prepare.

Breads, rolls, sweet rolls, and Danish pastries use yeast as the leavener. However, they differ in ingredients and the proportion of ingredients. They differ especially in the methods of preparation.

All products made with yeast have a pleasant, distinctive aroma, flavor, and texture. These differ from those of products leavened by other means.

BREADS AND ROLLS

There are many different kinds of yeast breads and rolls. Types of bread range from plain white bread to dark pumpernickel. There are hard rolls and very soft ones.

CHAPTER 17

Words to Remember

conditioner

diastase

fermenting

kneading

lean formula

makeup

maltase

maltose

mixing

mold inhibitors

panning

proofing

punching

resting

rich formula

Some white breads, such as French and Italian types, are very crusty with a rather coarse texture. However, most Americans prefer the soft-crusted white bread for sandwiches and toast.

Types of Breads

Breads differ according to the flours used. Bread made from whole wheat is sometimes called graham bread. It may be known by a brand name of a particular company. Some people prefer whole wheat bread to white bread because it has higher fiber content. It is also more chewy and flavorful. Many so-called health breads are made from whole wheat flour in combination with wheat germ, nuts, and meals such as oatmeal.

Other popular breads are pumpernickel and rye. Both of these are made from a mixture of rye and wheat flours. Frequently, caraway seeds are added for extra flavor. Rye breads have a firm texture and distinctive flavor. These are much liked for ham, cheese, and other sandwiches. Such breads are usually oval or round. They are well-browned with deep slashes on top.

Crusty French, Italian, and Vienna breads are shaped in long, narrow loaves. They have deep slashes, like rye bread. They are frequently sprinkled with poppy or sesame seeds.

Rolls may be hard or soft. Hard rolls are made from a dough similar to that used for crusty breads. Sometimes they are called dinner rolls because they are often served at that meal. They should be lightly browned and very crusty. They should have a soft center and a nutty, fresh taste.

Soft rolls are moist, tender, and slightly sweet. Made in a variety of shapes, they are served hot for breakfast, lunch, and dinner.

Ingredients

Table 17-1 compares the ingredients in four baked yeast products. These products are bread, soft rolls, sweet rolls, and Danish pastry. As you can see, flour, sugar, shortening, salt, and yeast are the com-

Table 17-1. Comparison of Ingredients in Baked Yeast Products

Ingredient	Bread		Soft Rolls		Sweet Rolls		Danish Pastry	
	Metric	Customary	Metric	Customary	Metric	Customary	Metric	Customary
Flour	1.8 kg	4 lb	1.6 kg	$3\frac{1}{2}$ lb	1.6 kg	$3\frac{1}{2}$ lb	1.6 kg	$3\frac{1}{2}$ lb
Sugar	15 g	$\frac{1}{2}$ oz	110 g	4 oz	170 g	6 oz	170 g	6 oz
Salt	20 g	$\frac{3}{4}$ oz	30 g	1 oz	20 g	$\frac{3}{4}$ oz	20 g	$\frac{3}{4}$ oz
Milk (nonfat)	110 g	4 oz	110 g	4 oz	55 g	2 oz	55 g	2 oz
Yeast	35 g	$1\frac{1}{4}$ oz	30 g	1 oz	30 g	1 oz	30 g	1 oz
Water	1 L	1 qt	1 L	1 qt	625 mL	$2\frac{1}{2}$ c	625 mL	$2\frac{1}{2}$ c
Shortening	110 g	4 oz	100 g	$3\frac{1}{2}$ oz	150 g	$5\frac{1}{4}$ oz	300 g	$10\frac{1}{2}$ oz
Eggs			110 g	4 oz	225 g	8 oz	225 g	8 oz

mon ingredients. In these particular yeast products, water mixed with dried milk is the liquid. But some breads use water alone.

Doughs made with water and very little shortening are said to have a *lean formula*. Those made with eggs, sugar, shortening, and milk are said to have a *rich formula*.

FLOUR

A high-gluten flour is needed for crusty breads and rolls. Such a flour is made from first clears. A slightly less strong flour is used for soft white bread. Such a flour might be patent flour mixed with first clears. Soft rolls use an all-purpose flour. The amount of gluten is the key.

SUGAR

Sugar is needed because it is a quick food for yeast. Crusty breads require very little sugar, while soft rolls require more. Notice the different amounts of sugar listed in Table 17-1. Bread has only 15 g [½ oz] of sugar, while soft rolls have 110 g [4 oz]. This is because sugar helps tenderize the gluten and retains moisture. This makes a softer product.

SHORTENING

Compare the amounts of shortening for the four baked products shown in Table 17-1. The bread has very little, the soft rolls a little less. The amount of shortening increases for sweet rolls. Danish pastries use double the amount of shortening used for sweet rolls. Crusty rolls and breads may have no shortening at all. However, some bakers like to add a small amount to delay *staling*, or drying out.

CONDITIONERS

A *conditioner* is added to change the structure of the product. Bakers generally add two conditioners to yeast doughs—enzymes and mold inhibitors.

As mentioned earlier, enzymes are substances produced by plant and animal cells. They make definite physical changes when mixed with another substance. *Maltase* (MOL-taze) and *diastase* (DIE-uh-STAZE) are the enzymes most commonly used in bakeries. When added to flour mixtures they turn some of the starch into a sugar called *maltose* (MOL-toze). Maltose has the following effects:

- It provides a quick food for yeast.
- It helps the dough rise.
- It shortens the rising time.
- It gives a better color to the finished product.
- It helps the product stay fresh longer.

Mold inhibitors prevent the growth of mold and bacteria. Calcium propionate or sodium propionate are the ones most commonly used in baked products. Bread containing these inhibitors will not mold, prolonging the shelf life. Large bakeries generally use mold inhibitors. Smaller bakeries specializing in food service usually do not need them. Their products are used promptly.

Conditioners have other effects. They encourage greater volume, better color, and finer grain and texture. Their use reduces rising time and produces a dough that is easier to handle. However, if too much conditioner is used, the product may be so moist that it cannot be used for sandwiches or toast. Many persons do not like the very moist, soft bread produced by the overuse of conditioners. The bread may be soft, pasty, and even soggy.

Stages of Production

Bread and rolls are produced by a series of steps, each with a definite name. These steps are explained here.

1. *Mixing* distributes the ingredients evenly and develops the strength of the gluten.

2. *Kneading* is a mixing process by which the dough is folded, pressed, and squeezed. This strengthens the gluten strands.

3. *Fermenting* is the rising of the dough.

4. *Punching* means folding and pressing the dough after fermentation.

5. *Resting* allows the dough to relax, making it easier to handle.

6. *Makeup* is shaping and preparing the dough for baking.

7. *Panning* is placing the dough in the pans for baking.

8. *Proofing* is the final rising of the dough before baking.

9. *Baking* is applying the heat of the oven to the dough. This process kills the yeast and hardens the gluten and starch strands. It drives off some of the moisture as steam and browns the sides and top.

Words to Remember

bucky dough	sponge
dough trough	sponge method
retard	straight method
ripe dough	young dough
short-time method	

MEASURING

As in most quantity cooking, the needed ingredients are weighed on a scale—the baker's scale in this case. The baker's scale is described in Chapter 16. To use the baker's scale:

1. Place the container for the ingredients on the platform to the left. The container may be a scoop, a pitcher, a bowl, or only a piece of waxed paper. The container will depend upon what you are measuring. Fig. 17-1.

2. Place the weights on the right side platform so that the scale balances.

17-1. Weighing milk on the baker's scale.

3. Move the weight on the beam to the desired grams (or ounces) you wish to weigh. The beam is graduated in grams or ounces, depending on the measurement system you are using. Most bakers still use the English, or customary, method. Scales graduated in this system weigh quantities up to ten pounds. As conversion to the metric system proceeds, these older scales will be replaced with the newer metric models.

4. Add ingredients to the container on the left until the scale balances.

MIXING

Because yeast is alive, certain precautions must be followed when working with it. Remember, absolute cleanliness is essential in all cooking procedures. Stray yeasts are sometimes called *wild yeasts.* These yeasts—and some bacteria—may ruin a batch of dough. Clean hands, hair confined in a net or cap, clean clothes, and sanitized equipment will help reduce the danger of contamination.

It is also essential to control temperature during mixing. Yeast grows fast between 28–32°C [82–90° F.]. It will die at temperatures over 60°C [140° F.]. Its growth is *retarded,* or slowed down, at temperatures below 15°C [60° F.]. Its growth is greatly retarded at temperatures normally found in refrigerators. The lower the temperature, the more the growth is retarded. Dough retarded in the refrigerator may be kept for several days. Dough may also be frozen and kept for several months without loss of quality.

Yeast breads and rolls may be produced by three methods of mixing. These methods are the straight, sponge, and short-time. These methods are similar—but there are also important differences.

Table 17-2 compares the three different methods of mixing. The *straight method* is used most often in food service. It is quick and produces an excellent product.

The *sponge method* is used in large commercial bakeries because the *sponge* can be set at night. A sponge is a thin mixture of yeast, liquid, and flour. It will be ready for the addition of the rest of the ingredients in the morning. It uses less yeast because the yeast can grow and develop over two fermenta-

Table 17-2. Comparison of Mixing Methods for Yeast Doughs

Straight Method	Sponge Method	Short-time Method
1. Place flour, sugar, salt, dry yeast, and nonfat milk solids in mixer. Mix thoroughly on low speed. 2. Add water mixed with melted shortening. Mix on low speed until combined. 3. Increase speed to medium and knead for 7 minutes. 4. Place in dough trough and allow to ferment until double in bulk—about 3 hours.	1. Mix the dry yeast with half the flour. Add the water and mix on low speed until well-blended. 2. Pour into the dough trough and allow to ferment until it collapses. 3. Return to mixer and add the sugar, salt, melted shortening, and dry milk solids. 4. Mix until well blended. 5. Add the rest of the flour and mix on low speed until combined. Increase the speed to medium and knead for 7 minutes. 6. Place in the dough trough and allow to ferment about $1\frac{1}{2}$ hours.	1. Place flour, sugar, salt, dry yeast, and nonfat milk solids in mixer. Mix thoroughly on low speed. 2. Add water mixed with melted shortening. Mix on low speed until combined. 3. Increase to medium speed and knead for 4 minutes. 4. Turn out on bench and shape as desired. 5. If desired, dough may be given a short preliminary fermentation before shaping.

tion periods. Sponges are adaptable to different situations because they may be held without loss of quality. However, the sponge method takes longer. It also requires two handlings, which increases labor costs.

The *short-time method* is used for soft dinner rolls. It is also used for small loaves of bread where a very soft, tender crust is desired. The finished product will have an open texture with a coarse grain. In this method, the dough is shaped before it is fully fermented. Bakers say the dough is "taken to the bench young." *Young dough* is dough that is shaped before it has doubled in bulk. After shaping, the proofing time is very short because of extra yeast and conditioners. The short fermentation and proofing times give this method its name.

Mixing and kneading may be done by hand. They can also be done automatically by using the bench,

floor, or horizontal mixers. The time needed for mixing and kneading will vary with the type of mixer and the strength of the flour. Generally, the dough is mixed until it clears the sides of the bowl. Dough is sufficiently kneaded when it springs back against the pressure of the hand, and the indentations slowly disappear.

During mixing, friction causes the temperature of the dough to rise. The longer the mixing time, the higher the temperature will rise. It is sometimes necessary to add ice water or chipped ice to keep the temperature within the desired limits. The ideal temperature during mixing is 22°C [72° F.].

Temperatures over 26°C [78° F.] cause over-fermentation, making the dough sticky and hard to handle. Bakers call such dough *bucky dough*. Bucky dough can also result from using green flour or flour that has not been bromated. (See pages 307–310.)

After mixing and kneading, the dough is placed in the dough trough or in bowls, lightly greased to prevent sticking. These are placed in the fermentation room. Humidity in the fermentation room is so high that it is usually unnecessary to cover the dough to prevent a crust from forming.

FERMENTATION

During the fermentation period, the yeast changes part of the starch into sugar. Enzymes and conditioners in the flour aid the yeast in this process. As the yeast feeds upon the sugar, it makes a gas, carbon dioxide. Control of the temperature and humidity is critical at this point. For best results, the temperature must be kept within the same limits as during the mixing. A humidity of 75 percent is best to keep a crust from forming on the dough.

Timing is also important. The gluten must have sufficient time to absorb the maximum amount of water. This is necessary if the dough is to be pliable and elastic, but not sticky. Dough that has fermented sufficiently is said to be fully ripe. Ripe dough has doubled in bulk. It gives way easily when the finger is inserted into the dough.

Dough that has been allowed to ferment too long will develop a sour taste. As fermentation proceeds, the yeast converts the sugar to alcohol and eventually to vinegar.

PUNCHING DOWN

Although the term *punch* is generally used, it is not really descriptive of the process. The dough is not punched. Rather, it is folded from the sides to the middle, driving out the gas. Punching helps the gluten relax and remixes the yeast with the starch so it can grow again. Punching may be omitted if the flour is weak or the dough is brought to the bench young.

RESTING

After punching, the dough is turned out on the bench to rest for ten to fifteen minutes. During this time, some fermentation takes place again. The gluten strands relax, and the dough becomes easier to shape.

Words to Remember

bloom	proofing cabinet
docking	panning
hearth	rounding
hearth breads	scaling
oven spring	shaping
proofing	

MAKEUP

The process of *makeup* includes *scaling, rounding, shaping, and panning.*

1. *Scaling.* The dough is divided into sections. These sections must be *scaled*, or weighed, to ensure that each section is the same size. To make a 454-g [1-lb] loaf of bread, the dough should weigh 510 g [1¼ lb]. The weight loss due to evaporation during baking is about 12 percent. The same amount of dough will make twelve dinner rolls or eighteen soft rolls.

2. *Rounding.* After scaling, each section is patted, pushed, and smoothed with the hands. It is formed into a round mound with a smooth top. The dough then rests ten minutes to prepare it for shaping.

3. *Shaping.* Figure 17-2 shows the steps in shaping a loaf of bread. Be careful to shape the loaf smoothly and evenly. Any irregularities will be twice as big after baking.

To shape hard rolls, divide the section into twelve equal pieces. Roll each one with the palms of the hands until smooth and round. Use both hands. Some hard rolls may be twisted for greater interest. The tops of the rolls may be dipped in egg mixed with water and poppy or sesame seeds.

Soft rolls are fun to shape. Each section is divided into eighteen pieces of equal size. Study Figs. 17-3 to 17-6 (Pages 330–333) to learn how to shape rolls in many interesting ways. A variety of shapes makes an intriguing service of rolls to the customer.

4. *Panning.* Panning is the process of placing the shaped dough in the pans for proofing and baking. Pans must be treated to prevent sticking. Some bakers prefer a salt-free shortening. Others mix oil and flour to grease the pans. The flour combines with

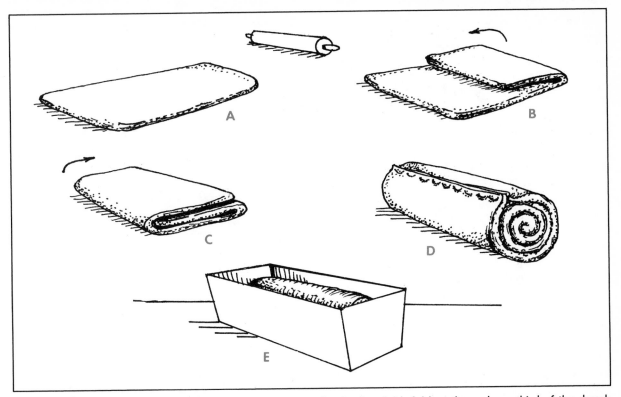

17-2. Shaping a loaf of bread. (A) Roll the dough. (B) Make the first fold, folding the end one-third of the dough over the middle one-third. (C) Make the second fold as shown. (D) Roll the dough tightly. (E) Pan the dough.

the oil during baking so the dough cannot touch the pan and stick. A few bakers may use a commercial spray derived from vegetable oil and containing a preservative.

Many bakers line bun pans with a silicone-treated paper, instead of using shortening. Using paper is a timesaver. The pans do not need to be greased before baking or washed when the baking is completed. The paper is expensive, but may be used many times.

Cornmeal is spread on the bake pans for hard rolls and crusty breads. As the dough rises, the cornmeal sticks to the bottoms of the loaves. The loaves are removed from the pan and slid onto the floor of the oven for baking. The cornmeal prevents the

bread from sticking. Bakers call the floor of the oven the *hearth*. Breads and rolls baked on the hearth are sometimes called *hearth breads*.

Hard rolls and crusty breads are *docked*. In docking, long slashes are cut across the width of the bread. These permit the steam to escape without breaking the crust.

PROOFING

Proofing is the final rising of the dough before baking. It requires warmer temperatures than the first fermentation period. Proofing is done in a *proofing cabinet*. Here, the temperature is maintained at about 38°C [100° F.]. The humidity is also very high—about 80 to 85 percent. To keep the

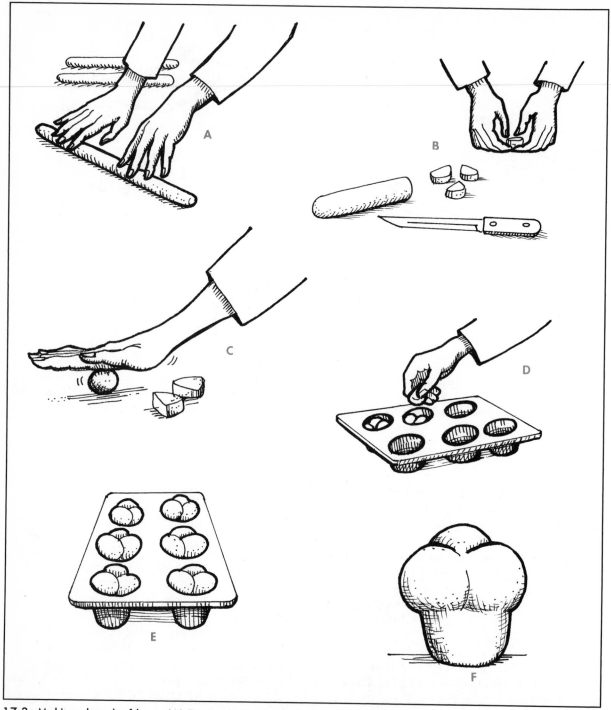

17-3. Making cloverleaf buns. (A) Form a long rounded strip. (B) Cut the strip into even chunks. (C) Round each chunk. (D) Place three rounds in each greased muffin cup. (E) Let rise, then bake. (F) Finished cloverleaf bun.

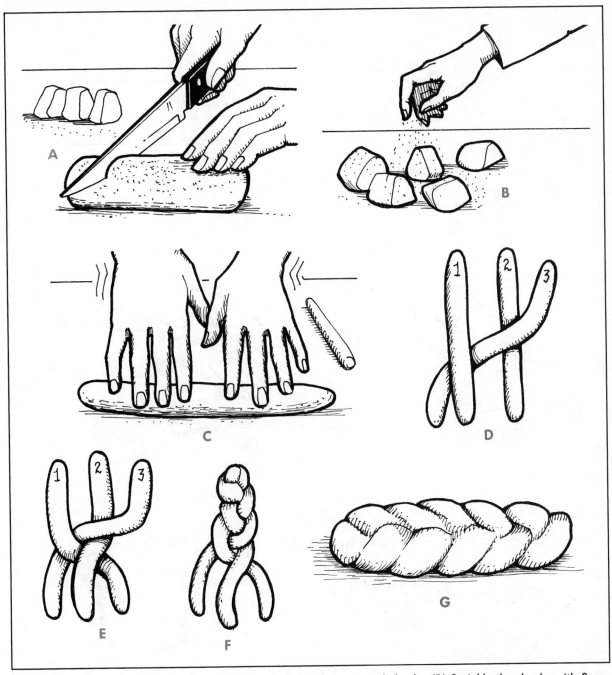

17-4. The braiding process. (A) Cut a thick round of dough into equal chunks. (B) Sprinkle the chunks with flour. (C) Roll each chunk into a long thin round. (D) Line up three rounded strips. Place strip number 3 over strip number 2 and under strip number 1. (E) Place strip number 1 under strip number 2. Continue alternating outside strips. Place strip number 3 over strip number 2 and under strip number 1. Continue in this fashion. (F) Seal each end of the braid. (G) The finished braid, with ends sealed.

17-5. Making butterflake fans. (A) Roll a square of dough spread with melted butter. (B) Slice into strips about 4 cm [1½ in] wide. (C) Divide strips into stacks of five or six. (D) Cut rolls about 4 cm [1½ in] wide. (E) Place in oiled muffin pans, cut side up. Let rise. (F) A baked butterflake fan.

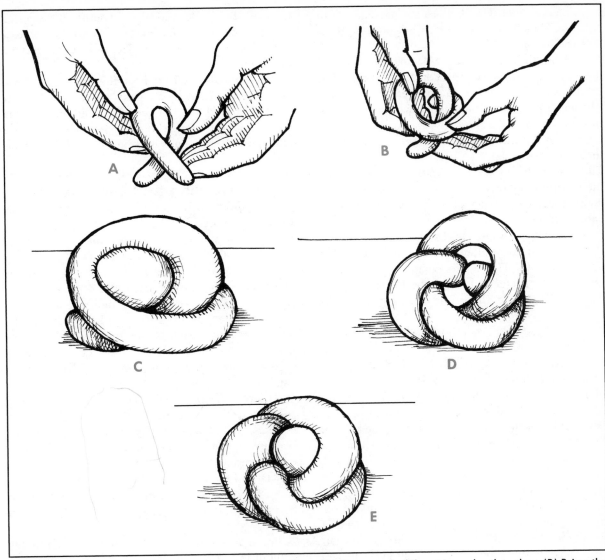

17-6. Making knots. (A) Form round strips as for braiding. Bend one end of the strip under the other. (B) Bring the top strip under and through the hole. (C) A single knot. (D) For a double knot, bring the other end over and through the hole. (E) A completed double knot.

high humidity, pans of water are heated slowly at the bottom of the proofing cabinet. Thus, water vapor circulates constantly as the dough proofs. The warmth and high humidity cause the dough to rise quickly, extending and softening the gluten strands. The outer surface remains smooth and soft. Proofing time is short, usually from fifteen to forty-five minutes. When the dough has doubled in size, it is ready for the oven.

BAKING

The dough, as it comes from the proofing cabinet, is very fragile. The slightest jar may cause it to collapse. Handle the pans gently as you slide them into the oven.

Preheat the oven before placing the pans of dough in it. Conventional and deck ovens should be preheated slightly above the desired temperature. The pans of unbaked dough will lower the temperature to the desired heat.

Preheat the carousel oven to the exact temperature. (The carousel oven is described in Chapter 16.) The pans of bread are constantly being loaded on the revolving shelves. The amount of unbaked dough placed in the oven at any one time is never enough to lower the temperature.

Some bakers prefer to bake bread at 218°C [425° F.] for fifteen minutes. They then reduce the heat to 190°C [375° F.] to complete the baking. Other bakers prefer to bake at the lower temperature for the whole time. The baking time is the same.

It is impractical to reduce the temperature in the carousel oven because of its large size and efficient insulation. The bread would be baked before the temperature dropped 10°C [50° F.]. Use the lower temperature for these large ovens.

The carousel oven has a very moist heat because of jets of water that turn to steam during the baking. Moist heat causes a product that is very soft on the inside with a thick, crisp crust.

During the first fifteen minutes of baking, the yeast grows quickly. The heat of the oven causes the carbon dioxide to expand suddenly. The sudden rising is called *oven spring*. It is one of the signs of a quality loaf of bread. The gluten and starch coagulate, making the product firm. The sugar in the dough causes the crust to brown and the bloom to develop. The *bloom* is the sheen or glossy look on the top of the product. It is another sign of quality.

Loaves weighing 510 g [1½ lb] will bake in about thirty-five minutes at 190°C [375° F.]. As mentioned, this will yield a 454-g [1-lb] loaf. Larger loaves will take a little longer.

Rolls, being smaller, are baked at 190°C [375° F.] for the entire time—about fifteen to thirty minutes. The actual time depends upon the size of the rolls. It also depends upon whether the sides of the rolls are touching. Sweet rolls are baked at a slightly lower temperature. The rich dough browns more quickly.

Most breads are baked for the full time. However, hard-crusted breads may be removed when partially baked, but not browned. The browning is completed just before serving to give a fresh-baked aroma and flavor. Rolls may be treated in the same manner.

Cooling and Storing

Yeast products are at their peak flavor and aroma immediately after baking. Proper storage is important because staling begins very soon after cooling.

When baked products are removed from the oven, they are placed on racks to cool. Loaves are taken from the baking pans at once to prevent *steaming*. As the pan cools, the moisture in the hot bread will condense. A soggy loaf may result. Smaller products, such as rolls, may be cooled in the pans. The products should be protected from cool air drafts during the cooling period. Such drafts may cause the bread and rolls to crack.

To prevent most breads and rolls from becoming stale, wrap them in moisture-proof wrappings after cooling. Do not wrap hard-crusted breads and rolls because it would soften the crust. Place them in open boxes and serve as soon as possible after baking. Hard breads and rolls stale very rapidly.

Store breads and rolls in a cool place. Refrigeration is not necessary unless the climate is hot and humid.

Bread and rolls may be frozen for a few months without loss of quality. They should be wrapped to prevent loss of moisture. Freeze them quickly and store at temperatures below −18°C [0° F.].

Words to Remember

creaming	steaming
Danish pastries	streusel
roll-in	three-fold
smear	wash

SWEET ROLLS, DOUGHNUTS, AND DANISH PASTRIES

Among the most popular breakfast items are warm, delicious cinnamon rolls, sticky buns, and Danish pastries. Fig. 17-7. Rolls made from very rich dough with a flaky texture are called *Danish pastries*. Many food service places have built their reputations on the service of these delightful baked products. Doughnuts are also well liked for breakfast and as a snack for coffee breaks.

Small products are called rolls or buns. Among these are nut and cinnamon rolls and raisin buns. Small products fried in deep fat are called raised doughnuts. Larger products baked in pans or shaped into rings are known as coffee cakes or kuchen.

Ingredients

Many sweet, baked goods may be made from the same basic recipe. Changing the shape, filling, flavoring, or topping creates an endless variety. The basic recipe for sweet dough is on page 341.

Sweet rolls, doughnuts, and Danish pastries are made from a rich formula dough. This dough has a high proportion of sugar, shortening, and eggs to the amount of flour. Refer to Table 17-1. Note that the basic ingredients of all yeast doughs are similar. However, the ingredient proportions and mixing methods are different. These differences make sweet

rolls, doughnuts, and Danish pastries sweeter, more tender, and less chewy.

FLOUR

An all-purpose flour or a mixture of bread and cake flours is used for sweet dough to reduce the amount of gluten. This results in a softer, less chewy product. Only the very best grade of flour should be used for sweet doughs. With sweet doughs, especially, flavor, color, and texture are important to the product's success.

SHORTENING

The shortening also must be of the highest quality. It must have a good flavor, since the taste of the product depends greatly on the flavor of the shortening. A quality hydrogenated shortening made for use in sweet rolls is often used. However, many bakers prefer a fine margarine for its flavor.

For Danish pastries, a special roll-in shortening is used. It is yellow to add richness to the appearance of the pastries. It will not become oily under the repeated roll-ins necessary for fine Danish pastries.

Refer again to Table 17-1, comparing the ingredients in different yeast products. Perhaps you noticed that Danish pastries have much more shortening than the sweet rolls. About half of the shortening is mixed with the dough. The other half is used for the *roll-in*, a process that makes Danish pastries flaky, instead of light and puffy. The recipe for Danish pastries on page 344 uses the sweet dough recipe as a base.

EGGS

Fortified eggs are usually used in sweet rolls to give added richness and color. As defined in Chapter 16, liquid or frozen eggs with extra egg yolks are called fortified eggs. The extra yolks give a tender, fine product.

SUGAR

Granulated sugar is used in the body of the dough, but powdered sugar is needed for the icing. Some recipes, however, call for a syrup such as honey. For instance, honey buns are made from a

17-7. Sweet rolls, strudel, and Danish pastries.

sweet dough with honey as the sweetener. The honey gives the buns an unusual flavor and a close-grained texture.

OTHER INGREDIENTS

• Nuts, particularly pecans, make delicious sweet rolls. Sticky, sweet pecan rolls are always popular.

• Many spices and flavorings are used, depending on the product desired. Cinnamon, nutmeg, vanilla, almond, lemon, and orange are just a few of the more usual ones.

Rich doughs cost much more than lean ones. Less rich doughs also give a larger number of servings. Therefore, each food service place must decide on how expensive a product it can afford to serve to its customers.

Methods of Mixing

Ingredients for sweet doughs must be thoroughly mixed without excess development of the gluten. Therefore, a different method of mixing is used for sweet dough than for breadmaking.

Following is the method for mixing sweet doughs.

1. Measure the shortening, sugar, salt, and flavorings. Place in the mixer bowl.

2. Cream on low speed, using the flat beater, until thoroughly mixed. *Creaming* means to beat together until fluffy. The term is usually applied to mixing sugar and shortening.

3. Add the dry milk solids. Cream again.

4. Add the eggs one at a time and beat on medium speed.

5. On low speed, gradually add about one-quarter of the flour. Mix the dough thoroughly until the flour disappears.

6. Add the water and mix until it disappears.

7. Sift the dried yeast with the rest of the flour. Add to the first mixture.

8. Using the dough hook, mix on slow speed until the flour disappears. Knead for three minutes on medium speed.

Take care not to overknead or the temperature will rise. Temperature control is critical in making sweet dough because of the low gluten content. If

the dough is over-mixed it may become tacky and difficult to handle.

At this point, the dough that is to be made into rolls or coffee cakes is separated from that to be used for Danish pastries. This is because they are handled differently during fermentation and makeup.

Sweet Rolls and Coffee Cakes
FERMENTATION

Because sweet dough has higher amounts of sugar, it requires less fermentation than bread dough. It is not allowed to double in size. The baker takes it to the bench young, when about three-fourths fermented. Such fermentation usually takes about one and one-half to two hours. Underfermented dough will give a better-tasting product with a finer texture. The recipe for sweet rolls on page 342 describes the method of handling sweet dough.

If sweet dough is to be retarded before makeup, it should be given only one-half to two-thirds fermentation. After the dough is placed in the refrigerator, it will still expand enough for makeup. Retarding the dough permits the baker to delay the makeup of the rolls. Thus, they can be served fresh-baked to the customers.

After fermentation, punch down the dough. Allow it to rest for at least fifteen minutes. Resting allows the gluten to relax. This makes it easier to roll and shape the dough.

MAKEUP

Figure 17-8 shows some of the many ways to shape sweet rolls for greater interest. Sweet rolls may also be varied by using different fillings or toppings. One filling that is always popular is a mixture of cinnamon and sugar. Others contain nuts, dates, or raisins. Many commercial fillings are excellent and save much time in makeup.

To shape for filled rolls, divide the dough and scale into 285-g [10-oz] sections. Round each section and roll out, using the rolling pin. The dough should be about 3 mm [$\frac{1}{8}$ in] thick.

Wash the rolled dough with water or a mixture of egg white and water. To *wash* means to spread the

17-8. Making cinnamon buns. (A) Roll a square of dough. Sprinkle with cinnamon and sugar. (B) Wash with water or a mixture of egg and water. (C) Slice the rolled dough. The slices should have a thickness of approximately 1.5 cm [½ in]. (D) Place in pan. Spread with melted butter and let rise. (E) Bake. Ice after baking.

liquid (the wash) thinly and evenly over the dough with a pastry brush. The wash binds the filling to the dough so it will not fall out when the dough is cut.

Roll up the dough as shown in Fig. 17-8. Cut into rolls with the dough scraper.

To make sticky pecan buns, prepare a *smear*. A smear is a sweet, thick mixture spread on the bottom of a pan before the dough is panned. A caramel smear contains brown sugar, liquid shortening, salt, corn syrup, and milk. Spoon the smear into the bottom of the greased cups in the muffin frames. Place a few pecans on the smear and top with a roll. Other smears may be used for variety, such as orange or maple.

Sweet dough is also used to make coffee cakes or kuchen. The dough is filled and rolled up as for rolls, but it is formed into a ring.

Dutch apple cake is made with a sweet dough base. A circle of sweet dough is pressed against the bottom and the sides of a cake pan. The dough is pricked to allow the steam to escape. Apple slices, sugar, and cinnamon are the topping for this popular coffee cake. Cherries, peaches, blueberries, or pineapple may be used instead of apples.

Sweet rolls and coffee cakes may have other toppings. *Streusel* (SHTROY-zul) topping, sweet and crumbly, is well liked. It is made of sugar, margarine, syrup, fortified eggs, and cake flour.

PROOFING

After makeup, proof until doubled in bulk. Rolls or coffee cakes without toppings should be spread with an egg wash before proofing. An egg wash gives them a glossy appearance after baking.

The proofing temperature should be 35–37°C [96–98° F.]. The humidity should be 80 percent to 85 percent.

If desired, sweet rolls and coffee cakes may be retarded before proofing. They will rise slowly while being retarded. They will require only a very short proofing before being ready for the oven. This is often done in food service places to ensure peak freshness when served.

Doughnuts

Doughnuts may be made from a sweet, yeast dough. Bring the dough to the bench young and roll about 1.3 cm [½ in] thick. Cut the doughnuts by

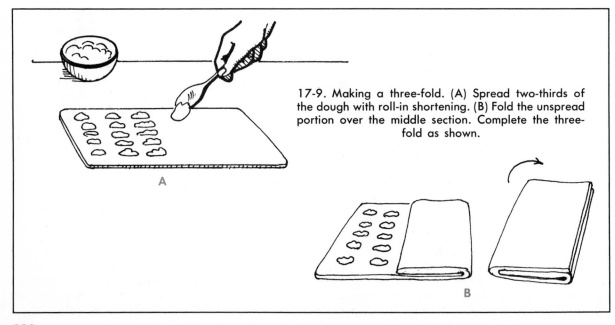

17-9. Making a three-fold. (A) Spread two-thirds of the dough with roll-in shortening. (B) Fold the unspread portion over the middle section. Complete the three-fold as shown.

hand so that each one weighs about 28–43 g [1–1½ oz].

For yeast doughnuts, the proofing time is very short–about ten to twenty minutes. The hole is gently pressed with the thumb and forefinger just before frying. The hot fat causes the doughnuts to rise instantly and brown very quickly. This makes a long proofing time unnecessary.

Review the section on deep-fat frying in Chapter 9. Yeast doughnuts are fried at 180°C [360° F.] for two minutes to two and one-half minutes.

After frying, yeast doughnuts are dipped in fine granulated sugar or a mixture of cinnamon and sugar. Sometimes they are glazed with a sugar syrup.

Danish Pastries

In making Danish pastries, it is very important to stop the mixing as soon as the ingredients are thoroughly blended. Do not knead because the gluten should not be developed. Too much mixing would also cause a temperature rise. Further mixing will take place during the roll-in. The dough should be at 18°C [65° F.] when taken from the mixer. The recipe on page 344 describes the method of handling sweet dough to make Danish pastries.

ROLL-IN PROCESS

The roll-in process consists of spreading shortening on the rolled dough. The dough is then folded so the shortening is in layers. This is done several times at intervals. It makes a very flaky yeast pastry.

After mixing, retard the dough for ten to thirty minutes to make it easier to handle during roll-in. The length of time for retarding depends upon the temperature of the dough when it comes from the mixer.

Bring the dough from the retarder or refrigerator and place on the bench. Roll with a rolling pin into an oblong about 1.3 cm [½ in] thick. To make a *three-fold*, spread two-thirds of the dough with the special roll-in shortening. Fold the unspread portion over the middle section. Fold the leftover section over the two folded sections. Fig. 17-9. You will now have three layers of dough and two layers of shortening. Retard for twenty to thirty minutes. Return

the dough to the bench. Repeat the roll-in process, making a three-fold without adding any more shortening. Retard before makeup for about thirty minutes.

MAKEUP

After the final roll-in, cut the dough into sections weighing about 285 g [10 oz]. Roll each section about 0.3 cm [⅛ in] thick by 20 cm [8 in] long.

Wash the dough with water or an egg white and water mixture. Spread with the filling, usually a ready-made almond or fruit paste.

Roll up the dough and cut into rolls with the dough cutter. Each roll should be about 2.5 cm [1 in] wide and weigh about 43–57 g [1½–2 oz] each. Place the rolls in a bun pan lined with silicone paper. Brush with an egg wash to encourage a golden brown crust. Proof at the same temperature and humidity as sweet rolls.

Snail-shaped Danish pastries are very attractive. Sometimes a cream filling or a spoonful of fruit jam is placed in the center of the roll. Follow the directions for shaping in Fig. 17-10.

Danish dough may be retarded after makeup until the time for baking. Danish pastries are best when served hot from the oven.

Baking

Sweet rolls, coffee cakes, and Danish pastries are baked at 190°C [375° F] until golden brown—about twenty to thirty minutes. Immediately after baking, almost all sweet products are glazed with a sugar and water syrup. The glaze improves the appearance and the keeping qualities of the products.

After the products have cooled, they may be iced. A mixture of powdered sugar, shortening, salt, and hot water is used.

Storage and Care of Baked Sweet Products

It may be necessary to hold sweet rolls, coffee cakes, and Danish pastries for serving. They should then be wrapped in moisture-proof wrappings and kept refrigerated. However, storage always brings some deterioration of quality. Baked products should be served as soon after baking as possible.

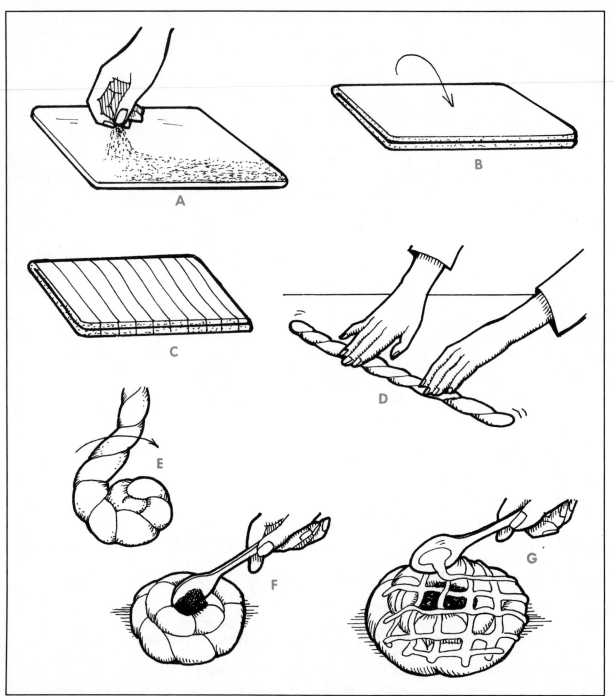

17-10. Making snail-shaped Danish pastry. (A) Roll an oblong of dough. Sprinkle with flour. (B) Fold over. (C) Slice into long strips. (D) Twist each strip. (E) Roll each strip into a snail shape. (F) Place jelly or jam in the center. (G) After baking, crisscross with icing.

Review the chapter. Answer the following questions to prepare yourself for the post-test. Check your answers with your teacher.

1. Define the *Words to Remember.*

2. What is the difference between a French bread and a regular loaf of white bread? Discuss the differences in ingredients, methods of preparation, and storage.

3. Why is a strong flour used in making bread?

4. What kind of flour is used to make sweet rolls, coffee cakes, doughnuts, and Danish pastries?

5. What is a conditioner? Name two conditioners used in baking and explain what they do.

6. Name the nine processes involved in making breads and rolls. Describe the purpose of each.

7. Name the three processes of mixing yeast dough and distinguish among them.

8. How does the process of mixing sweet rolls differ from that of mixing bread? Explain why they are mixed differently.

9. What process makes Danish pastries different than sweet rolls? Describe the process.

SWEET DOUGH FOR COFFEE CAKE, SWEET ROLLS, AND DANISH PASTRIES

Equipment
Bench mixer
Paddle attachment
Bowl
Scraper

Yield: 5.4 kg [12 lb]

Metric	Ingredients	Customary
1.8 kg	All-purpose flour	4 lb
900 g	Pastry flour	2 lb
450 g	Sugar	1 lb
450 g	Margarine	1 lb
110 g	Nonfat dry milk	4 oz
7 g	Nutmeg	$\frac{1}{4}$ oz
14 g	Butter flavoring	$\frac{1}{2}$ oz
7 g	Lemon flavoring	$\frac{1}{4}$ oz
28 g	Salt	1 oz
340 g	Dry yeast	12 oz
1 L	Water	1 qt
450 g	Liquid, whole eggs	1 lb
7 g	Yellow coloring	$\frac{1}{4}$ oz

(Method found on following page)

SWEET DOUGH FOR COFFEE CAKE, SWEET ROLLS, AND DANISH PASTRIES (Continued)

METHOD

1. **Combine** flours, sugar, margarine, dry milk, nutmeg, and salt in mixer bowl. Mix on low speed for 2 minutes.
2. **Dissolve** yeast in water in bowl.
3. **Add** yeast, flavorings, eggs, and coloring to mixture.
4. **Combine** on medium speed for 3 minutes.
5. **Complete** according to directions for specific product.

SWEET ROLLS

Equipment
Rolling pin
Baking pans

Yield: 48 sweet rolls
Temperature: 190°C [375° F.]
Time: 15–20 minutes

Metric	Ingredients	Customary
2.3 kg	Sweet dough	5 lb

METHOD

1. **Place** dough in bowl. Give dough three-fourths rise.
2. **Punch** and let rest.
3. **Scale** dough 28–56 g [1–2 oz] for each piece.
4. **Makeup, proof,** and **bake.**

Sweet Roll Varieties

Cinnamon Rolls
1. **Roll** dough into rectangle 1 cm [$\frac{3}{8}$ in] thick.
2. **Spread** with softened margarine.
3. **Sprinkle** with cinnamon and sugar.
4. **Roll** as for a jelly roll.
5. **Cut** 2.5-cm [1-in] slices.
6. **Place** cut side down on greased baking sheet. Allow 1.2 cm [$\frac{1}{2}$ in] between slices.
7. **Let rise** until doubled in size (about 45 minutes).
8. **Bake.**

Orange Rolls
1. **Roll** dough into rectangle 1 cm [$\frac{3}{8}$ in] thick.

2. **Spread** with softened margarine.
3. **Sprinkle** with sugar and grated orange rind.
4. **Roll up** like a jelly roll.
5. **Cut slices** 2.5 cm [1 in] thick.
6. **Place** cut side down on greased baking sheet. Allow 1.2 cm [$\frac{1}{2}$ in] between slices.
7. **Let rise** until doubled in size.
8. **Bake.**
9. **Glaze** immediately after baking with orange-flavored syrup.

CINNAMON KNOTS (SHORT-TIME METHOD)

Equipment
Mixer and bowl
Baker's scale
Rolling pin
Muffin pans

Yield: 396, depending upon size
Temperature: 190°C [375° F.]
Time: 15–25 minutes

Metric	Ingredients	Customary
4 L	Water	4 qt
450 g	Yeast	1 lb
900 g	Liquid eggs	2 lb
5 mL	Yellow coloring	1 t
30 mL	Vanilla	2 T
5.4 kg	Bread flour	12 lb
1.8 kg	Pastry flour	4 lb
110 g	Baking powder	4 oz
680 g	Sugar	1½ lb
1.4 kg	Shortening	3 lb
450 g	Nonfat milk	1 lb
110 g	Salt	4 oz

METHOD

1. **Warm** water to 27°C [80° F.]. Mix with yeast.
2. **Add** rest of ingredients to yeast in mixer bowl. Mix on medium speed for 1 to 1½ minutes.
3. **Scale** into 450-g [1-lb] pieces.
4. **Divide** each piece into 12 equal pieces, each 35 g [1¼ oz].
5. **Roll** each piece into strips about 10 cm [4 in] long.
6. **Dip** each roll into melted butter. Roll in cinnamon crunch topping. Tie in single knot.
7. **Place** in well-greased muffin pans.
8. **Let rise** until doubled in size.
9. **Bake.**

CINNAMON CRUNCH TOPPING

Metric	Ingredients	Customary
4.5 kg	Granulated sugar	10 lb
3.2 kg	Cake crumbs, sifted	7 lb
450 g	Cinnamon	1 lb
680 g	Margarine, melted	1½ lb

METHOD

1. **Mix** thoroughly.
2. **Store** in tightly sealed container in refrigerator.

DANISH PASTRIES

Equipment
Spreader
Rolling pin
Flat cookie sheet
Baking pan
Pastry brush

Yield: 48 rolls, 50 g [1¾ oz] each
Temperature: 190°C [375° F.]
Time: 15–20 minutes

Metric	**Ingredients**	**Customary**
2.3 kg	Sweet dough	5 lb
450 g	Special shortening or margarine	1 lb

METHOD

1. **Roll out** dough.
2. **Spread** with shortening.
3. **Make** three-fold and retard for 30 minutes.
4. **Make** three-fold two more times retarding 30 minutes between rolls.

5. **Retard** overnight.
6. **Make-up, proof,** and **bake.**
7. **Spread** pastries with light sugar syrup, using the pastry brush, 5 minutes before the end of the baking time.

To make snails or butterhorns

1. **Roll** dough in rectangle 1 cm [⅜ in] thick.
2. **Rest** 10 minutes.
3. **Cut** into strips 5 × 23 cm [2 × 9 in].
4. **Twist** strips, stretching as you twist.
5. **Coil** to form snail shape on baking pan. Allow 2.5 cm [1 in] between pieces.

6. **Place** a small amount of jelly or jam in center, if desired.
7. **Bake.**
8. **Glaze** before removing from oven.
9. **Frost** if desired, when cool.

Pies and Pastries

What Will You Learn?

When you finish studying this chapter, you should be able to do the following:
- Define and use the *Words to Remember*.
- Prepare and bake a variety of pastries that meet acceptable standards of excellence.
- Achieve a passing grade on the posttest.

Pastries are sometimes used as a base for appetizers and entrées. However, most persons think of pastry as a dessert—apple pie or flaky French desserts. The qualities of flakiness and tenderness set pastries apart from other baked products. Fig. 18-1. Pastries are among the most popular desserts on the menu.

PIES

The baker in charge of pastries, including pies, is sometimes known as the *pastry chef*. Pies are a type of pastry. They consist of an under crust, a filling, and often an upper crust. *Fruit pies* such as apple, peach, and berry are the most popular. Customers also like the *soft-filled pies*. Coconut, chocolate, and lemon are among the well-liked soft-filled pies.

Pies may be *single crusted* or *double crusted*. For variety, the top crust may be woven like a lattice, showing the filling. Single-crust pies with a sweet filling may be heaped with whipped cream, swirled with meringue, or topped with nuts.

Piecrusts

The most common piecrust is made from a mixture of flour, shortening, salt, and water. The crust may be flaky or mealy. This will depend upon the mixing method and the ingredient proportions. Piecrusts should have a delicate, nutlike flavor, and a light brown color.

CHAPTER

18

Unit 5: The Bakery

Durkee Foods

18-1. Light and flaky, pastries are a popular menu item, especially for breakfast.

Words to Remember

crimper
crimping
double-crusted pies
double-pan
fluting

fruit pies
pastry chef
single-crusted pies
soft-filled pies

Piecrusts may also be made from graham cracker crumbs mixed with sugar and melted shortening. The crumbs are pressed into a pie pan and baked. The crust should be lightly browned and firm, but slightly crumbly and tender.

Some specialty pies are made with a cookie or wafer crust prepared in the same manner. Nuts may also be used for further variety. Because nuts are expensive, they are usually mixed with crumbs.

EQUIPMENT

Some bakers believe a flaky crust can be made only by hand. Commercial piecrusts, however, are made by machine with very acceptable results. Small batches of pie dough can be made on the

bench mixer. Large bakeries will use the horizontal mixer.

If the baker prefers to mix by hand, a bowl is needed, along with a rolling pin, cutters, and the bench. In larger bakeries, the rolling out, trimming, and crimping will be done on the pie presser.

Most bakers now use aluminum pie pans. In them, the crust browns well and evenly. Some use pans coated with a shiny tin finish. These pans are cheaper than the aluminum pans. However, they must be treated to remove the shiny finish. A shiny finish will reflect the heat. This will cause a soggy bottom crust and prolong the baking time.

As in all baking procedures, the baker's scale is an absolute necessity. It is needed for accurate measuring of ingredients and for scaling the dough before rolling.

INGREDIENTS

The basic ingredients in pie dough are few—flour, shortening, salt, and water. Other ingredients may be added.

• *Flour.* For most crusts, a pastry flour is best—one with a low gluten content. Bakers usually prefer unbleached flour. It shrinks less in baking and produces a more tender crust with better color.

• *Shortening.* Fat is most important in pie-making because it affects the flavor, texture, and color of the finished product. In making pastry, more shortening is used in proportion to flour than in any other type of baking. The consistency of the shortening must be plastic so it can spread and separate the flour particles. However, it must not be so plastic that it will become oily. Oil spreads too much for fine piemaking. At one time, lard was considered the finest shortening for piemaking. It has the right plasticity to make a very flaky crust. However, pie dough made with lard is easily overmixed, making a tough crust. Some bakers still use it. Most, however, use a hydrogenated shortening made especially for pastry. This shortening mixes easily with flour and holds up well under automatic mixing. Some bakers add a small amount of butter to increase flavor and color.

Whatever shortening is used, it must be cool when used for piemaking. For best results, it should

346

be between 16–21°C [60–70° F.]. If the shortening is too cold, it will be hard to mix. If it is too warm, it will become oily and blend too thoroughly into the flour. Piecrusts made with shortening that is too warm will not be flaky.

- *Salt.* This essential ingredient is needed for flavor and control of the gluten formation. The salt should be very fine so it will dissolve instantly in the water.

- *Water.* Liquid is needed to hold the dough together during the rolling. It must be cold to slow down the gluten development during mixing. The cold water keeps all the ingredients cold so the shortening cannot become oily.

- *Additives.* Some recipes suggest the addition of dry milk powder to improve the browning. Others suggest the use of vinegar to make the crust more tender. Some recommend the addition of baking powder to improve the flakiness. Most chefs disapprove of such additions, feeling that they do not improve the quality of the crust. Some chefs, however, do add a small amount of corn syrup with the water. They feel it aids browning, improves flavor, and helps dry out the crust.

PROPORTION OF INGREDIENTS

On page 364 is a recipe for a fairly rich piecrust. It has 50 percent shortening. It is easier for a beginner to use than the richer formulas. As you read the Methods of Production, notice how this recipe employs the principles for successfully making a piecrust.

Table 18-1 shows the change in the proportions of flour, shortening, water, and salt according to the type of crust desired. Usually, the 70 percent shortening formula is used. However, some chefs prefer the 75 percent formula because the crust is flakier. Mealy dough requires less water and salt than the flaky type because the shortening is more thoroughly worked into the flour. Mealy doughs are less absorbent, but stronger, than flaky doughs. Therefore, they are used for bottom crusts. The flaky type is used for the top crust because it gives a more attractive appearance.

If a strong flour is used, the shortening must be increased to help tenderize the gluten. The proportion of water to flour stays the same. Notice the difference in the amounts in Table 18-2. Since shortening is more expensive than flour, most bakers will buy a flour with less gluten. Such a weaker flour requires less shortening.

METHODS OF PRODUCTION

While making piecrust, remember these important rules:

- The less water used, the more tender the crust.
- Excess water will cause shrinkage, toughness, and pale color.
- Insufficient water will make a dough hard to handle and result in cracking and splitting.
- Coarsely mixed flour and shortening will make a flaky crust. Well-mixed flour and shortening will make a mealy crust.
- Overmixing the dough will develop the gluten, resulting in a tough crust.

Many bakers have their favorite method of mixing pie doughs. The methods may vary slightly. The ones shown in Table 18-3 are those most generally used.

The flaky method requires ice water because the shortening must be kept cold. The shortening should be refrigerated until ready for use. Be especially careful not to overmix when using this method.

Notice there are three methods for making mealy dough. Methods Number 2 and Number 3 are easiest and foolproof for the beginner. They do not require ice water or refrigerated shortening.

COOKING TIP: *Remember, overmixing causes toughness. The amount of liquid is the most important factor in piemaking. Beginners frequently make one or two mistakes. Either they add more flour if the dough appears too sticky, or they add more water if it appears too dry. Either error results in overmixing and a tough crust. Accurate measurement will assure the exact amount of water needed for the shortening-flour mixture.*

RESTING

After the dough has been mixed, some bakers believe it should rest in a cool place for three to four

Table 18-1. Piecrust Formulas

Type Crust	Flour Metric	Flour Customary	Shortening Metric	Shortening Customary	Water* Metric	Water* Customary	Water* Percentage	Salt Metric	Salt Customary
70 Percent Shortening Formula									
Long flaky	4.5 kg	10 lb	3.2 kg	7 lb	1.6 kg	3½ lb	35%	165 g	5¾ oz
Medium flaky	4.5 kg	10 lb	3.2 kg	7 lb	1.4 kg	3 lb	30%	155 g	5½ oz
Mealy	4.5 kg	10 lb	3.2 kg	7 lb	1.2 kg	2¾ lb	27.5%	155 g	5½ oz
75 Percent Shortening Formula									
Long flaky	4.5 kg	10 lb	3.4 kg	7½ lb	1.6 kg	3½ lb	35%	165 g	5¾ oz
Medium flaky	4.5 kg	10 lb	3.4 kg	7¼ lb	1.4 kg	3 lb	30%	165 g	5¾ oz
60 Percent Shortening Formula									
Mealy	4.5 kg	10 lb	2.7 kg	6 lb	1.8 kg	4 lb	40%	150 g	5¼ oz
50 Percent Shortening Formula									
Very mealy and strong	4.5 kg	10 lb	2.3 kg	5 lb	1.8 kg	4 lb	40%	150 g	5¼ oz

*Water is not always measured in kilograms or pounds. However, when measuring large amounts measurement by mass or weight is sometimes easier.

Table 18-2. Shortening Changes Needed for Different Flour Types

Type Crust	Type Flour and Amounts	Shortening	Water*
Medium Flaky	Soft winter 4.5 kg [10 lb]	3.4 kg [7½ lb]	1.4 kg [3 lb]
	Hard winter 4.5 kg [10 lb]	3.6 kg [8 lb]	1.4 kg [3 lb]
	Hard spring 4.5 kg [10 lb]	3.9 kg [8½ lb]	1.4 kg [3 lb]
Mealy	Soft winter 4.5 kg [10 lb]	2.7 kg [6 lb]	1.4 kg [3 lb]
	Hard winter 4.5 kg [10 lb]	2.9 kg [6½ lb]	1.4 kg [3 lb]
	Hard spring 4.5 kg [10 lb]	3.2 kg [7 lb]	1.4 kg [3 lb]

*Water is not always measured in kilograms or pounds. However, when measuring large amounts, measurement by mass or weight is sometimes easier.

Table 18-3. Pie Dough Mixing Methods

Methods for Flaky Dough	Methods for Mealy Dough		
	Method Number 1	**Method Number 2**	**Method Number 3**
By hand 1. Measure flour into a bowl. 2. Cut half the shortening into the flour until in large lumps. 3. Add the rest of the shortening and cut in until mixture is coarse. The lumps should be about the size of small peas, each lump surrounded by flour. 4. Dissolve the salt in the ice water. Blend until the flour has taken up all the ice water.	**By hand** 1. Measure half the flour into a bowl and blend in all the shortening until like coarse cornmeal. 2. Add the rest of the flour and blend. 3. Dissolve the salt in the ice water and add to the flour mixture. 4. Blend until the flour takes up all the water.	**By hand** 1. Divide the flour into two parts. The first portion should be about five times the second. 2. Cut all the shortening into the larger portion of flour until like coarse cornmeal. 3. Add the water and the salt to the second portion of flour. Blend into a paste. 4. Blend the paste into the first mixture until all the liquid is absorbed.	**By mixer** 1. Cream shortening on medium speed. 2. Mix water and salt. 3. Gradually beat the water into the shortening until all the water is absorbed. 4. Add all the flour at once and mix until the flour is just moistened.
By mixer 1. Blend all the shortening with the flour on low speed for about 1 minute. 2. Dissolve the salt in the water. 3. Add the water to the flour and blend for 30 seconds.	**By mixer** 1. Blend all the shortening into half the flour for $1\frac{1}{2}$ minutes on low speed. 2. Add the rest of the flour and blend for 30 seconds. 3. Dissolve salt in water. 4. Add water to flour and blend for 30 seconds.	**By mixer** 1. Divide flour as in directions above. 2. On low speed, blend all the shortening into the larger portion of flour for 1 minute. 3. Add water and salt to second portion of flour. Blend to a smooth paste. 4. Add paste to flour and blend for 30 seconds.	

hours. The rest period gives the gluten a chance to absorb the water. It softens the gluten and makes the dough easier to roll. The rest period also helps reduce shrinkage during baking. Do not refrigerate the pie dough. The temperature is too cold. It will slow down the softening process. Pie dough kept in the refrigerator overnight will take a long time to become soft enough to handle. When taken from the refrigerator, the outside will quickly become sticky. The inside will still be hard.

However, pie dough with 75 percent shortening may be refrigerated for a short time before rolling. The lumps of shortening in this type of dough are rather large. They need to be kept quite firm.

MAKEUP

After resting, take the dough to the bench and scale it into 225-g [8-oz] pieces. Each piece will make one bottom or top crust for a 23-cm [9-in] pie. Experienced bakers may require only 170 g [6 oz] of dough. However, the larger piece can be handled more easily by beginners.

Pastry chefs in a restaurant will probably roll the dough by hand. Bigger operations will use a pie press.

For hand production, roll dough on a lightly floured, smooth surface or on a floured piece of canvas. The rolling pin is also floured to prevent sticking. Form the dough into a round ball. Flatten it with the palm of the hand, forming a disk. The rounder the disk, the more even the rolled dough will be. Starting at the center, roll lightly to the edges, forming a circle. Do not press hard with the rolling pin. Light, quick strokes are better than slow, heavy ones. Never roll back and forth or the dough will roll up on the pin. Turn the dough a quarter turn and roll again. Continue rolling and turning until the dough is about 3 mm [$\frac{1}{8}$ in] thick and slightly larger than the pan. Fig. 18-2. Check under the dough frequently to make sure it is not sticking. Dust lightly with flour as needed.

Fold the dough in half and place on the pan. Unfold and shape to the pan without stretching. Lift the dough and let the weight of the dough carry it gently into the bend of the pan. Fig. 18-3. Bring it up the sides and over the edge.

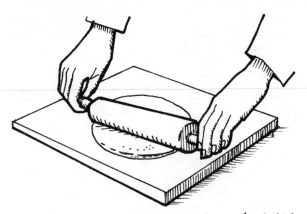

18-2. The dough should be about 3 mm [$\frac{1}{8}$ in] thick and slightly larger than the pan.

18-3. The weight of the dough should carry it into the bend of the pan.

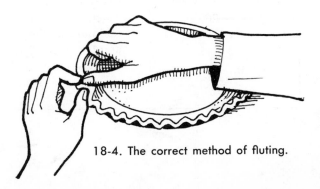

18-4. The correct method of fluting.

Single crusts. The edges of the piecrust may be finished by *fluting* or *crimping*. To flute, trim the edge with a knife about 13 mm [½ in] from the edge of the pan. Fold under the excess, making a thick rim. Using the thumb and index finger of one hand and the index finger of the other, make a wavy edge around the rim. Fig. 18-4. To crimp, bakers use a *crimper* or a fork. A crimper is a small tool that presses the edge of the crust against the rim of the pan. The tines of a fork may be used to press the crust against the edge of the pan.

Single crusts tend to shrink and puff up during baking. To allow the steam and air to escape from under the crust, dock the bottom and sides by piercing with a fork. Many bakers prefer to *double-pan*. In double-panning, the crust is baked between two pie pans. Figure 18-5 shows the technique for double-panning.

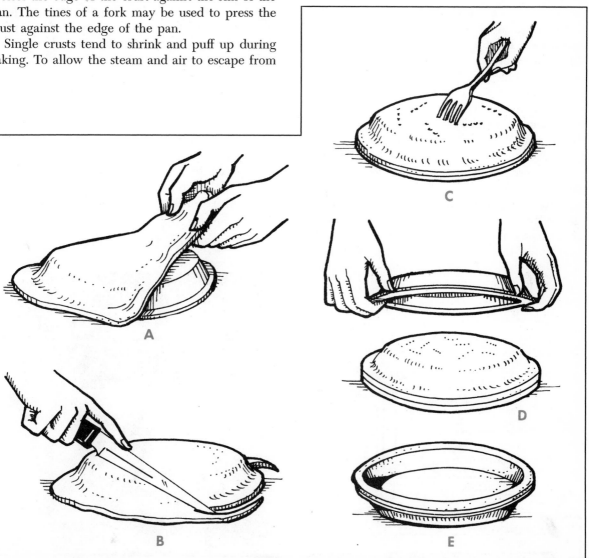

18-5. Double-panning. (A) Place rolled pie dough over outside of pie pan. (B) Trim the edges. (C) Dock the dough by piercing with a fork. (D) Cover piecrust with another pie pan. (E) Bake in oven.

Double crusts. After the pie is filled, dock the top crust by cutting several slits in the center. Fold it in half and unfold on top of the filling, centering the slits. Trim both crusts to the edge of the pan. Moisten the edge of the bottom crust with water. Seal it to the top crust by fluting or crimping.

For machine production, many bakeries use the pie presser. Fig. 18-6. The bottom crust or single crusts may be formed in the pie presser. However, the top crust is always rolled by hand.

The pie presser has a platform that can be raised or lowered. The top is a heated removable mold, shaped like a pie pan. The mold can be changed to fit the size of the pan. The piecrust is automatically rolled, trimmed, and crimped.

To operate the pie presser:

1. Place the scaled dough ball in the center of the pie pan. Fig. 18-7.

2. Place the pie pan on the platform. Fig. 18-8.

3. Be sure the mold is the same size as the pie pan.

4. Raise the platform, pressing the dough ball against the mold. The dough will not stick to the mold because the mold is slightly warm. Fig. 18-9.

5. Lower the platform and remove the pie pan.

6. Check to make sure there are no air pockets under the crust.

PIE WASHES

Bakers frequently use a *wash* to improve the color and finish of the top crust. Milk, cream, egg mixed with milk, or melted butter deepen the brown color and add shine to the crust. Some customers, however, object to the artificial-looking color and shine produced by egg washes. Milk, cream, or melted butter give a good color without the objectionable, artificial look. Melted butter also adds much to the tenderness and flavor of the crust.

Many bakers prefer to wash the top crust with water and sprinkle it with granulated sugar. The sugar adds sparkle to the crust and aids in browning.

USE OF PIE TRIMMINGS

If the dough is carefully scaled before rolling, there should be very few trimmings. Of course, the quality of the scrap dough has deteriorated because it has been worked during the rolling, developing

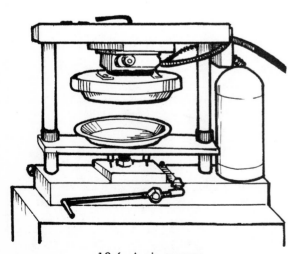

18-6. A pie presser.

18-7. Place the scaled ball of dough in the center of the pie pan.

18-8. Place the pie pan in the pie presser.

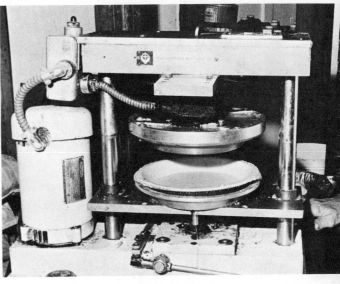

18-9. The pressed piecrust.

the gluten. Add trimmings to fresh dough with the water before resting. It is better to mix trimmings only with the dough used for the bottom crusts. This finished product does not need to be as flaky as the top crust.

EFFICIENCY OF PRODUCTION

Time-motion studies have shown that three cooperating workers can turn out a single-crust, filled pie, ready for baking, every minute and four seconds. Working alone, the three workers average a completed pie every three minutes. Obviously, if many pies are to be made, the production assembly line is most efficient.

The first worker rolls the dough and places it on the pan.

The second worker trims and flutes the crust.

The third worker fills the pie and places it on the rack for baking.

To make a two-crust pie, the assembly line would be modified as follows:

The first worker rolls the bottom crust and places it in the pan.

The second worker fills the pie.

The third worker rolls the top crust and places it on the pie.

The fourth worker trims and flutes the pie and places it on the rack for baking.

From the point of view of efficiency, the assembly line is practical. Pastry chefs, however, are proud of their work. Many would deeply resent becoming a part of an assembly line.

Words to Remember

cold-juice method	natural gums
cornstarch	pectin
homemade method	precooked starches
hot-juice method	wash
instant starches	waxy maize

Fruit Fillings

The kind of fruit, the thickener, other ingredients, and the method of preparation affect the quality of a fruit filling. Fruit pies should have the following characteristics:

- *Flavor*—a definite sweet fruit flavor.
- *Juiciness*—the juice should run slightly when the pie is served.
- *A firm bottom crust*—never soggy.
- *Appealing appearance*—a heavy, starchy filling is not appealing.
- *Well-filled*—when cut, the pie should appear to be well-filled with fruit. A high-quality pie will have a fruit to juice ratio of at least two to one by weight.

INGREDIENTS

- *Fruits.* Fruits may be fresh, frozen, or dried. Each type makes an excellent pie. In food service, fresh fruits are seldom used because they require much pre-preparation. Frozen or canned fruits, of course, require no pre-preparation. Dried fruits are soaked and usually cooked before being used as a filling.

Many pastry chefs have turned to canned, frozen, or prepared pie fillings. High labor costs have made it uneconomical to prepare fillings in the bake station. Some of the prepared fillings are of high quality. Others have been watered excessively, causing a flavorless pie with little fruit in proportion to juice.

- *Sugar.* Prepared fillings are usually pre-sweetened. For other fillings a fine granulated sugar is needed because it dissolves quickly.
- *Thickener. Cornstarch,* a white, powdery flour ground from corn, is usually used as a thickener for pie fillings. There are two types of cornstarch—regular and waxy maize.

Regular cornstarch, generally found in most kitchens, thickens easily, but the gel is cloudy. This is a disadvantage where a bright, clear color is desirable.

Waxy maize, a modified cornstarch, produces a clear gel. It also thickens at a lower temperature. Regular cornstarch thickens at 95°C [203° F.]. Waxy maize thickens at only 91°C [195° F.]. Most commercial pies are made with waxy maize as the thickener.

Instant starches, also called *precooked starches,* are used frequently. Such starches have been cooked and dried before packaging. They are particularly useful for pie fillings because they thicken without

cooking. Therefore, the fruit does not become mushy or lose flavor from overcooking.

- *Flavoring.* Some flavorings and spices may be used in fruit fillings. Cinnamon blends well with apples. A little almond extract deepens the flavor of cherry fillings.
- *Additives.* Commercial bakers frequently use additives to help thicken the juices while improving the clarity and brilliance of the color. Certain gums, natural or chemical, may be added to the filling. *Natural gums* are sticky substances given off by some trees and plants, but they may also be produced chemically. *Pectins* are a water-soluble carbohydrate found in ripe fruit. Pectins cause the jelly to form a gel. Powdered or liquid pectin may be added to pie fillings. They cause the juice to form a gel. Less cornstarch is needed.

METHODS OF PREPARATION

Fruit fillings are generally prepared by one of three methods—the so-called homemade method, the hot-juice method, and the cold-juice method. Each method gives a different type of filling. Although the homemade method is occasionally used, most bakers prefer the hot-juice or cold-juice method. The filling will not shrink, and the consistency of the juice can be controlled.

About 900 g [2 lb] of filling are needed for a 23-cm [9-in] pie.

By any method, fresh fruit must be mixed first with the sugar. It must then be allowed to stand for a short time to draw the juices.

Table 18-4 compares the methods of preparation for fruit pie fillings. The homemade method looks easiest, but it does not consistently give the best pie. As the fruit cooks, it forms a more compact mass, causing the filling to shrink. Sometimes, when the pie is cut, the top crust will be well above the filling level. Fruits vary in juiciness and tartness. Therefore, it is difficult to estimate the exact amount of sugar and thickener needed.

The hot-juice method is better. It uses waxy maize as the thickener.

The cold-juice method is excellent because it retains all the flavor of the fruit. It requires instant starch as the thickener.

Table 18-4. Fruit Pie Filling Preparation

Homemade Method	Hot-Juice Method	Cold-Juice Method
1. Mix the prepared fruit with the sugar, thickener, and flavorings. 2. Fill the bottom crust. 3. Dot with butter or margarine. 4. Put on top crust.	1. Drain the juice from the fruit and set fruit aside. 2. Mix the thickener with some of the juice, making a slurry. 3. Bring the rest of the juice to a boil. Stir in the slurry gradually. 4. Boil until thick, stirring all the time. 5. Cool slightly and pour over the fruit. 6. Fill piecrust. Put on top crust and bake.	1. Drain the juice from the fruit and set fruit aside. 2. Mix juice with sugar and instant starch. Stir until the juice is thick. 3. Mix with the fruit. 4. Fill the piecrust. Put on the top crust and bake.

Soft Fillings

Soft fillings are creamy, smooth, and puddinglike. Soft fillings are always placed in single piecrusts with a topping such as beaten egg white or whipped cream.

INGREDIENTS

At the end of this chapter, there are four recipes for soft pie fillings. These are vanilla cream, lemon, lemon chiffon, and pumpkin custard.

Cream pie fillings are made with a milk-egg base thickened with cornstarch or instant starch. In this example, vanilla is used as the flavoring. However, many different pies can be made by varying the flavors. Coconut, chocolate, butterscotch, and banana are a few of the delightful variations. Excellent mixes in many flavors are available and often used in food service.

Cream pie fillings are placed in a baked piecrust. Thus, no further baking is required. There is a recipe for cream pie filling on page 366.

Lemon pie filling has a water-egg yolk base. It may be thickened with cornstarch or instant starch. Egg yolks are needed to give a deep, lemony color.

The egg whites are used for the topping. There is a recipe for lemon pie filling on page 365.

Lemon-flavored pie fillings are available. However, they do not have the flavor of fillings made with fresh lemon juice.

Chiffon pie fillings are light, fluffy, and delicious because they contain beaten egg white or whipped cream. They are usually fruit flavored. Lemon, orange, strawberry, blueberry, and peach are a few of the flavors. Any recipe for cream fillings may be used for chiffon fillings by folding in whipped cream or beaten egg white.

Gelatin or cornstarch with gelatin is used to thicken chiffon fillings. Although cornstarch alone is sometimes used, the addition of gelatin keeps the filling firm.

The gelatin discussed in Chapter 8 and Chapter 21 is used for making chiffon pies.

The recipe for lemon chiffon pie filling is on page 366.

Custard pie fillings also have an egg-milk base but they use only eggs as the thickener. The filling is poured into an unbaked pie shell and baked. The recipe for pumpkin custard filling is on page 367.

Custard pies may be flavored with vanilla, coconut, lemon and many other flavors. In the example, pumpkin and spices are used to make a typically American pie. In the United States, pumpkin pie is traditional for the Thanksgiving feast.

To thicken properly, custard pies require at least 1.1 kg [2½ lb] of eggs for every 3.8 L [1 gal] of milk. A richer filling that never separates uses 285 g [10 oz] of sugar and ten eggs to every litre of milk.

Many bakers add precooked starch to help thicken the filling and prevent curdling. Special stabilizers made of egg white or tapioca may be used to bind the filling and make a smoother product.

METHODS OF PREPARATION

The methods of preparation for vanilla cream, lemon, and lemon chiffon are much the same. These fillings are thickened by cooking on top of the range. Notice that the cornstarch is always mixed with cold milk or water before being added to the hot liquid. This follows the principles of starch cookery explained in Chapter 20.

Eggs curdle very easily at high temperatures. Thus, a little of the hot mixture is mixed with the eggs before they are added to the rest of the hot liquid and cooked. Be careful not to overcook. About three minutes of cooking is all that is needed to cook the eggs.

When making the lemon filling, add the lemon juice and grated rind after the mixture is thick. The acid of the lemon juice may cause the starch to become runny. The filling should be cooled rapidly. Otherwise, the heat may quicken the action of the lemon juice on the starch.

The custard pie is thickened only by the cooked eggs. The piecrust shields the custard mixture from the heat of the oven. The pie filling is done when a knife inserted in the center comes out clean.

Specialty Pies

Parfait (par-FAY) *pie* is a variation of the chiffon pie. Soft ice cream is beaten into the fruit gel. The filling is poured into the pie shell and refrigerated.

A delicious lime pie may be made using sweetened condensed milk and lime juice. This pie requires no other thickener because the acid of the lime juice causes the milk to thicken. Egg whites beaten with sugar may be folded in for a lighter texture.

A double-crusted fruit pie baked in a deep dish is another specialty dish. It has a very thick filling. A pitcher of cream is served along with it.

Baked cookies, wafer, or nut crusts are used for other specialty pies. These may be filled with soft ice cream and flavored with different fruits. The pie is served frozen.

Baking of Pies

If a conventional oven is used, pies are baked at 218°C [425° F.] for ten minutes to set the crust. The temperature is then reduced to 177°C [350° F.] until the pie is done. However, in a carousel oven, common in bakeries, the heat of the oven cannot be reduced quickly enough. In these ovens, bake the pies at 182°C [360° F.] for the entire time. The cooking time is the same for both baking temperatures.

- Fruit pies (homemade method) take forty to fifty minutes.
- Fruit pies (hot-juice or cold-juice method) take twenty-five to thirty minutes.
- Custard pies take one hour.
- Single piecrusts take ten to twelve minutes.

Double-crust fruit pies are sometimes baked on sheet pans—a process known as *panning*. Panning catches the juices that may overflow, eliminating a messy oven-cleaning job. The pie pan and the sheet pan must be made of the same metal—for instance, aluminum on aluminum. Different metals conduct heat at different rates, interfering with the baking and browning.

COOKING TIP: *Remove berry pies before the juice boils. Blueberry pies, especially, tend to* blow. *This means that the juice tends to boil through the docking slits. This makes the pie less attractive.*

Frozen pies require special handling during baking to prevent a soggy bottom crust. Do not thaw. Bake frozen at 218°C [425° F.] for forty-five to fifty minutes. Frozen custard pies such as pumpkin will take a little longer to bake because of the very wet filling.

Words to Remember

à la mode	weeping
meringue	whipped cream

Toppings

One-crust pies, especially cream and chiffon types, are usually served with a fluffy topping. Toppings add greatly to the flavor and eye appeal of the pies.

MERINGUES

A *meringue* (muh-RANG) is a fluffy mixture of beaten egg whites and sugar. It is heaped lightly on the pie filling, swirled attractively, and browned in the oven. Meringues may be hard or soft, but only the soft type is used as a pie topping. A soft meringue should be very light, tender, and golden brown. It should cover the filling completely and be at least 5 cm [2 in] thick.

A meringue requires only three ingredients—egg whites, sugar, and cream of tartar. Sometimes a stabilizer is added to prevent the meringue from shrinking away from the pie filling.

The egg whites should be at room temperature for the greatest volume.

A very fine granulated sugar should be used. It dissolves easily, eliminating graininess. Some bakers use four parts of egg whites to three parts of sugar. Other bakers prefer a sweeter meringue. They use equal parts of egg white and sugar.

Cream of tartar is added to increase the acidity of the egg whites. It also makes a fluffier, more tender meringue.

The stabilizer can be tapioca, cornstarch, or one of the gum stabilizers.

Meringue mixes are also available with stabilizers already mixed in. They may be used with very good results if the directions are followed carefully.

To prepare a meringue, whip the egg whites on high speed until foamy. Add the cream of tartar and

stabilizer, if used. Whip to a good foam. Add the sugar gradually, whipping after each addition. Beat until the meringue stands in peaks and is glossy. Heap on a warm filling, swirling it attractively. About 140 g [5 oz] will make a liberal topping.

Meringues frequently *weep*, or *bleed*. Droplets of water gather under the meringue, causing it to slip. Stabilizers help prevent the formation of moisture. Weeping or bleeding also results from too much sugar, insufficient beating, or placing the meringue on a cold filling. A very thin slice of cake placed between the filling and the meringue will absorb any moisture. It will also prevent the meringue from slipping. Fig. 18-10. The cake does not affect the appearance or flavor because it is only about 6 mm [$\frac{1}{4}$ in] thick.

18-10. Jake cuts thin slices of cake to be placed between the meringue and the cream filling of pies.

WHIPPED CREAM

Whipped cream adds a luxurious quality to soft-filled pies. Chiffon, custard, and some specialty pies command higher prices if topped with whipped cream. Whipped cream may be purchased in aerosol cans. This type is not much used by pastry chefs because such foams do not hold up longer than a few minutes. Many bakers use mixes that are imitations of whipped cream. They are widely available under brand names. Evaporated milk and dry milk may also be whipped under certain circumstances.

For safety, only pasteurized cream should be used. Cream for whipping must be at least 30 percent butterfat. The higher the butterfat content, the more stable the whipped cream will be. However, all whipped creams will turn yellow, water, and lose volume about an hour after whipping.

Stabilized cream will not turn yellow. It will keep a fresh appearance for hours. To improve stability, pastry chefs use the following methods:

• Adding a stabilized liquid cream, similar to the liquid used in the aerosol cans, to the cream before whipping. Use 110 g [4 oz] per 1 L [1 qt] of cream.

• Mixing 42 g [1½ oz] of dry milk with each 1 L [1 qt] of cream twenty-four hours before whipping.

• Sifting instant gelatin with powdered sugar. Add 15 g [¼ oz] of gelatin for each 1 L [1 qt] of cream. Add after the cream is whipped.

After whipping, whipped cream is usually sweetened to taste with powdered sugar and vanilla. Powdered sugar adds more stability than granulated sugar.

To whip cream, a deep bowl is necessary for the best agitation. The bowl as well as the cream should be well-chilled—below 5°C [40° F.]. Either a wire whip or small mixer may be used for whipping.

Place the chilled cream in the cold bowl and whip on meduim speed until it forms peaks.

COOKING TIP: *Always watch the cream carefully when whipping. Overbeating will cause the butterfat to clump together, making the cream unusable.*

To whip mixes, mix the stabilizer with whole milk. Beat to stiff peaks. The sugar and flavoring are already in the mix. Mixes such as these are very stable, holding the foamy consistency for many hours. Many of them have a delicious flavor, close to genuine whipped cream. They also cost much less per serving.

Service

A 23-cm [9-in] pie will serve five generously and six adequately. Double-crust fruit pies are best served freshly baked and slightly warm. They are usually served alone, although a slice or wedge of Cheddar cheese sometimes accompanies apple pie. Deep-dish pies are served warm in a bowl with a pitcher of cream on the side. Some restaurants serve sweetened apple juice with apple pie. Many customers like to order pie *à la mode*. This is pie with a scoop of ice cream on top.

Chiffon and meringue pies are so eye-catching that they need no other garnishing. Custard pies are more appealing with a topping of whipped cream. Chiffon pies should always be served cold. They would be less firm at room temperatures. Serve meringue pies within a few hours of completion. Otherwise, the meringue loses its fresh appeal.

Care and Storage

All pies with a filling made of eggs and milk require special care. Like cream and egg sauces, they spoil quickly at room temperatures. It is best to bake pies daily, since their quality deteriorates rapidly. The top crust loses the flakiness characteristic of fine pastry. The bottom crust may become soggy. The best food service places do not serve day-old pie.

Words to Remember

à la king	fruit puff
chiffon	horn
choux paste	panning
cruller	patty shell
éclair	puff paste
four-fold	tartlet

OTHER PASTRIES

The pastry used for dessert pies is typically American. European pastries are usually made from choux paste or a variation of puff pastry.

Choux Paste

Choux (SHOW) *paste* is a very thick mixture of flour, eggs, and water. When baked, it forms a very light shell with a large hole in the center. The hole may be filled with a custard mixture or whipped cream for dessert. Sometimes the hole may be filled with a savory chicken, meat, or fish mixture and served as an appetizer.

When choux paste is formed with a scoop, it makes a cream puff. If formed with a pastry tube into an oblong, it makes an *éclair* (ay-CLARE). When formed into a doughnut and fried in deep fat, it makes a *cruller* (CRUH-ler).

On page 363 is a recipe for choux paste. Notice the ingredients.

- The *flour* must be of a high quality. Bread flour should be used for its gluten content.
- *Salt* and *sugar* add flavor and help the browning.
- The *shortening* is generally butter or margarine which add flavor and coloring.
- The *eggs* are fresh in the shell for adding one at a time.

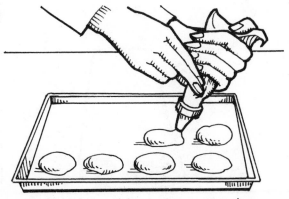

18-11. Forming éclairs using a pastry bag.

No leavener is added since the steam and air cause the paste to rise.

Choux pastry is easy to make. It is important to stir the thick paste over the heat until it leaves the sides of the pan and follows the spoon around. After the eggs are added, the paste should be smooth, shiny, and thick enough to form a ball.

For éclairs, using the pastry bag, scale about 55 g [2 oz] of choux pastry for each oblong. Fig. 18-11. For cream puffs, use the No. 20 scoop. Drop on a baking sheet about 5 cm [2 in] apart.

When placed in the oven, the high temperature causes steam to develop between the layers of fat. This pushes the paste up and out and leaves a large hole in the center. Expansion is completed in about fifteen minutes. However, it takes thirty-five to forty minutes to bake completely. The shell must be dried out so it will not collapse when cooled.

Crullers are fried until lightly browned in deep fat heated to 185°C [365° F.].

SERVING

Cut the puffs in half while still warm. Fill with a cream filling or sweetened whipped cream. After filling, frost éclairs with a thin chocolate icing.

Crullers are lightly dusted with a fine powdered sugar.

Small cream puffs are sometimes filled with a savory mixture and served hot as hors d'oeuvres.

CARE AND STORAGE

Once filled, éclairs and cream puffs must be kept refrigerated until served. The cream filling spoils very quickly, especially in warm weather. Like all pastries, those made from choux paste are best when freshly baked.

Puff Paste

Puff paste is known in Europe as the "paste of many leaves" because it forms leaves, or layers, of paper-thin pastry. It is very delicate, puffy, and light. Puff paste is used to form filled horns (sometimes called "lady locks"). It is also used for patty shells (used as a base for creamed dishes) and napoleons (a cream-filled dessert).

Unit 5: The Bakery

Puff paste is difficult and time-consuming to make. Prepared puff paste may now be purchased, ready to be shaped and filled. Many bakeries prefer to use the prepared product because of the high cost of labor. The making of fine puff paste is difficult for beginners.

INGREDIENTS

On page 364 is a recipe for puff paste. The ingredients are similar to those for choux paste, but the method of mixing is very different.

• The *flour* should be a high-gluten flour. The gluten is needed to form the many layers.

• The *shortening* should be a waxy, pliable margarine made specifically for puff paste. The weight of the shortening and the weight of the flour should be nearly equal.

• *Whole eggs* or *egg yolks* are added for flavor, color, and leavening action.

• *Cream of tartar* is needed to soften the gluten and make it more elastic.

• *Ice water* helps maintain the necessary cool temperature.

Note the lack of any specific leavener. The leavening action comes from the formation of steam, the expansion of air, and the bubbling of the melting fat.

METHOD OF PREPARATION

The method used for making puff paste is similar to that used for making Danish pastries. This method is the rolling-in method. As described in Chapter 17, the shortening is spread between the folds of dough and then rolled in. Each time the roll-in is repeated, the dough forms thinner and thinner layers. This makes the leaves of pastry paper-thin.

Between roll-ins, the dough must be allowed to rest in a cool room. This relaxes the gluten and prevents shrinkage. The dough and the shortening

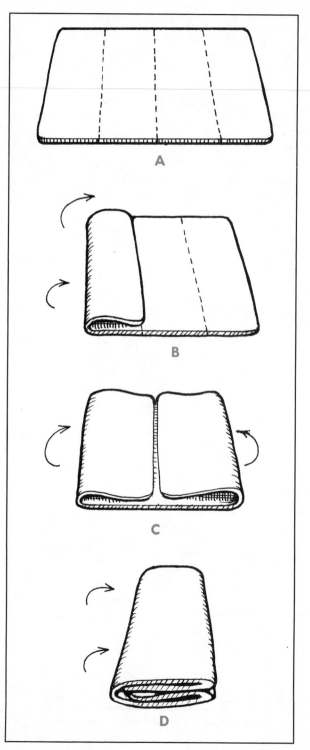

18-12. Making a four-fold. (A) Divide rolled dough with the eye into four equal parts. (B) Fold each end section over the closest middle section. (C) The end sections folded over the middle sections. (D) Fold in the middle, completing the four-fold as shown.

should be at the same temperature as the room—about 16°C [60° F.]. If the shortening is too cold, it will break through the dough. If it is too warm, it will become oily. The pastry will not be flaky. During the rests, spread the top of the dough with oil. Cover the dough with a piece of waxed paper or a bowl to prevent crust formation.

Puff paste may be made by two methods, each giving acceptable results. The first method is quicker than the second. The puff paste recipe uses the second method.

● *Method No. 1.* Sift dry ingredients into a bowl. Cut in all the shortening until the lumps of dough are the size of small eggs. Mix eggs and water and add to flour-shortening mixture. Mix lightly so shortening keeps its shape. Take to the bench. Give a four-fold without adding any more shortening.

To make a *four-fold*, roll and divide into fourths with the eye. Fold sections together, making four layers. Fig. 18-12. Cover and let rest for thirty seconds. Give three more four-folds at thirty-minute intervals. Cover and let rest between each roll-in.

● *Method No. 2.* Mix flour, regular shortening, water, eggs, and cream of tartar into a stiff dough. Let rest for thirty minutes. Scale 450 g [1 lb] for each roll-in. Make a three-fold. Roll the dough and divide into thirds with the eye. Fold one end third over the middle third. Fold over the other end third. (See page 338).

Roll and make a four-fold. Let dough rest thirty minutes between each roll-in. Roll a four-fold and let rest. Follow with three more four-folds at thirty-minute intervals. Shape as desired.

MAKEUP

● A *patty shell* is a pastry formed in a cup to hold a creamed mixture. It is made from puff paste. Fig. 18-13. To form *patty shells*, divide the dough into two equal parts. Roll one part about 7 mm [¼ in] thick on a floured board. Cut into rounds and

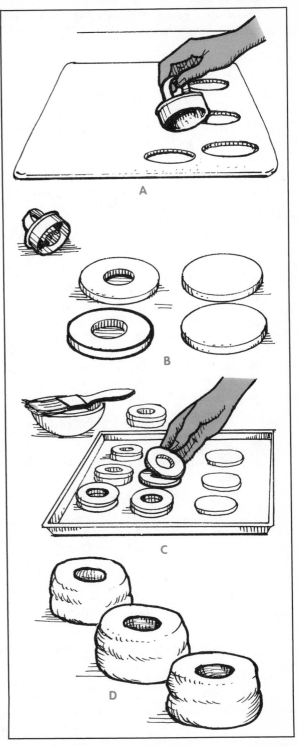

18-13. Making patty shells. (A) Cut solid rounds of dough. (B) Cut center holes in one-half of the rounds. (C) Spread solid rounds with butter. Place circles on top of rounds. (D) Baked patty shells.

place on a sheet pan. Roll the second part and cut the same number of rounds again. In these rounds, cut out the center with a smaller round, forming rings. Wash the rounds with water. Place the rings, floured side down, on top of them.

- To form *horns*, roll dough about 3 mm [⅛ in] thick and cut into strips about 3 × 38 cm [1¼ × 15 in]. Roll around a tube. Roll in granulated sugar before baking.

- *Fruit puffs* are pinwheels with a fruit center. To form *fruit puffs*, roll dough as for horns. Cut into 13-cm [5-in] squares. Wash with water. Cut from each corner almost into the center. Place a piece of glazed fruit in the center and fold corners in like a pinwheel. A variety of shapes may be made, as illustrated.

- *Tartlets* are small cups filled with fruit. To make *tartlets*, roll dough as for horns. Cut into rounds. Place in tartlet molds—a small, fluted mold. Press dough into flutes. Place fluted paper cups on top of the pastry to keep the pastry from puffing out of shape. Fill the cups with dried beans, peas, rice, or rock salt to weight them. These items are kept especially for this purpose in the bakery. They may be used again and again. Muffin tins may be substituted for tartlet molds.

BAKING

Bake puff pastries at 214–232°C [425–450° F.] for fifteen minutes until lightly browned. Good puff pastries will rise eight times their original size. Fig.

18-14. For instance, a patty shell measuring 1.3 cm [½ in] thick before baking may rise to almost 10 cm [4 in] high.

SERVING

Patty shells are filled with a creamed mixture and served as a luncheon entrée. Chicken served in this manner is called *chicken à la king*, meaning "fit for a king." It is a term used for foods served in a cream sauce with mushrooms, green peppers, and pimiento.

Small patty shells with a savory filling are served as hot hors d'oeuvres.

Horns are filled with a thick cream or fruit filling. Tartlets may also be filled with a cream filling and decorated with a bit of fruit and whipped cream.

In many fine restaurants, the pastry chef takes great pride in presenting to the customers a dessert tray of puff pastry delicacies.

CARE AND STORAGE

Puff paste may be made weeks ahead of time and kept under refrigeration. The shortening solidifies and there are no chemical leaveners or yeast to produce gas. For these reasons, the paste is actually improved by storage. The pastry chef bakes only those quantities needed. Thus, the customers are assured of fresh pastries. Once baked and filled, puff paste delicacies rapidly lose their fresh quality.

Durkee Foods

18-14. Properly made, a puff pastry should rise eight times its original size.

*How
Much
Have
You
Learned?*

Review this chapter. Answer the following questions to prepare yourself for the post-test. Check your answers with the teacher.

1. Define the *Words to Remember*. Use each one in a sentence.
2. Explain what makes pastry mealy or flaky.
3. Explain one method of making pastry. What is the most important factor in pie-crust making? Why?
4. What are the three methods for making a fruit filling? Describe each one.
5. What thickeners are used for fruit pies? Cream pies? Chiffon pies? Custard pies?
6. What is a meringue? How is it prepared?
7. What precautions should be observed in making whipped cream? How can whipped cream be stabilized?
8. What is choux paste? How is it prepared?
9. What is puff paste? How is it prepared?
10. What is meant by a four-fold?

CHOUX PASTE

Equipment
Saucepan
Stirring spoon
Mixer
No. 20 scoop
Pastry bag with plain tube
Bake pan

Yield: 50 puffs
Temperature: 205°C [400° F.]
Time: 35–40 minutes

Metric	Ingredients	Customary
500 mL	Water	2 c
5 mL	Salt	1 t
22 mL	Sugar	$1\frac{1}{2}$ T
450 g	Butter or margarine	1 lb
450 g	Bread flour	1 lb
16	Eggs	16

METHOD

1. **Place** water, salt, sugar, and butter in saucepan. Heat until butter melts. Bring to a boil.
2. **Add** flour in a steady stream, stirring all the time.
3. **Stir** until the paste leaves the sides of the pan and follows the spoon around.
4. **Remove** from heat.
5. **Place** in mixing bowl. Cool to 60°C [140° F.].
6. **Preheat** oven.
7. **Stir** eggs into paste one at a time on slow speed.
8. **Bag out** puffs on lightly greased pan, using pastry bag and plain tube or No. 20 scoop. Space about 5 cm [2 in] apart.
9. **Bake** until light and slightly browned.

PUFF PASTE

Equipment
Mixer and bowl
Rolling pin
Knife
Cutters for shaping

Yield: 50 items, depending upon size

Metric	Ingredients	Customary
1.4 kg	Bread flour	3 lb
15 mL	Cream of tartar	1 T
8 mL	Salt	$\frac{1}{2}$ T
1.1 kg	Butter, margarine, or roll-in shortening	$2\frac{1}{2}$ lb
250 mL	Fresh liquid eggs	1 c
1 L	Water (amount needed may vary)	4 c

METHOD

1. **Sift** dry ingredients into bowl.
2. **Cut in** all the shortening, using the hook, until the shortening is the size of small eggs.
3. **Mix** eggs and 750 mL [3 c] of water.
4. **Add** egg mixture to flour mixture. Mix lightly. Do not overmix. Add more water, up to 250 mL [1 c], if needed.
5. **Take** to bench. Give a four-fold.
6. **Rest** 30 seconds.
7. **Give** three more four-folds at 30-minute intervals.
8. **Cover** and let rest between each roll-in.
9. **Shape** as desired.

RICH PIECRUST (FLAKY METHOD—50 PERCENT SHORTENING)

Equipment
Bench mixer with paddle
Rolling pin
Pie pans

Yield: 108 single crusts; 66 double crusts (20-cm [8-in] pan)
Temperature: 221°C [430° F.].
Time: 6–8 minutes

Metric	Ingredients	Customary
3.2 kg	Pastry shortening	7 lb
1.6 kg	Margarine	$3\frac{1}{2}$ lb
5.7 kg	Pastry flour	$12\frac{1}{2}$ lb
2.9 kg	Pastry flour	$6\frac{1}{2}$ lb
1.1 kg	Pastry shortening	2 lb
340 g	Sugar	12 oz
340 g	Salt	12 oz
4.25 L	Ice water	4 qt 1 c

RICH PIECRUST (FLAKY METHOD—50 PERCENT SHORTENING)— Continued

METHOD

1. **Place** first amount of shortening, margarine, and flour in mixer bowl.
2. **Break** in with paddle on low speed. Turn switch on and off repeatedly until shortening is in lumps about the size of walnuts.
3. **Add** second amounts of flour and shortening. Break in as before until a coarse crumb is obtained—about 1 minute.
4. **Dissolve** sugar in water with salt.
5. **Add** to mixture, mixing on low speed until just blended.
6. **Let rest** in cool place for 3–4 hours.
7. **Roll,** pan, and bake.

LEMON PIE FILLING

Equipment
Saucepan
Bowl
Mixing spoon
Eggbeater

Yield: Eight 23-cm [9-in] pies

Metric	Ingredients	Customary
1.9 L	Water (hot)	2 qt
1.8 kg	Sugar	4 lb
340 g	Cornstarch	12 oz
950 mL	Water (cold)	1 qt
10 mL	Salt	2 t
340 g	Egg yolks	12 oz
110 g	Margarine	4 oz
10 mL	Grated lemon rind	2 t
625 mL	Lemon juice	$2\frac{1}{2}$ c

METHOD

1. **Bring** water and sugar to a boil.
2. **Mix** cornstarch with cold water. Add to boiling water, stirring all the time. Cook for 15 minutes.
3. **Beat** eggs with salt slightly. Add a little of the hot mixture to the eggs to warm them.
4. **Pour** egg mixture into hot mixture. Cook for 3 minutes.
5. **Add** margarine, lemon juice, and lemon rind.
6. **Cool** and fill piecrust.

CREAM PIE FILLING

Equipment
Double boiler   Mixing spoon
Bowl   Eggbeater

Yield: Eight 23-cm [9-in] pies

Metric	Ingredients	Customary
2.8 L	Milk (hot)	3 qt
1.4 kg	Sugar	3 lb
285 g	Cornstarch	10 oz
950 mL	Milk (cold)	1 qt
10 mL	Salt	2 t
510 g	Egg yolks	1 lb 2 oz
225 g	Margarine	8 oz
30 mL	Vanilla	2 T

METHOD

1. **Heat** first amount of milk in double boiler.
2. **Mix** cornstarch, sugar, and cold milk.
3. **Stir** cornstarch mixture slowly into hot milk. Cook 15 minutes.
4. **Beat** egg yolks with salt slightly. Add a little of the hot mixture to the eggs to warm them.
5. **Pour** egg mixture into the hot mixture. Cook for 3 minutes.
6. **Add** margarine and stir.
7. **Remove** from heat, cool slightly, add vanilla.
8. **Cool** and fill piecrust.

LEMON CHIFFON PIE FILLING

Equipment
Small bowl
Small saucepan
Double boiler
Wire whip
Bench mixer with whip attachment

Yield: Eight pies, each 23 cm [9 in]

Metric	Ingredients	Customary
90 mL	Gelatin	6 T
250 mL	Water	1 c
30 mL	Sugar	2 T
45 mL	Lemon rind	3 T
125 mL	Water	$\frac{1}{2}$ c
375 mL	Lemon juice	$1\frac{1}{2}$ c
28	Egg yolks	28
680 g	Sugar	$1\frac{1}{2}$ lb
28	Egg whites	28
450 g	Sugar	1 lb

LEMON CHIFFON PIE FILLING (Continued)

METHOD

1. **Soak** gelatin in water in small saucepan.
2. **Boil** first amount of sugar, lemon rind, water, and lemon juice in small saucepan until sugar is dissolved.
3. **Beat** egg yolks slightly in top of double boiler using wire whip. Gradually stir in second amount of sugar.
4. **Add** lemon mixture gradually. Cook over hot water until mixture begins to thicken.
5. **Remove** from heat and stir in gelatin. Stir until gelatin is dissolved. Cool.
6. **Refrigerate** until gelatin begins to set.
7. **Beat** egg whites in bench mixer to soft peaks. Add third portion of sugar, and beat until stiff but not dry.
8. **Fold** into gelatin mixture. Spoon into baked pie shells.
9. **Chill** for 4 hours before serving.
10. **Serve** with sweetened whipped cream swirled on top.

PUMPKIN CUSTARD PIE

Equipment
Bowl
Eggbeater
Unbaked pie shell

Yield: Eight 21-cm [9-in] pies
Temperature: 190°C [375° F.]
Time: 40–60 minutes

Metric	Ingredients	Customary
900 g	Brown sugar	2 lb
680 g	Granulated sugar	1½ lb
20 mL	Salt	4 t
40 mL	Cinnamon	8 t
20 mL	Ginger	4 t
10 mL	Cloves	2 t
16	Eggs	16
3 L	Canned pumpkin	3 qt
3 L	Evaporated milk	3 qt

METHOD

1. **Mix** sugar, salt, and spices in bowl.
2. **Beat** eggs. Add to spice mixture.
3. **Add** pumpkin. Mix well.
4. **Stir in** milk. Mix until smooth.
5. **Pour** into unbaked pie shell.
6. **Bake** at 190°C [375° F.] 40–60 minutes until set.

Cakes

What Will You Learn?

When you finish studying this chapter, you should be able to do the following:
- Define the *Words to Remember.*
- Prepare and bake butter, foam, and chiffon cakes that meet acceptable standards of excellence.
- Make up each cake for service, meeting acceptable standards of excellence.
- Achieve a passing grade on the posttest.

CHAPTER 19

The dictionary defines a cake as a mixture of flour, sugar, eggs, milk, and flavoring which is baked and often covered with icing. Every language has a word for cake for they have long been popular all over the world. From earliest times, *cakes* are mentioned in history. The Egyptians, Greeks, and Norse used cakes as a religious offering, for cakes were said to be "food for the gods." Today a moist, tender, sweet cake is among the most popular desserts offered on the menu.

There are many different kinds of cakes. Chocolate, spice, and fruit cakes are just a few of the endless varieties achieved by different flavorings and ingredients. Cakes may be baked in round, square, rectangular, or tube pans. They may be served with fresh fruit or iced with a sweet frosting. Some may have many layers with a sweet filling between the layers. For special occasions, cakes may be baked to resemble animals, trees, flowers, houses, or persons. A variety of color and flavor in the icings adds further interest.

SUCCESS FACTORS IN CAKE BAKING

Learning to make a perfect cake can be one of the greatest pleasures of baking. It is well worth the time and effort to achieve perfection.

Successful cake baking depends upon six factors.

Words to Remember

almond paste
balance
foam cake
formula
German sweet
   chocolate
gingerbread
high-ratio shortening

high-stability flour
petit fours
pound cake
shortened cake
upside-down cake
white cake
yellow cake

- A correct recipe.
- High-quality ingredients.
- Accurate weighing of ingredients.
- Correct pan size.
- Correct mixing methods.
- Correct baking temperature.

The Recipe

A cake is a very delicate product. Its quality depends first of all on a correct recipe.

A cake recipe is sometimes called a *formula* because each ingredient must be in correct proportion to the others. Even a small variation in one ingredient can change the quality of the cake. A formula with correct proportions of the ingredients, one to another, is said to be in *balance*. A balanced cake recipe, if followed accurately, will produce a perfect cake every time.

SOURCES FOR CAKE RECIPES

There are many sources for balanced cake recipes, or formulas. Most pastry chefs have a file of tested recipes. Some may be for "specialty of the house" cakes. Many restaurants have become famous through a cake recipe that has won applause from the customers.

Cookbooks of cake recipes are constantly being written for the bakery trade. Some may contain famous recipes from well-known eating places.

Companies that sell flour, shortening, and other ingredients to bakeries often maintain test kitchens. New recipes are developed and old ones revised and improved. These recipes are made available to bakers at no cost.

A careful baker will always try out a new recipe in small quantities first. A small error in the cake recipe may cause a large failure in the final product.

Ingredients

The highest-quality flour, shortening, sugar, eggs, leavener, and flavorings are needed for cakes. All ingredients should be at room temperature to produce a high-volume, fine-textured cake.

- *Flour.* A *high-stability flour* is needed. High-stability flour is a low-gluten flour that blends easily with the shortening to form a stable batter. A stable batter resists curdling. The stability promotes tenderness and fineness of grain. Batters made with this type of flour make a good product even if slightly overmixed or slightly undermixed.

Too much flour will cause a tough cake that cracks during baking. Too little flour will cause the cake to fall.

- *Shortening.* A *high-ratio shortening* is needed to absorb the sugar easily. A high-ratio shortening helps spread the fat throughout the sugar during the creaming process. It helps prevent curdling. With this type of shortening more sugar can be used in proportion to the shortening and flour. It produces a high-volume, very tender, very sweet cake with a fine grain and velvety texture. Although butter still gives the best flavor, it is more expensive and does not cream to as high a volume. Bakers frequently add artificial butter color and flavor to a cake.

Shortening should be at room temperature, but not melted. Melted shortening will not cream to a high volume.

Too little shortening will cause a tough cake with poor keeping qualities. Too much shortening will cause the cake to fall.

- *Sugar.* A fine, granulated sugar such as ultrafine or baker's special should be used. Fine sugar mixes more easily with the shortening during creaming. It produces a fine cake with more volume than that produced by coarser sugar. Sometimes part of the white sugar is replaced with brown sugar because of the flavor it gives.

Too much sugar will cause a dark-crusted cake. It may also cause the cake to fall. Too little sugar will cause a tough cake with poor keeping qualities.

	Size	Capacity
Rectangular		
	23 x 35 cm [9 x 13 in]	900 g [2 lb]
	30 x 51 cm [12 x 20 in]	1.8 kg [4 lb]
	46 x 66 cm [18 x 26 in]	3.6 kg [8 lb]
Round		
	23 x 4 cm [9 x 1½ in]	450 g [1 lb]
	25 x 4 cm [10 x 1½ in]	570 g [1 lb 4 oz]
Loaf		
	20 x 9 x 8 cm [8 x 3½ x 3¼ in]	450 g [1 lb]
	28 x 15 x 8 cm [11 x 6 x 3¼ in]	1.4 kg [3 lb]
Tube		
	25 x 10 cm [10 x 4 in]	6.75 g to 900 g [1½ to 2 lb]

Table 19-1. Size and Capacity of Cake Pans

• *Eggs.* Fresh eggs in the shell, fresh liquid eggs, frozen eggs, and dried eggs may be used. Most bakers prefer the liquid form.

Eggs are essential in cake baking. So-called "eggless" cakes are really quick breads. Since a very weak or soft flour is used in making cakes, eggs are needed to maintain the structure of the product.

A cake with too few eggs will be low in volume, coarse in texture, and have poor keeping qualities.

• *Liquid.* Usually, milk is used because it strengthens the structure of the cake and yet helps tenderize it. The milk may be fresh, canned or dried. Bakers prefer dried milk because it is easy to use and requires no refrigeration.

Too much liquid will cause a dense grain and too much shrinkage of the cake during baking. It will also cause fruits or nuts to sink to the bottom. Too little liquid will cause a tough cake.

• *Leavener.* Any of the leaveners may be used, except yeast. Some cakes depend on air and steam from beaten eggs for leavening power. In others, the main action comes from chemical leaveners. Baking powder is common, but baking soda with acid is also used.

Too much leavener will cause a very coarse cake with uneven grain, poor quality, and poor flavor. A cake with too little leavener will be flat with a dense grain.

Accurate Weighing of Ingredients

Accurate scales are of prime importance in cake baking to help keep the ingredients in proper proportion. Cakes of uniform quality cannot be made without them. The scales should weigh from grams to several kilos. Customary scales are graduated in ounces and pounds.

Pan Size

Scaling the batter into a pan of the correct size is also important to the final success of the cake. Too little batter in the pan will make a skimpy cake that browns too quickly. Too much batter may run over

Table 19-2 Basic Ingredients for Cake Batters

Shortened Cakes	Foam Cakes
Cake flour	Cake flour
Granulated sugar	Granulated sugar
Salt	Salt
Eggs	Eggs
Flavoring	Flavoring
Leavener (chemical)	
Milk	
Shortening	

the sides of the pan during baking. This will cause the cake to shrink in the middle.

Table 19-1 shows the usual sizes and capacities of cake pans. The largest pan is only 2.5 cm [1 in] in depth. It is seldom used except for jelly rolls since the corners may dry out before the center is done. Most bakers use the smaller pans because they have greater depth and straight sides.

Correct Mixing and Baking

There are several different methods of mixing batters for cakes. The method used is determined by the kind of cake and the ingredients.

Foam cakes require a different method of mixing than shortened cakes. A cake made with a high-ratio shortening is mixed differently than one made with regular shortening. The recipe will describe the mixing method to be used.

Recipes will also give the temperature for baking. Temperature affects the volume, texture, and color of the cake.

KINDS OF CAKES

There are two general types of cakes—*shortened* and *foam*. Table 19-2 compares the ingredients for each of these types.

So-called butter cakes are really shortened cakes because hydrogenated shortenings have widely re-

placed the use of butter. Shortened cakes use chemical leaveners.

Foam cakes may or may not contain shortening. They have a spongy texture because the main leavening action comes from the air and steam of the beaten eggs.

Shortened Cakes

A high-quality shortened cake should show these characteristics:
• Perfectly shaped with a top that is slightly rounded.
• Thin, tender, shiny, golden-brown crust.
• No cloudiness, dullness, or streaks on top.
• Moist, tender, velvety crumb.
• Fine grain.
• Good keeping qualities.
• Sweet, delicate, buttery flavor for plain, shortened cakes. Smooth, rich, chocolaty flavor for chocolate cakes with no hint of bitterness.

KINDS OF SHORTENED CAKES

All shortened cakes stem from the basic batter listed in Table 19-3. As you study the table, note the changes in the ingredients to make the different kinds of shortened cakes.
• *Gold, or yellow*—basic batter with fortified eggs or additional egg yolks.

Table 19-3. Basic Ingredients for Shortened Cake Batters

Basic Batter	Gold or Yellow Batter	Silver or White Batter	Chocolate Batter	Gingerbread Batter
Cake flour	Cake flour	Cake flour	Cake flour	Flour
Sugar	Sugar	Sugar	Sugar	Sugar
Salt	Salt	Salt	Salt	Salt
Eggs	Fortified eggs	Egg whites	Whole eggs	Whole eggs
Flavoring	Vanilla or lemon	Vanilla or almond	Vanilla	Molasses & spices
Leavener	Baking powder	Baking powder	Soda	Soda
Milk	Milk	Milk	Buttermilk	Buttermilk
Shortening	Shortening	Shortening, white	Shortening	Shortening
			Chocolate, cocoa, or German sweet chocolate	

- *Silver, or white*—basic batter with egg whites only and white shortening.
- *Chocolate*—basic batter flavored with chocolate, cocoa, or German sweet chocolate. *German sweet chocolate* is semisweet and highly prized for its delicate flavor.

As you read in Chapter 16, the color of chocolate cake depends upon the liquid and leavener that are used. Buttermilk and soda make a red cake. Sweet milk and baking powder make a dark brown cake.

- *Gingerbread*—basic batter with molasses and spices. Often, buttermilk and soda are used as the liquid and leavener. All-purpose flour may be substituted for cake flour.

In addition, several other varieties are often served.

- *Pound cake*—a fine-grained cake of rather solid consistency. Its name came from the original proportions of one pound each of shortening, sugar, and flour.
- *Upside-down cake*—basic batter poured over fruit sweetened with a sugar syrup. After baking, the cake is turned upside down. The fruit is on top.
- *Petit* (PET-e) *fours*—usually white cake baked in small oblongs. The small cakes are filled with a sweet filling. Each cake is covered with almond paste and dipped in icing. *Almond paste* is made from pulverized almonds. Since it is very time-consuming to make, it is usually bought ready-made.

A recipe for a basic shortened cake is on page 389.

MIXING METHODS

Shortened cakes are usually mixed by one of two methods—the blending method or the creaming method. The mixing method chosen depends on the ingredients and their proportion. Always follow the directions given for the recipe you are following.

Table 19-4 compares the two methods of mixing.

- *Blending method.* The blending method is used more often in food service than any other method. It gives a rich, sweet cake with a good shelf life. It takes less time than the creaming method. Sometimes this method is called the two-step method.

Table 19-4. Methods of Mixing Shortened Cakes

Blending Method	Creaming Method
1. Sift flour, baking powder, and salt into mixer bowl. Add shortening. Blend on low speed with the paddle for 5 minutes. Scrape down at least once.	1. Cream sugar, shortening, and vanilla in mixer bowl, using the paddle on low speed. Cream 10 minutes.
2. Mix eggs, milk and vanilla. Add half the mixture to ingredients in mixer bowl. Blend on low speed for 3 minutes. Scrape down.	2. Add eggs and cream 5 minutes.
3. Add sugar and blend for 3 minutes. Scrape down.	3. Sift flour, baking powder, and salt together.
4. Add remaining liquid and blend for 5 minutes, scraping down at least twice.	4. Add alternately with the milk to the creamed mixture, beginning and ending with dry ingredients. Scrape down at least once. Mix about 3 minutes until well blended.
5. Scale and pan in greased pans.	5. Scale and pan in greased pans.

	Angel Food	Sponge Cake (Warm Method)	Chiffon Cake

Table 19-5. Basic Ingredients for Three Types of Foam Cake	Egg whites
	Sugar
	Cake flour
	Salt
	Cream of tartar
	Vanilla or Almond
	   flavoring
		Fortified eggs
		Sugar
		Cake flour
		Salt
		Baking powder
		Vanilla or lemon
		Margarine
		Milk
			Whole eggs
			Sugar
			Cake flour
			Salt
			Baking powder
			Vanilla or other
			   flavoring
			Salad oil
			Water
			Cream of tartar

Never use it with regular shortening. It requires high-ratio shortening for success.

• *Creaming method.* The creaming method is also called the *conventional method*. It is more difficult and time-consuming than the blending method. However, many bakers believe it gives the best cake with the highest volume. Either regular or high-ratio shortening may be used with this method.

The batter in the blending method is thin. The batter in the creaming, or conventional, method is thick and fluffy.

The *muffin,* or *dump, method* is sometimes used for cakes. It is very quick but produces a coarse-grained, tough, dry cake. This method will be described in Chapter 20.

Mixes may be cheaper and better than producing cakes from "scratch." Most mixes contain all the ingredients except water. Some may require the addition of fresh eggs. The manufacturer's directions for adding ingredients, mixing, timing, and baking should be followed exactly.

Some large food service chains develop their own formulas for cakes. The formulas are given to a mill, which packages the mix under the name of the chain. This assures a uniform quality and taste to all cakes baked by that chain.

Other food service bake stations make their own mixes, ready for use as needed. Usually the blending method of mixing is used. After the dry ingredients

and shortening are blended, the mixture is stored in tightly covered containers. It is then stored in a cool place. Only the liquid and eggs need be added before baking.

Words to Remember

angel food cake   sponge cake
chiffon cake   sunshine cake
cold method   warm method
daffodil cake

Foam Cakes

Angel food, sponge, and *chiffon* cakes are types of foam cakes. Table 19-5 compares the ingredients for these three cakes. Although each has a basis of egg foam for leavening, they are very different from each other in taste, texture, and appearance. In addition to the egg foam, sponge and chiffon cakes have additional leavening from baking powder.

ANGEL FOOD CAKES

Angel food cakes are pure white because only the egg whites are used. They require very fine granulated sugar. Some recipes call for powdered sugar. Only the finest cake flour should be used for these delicate cakes. The cream of tartar helps stabilize the egg whites so they will retain air during mixing and baking. The acidity of the cream of tartar helps whiten the flour and reduce cake shrinkage during the cooling period.

The recipe for angel food cake is on page 388.

• *Mixing Method.* The mixing method may be found in Table 19-6. The success of the cake depends upon the correct mixing techniques.

Note that this particular method of mixing divides the sugar into two parts. Half the sugar is added to the beaten egg whites. The other half is sifted with the flour. Most pastry chefs believe this technique gives a higher, more tender cake. Other pastry chefs prefer to add all the sugar to the egg whites. When beating the egg whites, be careful not to overbeat. They should stand in peaks but should be glossy—never dry. Add the sugar gradually while beating. The weight of too much sugar at one time may flatten the egg whites.

Most pastry chefs fold in the flour with the hand. A spatula may be used, if preferred. Do not over-mix. Overmixing will make a tough cake. Fold until the flour disappears.

• *Variations of angel food cake.* Sunshine and daffodil cakes are variations of angel food. A *sunshine* cake contains some egg yolks as well as whites. The beaten egg yolks are added to the beaten egg whites after the sugar. Sunshine cakes are always flavored with lemon juice. A *daffodil* cake uses both yellow and white batter. The egg yolks are added to only half the batter. By alternating spoonfuls of yellow and white batter when filling the pans, a pretty yellow and white cake can be made.

Because it is difficult and time-consuming to make a fine angel food cake, many pastry chefs have turned to mixes or buying commercially made cakes. The mixes contain dried egg whites, which give a more stable foam. Therefore, the danger of overmixing is much less. The cost is about the same. The directions on the package must be followed exactly for best results.

Table 19-6. Methods of Mixing Three Types of Foam Cakes

Angel Food	Sponge (Warm Method)	Chiffon
1. *Sift* flour and half the sugar together four times. 2. *Place* egg whites in mixer bowl. Using the whip, beat on high speed until frothy. Add cream of tartar and salt. Beat to stiff peaks. 3. *Gradually add* half the sugar while beating. 4. *Add* flavorings and blend. Remove bowl from machine. 5. *Fold in* flour-sugar mixture until flour disappears. 6. *Scale and pour* into ungreased tube pan.	1. *Place* eggs in bowl and beat on high speed for 5 minutes. 2. *Weigh and sift* sugar. Add gradually to the eggs while beating. Beat for 10 minutes, scraping down the bowl at least three times. 3. *Heat* milk and melt margarine in it. 4. *Sift* flour, baking powder, and salt twice. 5. *Reduce speed* to low. Add the dry ingredients alternately with the milk to the egg mixture. Begin and end with flour. 6. *Scale and pour* into greased pans.	1. *Sift* flour, half the sugar, baking powder, and salt into bowl. Make a depression in center of flour mixture. 2. *Add* in this order: oil, egg yolks, water, and vanilla. Mix, using the paddle on low speed, until just blended. 3. *Place* egg whites and cream of tartar in a clean bowl. Using whip, beat on high until in soft peaks. Add rest of sugar gradually while beating. Beat to stiff peaks. 4. *Pour* first mixture into second mixture. Fold until blended. 5. *Scale and pour* into ungreased tube pan.

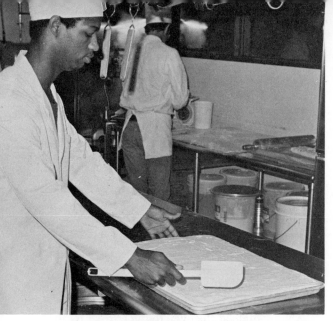
19-1. Reggie frosts a sheet cake.

The milk should be quite hot—just under the boiling point.

The batter will be thin. Pan immediately and bake, since the baking powder will begin to react from the heat of the milk.

This type of sponge cake may be baked in sheet pans or a tube.

CHIFFON CAKES

Chiffon cakes are newcomers to the family of foam cakes. Angel food and sponge cakes have been baked for hundreds of years, but chiffon cakes became popular about thirty years ago. They are extremely light, tender, moist, and delicious. In the last few years they have replaced angel food cake in popularity.

The ingredients and method of mixing for a chiffon cake may be found in Tables 19-5 and 19-6. Note that this type of cake uses salad oil. This gives the cake a good shelf life. The oil tenderizes and keeps the cake moist.

• *Mixing Method.* For success, the ingredients must be added in the order listed in Table 19-6. Chiffon cakes are easy to make because the batter is much more stable than that of angel food. It is not as sensitive to undermixing or overmixing.

Chiffon cakes may be made in many different varieties by adding chocolate, fruits, nuts, and many different flavorings. The method of mixing is always the same.

PANNING OF CAKES

All cake batters should be panned and baked immediately after mixing. Loss of air occurs if the mixture is allowed to stand. In shortened cakes or in sponge cakes using baking powder, the leavener will begin to react with the warmth and moisture. This causes loss of carbon dioxide.

Scale cakes according to the capacity of each pan as shown in Table 19-1.

Round cake pans are used for multiple-layer cakes. Although beautiful, these cakes require time for assembling, frosting, and serving. Many food service places prefer to serve single-layer cakes baked in rectangular pans. Fig. 19-1. Quantity cake recipes have been developed for different pan sizes.

SPONGE CAKES

Sponge cakes are golden yellow because of the large quantity of egg yolks. A fine sponge cake should have a high volume and a spongy texture. It should be sweet with a definite egg taste. The crust should be thin and golden brown. It may be flavored with vanilla, lemon, or other flavorings.

Sponge cakes may be made by two methods—the *cold method* or the *warm method.* The warm method is preferred. It makes a fine-grained, sweet cake with a good shelf life. Cakes made by the cold method are difficult to make, and they dry out quickly.

The ingredients for sponge cakes made by the warm method are listed in Table 19-5. Notice that margarine, baking powder, and milk are included. The margarine and milk add to the tenderness and the shelf life of the cake. Since fewer eggs are used, the baking powder assists in making a high volume cake.

• *Mixing Method.* The mixing method may be detailed in Table 19-6. While studying this method, be careful to follow these precautions.

All ingredients should be warm. Warm the sugar slightly in the oven. Warm the eggs over steam. For best results, the eggs should be about 50°C [120° F.].

Preparation and Filling the Pans

- *Shortened cakes*. Pans for shortened cakes need to be greased on the bottom and the sides. Use a commercially prepared pan grease or one prepared in the bakery. Some chefs use a mixture of one measure of shortening, one measure of oil, and one-half measure of flour. Others prefer to line the pans with silicone-treated paper.

Cake batters made by the blending method will spread easily to the corners of the pan because they are thin. Batters made by the creaming method are thick. Spread them evenly in the pans by using a spatula or the hand.

After filling each pan, rap it sharply on the bench. This settles the batter to the bottom of the pan and expels any air bubbles.

- *Foam cakes*. Angel food, sunshine, and chiffon cakes are baked in a deep, round pan with a tube in the center. The tube conducts the heat to the center of the large cake so that the outside and the inside will be done at the same time. The pan is ungreased to allow the delicate batter to climb up the sides.

Pour the batter into the pan very carefully. Turn the pan as you pour so it will fill evenly. Cut through the batter several times with a knife so no large air bubbles will be trapped under the batter. Bake immediately.

Unlike the other foam cakes, sponge cake made by the warm method requires a greased pan.

If the sponge cake is to be used for a jelly roll, it must have special handling. Jelly roll cakes are baked in large sheet pans. As discussed earlier, these pans are very shallow. They are too shallow for sheet cakes, but just right for jelly rolls. Grease the pan very heavily and sprinkle with flour to prevent sticking. A silicone liner may be used instead.

BAKING

During baking the cake goes through the following four stages:

1. The batter is quite liquid and rises rapidly.
2. The rising continues, bubbles form, and browning begins.
3. Rising is completed, eggs coagulate, and the starch hardens, forming the structure.
4. The crust turns golden brown and the cake shrinks from the sides of the pan.

Baking is critical to the cake's quality. While the cake is in the first two stages, jarring or vibration may cause the cake to fall. Even opening the oven door at this critical time may cause a failure.

Oven Temperature

An oven that is too hot will cause the cake to rise too fast. The grain will be coarse, the top cracked, and the crust too brown.

An oven that is too cool will cause a compact grain, a flat cake, and a sticky, colorless crust.

Uneven heat will cause a cake higher on one side than the other.

Always preheat the oven to the correct temperature before putting in the cakes. What is the correct temperature? Bakers do not always agree on the best temperature for baking cakes. Some bake all cakes at 190°C [375° F.]. They vary the time, but keep the temperature constant.

Other bakers believe that the temperature affects the volume, moisture, and grain of a cake. In selecting the temperature, they follow these rules:

- Bake shortened cakes made by the blending method at a higher temperature than those made by the creaming method. The thinner batter needs a higher temperature to evaporate the liquid.
- Bake chocolate cakes at a lower temperature because chocolate burns very easily.
- Bake large, thick cakes at a lower temperature so the inside and the outside will be done at the same time.
- Bake foam cakes at a much lower temperature. Bakers differ on the exact temperature they prefer.

Table 19-7 will help you judge the time and temperature needed for baking in a conventional oven. Table 19-8 gives the recommended times and temperatures for baking in a convection oven. As a beginner, follow the temperature and time given in the recipe.

Placement in the Oven

Place cake pans in the oven so they do not touch each other or the sides of the oven. Free circulation

Table 19-7. Cake Baking Temperatures and Times (at Sea Level)

Cake	Temperature		Time
	°C	°F.	
Shortened cakes			
Blended	190	375	See form of cake for time.
Creamed	177	350	
Chocolate	177	350	
Cupcakes	190	375	20 minutes
Layer cakes	See mixing method		25 minutes
Loaf cakes	177	350	45–60 minutes
Thick sheet cakes	177	350	35–40 minutes
Foam cakes			
Angel food	149–163	300–325	1 hour
Chiffon	149–163	300–325	1 hour
Sponge (warm method)	177	350	25 minutes

of air is necessary for an even distribution of heat. If a conventional oven is being used, place the oven rack about one-third up from the floor of the oven. The heat is most even there. The entire shelf of a carousel-type oven may be used. In a convection oven, the heat is even because the air is circulated by a fan. Hence, the placement of the cakes is not important. The whole oven may be used.

Some bakers bake a layer cake a little differently. A layer cake needs to be very moist, but the brown-

Table 19-8. Recommended Temperatures and Times for Baking (Convection Oven)

Type of Cake	Temperature		Time (in minutes)
	°C	°F.	

Shortened sheet cakes
45 x 65 x 2.5 cm [18 x 26 x 1 in]
  Scaled 2–2.7 kg [4½–6 lb] per pan
  Scaled 2.7–3.4 kg [6–7½ lb] per pan
	163–182
	168–177
		325–360
		335–350
			20–23
			22–25

Shortened sheet cakes 45 x 65 x 5 cm [18 x 26 x 2 in] Scaled 4.5 to 5.4 kg [10–12 lb] per pan	149–163	300–325	25–35
Foam sheet cakes 45 x 65 x 2.5 cm [18 x 26 x 1 in] Scaled 2.3–2.7 kg [5–6 lb] per pan	149–163	300–325	15–20
Foam, Loaf, or Tube Cakes	157–171	315–340	20–30
Cupcakes	177–204	350–400	6–12

ing is not important. The outside of the cake will be covered with frosting. To insure a moist cake, place the cake pan filled with shortened cake batter in a sheet pan partially filled with water. The water will steam during the baking. It will keep the cake very moist and prevent the sides from becoming brown and crusty.

Timing

Recipes always give the approximate time for baking a cake. The time can never be exact because it depends upon the oven temperature, the size of the pan, and the thickness of the batter.

As the time nears when the cake should be done, watch it carefully. When the cake is done, the bake station will be fragrant with the aroma of freshly baked cake. A time-honored method of testing the doneness is with a toothpick. It will come out clean when inserted into the middle of the cake. The cake will spring back when lightly touched with the finger. Be careful not to overbake. This will dry out the cake.

Adjustment for Altitude

Cake recipes are written to be baked at sea level. Therefore, they are affected by change in altitude because the air pressure decreases as elevation increases. Most formulas need no adjustment up to 914 m [3000 ft] above sea level. Above that, the leavening, sugar, liquid, and temperature must be modified.

Table 19-9 shows the changes needed in cake formulas from 914 m [3000 ft] to 2 134 m [7000 ft].

Each of these adjustments depends upon the richness of the cake formula and the proportion of one ingredient to another. A rich formula containing a high proportion of shortening, eggs, and sugar will require more adjustment than a lean formula.

When baking at high altitudes, bakers and pastry chefs must experiment in small quantities to find the exact amount of adjustment for each ingredient for a particular recipe. Once the recipe has been adjusted for altitude, success will follow each time the cake is baked.

Most cake mixes give the needed adjustment for altitude on the package.

Care and Storage

When cakes are removed from the oven, they are very fragile and break apart easily. Handle them according to these directions:

• *Shortened cakes* should cool in the pans on a rack for at least fifteen minutes. Shortened cakes should be removed from the pans while still warm so the bottom will not become soggy. Pound cakes require a longer period—about thirty minutes.

Loosen the sides of the cake with a spatula and turn the cake out on a rack. Turn the cake right-side-up on another rack. If a silicone liner was used, strip it off before righting the cake.

• *Foam cakes* should be inverted in the pan until cool. A tube pan has three "legs" so the cake will

Table 19-9. Guide for Cake-Baking at High Altitudes*

Adjustment	Altitude		
	914 m [3000 ft]	1 524 m [5000 ft]	2 134 m [7000 ft]
Reduce baking powder. For each teaspoon, decrease...	0.5 mL [$\frac{1}{8}$ t]	0.5–1 mL [$\frac{1}{8}$–$\frac{1}{4}$ t]	1 mL [$\frac{1}{4}$ t]
Reduce sugar. For each cup, decrease...	0–15 mL [0–1 T]	0–30 mL [0–2 T]	15–45 mL [1–3 T]
Increase liquid. For each cup, add...	15–30 mL [1–2 T]	30–60 mL [2–4 T]	45–60 mL [3–4 T]

*Adapted from Handbook of Food Preparation, American Home Economics Association, Washington, D. C.

not touch the bench while cooling. Do not remove the cakes from the pans until completely cool. Otherwise, they may break apart.

Sponge cakes for jelly rolls require special handling. Fig. 19-2. Place a clean towel on the bench. Spread it heavily with powdered sugar. Turn out the warm cake on the towel. Strip off the silicone lining, if used. Roll the cake loosely in the towel, using the towel to separate the roll. Unroll when cool. Spread with jelly. Roll up cake, using the towel to keep pressure even.

If the cakes are not to be made up immediately, they should be tightly wrapped when cool and stored in the refrigerator or freezer. If properly wrapped, cakes will keep for several days under refrigeration and several weeks if frozen. Unrefrigerated cakes mold very easily, especially in hot, humid weather.

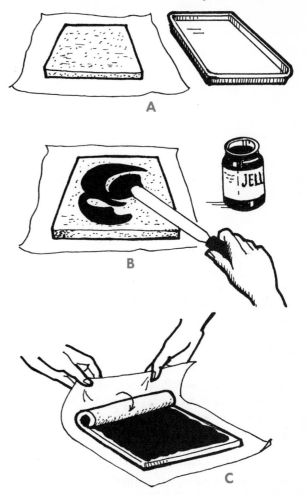

19-2. Making a jelly roll. (A) Spread a clean towel with powdered sugar. Turn out the warm cake on the towel. Roll up loosely, using the towel to separate the roll. (B) When cool, unroll and spread with jelly. (C) Roll up cake, using the towel to keep the pressure even.

Words to Remember

boiled frosting	icing
cake filling	pastry bag
creamed frosting	saturated solution
crystallization	simple icing
decorator's frosting	solution
decorator's wheel	sugar chef
fondant	supersaturated
frosting	solution
glaze	

FROSTING, ICING, AND DECORATING CAKES

Cakes may be prepared for service in different ways, but the type of makeup should be right for the kind of cake. For instance, some cakes such as angel food or pound may be served with fresh fruit and topped with whipped cream. A very rich, shortened cake may simply be dusted with powdered sugar.

To many persons, a cake is not a cake unless it is covered with a sweet frosting or icing. To some people, the terms *icing* and *frosting* are the same since both are made from a mixture of cooked or uncooked sugar, liquid, and flavoring. However, to a

baker, icing is thin and pourable. Frosting is thick, fluffy, and smearable.

A *cake filling* is a sweet, moist mixture spread between the layers of a cake to add flavor and moisture and to hold the layers together. It may be the same mixture as the frosting or a cream filling such as is used in pies. It may be a mixture of nuts, dried fruits, nonfat milk solids, sugar, and water.

Table 19-10. Amounts of Frosting to Use Per Cake

Cake Size	Type Frosting	Amount of Frosting	
		Filling	Sides and Top
Two layer			
23 cm [9 in]	Butter cream	110 g [4 oz]	325 g [11½ oz]
23 cm [9 in]	Boiled	70 g [2½ oz]	170 g [6 oz]
Sheet cake			
33 x 23 cm			
[13 x 9 in]	Butter cream		375 mL [1½ c]
66 x 48 x 3 cm			
[26 x 19 x 1 in]	Butter cream		1.5 L [6 c]

A *glaze* may be a thin coating of a sweet syrup, spread on the cake and broiled lightly in the oven. It may be poured over a hot cake, becoming firm as it cools and sealing the cake. A glaze may also be a sweet sauce, thickened with waxy maize and poured over a fruit topping to make it glossy and more appealing.

Frostings and icings are spread on cakes to improve appearance. While they add greatly to the eye appeal of the cakes, they also add flavor and richness. They add moisture and prevent cakes from drying out.

Frostings and icings demand the very best ingredients, especially in the choice of shortening. The highest quality butter or a shortening specifically developed for frostings should be used. Other rules to follow are:

• If powdered sugar is needed, use ultrafine or 10X.

• Use only the best flavorings. Cheap flavorings may destroy the quality of the cake.

• Be careful of coloring. Beginners tend to use shades that are too deep and vivid. Pastel tints and shades are more natural looking.

• Be sure the consistency of the frosting is right before spreading it on the cake. A frosting that is too thin will run. A frosting that is too thick may tear the cake surface during spreading.

• Use fresh fruit flavor whenever possible, but be careful of acids such as orange or lemon juice. They may cause the frosting to curdle.

Frostings are also used to decorate cakes for special occasions such as birthdays or anniversaries. Cake decorating may be very simple or extremely intricate. Cake decorating takes much time. Thus, highly decorated cakes are expensive.

Some restaurants and hotels may employ a sugar chef. A sugar chef has mastered the art and techniques of cake decorating. Such places usually specialize in banquets and receptions. On these occasions, elaborately decorated cakes are in demand.

A frosting should be liberal but not so heaped up that the cake is smothered by it. Table 19-10 shows the amounts of fillings and frostings needed for cakes of different sizes.

Uncooked Frostings and Icings

An uncooked icing is thin enough to be poured. An uncooked creamed frosting, however, is fluffy and thick enough to be spread. Another type of frosting, called decorator's frosting, is used only for special items such as rosettes on decorated cakes. Table 19-11 lists these three types.

• *Uncooked icings.* A thin, pourable icing is also called *simple, flat,* or *plain water icing.* It is a smooth mixture of liquid and powdered sugar. Warmed slightly, the icing may be spread on Danish pastries, sweet rolls, angel food cake, and sponge cake. It may be spread with a brush. Sometimes, it is poured over the top of the cake and allowed to run down the sides. Since this type of icing usually has no shortening, it dries and becomes brittle after a few hours. A variation may contain a small amount of shortening to prevent this drying out and prolong the shelf life.

- *Creamed frostings.* A *creamed frosting* is smooth, and fluffy. It is used more than any other type of frosting. It is easy to make, lends itself to decorating, and has a long shelf life.

It is made by two methods. The first is simpler to make but requires more shortening and heavy cream.

The second uses cornstarch and milk and so is less expensive. Frequently, milk powder is substituted for fresh milk.

Creamed frostings may be varied by using differ-

ent flavorings. Chocolate or cocoa, coffee, maple, and many other flavorings add variety.

Nuts or candied cherries may be added, especially in the portion to be used as a filling. The nuts may also be sprinkled over the top of the cake after frosting.

- *Decorator's frosting.* *Decorator's frosting* uses egg whites, shortening, and powdered sugar. It is too thick to be spread on a cake, but can easily be shaped into such items as rosettes, leaves, numerals, or letters. It dries very hard. Thus, the items can be placed on the cake after it has been frosted.

In humid weather, cornstarch may be added as a drier. Since the icing becomes dry and brittle, it

Table 19-11. Uncooked Icings and Frostings

| Simple Icing | Creamed Frosting | | Decorator's Frosting |
	Method Number 1	Method Number 2	
Ingredients Flavoring Water, milk, or fruit juice Powdered sugar **Method of Mixing** 1. *Mix* flavoring with liquid. 2. *Gradually add* powdered sugar to liquid. 3. *Blend* until smooth.	**Ingredients** Shortening Powdered sugar Vanilla Cream Salt **Method of Mixing** 1. *Cream* shortening, sugar, salt and vanilla on medium speed for 5 minutes. 2. *Add* cream and cream until light and fluffy.	**Ingredients** Shortening Sugar Cornstarch Milk Powdered sugar Vanilla **Method of Mixing** 1. *Cream* shortening with sugar on medium speed for 10 minutes. 2. *Combine* cornstarch and milk in saucepan. Heat to boiling, stirring all the time. Cook until thick. 3. *Cool.* 4. *Add* to creamed mixture. 5. *Add* powdered sugar and vanilla.	**Ingredients** Egg whites Shortening Powdered sugar **Method of Mixing** 1. *Place* all ingredients in mixer bowl. 2. *Beat* on medium speed until smooth, thick, and fluffy.

should be stored, tightly covered, in the refrigerator. If it becomes too stiff to work, thin it with a little water or egg white.

Mixes

Uncooked frostings are easily made. Thus, frosting mixes such as are found on the grocer's shelves are seldom used in food service. However, a commercially prepared fudge base is frequently used for a fluffy chocolate frosting. Only powdered sugar and water need be added. Follow the directions on the container.

Cooked Frostings and Sugar Cookery

Cooked frostings are much more difficult to make than uncooked frostings because cooked frostings involve the principles of sugar cookery. However, if you enjoy the artistry of cake frosting and decorating, you will be willing to learn the techniques for perfect cake frostings.

SUGAR COOKERY

Sugar dissolved in a liquid is the basis for most cooked frostings. The principles of sugar cookery concern how to dissolve large amounts of sugar in a liquid, and how to turn the dissolved sugar into a smooth, creamy mass for frostings or candies.

You need to know the following terms in order to understand sugar cookery.

- *Solution.* A *solution* consists of a solid dissolved in a liquid. In sugar cookery, a mixture of sugar is blended with a liquid, usually water or milk.
- *Saturated solution.* A solution holding as much dissolved sugar possible under certain conditions is a *saturated solution.*
- *Supersaturated solution.* When a saturated solution cools, it becomes *supersaturated.* It holds much more sugar than it normally could.
- *Crystallization.* As a supersaturated solution cools, it forms many crystals. This process is called *crystallization.* Crystallization is extremely important in making candies and frostings. Crystals may be of different sizes. Crystallization is a chain reaction. If large crystals are formed at the beginning, the succeeding crystals will be large. If small crystals are formed, the succeeding crystals will be small. Large crystals make a grainy, undesirable product. Small crystals make a smooth, creamy product.

Sugar dissolves easily in hot water. The hotter the water, the greater the amount of sugar that will dissolve in it. For instance, twice as much sugar will dissolve at 90°C [194° F.] as at 21°C [70° F.].

At sea level, water boils at 100°C [212° F.]. No matter how long you boil the water, the temperature will not rise any higher. However, sugar syrup can reach much higher temperatures than that. As the syrup boils, the water evaporates. The amount of sugar in the solution increases in relation to the amount of water. This causes the boiling point to rise, and the solution becomes saturated.

The amount of dissolved sugar in relation to the water can be judged by the boiling temperature. For this reason, a recipe may specify, "Cook the syrup to 113°C [235° F.]."

Different temperatures are needed for different products. Table 19-12 shows certain physical tests and the temperatures needed for different products. For instance, when a sugar solution reaches 111–112°C [232–234° F.], it will spin a thread. When a spoon is dipped into the hot syrup and held up so the liquid drips back into the pan, threads will float or spin off the drip. This test is often used for frostings.

Table 19-13 gives guides for adjustment for high altitudes. Since water boils at a lower temperature at high altitudes, the tests for sugar syrups must be adjusted.

Experienced cooks successfully use the tests shown in Table 19-12. However, a candy thermometer is the only accurate way to be sure the syrup has reached the correct temperature.

Sometimes, crystals may form on the sides of the pan during cooking. Since crystals will encourage the formation of other crystals, they should be removed. Cover the syrup when bringing it to a boil. The steam will wash down any crystals that may form. If any do remain, wipe them off with a damp cloth.

Certain ingredients may be added to sugar syrups to help form small crystals and a smooth product.

Table 19-12. Temperatures and Tests for Syrup*

Product	Temperature at Sea Level		Test	Description of Test
	°C	°F.		
Syrup	110–112	230–234	Thread	Syrup spins a 5-cm [2-in] thread when dropped from a fork or spoon.
Fondant	112–115	234–240	Soft Ball	Syrup, when dropped into very cold water, forms a soft ball that flattens on removal from water.
Boiled Frosting	112	234	Soft Ball	

*Adapted from *Handbook of Food Preparation*, American Home Economics Association, Washington, D.C.

Corn syrup may be cooked with the sugar and liquid. A small amount helps delay crystallization, and smaller crystals will be formed.

An acid such as cream of tartar or vinegar interferes with the crystallization and promotes smaller crystals. Cream of tartar is usually used for frostings. It helps keep them white and cuts a little of the sweetness. The acid must be measured carefully. Too much will keep the frosting from hardening.

When the syrup has reached the temperature specified in the recipe, it is cooled without stirring. Stirring hot syrup causes large crystals to form.

Table 19-13. Effect of Altitude on Boiling Point of Syrups

Temperature		Altitude	
°C	°F.	Metres	Feet
106	224	1 524	5000
108	226	1 219	4000
109	228	914	3000
110	230	610	2000
111	232	305	1000
112	234	Sea level	

Beating cool syrup causes small crystals to form, making a smoother product.

To review sugar cookery, remember these points:

• Add corn syrup, cream of tartar, or vinegar to the syrup before cooking.

• Wash down any crystals that may form on the sides of the pan.

• Do not stir while cooking.

• Cook to the right temperature.

• Cool the syrup without stirring.

• Beat vigorously when cool.

FONDANT

Fondant (FAHN-dunt) is a pure white icing that hardens when exposed to air. It is a sugar-water mixture boiled with cream of tartar to regulate the crystallization.

Table 19-14 gives the ingredients and method of cooking for fondant and other cooked frostings.

Some of the directions need a little more explanation. The directions say not to use an aluminum pan. Aluminum turns dark as it is used for cooking. The tarnish will come off in the fondant, turning it gray.

When putting the thermometer in the syrup, be careful that the bottom of the thermometer rests in the syrup and not on the pan itself. The temperature of the pan will be higher than that of the syrup.

Table 19-14. Cooked Frosting

Fondant	Boiled Frosting	
	Method Number 1	Method Number 2
Ingredients Granulated sugar Water Cream of tartar	**Ingredients** Granulated sugar Water Cream of tartar Egg whites	**Ingredients** Granulated sugar Water Cream of tartar Egg whites
Method of Cooking 1. *Mix* the sugar, water, and cream of tartar in a stainless steel saucepan with straight sides to hold the thermometer. Do not use aluminum. 2. *Cover* the pan and bring the syrup to a boil. Wash down the sides of the pan. 3. *Hook* the thermometer on the side of the pan and boil to 115°C [240° F.] without stirring. 4. *Pour* syrup into mixer bowl. 5. *Place* the bowl into a pan of cold water. Cool to 65°C [150° F.]. 6. *Beat* the syrup on high speed until it is stiff and white. 7. *Knead* by hand until smooth.	**Method of Cooking** 1. *Follow* the directions for making fondant. 2. *Place* the egg whites in the mixer bowl. 3. *Check* syrup temperature. When syrup is almost at 112°C [234° F.], beat the egg whites until stiff. 4. *Pour* the syrup in a thin stream over the egg whites, beating all the time. 5. *Beat* until the frosting stands in peaks.	**Method of Cooking** 1. *Follow* the directions for making fondant. 2. *Place* the egg whites in the mixer bowl. 3. *Start beating* the egg whites when the syrup has reached 112°C [234° F.]. 4. *Immediately pour* the syrup over the egg whites in a thin stream. 5. *Continue beating* until frosting stands in peaks.

The directions sound rather simple, but fondant takes much time and requires judgment for success. Many pastry chefs prefer to buy commercial fondant, which is packed in 18-kg [40-lb] cans. It is expensive. Purchased fondant will keep well if covered with a damp cloth. It may be thinned with water to the right consistency for use.

Fondant is used as a base for many frostings, but it may be used alone as an icing for small cakes such as petit fours. The cakes are dipped in the warm fondant and allowed to cool on a rack. After the fondant is hard, the cakes are decorated for service.

To prepare fondant for dipping, place it in a double boiler and heat to 38°C [100° F.], stirring all the time. The icing will become thin enough to flow freely over the item to be dipped. Do not allow the fondant to become too warm or it will lose its gloss.

Fudge frosting may be made with a fondant base. Combine commercially made fondant with butter, melted chocolate, and a small amount of evaporated milk. Increase to medium speed and beat for about four minutes. The frosting should be smooth, creamy, and fluffy. It should stand in soft peaks. It will not become brittle or hard.

BOILED FROSTINGS

Boiled frostings are also known as marshmallow, fluffy, or white mountain frostings. Egg whites are

Thomas J. Lipton, Inc.

Bundt cake, muffins, and ladyfingers are popular items on the menus of all food service operations. Served with hot tea, they provide an appealing snack.

384A

Thomas J. Lipton, Inc.

A popular beverage year-round, iced tea is especially suitable for the summer months.

General Foods

The preparation of pies, cakes, and puddings is the responsibility of the pastry chef. It takes skill and experience to prepare the desserts shown.

Oscar Mayer & Co.

The ingredients of a submarine sandwich can vary. Several kinds of meat may be used. Lettuce, tomato, and onion are usually added. One traditional characteristic is the shape of the roll.

384D

Uniformity and standardization are the keys to success in fast foods. Constant attention to such detail also helps ensure the quality of fast foods such as the hamburger shown below.

Burger King

19-3. Frosting a layer cake. The cake has been placed on a decorator's wheel.

In food service, the uncooked frostings and cooked frosting made from a commercial fondant base are used most often.

Frosting the Cake

Cakes need to be trimmed and shaped before frosting. If the crust is sticky or crumbly, remove it by placing a clean, damp cloth over the surface for a few moments. The crust should peel off easily.

Most professional bakers and pastry chefs use a *decorator's wheel* for frosting and decorating. A decorator's wheel is a plate on a turntable. The wheel revolves easily, permitting easy access to all sides of the cake, Fig. 19-3. A spatula is used to spread the frosting, Fig. 19-4.

LAYER CAKES

Place the bottom layer, top side down, on the plate. Spread the filling evenly to the edges. Place the second layer, right side up, on top. If more than two layers are used, trim the rounded top of the middle layer as flat as possible.

Spread a simple icing (see page 381) over the sides and the top of the cake. Fig. 19-5. Chill in the

used in addition to sugar syrup to give a very fluffy consistency. They may be made by two methods as shown in Table 19-14.

Method number 1 makes a frosting that hardens immediately after spreading on the cake. It is frequently used as a base for decorating a cake. By spreading with a wet spatula, the frosting can be made very smooth on top.

It is a rather difficult frosting to make because the egg whites must be beaten at the exact moment the correct temperature is reached in the sugar syrup. Judgment is required to know when the frosting has been beaten enough for spreading. If beaten too long, the frosting will become grainy and brittle.

Method number 2 makes a soft, swirly frosting that is very attractive. It hardens slowly, allowing more time for spreading on the cake. Since the frosting itself is very beautiful, it is seldom decorated.

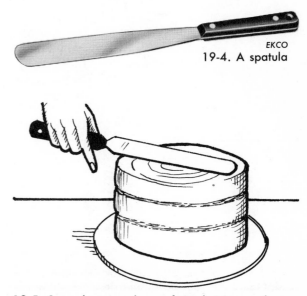

EKCO

19-4. A spatula

19-5. Spread an even layer of simple icing on the top and sides of the cake.

refrigerator until icing is hard. The icing protects the cake from the dragging effect of the thick frosting. The chilling makes the cake more firm.

Hold the spatula parallel to the sides. Frost the sides first, working from the bottom to the top. When the sides are completed, heap frosting on the top and spread it evenly. Fig. 19-6. Try to make the top as level as possible. Do this by building up the frosting on the sides. If a smooth frosting is desired, dip the spatula in warm water and smooth.

A smooth, dry top is needed for further decoration. However, a fluffy frosting looks better if it is swirled, accenting the fluffy texture.

FOAM CAKES

Foam cakes are more attractive with a light icing. For instance, a fudge fondant frosting on an angel food cake would overwhelm the delicate texture and flavor of the cake. The thin, chocolate icing described earlier would be a better choice. When frosting these delicate cakes, be careful not to exert too much pressure. Use a light touch.

A chiffon cake may have a thin icing or a butter cream frosting. Chiffon cakes, having a less spongy texture, can use a heavier frosting.

USE OF PASTRY BAG

A *pastry bag* may be used for decorating cakes. It is a tube made of cloth, plastic, or parchment paper folded and shaped like a cone. Paper is inexpensive and easily discarded. A different cone may be used for each color. Metal tips are used for the different designs. Using decorator's frosting, an experienced cake decorator can make beautiful rosettes, leaves,

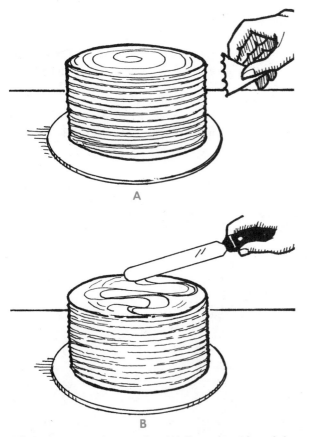

19-6. Frosting a layer cake. (A) Frost the sides of the cake. Notice the tool being used to make attractive ridges on the sides. (B) Swirl the frosting on the top of the cake.

19-7. Cakes can be decorated in a variety of ways.

and many other ornaments. The cake can be personalized with names, dates, and decorations for special occasions. Fig. 19-7. Cake decorating is not for everyone, but many find real joy in its artistry.

Care, Service, and Storage of Cakes

Since the frosting or icing seals in the moisture of cakes, they will stay fresh for several days. In humid weather, icings may become sticky through absorption of moisture from the air. To avoid this, drying ingredients such as cornstarch, flour, gelatin, or dry milk may be added to the frosting.

Great care must be taken in cutting the cake for service. Many cakes may be ruined by the wrong cutting techniques. For instance, angel food or true sponge cakes cannot be cut with a knife. The texture should be separated with a forklike cutter.

A layer cake should always be cut using a cake divider. Fig. 19-8. The use of a divider will ensure that each piece will be the same size. The cutting design depends upon the cake size, the shape, and the number of servings needed.

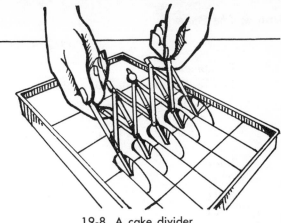

19-8. A cake divider.

Keep cakes under a plastic or metal cover while waiting for service. Once a cake is sliced, the exposed sides will dry out very quickly. To keep overnight, refrigerate in a tightly covered container.

Although frosted cakes may be frozen, the frosting will sweat during defrosting. This causes loss of quality. It is better to freeze the cake before it is frosted. Frost it the day it is to be served.

How Much Have You Learned?

Review this chapter. Answer the following questions to prepare yourself for the post-test. Check your answers with your teacher.

1. Name the six factors needed for successful cake baking. Briefly explain each one.
2. Identify the qualities needed by the following ingredients for successful cake baking: flour, sugar, shortening, eggs.
3. Describe the two methods for mixing shortened cakes.
4. How do angel food, sponge, and chiffon cakes differ from each other? Describe the method of mixing for each.
5. How are pans prepared for shortened cakes? For foam cakes?
6. Describe the four stages of cake baking.
7. How do you test the doneness of cakes?
8. Define *icing, frosting, filling,* and *glaze.* Give one example of each.
9. Name the three types of uncooked frostings and icings. Describe the methods of mixing each.
10. What is a supersaturated solution? How is it made?
11. What rules should be followed to assure a smooth, creamy, cooked frosting?
12. Why is a thermometer important in sugar cooking? If you do not have a thermometer, what tests can you use instead?
13. Why is cream of tartar added to sugar syrups?
14. Describe how to prepare and frost a layer cake.

BASIC ANGEL FOOD CAKE

Equipment
Bench mixer with balloon whip
Mixing spoon
Rubber spatula
3 tube pans, 25 cm [10 in]

Yield: 36 servings
Temperature: 165°C [325° F.]
Time: 1 hour

Metric	Ingredients	Customary
825 g	Sugar	1 lb 13 oz
370 g	Flour, cake	13 oz
1 L	Egg whites	1 qt
5 mL	Salt	1 t
23 mL	Cream of tartar	1½ T
15 mL	Vanilla	1 T
5 mL	Almond extract	1 t

METHOD

1. **Preheat** oven.
2. **Measure** sugar into two parts. The first part should weigh 225 g [8 oz]; the second part should weigh 600 g [1 lb 5 oz].
3. **Measure** flour. Sift with first amount of sugar three times.
4. **Add** salt to egg whites. Beat on high speed until foamy.
5. **Add** cream of tartar and flavorings. Beat on high speed until mixture is in stiff peaks but not dry.
6. **Add** second amount of sugar gradually. Beat until sugar disappears. Remove from beaters.
7. **Fold** the flour-sugar mixture into the egg whites. Use the spoon for folding. Fold until flour disappears.
8. **Pan** evenly into the three pans. Use spatula to scrape bowl.
9. **Cut** batter with spatula several times to remove large air bubbles.
10. **Bake.**

BASIC SHORTENED CAKE

Equipment
Bench mixer with paddle
Rubber spatula or scraper
2 cake pans 23 × 32 × 5 cm [9 × 13 × 2 in]

Yield: 30 servings
Temperature: 175°C [350° F.]
Time: 35–40 minutes

Metric	Ingredients	Customary
285 g	Shortening	10 oz
565 g	Sugar	1 lb 4 oz
250 mL	Eggs, liquid	1 c
15 mL	Vanilla	1 T
565 g	Flour, cake	1 lb 4 oz
30 mL	Baking powder	2 T
5 mL	Salt	1 t
675 mL	Milk	$2\frac{1}{2}$ c

METHOD

1. **Preheat** oven. Grease and flour pans.
2. **Cream** shortening and sugar for 15 minutes on medium speed. Scrape bowl with rubber spatula every five minutes.
3. **Sift** dry ingredients together while mixture is creaming.
4. **Reduce** to low speed. Add eggs and vanilla gradually.
5. **Increase** to high speed. Cream 5 minutes.
6. **Reduce** to low speed. Add one-third of the flour. Mix until flour disappears. Scrape down bowl.
7. **Add** half the milk. Mix until smooth. Scrape down bowl.
8. **Add** another third of the flour. Mix until flour disappears. Scrape down bowl.
9. **Add** rest of milk. Mix until smooth. Scrape down bowl.
10. **Add** rest of flour. Scrape down bowl. Mix one minute on medium speed.
11. **Pan** and bake.

Quick Breads and Cookies

What Will You Learn?

When you finish studying this chapter, you should be able to do the following:

- Define the *Words to Remember.*
- Prepare and bake a variety of quick breads that meet acceptable standards of excellence.
- Prepare and bake cookies from soft, semisoft, and stiff doughs that meet acceptable standards of excellence.
- Achieve a passing grade on the posttest.

CHAPTER 20

Quick breads are a bridge between yeast breads and cakes, having some of the qualities of both. They are often placed on the menu in place of yeast breads and rolls, offering variety and interest. They can be made quickly, thus their name.

Cookies hardly need to be defined. Most people are well acquainted with the small, sweet flat cakes. Crisp or chewy, soft or hard, they are popular with both children and adults.

QUICK BREADS

Quick breads are made with chemical leaveners, instead of yeast. They have a more tender, cakelike texture than yeast breads. Quick breads are extremely popular. Many of them are associated with Southern cooking at its finest. Beaten biscuits, cornbread, cornsticks, and cornpone have long been a part of Southern hospitality. But other regions of the United States have made contributions to these delicious hot breads. Bran muffins, johnnycake, popovers, scones, and Boston brown bread are just a few. Although they may be served at anytime, they are particularly suited to the breakfast menu.

Words to Remember

beaten biscuit
biscuit
dump, or muffin,
    method
johnnycake
loaf bread

muffin
popover
quick bread
scone
spoon bread

Remembering how long it takes to make yeast breads, you can readily understand how quick breads acquired their name. With the present emphasis on speed in food service, quick breads are gaining the importance in professional baking they deserve.

Kinds of Quick Breads

• *Biscuit.* A light, flaky, quick bread baked in small pieces. There is a recipe for baking powder biscuits on page 400.

• *Muffin.* A quick bread made with eggs and baked in small cup-shaped molds. There is a recipe for plain muffins on page 399.

• *Cornbread.* Similar to a muffin but slightly grainy because of the cornmeal. May be baked in muffin cups, as sticks, or in a cake pan.

• *Popover.* A very light, hollow muffin.

• *Scones.* A sweet, cakelike biscuit.

• *Beaten biscuit.* A flat, tender, flaky biscuit.

• *Johnnycake.* Cornbread flavored with molasses.

• *Spoon bread.* Cornbread made with white cornmeal and baked in a dish.

• *Loaf bread.* Made from batter similar to muffins, baked in loaf pans. There is a recipe for quick banana bread on page 401.

Ingredients

As you look at Table 20-1, you may notice that the ingredients are much the same for biscuits, muffins, and popovers.

• *Flour.* All-purpose flour is needed to give enough gluten for strength, but not enough to toughen.

• *Sugar.* Sugar tenderizes, adds flavor, and aids browning.

• *Milk.* Milk adds flavor, tenderizes the gluten, and aids browning.

• *Salt.* Salt is added for flavor.

These four ingredients are found in all quick breads. In addition, some breads contain shortening. Usually a hydrogenated shortening or margarine is chosen.

Eggs, also, are commonly used in quick breads. Eggs fresh in the shell or liquid eggs may be used.

PROPORTION OF INGREDIENTS

Since the ingredients are much the same for all quick breads, what makes the difference? It is in the

Table 20-1. Basic Ingredients for Biscuits, Muffins, and Popovers

Biscuits			Muffins			Popovers		
Metric	Ingredients	Customary	Metric	Ingredients	Customary	Metric	Ingredients	Customary
1.1 kg	Flour	2½ lb	1.1 kg	Flour	2½ lb	1.1 kg	Flour	2½ lb
110 g	Sugar	4 oz	225 g	Sugar	8 oz	30 mL	Sugar	2 T
450 g	Shortening	1 lb	450 g	Shortening	1 lb			
750 mL	Milk	3 c	1 L	Milk	1 qt	1.5 L	Milk	7 c
75 mL	Baking powder	5 T	60 mL	Baking powder	4 T			
15 mL	Salt	1 T	15 mL	Salt	1 T	15 mL	Salt	1 T
			225 g	Eggs	8 oz	900 kg	Eggs	2 lb

Table 20-2. Three Basic Methods for Mixing Quick Breads

Pastry, or Biscuit	Dump, or Muffin	Creaming, or Cake
1. *Sift* the flour, baking powder, and salt together in mixer bowl. 2. *Add* the shortening. Cut the shortening into the flour on low speed until the mixture is like coarse cornmeal. 3. *Add* the liquid. Blend the dough on low speed until a soft dough is formed.	1. *Sift* the flour, baking powder, sugar, and salt together. 2. *Melt* the shortening and mix with the milk. 3. *Dump* the milk into the dry ingredients. 4. *Mix* until the dry ingredients are moistened. The mixture will be lumpy.	1. *Cream* the shortening and sugar together on medium speed, using the paddle. 2. *Add* eggs and mix for 5 minutes. 3. *Sift* flour, baking powder, and salt. 4. *Add* dry ingredients alternately with the milk to the creamed mixture. Begin and end with flour.

proportion of the ingredients and in the method of mixing.

Refer to Table 20-1. Notice that all the breads take the same amount of flour. Look at the amounts of sugar. Biscuits have very little. Popovers have even less. But muffins have twice as much sugar as biscuits. Muffins are sweeter and more cakelike than biscuits.

Both biscuits and muffins contain the same amount of shortening. Popovers have none at all. Shortening makes tender biscuits and muffins. However, popovers need a strong structure to the crust, so they can pop and not collapse. Shortening would tenderize too much.

Milk is used in all three products, but look at the amounts. Biscuits take less milk than muffins. They also do not have the additional liquid from eggs. Now look at the amount of milk and eggs in the popovers. The popovers take almost three times as much milk and four times the amount of eggs as the muffins.

To understand why, you have also to look at the leavener. Notice that the popovers apparently have no leavener. But they do rise in the oven. They rise so suddenly that they are called popovers. Why? The large amount of liquid turns to steam and makes the popovers pop. This leaves a large hole in

the middle. The large amount of eggs adds structure to the popovers so the walls do not collapse.

Methods of Mixing

The ingredients and proportion of ingredients do not make all the difference in the three products. The method of mixing is important, too.

Table 20-2 compares the three methods of mixing quick breads.

The biscuit method of mixing is similar to that used for piecrusts. Biscuits are supposed to be flaky as well as tender. The shortening is cut into the dry ingredients, layering the flour with shortening. Just as in piecrust, the moist flour is left in soft, tender flakes when the shortening melts during baking. The method of mixing makes the difference.

When you were studying cakes, the *dump, or muffin, method of mixing* was mentioned as the less desirable way to mix a cake (Page 373). However, it is just right for quick breads. Quick loaf breads as well as muffins are frequently made by this very easy method. Be careful when mixing the milk and eggs into the dry ingredients. Mix only until the dry ingredients are just moistened. The batter will appear very lumpy. Overmixing will make flat-topped muffins with tunnels.

The creaming method is also often used for

loaves and muffins. It gives a finer texture and grain than the dump method.

Equipment

As always in baking, the baker's scale is needed for accurate measurement. Most quick breads are mixed on the bench mixer, using the paddle. Depending upon the type of quick bread to be made, a scraper, scoop, rolling pin, cutters, and bench scraper may be needed.

Baking sheets, loaf pans, or muffin frames may be used for baking quick breads.

Mixes

Mixes for all types of quick breads are available. Most of them are of a very high quality and produce excellent products, even by beginners. Only liquid and egg need be added. Their use is becoming much more common in food service because of the high-quality product and the saving in preparation time.

Some food service places prefer to make their own mixes. Recipes are easily found. The mixes can be made in quantity at considerable saving.

A basic quick mix contains flour, sugar, baking powder, salt, and shortening. All the ingredients are mixed on low speed until well blended, but coarse looking. The basic mix is stored in tightly covered containers. It may be used for biscuits, muffins, cornbread, and loaf breads by adding other ingredients as needed.

Mixes, correctly stored, will keep for several months.

Panning

• *Biscuits.* After mixing, take biscuit dough to the bench and knead lightly with the fingertips for about thirty seconds. Roll the dough lightly to the desired thickness. Biscuits will double in size during baking, so judge the thickness by the desired height after baking. Biscuits may be cut into rounds, but many pastry chefs prefer to cut the dough into squares. It eliminates rerolling the scraps. Place biscuits on greased baking sheets and wash tops lightly with an egg wash. If biscuits are placed with the sides touching, they will be high with soft sides. Placed apart, they will be browner and crisper.

After panning, let the biscuits stand for about twenty minutes before baking.

• *Muffins.* Muffins are usually baked in a fluted paper cup in a muffin frame. Pan, using a number 16 scoop. Bake immediately.

• *Popovers.* Popovers are baked in a heavy iron muffin pan, preheated in the oven before filling. The heated pan helps make the steam pop the bread.

Baking

Bake according to the time and temperature shown below.

Biscuits: 220°C [425° F.]—15 to 20 minutes.
Muffins: 205°C [400° F.]—20 to 25 minutes.
Popovers: 230°C [450° F.]—15 minutes.
Reduce heat to 190°C [375° F.]—30 to 40 minutes.
Loaf: 190°C [375° F.]—1 to $1\frac{1}{4}$ hours.

Care, Storage, and Service

Most quick breads do not keep well because they are made from a lean formula. Baked goods with a small amount of shortening always dry out quickly. They are at the peak of flavor and customer appeal when served hot from the oven. Biscuits, muffins, and popovers should never be served cold.

However, they can be frozen successfully and kept for several months. Reheat and serve as fresh breads.

Words to Remember

canvas liner   ladyfingers
cookie   macaroon
cookie gun

COOKIES

A *cookie* is a small sweet cake. There are thousands of varieties of cookies from all parts of the world. German springerle, English toffee squares, Chinese fortune cookies, and Moravian Christmas cookies are just a few.

However, in food service, cookie making is often limited to making a very few simple types. It is

393

much easier and cheaper to spread batter in a pan than to roll out the dough. Cutting a baked pan of cookie batter is quicker than cutting and baking individual cookies. For this reason, bar and square cookies are most often made in food service.

Decorated cookies are attractive, but they take too much time for most pastry chefs to bake them. They are made occasionally for special occasions such as an elaborated tea or reception.

Kinds of Cookie Dough

In Table 20-3, the ingredients and proportions used in making different kinds of cookie doughs are compared.

Many different kinds of cookies may be prepared from the following three basic types of dough:

• *Very soft.* A batter used for cookies to be spread and baked as one piece on a baking sheet. After baking, they are cut into bars or squares. Brownies, date sticks, and fruit bars are examples of cookies make from a soft batter.

• *Semisoft, or drop, dough.* A dough used for cookies dropped from a scoop or spoon onto a baking sheet. Chocolate chip, molasses, and soft chocolate cookies are examples of cookies make from a soft, moist dough.

• *Stiff, or rolled.* A dough used for cookies to be rolled or shaped in some manner. Refrigerator cookies are made from a stiff dough formed into long

rolls and chilled. Just before baking, the rolls are sliced and placed on a baking sheet.

The same dough may be put into a pastry bag or cookie press and formed into various shapes. Sometimes, these cookies are called pressed, bagged, or molded cookies.

The dough also may be rolled on a floured board or canvas liner. A *canvas liner* is a piece of heavy canvas used for rolling pastries and cookies. It helps prevent sticking. Various cookie cutters are used to make many interesting shapes.

Ingredients and Proportions

By referring to Table 20-1, you can see that the ingredients used for quick breads are also used for cookies.

• *Flour.* An all-purpose flour is usually used. Some cookies such as macaroons use no flour at all. A *macaroon* is a delicate cookie make from egg white, sugar, and ground almonds. For comparison of proportions, 1.36 kg [3 lb] of flour are used in the table for all cookies.

• *Shortening.* A hydrogenated shortening is used for most cookies. Margarine and, occasionally, butter may be needed for some plain cookies that depend upon the delicate flavor of the shortening for tastiness.

Notice the high proportion of shortening needed for stiff cookie dough. When chilled, the dough be-

Table 20-3. Comparison of Ingredients in Batters and Doughs

Very Soft Batter			Semisoft, or Drop, Dough			Stiff, or Rolled, Dough		
Metric	Ingredients	Common	Metric	Ingredients	Common	Metric	Ingredients	Common
1.4 kg	Flour	3 lb	1.4 kg	Flour	3 lb	1.4 kg	Flour	3 lb
680 g	Eggs	1½ lb	450 g	Eggs	1 lb	170 g	Eggs	6 oz
1.1 kg	Shortening	2½ lb	680 g	Shortening	1½ lb	1.4 kg	Shortening	3 lb
2.3 kg	Sugar	5 lb	1.4 kg	Sugar	3 lb	680 g	Sugar	1½ lb
	Salt			Leavener		250 mL	Milk	½ c
	Flavoring			Salt			Leavener	
				Flavoring			Salt	
							Flavoring	

comes much easier to handle because the shortening hardens. The shortening also helps the dough slip from the cookie press without sticking.

• *Eggs.* Eggs are required by all cookies for tenderness, flavor, and structure. Some may use whole eggs. Others may use only the whites or the yolks. For instance, macaroons use only the egg whites. *Ladyfingers* are made from a sponge cake mixture using fortified eggs. The dough is formed into elongated fingers using a pastry bag.

Recipes vary in the proportion of eggs to flour. More eggs produce a chewy cookie. Fewer eggs make a crisp one. Refer to Table 20-3. Notice the high proportion of eggs to flour in the very soft batter. Usually no leavener is used in these types of cookies. The leavening comes from the eggs. Soft dough cookies require less eggs than cookies made from the very soft batter. Stiff dough cookies use the least proportion of eggs. If more liquid is needed, milk is added to the ingredients.

• *Sugar.* Either white or brown sugar may be used. Some recipes for macaroons may require powdered sugar. A high ratio of sugar to shortening and flour makes a crisp cookie. Molasses and honey add flavor and a different consistency. Cookies made with either of these sweeteners will be soft because of the added moisture.

Notice how the proportion of sugar varies from soft to semisoft to stiff doughs. Cookies made from a semisoft batter are cakelike in consistency. The sugar does not make them crisp because they are so moist.

• *Leavener.* Chemical leaveners are most commonly used. All cookies spread during baking. The amount of spread can be controlled by the choice of leavener. Baking powder makes a "fat" cookie. Baking ammonia and soda will cause the dough to spread, making a thin, dry cookie. Other ingredients also affect the spread. A lean dough, one with less sugar and shortening, will spread less than a rich dough.

• *Other ingredients.* Salt and flavoring are needed in all cookies. The amount of salt is rather constant—about 5 ml [1 t] per 450 g [1 lb] of flour. Flavoring varies widely with the type of cookies. It may be chocolate, vanilla, spices, or many others.

The recipe should be followed carefully since it has been formulated to produce the type of cookie desired. Accurate weighing of ingredients and the correct method of combining will result in a fine product.

Equipment

The baker's scale is needed for cookie making as for all baking. In addition, the bench mixer and the paddle will be used. For some types of cookies, the whip will also be needed.

Depending upon the type of cookie, you may also need:

• Cookie cutters.
• French knife.
• Rolling pin.
• Pastry bag and tips.
• Cookie gun.
• Scraper.

Cookies are usually baked on a sheet pan lined with silicone paper. As explained in Chapter 16, the paper is specially treated with silicone for baking. It is also called parchment paper. The paper prevents sticking and the smell of burned grease during baking. It eliminates the need to wash the pan afterwards.

Methods of Mixing

Cookies are simple to make. The most often used method is the muffin, or dump, method. It is used to make soft-moist and semisoft doughs. The creaming method is most often used for stiff doughs since they require a high proportion of shortening. The foam method is best for macaroons and other similar cookies relying on eggs as the primary source of leavening.

Makeup

Cookies made from soft, moist batter or semisoft dough require no special makeup. They go from mixer to pan. Cookies from a stiff dough do require makeup. Thus, they are not produced in food service as frequently as the other types.

Stiff doughs always need refrigeration before makeup. This hardens the shortening and makes the dough easier to handle. Refrigerator cookies are

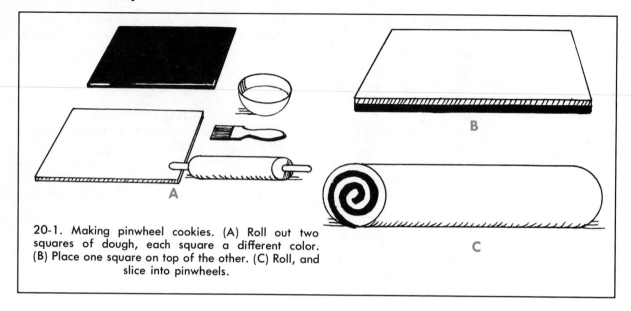

20-1. Making pinwheel cookies. (A) Roll out two squares of dough, each square a different color. (B) Place one square on top of the other. (C) Roll, and slice into pinwheels.

formed into long rolls and wrapped in waxed paper before refrigeration. A variety may be achieved by coloring part of the dough with chocolate or food coloring. Many interesting designs may be made, as shown in Figs. 20-1 and 20-2.

Molded cookies are pressed through the pastry bag or a cookie press onto a greased baking sheet.

To roll cookies, remove only as much chilled dough as you need for one rolling. Use a lightly floured board or canvas liner and a rolling pin. Roll lightly, checking under the dough occasionally to make sure it is not sticking. Cut into desired shapes with floured cutters. Fig. 20-3. Place the cutters as economically as possible to conserve the dough. Reworked dough will make a tougher, less desirable cookie.

Panning

Prepare the baking sheets by covering the bottom with silicone paper.

Allow for spreading by placing the cookies about 5 cm [2 in] apart on the sheet.

For bars and squares, spread thin for crisp cookies and thick for chewy ones. Raisins, nuts, choco-

late chips, and a variety of flavorings may be added for flavor and interest.

Although a spoon may be used, a scoop is best for depositing drop cookies on the baking sheet. The mechanical scraper on the scoop deposits the cookie dough cleanly. Also, the size of the cookie can be controlled. A number-30 scoop will make about a 28-g [1-oz] cookie. The cookies will be progressively smaller as the scoop number gets larger. A number-70 scoop will make a very small cookie. Large bakeries use an automatic cookie depositor.

Since macaroons are really drop cookies, they may also be deposited with a scoop. Some macaroons are improved if they are allowed to stand for thirty minutes before baking. Be sure to follow the recipe directions exactly.

Refrigerator cookies are panned after slicing. The slices may be thick or thin depending upon the need.

Baking

Time for baking is always approximate because cookies vary in size and thickness. Watch the cookies carefully and remove when lightly browned. Fig.

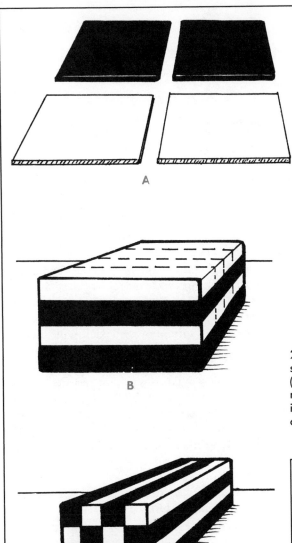

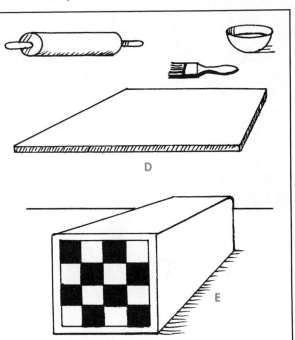

20-2. Making checkerboard cookies. (A) Roll four squares of dough, two of one color and two of another. (B) Place one piece of dough on top of the other, alternating the colors. Slice as shown. (C) Stack slices, making a checkerboard pattern. (D) Roll a long contrasting oblong of dough. (E) Wrap the dough around the checkerboard. Slice into cookies.

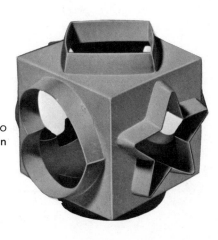

EKCO

20-3. Cookie cutters such as this one make cookies in a variety of styles.

20-4. Cookies bake quickly and evenly in the convection oven. Here, the cookies are being removed.

completed. They will become firm and turn crisp while cooling. Cut bars and squares as soon as they are removed from the oven.

Cookies should be cold before they are decorated or stored. Dry cookies may be stored in covered containers, but soft, moist cookies will stick together and crumble. Do not stack, but place them in a single layer in the container.

The crispness of cookies may be restored by placing in an oven at 107°C [225° F.] for about five minutes before serving.

Cookies lose their freshness quickly. It is better to bake often rather than depend on storage.

20-4. Chocolate cookies develop a burned flavor if baked too long. Use Table 20-4 to help judge when cookies are done.

Care and Storage

Cookies should be removed from the pans and placed on the rack to cool as soon as the baking is

Table 20-4. Temperatures and Times for Baking Cookies

Type	Temperature	Time
Moist, soft batter	175°C [350° F.]	20 to 30 minutes
Semisoft dough	227°C [440° F.]	8 to 12 minutes
Stiff dough		
Pressed cookies	175°C [350° F.]	15 minutes
Chocolate	165°C [325° F.]	12 minutes
Ball cookies	190°C [375° F.]	10 to 12 minutes
Refrigerated	190°C [375° F.]	10 to 12 minutes
Rolled cookies	190°C [375° F.]	15 minutes
Foam base		
Kisses	120°C [250° F.]	30 minutes
Chocolate meringue	150°C [300° F.]	about 25 minutes
Macaroons	175°C [350° F.]	10 minutes

Service

Cookies are often used as a base for desserts. For instance, ladyfingers may be placed around the edge of a mold. The inside is filled with whipped cream and gelatin. Brownies may be served a la mode with a chocolate sauce.

Cookies may be served by themselves for teas and receptions. They are often served with ice cream, sherbets, ices, fruit cups, puddings, and similar desserts. Cookies are always popular with customers. A tasty and eye-appealing cookie is sure to please.

How Much Have You Learned?

Review this chapter. Answer the following questions to prepare yourself for the post-test. Check your answers with your teacher.

1. What methods of mixing are used for quick breads?
2. What makes popovers pop? How are they mixed and baked?
3. Why are bar and square cookies most often made in food service?
4. What are the three types of dough used for cookies? Name at least one variety of cookie that can be made from each type.
5. How are cookie sheets prepared for baking? Can you depend upon the exact time for cookies to be done? Why?

PLAIN MUFFINS

Equipment
Bench mixer with paddle
Muffin cups
No. 20 scoop

Yield: 48 muffins
Temperature: 205°C [400° F.]
Time: 25 minutes

Metric	Ingredients	Customary
1.1 kg	Flour, all-purpose	$2\frac{1}{2}$ lb
225 g	Sugar	8 oz
75 mL	Baking powder	5 T
15 mL	Salt	1 T
250 mL	Eggs	1 c
450 g	Margarine	1 lb
1 L	Milk	1 qt

METHOD

1. **Preheat** oven. Grease muffin cups.
2. **Blend** flour, sugar, baking powder, and salt in mixer bowl.
3. **Beat** eggs slightly.
4. **Melt** margarine. Add to milk. Blend with eggs.
5. **Dump** wet ingredients into dry ingredients.
6. **Mix** just enough to moisten the dry ingredients. Batter will be lumpy.
7. **Scoop** batter using No. 20 scoop. Deposit one scoopful in each cup.
8. **Bake** for 25 minutes.

BAKING POWDER BISCUITS

Equipment
Bench mixer with hook attachment
Baking sheet
Biscuit cutter, 5 cm [2 in]

Yield: 100 biscuits
Temperature: 218°C [425° F.]
Time: 10–12 minutes

Metric	Ingredients	Customary
2.3 kg	Flour, all-purpose	5 lb
110 g	Sugar	4 oz
110 g	Baking powder	4 oz
28 g	Salt	1 oz
900 g	Margarine	2 lb
1.5 L	Milk	1½ qt

METHOD

1. **Preheat** oven. Oil baking sheets.
2. **Blend** flour, sugar, baking powder, and salt in mixer bowl.
3. **Cut in** margarine until mixture is like coarse cornmeal.
4. **Add** 1 L [1 qt] of milk. Mix cautiously. Add rest of milk if needed. Use enough milk to make a soft dough that can be kneaded.
5. **Knead** on floured bench for about 1 minute.
6. **Divide** into four pieces. Roll out to a thickness of 1.2 cm [½ in].
7. **Cut** with 5-cm [2-in] biscuit cutter.
8. **Place** on baking sheets so sides are touching.
9. **Brush** tops with milk. Let stand about 30 minutes.
10. **Bake** until lightly browned.

QUICK BANANA BREAD

Equipment
Bench mixer with paddle
Rubber spatula
French knife
3 loaf pans

Yield: 3 loaves
Temperature: 177°C [350° F.]
Time: 1 hour

Metric	Ingredients	Customary
285 g	Nuts, chopped	10 oz
565 g	Flour, all-purpose	$1\frac{1}{4}$ lb
45 mL	Baking powder	3 T
8 mL	Salt	$1\frac{1}{2}$ t
225 g	Margarine	$\frac{1}{2}$ lb
340 g	Sugar	$\frac{3}{4}$ lb
6	Eggs	6
875 mL	Bananas, mashed	$3\frac{1}{2}$ c

METHOD

1. **Preheat** oven. Grease and flour pans.
2. **Chop** nuts using French knife.
3. **Blend** flour, baking powder, and salt together.
4. **Mix** the nuts with half the flour mixture.
5. **Cream** margarine and sugar until fluffy. Add eggs. Cream two minutes on medium speed.
6. **Add** flour mixture and bananas alternately to creamed mixture, on low speed. Mix well.
7. **Add** floured nuts. Mix well.
8. **Divide** evenly in the loaf pans.
9. **Bake.**

Desserts and Dessert Sauces

What Will You Learn?

When you have finished this chapter, you should be able to do the following:
- Define and use the *Words to Remember*.
- Produce a variety of fruit desserts that meet the accepted standards of excellence.
- Produce a variety of puddings that meet the accepted standards of excellence.
- Produce a variety of frozen desserts that meet the accepted standards of excellence.
- Produce a variety of gelatin desserts that meet the accepted standards of excellence.
- Produce a variety of dessert sauces compatible with the desserts.
- Pass the posttest.

A dessert is a fitting climax to a good meal—the final touch for satisfaction. Many fine restaurants have built their reputations on a choice assortment of desserts, sure to please the customer. They often dramatize desserts by offering a choice of them on a tray or cart in a colorful fashion. Such merchandising tempts the diner to order dessert and helps increase the size of the sales check.

In many food service places, the dessert preparation is under the supervision of the pastry chef. Pies, cakes, and cookies are an important part of the dessert menu. Desserts however, also include fruits, gelatins, and frozen desserts. Fig. 21-1.

Morrison, Inc.

21-1. A dish of fresh strawberries topped with whipped cream is a delicious, but simple, dessert.

California Tree Fruit Agreement

21-2. Peaches and whipped cream add flavor and eye appeal to cream pie.

Words to Remember

bettys	dessert fritters
cobblers	fruit whips
compote	processed fruit
crisps	shortcakes

FRUIT DESSERTS

Colorful and delicious fruits make eye-appealing desserts. They are especially appealing to the diet-conscious person because they are light, nutritious, and low in calories.

Fresh Fruits

Fresh fruits in season are popular for desserts. Fresh fruits should be colorful, ripe, and in perfect condition. Imperfect fruit should be used for cooking.

Fresh fruits are often sliced and put on top of cakes, puddings, custards, and pies. Fig. 21-2.

PREPARATION

Fresh fruits to be served whole should be washed and dried. Polish apples, pears, and plums with a soft cloth.

Some fruits such as bananas, apples, and peaches darken when peeled and sliced. Mixing ascorbic acid or lemon juice with the sliced fruit will help prevent the discoloration. Sugar is also used to delay the darkening as well as to sweeten. Usually a simple syrup is used. It may be light or heavy as shown in Table 21-1.

Table 21-1. Sugar Syrups for Fruits (yield four litres, or one gallon)

Fruit	Syrup	Sugar		Water	
		Metric	Customary	Metric	Customary
Stewed	Light	1.4 kg	3 lb	3.8 L	3 qt 3 c
Compote	Medium	2.3 kg	5 lb	3.6 L	3 qt 2½ c
Preserves	Heavy	3.6 kg	8 lb	3.3 L	3 qt 1 c

Unit 5: The Bakery

To prepare a simple syrup, bring the water to a boil in a saucepan. Add the sugar and boil until clear. Cool before using.

Fresh fruit may be served as a compote. A *compote* (CAHM-pote) is a mixture of several kinds of fruit in a simple syrup. Fig. 21-3. Some chefs like to thicken the syrup slightly with cornstarch. Choose fruit with contrast in color, such as slices of red apple, bananas, green grapes, and cherries. Fig. 21-4.

Citrus fruits make a refreshing, colorful, and low-calorie dessert. Citrus fruit is peeled and sectioned for service as shown in Fig. 21-5. Section the fruit over a bowl to catch the juice. Be sure to remove all the seeds. Citrus fruit is usually served unsweetened.

CARE AND STORAGE

Fresh fruits, except bananas, need refrigeration for prime condition. Ripe fruits bruise easily, so handle carefully. Wash before storing. Berries, however, should be stored unwashed because they are very fragile. Wash just before serving.

SERVICE

Whole pears, apples, grapes, cherries, and other fresh fruit make a colorful display on the buffet table. Whole strawberries with fresh, green caps

21-4. All of these fruits are delicious for a fresh fruit compote.

may be arranged around a bowl of powdered sugar. A clear bowl of fresh citrus fruits, perhaps with cubes of watermelon, is also very attractive.

Compotes are usually served in a tall, rather flat, clear glass bowl to show off the beauty of the fruit.

Processed Fruits

Fruit which has been treated in some way to preserve it is called *processed fruit*. It includes canned, dried, frozen, and cooked fruit.

CANNED FRUITS

Canned fruits offer many varieties such as peaches, pears, cherries, apricots, berries, and mixtures of several different kinds of fruit. Food operators will usually order canned fruits in the No. 10 can. The number, or count, of the whole or half pieces is stated on the label. For instance, large peaches have a 22 count, but medium peaches have a 35 count.

Canned fruits are graded for quality by letters or descriptive names. Grade A, the top grade, is also known as Fancy. Only the finest grade should be

California Tree Fruit Agreement

21-3. Peaches, pears, and grapes in a sugar syrup are a light dessert.

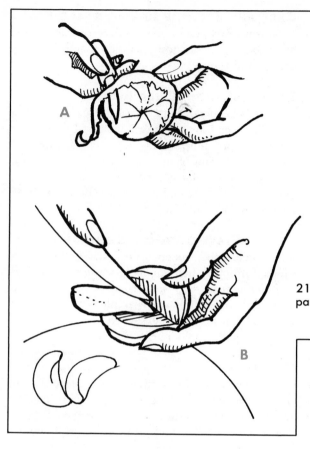

21-5. Sectioning an orange. (A) Peel orange, using a paring knife. (B) Cut out each section. (C) Discard the membrane.

selected for dessert service. Here, appearance and flavor are especially important.

DRIED FRUITS

Raisins, dried apricots, peaches, prunes, pears, and mixed fruits have been used as desserts in food service for a long time. They are easy to store and simple to prepare. Once considered inexpensive, they are no longer a low-budget item.

To prepare, cover the fruit with cold water in a saucepan. Let stand for four hours. Heat and simmer until tender. Do not boil, since boiling will toughen the fruit and cause it to disintegrate. Dried fruits are naturally sweet and require very little sugar. If more sweetness is desired, add the sugar after the fruit is cooked.

Dried fruits are graded and sold according to size. Select the largest size if the fruit is to be served whole or in a compote. The less expensive, smaller size may be chosen for purees and sauces.

FROZEN FRUITS

Frozen fruits are closest to fresh fruits in color and flavor. They are seldom served alone because they become mushy when defrosted. They are used to make many dessert items, such as fruit sauces, pies, and fillings.

Frozen fruits may be purchased dry or sugar packed. The ratio of sugar to fruits may vary from three parts or five parts of fruit to one part of sugar. All frozen fruits packed for food service show the sugar ratio on the package. If frozen fruit is substituted for fresh fruit, the sugar in the recipe should be decreased. Allowance must be made for the sugar added in freezing.

Frozen fruits should always be kept frozen until an hour before use. They lose quality rapidly once they are defrosted.

COOKED FRUITS

Fruits are seldom cooked on top of the range in food service. The time and labor involved make the product too expensive. Instead, canned or frozen fruits are substituted. Fresh fruits, however, are sometimes baked.

To bake apples, first core the apples. Peel the upper quarter of the apple and place it in the baking pan. Many chefs like to add some white wine to the bottom of the pan. Fill the core centers with brown sugar. Cinnamon and nuts may be added if desired. Brush the outside of each apple with honey or sugar syrup. Bake at 190°C [375° F.] for one hour or until tender. After cooking, the apples may be glazed with sugar syrup made of sugar, water, and red cinnamon candies.

For variety, fill the cavity with crushed pineapple. Make the sugar syrup with pineapple juice, instead of water.

Whole pears may also be baked. They are peeled but not cored. They may be baked in a honey syrup or in a mint-flavored sugar syrup, colored green.

Canned fruit may also be baked in the oven to make many delicious dishes. For instance, place canned pear halves on a baking dish. Beat egg whites until stiff and add mint jelly, slowly beating all the while. Spoon the meringue on top of each pear half. Brown lightly in the oven at 175°C [350° F.].

Scalloped, or escalloped, apples is another method of baking. Peel, core, and slice apples into a baking dish. Cover with a sugar sauce to which butter has been added. Bake one hour at 175°C [350° F.].

Broiled grapefruits are also served occasionally as dessert. Cut the grapefruit in half and remove the seeds. Loosen the sections, using the grapefruit knife. Fig. 21-6. Spread the halves with honey or brown sugar. Broil lightly until the honey or sugar boils and browns. Serve immediately.

21-6. A grapefruit knife.

CARE AND STORAGE OF PROCESSED FRUITS

Warm fruits should be served as soon as possible after cooking. Fruits to be served chilled should be cooled and refrigerated.

SERVICE OF PROCESSED FRUITS

Garnish cooked fruits attractively. A scoop of whipped cream or ice cream, a dessert sauce, or a sprinkling of chopped nuts adds to the appeal. A sprig of fresh mint blends well with many fruits and adds a dash of color contrast. Fruits of contrasting color may also be used, such as a cherry, a strawberry, or a slice of orange.

Fruit-based Desserts

Canned, dried, frozen, or fresh fruits can be combined with other ingredients to make rich desserts. Cobblers, crisps, bettys, shortcakes, fritters, turnovers, and fruit whips are examples of this type of dessert. Some are baked in the oven. Some are fried. A few require no cooking.

COBBLERS

Cooked fruit with a sweet sauce placed in the dish and covered with pie dough is called a *cobbler*. Individual baking dishes are used to make a cobbler. The cobblers are baked until the crust is golden brown. They are served hot from the oven.

Fruit dumplings are somewhat similar. Pie dough is rolled and cut into large squares. Fruit filling is placed in the center of each square. The corners are folded over the filling to the center. They are baked in the oven until brown and served hot.

CRISPS

Crisps are made from fruits in a sugar syrup, topped with a mixture of flour, nuts, sugar, and shortening. They are baked in the oven in a baking pan. Apples, peaches, pears, blueberries, and other fruits may be made into crisps. They are served with fruit sauce, whipped cream, or hard sauce. (See page 426.)

BETTYS

Bettys are made by spreading sweetened fruits between layers of cake crumbs. When baked, the bottom layer of cake crumbs is soft from the juice of the fruit. The top layer is brown and crisp. Bettys are an excellent way to use up leftover fruit and cake.

SHORTCAKES

Shortcakes may be made from rich biscuit dough or angel food cake. Sometimes a sponge cake is used as the base. The baked cake is split. Sweetened fresh fruit is spread between the layers. More fruit is heaped on top with a scoop of whipped cream as the final touch. Shortcakes are a typical American dessert, extremely popular during the strawberry and peach season.

DESSERT FRITTERS

Dessert fritters are pieces of fruit, such as apples and bananas, dipped in batter and fried in deep fat.

TURNOVERS

Puff paste is used to make turnovers. The rolled pastry is cut into squares. Place the sweetened fruit on one corner. Fold one-half over and form a triangle. Seal the edges with the fingers. Bake at 190°C [375° F.] for twenty to twenty-five minutes or until brown. Turnovers are often purchased from commercial sources and finished in the bake station for service.

FRUIT WHIPS

A *fruit whip* is made from sweetened, cooked fruit pulp mixed with either beaten egg whites or whipped cream. The whip is chilled before serving.

Words to Remember ———

baked soufflé	flan
creme brulée	thickeners
custard	trifle
dessert pudding	zabaglione

DESSERT PUDDINGS

A *dessert pudding* is a soft, sweet, thickened dessert, usually made with a milk base. Puddings are

Table 21-2. Ingredients in Puddings

Cornstarch Pudding	Tapioca Pudding	Rice Pudding	Bread Pudding
Milk	Milk	Milk	Milk
Cornstarch	Tapioca	Rice	Bread
Sugar	Sugar	Sugar	Sugar
Salt	Salt	Salt	Salt
Eggs	Eggs	Eggs	Eggs
Vanilla	Vanilla	Vanilla	Vanilla
Cold water		Margarine	Margarine
		Cinnamon	Cinnamon

easily made for quantity service. They are inexpensive and require little labor. Delicious puddings are popular with adults and children.

Pudding Ingredients

Table 21-2 shows the ingredients in four different puddings. Notice how similar the ingredients are for each of these puddings. What ingredients do they have in common?

- *Milk.* Fresh, canned, or dried milk may be used. Some recipes may call for light cream or whipping cream for extra richness.
- *Sugar.* Sugar is needed for flavor and sweetness. Although granulated sugar is most commonly used, some recipes may call for brown sugar, honey, molasses, or powdered sugar.
- *Salt.* Salt is needed for flavor.
- *Eggs.* Fresh eggs in the shell or fresh liquid eggs may be used. Eggs are needed for color and flavor and to help thicken the pudding. Puddings made with egg yolks are smoother than those made with whole eggs. Frequently, the recipe will direct the separation of yolks from the whites. The whites are beaten separately and folded into the pudding for fluffiness.
- *Flavoring.* Vanilla is often used alone or in combination with other flavorings. Chocolate- and butterscotch-flavored puddings also call for vanilla because the flavor of vanilla enhances the other flavorings.

Extracts easily lose their flavor and aroma during

cooking. Add the flavoring after cooking if the pudding is to be cooked on top of the range.

Thickeners

Look back at the ingredients listed for each pudding. Each pudding contains one different ingredient. This ingredient gives the pudding its name.

Cornstarch, tapioca, and rice belong to the cereal family. They are called *thickeners* because they thicken the pudding as it cooks. Bread also is a thickener because it has the ability to soak up such liquids as eggs and milk. Occasionally, other thickeners may be used such as farina (coarsely ground wheat) or cornmeal.

All thickeners except eggs contain starch. In Chapter 15 you learned to thicken sauces with flour, another member of the cereal family. Flour is used to thicken puddings occasionally. However, cornstarch gives a better flavor and smoother consistency.

STARCH COOKERY

Since the thickeners in dessert puddings are starches, you must follow the principles of starch cookery.

- Starch is composed of microscopic flecks called granules. The granules absorb liquid and swell when cooked. The swelling causes the product to thicken.

- The starch is mixed first with cold liquid to separate the granules and then heated for thickening. If uncooked starch were stirred directly into a hot liquid, the granules would clump together and form a lumpy product.

- As cooked starch cools, it thickens and forms a stable gel—one that remains thick when cold. For instance, a spoonful of pudding will keep its shape.

- Cooked starch mixtures may lose their thickness. Sometimes this is caused by cooking too long. Adding acid such as lemon juice before cooking will cause a pudding that is runny. Reread the discussion on making filling for lemon pies on pages 355–356. A frozen pudding may lose its thickness when unfrozen.

- Cooked starch mixtures tend to "weep" on cooling; that is, liquid slowly drains from the pudding as it cools. Stir the pudding occasionally while it cools to blend the liquid with the rest of the pudding.

MIXES

Possibly you may never make a pudding from "scratch" because most food service operations now use mixes. The ease of preparation and the high quality have made these products widely accepted in quantity food service.

Mixes may be of the instant variety or they may require cooking. Chapter 18 discussed the use of mixes for pie fillings. The same mixes are used for puddings. These instant mixes contain precooked starch and need only the addition of liquid to thicken.

Pudding mixes are easily varied through the addition of fruit, marshmallows, spices, and many other ingredients. With a little ingenuity, the pastry chef can offer a wide variety of desserts, even though they are made from a mix base.

Recently, puddings have become available in No. 10 cans. In the past, milk products were difficult to can. Now, the development of new techniques has made a better product possible. In the old canning process, water under pressure was used to heat slowly the products in the can. This killed the bacteria that might cause spoilage. In the new technique, the mixture is heated almost instantly to very high temperatures. It is pumped into sterile containers and sealed. Milk products sterilized by the new technique have a better, more natural flavor.

Frozen puddings are also available. The use of modified rice starch instead of cornstarch eliminates the "weeping" of the pudding when thawed. Frozen puddings may be kept for months if stored at −17°C [0° F.].

Equipment

Puddings are either cooked on top of the range, baked in the oven, or steamed. Each method requires its own equipment.

The top of the range is used for cornstarch and tapioca puddings and soft custards. Either a saucepan, double boiler, or bain-marie (for large amounts) may be used. Milk products scorch very easily. If cooked in a saucepan, they must be stirred constantly to prevent scorching. If a double boiler or bain-marie is used, the mixture is cooked over boiling water. This eliminates the need for constant stirring. The pudding cannot scorch.

Baking is used for rice, cornmeal, and bread puddings, and for baked custards. Frequently, the pan holding the pudding is set inside another pan filled with hot water. The water prevents the pudding from cooking too quickly.

Steaming is seldom used in food service. Occasionally, a Christmas plum pudding may be made, but usually they are purchased ready for service.

Sometimes juice cans are used to hold the puddings, but they look more festive if steamed in an attractive mold. The mold must have a cover to prevent condensation of steam in the pudding. The steamer shown in Fig. 21-7 is used for steaming puddings.

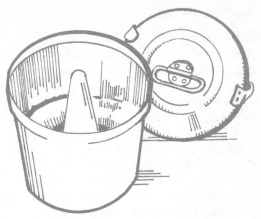

21-7. A mold for steaming puddings.

Methods of Production

Study Table 21-3. It compares the methods for producing puddings. Cornstarch and tapioca puddings are cooked on top of the stove. Rice and bread puddings are baked in the oven.

Table 21-3. Methods of Production for Puddings

Cornstarch Pudding (Top of Stove)	Tapioca Pudding (Top of Stove)	Rice Pudding (Baked)	Bread Pudding (Baked)
1. Blend cornstarch, sugar, salt and cold water. Heat the milk. Add to hot milk, stirring constantly. Cook until thick. 2. Beat eggs slightly. Add part of the hot mixture. Stir, and add the eggs to the rest of the hot mixture. Cook for about 3 minutes. 3. Remove from heat and add vanilla. 4. Cool and refrigerate.	1. Mix the tapioca, salt, and sugar with the milk. Cook in a double boiler about 15 minutes, or until tapioca is clear. Stir occasionally. 2. Beat the eggs slightly. Add part of the hot mixture to the eggs. Stir and add the eggs to the rest of the hot mixture. Cook for about 3 minutes. 3. Remove from heat and stir in vanilla. 4. Cool, stirring occasionally.	1. Mix rice, milk, sugar, cream, salt, and vanilla. 2. Beat the eggs slightly and mix with the rice. 3. Pour into greased baking dish or individual molds. Sprinkle with cinnamon and dot with margarine. 4. Place the baking dish in a larger pan. Pour water around the baking dish. 5. Bake at 149°C [300° F.] for 2 hours or until set.	1. Cut bread into cubes. 2. Combine milk, sugar, eggs, salt, flavoring, and melted margarine. 3. Soak bread cubes in milk mixture until bread has absorbed most of the milk. 4. Pour into greased baking dish. Sprinkle with cinnamon, dot with margarine. 5. Place baking dish in larger pan, filled with water. Bake at 149°C [300° F.] until set—about 1 hour. 6. Add sugar and mix well.

Top of the Stove Cooking

Notice that the method of production for cornstarch and tapioca puddings is almost alike. The method carries out the principles of starch cookery explained earlier.

When eggs are added to a hot mixture, a little of the hot mixture is first stirred into the eggs to dilute and warm them slightly. If they were poured directly into the hot mixture, they would cook too fast and curdle. After the eggs are added, the mixture is cooked for only three minutes—enough to cook the eggs but not to curdle them.

Cornstarch puddings will be thick after cooking. Tapioca puddings will still be thin, but they will thicken as they cool.

Baked Puddings

There are different methods of making baked rice pudding. The one illustrated here makes a very creamy, rich pudding. Because the rice is not cooked before baking, the pudding must be baked for a long time at a low temperature. Baking it in water keeps the egg mixture from cooking too fast and curdling. Note also that the sugar is added after the rice is cooked. If added with the uncooked rice, the rice will stay firm instead of becoming creamy.

The bread pudding is made by the same method. Because the bread does not need to be cooked until soft, the baking time is reduced to one hour.

Steamed Puddings

Steamed puddings are more cakelike in consistency. Like cakes, they contain shortening, sugar, eggs, flour, and soda. They also contain a heavy ratio of dried fruits and nuts. Bread crumbs are sometimes substituted for some or all of the flour. Because of the large amount of moisture in the fruit, little additional moisture is needed. Buttermilk is sometimes used as the liquid. The acidity of the buttermilk reacts with the soda to make the pudding rise. Steamed puddings are always very moist, waxy, and rather heavy.

Steamed puddings take much time to prepare. Thus, they are seldom prepared in the food service kitchens. For special occasions, such as Christmas, they are purchased ready to heat and serve.

Custards

A *custard* is a sweetened mixture of milk and eggs, thickened by the eggs. There are two kinds of custards—soft and baked. Sometimes a soft custard is incorrectly called a boiled custard. A custard should never be boiled because high temperatures will cause the egg to curdle. A baked custard is the same mixture as the soft custard, but it is baked in the oven until set.

Because of the ease of digestion and high nutritive quality, custards are often associated with foods served at hospitals or nursing homes. However, custards are delicious and frequently chosen as desserts by discriminating customers.

Excellent mixes for custards are on the market and frequently used in food service. Some contain precooked starch and thicken instantly when milk is added. Others require cooking. They are of such high quality that few food service places make custard from "scratch."

Since eggs are the thickener in custards, enough eggs must be used to form a stable pudding. Generally, the proportion of milk to eggs is four to one. Egg yolks may be substituted for whole eggs to make a richer, more yellow custard.

A true custard is thickened only with eggs, but other custards may use a combination of eggs and starch. These types are more commonly used in food service because they are easier to make, have more gloss, and cost less.

As discussed in Chapter 11, eggs thicken, or coagulate, when heated. Eggs cooked at a high heat for too long will be tough and will develop a greenish color. The critical point in making a custard is the coagulation of the eggs. A custard cooked too long at too high a heat will be rubbery and curdled. If the custard is removed from the heat too soon, it will be thin and watery. Proper control of the temperature and correct timing determine the quality of the custard.

Soft Custards

Soft custard is really a dessert sauce. Although vanilla is the most common flavor, chocolate, caramel, and other flavors may be used. A soft custard should be the consistency of heavy cream. It should be very smooth and velvety, sweet, and light yellow in color.

To prepare, scald the milk in the double boiler. Beat the eggs with the sugar, salt, and cornstarch, if used. Mix some of the hot milk with the eggs. Pour the egg mixture into the hot milk. Cook in the double boiler, stirring all the time. Eggs coagulate at 85°C [185° F.]. When coagulation is complete, the mixture will coat a clean spoon dipped into the center. Remove immediately from the heat and pour into a stainless steel bowl to cool. Do not use aluminum, since it will cause the custard to develop a grayish cast.

RELATED DISHES

Soft custards have foreign cousins with exotic names. For instance:

• *Creme brulée* (brew-LAY). A rich, soft custard made with brown sugar and cream—the French cousin. Served with crisp, broken caramelized sugar on top.

• *Zabaglione* (ZAHB-ul-YO-knee). A soft custard flavored with wine and whipped constantly during cooking to make it fluffy. Whipped cream is folded in before serving, and it is served warm—the Italian cousin.

• *Trifle.* Soft custard poured over cake that has been spread with jam. Served with whipped cream—the English cousin.

• *Floating island.* Islands of meringue, floated on soft custard and browned lightly under the broiler—a favorite with children. The meringue may be flavored and colored if desired.

BAKED CUSTARDS

To make a baked custard, use the same recipe and method of mixing as for soft custard. To reduce the baking time, the temperature of the custard should be about 60°C [140° F.] when it goes into the oven. Baked custard that separates during baking is overcooked.

Pour the mixture into a buttered baking dish. Butter is used because of its flavor. Sprinkle the top with grated nutmeg. Set the baking dish into a larger dish and fill the larger dish with boiling water. Place in the oven and bake one hour at 165°C [325° F.] or until a knife comes out clean when inserted in the center.

A baked custard should be tender, quivery, but firm enough to hold its shape when spooned for serving. The top should be delicately browned.

> COOKING TIP: *Overbaking or too hot an oven will cause the custard to water, or "weep."*

Baked Soufflés

A *baked soufflé* is a light puffy dessert leavened by beaten egg whites. It is baked in a fluted ceramic dish of the exact size for the proportions of the recipe. Although some dessert soufflés may be flavored with fruit or liqueurs, chocolate is by far the most popular flavoring.

A baked soufflé is extremely delicate and difficult to make. If not made correctly, it may collapse before it is served.

Soufflés may be made by two methods as shown in Table 21-4. One is made with a pudding base and the other with milk, eggs, and flour. The pudding base soufflé is much easier and does not collapse. It is often used in food service.

Care and Storage of Puddings, Custards, and Soufflés

All puddings with milk-egg base require very careful storing and care. The danger of food poisoning in such a mixture was discussed in Chapter 15. Staphylococcus bacteria grow very fast in this mixture when the mixture is lukewarm. Cool all puddings rapidly in the refrigerator. Cover to prevent a scum from forming and stir occasionally while cooling. Keep refrigerated until serving time.

Puddings and custards continue to cook if they are removed from the heat and not cooled immediately. This can cause overcooking and curdling, especially in custards. This is another good reason for cooling puddings and custards rapidly.

Puddings and custards cannot be frozen successfully. The freezing temperature will cause the pudding to separate and "weep."

Steamed puddings are more like baked products since they are not a milk-egg mixture. Stored in

Table 21-4. Baked Soufflés

French Method	Pudding Method
Ingredients Milk Eggs Flour Butter Sweet flavoring **Method** 1. **Butter** soufflé dish and dust lightly with flour. 2. **Heat** milk. 3. **Separate** the egg yolks in one bowl and whites in another. 4. **Beat** egg yolks with flour until thick. 5. **Stir** in hot milk slowly. Return egg milk mixture to heat. Cook until thick, stirring all the time. 6. **Add** flavoring. 7. **Beat** egg whites until in soft peaks. Fold half the egg whites into the batter. Fold the remainder into the batter. 8. **Pour** into soufflé dish. Smooth top with knife. 9. **Bake** in oven at 232°C [450° F.] for 15 minutes. Using the tip of a knife, cut around the edge of the soufflé toward the bottom. 10. **Reduce** heat to 204°C [400° F.] and bake 15 minutes until golden brown. 11. **Serve** immediately.	**Ingredients** Pudding mix made with cream Eggs **Method** 1. **Butter** soufflé dish lightly and dust with flour. 2. **Make** pudding mix. 3. **Separate** eggs, yolks in one bowl and whites in another. 4. **Beat** egg yolks until thick. 5. **Stir** hot pudding slowly into egg yolks. Return mixture to heat and cook for 3 minutes, stirring all the time. 6. **Cool** to room temperature. 7. **Beat** egg whites to soft peaks. Fold pudding mixture into egg whites. Fold just until blended. 8. **Pour** into soufflé dish. Smooth top with knife. 9. **Place** soufflé dish in pan of hot water. 10. **Bake** in oven at 163°C [325° F.] for $1\frac{1}{2}$ hours. 11. **Serve** immediately or set aside until later.

the original container on a shelf in a cool, dry room, they keep very well for several weeks. Too much humidity may cause molding.

Soufflés are usually served promptly, so storage is not a problem.

Service of Puddings, Custards, and Soufflés

Milk-based puddings are frequently served with colorful canned or fresh fruit topping. A dab of whipped cream adds to their appeal. A dessert sauce may be used on firm puddings such as baked custard. Caramel sauce is especially good on *flan* (FLAHN), a Spanish form of baked custard. Fruit sauces also add flavor and color. Every effort should be made to serve puddings and custards attractively so the customer will not feel that the dessert is "just a pudding."

Plain bread pudding may be served with lemon sauce or topped with meringue. Brown the meringue before serving. Fruit, caramel sauce, and a scoop of whipped cream add to the appeal of these economical desserts.

Steamed puddings are usually served with a hard sauce or a lemon, orange, or supreme sauce. (See pages 426–427.) Reheat the pudding before it is served since these puddings are best served warm. Slice with a serrated knife.

A high, puffy soufflé is a spectacular dessert and needs only a topping of whipped cream to add to its beauty.

Words to Remember

ambrosia	snow
Bavarian cream	Spanish cream
bloom	sponge
charlotte	whip
Russian cream	

GELATIN DESSERTS

Gelatin is frequently used for desserts as well as salads. It was discussed in detail as a base for salads on pages 151–152. The same principles apply in its use for desserts. Gelatin desserts are colorful, flavorful, low in cost, and a light ending to a heavy meal. They are very popular. Many pastry chefs use gelatin as a means to use up fruits, fruit juices, cookie crumbs, and bits of cake leftover from production. For instance, leftover fruit cocktail may be congealed in fruit-flavored gelatin for dessert.

Gelatin

Both flavored and unflavored gelatin are used for dessert production. Strawberry, raspberry, and cherry are the most popular. Lemon is the second most popular because it forms a base for orange-colored fruits such as peaches and apricots. Orange and lime flavors provide variety and color. New flavors are now on the market. Some of them are fortified with iron and vitamins A and C to make them more nutritious. Grape, grapefruit, and black raspberry are among the newer flavors.

• *Flavored gelatin.* The quality of flavored gela-

tin is most important, especially in dessert production. The flavor is important, but so is the gelling property called the *bloom.* Bloom is measured in numbers. The higher the number, the greater the gelling capacity. A bloom count of at least 200 is essential to form a gel firm enough for desserts. Inexpensive gelatin may seem like a bargain. However, if the bloom count is so low that the gelatin will not stand up, it is not suitable for use. Cheaper flavored gelatins may be strengthened by mixing with unflavored gelatin before dissolving in hot water.

Gelatin should be used promptly. If stored on the shelf for several months, it gradually loses its bloom count. The chef may suddenly find that the gelatin did not make a firm gel.

Gelatin must be dissolved completely to be successful. Most directions for flavored gelatin mention only warm water is needed to dissolve the gelatin. Pastry chefs prefer to use boiling water instead because of unfortunate experiences with water less than boiling. The gelatin must be completely dissolved. Undissolved gelatin may appear in the desserts as streaks of granular, ropy material. The gel may not be strong enough to serve. To be sure the gelatin is completely dissolved, bring half the needed liquid to a boil, and add the gelatin. Stir until the gelatin is completely clear. Add the remaining liquid cold. As an alternate, quick method, the gelatin may be dissolved in one-fourth the hot liquid and the rest of the liquid added in the form of shaved ice.

• *Unflavored gelatin.* This form of gelatin may be purchased in sheets or powdered. Chefs overwhelmingly prefer the powdered form because it is easy to use. It must be measured very carefully.

Unflavored gelatin must first be soaked in cold water before dissolving in hot water.

Unflavored gelatin is also rated according to its bloom. For a firm gel, use 680 g [1½ lb] of flavored gelatin and 70 g [2½ oz] of plain gelatin per 3.8 L [1 gal] of liquid.

Gelatin Dessert Ingredients

Gelatin desserts require very few ingredients.

• *Sugar.* Granulated sugar is used to sweeten

those desserts made with unflavored gelatin. Flavored gelatin already contains the sugar.

• *Fruit.* Any fruit except fresh pineapple may be used with gelatin. Fresh pineapple, including its juice, contains an enzyme that prevents the gelling of the mixture. Canned pineapple and juice may be used, since the canning process kills the enzyme.

The fruit should blend with the flavor of the gelatin. Cherries should be matched with cherry gelatin, strawberries with strawberry gelatin. Lemon and orange may be used as the base for all orange and yellow fruits.

Fruit juices may be substituted for all or part of the liquid, adding much flavor to the desserts. For certain desserts, a hot pudding or soft custard is used as the liquid for dissolving the gelatin. Notice the ingredients for Bavarian creams and Spanish creams.

• *Egg whites and whipped cream.* Beaten egg whites are folded into gelatin mixtures for lightness and beauty. Whipped cream adds richness, flavor, and smooth texture. Some recipes may call for softened ice cream, whipped and folded into the gelatin mixture. Ice cream adds flavor and fluffy texture to the desserts. Its coldness hastens the gelling of the desserts.

• *Bases.* Many of the spectacular desserts use a cake as a base for the desserts. Notice the use of ladyfingers in the charlotte. Sponge cake or angel food cake may also be torn into small pieces and folded into the gelatin.

Equipment

The beauty of gelatin desserts depends in great measure on the molds used for setting the gel. Of course, gelatin may be molded in plain baking pans and cut into squares for service. However, for truly dramatic, elegant service, a variety of molds is required. A few of these beautiful molds are shown in Fig. 21-8.

Gelatin desserts may be molded directly in the serving glassware. Parfait, sherbert, and wine glasses and glass bowls are just a few that add beauty and distinction to gelatin desserts.

Methods of Production

The methods of production for gelatin desserts are given in Table 21-5. Once you have learned to make clear gelatin and fruit gelatin, the other deserts are simple.

GELATIN-BASED DESSERTS

• *Whips.* A *whip* is a clear gelatin that has been whipped after it is partly set.

COOKING TIP: *If the gelatin has not set long enough before being whipped, the whip will not hold. The dessert may collapse. Notice the suggested method. Place the bowl holding the gelatin in another bowl with cracked ice to keep the gelatin fairly firm.*

• *Sponges, or Snows.* A sponge, or snow, is a clear gelatin dessert with beaten egg white folded in.

• *Bavarian creams.* A Bavarian cream is a smooth, velvety, delicate dessert made with gelatin and whipped cream. Bavarian creams, molded in a beautiful mold, make spectacular desserts. There are two types of Bavarians—the original, or true, Bavarian and the fruit Bavarian.

The true Bavarian has a soft custard base, molded with gelatin. Whipped cream is folded in when partially set. Fruit Bavarians are made with fruit juice, instead of custard. Crushed fruit and whipped cream are folded in when partially congealed.

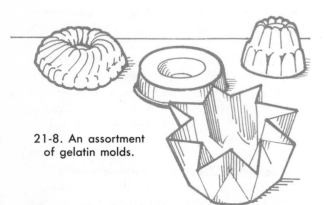

21-8. An assortment of gelatin molds.

Table 21-5. Methods of Preparation for Gelatin Desserts

To prepare clear gelatin	Bring water to a boil. Dissolve flavored gelatin in hot water. Cool, mold, and refrigerate until set. For unflavored gelatin, soak in cold water for 5 minutes and dissolve in hot fruit juice. Cool and mold. Refrigerate until set.
To add fruit	When gelatin is partly set, about the consistency of unbeaten egg whites, stir in the chopped fruit. Mold. Refrigerate until set.
To whip	When gelatin is partly set, place bowl in larger bowl of cracked ice. Whip with beater until white and frothy. Mold. Refrigerate until set.
To add whipped egg whites or whipped cream	When gelatin is partly set, whip egg whites to stiff peaks. Whip gelatin into the whites. Mold, and refrigerate until set. Whip cream just until stiff. Do not overbeat. Fold into gelatin. Mold. Refrigerate until set.

A high-bloom count gelatin must be used when making Bavarians. It must have at least a 200-bloom count to stabilize the whipped mixture so it will stay firm during service.

Chill Bavarians for at least four hours before service.

• *Charlottes.* A *charlotte* is a Bavarian flavored with kirsch (a black cherry liqueur) or maraschino. The mold is lined with ladyfingers or cake. A *Charlotte Russe* is considered one of the most elegant desserts. It uses a soft custard base and heavy cream. For service, it can be beautifully decorated with fresh fruits.

• *Spanish creams.* A *Spanish cream* is similar to a true Bavarian. It does not have whipped cream folded into it, but the base is a soft custard. Sometimes a cornstarch pudding is molded and called a Spanish cream.

• *Russian creams.* A Russian cream contains no eggs. The gelatin is dissolved in hot, sweetened cream. When partly set, whipped, sour cream is folded in. It is pure white, velvety smooth, and slightly cheesy in taste.

• *Ambrosia.* Ambrosia also has a soft custard base. After the soft custard begins to set, a meringue made of beaten egg whites and sugar is folded in.

The mixture is poured over cubed angel food cake. Frequently, the mixture is layered in a mold with crushed pineapple.

• *Mousse.* A mousse is also a true Bavarian frozen in a mold without stirring.

• *Soufflés.* Soufflés may also be made with gelatin. This type of soufflé is often made in food service because it is easier to prepare. It is also more stable than the baked soufflé described earlier. A baked soufflé may collapse when served. Gelatin soufflés, however, may be made well in advance and will never fall.

A soft custard may be used as the base, but beaten egg whites and whipped cream are used to make it very fluffy. The flavor of the base must be strong because of the great volume added by the egg whites and whipped cream. For instance, a base for chocolate soufflé must be very chocolaty. The chocolate flavor must still be distinct when the egg whites and whipped cream are folded in.

Soufflés must always rise above the mold to form the characteristic soufflé shape. Choose a fluted, round mold, either single-serving size or large enough for several persons. Extend the top of the mold with a collar of aluminum foil bound firmly to the mold rim. Fill the mold to the top of the foil.

Just before serving, remove the foil so the soufflé extends above the mold edge. Soufflés may be molded directly in the serving glasses. Extend the rim of the glass with aluminum foil in the same manner.

PRINCIPLES OF GELATIN COOKERY

Gelatin desserts will always be successful if you remember the following basic principles:

- Soak unflavored gelatin in cold water before dissolving.
- Be sure liquid is hot enough to dissolve the gelatin completely.
- Chill the gelatin mixture until partly set before adding fruit, beaten egg whites, or whipped cream.
- Allow gelatin to chill at least four hours before service.

Care and Storage

Since gelatin desserts require at least four hours for a firm set, they are usually molded the night before. The pastry chef is usually busy during the day making such desserts as pies, cakes, and others that are better served the same day when baked. Making gelatin desserts the night before is good management of time and labor.

Gelatin desserts should be covered in the refrigerator. This prevents the absorption of odors and tastes. It also prevents the gelatin from drying out. Because gelatin desserts soften gradually at room temperature, they should be refrigerated until serving time.

Service

To unmold gelatin desserts, dip the mold quickly into very hot water. Place the serving dish on top of the mold. Quickly invert on the serving dish. The hot water softens the gelatin on the inside of the mold, allowing it to slip out.

COOKING TIP: *Judgment comes with experience. Too long a time in the hot water will liquefy the gelatin, making sloppy service. Too short a time makes it difficult to remove the dessert.*

Gelatin desserts are usually spectacular and need very little garnishing. Serve fruit gelatins with soft custard or a dab of whipped cream. Bavarians may be garnished with fresh fruits that match the flavoring. For instance, orange-flavored Bavarian may be garnished with slices of mandarin oranges. Russian creams are attractive and tasty when garnished with fresh strawberries or raspberries. Mounds of whipped cream are brightened with a cherry.

Soufflés, traditionally, are garnished more elaborately. For instance, chocolate soufflés may be sprinkled with chocolate shavings. They may be decorated with whipped cream rosettes and chopped nuts.

Gelatin desserts are usually served on clear glass plates or in stemmed glassware. Clear glass shows off the beauty and delicacy of the desserts, making them more eye-catching to the customers.

Words to Remember

à la mode	overrun
baked Alaska	parfait
bombe	peach Melba
coupe	sherbets
dipper well	soda
glacé	sundae
ice milk	vacherin
ices	

MERINGUES

There are two types of meringues—soft and hard. Soft meringues were discussed on page 357 as a topping for pies. Soft meringues are also used to garnish puddings, cakes, and ice-cream-based desserts.

A hard meringue is used as a shell to hold desserts. For instance, hard merginue shells may be filled with ice cream and topped with sliced strawberries and whipped cream. Experienced pastry chefs make glamorous desserts using meringue shells as the base. The meringues may be shaped like a swan, a basket, a nest, or a shell. This dessert is called *vacherin* (VASH-ur-EN) and is a favorite in first-class restaurants.

Hard meringues are rather tricky to make. Much more sugar is used in proportion to egg white than for a soft meringue. The usual proportions are 900 g [2 lb] of sugar for each 450 g [1 lb] of egg white. Because of the high proportion of sugar, some water is needed to help dissolve the sugar. Vinegar, lemon juice, or cream of tartar is also added as a stabilizer.

To make a hard meringue, beat the egg whites to a soft foam. Add the stabilizer and the water. Add half the sugar gradually, beating to a stiff foam. It should stand in stiff peaks. Fold in the rest of the sugar by hand, being careful not to agitate too much. The foam is very tender, and too much agitation will cause loss of air. Remember that the trapped air is the only leavener.

Using a pastry bag, form shells or nests on silicone-paper-lined baking sheets. Bake in a preheated oven at 135°C [275° F.] for one and one-half hours or at 177°C [350° F.] for fifty minutes. Some pastry chefs prefer to make the shells the night before. They preheat the oven to 163°C [325° F.], place the meringues in it, and turn off the oven. The meringues bake all night as the oven gradually cools. Meringues must be dry—but not so dry that they shatter when removed from the pans.

FROZEN DESSERTS

Frozen desserts include ice cream, ice milk, ices, and sherbets. Many delightful desserts are based on them. Most food service operations buy the frozen product commercially and construct elaborate desserts using them as the base. A few places make their own for specialty items, for the holiday seasons, or special occasions. Frozen desserts are among the most popular on the menu.

Frozen Dessert Ingredients

Most frozen desserts are based on commercially made ice cream. Ice creams vary in quality and price. For best results, the highest quality within the allowable price range should be purchased.

Cleanliness and sanitation are the first essentials to be considered. The manufacture of frozen products is governed by state and local laws. These vary considerably. Ice cream, ice milk, and sherbets should be made only from pasteurized milk or cream.

Another quality factor is the amount of *overrun*. Overrun refers to the amount of air beaten into the product during freezing. A certain amount of overrun is necessary for a smooth texture and light body. However, too much overrun lowers the quality of the product. It causes frothiness. Too little overrun gives a coarse texture and makes a heavy product. Weight is an indication of the amount of overrun. Specifying the minimum weight in proportion to volume is one way to be sure of receiving a high-quality product. Ice cream should weigh a minimum of 2 kg [4.5 lb] per 3.8 L [1 gal]. Ices and sherbets should weigh 2.7 kg [6 lb] per 3.8 L [1 gal].

ICE CREAMS

An ice cream must contain at least 10 percent butterfat by federal regulation. If the ice cream contains ingredients with no butterfat content, the requirement is reduced to 8 percent. For instance, fudge royale ice cream contains chocolate syrup. Because chocolate syrup contains no butterfat, the requirement for this type of ice cream would be 8 percent butterfat.

Philadelphia ice cream is made from a mixture of light cream, sugar, flavoring, and a stabilizer. French ice cream is made from a soft custard base.

Ice cream may be combined with fruits, nuts, cookie or cake crumbs, and flavorings such as chocolate, vanilla, or peppermint. For example, ice cream royale has syrup stirred into it when partially frozen. Peppermint stick candy may be crushed and mixed in for another delightful variety.

Ice cream currently is sold in two and one-half and five-gallon containers. Probably, it will soon be packed in ten- and twenty-litre containers.

The quality of ice cream is judged according to the following standards:

• *Flavor*—pleasant and true, with proper acidity and sweetness.

• *Appearance*—bright, smooth, and glossy.

• *Body and texture*—smooth fine-grained and creamy. Never watery, icy, gummy, or frothy. Body refers to the way it feels in the mouth. It should feel

Table 21-6. Scoops for Serving Ice Cream

Service	Size Scoop	Number of Servings per 3.8 L [1 gal]
À la carte	12	22 to 26
Sundaes	16	31 to 35
À la mode	20	38 to 42
	24	47 to 51
Parfaits	30	58 to 62

slightly firm and very smooth, but not pasty or cottony.

• *Color and packaging*—delicate colors according to the flavor, but not artificial looking. There should be no holes or tunnels in the ice cream after packaging.

• *Melting quality*—melts completely to a liquid. Inferior products will still retain their shape when melted.

ICE MILKS

Ice milks contain from 2 to 7 percent butterfat. By federal regulation, they must have at least 11 percent milk solids.

They should meet the same quality standards as ice cream. However, they will be slightly more grainy because of the reduced butterfat content. They are packed in containers of the same size as those used for ice cream.

ICES

Ices are sweetened fruit juices that have been frozen. They should have the true fruit flavor and color. Many ices are over-colored, giving them an artificial look.

SHERBETS

Sherbets are sweetened fruit juices with milk used as part of the liquid. They usually have beaten egg whites mixed in the liquid for added volume. Sherbets are becoming more popular for dessert as diet-conscious customers ask for lighter desserts.

MIXES

Although most food service operations buy their frozen products, a few make their own mixes or buy commercially made mixes. Mixes may be purchased for Philadelphia, French, and most other varieties of ice cream. The quality is high. Some chain operations make their own ice creams in a commissary and deliver them to the chain restaurants. In this way they control quality and price, while offering a good variety.

Equipment

Most food operations do not make their own ice cream because of the expensive equipment required. Mixing vats, pasteurizers, homogenizers, and filters are needed to make mixes. Freezers and hardening cabinets are needed to freeze and store the ice cream. The equipment is not only expensive but also requires trained labor to operate it and space to maintain it. For these reasons, most food service managers believe it is cheaper to buy high-quality frozen products ready to serve or to be made into a variety of desserts. A storage cabinet, however, is needed to keep the products at the correct temperature for prolonged storage. Temperatures should be below $-18°C$ [$0°$ F.]. Cabinets for immediate service should be a little warmer—about $-14°$ to $-9°C$ [$8°$ to $15°$ F.].

Different size scoops are needed for portion control as shown in Table 21-6.

Ice-Cream-Based Desserts

Many desserts are based on ice cream and sherbets. Ices and sherbets are usually served alone or with a cookie alongside. Ice cream, since it is richer and holds up better, is used for many delicious desserts. Some of them are very elaborate and spectacular.

À LA MODE SERVICE

When a scoop of ice cream is served on top of a piece of cake or pie, the dessert is called *à la mode*. Such a dessert might be a slice of angel food cake with a scoop of strawberry ice cream. It might be apple pie with vanilla ice cream. À la mode desserts are always popular.

SUNDAES

Sauce on ice cream makes a *sundae*. There are many variations, some simple, some elaborate. Almost any dessert sauce may be used to make a sundae. A sundae may be topped with whipped cream and possibly a sprinkle of chopped nuts and a cherry.

Sundaes may be hot or cold. A chocolate sundae may be served with cold chocolate sauce or hot fudge sauce.

For a more elaborate dessert, a split banana may be placed in a long glass dish with two or three scoops of ice cream on top. All may be the same flavor or each one a different flavor. Topped with chocolate sauce, whipped cream, and a cherry, this dessert is called a banana split.

An exotic dessert is cherries jubilee. This dessert is always prepared in front of the customer. A Bing cherry sauce is prepared in a chaffing dish at the table. Cherry brandy is poured into the hot sauce and flamed. The flaming brandy adds a delightful and unusual flavor to the sauce. Poured over vanilla ice cream and served to the customer with a flourish, it never fails to please.

PARFAITS

A *parfait* (par-FAY) consists of several scoops of ice cream layered with fruit sauce in a tall, narrow glass. In Table 21-5, you may notice that parfaits require the small scoop to fit the narrow glasses. Parfaits are topped with swirled whipped cream and chopped nuts. They are garnished with fruit to match the sauce. Although simple and economical to prepare, most customers consider them a special dessert.

SODAS

An ice cream *soda* is a mixture of ice cream, carbonated water, syrup, whipped cream, and garnish. They are popular in ice cream parlors and fast food places. Occasionally, they may be served in restaurants.

COUPES

A *coupe* (COOP) is made by pressing ice cream in a stemmed glass. A small amount of sweetened fruit is placed on top and covered with matching sauce. Whipped cream is circled around the rim so the fruit and syrup show in the middle. Coupes are frequently made with the same liqueurs as the sauce and named for famous persons.

PEACH MELBA

Peach Melba was named for a well-known opera singer. It is simple to prepare. A scoop of ice cream is placed on a slice of sponge cake. A peach half is added and topped with whipped cream. This is covered with slivered almonds and Melba sauce. (See page 424.)

MOUSSE

Mousse, described in the section on gelatin desserts, may also be made without gelatin. However, it is then more difficult to achieve a smooth, creamy, product. A mousse is the base for many luxurious desserts, such as bombe, glacé, and biscuit Tortoni.

To prepare the mousse base, you need only sugar, water, and egg yolks. Boil the sugar and water together until the temperature reaches 115°C [240° F.]. Cool slightly. Beat the egg yolks until very thick and lemon colored. Gradually pour the syrup on the egg yolks in a thin stream, beating all the time. Beat until cold. Pour into a jar and refrigerate. This base will keep for a week or longer under refrigeration.

- A *bombe* (BOMB) is a mousse mixture frozen in a spherical or dome shape—hence its name. To make a bombe, line the mold with vanilla ice cream, pressing the ice cream firmly against the sides of the mold. Freeze quickly until solid. Add frozen fruit and whipped cream to the mousse base. Fill the center of the bombe and freeze. Unmold for serving. Decorate with fresh fruit and whipped cream.

- *Glacé* (glah-SAY) is the French word for "ice cream." In American usage, it is a mousse base mixed with a flavoring such as rum or brandy. Whipped cream is folded in, and the mixture is frozen in paper soufflé cups. Before serving, it is decorated to match the flavoring and served in the cups in which it was frozen.

- *Biscuit Tortoni*, in spite of its name, is not related in any way to the biscuits baked in the oven.

To prepare, add rum and crushed macaroons to the mousse base. Fold in whipped cream and fill the tortoni cups. These are fluted paper cups about the size of a large muffin. Use the pastry tube with the star point to fill the cups so the mixture is swirled. Sprinkle with more crushed macaroons and top with a cherry. Freeze.

BAKED ALASKA

One of the most spectacular desserts, baked Alaska is made on a sponge cake base. To prepare, cut an oblong sponge cake into four slices the exact size of a litre [quart] brick of ice cream. Make a soft meringue of sugar and egg whites. Cover the bottom, sides, and top of the brick of ice cream with the sponge cake slices. Spread the whole with thick meringue. Sprinkle with slivered almonds, and brown in a hot oven. Serve immediately.

The sponge cake and meringue act as insulation, keeping the heat of the oven away from the ice cream. Many fine restaurants and hotel dining rooms like to serve baked Alaska with a flourish. For a banquet, the waiters march into the darkened banquet hall carrying the baked Alaskas lighted with candles. It always receives a storm of applause. This is good merchandising for an inexpensive dessert commanding a high price.

ICE CREAM PIES

An ice cream pie is another eye-appealing dessert. It may be bought commercially or prepared in

21-9. A crêpe pan.

the kitchen. Either a baked pie shell or a crust made of graham crackers or cookie crumbs may be used as the base. To prepare, fill the baked crust with softened ice cream, allowing 720 mL [1½ pt] of ice cream for each pie. Use one flavor or layer two or three different flavors. After filling the pie, cover and immediately place in the freezer. For service, ice cream pies may be garnished with whipped cream and fresh fruit. Sometimes they are covered with a meringue and browned in the oven like a baked Alaska.

Care and Storage of Ice-Cream-Based Desserts

All frozen products must be kept frozen hard for prolonged storage. They should always be tightly covered to prevent drying out. Ice cream that has softened and been refrozen loses volume and develops a dense, solid consistency. It will serve fewer portions.

Service

Ice creams and other frozen products should be transferred to a slightly warmer cabinet several hours before service. For best service, the temperature should be kept at $-14\,°C$ to $-9\,°C$ [8° F. to 15° F.]. The ice cream should be just soft enough to cut easily with a scoop. Scooping hard ice cream demands too much pressure. It is also difficult to fill the scoop completely. Very soft ice cream will melt before it is served to the customer.

Proper dipping is important in the number of portions from each carton of ice cream. The dipper or scoop should have a sharp edge and be free from nicks. Always keep the scoop in the *dipper well* between servings. A dipper well is a narrow cylinder filled with cold, running water. Be sure to tap the dipper against a pad or paper towel to remove excess water before using it. Water will cause ice crystals to form in the ice cream.

Using a circular motion, dip close to the sides of the carton around the surface until the dipper is full. Release the scoop of ice cream into the serving glass. Continue to scoop in a circular motion, removing the ice cream a layer at a time. Lower the level of the ice cream evenly for more portions. This maintains the texture and prevents the formation of ice crystals.

Words to Remember

crêpe	hard sauces
crêpe pan	Melba sauce
crêpe Suzette	rich sauces
custard sauces	supreme sauces
fruit sauces	

CRÊPES

A *crêpe* (CRAPE) is a very thin pancake, browned on one side, rolled, and served hot. A *crêpe pan* is usually used. Fig. 21-9. Some chefs, however, use a small round grill. The grill is used especially in restaurants that feature many different kinds of crêpes. It is kept hot all the time, ready for instant use.

A thin batter of flour, milk, eggs, salt, and melted butter is all that is needed for the crêpe base. The batter is very thin and spreads easily over the grill, browning almost instantly. Crêpes are usually filled before rolling.

Usually a sweet filling is used for dessert crêpes. A butter cream, fruit preserve, conserve, jelly, sour cream, sweet pudding, or sauce might be used.

A *crêpe Suzette*, a well-known dessert crêpe, is filled with orange butter cream. Orange liqueur is poured over the crêpe while it is still in the pan. The brandy is flamed. The crêpe Suzette is always flamed in front of the customers.

DESSERT SAUCES

Purchased dessert sauces are usually served in most food service places. The high cost of labor makes it cheaper to buy them ready to serve, rather than making them in the kitchen. However, as a professional cook, you need to know how to make some fine dessert sauces.

Purposes of Sauces

The purposes of sauces are to:
- Improve appearance.
- Enhance flavor.
- Add variety and contrast in flavor and color.
- Increase customer appeal.

Types of Sauces

Dessert sauces may be divided into five general types—rich, fruit, hard, supreme, and custard. Custard sauces were discussed on pages 410-411. The others will be described here.

RICH SAUCES

Rich sauces include such favorites as chocolate, butterscotch, and marshmallow. Most food service places buy canned ready-made sauces. A few may prefer to make their own.

- A *chocolate sauce* should have a true chocolate flavor and a rich, dark brown color. Two kinds are generally used in food service—chocolate syrup and chocolate fudge. Either may be made with baking chocolate or cocoa.

The chocolate-syrup type may be made using the recipe on page 425. The syrup is dark and smooth with a rich chocolaty taste. It is easy to make.

A chocolate fudge sauce is much more difficult. It requires boiling to a definite temperature—110°C [230° F.]. It is apt to become grainy if stirred too much. If overcooked, the sauce may turn into candy. A beginner will be more successful following the recipe for chocolate syrup.

- *Butterscotch sauce* is made from brown sugar, dark corn syrup, cream, sugar, butter, and salt. The brown sugar and corn syrup give it the butterscotch flavor. Like chocolate fudge, it is difficult to make for a beginner. It also requires boiling to an exact temperature. The temperature is even higher than that needed for chocolate fudge sauce. Reread the discussion of sugar cookery in Chapter 19 before attemping the more difficult sauces.

- *Marshmallow sauce* is made from gelatin, sugar, corn syrup, hot water, and vanilla. Although the syrup must be boiled, the required temperature is lower than that for butterscotch or chocolate fudge sauces. The gelatin dissolves in the hot syrup and helps thicken the sauce. When beaten, it becomes white, light, and fluffy.

FRUIT SAUCES

There are as many *fruit sauces* as there are kinds of fruits. Lemon, orange, cherry, pineapple, raspberry, and strawberry are just a few of the fruits used to make these useful and popular sauces.

- *Melba sauce* makes the peach Melba dessert famous. The recipe is on page 424. It contains raspberries and currant jelly. It is thickened with cornstarch.

- *Lemon and orange sauces* are used on puddings, gelatins, and cakes such as gingerbread. They are sweet sauces, thickened with cornstarch and eggs and flavored with lemon or orange.

On page 425 is a recipe for orange sauce. The method of preparation is much the same as making a filling for a pie. Notice that the cornstarch is mixed with the sugar, salt, and water before being added to the hot juice. Perhaps you remember that this technique prevents the cornstarch from lumping. Also notice that the lemon juice is added after the cornstarch has thickened the mixture. As you have read previously, the acidity of lemon juice can lessen the thickening power of the cornstarch.

Other fruit sauces such as cherry, cider, peach, or apricot are made in the same way. If whole or pieces of fruit are part of the sauce recipe, they are added after the juice is thickened. Coloring is often added to fruit sauces to make them even more attractive.

HARD SAUCES

Hard sauce is similar to frosting. It is used as a topping for plum puddings, fruitcakes, ginger-

breads, and steamed puddings. Hard sauces are made from butter, confectioner's sugar, eggs, vanilla, and flavoring.

Some hard sauces call for the addition of boiling water. Beaten egg white is folded in after the hard sauce is prepared. This type of hard sauce is actually rather soft.

On page 426 is a recipe for a hard sauce that is very firm. The only liquid is a small amount of cream and the eggs. When refrigerated, this type of hard sauce is very similar to a butter cream frosting.

Hard sauces are frequently flavored with rum or brandy. Usually a pastry bag is used to apply the garnish to the pudding or cake.

SUPREME SAUCES

Supreme sauces are foamy sauces made with beaten egg whites or whipped cream or both. They may be flavored with fruits, extracts, or liqueurs.

On page 427 is a recipe for a plain supreme sauce. Like the hard sauce, it requires no cooking and is very easy to make.

Some supreme sauces require the addition of fresh fruits. Strawberries, raspberries, or other juicy fruits may be selected. The fruit is cooked before being mixed with the sauce.

Care and Storage of Sauces

Sauces containing eggs should be used the same day they are made. Egg sauces spoil very quickly. Unless they are to be served warm, all sauces should be refrigerated until ready to be served. Fruit sauces will keep for several days under refrigeration.

Service

The sauce should be compatible with the dessert. For example, strawberry sauce might be served on strawberry dessert. However, blending of flavors makes for more interest. Chocolate sauce is sometimes served on peppermint ice cream. The raspberry-currant mixture is blended with peaches in the peach Melba.

Although the serving of sauce should be generous, it should not "drown" the dessert. Be careful to make a neat-looking dessert. A sauce can easily spill over the dish, making a sloppy serving.

**How
Much
Have
You
Learned?**

Review this chapter. Answer the following questions to prepare yourself for the posttest. Check your answers with the teacher.

1. Define at least 75 percent of the *Words to Remember*. Use each word in a sentence.

2. Name the four types of dessert fruits and give an example of a dessert made from each type. Select a fruit-based dessert and describe its preparation.

3. Explain the principles of fruit cookery. Select one method of cooking fruit and describe the preparation of a fruit by this method.

4. Explain the principles of starch cookery.

5. Select one type of pudding and describe its preparation.

6. How are eggs added to a pudding? Why are special precautions needed? Apply these precautions to cooking soft custard.

7. How are custards and puddings with milk-egg base stored? Why?

8. How is fruit-flavored gelatin dissolved? How is plain gelatin dissolved? How important is temperature? What will happen if the gelatin is not thoroughly dissolved?

9. How is fruit added to gelatin? Why?

10. Describe the preparation of Bavarian Cream. What is the difference between a true Bavarian and a fruit Bavarian?

11. Is it easier to make a baked soufflé or a gelatin soufflé? Why?

12. How long before serving time should a gelatin dessert be made? Why?

13. Describe the preparation of a hard meringue.

14. Name five points for judging the quality of ice cream. Explain each one.

15. Describe the correct method for scooping ice cream for service.

16. Name the five types of dessert sauces. Select one and describe its preparation.

References

Books

Amendola, Joseph, and Lundberg, Donald. *Understanding Baking.* Boston: CBI Publications, 1973.

Amendola, Joseph, and Wilkinson, Jule. *Baking Recipes.* Boston: Cahner's, 1974.

Barrows, A. B. *Everyday Production of Baked Goods.* Boston: Cahner's, 1975.

Cote, Patricia. *People, Food, and Science.* Boston: Ginn and Co., 1968.

Fance, Wilfred. *The International Confectioner.* London: Virtue and Co., 1968.

Folsom, LeRoi. *The Professional Chef.* Boston: CBI Publications, 1974.

Haines, Robert G. *Food Preparation for Hotels, Restaurants, and Cafeterias.* Chicago: American Technical Society, 1973.

Hardwick, Geraline B., and Kennedy, Robert L. *Fundamentals of Quantity Food Preparation: Desserts & Beverages.* Boston: Cahner's, 1975.

Kotschevar, Lendel H. *Standards, Principles, and Techniques in Quantity Food Production.* Boston: Cahner's, 1973.

Ray, Mary F., and Lewis, Evelyn J. *Exploring Professional Cooking*. Peoria, Ill.: Chas. A. Bennett Co., Inc., 1976.

Terrell, Margaret E. *Large Quantity Recipes*. Philadelphia: J. B. Lippincott Co., 1975.

Manufacturers' Books and Booklets

Durkee's Baking Formula Book. Cleveland: Durkee Food Service Group.

Baker's Aid. Minneapolis: Russell Miller-King Midas Mills.

Bakery Service. Cincinnati: Procter and Gamble Co.

Cake and Pastry Fillings. LaGrange, Ill.: Sokol and Co.

Chiffon Cakes. Fullerton, Calif.: Hunt-Wesson Foods.

Films

The Amazing Art of Flour Milling. R. J. S. Carter Co., 404 National Building, Second Avenue and Sixth Street South, Minneapolis, Minn.

MELBA SAUCE

Equipment
Double boiler
Wire whip
Sieve or china cap

Yield: 750 mL [3 c]

Metric	Ingredients	Customary
250 mL	Currant jelly	1 c
500 mL	Raspberries (frozen)	2 c
10 mL	Cornstarch	2 t
3 mL	Salt	$\frac{1}{4}$ t

METHOD

1. **Defrost** raspberries. Force through sieve or china cap.
2. **Combine** all ingredients in top of double boiler. Blend thoroughly.
3. **Cook** over hot water until thick and clear. Cool.

CHOCOLATE SAUCE

Equipment
Double boiler
Wire whip

Yield: 1.5 L [1½ qt]

Metric	Ingredients	Customary
340 g	Chocolate, bitter	12 oz (12 squares)
340 g	Butter or margarine	12 oz
90 mL	Corn syrup	6 T
600 g	Sugar	1 lb 5 oz
410 g (1 can)	Milk, evaporated	14½ oz (1 can)
5 mL	Vanilla	1 t

METHOD

1. **Melt** chocolate and butter in top of double boiler over hot water.
2. **Add** corn syrup. Stir with wire whip.
3. **Add** half the sugar. Stir until dissolved.
4. **Add** half the milk. Stir.
5. **Add** the rest of the sugar. Stir until dissolved.
6. **Add** the rest of the milk and flavoring. Blend thoroughly.

ORANGE SAUCE

Equipment
Saucepan
Bowl
Wire whip

Yield: 1.5 L [1½ qt]

Metric	Ingredients	Customary
875 mL	Orange juice	3½ c
30 mL	Orange rind	2 T
90 mL	Cornstarch	6 T
560 mL	Sugar	2¼ c
1 mL	Salt	¼ t
375 mL	Water, cold	1½ c
30 mL	Lemon juice	2 T
115 g	Butter or margarine	4 oz

(Method found on following page)

ORANGE SAUCE (Continued)

METHOD

1. **Bring** orange juice and orange rind to boil in saucepan.
2. **Mix** cornstarch, sugar, and salt in bowl.
3. **Blend** with cold water using wire whip.
4. **Stir** cornstarch mixture slowly into boiling juice. Stir vigorously with wire whip.
5. **Boil** until thick, stirring all the time.
6. **Reduce** heat. Simmer for 2 minutes.
7. **Remove** from heat and add lemon juice and butter. Stir.
8. **Cool,** stirring occasionally.

HARD SAUCE

Equipment
Bench mixer
Paddle attachment

Yield: 1.5 L [1½ qt]

Metric	Ingredients	Customary
225 g	Butter or margarine	8 oz
450 g	Sugar, confectioners'	1 lb
60 mL	Cream, half and half	4 T
5 mL	Flavoring (vanilla, rum, or brandy extract)	1 t

METHOD

1. **Cream** butter on middle speed until light and fluffy.
2. **Reduce** to low speed. Add sugar gradually.
3. **Increase** to high speed. Cream until very light.
4. **Reduce** to low speed. Gradually add cream and flavoring.
5. **Increase** to high speed. Cream for 5 minutes.
6. **Chill** in refrigerator.

SUPREME SAUCE

Equipment
Bench mixer
Whip attachment
2 bowls for mixer

Yield: 1.25 L [1¼ qt]

Metric	Ingredients	Customary
500 mL	Cream, whipping	1 pt
4	Eggs	4
45 mL	Flavoring (rum, brandy, lemon, or vanilla extract)	3 T
450 g	Sugar, confectioners'	1 lb

METHOD

1. **Beat** cream until stiff in first bowl. Set aside.
2. **Beat** eggs in second bowl on high speed until thick and fluffy.
3. **Reduce** to second speed. Add sugar gradually.
4. **Beat** on high speed until very fluffy.
5. **Add** flavoring.
6. **Reduce** to low speed. Add whipped cream. Blend thoroughly.

Fast Foods

Donald Breitkreutz, Group Director of Training, Burger King University, Burger King Corporation, Miami, Florida.

MEET THE CONSULTANT

Don Breitkreutz, blue-eyed, friendly, and enthusiastic, is a man in love—in love with his job. He has been involved in this love affair for fourteen years.

When Don graduated from high school, he was not sure what he wanted to do with his life. He didn't want to go to college. He didn't have the money for it, anyway. He had worked part-time while at school and during the summers since he was twelve years old. Born in South Dakota, famous as a dairy state, he found

428

jobs in the dairies wrapping butter and washing milk bottles. He worked as a stockboy in supermarkets and as a dishwasher in restaurants. He always seemed to find jobs connected with foods.

After graduating from high school, he took a job in Nebraska in a candy factory. He made the candy and learned the fine art of dipping chocolates. After nine years, he felt there was no future for him in Nebraska. He had married and was looking for opportunities to get ahead. He moved to Washington, D.C., taking another job in a candy company. The pay was low, and Don needed more money to support his growing family.

He noticed that a well-known fast-food chain was opening a new restaurant near his home. He applied for a part-time job and was trained to make milk shakes. When the restaurant opened, Don was frantically trying to keep up with the demand. He noticed a man wearing a company blazer standing nearby checking all operations. In his hurry, Don made a "short" milk shake, and capped it. Immediately the man stepped forward, tapped him on the shoulder, and said, "We don't do things that way. All shakes must be exactly alike."

Don says, "At that moment, I fell in love—in love with fast foods. If they were that particular, this was the place for me." He quit his job with the candy company and worked full-time at the fast-food restaurant.

Soon he became swing manager. The swing manager is the person who takes over the responsibility when the manager is gone. Not long after, he began training for management. He was placed in a restaurant near Washington, D.C. In one year, he had greatly increased the business and caught the eye of the regional manager. He had a friendly manner and obvious enthusiasm. These qualities, plus his ability to manage people and keep a cool head during emergencies, helped to advance him swiftly. He was promoted to regional training supervisor. In this job, he had to talk to all kinds of people.

Five years later, he was sent to the training school near Chicago as a professor. He liked this job. He really enjoyed teaching, and he was happy not to be traveling so much. Within a few months, he was made dean of the training school. He upgraded the staff and instituted stiffer courses. He introduced the use of color film slides and other illustrations to picture every step of fast foods. While he was dean, the facilities doubled and the enrollment greatly increased.

He had an itchy foot, however. When he was offered a job with another food chain that gave him the chance to travel in the Far East, he took it. The company was opening many new restaurants in Japan. Don's job was to help plan them, train the workers, and supervise the management. This exposed him to new cultures and enlarged his interests.

Along the way he picked up new responsibilities. He moved into product and equipment development. He drew up specifications for hamburgers, buns, sauces, and other foods sold in the restaurants. In fast foods, standardization is the key to profit. Each hamburger served must be exactly like any other.

"This is one of the fascinating aspects of fast foods," says Don. "You try to remove the element of human error as much as possible. The customer must be sure to receive the same quality of food, served in the same manner, and in the same type of facility no matter what part of the country. Standardization is the only way to control costs."

He also designed functional layouts for the kitchens and serving areas so the food would flow smoothly from the time of arrival, through production, to service. Perhaps you remember the phrase *mise en place* from Chapter 1. This phrase is meaningful in fast foods also.

"Let the students in food service know of the opportunities in fast foods," says Don Breitkreutz. "If they fall in love with the concept, as I did, they can go far. Just start at the bottom and take advantage of every opportunity to learn more. The opportunities are there, just waiting for them."

Fast Foods

CHAPTER

22

What Will You Learn?

When you finish studying this chapter, you should be able to do the following:
- Identify the types of operations that feature fast foods.
- Prepare hamburgers, steaks, fried chicken, fried fish, french fried potatoes and onions, and pizza using the techniques used in fast food operations.
- Pass the posttest.

Fast foods are not new to food service. Most restaurants have a short-order cook whose job is to broil, grill, and fry foods quickly to order.

What is new is the standardized production in thousands of chain restaurants all over the country. Only twenty-five years ago, the fast-food industry was just beginning. Today, it is a twenty-five billion dollar industry catering to the demands of millions of people.

WHAT ARE FAST FOODS?

A short-order cook grills a hamburger and serves it on a bun to the customer sitting on a stool at the counter. A driver of a car goes to the drive-in window and buys a bucket of fried chicken for a party. To feed her family, a busy mother picks up a pizza on her way home from work. A family traveling far from home orders hamburgers, French fries, and milk shakes at a serving counter. Then, seated in a booth, they eat a quick lunch. All of these foods are *fast foods*. Fast foods are foods that are served within a few minutes after the order for them has been given.

Why the Demand for Fast Foods?

The demand for fast foods arises from the changing habits of the American people. A habit is just a customary way of doing things. American habits in eating and life-style are different than they were twenty-five years ago.

Words to Remember

assembly table	franchising
commissary	franchisor
distribution center	licensee
dressing	product mix
fast foods	short-order cook
FIFO	stoning
franchisee	

Americans have always been a people in a hurry. The pace of living is fast and hectic. However, until twenty-five years ago eating out was fairly relaxing. It was "dining out"—an occasion for leisurely enjoyment. Now that seems to be changing.

A waitress with many years experience says she always enjoyed giving good service at a table set with polished silverware, gleaming crystal, and folded cloth napkins. Now people seem to want to eat and run. She says, "They ask how long it will take to prepare a certain dish. How quickly can it be served? They want the dessert on the table while they are gulping the first course. Where are they going in such a hurry?"

The tremendous growth of fast foods stems in part from this demand by many people for quick service. The service is demanded even if it means service with paper cartons, paper cups, plastic spoons, and plastic forks. Everything is disposable, except the tray.

Another reason for the growth of fast foods is the increased number of travelers. Fast foods make it easy for travelers to eat on the way. Fast-food chains may not offer gourmet food, but they are usually clean and conveniently located. The menu may be limited, but the food is relatively inexpensive and quickly served. The surroundings are familiar. Fast foods appeal to those traveling far from home. Fig. 22-1.

Fast food also meets the needs of people other than travelers. A poll shows that 80 percent of the people eating in a well-known food chain live or work within a few miles of the restaurant. Fast-food restaurants in downtown office centers cater to office personnel. Even fast-food restaurants in the out-lying suburbs find that many customers are repeaters. They tend to come to the same place day after day.

Recently, the fast-food companies have been making great efforts to attract families as customers. They are providing more attractive sit-down space. They offer high chairs for the little ones, a more varied menu, and clean restrooms. Children quickly recognize the trademark names and clamor to eat there. The food appeals to them. The quick service keeps them from becoming restless.

The fast-food industry also satisfies the American appetite for snacks. Many Americans, especially the young, like to snack. So they snack on doughnuts, hamburgers, fried chicken, hot dogs, tacos, and French fries.

GROWTH OF FAST FOODS

The fast-food industry is one of the fastest growing industries in the United States. It is rapidly spreading all over the world. More and more people are choosing fast foods. In choosing fast foods, they are choosing a different type of place for dining.

Many food service professionals see fast foods as a threat. However, diners who preferred more leisurely dining, with table service, still prefer that type of service. Those who are looking for quick,

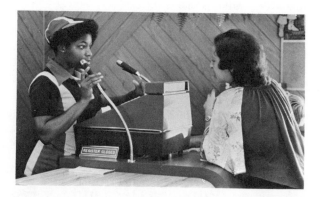

Burger King, Inc.

22-1. Fast-food restaurants are conveniently located. Since they serve food quickly, they appeal to travelers and people who work close by.

Burger King, Inc.

22-2. Managers of fast-food restaurants are trained in the techniques of fast-food preparation. Here, Donald Breitkreutz instructs a class.

inexpensive food are changing to fast-food restaurants.

Franchising

Much of the quick growth of fast food is due to *franchising*. Franchising is also called *licensing*. It means granting to an individual or group of individuals the right to market a product with full use of the company name. The individual or group of individuals is called the *franchisee* or *licensee*. The company is the *franchisor* or *licensor*.

In return for the right to use the company name, the franchisee must fulfill certain obligations, such as:

• Meeting certain financial obligations. The required amount varies widely.

• Meeting company standards in production and service of foods.

• Using company-designed facilities and trademarks.

• Following company policies regarding cleanliness, decor, uniforms, and production methods.

For instance, a large company marketing hamburgers under a trademark may need more outlets. They may not have enough money to build the facilities, pay the managers, and market the hamburg-

ers. For a fee, they sell to an individual the right to open a restaurant using the company name. This person is also granted the right to sell the hamburgers under the trademark. This is a *franchise*.

Many fast-food restaurants operating under company names are franchisees or licensees. Franchises may be good or bad, depending upon the integrity of the company and the ability of the franchisee. As in every industry, there are "fly-by-night," unscrupulous people who encourage an individual to buy a franchise with promises of big money to be made. Once the front money has been paid, the franchisee is left to sink or swim—usually to sink into bankruptcy and despair.

On the other hand, reputable companies consider the franchisee as a partner in selling their products. They recognize their responsibilities and offer help in the following ways:

• By providing attractive facilities that are readily recognizable, on a site with customer potential. Before building a restaurant, a reputable company makes a survey to make sure there are enough prospective customers to make the restaurant profitable. The facilities may be rented to the franchisee for a reasonable price, or the franchisee may own the building and the land.

• By training the franchisee in proper management practices and offering further training, as needed. Fig. 22-2.

• By setting specifications for standardized products and equipment so cost can be controlled. Many franchisors also own equipment companies and rent the equipment to the franchisee.

• By helping the franchisee find purveyors for product ingredients when necessary. Many companies own commissaries from which the necessary supplies are distributed.

• By helping the franchisee with legal problems.

• By checking the standards of the operation and making suggestions for improvements. Many companies review the performance in detail every three months to a year.

• By being always available in case of trouble.

• By furnishing field consultants.

• By providing information about such important matters as local health codes.

• By constant communication with the franchisee.

The company generally has little or no control over menu pricing or employee pay rates. This varies among the franchisees and from region to region. Competition among franchisees located close together affects prices and wages. The franchisee is free to hire and fire managers and other employees.

One company executive said, "I tell our franchisees they are paying a lot of money for their franchises. If they don't ask us to send somebody out there when they have a problem, they're foolish."

The company has the right to enter the premises and inspect at any time. If the franchisee is not following company policies, or the products are not up to standards, suggestions for improvement are made. If such suggestions are not followed, the franchise may be terminated. Such drastic action is usually not needed, since the franchisee is interested in making money. More profit will generally be made by following company policies.

Of course, even the best company cannot promise a profitable venture if the franchisee does not meet his or her responsibilities.

Company-owned Restaurants

As fast-food chains have become bigger, more money has become available for expansion. Some of the companies are buying back franchises. Company-owned restaurants are usually more profitable for the franchisor because the company reaps all the profits. The company controls the management. The company is responsible for all aspects of the operation. In most of the national chains, about 25 percent of the outlets are company owned. In one company, 90 percent of the oulets were under franchise in 1978, but they expect to have less than 50 percent under franchise by 1980. Company-owned restaurants are used to test new products, equipment, and procedures before implementing them nationally.

Commissaries

A *commissary* is a central kitchen or distribution point where food may be purchased, prepared, and held in storage in quantity. Some commissaries prepare no food. They are merely warehouses to hold fresh, frozen, canned, or packaged food and supplies to be distributed to the outlets. They are called *distribution centers*. In other commissaries, extensive food preparation may be done.

Some of the commissaries or distribution centers may be owned by a branch or subsidiary of the fast-food company. They service only the outlets belonging to the chain. For example, they may buy wholesale cuts of beef, portion them, freeze the portions, and deliver them to the restaurants. They may buy fresh chickens, portion them, and deliver them. They may prepare potatoes for French frying. They may bread items such as fish to make them ready for frying.

Other commissaries may service many different fast-food outlets, performing the same services for all as ordered. For instance, the commissary may sell frozen steaks complete with grid marks to many food service places.

Commissaries may send specifications for roll mix to a flour milling company. The mix is made up at the mill according to specifications. It is packaged under the name of the company operating the commissary and delivered to the commissary. From there it is distributed to the food service outlets for makeup.

Some commissaries purchase raw coffee beans. They roast, grind, and blend their own coffees. They may package teas as well as coffees under their own brand name.

TYPES OF FAST-FOOD OPERATIONS

Perhaps the concept of fast foods began with the cafeterias where service was drastically cut, permitting self-service. Perhaps it began with the coffee shops with limited service and limited menu. It has come to full operation with the huge chains offering standard food, in standard surroundings, cooked and served under standard conditions.

Short-Order Cook

Many restaurants offering full service and a varied menu employ a *short-order cook*. In a chain restaurant, this versatile cook may preside over a compact, highly efficient kitchen in full view of the customers.

The heart of the kitchen is the cutting board. Here, the cook works more often and longer than in any other section. Vegetables are chopped, sandwiches assembled, and simple salads are prepared on the cutting board. For efficiency, the grill should be on one side of it and the garnish table on the other. All equipment should be within a few steps of the cutting board. Fig. 22-3.

FOODS PREPARED BY THE SHORT-ORDER COOK

Almost all quick foods are prepared by this cook. Following is a partial list.

- Minute steaks.
- Hamburgers.
- Hot dogs.
- Eggs, all kinds.
- Bacon, sausages.
- Hot sandwiches.
- Cold sandwiches.
- Simple salads.
- Toast.
- Pancakes, French toast.
- French fries.
- Fried onions.

To speed service, the short-order cook may use many convenience foods. These foods also help give variety to the menu, save labor costs, and conserve storage space. Some of these are listed below.

- *Frozen foods* such as sliced potatoes, hashed brown potatoes, onions, hamburger patties, steaks, vegetables.
- *Refrigerated foods* such as precut salad greens, coleslaw, sandwich mixes, salad dressings.
- *Dehydrated and freeze-dried foods* such as instant potatoes, onions, and garlic.
- *Ready-to-heat foods* such as fried chicken, preblanched steaks, and presliced roast beef.
- *Mixes* for gravies, sauces, hot breads, and rolls.
- *Packaged seasonings.*

EQUIPMENT

Refer to Chapter 2 for pictures and descriptions of the following large pieces of equipment.

22-3. A short-order cook prepares a hamburger plate. Notice the arrangement of the ingredients and equipment.

- Grill or broiler.
- Deep fryer.
- Waffle iron.
- Toaster.
- Food slicer.
- Infrared lamps.
- Microwave oven.
- Drawer-type refrigerator.

In addition, small equipment is needed. Perhaps the most important is the French knife. The cook uses this for all chopping and most slicing operations. Other tools that are used include:

- Turner.
- Spatula.
- Rubber scraper.
- Tongs.
- Scoops.

435

- Measuring spoons.
- Spreading knife.
- Wire whip.
- Egg rings.

METHODS OF COOKING

During the quiet morning hours, the short-order cook does the necessary prepreparations such as chopping lettuce, slicing onions and tomatoes, preparing garnishes, and setting up the garnish table.

• *Grilling*. The grill needs to be preheated. If several types of foods are to be grilled, different temperatures are needed. For instance, eggs should be cooked at 149°C [300° F.], hamburgers at 177°C [350° F.] and pancakes at 190°C [375° F.]. To ensure these varied temperatures, a grill with thermostatic control on each side in needed.

Notice Fig. 22-4. Although the surface is a unit, the grill is divided into two separate temperature zones. Each has its own thermostat.

To operate this grill follow these directions:

1. Set the left temperature at 149°C [300° F.].
2. Set the right temperature at 204°C [400° F.].

When preheated, the far left of the grill will be at low heat, just right for eggs. The far right will be at high heat, just right for pancakes. The middle of the grill will vary from 163°C [325° F.] on the left to 190°C [375° F.] on the right. This temperature range is just right for meats such as minute steaks, hamburgers, and bacon.

Follow the directions for grilling found on pages 190–191.

CARE OF GRILL

A short-order cook must keep the grill clean. After each use, the grill should be scraped clean of bits of food. Any excess grease should be wiped off.

Every twenty-four hours, the grill should be *stoned*, or scrubbed with a pumice stone. In stoning, follow these directions:

1. Heat grill to 175°C [350° F.].
2. Pour 125–250 mL [$\frac{1}{2}$–1 c] of old oil on the grill.
3. Scrub with the pumice stone, using a circular motion. Overlap each motion and cover the surface thoroughly. Pay particular attention to the back of the grill.
4. Loosen any stuck particles with a grit cloth.
5. After all burned particles are loosened, wipe them up with paper towels. Water may be used, but no scouring powder.
6. Empty the grease drawer and wash it.

Fast Foods and Nutrition

Are fast foods nutritious? Many well-known nutritionists are concerned about this question. School food service is particularly concerned. They have noticed that whenever students are permitted to leave the school grounds at lunchtime, they flock to the nearby fast food restaurants.

According to recent surveys, teenagers have the poorest nutrition of any age bracket. Nutritionists worry about the eating of fast foods. Some of them do not rate very high nutritionally. Of course, it depends upon the choice. A hot dog and a coke have low nutritional value. On the other hand, two pieces of fried chicken, coleslaw, potatoes, and gravy supply a good amount of the needed nutrients. So does a piece of pizza. School lunch personnel point to the high nutritional quality of the Type-A lunch. However, how much of that lunch is thrown into the garbage? A Type-A lunch must contain:

- 57 g [2 oz] meat or other protein.
- 175 mL [$\frac{3}{4}$ c] vegetables or fruit.

	149°C 300° F. Eggs	163–190°C 325–375° F. Hamburgers Steaks	204°C 400° F. Pancakes
22-4. Varying temperatures for grilling.			

Front of Grill

Burger King, Inc.
22-5. A conveyor chain broiler.

- 250 mL [1 c] milk.
- One slice bread or rolls.

KINDS OF SPECIALIZED FOODS

More fast-food restaurants specialize in hamburgers than in any other food. Pizza and fried chicken rank second in popularity. There are also steak houses and fish-and-chip places.

The fast-food restaurants have expanded the menu to include such side dishes as coleslaw, fried onions, corn-on-the-cob, and French fries. Simple desserts are often offered, as well as beverages.

Hamburgers

The hamburger began fast-food service because it can be cooked quickly and is very popular. Hamburgers consist of the patty, the bun, and the dressing.

INGREDIENTS

- *Patty.* Hamburger patty sizes are standardized. They are all-beef, preportioned, and delivered fresh or frozen in cartons. The exact weight is specified, usually in one of the following weights:
  - 57 g [2 oz]—The weight used most often.
  - 85 g [3 oz].
  - 113 g [4 oz].
  - 198 g [7 oz].

Thickness is specified also. Preportioned patties are essential for quick service. They eliminate waste and save labor and time.

- *Bun.* Many fast-food chains use local bakeries to supply the buns. The weight, height, and diameter must be exactly as specified. Buns may be plain or seeded. The sesame seed bun is very popular. The bun must have a firm texture so it will not fall apart while being eaten.

- *Dressing.* The frills put on the hamburger are called the *dressing,* or *condiments.* They vary among the different companies, but essentially they are very much alike. The pickles and onions are presliced. The lettuce is already washed and shredded when delivered from the commissary or distribution center. Catsup and mustard are in dispenser bottles or portion control equipment. The mayonnaise is in a container ready for spreading. Not all chains offer tomatoes. If available, they are the only part of the dressing that is prepared on the premises.

Some restaurants prefer to offer small packets of catsup, mustard, salt, and pepper at the serving counter.

EQUIPMENT

Either a grill or a broiler is used to cook the hamburgers. A warmer/steamer, assembly table, and warmer/serving shelf are also needed. A spreading knife is used at the assembly table.

Some persons prefer the grilled hamburger. Grilling caramelizes the slight amount of sugar in meat, adding to the flavor. Other customers prefer broiling and the flavor developed by the open flame.

- *Grill.* This useful piece of equipment has already been described on pages 50–51.

- *Broiler.* Some fast-food restaurants may use the open broiler described on page 51. Most fast-food restaurants use a conveyor chain broiler. Fig. 22-5.

Burger King, Inc.

22-6. Placing hamburger patties on the conveyor chain broiler. Notice that the buns are toasted in a separate section.

Burger King, Inc.

22-7. Broiled patties and toasted buns are taken from the conveyor chain broiler.

The conveyor chain broiler is usually divided into two sections, side by side. One side is used for broiling the patties. The other side is used for toasting the buns. Fig. 22-6. The chain belt on both sections is endless. The flame is on top and bottom for the one used for the patties. Thus, both sides are broiled at once.

The worker places the hamburger at one end. It is deposited in a basket or tray at the other end. Fig. 22-7. The presliced buns are opened and also placed on a conveyor that deposits them in a basket or tray after toasting. Toasting warms the bun and seals the inner surface. Thus, the bun will not become soggy from the meat juices. Toasting also improves the flavor.

• *Assembly table.* The hamburgers are dressed and wrapped on the assembly table—a long table leading to the serving counter. The surface of the assembly table may be stainless steel or wood. Fig. 22-8.

• *Warmer/steamer.* The warmer/steamer makes it possible to keep ready a warm supply of hamburgers. The warmer is a small box heated by steam. The steam keeps the sandwich from drying out. The sandwich stays warm until ready to be dressed. Fig. 22-9.

METHODS OF COOKING

One of the reasons for disdain of fast foods by professional cooks it that there is really no need for

Burger King, Inc.

22-8. The assembly table.

Burger King, Inc.

22-9. Hamburgers are placed in the warmer/steamer. The maximum holding time is ten minutes.

a highly developed skill in cooking. Standardization has taken the guesswork out of production. The skill is in management.

Timing. Every fifteen minutes in many fast-food restaurants, the manager gets a reading from the computer cash register. This reading gives the number of hamburgers, French fries, and other menu offerings sold in the previous fifteen minutes. Checking these statistics over several days, the manager knows how many sandwiches of each type will probably be sold at different times of the day. This is known as *product mix.* Such information is essential to prevent waste. Sandwiches must be made ahead of time for quick service. However, they must not be made so far ahead that they are no longer fresh. As you read the following, notice how important timing is to the manager.

- *Grilling.* See pages 190–191.

- *Broiling.* About a half hour before opening time, the manager turns on the broiler. After preheating, the broiler must be tested. Several experimental patties are cooked until the broiler turns out a properly broiled patty. A stopwatch may be used to time the patty from the time it enters the broiler until it is deposited in the basket. Once the heat is correct, the broiler is ready to use. The statistics tell the manager how many hamburgers should be broiled in any fifteen-minute period. These statistics are posted by the manager on a chart. The broiler

Burger King, Inc.

22-10. Fast-food preparation is standardized. The ingredients in this hamburger are placed on the bun in a certain sequence.

operator follows this chart. If the broiler has more than one meat chain, only one of the chain broilers is used during slow times. During busy times, both broiler chains are working at top speed.

The worker at the other end of the broiler places the broiled patty between the toasted bun and places it in the warmer/steamer.

- *Warming.* Preassembled hamburgers must not stay in the warmer/steamer longer than ten minutes. Quality is high up to that point but deteriorates rapidly after that. Sandwiches held longer than ten minutes must be discarded—an expensive waste. Workers must learn to follow that well-known rule of storage—*first in, first out.* The workers call it *FIFO* and soon become used to that abbreviation. The hamburgers are rotated—the ones put in first are taken out first.

- *Assembling.* The assembly of each sandwich is also standardized. Fig. 22-10. Workers are trained to place the hamburger in the bun on the paper wrapping in a certain way. This makes it easy to add the dressing and wrap the sandwich securely. No deviation is permitted unless requested by the customer. For instance, the customer may say, "No pickles and onions, please."

For example, four pickle slices may be placed on a sandwich and topped with shredded lettuce and sliced onions. Workers are trained to recognize the correct dressing amount by appearance, rather than by weight. In training workers, the manager demonstrates the assembling of the sandwiches. The use of correct ingredient amounts is stressed. The workers practice until they can easily judge the right amount.

The top of the bun is spread with mayonnaise. If used, the lettuce and tomato are placed on the mayonnaise. Catsup is added, and the sandwich is securely wrapped.

Each fast-food company offers a variety of hambugers with different dressings. Some have two hamburger patties in a three-piece bun. As a worker, you must know the ingredients. You must know the amount and type of dressing to use on each kind of sandwich on the menu.

- *Serving.* The completed sandwich is placed on the warming/serving shelf behind the serving counter. Infrared bulbs keep the food warm. Fig. 22-11. There is a definite order for placing the sandwiches here. Each type is separated from the others. The sandwiches made first are placed closest to the serving counter. The completed sandwich cannot stay on the warming shelf longer than ten minutes. Otherwise, it must be discarded. The workers must place the sandwiches in order, so the counter server will know which ones to serve first.

Without knowing how many of each sandwich type will be sold each fifteen minutes, the manager would not be able to control production. During the lunch and dinner hours, the sandwiches will be sold as fast as they can be made. The time between is the slack time. Then, the manager must be sure to have enough sandwiches to satisfy the demand, but not enough to cause waste.

Words to Remember

calibrating

Steaks

In response to customer demand for less expensive steak dinners, the fast-food steak houses were born. The lower-priced steak dinners have become very popular.

TYPES OF STEAKS

To satisfy the demand for less expensive steaks, the lower grades of beef are used. You probably remember reading in Chapter 4 that the lower grades of meat are just as nutritious as the higher grades. They may be even more flavorful, but not as tender. To make them more tender, they are tenderized before they are frozen. (See page 175 for methods of tenderizing.)

Like the hamburger patties, the steaks must meet exact specifications. Following are the specifications for T-bone steaks.

- No more than 1.2 cm [$\frac{1}{2}$ in] fat cover.
- Tail no longer than 5 cm [2 in].
- Tenderloin at least 3 cm [$1\frac{1}{4}$ in] wide.
- Portion: 340–395 g [12–14 oz].
- Packing: 61–64 count in a 23-kg [50-lb] case.

Other cuts may be offered, such as boneless New York strip, top sirloin butt, and rib eye. Ground beef patties may be offered. Each of these must meet similar specifications.

EQUIPMENT

Some steak houses may grill the steaks, but most broil them. They may use a continuous broiler similar to the one used for hamburgers. However, many steak houses prefer a long, open broiler. The customers enjoy seeing the steaks being broiled. See page 51 for a description of an open broiler.

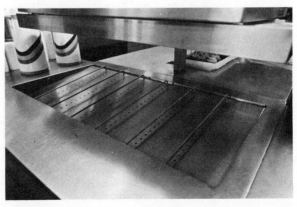

Burger King, Inc.
22-11. Infrared warmers.

The broiler cook needs the following small equipment.

- *Tongs* for turning the steaks.
- *Spatula* or *turner* for turning the hamburgers.
- *Wire grid brush* and *wire scraper* for cleaning the grids between broilings.
- *Putty knife* for cleaning at the end of the day.
- *Corn whisk broom* to brush off pieces of burned steak.
- *Asbestos gloves* to protect the hands of the workers from the hot fire of the broiler.
- *Salt and pepper shakers* for seasoning the steaks.

CAUTION

Sometimes the broiler fire flares up as the grease drips into the fire. A box of soda and salt should be available to put out the flare-up. When sprinkled on an open flame, either of these ingredients will smother the flames.

METHODS OF COOKING

The broiler cook is responsible for thawing the steaks, broiling them, and taking care of the broiler.

- *Thawing.* To thaw steaks, follow these directions:

1. Remove steaks from the freezer. Steaks are packed in plastic sleeves so they can be easily separated. Place like steaks on separate trays. For instance, T-bone is placed on one tray, rib eye on another and so on. Do not stack one tray on top of the other—the steaks cannot thaw evenly. Place a paper on each tray with the time marked on it. Check the carton carefully to be sure all steaks have been removed.

2. Place trays in walk-in refrigerator. Move steaks left-over from the day before to the front. Place steaks to be thawed in back.

3. After thawing, remove sleeves and transfer steaks to undercounter refrigerator, ready for broiling. *Remember, FIFO—first in, first out.*

4. At the end of the day, return any unused steaks to the walk-in refrigerator. Use these first the next day.

- *Broiling.* The second job of the broiler cook is to preheat the broiler. This takes about one hour. Most broilers are in two sections. One is set at high heat—288°C [550° F.]. The other section is set at a much lower heat 88–105°C [190–220° F.]. A thermometer is built in the broiler to check the heat. Checking the heat with a thermometer is called *calibrating.*

While the broiler is preheating, the broiler cook should check to make sure all needed tools are on hand. Once the broiling starts, there is no time to look for tools. Mise en place, remember?

Each fast-food chain has a definite system for placing the steaks on the broiler. The system must be followed. Using it, the broiler cook will always know where a particular kind of steak has been placed. The cook will also know the degree of doneness it has reached. The hottest side of the broiler is used for browning the steaks. The cooler side is used for keeping the steaks warm until ordered by the customer. After being ordered, the steak is moved to the hot side again for finishing. Customers expect steaks to have the degree of doneness they ordered. Only by following a definite system can the broiler cook prepare such a steak. Figure 22-12 suggests how a broiler might be divided.

To broil a steak, follow these directions:

1. Check that steak is completely thawed. Partially frozen steaks take longer to cook.

2. Place steaks individually on the broiler, following the system you have learned. Never dump several steaks on at once and then spread them apart. Grid marks are set as soon as the steaks hit the grid. Grid marks must have a definite pattern as discussed in Chapter 9. See page 189.

3. Cook each steak to order.

4. Do not poke, press, or handle the steaks. These practices cause loss of juices.

5. Turn steaks when blood seeps through to the top side.

6. Rare steaks are turned only once and have grid marks going only one way.

7. Well-done steaks are turned three times and have grid marks at right angles to each other on both sides.

8. Season just before serving.

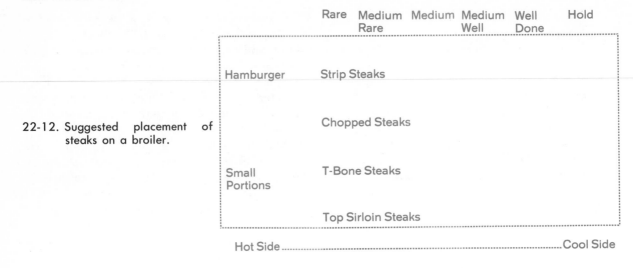

22-12. Suggested placement of steaks on a broiler.

See pages 180 and 190 for ways of recognizing the different degrees of doneness. However, since the steaks are standardized in weight and thickness, the broiling time for each type of steak should be the same.

• *Care of broiler.* Use the wire grid brush to clean the grids between broilings. Bits of steak left on the grids will char. They will give an undesirable flavor to the next steak.

After the dinner hours, clean the grids thoroughly with the wire scraper. Use the putty knife to loosen any burned-on bits of meat. Finish with the wire brush and wipe clean with the damp towel. Empty the grease drawer.

Words to Remember ————

breader/sifter   warming cabinet
pressure fryer

Fried Chicken

Deep-fried chicken as a fast food was introduced about twenty-five years ago.

Individual portions of fried chicken may be eaten for lunch, dinner, or as a snack. It is also sold by the bucket or barrel to take home.

INGREDIENTS

The ingredients consist of chicken, breading, and the shortening for frying.

• *Chickens.* The chickens must meet the specifications of the fast-food chains. The specifications may vary, but the largest chain specifies 1.1–1.4 kg [2$\frac{1}{2}$–3 lb] for each chicken, divided into exact serving portions. Each portion must have about the same proportion of meat to bone. Fresh chickens are preferred, packaged two chickens in a plastic bag. The customer may be given a choice of white or dark meat.

• *Breading.* In most fast-food outlets, breading is done on the premises. The breading recipe is *proprietary;* that is, the seasoning recipe is owned by the company and kept secret. The wash is a mixture of milk powder, water, and, sometimes, egg.

• *Shortening.* A special frying compound is usually made from an all-vegetable base. It is specially made to resist the high heat of frying without disintegrating. Some places may use oil, but most use a solid compound.

EQUIPMENT

There are several important pieces of equipment used for the fast-food production of fried chicken—the breader/sifter, the pressure fryer, and the warming cabinet.

Burger King, Inc.
22-13. A warming cabinet for fish and chicken.

• *Breader/sifter.* The breader/sifter is an oblong, stainless steel pan about 25 cm [10 in] deep. The bottom of the pan can be opened, revealing a sieve underneath for sifting the breading material into another pan.

• *Pressure fryer.* The pressure fryer is pictured in Fig. 22-15. It has a heavy lid that clamps down, increasing the pressure on the hot fat. It has a thermostat and a timer. The pressure is automatically released when the cooking time is completed. The stainless steel basket is made in four tiers. The tiers can be spread out for easy loading. They can be folded together to fit into the fryer during cooking.

• *Warming cabinet.* The warming cabinet is a heated cabinet to keep the chicken at a steady 60°C [140° F.] after frying until served. Fig. 22-13.

METHODS OF COOKING

In many fast-food restaurants featuring fried chicken, open-fried and pressure-fried chicken are offered.

• *Open-fried chicken.* Open-fried chicken is fried in an open frying kettle similar to that used for French fries. Fig. 22-14. The chicken has a rough, crunchy crust.

To prepare the chicken, it is first marinated in a seasoned, acid mixture. The formula is secret. Although chicken is naturally very tender, the marinade shortens the cooking time. It also makes the chicken juicier.

The marinade is drained from the chicken. Then the chicken is placed in the flour breading mixture. The worker mixes the chicken with the flour, removes it, and places it in a colander. The excess breading is shaken off. The chicken is then dipped in the wash, a weak mixture of milk and water. After the wash, the worker rebreads the chicken and again shakes off the excess breading.

After breading, the chicken is placed in the fryer basket and lowered into the hot fat. It takes twelve minutes at 175°C [350° F.] to fry the chicken to a golden brown.

While the chicken is frying, the worker returns to the breader/sifter. The wash dripping from the chicken mixes with the breading material, forming dough balls. These are sifted out so the breading can be used again.

Burger King, Inc.
22-14. Deep-fat fryers.

• *Pressure-fried chicken.* Pressure-fried chicken is not marinated first. It is dipped in a wash of water, milk, and egg and then into a seasoned breading mixture. The seasoning is a jealously guarded secret since its flavor distinguishes one kind of fried chicken from another.

After the excess breading has been shaken off, the chicken is placed on the tiers of the frying basket. Fig. 22-15. Each tier swings out for easy loading. The chicken is loaded in the tiers separated according to parts. The white meat is placed on one tier and the dark meat on another tier. The basket is folded together and lowered into the fat. When the lid is clamped down, the sizzling sound of the pressure building up can be heard. The chicken is cooked at 135°C [275° F.] for twelve minutes. Although the temperature is lower than that for open frying, the chicken cooks in the same time. The pressure drives the heat into the chicken.

When the cooking is completed, the pressure is automatically released, letting a cloud of steam into the kitchen. Ventilating hoods over the fryers remove the steam. If desired, the operator can manipulate the valve to release the steam more quickly.

After draining a few minutes, the chicken is placed on the serving pass-through under infrared heat if it is to be served shortly. If it will be held longer than ten minutes, it is placed in the warming cabinet.

Kentucky Fried Chicken

22-15. A pressure fryer.

CARE OF SHORTENING

As you read in Chapter 9, fat is expensive. When under constant use, as in frying chicken for fast foods, the proper care of it becomes even more important. Reread the directions on page 196 for daily filtering procedures. Also check the precautions to keep the hot shortening from disintegrating.

Words to Remember

flash frozen   tempering
tartar sauce

Fried Fish

Fish and chips is a fast food that came to us from England. In the small fishing villages that dot the coast of England, fish and chips has been a delightful specialty food from the sea. The first recorded fish and chips place was opened by Malins in London, England, in 1865. Malins used any inexpensive fish, cut it into chunks, and fried it. Soon Malins fried chunks of potatoes, too, to go along with the fish. Two cones were made of newspaper—one for the fish and one for the potatoes. It was strictly a take-out food, to be eaten in the local pub or munched while walking on the boardwalk.

Fish and chips became very popular in England. Its popularity spread to Canada and the United States. There are now about 14,000 fast-food places serving fish and chips in England, Canada, and the United States. While fried fish cannot compete with hamburgers, chicken, or pizza in popularity, it has been very well accepted. Many of the biggest chains serving fast-food hamburgers offer fish sandwiches as well.

Fish sandwiches are composed of three parts—the fried fish, the bun, and the garnish, or dressing.

• *Fish.* Saltwater fish that holds its shape is chosen for fish dinners and fish sandwiches. Ocean perch, pollock, whiting, or cod are used. Cod is preferred. It is plentiful, pure white, and flavorful, with a firm but tender texture.

The largest of the fast-food fish chains buy cod from Iceland. The cod is pressed into blocks and *flash frozen.* Flash freezing means to dip the fish into liquid air so it is frozen instantly. At the commissary the blocks are cut into 55-g [2-oz] portions.

• *Oil.* Oils from a vegetable base are usually chosen. Peanut oil is often used because it holds up well under high heat and does not transfer the fishy taste. It has no cholesterol, a fat associated with heart disease. This fact is used as a selling point for fish.

• *Bun.* The bun is usually round and meets the same specifications as the bun for hamburgers.

• *Breading.* The breading consists of cornmeal, and a batter made from a mix.

• *Dressing.* Fish sandwiches are made more attractive by the garnishing. *Tartar sauce*—a mixture of mayonnaise, chopped pickles, and other ingredients—is spread on the bun, unless the customer requests otherwise. Some restaurants use a cheese sauce as the dressing. Both the tartar sauce and the cheese sauce are delivered from the commissary ready for use.

Carrying out the English tradition of fish and chips, a bottle of malt vinegar is provided.

Lettuce, tomato slices, parsley, and other colorful garnishes may be served alongside the sandwich.

EQUIPMENT

Ordinary deep fryers are used for frying fish. Since fish fries so quickly, there is no need for pressure fryers. The fish fryers are usually not automatic; that is, the fish is not placed in a basket and automatically lowered into the fat. The batter would stick to the basket, preventing the fish from floating as it fries.

A slotted lifter is used to remove the fish from the hot fat.

METHOD OF COOKING

In the morning, the fish is removed from the freezer and placed in a defrosting cabinet. The fish is brought from $-18°C$ to $-3°C$ [0° F. to 26° F.]. It is still frozen, but not at a hard freeze.

• *Tempering.* In tempering, the fish is marinated in a salty solution for a short time to prepare it to receive the dusting compound.

• *Dusting.* The fish is dusted or spread lightly with cornmeal. The cornmeal helps the batter cling to the fish.

• *Dipping.* The fish is dipped in batter and drained.

• *Frying.* The fish is fried at $180°C$ [360° F.] for three minutes or until three corners float.

• *Dressing.* The bun for a fish sandwich is spread top and bottom with tartar sauce or cheese sauce.

• *Warming.* The fish is placed on the bun, dressed with lettuce, and kept under infrared heat at a steady $60°C$ [140° F.] until served, but never longer than fifteen minutes.

SERVING

Fried fish is often served as a sandwich, but it may also be part of a lunch or dinner. French fries (the chips) and coleslaw usually make up the dinner.

Oysters, clams, shrimp, and breast of chicken are frequently offered on the menu. They are fried in deep oil, as are the fish.

CARE OF OIL

To increase the life of the oil, an additive is put in the oil every night. The oil is first filtered to remove bits of fish and breading. The additive is a chemical that keeps the oil in a liquid state. It also prevents deterioration and the development of off-flavors.

French Fries and Fried Onions

French fries are as important to fast foods as the sandwich they almost always accompany. The frying of potatoes and onions has become very exact. Thus, their quality is often higher in fast-food restaurants than in many full-service restaurants.

INGREDIENTS

• *Potatoes.* The potatoes are prepared in the commissary. Idaho bakers are preferred because of their mealy texture after frying. The potatoes are delivered to the restaurant preblanched, frozen, and ready to cook. They are delivered in large plastic bags. Each bag fills four fryer baskets.

• *Onions.* The onions also are breaded, frozen, and ready to cook. Large, sweet, Spanish onions make the best fries.

• *Shortening.* All vegetable oils or fats may be

used. Many operations prefer a mixture of animal and vegetable fats. They believe the animal fat adds flavor. The fat contains additives that keep it from turning rancid. The additives also help the fat withstand the high heat of frying without breaking down.

EQUIPMENT

• *Fryer.* See page 53.

• *Holding rack.* After the frying baskets are filled with the frozen potatoes, they are placed in a holding rack close to the fryer.

• *Skimmer.* A skimmer is needed for lifting out the onions.

METHOD OF COOKING

French fries and onions must be freshly fried for best quality.

• *French fries.* The worker divides the frozen potatoes from one plastic sack among four frying baskets and places them in the holder. Care must be taken not to put out the potatoes too soon, or they will be limp when fried. However, enough potatoes must be on hand in frying baskets to fill the needs. The worker follows the schedule made out by the manager.

The worker turns on the fryer and sets the thermostat at 170–180°C [340–360° F.]. A light goes on while the fat is heating. When it goes out, the fat has reached the correct temperature. The worker places the loaded basket in the lowering position and pushes the button. The basket should not hang over the fat, waiting to be lowered. Timing is also automatic. The basket should be shaken occasionally so the potatoes will not stick together during frying. At the end of the cooking time, a buzzer sounds and the basket rises above the fat. The French fries drain a few minutes. Then the worker packages them in small bags and places them on the warming shelf. They should be held there only ten minutes and discarded after that time.

• *Fried onions.* Because the breading would become soggy, onions are not allowed to defrost. They are not loaded into a basket because the breading might stick to the basket. Instead, they are fried directly in the hot fat and lifted out with a skimmer.

They are also packaged in small bags and placed on the warming shelf.

Frequently, one worker will be responsible for frying fish, chicken, onions, potatoes, and the fried pies that are popular for dessert. During the lunch and dinner hours, the service keeps the worker constantly busy.

Words to Remember

dusting powder	staging
food release	traveling convection
hearth	oven
peel	

Pizza

Borrowed from Naples, Italy, pizza has become almost as popular as hamburgers and fried chicken. In Naples, pizza is made with a thin crust and little sauce so it can be rolled and eaten with the fingers. In the United States and Canada the crust has been thickened. There is more sauce. The toppings are varied.

Recent surveys show pizza to be second to hamburgers in popularity. Pizza has another point in its favor. In a study made of the nutritional value of fast foods, pizza proved to be the most nutritious. Pizza is especially popular with those persons in the twenty-one to thirty-four age bracket.

Pizzas may be many sizes and shapes. The smallest are often used as hot hors d'oeuvres. The largest serve eight to twelve persons. The shape may be round, square, or rectangular. Round is the conventional and most popular form.

INGREDIENTS

Pizza is composed of the crust, sauce, cheese, and the topping. Table 22-1 gives storage information for pizza ingredients.

• *The crust* may be thin and crisp or thick and chewy. Fig. 22-16. It is made from lean dough, leavened with yeast. A high-gluten flour is needed for the thick and chewy crust. The flour for the thin and crisp crust may be all-purpose flour. Oil is added to

| | Temperature | | Shelf Life |
Ingredient	°C	°F.	
Crusts, Sauces, and Cheeses			
Cheese, frozen	−18	0	2 months
Cheese, thawed	2–5	35–40	7–10 days
Crust, thick	2–5	35–40	24 hours
Crust, thin	18–24	65–75	24 hours
Sauce, mixed	2–5	35–40	4 days
Toppings			
Anchovies, opened	2–5	35–40	7 days
Bacon bits, opened	2–5	35–40	14 days
Beef, ground	2–5	35–40	7 days
Canadian bacon	2–5	35–40	5 days
Green pepper, sliced	2–5	35–40	24 hours
Italian sausage	2–5	35–40	7 days
Onions, sliced	2–5	35–40	24 hours
Pepperoni	2–5	35–40	7 days
Pork, ground	2–5	35–40	7 days
Shrimp, opened	2–5	35–40	3 days

Table 22-1. Storage of Pizza Ingredients

the crisp crust to tenderize. Some companies add a little sugar to make the crust even more tender. Tables 22-2 and 22-3 give scaling information for the two types of pizza crust.

• *The sauce* is similar to the Italian sauce described in Chapter 15. Most pizza served in fast foods has a sauce made from a "secret recipe." On page 453 is a recipe for pizza sauce. It contains tomato sauce, tomato paste, and seasonings. The commissaries serving fast food companies deliver No. 10 cans of tomato sauce and paste made to order. Other companies cannot make exactly the same sauce and paste. The seasonings are also delivered in a seasoning bag called a "goodie bag." The seasonings vary among the companies. Most contain thyme, sage, sweet basil, oregano, garlic, and onions.

• *The cheese* may be mozzarella or Cheddar. Provolone is also used. The cheese is bought locally and may be fresh or frozen. Mozzarella makes the

Pizza Hut, Inc.
22-16. Thick-crusted pizza on the left; thin-crusted pizza is on the right.

Table 22-2. Scaling Dough, Sauce, and Cheese (Pizza with Thin and Crisp Crust)

Pizza Size	Dough		Sauce		Cheese	
	Metric	Customary	Metric	Customary	Metric	Customary
Very small	105 g	$3\frac{3}{4}$ oz	75 mL	$\frac{1}{2}$ c	55 g	2 oz
Small	170 g	6 oz	150 mL	$\frac{2}{3}$ c	85 g	3 oz
Medium	275 g	$9\frac{3}{4}$ oz	205 mL	$\frac{3}{4}$ c plus 2 T	140 g	5 oz
Large	370 g	13 oz	280 mL	1 c plus 2 T	200 g	7 oz

authentic Italian pizza, but Cheddar is often substituted. Many people prefer it, and it is less expensive.

• *The topping* makes the pizza and gives it its name. Pepperoni sausage, Italian sausage, mushrooms, anchovies, shrimp, black olives, and ground beef are just a few of the endless varieties. Fresh vegetables such as green peppers and sweet onions add color and flavor. Fig 22-17.

The following items are also needed:

• *Olive oil* adds the real Italian flavor and may be spread on the pizza before baking. Because it is expensive, other oils are often substituted.

• *Dusting powder* is a mixture of Parmesan cheese and crushed oregano.

• *Food release* is a mixture of vegetable oil, alcohol, and lecithin sprayed on the baking pans to prevent the pizza from sticking.

EQUIPMENT

• *Vertical mixer* for mixing the dough.

• *Sheeter* for automatically rolling and cutting the dough. It is used only for thin crusts.

• *Small equipment* such as pizza pans, spoons for stirring, portion scales, measuring cups, ladles, rubber spatulas, dough cutters, wire whisks.

• *Ovens* are usually deck ovens with heavy bottoms called the *floor* or the *hearth*. Pizzas are baked at very high temperatures, 290°C [550° F.]. When completely filled the large fast ovens can bake 180 pizzas an hour. A single pizza will bake in six minutes.

• *Traveling convection ovens* are the newest ovens for baking pizza. They are called travel ovens because the pizza travels on a conveyor belt as it bakes. It is similar to the conveyor belt broiler described earlier in this chapter. The travel ovens are

Table 22-3. Scaling Dough, Sauce, and Cheese (Pizza with Thick and Chewy Crust)

Pizza Size	Dough		Sauce		Cheese	
	Metric	Customary	Metric	Customary	Metric	Customary
Very small	170 g	6 oz	75 mL	5 T	65 g	$2\frac{1}{4}$ oz
Small	270 g	$9\frac{1}{2}$ oz	125 mL	$\frac{1}{2}$ c	100 g	$3\frac{1}{2}$ oz
Medium	450 g	16 oz	175 mL	$\frac{3}{4}$ c	170 g	6 oz
Large	595 g	21 oz	250 mL	1 c	225 g	8 oz

Pizza Hut, Inc.

22-17. Pizza toppings can be garnished with many different foods. This pizza has been garnished with sliced mushrooms and sliced green pepper.

Sparta Brush Co.

22-18. A pizza oven brush. This brush has bristles and a scraper. The scraper cleans off particles that may be stuck to the floor of the oven. The bristles brush off the crumbs.

usually divided into three sections, each with its own door. Each section has its own speed of travel. As in all convection baking, the baking is very fast. One section may be set to cook the thin-crusted pizzas with quick cooking toppings in three minutes. The middle one will cook a pizza with a medium-thick topping in six minutes. The third section is for thick and chewy crusts. This one takes fifteen minutes. Some operators of these fast ovens place foil underneath the pans. The foil reflects the heat to the bottom of the pan and causes the crust to brown quickly.

- A *wooden paddle,* called a *peel,* is used to remove the pizza from the oven.
- *Ladles* are used for accurate measurement of the sauce.

- *Asbestos gloves* are worn by the workers to shield the hands from the intense heat of the ovens.
- The *pizza oven brush* is used to clean the oven floor after the baking is finished. Fig. 22-18.

METHOD OF COOKING

Pizza must be hot, tasty, and freshly baked. Some pizza places buy totally prepared, frozen pizzas that only need to be baked. Others prepare pizza from convenience foods supplied by the company commissary. Still others prepare pizza from scratch. Pizza preparation methods are listed in Table 22-4.

Preparation of the Crust

The preparation of thin pizza crust is detailed in the recipe on page 454. Notice that the method of preparation follows the principles of yeast baking (Chapter 17).

After mixing, the thin crust mixture is rather crumbly. Excess moisture will make a tough crust. Notice that it has less water and yeast than the thick crust. It must rise for six hours at room temperature.

The thick crust mixture is a typical, stretchy yeast dough. Since it contains more water and yeast than the thin dough, it will begin to rise during the mixing. The rising is retarded in the refrigerator so it will not overrise. The recipe for thick pizza crust is on page 455.

Both kinds of crust are portioned by weight. The thin crust mixture is portioned as needed after ris-

Table 22-4. Making Pizza By Three Methods

Frozen Pizza	Convenience Food Pizza	Pizza from Scratch
Microwave Method 1. *Place* frozen pizza on absorbent paper. 2. *Heat* on high for about 1 minute. Check manufacturer's directions, since time varies with different models. **Convection Oven Method** 1. *Heat* oven to 260°C [500° F.]. 2. *Place* pizza in pan in oven and bake until hot and bubbly—about 5–6 minutes.	1. *Remove* crust from refrigerator or freezer. 2. *Spread* with olive oil. 3. *Spread* with prepared sauce (250 mL [1 c] per pizza). 4. *Garnish* as desired. 5. Sprinkle with cheese (125 mL [$\frac{1}{2}$ c] per pizza). 6. Bake 5–6 minutes at 315°C [600°F.]	**Prepare Crust** 1. *Mix* flour, sugar, and salt on first speed of mixer. 2. *Dissolve* yeast in water and add to flour mixture. Add shortening. 3. *Knead* until smooth on first speed. 4. *Let rise* two hours. 5. *Punch down* and let rest 45 minutes. 6. *Roll out* and place in pans. 7. *Spread* with olive oil. **Prepare Sauce** 1. *Combine* all ingredients in steam-jacketed kettle. 2. *Simmer* for 15 minutes. 3. *Remove* from kettle and cool. 4. *Spread* sauce on crust (250 mL [1 c] per pizza). **Garnish** 1. *Top* as desired. 2. *Spread* with olive oil and shredded mozzarella cheese (125 mL [$\frac{1}{2}$ c] per pizza). 3. *Bake* at 315°C [600° F.] for 5–6 minutes. Time and temperature are approximate. Check manufacturer's directions.

ing. It is immediately placed in the sheeter to be rolled automatically.

The thick crust mixture is portioned into patties before rising. Each patty will make one thick crust. Special plastic storage containers hold the patties in the refrigerator. As needed, the patties are placed in the prepared pizza pans. The dough is spread in the pans by hand, using the fingers and the heel of the palm.

Pizza pans are prepared by spraying with food release before putting in the crust.

Preparation of the Sauce

The recipe for pizza sauce on page 453 is very simple to prepare. Notice that the sauce must be stored for at least four hours before using. The seasonings have been partially cooked to speed the flavor release.

Ladles of different sizes are provided to measure the sauce. Usually the ladles measure:

- 55 mL [2 fl oz].
- 90 mL [3 fl oz].
- 180 mL [6 fl oz].
- 200 mL [7 fl oz].

Distribute the sauce evenly over the crust, using a spoon.

Preparation of the Cheese

The cheese may be purchased sliced or diced, frozen or unfrozen. Unfrozen cheese must be kept in the refrigerator until used. Frozen cheese must be defrosted before use. This process takes about three days. It takes that long for the moisture to be redistributed throughout the solids of the cheese so it is like fresh cheese.

The amount of cheese to be placed on the pizza is specified by the company. Place the cheese on top of the sauce. Be careful not to cover the bare crust around the edge. Most fast-food companies specify the exact way the cheese should be placed on top of the pizza sauce.

Preparation of Pizza Toppings

The exact amount of topping is also specified by the company. The order in which it is placed on the pizza is usually as follows:

1. *Additional cheese* for a cheese pizza.
2. *Sliced meat* such as pepperoni sausage spread evenly over the surface.
3. *Vegetables* such as sliced onions, green peppers, mushrooms, olives, and hot peppers.
4. *Ground meat* such as beef, pork, or Italian sausage.
5. *Dusting powder* as a finishing touch.

Garnishes for Pizza

Try some of these garnishes to vary the pizza.

- Sauté ground beef and minced onions with garlic. Spread on pizza and cover with sauce. Top with green pepper rings and small whole mushrooms and cheese.
- Slice pepperoni sausage very thin. Place on top of the sauce. Add sliced mushrooms. Spread lightly with olive oil, and sprinkle with mozzarella.
- Substitute thin slices of salami for the pepperoni sausage.

BAKING THE PIZZA

Both types of crusts are baked directly on the hearth. Large pizzas should be placed toward the back of the oven. Smaller pizzas should be placed in front since they will take less time to bake. Sometimes the pizza will form bubbles as it cooks. The pizza with the thick and chewy crust will not form as many bubbles as the pizza with the thin crust. The baker should check for bubbles at the end of five minutes of baking. The surface of the bubbles should be gently broken using the cutter. The ingredients should be spread gently over the bubbles so they do not show. Check again for bubbles after seven minutes.

Pizza is done when:

- The crust is lightly browned.
- The cheese no longer is runny.
- The top is well-cooked.

Cooking time will vary from eight to fifteen minutes. The length of time depends upon the following factors:

- The size of the pizza.
- The thickness of the crust. Thin crusts will cook faster than thick crusts.
- The amount of topping. Thick toppings take longer than thin toppings.
- The number of pizzas in the oven. The oven will have a lower temperature when filled with pizzas.
- The number of times the oven is opened. Heat escapes each time the oven door is opened.

Beginners tend to overcook pizza. Overcooked pizza is dry. There is a specific moment when the pizza should be removed from the oven. Experience will tell you when. Remember, the pizza will continue to cook during the staging time.

STAGING

Staging means allowing the pizza to stand on top of the oven for about thirty to forty-five seconds before cutting. This is especially important for thick-crusted pizzas. Staging permits the pizza to harden slightly, making it easier to cut.

CUTTING THE PIZZA

Round pizza is usually cut into pie-shaped pieces. The cutter is a saw-toothed wheel set in a handle. Usually a divider is used to guide the cutter. It is divided into four sections for the smallest pizza, and into six sections for the small pizza. The medium and large pizzas are divided into eight and twelve sections respectively.

Be sure to cut completely through the crust. Pizzas are very difficult to cut when they cool. Serve pizzas as soon as they are cut.

STORING

Cooked pizzas cannot be stored without great loss of quality. Uncooked pizzas may be tightly wrapped in plastic film and frozen.

The separated parts of the pizza may be stored in the refrigerator for a limited time.

Burger King, Inc.

22-19. Fried apple pies.

Salads and Desserts

To make a more complete meal, some fast food chains have added salads to their offerings. Usually it is *coleslaw,* a finely chopped cabbage mixed with salad dressing. Coleslaw stays fresh for several days if refrigerated. It is often delivered from the commissary in large jars, ready-for-service.

Recently, some fast-food chains have added salad bars. The salads offered are simple. Torn lettuce, sliced tomatoes, onions, a choice of dressings, and toppings such as bacon bits and cheese are usually offered. Salad bars add substantially to the nutritive value of the fast-food offerings.

Desserts are not a big part of the menu offerings in fast foods. Some chains offer fried pies which have proved quite popular. Fig. 22-19. Frozen apple and cherry tarts are fried quickly in deep fat, wrapped, and kept hot on the serving shelf. Shelf life is forty-five minutes.

How Much Have You Learned?

Review this chapter. Answer the following questions to prepare yourself for the posttest. Check your answers with your teacher.

1. Define the *Words to Remember.*

2. How do modern fast foods differ from those prepared in short-order cooking?

3. Give at least three reasons for the growth of the fast food industry.

4. What is a franchise? Who is the franchisee? Who is the franchisor? What is another name for franchise? Discuss the advantages and disadvantages of franchises.

5. What is a commissary? What is the connection of commissaries to fast foods?

6. How should a short-order kitchen be organized?

7. Explain the temperature settings on a grill for short-order cooking. Demonstrate how to clean a grill.

8. Name and describe the three parts of a hamburger.

9. How does a conveyor chain broiler operate? How is the broiler prepared in the morning for broiling?

10. What is a warmer? How is it used?

11. Why are specifications important for steaks? How are the frozen steaks prepared for broiling?

12. Describe a system for identifying the type of steak and degree of doneness while broiling.

13. Describe the care of the broiler during broiling and after the broiling is over.

14. What is the difference between a regular deep fryer and the pressure deep fryer.

15. Explain how to care for fat used in deep frying.

16. Describe two methods for preparing the chicken for frying.

17. What kind of fish is mostly used for fast foods? Why?

18. Describe the preparation of fish for frying. Are pressure fryers used for fish? Explain your answer.

19. Describe the four parts of a pizza.

20. What type of oven is used to bake pizza?

21. Why should a high-gluten flour be used for making pizza?

PIZZA SAUCE

Yield: 100 servings

Equipment
Can opener
Stockpot
Rubber spatula
Wire whip
Storage containers

Metric	Ingredients	Customary
12 kg	Tomato puree	3 No. 10 cans
4 kg	Tomato paste	1 No. 10 can
4 kg	Water	1 No. 10 can
1	Spice bag	1

METHOD

1. **Open** and empty cans of tomato puree and tomato paste into stockpot.
2. **Rinse** each can with water. Empty water into one of the cans. Fill can to top with water and add to tomato mixture.
3. **Add** contents of spice bag.
4. **Mix** thoroughly with wire whip.
5. **Pour** sauce into storage containers.
6. **Store** for at least 4 hours before using.

PIZZA DOUGH (THIN AND CRISP)

Equipment   **Yield:** Depends on size of pizza
Thermometer
Portion scales
Rubber spatula
Mixer with bowl
Measuring cups
Dough container

Metric	Ingredients	Customary
4.5 L	Water, warm	$4\frac{1}{2}$ qt
115 g	Yeast, dry	4 oz
500 mL	Oil	2 c
255 g	Salt	9 oz
11.5 kg	Flour	25 lb

METHOD

1. **Pour** measured water into mixing bowl. Adjust temperature to 41°C [105° F.].
2. **Sprinkle** yeast on top of water. Mix with rubber spatula about 2 minutes.
3. **Add** oil and salt. Mix with rubber spatula about 1 minute.
4. **Add** flour. Mix on low speed using paddle for 3 minutes.
5. **Place** dough in lightly greased container.
6. **Cover** and let rise at room temperature for 6 hours.
7. **Portion** according to chart.
8. **Place** dough in sheeter as needed for automatic rolling.

PIZZA DOUGH (THICK AND CHEWY)

Equipment

Yield: Depends on size of pizza

Thermometer
Portion scales
Rubber spatula
Measuring cups
Dough patty storage containers
Dough cutter
Dough mixer with bowl

Metric	Ingredients	Customary
6.5 L	Water, warm	6½ qt
170 g	Yeast	6 oz
255 g	Salt	9 oz
11.5 kg	Flour	25 lb

METHOD

1. **Pour** measured warm water into mixing bowl. If necessary, cool to 41°C [105° F.] by stirring.
2. **Sprinkle** yeast on water. Mix with rubber spatula for 2 minutes.
3. **Add** salt. Stir with rubber spatula for 2 minutes.
4. **Add** flour. Mix on low speed for 5 minutes.
5. **Oil** storage containers.
6. **Portion** dough, using dough cutter. Check weight on portion scales according to chart.
7. **Form** into patties about 7.5 cm [3 in] thick.
8. **Store** in patty containers in refrigerator for 6 hours.

Beverages

When you finish studying this chapter, you should be able to do the following:

- Define the *Words to Remember.*
- Prepare coffee by two methods that meet the standards for acceptable service.
- Prepare tea that meets the standards for acceptable service.
- Demonstrate the correct way to draw a sample milk shake and test for consistency and flavor.
- Demonstrate the correct way to dispense a soft drink.
- Demonstrate how to clean the coffee makers and the milk shake dispensers.
- Pass the posttest.

CHAPTER

23

Beverages are common to all food service, but they play an important part in fast foods also. Many beverages, such as milk, soft drinks, and fruit juices, require no preparation. Others, such as coffee, need some simple preparation. Coffee, hot tea, iced tea, hot chocolate, and milk shakes are the prepared beverages most often found in fast foods.

COFFEE

Americans drink more coffee than any other beverage. Over 15 billion cups of coffee are drunk in the United States each year. This is an average of almost three cups of coffee per person per day. Coffee has been consistently the favorite snack-time beverage.

Since coffee is so popular, Americans have a right to expect a good cup of coffee. However, nothing served in restaurants causes more complaints than coffee. The quality and quantity of coffee served influences the judgment of the entire restaurant. Customers demand good taste in coffee. Bland coffee is usually the result of poor coffee making practices. The flavor of ground coffees does not vary much among the well-known brands.

Words to Remember

activated charcoal	green tea
black tea	milk stone
brewed	oolong tea
brewer	seat line
caffein	steep
decanter	urn
dispenser	

When the flavor of an ingredient is extracted by water the process is called *brewing*. Coffee is brewed.

Ingredients

• *Coffee*. This popular beverage is made from coffee beans grown mostly in the countries of Central and South America. The best coffees are grown in the higher altitudes where the days are hot and the nights cool. Some coffees are dark in color, rich in flavor, and heavy in aroma. Others are much lighter. Different coffees are blended to produce the desired characteristics of color, flavor, and aroma.

Coffee is shipped as green beans. It is roasted to give it the dark brown color and familiar coffee taste and smell. Once coffee has been roasted, it quickly loses its quality. Coffee should be wrapped in airtight packages as soon as possible after roasting.

To extract the color, flavor, and aroma, the roasted coffee bean is ground. Each method of brewing requires a specific grind for best results. If the grind is too coarse, the coffee will be weak. If the grind is too fine, the coffee will be murky.

Most restaurant chains specify the exact blend, grind, and packaging of the coffee used in each outlet. A few chains roast, blend, and grind their own coffee.

• *Water*. Water makes up 98 percent of the body of the coffee. Poor quality water can ruin coffee. The water should be slightly hard and not artificaly softened. Water with an undesirable taste or water high in chlorine or iron should be filtered through *activated charcoal*. Activated charcoal is specially

treated charcoal that removes sediment and foreign tastes or odors from water.

• *Instant coffee*. Freeze-dried, granulated coffee is easy to use, but most customers want and expect "real" coffee in food service. Caffein is a stimulant found in coffee, tea, and chocolate. Some people do not like beverages containing *caffein*. Thus, brand-name decaffeinated coffee in packages for one cup is often offered to customers who prefer that type. Hot water is served in a pitcher to dissolve the instant coffee.

Equipment

Whatever equipment is used, it must be absolutely clean. Coffee contains an oil that collects on the sides of urns, giving the coffee a bitter taste. Daily cleaning will prevent off-flavors and odors.

Electric urns are difficult to clean because of the faucets and water pipes. Fig. 23-1. Special brushes

Cecilware Corp.

23-1. An automatic coffee urn.

are needed to fit into these hard-to-clean places. Fig. 23-2.

The brewers are easy to clean. Since the servers are made of glass with rounded sides, they can be washed as easily as a dish.

In food service, coffee is usually brewed in a large electric urn or in small brewers.

• *Electric urns.* An *urn* is a container with a faucet. There are three types of electric urns, the manual, the semiautomatic, and the fully automatic. Since use of the manual urn involves pouring boiling water (a dangerous operation) and is very slow, it is not used in fast-food operations. The semiautomatic urn also is not fast enough.

The fully automatic urn is connected to a source of hot water. A filter basket fits in the top. The coffee is premeasured and poured into the filter basket. A push of the button starts the coffee brewing. It automatically shuts off when the brewing is completed.

• *Coffee brewers.* A *brewer* is a container, usually made of glass, used for brewing coffee and, sometimes, tea. This type of coffee maker is very popular. It is rapidly replacing the large urns. The coffee is brewed directly into the server. Fig. 23-3. The customer can see the coffee being made at frequent intervals. This assures the customer of the coffee's freshness.

The coffee brewer is hooked up to water and electricity. The coffee is in premeasured bags. A fluted paper filter is placed in the filter cup and filled with coffee. The filter goes on top of the server. When the button is pushed, the hot water automatically drips through the coffee into the serving *decanter*. Decanter is another name for a server. When the server is full, the water shuts off.

To make good coffee by the brewing method, follow these directions:

1. Use the correct amount of coffee.
2. Spread coffee evenly in the filter chamber.
3. Check water temperature. It should be at least 88°C [190° F.].
4. Check brewing time. The decanter or server should be filled in three to four minutes.
5. Remove grounds immediately.
6. Serve only fresh coffee. Do not hold longer than one hour.

HOT CHOCOLATE AND COCOA

Since the demand for hot chocolate or cocoa is much less than for coffee, most restaurants keep packages of instant cocoa on hand. The quality is high and the preparation simple. Instant cocoa is a blend of cocoa, sugar, and milk solids. The cocoa has been specially treated so it will mix easily and smoothly with hot water. Hot chocolate or cocoa is usually served with a small scoop of whipped cream.

TEA

Tea comes from the leaves of a bush that grows in Japan, China, other parts of the Orient, and South America. The top leaves on the tips of the branches make the highest quality tea. Tea is picked by hand. It is then dried, rolled, and dried again. Tea is very popular in England, Scotland, Ireland, Canada, Australia, and throughout the Orient. It is rapidly becoming more popular in the United States.

Iced tea is a well-liked beverage in the United States, especially during the summer months. However, in the Orient, where tea originated, it is unknown.

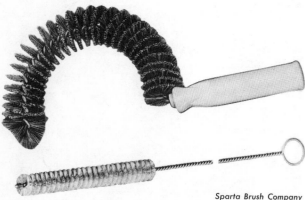

Sparta Brush Company
23-2. Brushes for cleaning coffee urns.

Bunn-O-Matic Corp.
23-3. An automatic coffee brewer.

Ingredients

There are three general types of tea—*green, oolong,* and *black.* Each of these types may be purchased under many different names.

- *Green tea.* This is the type generally served throughout the Orient. After the tea is dried and rolled, green tea is steamed to prevent it from fermenting. The brew from green tea is very pale and slightly green in color. It is not very popular in the United States, except in places featuring Japanese or Chinese cuisine.
- *Oolong tea.* This is partially fermented tea with a light color, taste, and aroma.
- *Black tea.* This is the type generally preferred by Americans and other English-speaking people. In the Orient, black tea is called English tea. Black tea is allowed to ferment by spreading it on trays under humid conditions. The fermentation give the tea the characteristic aroma, dark color, and deep flavor associated with tea in this country. After fer-

mentation, black tea is fired to stop the fermentation. Only black tea is used to make iced tea.

Tea may be purchased loose by the kilogram or pound or in tea bags. Tea bags are almost always used in food service. Small bags, each holding enough tea for a two-cup pot, are used for hot tea. For iced tea, large tea bags holding 28 g [1 oz] of tea may be used. Each large bag will make twenty servings of tea. However, instant tea is popular because it is convenient and saves ice. It may be either plain in flavor or flavored with lemon and sugar.

Equipment

Tea requires a source of boiling water. The jacket around the coffee urn may be used. A dispenser of boiling water on the electric brewer can also be used.

An instant dispenser for iced tea is a most economical piece of equipment. Iced tea is a good profit item, and a dispenser makes it easy to make. Be sure the dispenser does not have brass locknuts and washers, since tea interacts with this metal. Neoprene washers and stainless steel locknuts are best.

459

Clean the faucets often. Wash the dispenser every day by flushing with clean, cold water.

Methods of Making Tea

Tea is *brewed*. To brew means to soak or *steep* in very hot water to extract the color, flavor, and aroma.

Water temperature of not less than 82°C [180° F.] is required for extraction. Although the temperature is close to boiling, the water used for tea must not be boiled. Boiling makes a bitter tea.

Tea should be steeped for about five minutes or less. Some people, especially Americans, prefer a shorter steeping time. If the water is the proper temperature, the desirable color, flavor, and aroma will be produced in five minutes. Longer steeping will result in a bitter flavor.

Tea is very simple to make, but it is difficult to get a good cup of tea in almost any restaurant. A good cup of tea requires freshly boiling water, a preheated tea pot, and preheated cup—not a pot of tepid water with a tea bag alongside.

To make hot tea for individual service, follow these directions:

1. Allow one tea bag for each pot holding two teacups.

2. Rinse pot with very hot water.

3. Place tea bag in pot and fill with boiling water.

4. Serve immediately. The customer will control the steeping time.

DOUBLE-STRENGTH TEA

When hot tea is to be served in large quantities, double-strength tea is usually prepared. When served, two teapots are needed. One is filled with the hot, double-strength tea. The other is filled with very hot water. At service, a teacup is filled half with the strong tea and half with the hot water.

Double-strength tea is also used for making iced tea. The melting ice will dilute the tea.

To make double-strength tea, follow these directions:

1. Use the 28-g [1-oz] tea bags, one for each 2 L [½ gal] of strong tea.

2. Place tea bag in pitcher and pour 1 L [1 qt] of boiling water over it.

3. Let steep for six minutes.

4. Pour hot tea into 1 L [1 qt] of cold water.

For instant tea, follow the directions on the packet.

MILK SHAKES

Milk shakes are favorites in fast foods, especially with the young. In the American West, more than half of those eating in fast-food restaurants prefer milk shakes with their food. In the Midwest and South, the percentage is almost as high. It seems customers of all ages, no matter where they live, like milk shakes. One fast-food chain sells more than 300 million shakes in one year. Milk shakes are almost as American as hamburgers. Milk shakes are high in nutrients, adding much good nutrition to fast foods.

Milk shakes may be made to order or prepared in advance and held in the freezer. Most milk shakes in fast foods are prepared in an automatic dispenser.

Ingredients

The ingredients of a milk shake are simple—milk, ice cream, and a flavor. Most places offer three flavors—vanilla, chocolate, and strawberry. Chocolate is by far the favorite.

The thickness of the ready-made dispenser milk shakes is not due to the amount of ice cream. A stabilizer similar to those mentioned on page 358 is added to increase the thickness and make the foam stable. The stabilizer greatly enhances the apparent richness of the shake.

Equipment

For milk shakes made to order, a blender is used. The blender smoothly mixes the milk, ice cream, and flavoring. It is difficult to control the quality of milk shakes made to order. It is easy for the worker to put in a little more or less of the ingredients. Thus, the quality of the shakes is not consistent. Lack of consistency causes customer dissatisfaction and leads to less profit.

Fast foods use the multiflavor, automatic dispenser. Fig. 23-4. In the newest type, the operator selects the flavor, pushes the button, and holds the container under the serving spout. The machine automatically ejects the right amount of syrup into the cup as it is being filled. It takes about six to seven seconds to make a milk shake. In some of the older machines, the syrup is put in the cup by hand before it is filled.

Methods of Making Milk Shakes

The key to quality control when using the automatic dispenser lies in following the manufacturer's directions exactly. Be especially careful to follow the daily start-up procedure as outlined in the operator's manual.

In addition to the instructions in the manual, follow these tips.

1. When the machine is ready for operation, draw a sample shake. Test for consistency. Most machines have a control, so the shake can be made as thick as desired.

2. Check the flavor and color by drawing a sample shake of each flavor. Increase or decrease the amount of syrup to get the flavor and color desired. Generally 28–43 g [1–1½ oz] of syrup will flavor a 470-mL [1-pt] serving.

3. Make sure you have correct cup size. Use 454-g [16-oz] size if not specified.

4. Lift plunger all the way up so cup will fill faster.

5. Fill to *seat line*. Close to the top, each cup has a mark called a seat line. The seat line ensures that all shakes will be the same size.

6. Cap and mark flavor on top with grease pencil.

When adding flavor not included in the automatic dispenser, use vanilla shake. Put 28 g [1 oz] of flavoring in cup. Fill with vanilla shake 1.3 cm [½ in] below seat line. Raise cup to blender shaft. Depress switch for few seconds to mix. Shake will rise to seat line.

Care of Dispenser

Milk stone is a deposit that forms inside any piece of equipment used with dairy products. It harbors

Taylor

23-4. An automatic milk shake dispenser.

bacteria and must be removed every night. Following the manufacturer's instructions, dismantle the dispenser. Clean thoroughly with a special milk stone remover. Rinse with cool water. Recharge the cleaned dispenser in the morning.

SOFT DRINKS

Soft drinks are usually sold in three cup sizes: small (12 oz), medium (16 oz), and large (24 oz). Eventually, metric cup sizes will be introduced.

In filling cups with soft drinks, follow these tips:

1. Fill cup exactly one-half full with ice unless customer requests otherwise.

2. Tilt cup when dispensing to reduce foam.

3. Mark lid with drink flavor, using grease pencil.

Unit 6: Fast Foods

How Much Have You Learned?

Review this chapter. Answer the following questions to prepare yourself for the posttest. Check your answers with your teacher.

1. Define the *Words to Remember*.
2. Describe the steps for making coffee in a coffee brewer.
3. Describe the steps for making hot tea.
4. Describe the steps for making double-strength tea.
5. What is the best water temperature for making tea? How long should tea be steeped?
6. How do you test an automatic milk shake dispenser before beginning service? How do you clean the dispenser?

References

Hardwicke, Geraline B., and Kennedy, Robert. Fundamentals of Quantity Food Preparation: *Desserts and Beverages*. Boston: Cahner's, 1975.

Haines, Robert G. *Food Preparation for Hotels, Restaurants, and Cafeterias*. Chicago: American Technical Society, 1973.

Kotschevar, Lendel H. *Standards, Principles, and Techniques in Quantity Food Production*. Boston: Cahner's, 1973.

Ray, Mary F., and Lewis, Evelyn J. *Exploring Professional Cooking*. Peoria, Ill.: Chas. A. Bennett Co., Inc. 1980.

Index

Index

Lisa
Weber

Index

Index

Index